LET'S GO

■ THE RESOURCE FOR THE INDEPENDENT TRAVELER

"The guides are aimed not only at young budget travelers but at the indepedent traveler; a sort of streetwise cookbook for traveling alone."
—*The New York Times*

"Unbeatable; good sight-seeing advice; up-to-date info on restaurants, hotels, and inns; a commitment to money-saving travel; and a wry style that brightens nearly every page."
—*The Washington Post*

"Lighthearted and sophisticated, informative and fun to read. [Let's Go] helps the novice traveler navigate like a knowledgeable old hand."
—*Atlanta Journal-Constitution*

"A world-wise traveling companion—always ready with friendly advice and helpful hints, all sprinkled with a bit of wit."
—*The Philadelphia Inquirer*

■ THE BEST TRAVEL BARGAINS IN YOUR PRICE RANGE

"All the dirt, dirt cheap."
—*People*

"Anything you need to know about budget traveling is detailed in this book."
—*The Chicago Sun-Times*

"Let's Go follows the creed that you don't have to toss your life's savings to the wind to travel—unless you want to."
—*The Salt Lake Tribune*

■ REAL ADVICE FOR REAL EXPERIENCES

"The writers seem to have experienced every rooster-packed bus and lunar-surfaced mattress about which they write."
—*The New York Times*

"A guide should tell you wha* . . . destination. Here Let's Go shines."
Tribune

"[Let's Go's] devoted updater ... de, and trek the trail). Learn how to fis
& Wine

D1041018

LET'S GO PUBLICATIONS

TRAVEL GUIDES

Alaska 1st edition **NEW TITLE**
Australia 2004
Austria & Switzerland 2004
Brazil 1st edition **NEW TITLE**
Britain & Ireland 2004
California 2004
Central America 8th edition
Chile 1st edition
China 4th edition
Costa Rica 1st edition
Eastern Europe 2004
Egypt 2nd edition
Europe 2004
France 2004
Germany 2004
Greece 2004
Hawaii 2004
India & Nepal 8th edition
Ireland 2004
Israel 4th edition
Italy 2004
Japan 1st edition **NEW TITLE**
Mexico 20th edition
Middle East 4th edition
New Zealand 6th edition
Pacific Northwest 1st edition **NEW TITLE**
Peru, Ecuador & Bolivia 3rd edition
Puerto Rico 1st edition **NEW TITLE**
South Africa 5th edition
Southeast Asia 8th edition
Southwest USA 3rd edition
Spain & Portugal 2004
Thailand 1st edition
Turkey 5th edition
USA 2004
Western Europe 2004

CITY GUIDES

Amsterdam 3rd edition
Barcelona 3rd edition
Boston 4th edition
London 2004
New York City 2004
Paris 2004
Rome 12th edition
San Francisco 4th edition
Washington, D.C. 13th edition

MAP GUIDES

Amsterdam
Berlin
Boston
Chicago
Dublin
Florence
Hong Kong
London
Los Angeles
Madrid
New Orleans
New York City
Paris
Prague
Rome
San Francisco
Seattle
Sydney
Venice
Washington, D.C.

COMING SOON:
Road Trip USA

LET'S GO

SOUTHWEST USA
ADVENTURE GUIDE

CHARLES L. BLACK EDITOR
ROBERT CACACE ASSOCIATE EDITOR

RESEARCHER-WRITERS
KRISTIN HOELTING
LUCAS LAURSEN
BRENDAN J. REED
TAYLOR TERRY
BRYDEN SWEENEY-TAYLOR

ELIZABETH H. PETERSON MAP EDITOR
LAUREN E. BONNER MANAGING EDITOR

ST. MARTIN'S PRESS ❧ NEW YORK

Maps by David Lindroth copyright © 2004 by St. Martin's Press.

Distributed outside the USA and Canada by Macmillan.

ISBN: 0-312-31998-3

First edition
10 9 8 7 6 5 4 3 2 1

Let's Go: Southwest USA Adventure Guide is written by Let's Go Publications, 67 Mount Auburn Street, Cambridge, MA 02138, USA.

CONTENTS

MAPS

HOW TO USE THIS BOOK

ORGANIZATION: Discover gives an overview of why people come to the Southwest, what to expect, and what not to miss; it should give you a broad idea of your itinerary and its goals. **Life & Times** supplies background on the history, art, and culture of the region, referencing other resources as well. **Essentials** lays out the nitty-gritty travel particulars—reading it carefully could save you a lot of inconvenience later on. The new and improved **Alternatives to Tourism** offers a wealth of ideas on how to enrich your trip with volunteering, work, and study. **The Great Outdoors** explains the public land system and offers advice on all things outdoors, from gear to wildlife to safety. Travel coverage begins with a special Grand Canyon chapter and proceeds state by state.

THE INSIDE SCOOP. Dispersed throughout the guide are black sidebars designed to give a peek into the experience of traveling in the Southwest, the cultural and outdoor opportunities of a particular spot, and the issues affecting towns and regions. Three **articles** go even further in-depth; see p. 91, 131, and 417.

COVERAGE. Within each destination, the most essential information comes first. After a short intro, **Transportation** explains how best to reach a given destination, while **Orientation & Practical Information** explain how to get around and where to go for essential services (police, post office, etc.) and info. Finding **accommodations** is the next logical step. The attractions you came for—in most cases **outdoor activities**—are listed and described in depth toward the end of each section.

PRICES. All accommodations and food listings are ranked by value; our researchers' absolute favorites get the *Let's Go* **thumbs-up** (🖐). Since the best value does not always mean the cheapest price, we've incorporated a system of five **price ranges** (❶ through ❺) to indicate what to expect—see the chart on p. xiv.

PHONE CODES & NUMBERS. Area codes appear opposite the name of the region and are denoted by the ☎ icon, as are phone numbers within the coverage proper.

WHEN TO USE IT

2 MONTHS BEFORE. Discover the Southwest USA—browse individual destination coverage and design your itinerary. Scan **Essentials** to start taking care of logistics, such as visas, reservations, financial planning, and ticket buying.

1 MONTH BEFORE. Take care of **travel insurance**, and think about how much financial flexibility you'll need. Make a list of **essential gear** (see **Equipment,** p. 63) and start shopping. Make sure you understand the logistics of your route.

2 WEEKS BEFORE. Leave an itinerary and photocopies of important documents, including credit cards, with someone at home. Make yourself a list of important numbers and hotlines. Read the **Life & Times** and **Great Outdoors** sections, and make sure you have the supplies you'll need.

A NOTE TO OUR READERS The information for this book was gathered by *Let's Go* researchers from May through August of 2003. Each listing is based on one researcher's opinion, formed during his or her visit at a particular time. Those traveling at other times may have different experiences since prices, dates, hours, and conditions are always subject to change. You are urged to check the facts presented in this book beforehand to avoid inconvenience and surprises.

ABOUT LET'S GO

GUIDES FOR THE INDEPENDENT TRAVELER

Budget travel is more than a vacation. At *Let's Go*, we see every trip as the chance of a lifetime. If your dream is to grab a knapsack and a machete and forge through the jungles of Brazil, we can take you there. Or, if you'd rather enjoy the Riviera sun at a beachside cafe, we'll set you a table. If you know what you're doing, you can have any experience you want—whether it's camping among lions or sampling Tuscan desserts—without maxing out your credit card. We'll show you just how far your coins can go, and prove that the greatest limitation on your adventure is not your wallet, but your imagination. That said, we understand that you may want the occasional indulgence after a week of hostels and kebab stands, so we've added "Big Splurges" to let you know which establishments are worth those extra euros, as well as price ranges to help you quickly determine whether an accommodation or restaurant will break the bank. While we may have diversified, our emphasis will always be on finding the best values for your budget, giving you all the info you need to spend six days in London or six months in Tasmania.

BEYOND THE TOURIST EXPERIENCE

We write for travelers who know there's more to a vacation than riding double-deckers with tourists. Our researchers give you the heads-up on both world-renowned and lesser-known attractions, on the best local eats and the hottest nightclub beats. In our travels, we talk to everybody; we provide a snapshot of real life in the places you visit with our sidebars on topics like regional cuisine, local festivals, and hot political issues. We've opened our pages to respected writers and scholars to show you their take on a given destination, and turned to lifelong residents to learn the little things that make their city worth calling home. And we've even given you Alternatives to Tourism—ideas for how to give back to local communities through responsible travel and volunteering.

OVER FORTY YEARS OF WISDOM

When we started, way back in 1960, Let's Go consisted of a small group of well-traveled friends who compiled their budget travel tips into a 20-page packet for students on charter flights to Europe. Since then, we've expanded to suit all kinds of travelers, now publishing guides to six continents, including our newest guides: *Let's Go: Japan* and *Let's Go: Brazil*. Our guides are still annually researched and written entirely by students on shoe-string budgets, adventurous travelers who know that train strikes, stolen luggage, food poisoning, and marriage proposals are all part of a day's work. Even as you read this, work on next year's editions is well underway. Whether you're reading one of our new titles, like *Let's Go: Puerto Rico* or *Let's Go Adventure Guide: Alaska*, or our original best-seller, *Let's Go: Europe*, you'll find the same spirit of adventure that has made *Let's Go* the guide of choice for travelers the world over since 1960.

GETTING IN TOUCH

The best discoveries are often those you make yourself; on the road, when you find something worth sharing, please drop us a line. We're Let's Go Publications, 67 Mt. Auburn St., Cambridge, MA 02138, USA (feedback@letsgo.com).

For more info, visit our website: www.letsgo.com.

RESEARCHER-WRITERS

Kristin Hoelting   *Colorado, NW New Mexico, & East Utah*

Alaska native Kristin brought her love and concern for the outdoors to every mountain village on her route. Given her environmental studies degree and extensive outdoors leadership experience, Kristin's enthusiasm for all things backcountry comes as no surprise, nor does her penchant for accurate research. Charming her way through the Southwest with her cheerfulness, Kristin earned the respect of her editors with reliability and thoughtfulness.

Lucas Laursen   *Southern California & Arizona*

SoCal native Lucas savored the opportunity to explore the natural playgrounds of his own backyard. His vast outdoors experience—from leading an outdoor youth group to climbing 14,000 ft. peaks—helped him sniff out adventure and report back with an impressive eye for detail and good stories. Stumbling through nighttime Tempe or avoiding wash-outs in the Eastern Mojave, Lucas brought a youthful exuberance to the sometimes lonely life on the road.

Brendan J. Reed   *Utah & Grand Canyon*

An aspiring, inspiring man of letters, Brendan translated his passion for the written word into research and writing of remarkable intensity. He braved the brutal summer heat to search for adventure in the nooks and crannies of Utah's national parks. Whether cruising desert highways in a huge diesel rig or waxing poetic in Dinosaur National Monument, Brendan lived the Southwestern vibe to its fullest and let his editors live it too, through his vivid writing.

Bryden Sweeney-Taylor   *Nevada & California*

With three tours of duty under his belt (*Southwest '02, South Africa '03, Hawaii '03*), Bryden understands the spirit of *Let's Go*. This Deep Springs College graduate knows all the tricks of the trade, and it shows in his thoroughness—rivaled only by the meticulousness of his writing. An editor waits for Bryden's copy like a connoisseur waits for vintage wine. Bryden's ability to put the scents of his travels on paper is always worth the wait.

Taylor Terry   *New Mexico & West Texas*

Not even a forest fire could slow Taylor's progress through New Mexico and West Texas, all the while using a discerning eye to make sure every hostel and taco stand was beyond reproach. From climbing peaks near Taos, to munching chile peppers and soaking in the hot springs of Truth or Consequences, Taylor took it as his job to live it up in Southwestern style. His observations reflected a sensitivity to all facets of Southwestern culture.

Jay Gierak   *Partial coverage of Las Vegas*

Andrew Price   *California*

CONTRIBUTING WRITERS

Claudia Cyganowski graduated from Harvard University with a degree in Astronomy. She has participated in archeological field research in Southwestern Colorado and Copán, Honduras, and has researched the significance of astronomy and the calendar in classic Maya society, the Zapotec hieroglyphic writing system, and other archaeological topics.

Eric Henson is a member of the Chickasaw Nation and a Research Fellow at the Harvard Project on American Indian Economic Development. A skilled economist, he holds a BBA in economics from the University of Texas at San Antonio, an MA in economics from Southern Methodist University, and he will earn an MPP from Harvard's Kennedy School of Government. He has worked at Haver Analytics and Fidelity Investments, and is currently a senior consultant at Lexecon, Inc.

Mark Kirby attended Deep Springs, one of the few colleges in the US that includes mending fences in their curricula. His cowboy training gave him the skills to cover the Grand Canyon, Utah, and northern Nevada for *Let's Go: Southwest USA 2002*, the inaugural year of the Southwest book. He's gone on to routes in New Zealand and Alaska, and in the fall of 2003 he will begin work at National Geographic's *Adventure* magazine.

Evan North researched Utah for the 2003 edition of *Let's Go: Southwest USA*.

Jonathan Sherman researched New Mexico and Texas for the 2003 edition of *Let's Go: Southwest USA*.

NEVADA
pp. 196-244

UTAH
pp. 245-331

COLORADO
pp. 332-376

GRAND CANYON
pp. 73-93

CALIFORNIA
pp. 157-195

NEW MEXICO
pp. 377-445

ARIZONA
pp. 94-156

WEST TEXAS
pp. 446-466

Southwest USA
Chapter Overview

ACKNOWLEDGMENTS

LET'S GO

CHARLIE THANKS: Rob—I couldn't have asked for a better colleague and buddy. Lucas, Kristin, Brendan, Bryden, and Taylor, whose dedication and enthusiasm form the core of this guide (*LG*'s only "best" guide; cf. Alaska Ack.). Lauren, for laughing and still believing in us (and for the opportunity). With love and thanks to Suzanne for inspiration, understanding, and so much more. Greg, for hours of laughter and stomping around. Jennie, for believing (in?) me. Elizabeth, for endless patience. Cutmasters Dusty and Greg. *Sine qua non:* Amelia, Emma, Jeff, Nitin, Steve, Tor, Megan. Hallball, the 3rd fl. for getting out of the way. Lloyd Christmas, for genius. With love to Mom, Dad, Heidi, Topher, Scout, CH.

ROB THANKS: Charlie Black, for supplying a great vision for the book, an accommodating managerial style, 10 year-old whiskey, and a great time. Brendan, Bryden, Kristin, Lucas, and Taylor, for their tireless work and wonderful research, all of this book's successes are due to you. The failures are Charlie's. Thanks to Regis, Eliot gang, 44 and its very bright future, SAE, Seaside, Eric Henson, Elizabeth Peterson, Sussudio, Pat Blanchfield, Chris Reisig, City Pod, AK, CA, hallball, Harry Dunn, Mr. and Mrs. Bartley, Jon Dienstag, Hickey, Damien, Joe, Gattman, P, Steph, Fayerweather on whole wheat, and Ol' Blue Eyes. Special thanks to the Chuckwagon, Lauren, Sam, Parker, John Barkett, Megan, Mom, Dad, Dani, and Mike.

ELIZABETH THANKS: Nathaniel, for being an amazing map manager. My fellow mappers, for making it an awesome summer. And of course, Charlie and Rob, for being great editors.

LAUREN THANKS: Brian, Ian, and Jamie at Daedalus, for keepin it real. For rizzle.

Editor Charles L. Black
Associate Editor Robert Cacace
Map Editor Elizabeth H. Peterson
Managing Editor Lauren E. Bonner
Typesetter Ankur Ghosh

Publishing Director
Julie A. Stephens
Editor-in-Chief
Jeffrey Dubner
Production Manager
Dusty Lewis
Cartography Manager
Nathaniel Brooks
Design Manager
Caleb Beyers
Editorial Managers
Lauren Bonner, Ariel Fox,
Matthew K. Hudson, Emma Nothmann,
Joanna Shawn Brigid O'Leary,
Sarah Robinson
Financial Manager
Suzanne Siu
Marketing & Publicity Managers
Megan Brumagim, Nitin Shah
Personnel Manager
Jesse Reid Andrews
Researcher Manager
Jennifer O'Brien
Web Manager
Jesse Tov
Web Content Director
Abigail Burger
Production Associates
Thomas Bechtold, Jeffrey Hoffman Yip
IT Directors
Travis Good, E. Peyton Sherwood
Financial Assistant
R. Kirkie Maswoswe
Associate Web Manager
Robert Dubbin
Office Coordinators
Abigail Burger, Angelina L. Fryer,
Liz Glynn

Director of Advertising Sales
Daniel Ramsey
Senior Advertising Associates
Sara Barnett, Daniella Boston
Advertising Artwork Editors
Julia Davidson, Sandy Liu

President
Abhishek Gupta
General Manager
Robert B. Rombauer
Assistant General Manager
Anne E. Chisholm

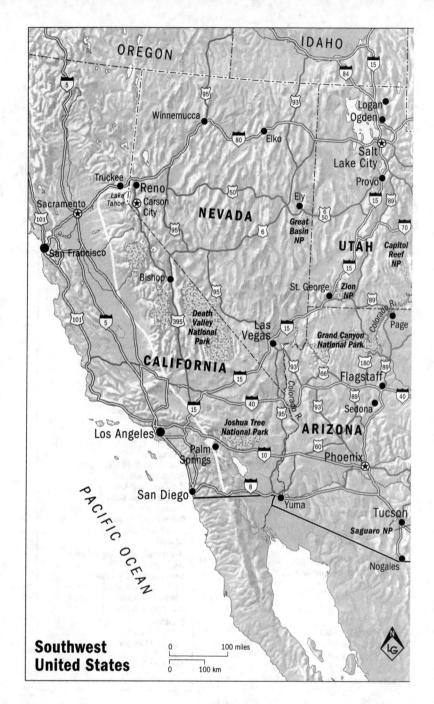

Southwest United States

0   100 miles

0   100 km

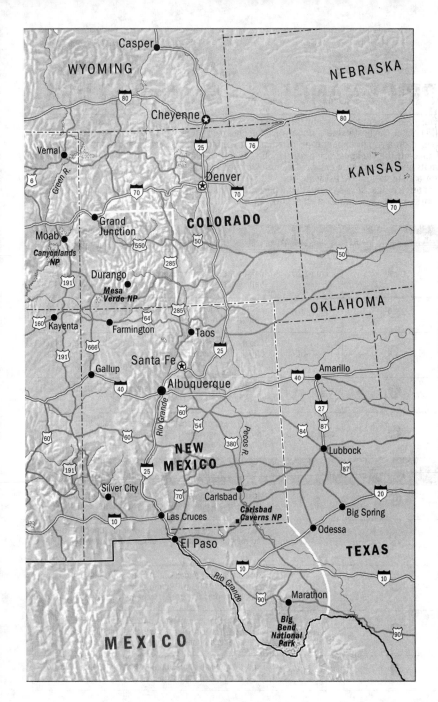

PRICE RANGES >> Southwest USA

Our researchers rank establishments by value; our favorites get the Let's Go thumbs-up (🖐). Since the best value is not always the cheapest price, we have a system of price ranges based on a rough expectation of what you will spend. For **accommodations,** we base the range off the cheapest price for which a single traveler can stay for one night. For **restaurants** and other dining establishments, we estimate the average amount you would spend for a meal. Below we list what you will *typically* find in the Southwest at the corresponding price range; keep in mind that a particularly expensive ice cream stand may still only be marked a ❷, depending on what you will spend.

ACCOMMODATIONS	RANGE	WHAT YOU'RE LIKELY TO FIND
❶	Free-$20	Camping; most dorm rooms, such as HI or other hostels or university dorm rooms. Expect bunk beds and a communal bath; you may have to provide or rent towels and sheets.
❷	$20-40	Lower-end motels, but often good value. Expect a private bathroom, towels, and TV.
❸	$40-60	Chain motels and hotels A small room with a private bath. Should have decent amenities, such as phone and cable TV. Breakfast may be included in the price of the room.
❹	$60-80	Similar to 3, but may have more amenities or be in a more touristed area.
❺	$80 and up	Large hotels or upscale chains, especially in ski resort towns and large cities. If it's a 5 and it doesn't have a hot tub, you've paid too much.
FOOD	RANGE	WHAT YOU'RE LIKELY TO FIND
❶	$1-7	Mostly street-corner stands, pizza places, or fast-food joints. Lots of good Mexican food falls in this range.
❷	$7-12	Sandwiches, appetizers at a bar, or low-priced entrees. You may have the option of either sitting down or getting take-out to go.
❸	$12-16	Mid-priced meat-based entrees, possibly coming with a soup or salad. Tip will bump you up a couple dollars, since you'll probably have a waiter or waitress.
❹	$16-20	A somewhat fancy restaurant or a steakhouse. Either way, you'll have a special knife. Few restaurants in this range have a dress code, but some may look down on t-shirt and jeans.
❺	$20 and up	Food with foreign names and a decent wine list. Dress to impress, and don't order PB&J.

DISCOVER THE SOUTHWEST USA

While the vastness of the Southwestern desert, the dramatically colored canvas of Arizona's red rock, sandstone, scrub brush, and pale sky, and the breathtaking vistas from Utah's mountains all invite contemplation, awe, and photo-ops, the opportunity for mild and extreme outdoor activities defines a side of the region that Kodak cannot capture. Be it hiking in Zion National Park, biking near Moab, bouldering at Hueco Tanks, rafting the Colorado, backpacking the remote Gila Wilderness, or skiing the slopes of northern Utah, the rich and varied potential for outdoor adventure is unparalleled.

WHEN TO GO

Most tourists and vacationers descend upon the Southwest's sights during the summer, when the Grand Canyon and other national parks strain to accommodate the influx of visitors. However, during the summer, some of the low desert sights along the southern periphery of the Southwest are simply too hot to enjoy. In the winter, ski season heats up and even the high deserts don a layer of sparkling white on their red-rock formations. Meanwhile, the low deserts along the Mexican border afford a mild refuge of year-round warmth. All things considered, the best time to catch the region at its best may well be spring, when the Grand Canyon is not yet packed, the low deserts sport blooming wildflowers, and the high deserts have already emerged from winter's snow and ice. Fall can also be rather mild.

THINGS TO DO

NATURE'S PLAYGROUND

HIKING & BACKPACKING (HIGH & LOW). The sheer number of destinations and variety of terrain can make hiking the Southwest a confusing proposition. The upside: if you know what you want, you can find it. In Utah, red-rock turrets and the amazing Narrows Trail of **Zion** (p. 272) contrast with astounding slickrock and the Turret Arch Trail found in **Arches** (p. 280). Go off the beaten path in popular **national parks** by making a rim-to-rim trek through the **Grand Canyon** (p. 73) or by hiking **Death Valley** (p. 172) and its myriad washes in winter. The **Weminuche Wilderness** between **Durango** (p. 333) and **Creede** (p. 352) boasts alpine hiking galore. Great opportunities for long **backpacking** treks exist in the well-trod **Pecos Wilderness** (p. 399), the **Gila National Forest** (p. 428), and in the hidden **Great Basin National Park,** NV (p. 239). For a little of everything, **Big Bend** (p. 458) fits the bill, with great hikes both in the high Chisos Mountains and in the lowlands along the Río Grande. For more hiking and backpacking opportunities, see **In the Middle of Nowhere** (p. 3).

MOUNTAIN BIKING. The secret's out. Everyone knows that **Moab** (p. 272) and its slickrock has the best mountain biking in the West. Of course, **Durango** (p. 333) is right behind, offering trails in the foothills and mountains north of town. Not as

TOP 10 MUST-DOS

In the Southwest, adrenaline flows like wine and adventurers instinctively flock like the salmon of Capistrano.

1. Hike the Grand Canyon (p. 73). Drop down the South Kaibab Trail to the deepest depths of Nature's magnum opus.

2. Mountain bike Moab (p. 272). Make the pilgrimage to the Mecca of mountain biking for trails like you never imagined.

3. Explore Zion's Narrows (p. 305). It may take a guide, but navigating these slot canyons is an experience you won't forget.

4. Ski Utah's slopes (p. 254). It's no mystery why the Winter Olympics came: world-class skiing is standard.

5. Monument Valley on horseback (p. 136). You'll feel like John Wayne in the quintessential scenery of the West.

6. Havasupai Waterfalls (p. 82). The ethereal cascades on the Havasupai Reservation easily merit a trek in from the South Rim.

7. Rock out at Joshua Tree (p. 158). Endless bouldering awaits among the austere trees behind the name.

8. Party in Tempe (p. 103) The wildest area in the Southwest is arguably the party scene at ASU.

9. Ice climb Ouray (p. 350). Sharpen your ice axe, learn what "crampons" are, and experience the frosty side of getting vertical.

10. A night on the town: Vegas (p. 197). Sidle up and throw the bones: Lady Luck lives in Sin City.

well-known are the singletrack trails near **Taos** (p. 404), **Crested Butte** (p. 371), and **Flagstaff,** especially around **Sedona** (p. 120). The miles of trail surrounding **Lake Tahoe** (p. 223) promise enough riding to exhaust anyone, whatever your skill level.

CLIMBING. Adventurous travelers know they can count on **Moab** (p. 272) for awesome climbing, but the massive boulders of **Joshua Tree** (p. 158) offer the true paradise, providing fodder for thousands of climbers at a time. **Zion National Park** (p. 299), **Hueco Tanks** (p. 451), **Black Canyon** (p. 369), **Unaweep Canyon** (p. 367), and the **Bishop** (p. 188) area round out the Southwest's best climbing spots. **Ouray** (p. 350) invites climbers to scale walls of frozen water, making it the region's premier ice climbing destination.

RIVER RUNNING. The wild rivers that rage in the Southwest carve the region's canyons, but they also bear brave rafters and kayakers down their rapids. The **Green and Yampa Rivers** in **Dinosaur National Monument** (p. 263) are among the area's most scenic rivers, though they require permits. The Gunnison roars through **Black Canyon** (p. 369), near Montrose, and the **Río Grande** provides entertaining rapids through **Taos Box** (p. 411) but peters out by the time it reaches **Big Bend** (p. 458). The **Colorado** runs near **Moab** (p. 272) and careens through the **Grand Canyon** (p. 73).

SKIING. Even before it received the Olympic nod, the **Salt Lake City** area claimed to have the greatest snow on earth. The best skiing is located near **Park City** (p. 252) and **Ogden.** In southwestern Colorado, **Telluride** (p. 344), **Purgatory** (p. 341), **Silverton** (p. 341), and **Crested Butte** (p. 371) all have first-rate slopes. **Taos Ski Valley** (p. 410) is strictly for experts, boasting some of the region's most difficult terrain. The numerous peaks that ring **Lake Tahoe** (p. 227), also a former Olympic host, provide powder for top-notch skiing that straddles two states.

SPELUNKING. If you've had enough of the Southwest's sun, its **subterranean wonders** will cool you off and stun you with intricate beauty. **Carlsbad Caverns** (p. 442) is the most developed of the lot; **Lehman Cave** (p. 242) is the least-visited. Other regional caves include **Timpanogos Cave** (p. 326), **Kartchner Caverns** (p. 145), and **Lava River Cave** (p. 116).

SCINTILLATING SCENERY. Though experiencing many of the Southwest's wonders requires hiking boots or harnesses, other regional highlights involve merely snapping a few photos and taking in the impressive view. The granddaddy of all views, the **Grand Canyon** (p. 73), won't disappoint, but if you are looking for less-crowded canyon rim vistas, you

might check out **Canyon de Chelly** (p. 130) or **Black Canyon of the Gunnison** (p. 369). Other canyon wonders include the falls of **Havasupai Reservation** (p. 82) and the hoodoos of **Bryce Canyon** (p. 307). Rounding out the most spectacular photo-ops in the Southwest are the otherworldly volcanic pillars of **Chiricahua** (p. 155) and the alpine majesty of the **Ruby Mountains** (p. 232). Look for awe-inspiring scenic drives, like the **Apache Trail** (p. 107), throughout this guide.

IN THE MIDDLE OF NOWHERE

If you're looking for unspoiled land to play modern-day adventurer or fulfill your extreme backcountry urges, the Southwest is the best place south of Alaska to find untrammelled wilderness. Though the Southwest's **deserts** should not be explored without precaution (see **The Desert & You**, p. 66), a backcountry trip into arid climes will appeal to solitude-seeking travelers and stringent ascetics. **Grand Staircase-Escalante National Monument** (p. 314) offers almost two million acres of sandstone narrows and sedimentary stair-steps down toward Lake Powell. The **Black Rock Desert** (p. 216) features the **Burning Man** (p. 218), immense stretches of playa, and some of the most remote canyons and mountains in the nation. To the southwest, occasional dirt roads mark **Mojave National Preserve** (p. 170), but the park's cinder cones and sand dunes are set amid large chunks of desert wilderness. On the Mexican border, **Organ Pipe National Monument** (p. 148) presents visitors with great winter biking through stands of cacti. Finally, eastern Utah's vast **Canyonlands National Park** (p. 285) is criss-crossed only by the occasional four-wheel-drive road, making it a true backpacker's delight.

While the Southwest is known for its deserts, its **mountain wilderness** deserves equal attention. The scrubby **Guadalupe Mountains** (p. 452) make for an unknown, sparsely traveled desert in the sky. In the heavily developed Colorado Rockies, the **Weminuche Wilderness** (p. 338) is a haven of tranquility from strip-mall civilization. East of Salt Lake City, is the **Uinta Wilderness** (p. 269), which also provides an alternative to the heavily-trafficked trails of the Wasatch Range. Finally, Nevada's rugged **Ruby Mountains** (p. 232) are a still-glaciated range of jagged peaks and placid alpine lakes, perhaps the most rugged of the Southwest's several alpine ranges.

ARCHAEOLOGY

Cradling some of the oldest ancient cultures in North America, the Southwest offers great opportunities to explore remnants of the past. One of the best sites is **Canyon de Chelly** (p. 130), home to indigenous peoples for almost five millennia. **Chaco Culture National Historical Park** (p. 415), maintains the first great settlement of the Ancestral Puebloans, dating to the 9th century. Encompassing 33,000 acres of wilderness with 70 miles of trails, **Bandelier** (p. 398) features spectacular cliff dwellings and stone houses. **Mesa Verde** (p. 356) is the only national park set aside exclusively for archaeological remains and offers views of 13th-century Ancestral Puebloan cliff dwellings. In Utah, the **Nine-Mile Canyon** (p. 261) houses the world's most concentrated collection of prehistoric rock art, dating to the first century AD. Several locales serve not only as archaeological sites, but also as sites of contemporary inhabitation. **Taos Pueblo** (p. 408) contains homes between 700 and 1000 years old and is the oldest continuously inhabited settlement in the US.

CITIES

TUCSON, ARIZONA. Arguably the cosmopolitan center of Arizona, Tucson offers world-class museums, entertainment, a diverse population, and bustling nightlife. The local outdoors attractions of **Saguaro National Park** (p. 145) and **Sabino Canyon**

DISCOVER

■ LET'S GO PICKS

BEST PLACE TO SEE GROWN MEN CRY: Every January, cowboys and ranchers stampede into Elko, NV for the annual **Cowboy Poetry Festival** (p. 234), drawing herds of admirers.

BEST PLACE TO HEAR THE SAND SING: Visit the dunes of **Eureka Valley** (p. 191) near **Bishop,** CA, or the **Mojave National Preserve** (p. 170) and listen for the deep hum created by friction in the sand beneath your feet.

BEST PLACE TO SHARE THE TRAIL WITH A PRO: Tie—**Moab,** UT (p. 272) may have eclipsed **Durango,** CO (p. 333) as the mountain bike capital of the US, but both towns cater to biking fanatics and feature some of the country's most thrilling rides.

BEST PLACE TO BE IN A WESTERN: Immortalized on Hollywood celluloid, the landscapes of **Monument Valley,** AZ (see p.136) and **Lone Pine,** CA (p.183) have served as sets for loads of films, including *Bonanza* and *Rawhide* in Lone Pine and *Stage Coach* in Monument Valley.

BEST PLACE TO GO WILD: Most describe the week-long **Burning Man** festival as "indescribable." In late summer, Nevada's **Black Rock Desert** morphs into a thriving city, ruled only by a sense of fun, abandon, and community. See p. 218; better yet, just go.

BEST PLACE TO PRETEND YOU'RE AN OLYMPIAN: Plummet lightning-fast down the year-round **bobsled** course or try your hand at **freestyle aerial jumping** into Olympic Park's splash pool (p. 252), both in Salt Lake City, UT, of course.

BEST PLACE TO STUMBLE UPON ANCIENT RUINS: Southwestern Colorado's excellent **Mesa Verde National Park** (p. 356) brims with haunting Pueblo ruins, but you have to hike in and find them yourself.

BEST PLACE TO SOLVE YOUR PROBLEMS: Tie—For perplexing bouldering problems, **Joshua Tree National Park** (p. 172) and **Hueco Tanks** (p. 451), near El Paso, are rock gardens *par excellence*.

BEST HIKING FOR NIGHTOWLS: On full moon summer nights, **White Sands National Monument** (p. 432) stays open late. Doff your boots, climb the dunes, and howl at the moon.

BEST PLACE TO ISSUE AN ULTIMATUM: Kick back, relax, and play some hardball "truth or dare" in the awesome hot springs of **Truth or Consequences,** NM (p. 421).

BEST PLACE TO HAVE A CLOSE ENCOUNTER: With its annual UFO Festival, **Roswell,** NM (p. 438) is famously crazy about aliens. If a UFO crashed near your town, you would be too.

(p. 147) make easy daytrips, while longer treks lead to **Organ Pipe Cactus National Monument** (p. 148), hikes in the **Coronado National Forest** (p. 149), Mexican **border towns,** and the thriving small town of **Bisbee** (p. 153).

ALBUQUERQUE, NEW MEXICO. The **Sandía** (p. 384) and lesser-known **Manzano Mountains** (p. 386) tower over the city to the west, seeming to watch over the historic buildings of Albuquerque's **Old Town** (p. 382) as well as the city's many delicious restaurants in all price ranges. These surrounding mountains offer plentiful hiking, biking, and skiing opportunities for the tourists who fly or drive into Albuquerque each day.

PHOENIX, ARIZONA. The hub of all hubs, sprawling Phoenix is the most convenient destination for flights headed to the Southwest. Nearly equidistant from both Flagstaff and Tucson, this city can easily be the first stop on any journey to the state of Arizona (or elsewhere in the Southwest). Take the time to explore Phoenix's own gems before setting out into the wilds of the rest of the region: visit Frank Lloyd Wright's **Taliesin West** (p. 105), drive the nearby **Apache Trail** (p. 107), and wander through the **Heard Museum** (p. 104).

SANTA FE, NEW MEXICO. Though the city's accommodations and food are pricey, hiking in the **Pecos Wilderness** (p. 399), biking near **Los Alamos** (p. 401), viewing **Bandelier's** (p. 398) dwellings, and visiting pueblos on the **High Road** (p. 397) provide sufficient escape from the city's glitz and glamor.

SALT LAKE CITY, UTAH. Host to the 2002 Olympics, Salt Lake City has undergone a facelift over the past several years, and now, with premier **skiing** and **rock climbing** near **Park City** (p. 252), a host of new ethnic restaurants, and an improving nightlife, SLC is ready to become a tourist city of a new-and-improved order. And remember, the **Uintas** (p. 270) and **Dinosaur National Monument** (p. 263) are only a hop, skip, and a jump away.

LAS VEGAS, NEVADA. The gloriously overdone city of sin, filled with grandiosely outfitted casinos and entertainment spectaculars, offers enough decadence for a lifetime. Balance out your time with a visit to the water sport paradise of **Lake Mead** (p. 209), a visit to **Red Rocks** (p. 208), and a tour of **Hoover Dam** (p. 209).

SUGGESTED ITINERARIES

NEW MEXICO (2 WEEKS)

drag at high noon in Billy the Kid's hometown. To the east, **White Sands National Monument** (p. 432) evokes lunar expanses with its rolling sand dunes. Camping here is a coveted privilege, but worth it, so be sure to arrive early. Even farther east, near the Texas border, the **Carlsbad Caverns** (p. 442) promise hours of harrowing spelunking. During the summer, dusk brings a magnificent spectacle as thousands of bats storm from Carlsbad's caves in search of a midnight snack. Return to the light of day and strike out north for artsy **Taos** (p. 404), one of New Mexico's funkiest cities.

NEW MEXICO (2 WEEKS)

After your plane (or hot air balloon) touches down in **Albuquerque** (p. 378), scoot west to the fascinating rock inscriptions, lava tubes, and natural arches of the **El Malpais and El Morro National Monuments** (p. 420). The monuments pass crazy lava terrain, imposing arches, and centuries-old rock art. Soak off a hard day's hike in the hot-springs-heavy **Truth or Consequences** (p. 421), one of New Mexico's quirkiest little towns, with the name to prove it. Glimpse the ancient stone and timber pueblos of the **Gila Cliff Dwellings** (p. 430) from behind the wheel, but be prepared to step out of your rig in the **Gila National Forest** (p. 428), the Southwest's largest. The nearby town of **Silver City** (p. 426) grants a look into the Old West, and it still takes some guts to walk down the main

CALI, NEVADA, & UTAH (3 WEEKS)

CALI, NEVADA, & UTAH (3 WEEKS)

Tent in tow, fly into **Phoenix** (p. 95), Arizona, the major hub city of the Southwest. From there, take off straight across the desert to California for some bouldering in legendary **Joshua Tree National Park** (p. 158). The spooky trees that give the park its name surround some of the best granite problems in the country. Next, head north for the desolate solitude of **Death Valley National Park** (p. 172), though the typically record-setting summer heat may have you wishing it was winter or fall. Nearby along the border between California and Nevada is majestic **Lake Tahoe** (p. 223), which draws travelers in every season. From excellent cross-country skiing to spring and summertime canoeing, Tahoe and the villages that ring its crystal blue waters have it all, including several glitzy casinos. Tear east along I-80 into Nevada and pull into **Elko** (p. 232), a bustling old mining town where the cowboys are free to sip cosmopolitans. The jagged **Ruby Mountains** (p. 232) flank the outskirts of this booming northern Nevada hub, sheltering one of the Southwest's best-kept secrets within their pristine alpine peaks. From Elko, head out to Utah, stopping by the capital, **Salt Lake City** (p. 246), for some good, clean family fun before bombing down the slopes of the numerous world-class **ski mountains** nearby (p. 252). Some of the best powder in the world sits on these peaks, which recently hosted the 2002 Winter Olympics. Heading southeast in the state, don't even think of missing the top-notch biking on the slickrock trails of **Moab** (p. 272); if you prefer to set out on foot rather than on two wheels, Moab allows adventurers to hike, backpack, and canyoneer in some of the most rugged terrain the West has to offer. Just outside of town is **Canyonlands National Park** (p. 285), which will prime you for the miles of canyon country to come on your trip. Back west, a visit to three of the most magnificent natural locales in the entire country awaits. **Grand Staircase-Escalante** (p. 314) sprawls across the countryside in wild, untrodden leaps and bounds, while **Bryce Canyon** (p. 307) tempts your curious nature with its mysterious hoodoos. Crowded **Zion** (p. 299) somehow accommodates the seemingly endless hordes of tourists who visit it every year—the park's limit-testing canyoneering opportunities may have something to do with this. Catch your breath as you head across into Arizona, where the mother of all views (and tourist destinations) awaits: the famous **Grand Canyon** (p. 73).

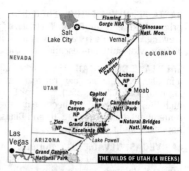

THE WILDS OF UTAH (4 WEEKS)

THE WILDS OF UTAH (4 WEEKS)

Tour the sites, both religious and secular, of **Salt Lake City** (p. 246), or follow the paths of Olympians at nearby **ski mountains** (p. 252). The peaks thrill in any season, but winters promise to be unforgettable. To the east, the town of **Vernal** (p. 258) caters to travelers eager to run the Green River in the awesome **Dinosaur National Monument** (p. 263). Some of the best rapids in the West lie along the waterway in the middle of a vast archaeological wonderland. Just north, anglers lure world-class trout at the reservoir in **Flaming Gorge National Recreation Area** (p. 266). Cruise the longer-than-advertised **Nine-Mile Canyon** (p. 261) on your way to experiencing Mother Nature's more creative side at **Arches** (p. 280) and **Canyonlands National Parks** (p. 285). Delivering on its name, Arches boasts the richest collection of rock arches in the world. Canyonlands, to the south, protects some of the most desolate expanses of southern Utah, providing three areas for backcountry exploration. Near the parks, **Moab** (p. 272) attracts biking enthusiasts from all over to tear across its famed slickrock trails. The gravity-defying spans of **Natural Bridges National Monument** (p. 296) make miles of hard rock appear as malleable as clay, as arches launch themselves over running rivers below. **Capitol Reef** (p. 320), known for its dome-shaped rock structure, tempts the sweet tooth in all of us with a campground where visitors eat fresh fruit right off the trees. Rugged and gorgeous **Bryce National Park** (p. 307) and **Grand Staircase-Escalante National Monument** (p. 314) are a hiker or backpacker's dream. Grand Staircase represents 1.9 million acres of barely explored wilds, offering some of the best four-wheeling in the West. Bryce's downright odd hoodoo rock formations are sure to be one of the more memorable aspects of your trip. Next, set your bearings southwest because the Mormon pioneers might not have been wrong in calling the **Zion National Park** (p. 299) region the "promised land." Straddling the Utah-Arizona border, the blue stretches of **Lake Powell** (p. 87) disappear behind innumerable canyons lining its shores. Follow the canyons from Lake Powell until you meet one that seemingly never ends: the **Grand Canyon** (p. 73), perhaps the country's greatest attraction. The more rugged and untrodden North Rim is a good bet for those looking to beat tourist throngs. End your odyssey in the wildest place that the Southwest has to offer: **Las Vegas** (p. 197).

A LITTLE OF EVERYTHING (4-5 WEEKS)

Get a cheap airfare to **Las Vegas** (p. 197) and gamble away what you saved. Set out east to two of Arizona's coolest destinations: **Flagstaff** (p. 111) and **Sedona** (p. 120), home to free-spirited folk, and their outdoor activities are some of the best around. Just north, the **Grand Canyon** (p. 73) unfailingly delights each traveler who stands on its rim, forgetting that he's on the ground and gazing over miles of painfully beautiful desert and canyon. Next, cut north into Utah. **Capitol Reef** (p. 320) combines

all the attractive, eccentric features of southern Utah's national parks in one area. Pick up more film and head to **Moab** (p. 272) for mountain biking and **Canyonlands** (p. 285) and **Arches National Parks** (p. 280). Backcountry delights abound in two of Utah's more remote national parks. Saddle up again and take sheer delight in the mountains of **Durango** (p. 333). From here, a trip to the archaeological nirvana of **Mesa Verde National Park** (p. 356) allows you to hike among ancient ruins. Head south to the otherwordly formations of **El Malpais** and **El Morro National Monuments** (p. 420). The stunning dunes of **White Sands National Monument** (p. 432) roll to the southeast, where camping under the moon will surely be a highlight. Along the Texas border, **Carlsbad Caverns** (p. 442) shelter an enormous underground world of caves and rock formations. Don't forget your flashlight! A little farther south, **Guadalupe Mountains National Park** (p. 452) lies just over the Texas border, offering fantastic, remote hiking. One of the Southwest's wackiest destinations, **Roswell** (p. 438) claims to be the site of a UFO crash landing. You'll feel like you're in another world when you witness how much the town revolves around extra-terrestrials. In **Santa Fe** (p. 388), evidence of early European civilization blends with modern art in one of the state's most intriguing spots. The authentic Mexican food at the Farmer's Market is worth a taste.

A LITTLE OF EVERYTHING (4-5 WEEKS)

LIFE & TIMES

While the Southwest is best known for its dramatic landscape and recreational activities, its kaleidoscopic mix of cultures is just as intriguing. The history of this multi-culturalism's rise is one of struggle and strife, as Anglo and Spanish colonial powers fought for centuries to stake their claims in the region, wresting its lands and resources from the Native peoples who had lived here in relative peace. The influences of this three-way clash are still very present throughout the Southwest, and the legacy of the American frontier stretches on into the twenty-first century, bringing many to the Southwest who simply want to escape mainstream culture. True to the eccentric spirit of the land, the Southwest calls itself home to hippies, cowboys and cowboys-at-heart, New Age spiritualists, Native Americans, Mexicans and Mexican-Americans, government scientists, aging conservatives, liberal outdoor junkies, transplanted suburban families, and droves of tourists who have rambled their way here, to the true American desert.

HISTORY

PRE-EUROPEAN SOUTHWEST (BEFORE 1492)

Archaeologists now estimate that the first Southwesterners were big game hunters who arrived in the Southwest at least 25,000 years ago, having crossed over from Asia along the frozen Bering Strait near present-day Alaska. Knowledge of the earliest distinct culture was solidified in the 1930s, when the discovery of prehistoric spear points provided concrete evidence of the Clovis people, a society of hunters and gatherers who settled in the Southwest around 9500 BC. Over the next several centuries, drastic environmental changes transformed the region into the desert land that we associate with the Southwest today. Evidence suggests that by 3500 BC, the region's dwellers had capitalized on the warmer climate to begin agricultural civilizations.

Between 500 and 100 BC, three major cultures surfaced in the area that we now call the Southwest. From around 500-300 BC, the **Mogollon** people arrived at the Arizona/New Mexico border and established what may have been the region's first true farming civilization. While the Mogollon culture seems to have died out around AD 1200, it is likely that the Mogollon may have survived to become the modern **Zuni**. The **Hohokam,** a second farming culture, migrated from modern-day Mexico around 300 BC and settled farther west in southern Arizona. With the help of highly advanced agricultural and technical innovations, they expanded their civilization into the Tucson Basin, the Phoenix area, and even to modern-day Flagstaff, peaking in prosperity between AD 1100 and 1200. The last of these three major civilizations the **Ancestral Puebloans** emerged around 100 BC in the Four Corners area, and moved from a foraging way of life to farming around AD 400, adopting the pueblo pattern of living around AD 700. The Ancestral Puebloans, formerly known as the **Anasazi,** flourished in the Great Pueblo Period, from AD 1100-1300, before their mysterious decline in the 13th century. While the notion of the Anasazi "disappearance" is common, it is more likely that they migrated from the Four Corners region and provided the ancestry of modern-day pueblo-inhabiting Native Americans, such as the Hopi.

The most recent additions to the civilizations of the Southwest prior to the arrival of Europeans were the nomadic tribes of the **Navajo** and the **Apache,** known in Navajo language as *Dineh.* The **Dineh,** originally inhabitants of the subarctic, most likely arrived in the Southwest around AD 1450. Tension immediately developed between the nomads and settled agricultural peoples. Though the Navajo subsequently developed a lifestyle that was relatively settled in comparison to the nomadic Apache, both civilizations remained at odds with the Pueblo Indians.

THE ERA OF THE SPANISH

After four survivors from a 1527 Spanish shipwreck off the coast of Florida spent nine years traveling west, ultimately arriving in the town of Culiacán in New Spain, they came with tales of the gold-filled **"Seven Cities of Cibola,"** otherwise known as the adobe pueblos of New Mexico. Fascinated by these tales, the Spanish government sent **Francisco Vásquez de Coronado** on a mission to conquer the land in 1540. Equipped with hundreds of soldiers and horses, Coronado made his way to Zuni territory on an expedition which marked the beginning of the Spanish era of the Southwest. However, the government of New Spain did not officially begin its period of colonization until the turn of the 17th century, at which point the influx of soldiers and horses came accompanied by fleets of priests on a mission to pacify and Christianize the Indians.

Although the Spanish occupation of the Southwest was based on the themes of assimilation and Christianization rather than the theme of annihilation that characterized the later Anglo-American presence, the relationship between Native tribes and Spanish settlers was less than peaceful. The Spanish encouraged active slave trading, brought disease, occupied native land, and often violently repressed the practice of indigenous religious beliefs. In return, Native American groups, including the Puebloans, the Apaches, and the Navajos, often mounted determined resistance, as was seen especially in the Pueblo Revolt of 1680, when the Puebloans managed to drive the Spanish from Santa Fe for several years. Due to factionalism among the Puebloans, however, the Spanish were able to achieve reconquest in 1692 and maintained power for the next 125 years, until Mexico gained independence from Spain in 1821.

ANGLO EXPANSION

While tensions between the United States and Mexico continued to grow, religious tensions within the US forced the Mormons westward. Joseph Smith, who founded the Church of Jesus Christ of Latter-day Saints in New York in the early-1830s, was killed in an instance of religious persecution in 1844. The religion's new leader, Brigham Young, set off for the West in search of both freedom of worship for Mormons and the idyllic lands described by adventurer John Fremont. In 1847, Young and 148 followers charted a course along the Oregon Trail and settled at the Great Salt Lake.

Although the Mormons found a haven in the wild expanses of the West, the region proved too small for neighboring countries contesting its settlement. The US declared war on Mexico in May 1846 and three months later claimed New Mexico as American land. One year prior, the US had annexed the Republic of Texas, an independent nation comprising present-day Texas that had won its independence from Mexico in 1836. In 1848, the **Treaty of Guadalupe Hidalgo** ceded a large portion of Southwestern land to the US. Five years later, the **Gadsden Purchase** added the remaining portions of what is today known as Arizona and New Mexico. By 1853, Mexico had ceded the territories that would eventually make up southwestern Texas, Arizona, New Mexico, Utah, Nevada, and California.

The US encroached on Native lands and life with political and military aggression. The creation of the Bureau of Indian Affairs in 1824, and its inclusion as a wing of the War Department, gave the government sweeping control over Western lands and served as an auger of tumultuous times to come. Andrew Jackson's massive force marched tribes such as the Cherokee and Choctaw on the **Trail of Tears** (from the Southeastern United States to what is now Oklahoma) in the 1830s. The 1850s saw the US government build **Fort Defiance** on Navajo land, forcing Navajos to negotiate for their own land and water. Anger over this and other encroachments led to the **Navajo-Apache Wars,** which pitted the Navajo in Arizona and Apache in New Mexico against the federal government for the next 20 years.

Between 1863 and 1864, in one of the most tragic and infamous events of the Navajo-Apache Wars and all of American history, **Kit Carson** rounded up over 8000 Navajo and led them on the **Long Walk.** This "walk," a winter-long death march during which people starved and were shot for walking too slowly, ended at the concentration camp at Bosque Redondo, where many Navajo and Apache died. In 1868, the Navajo signed the **Treaty of Bosque Redondo** with the US government, through which they were allowed to return to their land and received a scant 10% of their original territory. In exchange, they agreed not to conduct war against the US, not to carry firearms, and to send their children to white schools, where they would be forced to learn English and assimilate with every aspect of white culture.

In part because the land the Navajo received was unfit for grazing and lacked suitable water sources, the treaty set off a new period of **Navajo-Hopi land disputes.** Since the Hopi did not participate in the wars, they were not included in the dubious terms of the treaty, and the lands that were designated as the Navajo Reservation land conflicted with the lands that the Hopi had called home for centuries. In 1882, the government set boundaries around a 2.5 million acre area enclosed in Navajo land for the Hopi Reservation.

While Native Americans struggled for rights to life and land, Anglo settlement in Arizona and New Mexico continued in full-force, and with it the booming industries of mining and the railroad. Despite the fact that the region was becoming increasingly profitable and established within the US economy, statehood for Arizona and New Mexico was put off for longer than any of the other states in the contiguous US, largely as a result of the anti-Hispanic racism that prevailed in Congress and many American minds. Both states joined the Union in 1912.

TODAY

Throughout the 20th century, Native Americans struggled to defend their rights of access and ownership to the natural resources on their reservations, while the US government sought to reap the economic benefits of Southwestern land.

MINING

While agriculture has always provided a backbone for Southwestern economies, the 20th century introduced mainlining as the other lifeline of the economy. Two years after oil was discovered on the Navajo Reservation in 1922, Congress passed the **Indian Oil Leasing Act,** which gave the states royalties from all oil produced on Indian lands. The barren land granted to the Navajos had proven valuable to US interests after all, and the discovery ushered in another century of conflict. In 1937, **coal** and **natural gas** were also found on the Reservation, and the 1938 **Indian Lands Mining Act** gave the US Bureau of Indian Affairs broad powers over all the Reservation's natural resources. Huge mining projects were underway on indigenous land several years before Arizona Indians were even granted the right to vote in US elections in 1948.

LAND RIGHTS

Land-use controversy is not, of course, limited to conflicts between the US government and Native Americans. Environmentalists concerned with the effects of mining and damming, and with the preservation of endangered species and habitats, have time and again butted heads with locals who value the economic benefits of such projects and ideologically resent the government regulation of local land. Throughout the 20th century, several **Sagebrush Rebellions** arose throughout the Southwest as protests against federal land regulation laws, demanding more area land for private use.

WATER

The struggle for ownership and access to water supplies is one that has taken center stage on many fronts. Not only do water rights provide fodder for the continual struggles of Native Americans seeking to gain and maintain control of the water on their lands, but it has sparked ongoing controversy between private economic interests and environmentalists. Recently, farmers and fishermen have tangled with preservationists who long to close off certain waterways in an effort to protect endangered species of fish and other wildlife. Between August 2001 and August 2002, the Southwest experienced its driest year in recorded history and felt the effects of forest fires in dozens of parks and wilderness areas. Despite the regional shortage, water use in burgeoning cities is increasing dramatically and threatening the survival of the ecosystem.

THE NUCLEAR AGE

The first atomic bomb was detonated at the **Trinity site,** northwest of Alamogordo, New Mexico, on July 16, 1945. With wide-open spaces and a relatively sparse population, many areas of the Southwest seemed and continue to seem the perfect locales for nuclear power plants, and many Southwesterners embraced the local presence of atomic power for its jobs and revenue. At the same time, the environmental costs of nuclear research stations and power plants appear to be immense, and concerns over issues including **nuclear waste disposal** and **transport** have created constant controversy. In 1951, Nevada welcomed a nuclear test site to the state, but today many Nevadans are singing a different tune as **Yucca Mountain** (90 miles from Las Vegas) readies itself to serve as a depository for highly radioactive nuclear waste despite substantial legal resistance by state lawmakers.

OTHER WORLDS

In the 1950s, a remote tract of land on Groom Lake dubbed **Area 51** by the federal government became a symbol for alleged US government UFO cover-ups after tales of **UFO sightings** surfaced. In 1947, an unidentified flying object allegedly crashed down in the town of **Roswell,** New Mexico (p. 438) and was then alledgedly snatched by the US government as part of an elaborate conspiracy to cover up evidence of extraterrestrial life.

GO WEST, YOUNG MAN

A population boom has left New Mexico with more than three times as many residents as in 1940, and the Arizona population has multiplied by an astounding ten times in the same period. Over the last 25 years, Nevada has been the fastest growing state in the country, and the city of Las Vegas, born less than 100 years ago, is now home to over one million people. Recently, the 2002 Winter Olympics in Salt Lake City drew unprecedented attention to Utah.

LIFE & TIMES

PEOPLE

DEMOGRAPHICS

The Southwest was the last region of the continental United States acquired by the American government and thus the last part of the United States exposed to Anglo colonization and development. This historical fact has visible manifestations in the demography of the Southwest. Whereas in much of the United States Native peoples have been reduced to tiny proportions of the population, in the Southwest large-scale Native communities have survived into the present, maintaining their traditional pueblo culture and way of life.

Similarly, Mexico's stake in the region is visible in the population of the Southwest; to a greater extent than anywhere else in the US, Spanish is a public language, and Mexicans and Mexican-Americans form a sizeable portion of the community. Even within the Mexican-American community, diversity is the rule; some Mexican-Americans are recent immigrants, while others' families have histories in the area older than the United States. Economically, some individuals and communities have thrived, while others still struggle toward the American dream.

Though not a large presence, the Basque people, hailing from the area around the Pyrenees of northern Spain and southern France, bring to the Southwest their unique cuisine and sheep-herding culture. Nevada and California claim two of the three largest concentration of Basques in the US. The mountainous areas of these two states nurtured favorable conditions for the Basques to continue herding.

Even the Anglo settlement in the Southwest is distinguished by considerable diversity. At roughly the same time the Mormons were making their historic pilgrimage to Utah, a mid-19th century gold and silver rush created a Southwestern culture of outlaws and opportunists. Cheap land and isolation soon brought more newcomers and increased the region's agricultural focus. The 20th century saw a large-scale migration of artists, new-age spiritualists, extreme sports enthusiasts, and other counter-culturalists to the area. Today, the Southwest is truly one of the most multi-faceted regions of a nation known for its melting-pot diversity.

CULTURE

FOOD & DRINK

Southwestern cuisine emerged from a blend of **Mexican, Spanish,** and **Native American** cooking, so traveling in the region will certainly bring you your fill of burritos, tacos, and enchiladas. Still, you'll find these Mexican tortilla-based entrees balanced out with the **Three Sisters** of corn, beans, and squash, all traditionally grown by Southwestern tribes. When traveling through reservations, be sure to try **Navajo fry bread,** not unlike the indulgent fried dough found at fairs and carnivals.

Stemming from this blend of culinary traditions is **Tex-Mex** food, a synthesis of Old and New World ingredients that dominates the menus of the Southwest. An amalgam of Northern Mexico's peasant fare and Texas cowboy favorites, Tex-Mex obeys the American tradition of being both native to its region while foreign in its roots. The tortillas, rice, and beans typically associated with Tex-Mex are stamples of Mexican cuisine, while the meat and chili used in many dishes are descendants of the hearty cuisine of Texas and long-haul cowboys. The growing popularity of Mexican food is evidence of the success of this fusion style; most items served at Mexican restaurants are actually not traditional dishes but examples of the Tex-

Mex tradition. While eateries serving burritos, nachos, and tacos are spring up all over the US, the Southwest claims the cuisine's most authentic outposts.

Chiles are perhaps the most famous of all Southwestern foods. More than any other item, this one ingredient is synonymous with and emblematic of Southwestern cuisine. The heat of a chili is measured in **Scoville Units.** While the bell pepper measures in with a rating of 0, the red habanero has been tested at 577,000 Scoville Units. The jalapeño pales in comparison, at about 5000. Be prepared to hear the same question over and over when ordering in restaurants: red or green? This refers to the color of the chiles that will be used in your meal. A combination of the two can be referred to as "Christmas."

CUSTOMS & ETIQUETTE

The standards for civil behavior in the Southwest are much the same as those for the rest of the country. Bargaining is futile, except in the purchase of real-estate and automobiles.

UTAH

Most of Utah's inhabitants are Mormons, who comprise over 70% of the total population of the state. The prevalence of the religion and devotion of its followers make Utah a uniquely more wholesome place than the other Southwestern states, especially more than traditionally free-wheeling California. Mormonism strictly forbids the consumption of alcohol, caffeine, nicotine, illicit drugs, and premarital sex. The Mormons will help you keep away from the bottle. The only spirit widely sold in Utah is watered down beer (3% alcohol by volume), and only "private clubs" can serve liquor. Local entrepreneurs have found ways to stretch the definition of "private club," so regular bars exist, but with cover charges and bizarre entry rituals. Dress is more modest in Utah than in other parts of the country; revealing clothing will fetch disapproving grimaces. Mormons are scrupulous about clean language, especially respect for the Lord's name, so avoid profanity. The Sabbath is also treated more seriously in Utah than in other parts of the US, so expect stores to be closed on Sunday and people to be less willing to work or play.

NATIVE RESERVATIONS

Crossing into a Native American reservation entails not only a change of administrative jurisdiction but also a wholesale change of culture. In the Southwest especially, Native Americans have resisted encroachment by Anglo culture onto their reservations and have preserved a distinct society. Customs and social mores vary from people to people; be aware of which tribe's land you're visiting and learn what behavior is expected of you ahead of time. Generally speaking, it doesn't hurt to dress conservatively and to be reserved in speech and demeanor. Visitors to the Navajo reservation should expect locals to be more withdrawn than their Anglo counterparts. Eye contact and chattiness are thought to be disrespectful, and many outsiders confuse Navajo politeness with standoffishness. Hopi tradition forbids the depiction of people in any medium; if you plan to visit the Hopi, leave your cameras and recorders behind.

THE ARTS

The highly distinctive aesthetic of the Southwest is the product of Native communities, its awesome natural landscape, and the numerous famous artists that it has attracted and inspired. Characterized by its earthy, organic qualities, Southwestern art gets as close to the spirit of the natural world as any other art in the US.

ARCHITECTURE

In part because of his innovative work throughout the Southwest, **Frank Lloyd Wright** forever changed thinking about architecture both in America and, to a lesser extent, around the world. Wright believed that designs for living spaces should be more "organic," or representative of their surroundings. Wright designed several buildings in Phoenix, including the Biltmore, and he established his school of architecture, Taliesin West, on the outskirts of the city. **Paolo Soleri,** a follower of Wright, studied at Taliesin West and established his own architectural project in Arizona called **Arcosanti** (see p. 126). About midway between Phoenix and Flagstaff, this planned community is Soleri's response to the fragmentation and isolation of modern America. He designed this communal townsite to blend in with the desert and foster a healthier, more organic lifestyle.

FINE ARTS

In Taos in 1915, a group of artists led by **Joseph Sharp** were enchanted by the beauty of the region and determined to share the area and its art with the rest of the American public. With this in mind, they decided to found the **Taos Society of Artists.** Though the group disbanded in 1927, their effort was not in vain. Ever since, Taos has been a thriving artistic community that still feeds on the natural beauty of the area.

At about the same time as the Taos group was forming out West, **Georgia O'Keeffe** was studying and teaching art in New York City. It was an apprenticeship that would soon find its inspiration in New Mexico, and though she lived on the east coast for much of her life, O'Keeffe became more and more infatuated with the Southwest. She finally moved there permanently after her husband (Alfred Stieglitz) died in 1946, and she spent the rest of her days in Abiquiu, southwest of Taos. She claimed to take her inspiration from the pure colors and forms she found in the high desert, and certainly, her large (and largely suggestive) flower canvases are singularly emblematic of Southwestern art for many.

As O'Keeffe is known for her flowers, so **Ansel Adams** is known for his black-and-white landscape photography. Though Adams is probably most remembered for his photos of Yosemite National Park and the High Sierra, much of his work was actually done within the boundaries of the Southwest. Commissioned to photograph the conditions of national parks by the Department of the Interior 1933-1942, he ventured across seven Western states with a stipend of $22 per day. In 1946, the Guggenheim gave Adams his first grant to photograph US national parks. Images of the Grand Canyon and a panorama of the Panamint Mountains from Badwater in Death Valley are among the Southwestern images he made famous.

Long before transplanted modernists were a presence in the Southwest, the landscape served as the medium and inspiration for the region's Native artists. Ancient native artwork bears witness to this fact still, as **petroglyphs** carved into rocks by the region's first inhabitants date back eons. The roots of **modern Native American art,** however, lie in the early 19th century. Though interactions with the United States varied greatly among Native peoples, the Government's aggressive removal policies created an occasion for Native American tribes to define themselves in relation to white America as a means of cultural preservation.

At the turn of the twentieth century, an archaeological discovery set in motion the career of one of the most famous Native American artists, **Maria Martinez.** Martinez, a member of the San Idelfonso Pueblo north of Santa Fe, was approached by archaeologists and asked to replicate ancient **pottery** samples. She lived at San Ildelfonso with her husband Julian for all of her almost century-long lifetime. Together, they perfected a technique for producing pottery that they shared freely with others and gained world-wide fame.

Two groups created early modern paintings in the late 1910s and 20s. One was led by **Carl Sweezy, Ernst Spybuck,** and the **Kiowa Five,** a group of Kiowa artists from Oklahoma including Spenser Asah, Jack Hokeah, Stephen Mopope, Lois Smokey, Monroe Tsatoke, and James Auchiah. Sweezy and Spybuck helped bring Native American art to an appreciative international market. The Kiowa Five—six before Smokey left—painted flat, 2D pictures of traditional native life and were active in aspects of native culture, especially dance. By the 1960s and 70s, artists like T.C. Cannon and Fritz Scholder pushed the genre in a more political direction, placing emphasis on individual pride in Native American cultural heritage.

Since the mid-80s, Native American painting has embraced many characteristics of postmodernism. Among the first Native American artists to utilize postmodern themes was **George Longfish,** whose highly political paintings, like other postmodern works, employ art as an occasion for moral performance in the form of resistance to cultural assimilation. Alongside modern developments in painting, traditional forms continue to thrive as a mainstay in Native American art, and both have gained an enormous following. The Southwest is the best region in the US for viewing traditional and modern Native American art. Both the Heard Museum of Phoenix and the Museum of New Mexico in Santa Fe display large collections of Native American art, while numerous festivals in the Southwest are dedicated solely to this growing genre.

LITERATURE

From frontier novels to naturalists' escapades to Native Americans' struggles, the literature of the Southwest is multi-faceted, layered with the experiences of different eras and cultures. These are just a few of the books integral to the development and flourishing of the regional canon:

Mark Twain, *Roughing It* (1872). Between 1861 and 1866, Twain (a.k.a. Samuel Clemens) traveled west through Salt Lake City and the Nevada desert, all the way to San Francisco, documenting his personal experiences with the West Coast silver rush.

John Wesley Powell, *Canyons of the Colorado* (1875). A travelogue and adventure story of Powell's trips down the Green and Colorado Rivers from 1867 to 1875. This account and Powell's exploration were an inspiration for many latter-day Western writers, including Wallace Stegner and Edward Abbey.

Zane Grey, *Riders of the Purple Sage* (1912). Set in the Mormon country of southern Utah, the most popular of Grey's novels focuses on the life of Jane Witheersteen, a beautiful, rich Western cattle heiress forced to make crucial decisions about her lifestyle and religion in the heat of a vicious town power struggle.

Willa Cather, *Death Comes for the Archbishop* (1927). Using historical letters from the period, Cather describes the efforts of two Catholic priests to spread the faith in New Mexico. Beginning in Santa Fe in 1951, the novel is laden with descriptions of the region's stark desert features.

Louis L'Amour, *Hondo* (1953). L'Amour is the prolific modern-day master of the "Cowboys and Indians" genre, taking up the mantle of the Western novel. This novel and his many others are a quick and easy read.

Edward Abbey, *Desert Solitaire* (1968). Documenting his experience as a ranger in Arches National Park, Abbey's work revels in the stark desert landscape and struggles to redefine the relationship between man and nature on a personal level. Abbey's later novel, *The Monkey-Wrench Gang* (1975), is a comic yet fanciful novel about eco-terrorists and their run-ins with Western infrastructure.

Larry McMurtry, *Lonesome Dove* (1986). Follows the story of Gus and Call, two ranchers living in a small Texas border town. McMurtry skillfully captures the rich landscape and tenuous existence on the frontier.

Tony Hillerman, *Skinwalkers* (1986). Sergeant Jim Chee and Lieutenant Leaphorn are the crime-solving heroes of Hillerman's series of mystery thrillers. Along the way, Hillerman skillfully weaves into his plots a taste of Navajo culture and mysticism.

Terry Tempest Williams, *Refuge* (1991). An environmentalist-*cum*-lyricist, Williams tells the story of her mother's fight with cancer side-by-side with her account of the flooding of the Great Salt Lake, an event which threatened the lake's saline ecosystem.

MUSIC

Navajo music plays a vital ceremonial role. Music during these ceremonies is mostly vocal and reflects aspects of the Navajo environment, including gods, animals, and features of the land. **Chants,** comprising seveural songs and scores of lines, are sung during ceremonies and are belieived to have healing powers. Eschewing harmony, these syllabic chants are significant not only for the narrative contained within them but for the jarring sounds that they create. Modern Navajo music contains influences of country music more conventionally associated with the region. **Country** grew out of folk traditions in the American South, as musicians composed songs about personal experiences, using instruments such at the fiddle, violin, banjo, and guitar to accompany the vocals. Near the southern border of the US, the **mariachi** culture shows the influence of Mexican music. "Mariachi" originally meant musician, but after centuries of evolution, it has come to define a style of music, dress, and living that was adopted from the Mexican tradition of the traveling musician. Performing around the Southwest, Mariachis use harps, violins, and the vihuela, a small, rhythmic, guitar-like instrument.

FILM

Nowhere does the Southwest find its cinematic backbone as memorably as in **Westerns.** The genre's plot is commonly one of good and evil, featuring the stereotypically wild, untamed West as the playground for either the surly, introspective loner, or the tough-talking, vigilant defender of peace, all amid the chaos of barbaric Indians, sinister thieves, and corrupt local politicians. Westerns have existed since the earliest days of the silver screen and have varied widely in terms of quality, budget, and prominence. The careers of tough guys John Wayne and Clint Eastwood were solidified in the Hollywood-fashioned desert environs of the Southwest, while directors such as John Ford introduced themes that would recur in scores of films to come. Some of the most memorable include:

Stagecoach **(1939).** Considered a ground-breaking film that reinvented the genre of the Western and raised it out of the dubious "B" designation, this John Ford film depicts nine stagecoach passengers, each forced to navigate dangerous adventures and reveal their true character, all against the backdrop of Monument Valley.

Gunfight at the OK Corral **(1957).** Burt Lancaster and Kirk Douglas star in this movie that relives the legendary relationship between Wyatt Earp and Doc Holliday.

True Grit **(1969).** John Wayne received the Oscar for Best Actor for his role as a no-nonsense marshall in this movie based on the novel by Charles Portis.

Easy Rider **(1969).** Peter Fonda and Dennis Hopper star in this classic 1960s counterculture road-tripping adventure.

The Milagro Beanfield War **(1988).** In this Robert Redford movie based on the novel by John Nichols, a New Mexican town supports a farmer who unintentionally irrigates his land with water owned by a rich entrepreneur.

Tombstone **(1993).** Val Kilmer and Kurt Russell star in a more current interpretation of the Earp-Holliday duo and their southern Arizona hangout, Tombstone.

Leaving Las Vegas **(1995).** This tragic and disturbing romance starring Elizabeth Shue and Nicholas Cage captures the darker side of the glittering city.

Smoke Signals **(1998).** Two Navajo young men living in Idaho, Victor and Thomas Builds-the-fire, travel to Arizona to retrieve the remains of Arnold, who was Victor's father and the man who saved Thomas Builds-the-fire's life at early age. The two have very different visions of Arnold, which they debate along the way.

SPORTS & RECREATION

Traditional outdoor sports like hiking and mountain biking dominate the imagination of most travelers to the Southwest, and much of this book is devoted to exploring their function in the region. Yet more than any other area in the US, the Southwest furnishes opportunities to watch and, for the brave, experience, the sports the mainstream overlooks.

Born from a fusion of Hispanic *vaquero* and American cowboy traditions, rodeo rose to popularity largely in the Southwest in the late 19th and early 20th centuries and continues to thrive throughout the region as a spectator sport. Thousands pour into arenas for weekly events on the **Professional Rodeo Cowboys Association (PRCA) Tour** to watch events like team roping, bareback riding, saddle bronc riding, and a crowd favorite, bull riding. Each December, the PRCA holds its championship, the **Wrangler National Finals Rodeo,** in Las Vegas, and sponsors other events across the Southwest which are surprisingly accessible to fans in any budget range. For information about PRCA events visit www.prorodeo.com.

Considering its dramatic and wildly diverse landscapes, it's no surprise that the Southwest is the birthplace of many of the world's most unconventional sports, most of which are directly inspired by regional features. **Kiteboarding,** in which boarders are propelled by kites instead of motor boats, popped up at Lake Tahoe. The windswept saltflats of Nevada have inspired **landsailing** in lightning-fast three-wheeled vehicles powered by sail. Amateur **canyoneers** hike, scramble, swim, and rappel through the labyrinthine canyons of Utah, while **balloonists** in Albuquerque float dangerously close to the sun. The legacy of frontier culture is, in part, an undying urge to stretch limits, and this spirit continues to inspire Southwesterners as they look for new ways to appreciate their unique lands.

ADDITIONAL RESOURCES

GENERAL HISTORY

Marc Reisner, *Cadillac Desert* **(1986).** A jarring look at the no-holds-barred struggle for scarce water in the West. The author focuses on the story of L.A., the great Western water parasite.

Richard White, *'It's Your Misfortune and None of My Own': A New History of the American West* **(1993).** This is a history of the relationships between whites and Native Americans in the West by one of the foremost historians in the field.

Robert S. McPherson, *The Northern Navajo Frontier, 1860-1900: Expansion Through Adversity* **(2001).** McPherson traces the success and failures of the Navajo in dealing with the Federal Government.

Steven G. Hyslop, *Bound for Santa Fe: The Road to New Mexico and the American Conquest, 1806-1848* **(2002).** Hyslop presents an in depth historical examination of the actions leading up to the Treaty of Guadalupe Hidalgo.

TRAVEL NARRATIVES

As the home of Route 66, Las Vegas, and vast expanses of untouched land, the Southwest has proved an ideal inspiration and setting for various travel narratives written over the years. Below are some of the premier works of this genre that employ the Southwest as a setting.

Woody Guthrie, *Bound for Glory* (1943). In this autobiographical work, the legendary American folk singer recounts his life and travels across the United States including numerous trips through the Southwest.

Jack Kerouac, *On the Road* (1957). One of America's first beatniks, Kerouac recalls his trips on Route 66 across the Southwest to California.

Hunter S. Thompson, *Fear and Loathing in Las Vegas* (1971). In this "new journalism" classic, Thompson explores Vegas in all of its decadence and depravity.

DOCUMENTARIES

Various documentaries aim to capture the vibrant culture and environments of Southwestern communities. Search www.powwowcountry.com to purchase some of the selections below:

***The Shadow Catcher: Edward S. Curtis and the North American Indian* (1974).** Critical account of Curtis's interaction with natives in the Southwest, whom he wrote about and photographed for 32 years. Includes some of Curtis's original footage.

***Chulas Fronteras and Del Mero Corazon* (1976)** Depicts the life of southern Texas musicians steeped in Mexican tradition. Focuses on all aspects of daily life, from working to socializing.

***The Pueblo Peoples: First Contact* (1990).** Describes the first contact between Native Americans of the Southwest and Spanish conquistadores.

***America's Canyon Country* (1992)** Traces the development of canyon country in the Southwest, with some mention of the people that inhabit the area.

HOLIDAYS & FESTIVALS

NATIONAL HOLIDAYS

2004	2005	US HOLIDAY
Jan. 1	Jan. 1	New Year's Day
Jan. 19	Jan. 17	Martin Luther King, Jr. Day
Feb. 16	Feb. 21	Presidents' Day
May 31	May 30	Memorial Day
July 4	July 4	Independence Day
Sep. 6	Sep. 5	Labor Day
Oct. 11	Oct. 10	Columbus Day
Nov. 11	Nov. 11	Veterans Day
Nov. 25	Nov. 24	Thanksgiving
Dec. 25	Dec. 25	Christmas Day

FESTIVALS IN THE SOUTHWEST

MONTH	FESTIVAL
January	**National Cowboy Poetry and Music Festival,** Elko, NV (p. 234)
	Sundance Film Festival, Park City, UT (p. 327)
February	**National Date Festival,** Indio, CA (p. 168)
March	**Cowboy Poetry Festival,** Alpine, TX (p. 455)
April	**Gathering of Nations Powwow,** Albuquerque, NM (p. 378)
May	**Telluride International Film Festival,** Telluride, CO (p. 347)
June	**Telluride Bluegrass Festival,** Telluride, CO (p. 347)
	Utah Shakespearean Festival, Cedar City, UT (p. 329)
July	**UFO Festival,** Roswell, NM (p. 440)
	Artown Festival, Reno, NV (p. 214)
August	**Jazz Celebration,** Telluride, CO (p. 347)
	Indian Market, Santa Fe, NM (p. 393)
	International Bat Festival, Carlsbad, NM (p. 440)
September	**Blues and Brews Festival,** Telluride, CO (p. 347)
	Burning Man, Black Rock Desert, NV (p. 218)
	Marfa Lights Festival, Alpine, TX (p. 455)
October	**Hot Air Balloon Rally,** Albuquerque, NM (p. 383)
November	**49ers Encampment Festival,** Death Valley, CA (p. 172)
	Festival of the Cranes, Socorro, NM (p. 424)

LIFE & TIMES

ESSENTIALS

FACTS FOR THE TRAVELER

ENTRANCE REQUIREMENTS
Passport (p. 21). Required for citizens of all foreign countries except Canada.
Visa (p. 21). Visitors from most of Europe, Australia, and New Zealand can travel in the US for up to 90 days without a visa, although you may need to show a return plane ticket. Citizens of South Africa need a visa.
Inoculations: (p. 28).
Work Permit (p. 21). Required for all foreigners planning to work in the US.
Driving Permit (p. 43). Required for all those planning to drive.

EMBASSIES & CONSULATES

US EMBASSIES & CONSULATES ABROAD

Contact the nearest embassy or consulate to obtain information regarding visas and permits to the US. Offices are open during limited hours, so call well before you depart. The US State Department provides contact information for US diplomatic missions via the Internet at http://foia.state.gov/MMS/KOH/keyofficers.asp. Foreign embassies in the US are located in Washington, D.C., but there are consulates in the Southwest that can be helpful in an emergency. For a more extensive list of embassies and consulates in the US, consult the website www.embassy.org.

Australia: Embassy: Moonah Pl., Yarralumla **(Canberra)**, ACT 2600 (☎02 6214 5600; http://usembassy-australia.state.gov/consular). **Other Consulates: Sydney, Melbourne,** and **Perth.**

Canada: Embassy: Consular Section, 490 Sussex Dr., **Ottawa**, P.O. Box 866, Station B, Ottowa, Ontario K1P 5T1(☎613-238-5335; www.usembassycanada.gov). **Other Consulates: Calgary, Halifax, Montréal, Toronto,** and **Vancouver.**

Ireland: Embassy: 42 Elgin Rd., Ballsbridge, **Dublin** 4 (☎01 668 8777 or 668 7122; fax 668 9946; www.usembassy.ie).

New Zealand: Embassy: 29 Fitzherbert Terr. (mailing address: P.O. Box 1190), Thorndon, **Wellington** (☎04 462 6000; http://usembassy.org.nz). **Other Consulate: Auckland.**

South Africa: Embassy: 877 Pretorius St., **Pretoria**, P.O. Box 9536, Pretoria 0001 (☎012 342 1048; http://usembassy.state.gov/pretoria). **Other Consulates: Cape Town, Durban,** and **Johannesburg.**

UK: Embassy: 24 Grosvenor Sq., **London** W1A 1AE (☎020 7499 9000; www.usembassy.org.uk). **Other Consulates: Belfast** and **Edinburgh.**

CONSULAR SERVICES IN THE SOUTHWEST

Australia: 2049 Century Park E, 19th fl. of Century Plaza Towers between Olympic Blvd. and Santa Monica Blvd., **Los Angeles,** CA 90067 (☎310-229-4800).

Canada: 550 S. Hope St., 9th fl., **Los Angeles,** CA 90071 (☎213-346-2700; inglstd@dfait-maeci.gc.ca).

Ireland: Honorary Consulate at 920 Schelbourne St., **Reno,** NV 89511 (☎/fax 775-853-4497; bbrady@nvbell.net).

New Zealand: 1379 N. Brookhurst Circle, Centerville, **Salt Lake City,** UT 84014 (☎801-296-2494; fax 296-1523).

South Africa: 2272 Ridgewood Way, **Bountiful,** UT 84010 (☎801-266-7867).

UK: 15249 N. 59th Ave., **Glendale,** AZ 85306 (☎602-978-7200).

DOCUMENTS & FORMALITIES

PASSPORTS

REQUIREMENTS. All foreign visitors except Canadians need valid passports to enter the US and re-enter their own country. The US does not allow entrance if the holder's passport expires in under six months; returning home with an expired passport is often illegal and may result in a fine. Canadians need to demonstrate proof of citizenship with documents such as a citizenship card or birth certificate.

NEW PASSPORTS. Citizens of Australia, Canada, Ireland, New Zealand, and the United Kingdom can apply for a passport at any post office, passport office, or court of law. Citizens of South Africa can apply for a passport at any Home Affairs office. Any applications must be filed well in advance of the departure date, although most passport offices offer rush services for a very steep fee.

PASSPORT MAINTENANCE. Photocopy the page of your passport with your photo, as well as your visas, traveler's check serial numbers, and any other important documents. Carry one set of copies in a safe place, apart from the originals, and leave another at home. Consulates also recommend that you carry an expired passport or an official copy of your birth certificate separate from other documents. If you lose your passport, notify local police and the consulate of your home government right away. In some cases, a replacement may take weeks to process, and it may be valid for only a limited time. Any **visas** stamped in your old passport will be irretrievably lost. In an emergency, ask for **temporary traveling papers** that will permit you to re-enter your home country.

VISAS, INVITATIONS, & WORK PERMITS

VISAS. Citizens of South Africa and most other countries need a visa in addition to a valid passport to enter the US. See http://travel.state.gov/visa_services.html and www.unitedstatesvisas.gov for more information. To obtain a visa, contact a US embassy or consulate. Recent security measures have made the visa application process more rigorous and lengthy; apply well in advance of your travel date.

Canadian citizens do not need a visa to enter the US. Citizens of Australia, New Zealand, and most Western European countries can waive US visas through the **Visa Waiver Program** if they are traveling only for business or pleasure (*not* work or study), are staying for fewer than **90 days,** have proof of intent to leave (e.g., a return plane ticket), possess an I-94W form (issued at the airport), are traveling on particular air or sea carriers, or possess a machine readable passport. See http://travel.state.gov/vwp.html for more information. If you lose your I-94W form, replace it by filling out form I-102, although it is unlikely that the form will be replaced within the time of your stay. Get the form from the **Bureau of Citizenship and Immigration Services** (**BCIS;** ☎800-870-3676; www.bcis.gov; form request www.bcis.gov/graphics/formsfee/forms/i-102.htm). **Visa extensions** are sometimes granted with a completed I-539 form; call the forms request line (☎800-870-3676) or get it online at www.immigration.gov/graphics/formsfee/forms/i-539.htm.

All travelers, except Canadians, planning a stay of more than 90 days also need to obtain a visa. Admission as a visitor does not include the right to work, which is authorized only by a **work permit.** Entering the US to study requires a special visa. For more information, see **Alternatives to Tourism,** p. 50.

IDENTIFICATION

When you travel, always carry two or more forms of identification with you, including at least one photo ID; a passport or a driver's license with birth certificate is usually adequate. Never carry all your IDs together. Split them up in case of theft or loss, and keep photocopies of them in your bags and at home.

TEACHER, STUDENT, & YOUTH IDENTIFICATION. The **International Student Identity Card (ISIC),** the most widely accepted form of student ID, provides discounts on sights, accommodations, food, and transport; access to a 24hr. emergency helpline (in North America call ☎ 877-370-4742; elsewhere call US collect ☎ 715-345-0505); and insurance benefits for US cardholders (see **Insurance,** p. 30). The ISIC is preferable to an institution-specific card (university ID). Applicants must be degree-seeking students of a secondary or post-secondary school and must be at least 12 years of age. Because of the proliferation of fake ISICs, some services (particularly airlines) require additional proof of student identity, such as a school ID or a letter signed by your registrar and stamped with your school seal.

The **International Teacher Identity Card (ITIC)** offers teachers the same insurance coverage and similar, but limited, discounts. For travelers who are 25 years old or under but are not students, the **International Youth Travel Card (IYTC;** formerly the **GO 25** Card) offers many of the same benefits as the ISIC.

Each of the cards costs around $22. ITIC cards are valid for 16 months; ISIC and IYTC cards are valid for one year. Many student travel agencies (see p. 39) issue the cards, including STA Travel in Australia and New Zealand; Travel CUTS in Canada; USIT in the Republic of Ireland and Northern Ireland; SASTS in South Africa; Campus Travel and STA Travel in the UK; and Council Travel and STA Travel in the US. For more information, contact the **International Student Travel Confederation (ISTC),** Herengracht 479, 1017 BS Amsterdam, The Netherlands (☎ +31 20 421 28 00; www.istc.org).

CUSTOMS

Upon entering the US, you must declare certain items from abroad and pay a duty on the value of those articles that exceeds the US customs allowance. Goods and gifts purchased at duty-free shops abroad are not exempt from duty or sales tax at your point of return and thus must be declared as well; "duty-free" merely means that you do not pay tax in the country of purchase. Upon returning, you must declare all articles acquired abroad and pay a duty on the value of articles in excess of your home country's allowance.

CURRENCY & EXCHANGE

The currency chart below is based on August 2003 exchange rates between US dollars (US$) and Australian dollars (AUS$), Canadian dollars (CDN$), Irish pounds (IR£), New Zealand dollars (NZ$), South African Rand (ZAR), British pounds (UK£), and European Union euros (EUR€). Check financial websites such as www.bloomberg.com and www.xe.com for the latest exchange rates.

It is usually cheaper to convert money in the US than at home, but be sure to bring enough dollars to last for the first 1-3 days of your trip. Since you lose money with every transaction, **convert large sums** (unless the currency is depreciating rapidly), **but no more than you'll need.** If you use traveler's checks or bills, carry some

EXCHANGE RATES	AUS$1 = $0.66	US$1 = AUS$1.53
	CDN$1 = $0.72	US$1 = CDN$1.39
	IR£1 = $1.44	US$1 = IR£0.70
	NZ$1 = $0.59	US$1 = NZ$1.70
	ZAR1 = $0.14	US$1 = ZAR7.40
	UK£1 = $1.60	US$1 = UK£0.62
	EUR€1 = $1.13	US$1 = EUR€0.89

in small denominations for times when you have to exchange money at disadvantageous rates, but bring a range of denominations since charges may be levied per check cashed. Store your money in a variety of forms.

TRAVELER'S CHECKS

Traveler's checks are one of the safest and least troublesome means of carrying funds. American Express and Visa are the most widely recognized brands; many banks and agencies sell them for a small commission. Check issuers provide refunds if the checks are lost or stolen, and many provide additional services, such as toll-free refund hotlines abroad, emergency message services, and stolen credit card assistance. Traveler's checks are readily accepted in the US.

American Express: Checks available with commission at select banks, at all AmEx offices, and online (www.americanexpress.com; US residents only). AmEx cardholders can also purchase checks by phone (☎888-269-6669). AAA (see p. 43) offers commission-free checks to members. Checks available in US, Australian, British, Canadian, Japanese, and EU currencies. *Cheques for Two* can be signed by either of 2 people traveling together. For purchase locations or more information contact AmEx's service centers: In the US and Canada ☎800-221-7282; in the UK ☎0800 587 6023; in Australia ☎800 68 80 22; in New Zealand 0508 555 358; elsewhere US collect ☎+1 801-964-6665.

Visa: Checks available (generally with commission) at banks worldwide. For the location of the nearest office, call Visa's service centers: In the US ☎800-227-6811; in the UK ☎0800 51 58 84; elsewhere UK collect ☎+44 020 7937 8091. Checks available in US, British, Canadian, Japanese, and European Union currencies.

Travelex/Thomas Cook: In the US and Canada call ☎800-287-7362; in the UK call ☎0800 62 21 01; elsewhere call UK collect ☎+44 1733 31 89 50.

CREDIT, DEBIT, & ATM CARDS

Where they are accepted, credit cards often get superior exchange rates. They may also offer services such as insurance or emergency help, and are sometimes required to reserve hotel rooms or rental cars. **MasterCard** and **Visa** are the most widely accepted; **American Express** cards work at AmEx offices, major airports, and some ATMs. **ATMs** are widespread in the Southwest, and, depending on the system your home bank uses, you can probably access your bank account from the US. ATMs get the same wholesale exchange rate as credit cards, but there is often a limit on the amount of money you can withdraw per day (around $500). A withdrawal surcharge of $1-5 is not uncommon. **Debit cards** are as convenient as credit cards but have a more immediate impact on your funds. A debit card can be used wherever its associated credit card company (usually Mastercard or Visa) is accepted, but the money is withdrawn directly from the holder's checking account. Debit cards often also function as ATM cards and can be used to withdraw cash from banks and ATMs throughout the US. The two major international money networks are **Cirrus** (to locate ATMs, US ☎800-424-7787 or www.mastercard.com) and **Visa/PLUS** (to locate ATMs, US ☎800-843-7587 or www.visa.com).

GETTING MONEY FROM HOME

If you run out of money while traveling, the easiest and cheapest solution is to have someone back home make a deposit to your credit card or ATM card. It is also possible, however, to arrange a **bank money transfer,** which means asking a bank back home to wire money to a bank in the Southwest. This is the cheapest way to transfer cash, but it's also the slowest, usually taking several days or more. Note that some banks may only release your funds in local currency, potentially sticking you with a poor exchange rate; inquire about this in advance. Money transfer services like **Western Union** are faster and more convenient than bank transfers—but also pricier. Western Union has many locations worldwide. To find one, visit www.westernunion.com or call in the US☎800-325-6000, in Canada ☎800-235-0000, in the UK ☎0800 83 38 33, in Australia ☎800 501 500, in New Zealand ☎800 27 0000, in South Africa ☎0860 100031. Money transfer services are also available at **American Express** and **Thomas Cook** offices.

COSTS

The most significant expense of your trip will probably be your round-trip (return) **airfare** to the Southwest (see **Getting to the Southwest: By Plane,** p. 39). Renting a car will be another major expense, but perhaps a wise decision since much of the Southwest is accessible only by car. Before you go, calculate a reasonable daily **budget** that will meet your needs. Don't forget to factor in emergency funds (as much as $200).

STAYING ON A BUDGET. Accommodations start at about $12 per night in a hostel bed, while a basic sit-down meal costs $8-10 depending on the region. If you stay in hostels and prepare your own food, you'll probably spend from $30-40 per person per day. Camping opportunities abound in the Southwest and are often the cheapest option, with prices ranging from free to as much as $20 for a tent site (see **The Great Outdoors,** p. 60). A slightly more comfortable day (sleeping in hostels/guesthouses and the occasional budget hotel, eating one meal a day at a restaurant, going out at night) would run $50-65; for a luxurious day, the sky's the limit. **Gas** prices in the US have risen over the past year but still remain lower than they are in Europe. A gallon of gas now costs about $1.60 (42¢ per L), but prices vary widely according to state gasoline prices.

TIPS FOR SAVING MONEY. Since saving just a few dollars a day over the course of your trip might pay for days or weeks of additional travel, the art of penny-pinching while traveling is well worth learning. Take advantage of **freebies:** for example, museums will typically be free once a week or once a month, and cities often host free open-air concerts and cultural events (especially in the summer). You'll find great hiking and biking for free, and if you're going to be visiting a few national parks, a **National Parks Pass** can easily save you $50 or even $100. Bring a sleeping bag (see p. 63) to save on sheet charges in hostels, and do your **laundry** in the sink (where permitted). You can split **accommodations** costs (in hotels and some hostels) with trustworthy fellow travelers; multi-bed rooms are always cheaper per person than singles. Of course, with few exceptions, camping will always be the least expensive option, and you can quickly make up for the cost of a tent after a few weeks of traveling. Visits to the supermarket, instead of restaurants, can save you a bundle.

TIPPING & BARGAINING

Tipping is expected by service staff in the US. The customary tip for waitstaff and cab drivers is 15-20%. Tips are not included in restaurant bills unless you are in a party of six or more (the bill will refer to a "gratuity"). At the airport and in hotels, porters expect at least $1 per bag. Outside of flea markets, bargaining is frowned upon and fruitless in the US.

EMERGENCY = 911. For emergencies in the US, dial **911.** This number is toll-free from all phones, including coin phones. In a very few remote communities, 911 may not work. If it does not, dial 0 for the operator and request to be connected with the appropriate emergency service. In national parks, it is usually best to call the **park warden** in case of emergency. *Let's Go* lists emergency contact numbers where 911 is not applicable. If you are calling from a cellular phone, be sure to tell the 911 dispatcher your exact location. Due to the vagaries of cellular networks, you may not be connected to the closest call center.

TAXES

Sales tax is similar to the European Value-Added Tax but is generally not included in advertised prices. Southwestern state sales taxes range from 5-8% depending on the item and the state; in some states, groceries are not taxed.

SAFETY & SECURITY

Although the vast majority of the Southwest is sparsely populated, the few urban areas are among the most crime-ridden in the nation. One should be particularly cautious when visiting Phoenix, Albuquerque, Las Cruces, El Paso, Gallup, and towns outlying the Navajo Nation. However, the conscientious traveler should have no problems if he abides by a few basic guidelines and by common sense. For info on outdoors safety, see **The Great Outdoors,** p. 60.

BLENDING IN. Tourists are vulnerable to crime because they often carry large amounts of cash and are not as street-savvy as locals. Try to blend in as much as possible, taking your fashion cues from the locals. The gawking camera-toter is a more obvious target than the low-profile traveler. Also, carry yourself with confidence. Check maps in shops or restaurants rather than on the street.

EXPLORING. Extra vigilance is always wise, but there is no need to go overboard when exploring a new city or region; familiarize yourself with your surroundings before setting out. Find out about **unsafe areas** from tourist offices, hotel and hostel managers, and locals whom you trust. You may want to carry a **whistle** to attract attention in an emergency. Whenever possible, *Let's Go* warns of unsafe neighborhoods and areas. When walking at night, stick to busy, well-lit streets and avoid dark alleyways. Don't cross through parks, parking lots, or other large, deserted areas. Buildings in disrepair, vacant lots, and unpopulated areas are all bad signs. The distribution of people can reveal a great deal about the relative safety of the area; look for children playing, women walking in the open, and other signs of an active community. Keep in mind that a district can change character drastically between blocks. Be sure that someone at home knows your itinerary and **never admit that you are traveling alone.** Ultimately, go with your gut: if you feel uncomfortable where you are, leave as quickly and directly as you can.

GETTING AROUND. Driving in the Southwest is generally safe, though desert driving requires some extra precautions (see **The Desert and Your Car,** p. 67). Study route maps before hitting the road, and consider bringing a few spare parts. For long drives in desolate areas, invest in a cellular phone and a roadside assistance program (see p. 43). It is also a good idea to drive during the day because you can get help faster and avoid trouble in city streets at night. In larger cities such as Phoenix and Albuquerque, park your vehicle in a garage or well traveled area, and secure it with a steering wheel locking device. **Sleeping in your car** is one of the most dangerous (and often illegal) ways to get rest. **Public transportation** across

ESSENTIALS

states (buses and trains) is generally safe. Occasionally, stations can be dangerous; *Let's Go* warns of these stations where applicable. If possible, avoid using public transportation late at night unless you are in a large group. The cost of a **taxi** fare is far less than that of your personal well-being. *Let's Go* does not recommend **hitchhiking** under any circumstances, particularly for women. Hitching is especially dangerous in the Southwest, with its vast lengths of remote and seldom-traveled highways—see **Getting Around**, p. 41, for more info.

SELF DEFENSE. There is no sure-fire way to avoid all the threatening situations you might encounter, a self-defense course will give you concrete ways to react to unwanted advances or aggression. **Impact, Prepare, and Model Mugging** can refer you to self-defense courses in the US (☎ 800-345-5425; www.impactsafety.org). Workshops (2-3hr.) start at $50; full courses (20hr.) run $350-500.

TERRORISM. The September 11, 2001 terrorist attacks in the Eastern US have awakened Americans to the potential for further domestic terrorist activities. Terrorists often target popular landmarks; however, the threat of an attack is rarely specific enough to warrant avoiding certain places or modes of transportation. Stay aware of developments in the news and watch for alerts from federal, state, and local law enforcement officials. Also, allow extra time for airport security and remember that sharp objects in your carry-on luggage will be confiscated. For more information, visit www.terrorismanswers.com and the Department of Homeland Security at www.ready.gov. The box on **travel advisories** (p. 27) lists offices to contact and webpages to visit to get the most updated list of your home country's government's advisories about travel.

FINANCIAL SECURITY

PROTECTING YOUR VALUABLES. Theft in the US is most common in big cities and at night.Don't keep all your valuables (money, important documents) in one place, and always make **photocopies.** Carry one copy separately and leave another copy at home. Label every piece of luggage both inside and out. *Don't put a wallet with money in your back pocket.* Never count your money in public and carry as little as possible. If you carry a **purse,** buy one with a secure clasp. Secure packs with small combination padlocks that slip through the two zippers. A **money belt** is the best way to carry cash; you can buy one at most camping supply stores. Alternatively, a nylon, zippered pouch with a belt that sits inside the waist of your pants or skirt combines convenience and security. A **neck pouch** is equally safe, although far less accessible and discreet. Keep a small cash reserve—about $50—separate from your primary stash, perhaps sewn into or stored in the depths of your pack, along with your traveler's check numbers and important photocopies.

CON ARTISTS & PICKPOCKETS. In large cities **con artists** often work in groups, and children are among the most effective. Beware of certain classics: sob stories that require money, rolls of bills "found" on the street, mustard spilled (or saliva spit) onto your shoulder to distract you while they snatch your bag. **Never let your passport and your bags out of your sight,** especially near the Mexican border. Beware of **pickpockets** in city crowds, especially on public transportation. Also, be alert in public telephone booths: if you must say your calling card number, do so very quietly; if you punch it in, make sure no one can look over your shoulder.

ACCOMMODATIONS & TRANSPORTATION. Never leave your belongings unattended. Bring your own **padlock** for hostel lockers, and don't ever store valuables in any locker. Be particularly careful on **buses** and **trains;** horror stories abound about determined thieves who wait for travelers to fall asleep. Carry your backpack in front of you where you can see it. When alone, never stay in an empty train com-

TRAVEL ADVISORIES. The following government offices provide travel information and advisories by telephone, by fax, or via the web:

Australian Department of Foreign Affairs and Trade: ☎1300 555 135, in Australia; ☎612 6261 1111 from outside; www.dfat.gov.au.

Canadian Department of Foreign Affairs and International Trade (DFAIT): In Canada and the US call ☎800-267-8376, elsewhere call ☎613-944-4000; www.dfait-maeci.gc.ca. Call for their free booklet, *Bon Voyage...But.*

New Zealand Ministry of Foreign Affairs: ☎04 439 8000; www.mft.govt.nz/ travel/index.html.

United Kingdom Foreign and Commonwealth Office: ☎0870 606 0290; fax 020 7008 0155; www.fco.gov.uk.

US Department of State: ☎202-647-5225; http://travel.state.gov. For *A Safe Trip Abroad*, call ☎202-512-1800.

partment, and lock your pack to the luggage rack. Always sleep on top bunks with your luggage stored above you (if not in bed with you), and keep your valuables hidden on your person. If traveling by **car,** don't leave valuables in it while you are away. Drivers should take necessary precautions against **carjacking,** which has become one of the most frequently committed crimes in the US. Carjackers, who are usually armed, approach their victims in their vehicles and force them to turn over the automobile. They prey on cars parked on the side of the road or stopped at red lights. If you pull over on the side of the road, keep your doors locked and windows up at all times. Do not under any circumstances pull over to help a car in the breakdown lane; call the police instead.

DRUGS & ALCOHOL

The drinking age in the United States is 21 and drinking-related laws are strictly enforced. Most areas restrict where and when alcohol can be sold, and youthful travelers can expect to be asked to show photo ID when purchasing it. **Never drink and drive**—you risk your own life and those of others, and getting caught results in imprisonment and fines. It is illegal to have an open bottle of alcohol in a car even if you are not driving. Possession of illegal narcotics such as marijuana, heroin, and cocaine carries severe punishments. If you have prescription drugs, keep a copy of the prescriptions, especially at border crossings. You must be at least 18 years old to buy cigarettes.

HEALTH

Common sense is the simplest prescription for good health while you travel. Luckily, the US has an excellent healthcare system and travelers can usually be treated easily for injuries and health problems. Travelers complain most often about their gut and their feet, so take precautionary measures: drink lots of fluids to prevent dehydration and constipation, and wear sturdy, broken-in shoes and clean socks.

BEFORE YOU GO

In your **passport,** write the names of any people to be contacted in a medical emergency and list allergies or medical conditions. Matching a prescription to a foreign equivalent is often difficult, so carry prescriptions or a statement from your doctor with the brand name, manufacturer, chemical name, and dosage. Keep medication with you in your carry-on luggage. For tips on packing a basic **first-aid kit,** see p. 31.

ESSENTIALS

IMMUNIZATIONS & PRECAUTIONS

Travelers should make sure that the following vaccines are up to date: MMR (for measles, mumps, and rubella); DTaP or Td (for diptheria, tetanus, and pertussis); OPV (for polio); HbCV (for haemophilus influenza B); HBV (for hepatitis B); and Varicella (for chickenpox, for those who are susceptible). For recommendations on immunizations and prophylaxis, consult the CDC (see below) in the US or your home country's equivalent, and check in with your doctor.

USEFUL ORGANIZATIONS & PUBLICATIONS

The US **Centers for Disease Control and Prevention** (**CDC; ☎**877-FYI-TRIP/394-8747; fax 888-232-3299; www.cdc.gov/travel) maintains an international traveler's hot-line and website. Their *Health Information for International Travel*, an annual rundown of disease, immunization, and health advice, is $29 via the Public Health Foundation (**☎**877-252-1200) or free online. Consult the appropriate agency of your home country for information on health, and entry requirements for various countries (see **Travel Advisories,** p. 27). For information on health and other travel warnings, call the **Overseas Citizens Services** (**☎**202-647-5225, 888-407-4747 M-F 8am-8pm; after-hours 202-647-4000), or contact a passport agency, embassy, or consulate abroad. US citizens can send a self-addressed, stamped envelope to the Overseas Citizens Services, Bureau of Consular Affairs, Room 4811, US Department of State, Washington, D.C. 20520-4818. For information on medical evacuation services and travel insurance firms, see the US government's website at http://travel.state.gov/medical.html or the **British Foreign and Commonwealth Office** (www.fco.gov.uk). For information on travel health, including a country-by-country overview (and a list of travel clinics in the USA), try the **International Travel Health Guide,** by Stuart Rose, MD ($25; www.travmed.com). For general health info, contact the **American Red Cross** (**☎**202-303-4498; www.redcross.org).

MEDICAL ASSISTANCE ON THE ROAD

Medical care in the US is among the best in the world. In case of medical emergency, dial **☎911** from any phone and an operator will dispatch help. Emergency care is also available in the Southwest at any hospital emergency room on a walk-in basis. If you do not have insurance, you will have to pay for medical care (see **Insurance,** p. 30). Appointments are required for non-emergency medical services. Those with medical conditions (such as diabetes, allergies to antibiotics, epilepsy, heart conditions) may want to obtain a **Medic Alert** membership (first year $35, annually thereafter $20), which includes a stainless steel ID tag, among other benefits. Contact the Medic Alert Foundation, 2323 Colorado Ave, Turlock, CA 95382, USA (**☎**888-633-4298; outside US **☎**209-668-3333; www.medicalert.org).

ENVIRONMENTAL HAZARDS

Heat exhaustion and dehydration: Heat exhaustion leads to nausea, excessive thirst, headaches, and dizziness. Prevent it by drinking plenty of fluids, eating salty foods, and avoiding dehydrating beverages. Continuous heat stress can eventually lead to heat-stroke, characterized by a rising temperature, severe headache, delirium, and cessation of sweating. Victims should be cooled off with wet towels and taken to a hospital immediately. Heat exhaustion is a year-round problem in certain areas of the Southwest.

Sunburn: If you spend time near water, in the desert, or in the snow, sunburn will be a risk, even when its cloudy. If you get sunburned, drink more fluids than usual and apply an aloe-based lotion. Severe sunburns can lead to sun poisoning, characterized by fever, chills, nausea, and vomiting. Sun poisoning demands immediate medical care.

Hypothermia and frostbite: A rapid drop in body temperature is the clearest sign of overexposure to cold. Victims may also shiver, feel exhausted, have poor coordination or slurred speech, hallucinate, or suffer amnesia. **Do not let hypothermia victims fall**

asleep. To avoid hypothermia, keep dry, wear layers, and stay out of the wind. When the temperature is below freezing, watch out for frostbite. If skin turns white or blue, waxy, and cold, do not rub the area. Drink warm beverages, stay dry, and slowly warm the area with dry fabric or steady body contact until a doctor can be found.

High altitude: To avoid altitude sickness, allow your body a couple of days to adjust to less oxygen before exerting yourself. Altitude sickness/Acute Mountain Sickness (AMS) is characterized by headaches, loss of appetite, fatigue, nausea, dizziness, and confusion. Those suffering from AMS should stop ascending and seriously consider descending in altitude. AMS is a risk in any high altitude region.

INSECT-BORNE DISEASES

Many diseases are transmitted by insects—mainly mosquitoes, fleas, ticks, and lice. Be aware of insects in wet or forested areas, especially while hiking and camping; wear long pants and long sleeves, tuck your pants into your socks, and buy a mosquito net. Use insect repellents containing DEET and soak or spray your gear with permethrin (licensed in the US for use on clothing). To stop the itch after being bitten, try Calamine lotion or topical cortisones. **Lyme Disease** is a bacterial infection carried by ticks and marked by a circular bull's-eye rash of 2 in. or more. Later symptoms include fever, headache, fatigue, and aches. Antibiotics are effective if taken early. Left untreated, Lyme can cause problems in joints, the heart, and the nervous system. Ticks, responsible for Lyme and other diseases, are a particular danger in the mountains. If you find a tick attached to your skin, grasp the head with tweezers as close to the skin as possible and apply slow, steady traction. Removing a tick within 24 hours greatly reduces the risk of infection. Do not try to remove ticks by burning them or coating them with solvents.

OTHER INFECTIOUS DISEASES

In the Southwest, the risk of food poisoning is low and can be further reduced by eating only at clean, respectable establishments. When visiting Mexico, further precautions are necessary, as the water is generally not to be trusted. When camping, bring water, or purify stream water by bringing it to a rolling boil for three minutes or treating it with **iodine tablets;** note, however, that some parasites such as *giardia* have exteriors that resist iodine treatment; boiling is more reliable. Wash your hands before eating, or use an anti-bacterial liquid hand cleaner.

Traveler's diarrhea: Results from drinking untreated water or eating uncooked foods. Symptoms include nausea, bloating, and urgency. Try quick-energy, non-sugary foods with protein and carbohydrates. Over-the-counter anti-diarrheals (e.g., Imodium) may help. The most dangerous side effect is dehydration; drink lots of water. If you develop a fever or your symptoms don't go away after 4-5 days, consult a doctor.

Parasites: Microbes, tapeworms, etc. that hide in water and food. **Giardiasis,** for example, is acquired by drinking untreated water from streams or lakes. Symptoms include swollen glands or lymph nodes, fever, rashes or itchiness, and digestive problems. Boil water, wear shoes, and eat only well cooked food.

Rabies: Transmitted through the saliva of infected animals; fatal if untreated. By the time symptoms (thirst, malaise, fever, headache and muscle spasms) appear, the disease is in its terminal stage. If you are bitten, wash the wound thoroughly, seek immediate medical care, and try to have the animal located. A rabies vaccine, which consists of 3 shots given over a 28-day period, is available but is only semi-effective.

Hepatitis B: A viral infection of the liver transmitted via bodily fluids or needle-sharing. Symptoms, which may not surface until years after infection, include jaundice, loss of appetite, fever, and joint pain. A 3-shot vaccination sequence is recommended for health-care workers, sexually-active travelers, and anyone planning to seek medical treatment abroad; it must begin 6 mo. before traveling.

Hepatitis C: Like Hepatitis B, but the mode of transmission differs. IV drug users, those with occupational exposure to blood, hemodialysis patients, and recipients of blood transfusions are at the highest risk, but it can also be spread through sexual contact or sharing items like razors and toothbrushes that may have traces of blood on them.

AIDS, HIV, & STDS

For detailed information on **Acquired Immune Deficiency Syndrome (AIDS)** in the US, call the **US Centers for Disease Control's** 24hr. hotline at ☎800-342-2437, or contact the **Joint United Nations Programme on HIV/AIDS (UNAIDS),** 20, ave. Appia, CH-1211 Geneva 27, Switzerland (☎+41 22 791 3666; fax 22 791 4187; www.unaids.org). The Council on International Educational Exchange's website (www.ciee.org/Isp/safety/travelsafe.htm) posts their pamphlet *Travel Safe: AIDS and International Travel,* along with links to other resources. According to US law, HIV positive persons are not permitted to enter the US. However, HIV testing is conducted only for those who are planning to immigrate permanently. Travelers from areas with particularly high concentrations of HIV positive persons or those with AIDS may be required to provide more info when applying.

Sexually transmitted diseases (STDs) such as gonorrhea, chlamydia, genital warts, syphilis, and herpes are easier to catch than HIV and can be as dangerous. **Hepatitis B** and **C** can also be transmitted sexually (see p. 29). Though condoms may protect you from some STDs, oral or even tactile contact can lead to transmission. If you think you may have contracted an STD, see a doctor immediately.

WOMEN'S HEALTH

Women traveling in unsanitary conditions are vulnerable to **urinary tract** and **bladder infections,** common but uncomfortable bacterial conditions that cause a burning sensation and painful (sometimes frequent) urination. Over-the-counter medicines can sometimes alleviate symptoms, but if they persist, see a doctor. **Vaginal yeast infections** may flare up in hot and humid climates. Wearing loosely fitting trousers or a skirt and cotton underwear will help, as will over-the-counter remedies like Monostat or Gynelotrimin. Bring supplies from home if you are prone to infection. Since **tampons, pads,** and reliable **contraceptive devices** are sometimes hard to find when traveling, bring supplies with you.

INSURANCE

Travel insurance generally covers four basic areas: medical/health problems, property loss, trip cancellation/interruption, and emergency evacuation. Although your regular insurance policies may extend to travel-related accidents, consider purchasing travel insurance if the cost of potential trip cancellation/interruption or emergency medical evacuation is greater than you can absorb. Prices for travel insurance purchased separately generally run about $40 per week for full coverage, while trip cancellation/interruption may be purchased separately at a rate of about $5.50 per $100 of coverage. **Medical insurance** (especially university policies) often covers costs incurred abroad; check with your provider. **Canadians** are protected by their home province's health insurance plan for up to 90 days after leaving the country; check with the provincial Ministry of Health or Health Plan Headquarters for details. **Homeowners' insurance** (or your family's coverage) often covers theft during travel and loss of travel documents (passport, plane ticket, etc.) up to $500. **ISIC** and **ITIC** (see p. 22) provide basic insurance benefits, including $100 per day of in-hospital sickness for up to 60 days, $3000 of accident-related medical reimbursement, and $25,000 for emergency medical transport. Cardholders have access to a toll-free 24hr. helpline (run by the insurance provider **Travel-Guard**) for medical, legal, and financial emergencies (US and Canada ☎877-370-4742). **American Express** (US ☎800-528-4800) grants some cardholders automatic car rental insurance (collision and theft, but not liability) and ground travel accident coverage of $100,000 on flight purchases made with the card.

INSURANCE PROVIDERS. STA (see p. 39) offers supplemental coverage. Other private providers in the US and Canada include: **Access America** (☎866-807-3982; www.accessamerica.com); **Berkely Group** (☎800-797-4514; www.berkely.com); **GlobalCare Insurance Services Inc.** (☎800-821-2488; www.globalcare-cocco.com); and **Travel Assistance International** (☎800-821-2828; www.travelassistance.com). Providers in the **UK** include **Columbus Direct** (☎020 7375 0011; www.columbusdirect.co.uk). In **Australia**, try **AFTA** (☎02 9264 3299; www.afta.com.au).

PACKING

Pack lightly: Lay out only what you absolutely need, then take half the clothes and twice the money. If you plan to do a lot of hiking, see **Camping**, p. 62.

LUGGAGE. If you plan to cover most of your itinerary by foot, a sturdy **internal frame backpack** is unbeatable. (For the basics on buying a pack, see p. 63.) Toting a **suitcase** or **trunk** is fine if you plan to live in one or two cities or can store things in your car, but otherwise can be burdensome. In addition to your main piece of luggage, a **daypack** (a small backpack or courier bag) is a must.

CLOTHING. For travel in alpine areas, pack layers of clothing—mornings and evenings tend to be cold year-round, while days can vary drastically. A sweater and light jacket or windbreaker may be necessary even in mid-summer. From late fall to early spring, be sure to bring a rain jacket (Gore-Tex® is both waterproof and breathable) or umbrella and a mid-weight jacket or heavy sweater. Wherever you go, **sturdy shoes** and **thick socks** can save your feet. **Flip-flops** or waterproof sandals are crucial for grungy hostel showers. You may also want to add one outfit beyond the jeans and t-shirt uniform, and maybe a nicer pair of shoes if you have the room.

TOILETRIES. Toothbrushes, towels, cold-water soap, talcum powder (to keep feet dry), deodorant, razors, tampons, and condoms are all readily available. If you wear **contact lenses,** bring an extra pair as well as back-up glasses. Also bring a copy of your prescription in case you need emergency replacements.

CONVERTERS & ADAPTERS. In the United States, electricity in outlets is standardized at 120 volts AC. **International travelers** using 220/240V electrical appliances should buy an **adapter** (which changes the shape of the plug) and a **converter** (which changes the voltage; $20). Don't make the mistake of using only an adapter (unless appliance instructions explicitly state otherwise). For more info, visit http://kropla.com/electric.htm.

FIRST-AID KIT. For a basic first-aid kit, take along the following supplies: bandages, pain reliever, antibiotic cream, a thermometer, a pocket knife or multi-tool, tweezers, moleskin, decongestant, motion-sickness remedy, diarrhea or upset-stomach medication (Pepto Bismol or Imodium), an antihistamine, sunscreen, insect repellent, and burn ointment.

FILM. Camera stores abound in the Southwest, offering many film and developing options. Less serious photographers may want to bring a **disposable camera** or two. Despite disclaimers, airport security X-rays *can* fog film, so buy a lead-lined pouch at a camera store or ask security to hand-inspect it. Always pack film in your carry-on luggage, since higher-intensity X-rays are used on checked luggage.

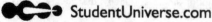

OTHER USEFUL ITEMS. For safety purposes, you should bring a **money belt** and small **padlock. Quick repairs** of torn garments can be done on the road with a needle and thread; also consider bringing electrical tape for patching tears. If you want to do **laundry** by hand, bring detergent, a small rubber ball to stop up the sink, and string for a makeshift clothes line. **Other things** you're liable to forget: an umbrella, an **alarm clock,** safety pins, ear plugs, garbage bags, and a flashlight.

ACCOMMODATIONS

HOSTELS

Hostels are generally laid out dorm-style, often with large single-sex rooms and bunk beds, although some offer private rooms for families and couples. They sometimes have kitchens and utensils for your use, bike or moped rentals, storage areas, transportation to airports, breakfast, and laundry facilities. Drawbacks can include daytime "lockout" hours, curfews, lack of reservations, imposition of a maximum stay, or a requirement that you do chores. In the Southwest, a dorm bed in a hostel will average around $15-20 and a private room around $40-50.

HOSTELLING INTERNATIONAL

Joining a youth hostel association in your own country (listed below) automatically grants you membership privileges in **Hostelling International (HI),** a federation of national hostelling associations. There are HI hostels scattered throughout the Southwest, and many accept reservations via the **International Booking Network,** which takes reservations online and over the phone (☎202-783-6161; www.hostel-booking.com). HI's umbrella organization's web page (www.iyhf.org), which lists the web addresses and phone numbers of all national associations, is a good place to start your research, and www.hostels.com/us.southwest.html has listings of Southwestern hostels and other resources. Most HI hostels honor **guest member-ships**—a blank card with space for six validation stamps. Each night you'll pay a nonmember supplement (one-sixth the membership fee) and earn one stamp; get six, and you're a member. A membership benefit is the Free Nites program, which allows you to gain points toward free rooms. Most student travel agencies (see p. 39) sell **HI cards,** as do the hostelling organizations below. All prices listed are for **one-year memberships** unless otherwise noted.

Australian Youth Hostels Association (AYHA; www.yha.org.au). AUS$52; under 18 AUS$16.

Hostelling International-Canada (HI-C), 205 Catherine St. #400, Ottawa, ON K2P 1C3 (☎613-237-7884; www.hihostels.ca). CDN$35; under-18 free.

An Óige (Irish Youth Hostel Association), 61 Mountjoy St., Dublin 7 (☎830 4555; www.irelandyha.org). €25; under-18 €10.5.

Youth Hostels Association of New Zealand (YHANZ), P.O. Box 436, 166 Moorhouse Ave., Moorhouse City, Christchurch (☎03 379 9970; www.yha.org.nz). NZ$40; under-18 free.

Hostels Association of South Africa, 3rd fl. 73 St. George's House, Cape Town 8001 (☎021 424 2511; www.hisa.org.za). R79; under-18 R40.

Scottish Youth Hostels Association (SYHA), 7 Glebe Crescent, Stirling FK8 2JA (☎ 870 1 55 32 55; www.syha.org.uk). UK£6; under-18 £2.50.

Youth Hostels Association (England and Wales), Trevelyon House, Dimple Rd., Matlock, Derbyshire DE4 3YH, UK (☎01629 5962600; www.yha.org.uk). UK£13.50; under-18 UK£6.75.

KEEPING IN TOUCH

BY MAIL

DOMESTIC RATES

First-class letters sent and received within the US take 1-3 days and cost 37¢, **Priority Mail** packages up to 1 lb. generally take 2 days and cost $3.85, up to 5 lb. $5.85-12.15. **All days specified denote business days.** For more details, see www.usps.com.

SENDING MAIL HOME FROM THE SOUTHWEST

Airmail is the best way to send mail from the US; letters or packages sent by airmail generally take 5-7 days to arrive. **Aerogrammes,** one form of airmail, are printed sheets that fold into envelopes and are available at post offices. Write *"par avion"* or "air mail" on the front. Most post offices will charge exorbitant fees or simply refuse to send aerogrammes with enclosures. Letters sent by regular airmail cost 60-80¢, packages up to 1 lb. run $13-17, and packages up to 5 lb. are $17-28. **Surface mail** is the cheapest and slowest way to send mail. It takes one to three months to cross the Atlantic and two to four to cross the Pacific.

SENDING MAIL TO THE SOUTHWEST

Mark envelopes "air mail" or *"par avion,"* or your letter or postcard will never arrive. In addition to the standard postage system, **Federal Express** (Australia ☎ 13 26 10, US and Canada ☎ 800-247-4747, New Zealand ☎ 0800 73 33 39, UK ☎ 0800 12 38 00; www.fedex.com) handles express mail services from abroad to the US, as well as within the country. For example, they can get a letter from New York to Los Angeles in 2 days for $10.76, and from London to New York overnight for $27.78.

RECEIVING MAIL IN THE SOUTHWEST

There are several ways to arrange pick-up of letters while you are abroad. Mail can be sent via General Delivery to almost any city or town in the Southwest with a post office. Address General Delivery letters like this: Ned FLANDERS, General Delivery, Flagstaff, AZ 86004, USA. The mail will go to a special desk in the central post office, unless you specify one by street address or postal code. Bring your passport or other photo ID for pick-up. If the clerks insist that there is nothing for you, have them check under your first name as well. **American Express's** travel offices throughout the world offer a free Client Letter Service (mail held up to 30 days and forwarded upon request) for cardholders who contact them in advance.

BY TELEPHONE

CALLING HOME FROM THE SOUTHWEST

A **calling card** is probably your cheapest bet. Calls are billed collect or to your account. You can frequently call collect without having a company's calling card: call their access number and follow instructions. To **call home with a calling card,** contact the operator for your service provider by dialing the toll-free access number. You can often also make **direct international calls** from pay phones, but they're expensive. Occasionally, prepaid phone and credit cards can be used for international calls, but they are less cost-effective (see **Placing International Calls,** p. 38).

Let's Go has recently partnered with **ekit.com** to provide a calling card that offers a number of services, including email and voice messaging. Before purchasing any calling card, always be sure to compare rates with other cards, and to make sure it serves your needs (a local phonecard is generally better for local calls, for instance). For more information, visit www.letsgo.ekit.com.

CALLING WITHIN THE SOUTHWEST

The simplest way to place a local phone call within the Southwest, is to use a coin-operated phone; in the Southwest, these calls cost 35¢ from any public phone. **Prepaid phone cards,** which carry a certain amount of phone time depending on the card's denomination, are the best option for placing international calls or US long-distance calls. Prepaid cards save time and money in the long run, though the cards require a 25¢ surcharge when used from pay phones. There are usually multiple denominations of prepaid cards (for various countries) readily available at convenience stores, pharmacies, and other locations throughout the Southwest.

TIME DIFFERENCES

The majority of the Southwest is on **Mountain Standard Time** (GMT/UTC minus seven hours) including all of Utah, Colorado, and New Mexico. Arizona is an anomaly in the States, as the vast majority of the state does not observe Daylight Savings Time. Therefore, while Arizona abides by Mountain Time during the winter months, in the summer it is on **Pacific Standard Time,** along with Nevada and California. The entire Navajo Nation is in Mountain Time year-round, so it is one hour off from the rest of Arizona in the summer. To add to the confusion, the Hopi Reservation, enclosed within the Navajo Nation, sticks with the rest of Arizona, spending half the year on Mountain Time and the other half on Pacific Time. For a visual clarification of this confusing system, check the time zone map on the inside of the back cover of this book.

BY EMAIL & INTERNET

Though in some places it's possible to forge a remote link with your home server, in most cases this is a much slower (and more expensive) option than using free **web-based email accounts** (such as www.hotmail.com and www.yahoo.com). Travelers with laptops can call an Internet service provider via a **modem.** Long-distance phone cards intended for such calls can defray normally phone charges; check with your long-distance provider. Most Southwestern cities have public libraries with free Internet terminals. Establishments offering **Internet access** are listed in the Practical Information sections of major cities. Various websites **(www.cyberia-cafe.net/cyberia/guide/ccafe.htm; www.cybercaptive.com)** may be helpful in locating cybercafes in the Southwest and other regions of the US.

PLACING INTERNATIONAL CALLS. To call the US from home or to call home from the US, dial:

1. The **international dialing prefix.** To dial out of **Australia,** dial 0011; **Canada** or the **US,** 011; the **Republic of Ireland, New Zealand,** or the **UK,** 00; **South Africa,** 09.

2. The **country code** of the country you want to call. To call **Australia,** dial 61; **Canada** or the **US,** 1; the **Republic of Ireland,** 353; **New Zealand,** 64; **South Africa,** 27; the **UK,** 44.

3. The **city/area code.** *Let's Go* lists the city/area codes for cities and towns in the Southwest opposite the city or town name, next to a ☎.

4. The **local number.**

GETTING TO THE SOUTHWEST

BY PLANE

If your plans are flexible enough to deal with the restrictions, courier fares are the cheapest. Tickets bought from consolidators and standby seating are also good deals, but last-minute specials, airfare wars, and charter flights often beat these fares. The key is to be flexible, and to ask persistently about discounts. Students, seniors, and those under 26 should never pay full price for a ticket.

AIRFARES

It is cheapest to travel midweek (M-Th morning), as round-trip prices are often bumped up $40-50 on the weekend. Traveling with an "open return" ticket or arriving in and departing from different cities ("open-jaw") can be pricier than round-trip flights. Patching one-way flights together is the most expensive way to travel. Flights from or to major cities such as Phoenix, Salt Lake City, Las Vegas, and Albuquerque tend to be cheaper.

BUDGET & STUDENT TRAVEL AGENCIES

While knowledgeable agents specializing in flights to the Southwest can make your life easier, they may not spend the time to find you the lowest possible fare—they get paid on commission. Travelers holding **ISIC and IYTC cards** (see p. 22) qualify for big discounts from student travel agencies. Most flights from budget agencies are on major airlines, but in peak season some may sell seats on less reliable chartered aircraft.

USIT, 19-21 Aston Quay, Dublin 2 (☎01 602 1600; www.usitworld.com). Ireland's leading student/budget travel agency has 22 offices throughout Northern Ireland and the Republic of Ireland. Offers programs to work in North America.

CTS Travel, 30 Rathbone Pl., London W1T 1GQ, UK (☎020 7290 0630; www.ctstravel.co.uk). A British student travel agency with offices in 39 countries including the US: Empire State Building, 350 Fifth Ave., Suite 7813, New York, NY 10118 (☎877-287-6665; www.ctstravelusa.com).

STA Travel, 7890 S. Hardy Dr., Ste. 110, Tempe AZ 85284 (24hr. reservations and info ☎800-781-4040; www.sta-travel.com). A student and youth travel organization with over 150 offices worldwide (check their website for a listing of all their offices), including US offices in Boston, Chicago, LA, New York, San Francisco, Seattle, and Washington, D.C. Ticket booking, travel insurance, rail passes, and more. In the UK, walk-in office 11 Goodge St., **London** W1T 2PF (☎020 7436 7779). In New Zealand, Shop 2B, 182 Queen St., **Auckland** (☎09 309 0458). In Australia, 366 Lygon St., **Carlton** Vic 3053 (☎03 9349 4344).

Travel CUTS (Canadian Universities Travel Services Limited), 187 College St., **Toronto,** ON M5T 1P7 (☎416-979-2406; www.travelcuts.com). Offices across Canada and the United States in Seattle, San Francisco, Los Angeles, New York and elsewhere. Also in the UK, 295-A Regent St., **London** W1B 2H9 (☎0207 255 2191).

COMMERCIAL AIRLINES

The commercial airlines' lowest regular offer is the **APEX** (Advance Purchase Excursion) fare, which provides confirmed reservations and allows "open-jaw" tickets. Generally, reservations must be made seven to 21 days ahead of departure, with seven- to 14-day minimum-stay and up to 90-day maximum-stay restrictions. These fares carry hefty cancellation and change penalties (fees rise in summer).

Book peak-season APEX fares early; by May you will have a hard time getting your desired departure date. Use **Microsoft Expedia** (www.expedia.com) or **Travelocity** (www.travelocity.com) to get an idea of the lowest published fares, then use the resources outlined here to try and beat those fares.

AIR COURIER FLIGHTS

Those who travel light should consider courier flights. Couriers help transport cargo on international flights by using their checked luggage space for freight. Couriers must travel with carry-ons only and deal with complex flight restrictions. Most flights are round-trip only, with short fixed-length stays (usually one week) and a limit of a one ticket per issue. Most flights also operate only out of major gateway cities (e.g., Phoenix). Generally, you must be over 21 (in some cases 18). In summer, the most popular destinations usually require an advance reservation of about two weeks (you can usually book up to two months ahead). Super-discounted fares are common for "last-minute" flights (three to 14 days ahead).

STANDBY FLIGHTS

Traveling standby requires considerable flexibility in arrival and departure dates. Companies dealing in standby flights sell vouchers rather than tickets, along with the promise to get to your destination (or near your destination) within a certain window of time (typically 1-5 days). You call in before your specific window of time to hear your flight options and the probability that you will be able to board each flight. You can then decide which flights you want to try to make, show up at the appropriate airport at the appropriate time, present your voucher, and board if space is available. Vouchers can usually be bought for both one-way and round-trip travel. You may receive a monetary refund only if every available flight within your date range is full; if you opt not to take an available (but perhaps less convenient) flight, you can only get credit toward future travel. Carefully read agreements with any company offering standby flights as tricky fine print can leave you in a lurch. To check on a company's service record in the US, call the Better Business Bureau (☎212-533-6200). It is difficult to receive refunds, and clients' vouchers will not be honored when an airline fails to receive payment in time.

TICKET CONSOLIDATORS

Ticket consolidators, or "bucket shops," buy unsold tickets in bulk from commercial airlines and sell them at discounted rates. The best place to look is in the Sunday travel section of any major newspaper (e.g., *The New York Times*), where many bucket shops place tiny ads. Call quickly, as availability is typically extremely limited. Not all bucket shops are reliable, so insist on a receipt that gives full details of restrictions, refunds, and tickets, and pay by credit card (in spite of the 2-5% fee) so you can stop payment if you never receive your tickets. For more info, see www.travel-library.com/air-travel/consolidators.html.

FROM THE US & CANADA. Travel Avenue (☎800-333-3335; www.travelavenue.com) searches for best available published fares and then uses several consolidators to attempt to beat that fare. Other consolidators worth trying are **Interworld** (☎305-443-4929; fax 443-0351); **Pennsylvania Travel** (☎800-331-0947); **Rebel** (☎800-227-3235; www.rebeltours.com); and **Travac** (☎800-872-8800; fax 212-714-9063; www.travac.com). Other consolidators on the web include the **Internet Travel Network** (www.itn.com); **Travel Information Services** (www.tiss.com); **TravelHUB** (www.travelhub.com); and **The Travel Site** (www.thetravelsite.com). Keep in mind that these are just suggestions to get you started; *Let's Go* does not endorse any of these agencies. As always, be cautious, and research companies before you hand over your credit card number.

FLIGHT PLANNING ON THE INTERNET. Many airline sites offer special last-minute deals on the Web. Other sites do the legwork and compile the deals for you—try www.bestfares.com, www.flights.com, www.lowestfare.com, www.onetravel.com, and www.travelzoo.com.

StudentUniverse (www.studentuniverse.com), **STA** (www.sta-travel.com), and **Orbitz.com** provide quotes on student tickets, while **Expedia** (www.expedia.com) and **Travelocity** (www.travelocity.com) offer full travel prices. **Priceline** (www.priceline.com) allows you to specify a price, and obligates you to buy any ticket that meets or beats it; be prepared for antisocial hours and odd routes. **Skyauction** (www.skyauction.com) allows you to bid on both last-minute and advance-purchase tickets.

An indispensable resource on the Internet is the *Air Traveler's Handbook* (www.cs.cmu.edu/afs/cs/user/mkant/Public/Travel/airfare.html), a comprehensive listing of links to everything you need to know before you board a plane.

CHARTER FLIGHTS

Charters are flights a tour operator contracts with an airline to fly extra loads of passengers during peak season. Charter flights fly less frequently than major airlines, make refunds particularly difficult, and are almost always fully booked. Schedules and itineraries may also change or be cancelled at the last moment (as late as 48 hours before the trip, and without a full refund), and check-in, boarding, and baggage claim are often much slower. However, they can also be cheaper.

Discount clubs and **fare brokers** offer members savings on last-minute charter and tour deals. Study contracts closely; you don't want to end up with an unwanted overnight layover. **Travelers Advantage,** Trumbull, CT, USA (☎877-259-2691; www.travelersadvantage.com; a US$60 annual fee includes discounts and cheap flight directories), can provide more information.

GETTING AROUND

BY TRAIN

Trains are one of the least expensive (and most pleasant) ways to tour the Southwest, but discounted air travel is faster and may be cheaper. You can save money by purchasing your tickets far in advance, so plan ahead and make reservations early. It is essential to travel light on trains; not all stations will check baggage.

AMTRAK

Amtrak is the only passenger train service in the Southwest via its **Southwest Chief** and **Sunset Limited** lines. (☎800-872-7245; www.amtrak.com. Albuquerque to L.A.: 15hr., $96; Albuquerque to Flagstaff: 4hr., $84; Tucson to L.A.: 10hr., $61.) The Southwest Chief line runs parallel to Rte. 66/I-40 and the Santa Fe railroad line, via **Albuquerque** (p. 378), **Gallup** (p. 418), **Flagstaff** (p. 111), and **Williams** on its way to Los Angeles. The Sunset Limited Line runs just north of the border, serving cities including San Antonio, El Paso, Tucson, and L.A. Train travel to Phoenix is arranged through a bus connection to Tucson. Cities on the Amtrak line have ticket offices, but tickets must be bought through an agent in some small towns. Amtrak's website lists up-to-date schedules, fares, and arrival and departure info, and makes reservations. Discounts on full rail fares are given to senior citizens (10% off), students with a Student Advantage card (15% off; visit amtrak.com to

ESSENTIALS

purchase the $20 card), travelers with disabilities (15% off), children 2-15 accompanied by an adult (50% off), and children under 2 (free). Active-duty veterans may enroll in the **Veterans Advantage** program, which provides discounts from 15 to 50% for an annual fee ($20). Amtrak's "Rail SALE" allows travelers to save up to 90% on certain trips. The **Air-Rail Vacations** program (☎ 877-YES-RAIL), offered in conjunction with United Airlines, allows you to travel in one direction by train and return by plane. The train portion of the journey can last up to 30 days and include up to three stopovers. A multitude of variations are available.

BY BUS

Buses offer the most frequent service between cities and towns in the Southwest. Often a bus is the only way to reach smaller locales without a car. In rural areas, however, bus lines tend to be sparse. *Russell's Official National Motor Coach Guide* ($16) is invaluable in constructing an itinerary. Updated each month, *Russell's Guide* has schedules of every bus route in the US and Canada. *Russell's* also publishes two semiannual supplements, which are free when ordered with the main issue: a Directory of Bus Lines and Bus Stations, and a series of Route Maps ($9 each if ordered separately). To order any of the above, write **Russell's Guides, Inc.,** P.O. Box 178, Cedar Rapids, IA 52406 (☎319-364-6138; fax 362-8808).

GREYHOUND

Greyhound (☎800-231-2222; www.greyhound.com) operates the largest number of routes in the US, though local companies may provide more extensive services within specific regions. Schedules are available at any Greyhound terminal, on the website, or by calling the 800 number. Reserve with a credit card over the phone at least 10 days in advance, and the ticket can be mailed anywhere in the US. Otherwise, reservations are available only up to 24hr. in advance. You can buy your ticket at the terminal, but arrive early. **If boarding at a remote "flag stop," be sure you know exactly where the bus stops.** Call the nearest agency and let them know you'll be waiting and at what time. Catch the driver's attention by standing on the side of the road and flailing your arms wildly—better to be embarrassed than stranded. If a bus passes (usually because of overcrowding), a later, less-crowded bus should stop. Whatever you stow under the bus must be clearly marked; get a claim check for it and make sure your luggage is on the same bus as you.

Advance purchase fares: Reserving space far ahead of time ensures a lower fare, but expect smaller discounts June 5-Sept. 15. Fares are often lower for 14-, 7-, and 3-day advance purchases. For 3-day advance purchase M-Th, 2 people ride for the price of 1 ticket. Call for up-to-date pricing or consult their web page.

Discounts on full fares: Senior citizens with a Greyhound Senior Club Card (10% off), children ages 2-11 (50% off), Student Advantage card holders (up to 15% off), disabled travelers and their companions receive two tickets for the price of one, and active and retired US military personnel and National Guard Reserves (10% off with valid ID). With a ticket purchased three or more days in advance during the spring and summer months, a friend can travel along for free (with some exceptions).

Ameripass (☎800-454-7277): Allows adults unlimited travel through the US. 7-day pass $229; 10-day pass $279; 15-day pass $349; 30-day pass $459, 45-day pass $519; 60-day pass $625. Student discounts available. Children's passes are half-price. **Coaches, Vermont Transit, Carolina Trailways,** and **Valley Transit** are Greyhound subsidiaries, and as such will honor Ameripasses; actually, most bus companies in the US will do so, but check for specifics.

International Ameripass (☎ 800-454-7277): For travelers from outside North America. 7-day ($219), 10-day ($269), 15-day ($329), 30-day ($439), 45-day ($489), or 60-day ($599). Not available at the terminal; they can be purchased in foreign countries at Greyhound-affiliated agencies; telephone numbers are listed on the website. Passes can also be ordered at the website or purchased by calling ☎ 800-229-9424 in the US.

BY CAR

Driving is the most convenient way of getting around the Southwest and also probably also the most enjoyable. Since most cities and even many smaller towns, true to the Western-sprawl school of urban planning, cannot be explored without wheels, and since almost everyone has wheels, there is little public transportation. Gas and car rentals are inexpensive in the Southwest. Roads are wide, straight, and laid out logically—all the more reason to go by car if possible.

INTERNATIONAL DRIVING PERMITS

If you do not have a US or Canadian license, you may want an International Driving Permit (IDP)—it can help with police if your license is not written in English. You must carry your home license with your IDP at all times. You must be 18 to obtain an IDP, which is valid for a year and must be issued in the country of origin.

CAR INSURANCE

Insurance is mandatory for all drivers in the US. If you're renting a car, make sure the rental agreement provides it if you don't already have it, and ask whether the price includes insurance against **theft and collision.** Most credit cards cover standard insurance. **American Express** offers its cardholders secondary insurance if the reservation is made and paid for with the card (☎ 800-638-1670). If you rent, lease, or borrow a car, you will need a **green card,** or **International Insurance Certificate** to certify that you have liability insurance and that it applies abroad. Green cards can be obtained at car rental agencies, car dealers (for those leasing cars), and some travel agents and border crossings. If you are driving a conventional vehicle on an **unpaved road** in a rental car, you are almost never covered by insurance.

AUTOMOBILE CLUBS

Most automobile clubs offer free towing, emergency roadside assistance, travel-related discounts, and random goodies in exchange for a modest membership fee. Travelers should strongly consider membership if planning an extended roadtrip.

◪ **American Automobile Association (AAA;** ☎ 800-222-4357 road service, 800-564-6222 to sign up; www.aaa.com). Provides emergency road service. Free trip-planning services, maps, and guidebooks, and 24hr. emergency road service anywhere in the US, free towing and commission-free AmEx Traveler's Cheques. Discounts on Hertz car rental (5-20%), Amtrak tickets (10%), and various motel chains and theme parks. Basic membership $48, Associate Membership $25.

Mobil Auto Club, 200 N. Martingale Rd., Schaumbourg, IL 60174 (info ☎ 800-621-5581; emergency service 800-323-5880). Benefits include locksmith reimbursement, towing (free up to 10 mi.), roadside service, and car-rental discounts. $8 per month covers you and another driver.

ON THE ROAD

A good US road atlas, such as Rand McNally's (available at bookstores and gas stations, $11), is essential for road-trippers. Research gas station availability before you set out, and make sure you have all the tools mentioned in **The Desert and Your**

Car (p. 67). Those traveling long stretches of road may want to consider purchasing a **cell phone**. In more sparsely populated areas of the Southwest, cell service is sporadic at best, but most phones should get reception on major thoroughfares. While driving, buckle up—**seat belts are required by US law. Speed limits** on interstates throughout most of the Southwest are 70-75 m.p.h. Local police and state troopers make frequent use of radar to catch speed demons, so be attentive when zipping along the interstates. The region has many unpaved and often unmapped roads. Avoid seeking shortcuts on unmarked rural roads.

RENTING

Car rental agencies fall into two categories: national companies with hundreds of branches, and local agencies that serve one city or region. National chains usually allow you to pick up a car in one city and drop it off in another (for a hefty charge, sometimes over $1000). Steep prices (a compact car rents for $25-45 per day) and high minimum ages for rentals (usually 25) are the drawbacks. Most branches rent to ages 21-24 with an additional fee, but policies and prices vary. **Alamo** (☎ 800-327-9633; www.alamo.com) rents to ages 21-24 with a major credit card for an additional $20 per day; **Enterprise** (☎ 800-736-8222; www.enterprise.com) rents to ages 21-24 with a variable surcharge; and **Dollar** (☎ 800-800-4000; www.dollar.com) and **Thrifty** (☎ 800-367-2277; www.thrifty.com) do likewise for varying surcharges. **Rent-A-Wreck** (☎ 800-944-7501; www.rent-a-wreck.com) specializes in supplying vehicles that are past their prime for lower-than-average prices; a bare-bones compact less than eight years old rents for around $20 to $25. There may be an additional charge for a **collision and damage waiver** (**CDW;** usually about $12-15 per day). Major credit cards (including MasterCard and American Express) will sometimes cover the CDW if you use their card to rent a car; call your credit card company for specifics.

AUTO TRANSPORT COMPANIES

These services match drivers with car owners who need cars moved from one city to another. Travelers give the company their desired destination, and the company finds a car that needs to go there. Expenses include gas, tolls, and living expenses. Some companies insure their cars; with others, a security deposit covers breakdowns and damage. You must be over 21, have a valid license, and agree to drive about 400 mi. per day on a fairly direct route. **Auto Driveaway Company** (☎ 800-346-2277 or 312-341-1900; www.autodriveaway.com) and **Across America Driveaway** (☎ 800-619-7707; www.schultz-international.com) are two popular companies.

BUYING

Adventures on Wheels (☎ 732-495-0959 or 800-943-3579; adventuresonwheels.com) sells motorhomes, minivans, station wagons, and compact cars, organizes registration, and provides insurance. Cars with a buy-back guarantee start at $2500. Buy a camper for $6500, use it for six months, and sell it back for $3000-4000. Offices are in New York/New Jersey, Los Angeles, San Francisco, Las Vegas, Denver, and Miami. Vehicles can be picked up at one office and dropped off at another.

BY BICYCLE

Before you pedal furiously along the byways of America, remember that safe and secure cycling requires a quality helmet and lock. Some U-shaped **Kryptonite** locks ($30-90) carry insurance against theft for one or two years if your bike is registered with the police. For biking gear, the **Bike Nashbar** catalog, P.O. Box 1455, Crab Orchard, WV 25827 (☎ 800-627-4227), will beat any nationally advertised in-stock price by 5¢ and ships anywhere in the US or Canada, and their techline

(☎800-888-2710; open M-F 8am-6pm ET) fields questions about repairs and maintenance. For maps and info, the national, non-profit **Adventure Cycling Association**
(☎800-755-2453; www.adv-cycling.org) researches routes and organizes bike tours
(75-day Great Divide Expedition $2800, 6-9 day trip $650-800; membership $30).

BY MOTORCYCLE

The burly leather and wind-in-your-face thrill of motorcycle culture has built a cult
following, but motorcycle riding is the most dangerous roadtop activity. Safety
should be your primary concern. Helmets are required by US law; wear the best
one you can find. Contact the **American Motorcyclist Association,** 13515 Yarmouth
Dr., Pickering, OH 43147 (☎800-262-5646; www.ama-cycle.org), the linchpin of US
biker culture. A full membership ($39 per year) includes a subscription to the
informative *American Motorcyclist* magazine, discounts on insurance, rentals,
and hotels, and a patch for your riding jacket. And of course, take a copy of Robert
Pirsig's *Zen and the Art of Motorcycle Maintenance* (Bantam, $8) with you.

BY THUMB

Hitchhiking involves entrusting your life to a randomly selected person, risking
theft, sexual harassment, assault, and unsafe driving. While this may be compara-
tively safe in some areas of Europe and Australia, it is *not* safe in the US, and especially not in the Southwest. *Let's Go* strongly urges you to find other means of
transportation and to avoid situations where hitching is the only option.

SPECIFIC CONCERNS

WOMEN TRAVELERS

Women traveling solo inevitably face some additional safety concerns, but it's easy
to be adventurous without taking undue risks. Consider staying in hostels that offer
single rooms that lock from the inside or in religious organizations with rooms for
women only. Stick to centrally located accommodations and avoid solitary late-
night treks or metro rides, and carry extra money for a phone call, bus, or taxi.
Hitchhiking is never safe for women, even for two women traveling together. When
on overnight or long train rides, choose a compartment occupied by women or couples. If you're lost, approach older women or couples for directions. The less you
look like a tourist, the better off you'll be. Dress conservatively, especially in rural
areas. Trying to fit in can be effective, but dressing to the style of an obviously different culture may cause you to be ill at ease and a conspicuous target. Wearing a
wedding band may help prevent unwanted overtures.

Your best answer to verbal harassment is no answer at all; feigning deafness, sitting motionless, and staring straight ahead will do a world of good that reactions
usually don't achieve. The extremely persistent can sometimes be dissuaded by a
firm, loud, and very public "Go away!" Don't hesitate to seek out a police officer or
a passerby if you are being harassed. Memorize the emergency numbers in places
you visit, and consider carrying a keychain **whistle.** A self-defense course will prepare you for a potential attack and raise your level of awareness of your surroundings (see **Self Defense,** p. 26). For general information, contact the **National
Organization for Women (NOW),** 733 15th St. NW, 2nd Floor, Washington, D.C. 20005
(☎202-628-8669; www.now.org), which has branches across the US that can refer
women travelers to rape crisis centers and counseling services.

TRAVELING ALONE

There are many benefits to traveling alone, including independence and greater interaction with locals. But any solo traveler is a vulnerable target of harassment and theft. Try not to stand out, look confident, and be especially careful in deserted or very crowded areas. If questioned, never admit that you are traveling alone. Maintain regular contact with someone at home who knows your itinerary. For more tips, pick up *Traveling Solo* by Eleanor Berman (Globe Pequot Press, $18) or subscribe to **Connecting: Solo Travel Network**, 689 Park Road, Unit 6, Gibsons, BC V0N 1V7, Canada (☎604-886-9099; www.cstn.org; membership $35). To link up with a tour group, try **Contiki Holidays** (888-CONTIKI; www.contiki.com), which offers a variety of packages designed for 18- to 35-year-olds. Tours include accommodations, transportation, guided sightseeing and some meals; most average about $75 per day.

OLDER TRAVELERS

Senior citizens are eligible for a range of discounts on transportation, museums, movies, theaters, concerts, restaurants, and accommodations. If you don't see a senior citizen price listed, ask. The books *No Problem! Worldwise Tips for Mature Adventurers*, by Janice Kenyon (Orca Book Publishers; $16) and *Unbelievably Good Deals and Great Adventures That You Absolutely Can't Get Unless You're Over 50*, by Joan Rattner Heilman (NTC/Contemporary Publishing; $15) are excellent resources. The monthly newsletter, *The Mature Traveler*, P.O. Box 1543, Wildomar, CA 92595 (☎909-461-9598, www.thematuretraveler.com, subscription $30), has deals, discounts, tips, and travel packages for the senior traveler. Many tour agencies cater to older travelers as well. **Elderhostel**, 11 Ave. de Lafayette, Boston, MA 02111 (☎877-426-8056; www.elderhostel.org), has useful info and organizes one- to four-week educational adventures for those 55+. **Walking the World**, P.O. Box 1186, Fort Collins, CO 80522 (☎800-340-9255; www.walkingtheworld.com), runs walking-focused trips for travelers 50+ in the Southwest.

BISEXUAL, GAY, & LESBIAN TRAVELERS

Some of the Southwest's more cosmopolitan communities, such as Tucson and Phoenix in Arizona and Las Vegas in Nevada, have thriving gay and lesbian communities; many college towns in the region are also quite gay-friendly. Nevertheless, incidents of homophobia are all too common. Attitudes toward gay and lesbian travelers will vary greatly throughout the region, from state to state and town to town. However, BGLT travelers should feel confident and safe traveling in all parts of the Southwest. BGLT travelers who experience harassment should immediately report incidents to the police. *Let's Go* includes local gay and lesbian info lines and community centers when available, and **Out and About** (www.planetout.com) publishes a newsletter addressing travel concerns. **Giovanni's Room**, 1145 Pine St., Philadelphia, PA 19107 (☎215-923-2960; www.queerbooks.com), is an international lesbian/feminist and gay bookstore that stocks many (including some of those below) and offers mail-order service.

TRAVELERS WITH DISABILITIES

Federal law dictates that all public buildings should be handicapped accessible, and recent laws governing building codes make disabled access more the norm than the exception. However, traveling with a disability still requires planning and flexibility. Those with disabilities should inform airlines and hotels of their disabilities when making reservations; some time may be needed to prepare special accommodations. Call ahead. US Customs requires a certificate of immunization against rabies for **guide dogs** entering the country.

> **FURTHER READING: BISEXUAL, GAY, & LESBIAN**
>
> *Spartacus International Gay Guide 2003-2004*, Spartacus Travel Team ($33).
> *Damron Men's Guide, Damron Road Atlas, Damron's Accommodations,* and *The Women's Traveller*, Damron Travel Guides (☎800-462-6654; www.damron.com; $14-19).
> *Ferrari Guides' Gay Travel A to Z, Ferrari Guides' Men's Travel in Your Pocket,* and *Ferrari Guides' Inn Places*, Ferrari Pub. (www.ferrariguides.com; $16-20).
> *The Gay Vacation Guide: The Best Trips and How to Plan Them*, Mark Chesnut. Kensington Publishing Corporation ($15).
> *Gayellow Pages USA/Canada*, Frances Green. Gayellow Pages (www.gayellowpages.com; $16).

In the US, Amtrak and major airlines will accommodate disabled passengers if notified at least 72 hours in advance. Hearing-impaired travelers can contact Amtrak using teletype printers (☎800-523-6590 or 800-654-5988). Greyhound buses will provide free travel for a companion; if you are alone, call Greyhound (☎800-752-4841) at least 48 hours, but no more than one week, before you leave, and they will assist you. For information on transportation availability in individual US cities, contact the local chapter of the Easter Seals Society.

If you are planning to visit a national park or attraction in the US run by the National Park Service, get a free **Golden Access Passport**, available at all park entrances and federal offices whose functions relate to land, forests, or wildlife. It entitles disabled travelers and their families to free park admission and a 50% discount on all campsite and parking fees. For further reading, check out *Resource Directory for the Disabled*, by Richard Neil Shrout (Facts on File; $45).

USEFUL ORGANIZATIONS & TOUR AGENCIES

Mobility International USA (MIUSA), P.O. Box 10767, Eugene, OR 97440 (voice and TDD ☎541-343-1284; www.miusa.org). Sells *A World of Options: A Guide to International Educational Exchange, Community Service, and Travel for Persons with Disabilities* ($35), and provides other useful travel info.

Society for Accessible Travel & Hospitality (SATH), 347 Fifth Ave., #610, New York, NY 10016 (☎212-447-7284; www.sath.org). An advocacy group that publishes free online travel information and the travel magazine *OPEN WORLD* ($18, free for members). Annual membership $45, students and seniors $30.

Directions Unlimited, 123 Green Ln., Bedford Hills, NY 10507 (☎800-533-5343). Books individual and group vacations for the physically disabled; not an info service.

The Guided Tour Inc., 7900 Old York Rd., #114B, Elkins Park, PA 19027 (☎800-783-5841; www.guidedtour.com). Organizes travel programs for persons with developmental and physical challenges in the Southwest and elsewhere in the United States.

MINORITY TRAVELERS

Racial and ethnic minorities sometimes face blatant and, more often, subtle discrimination and/or harassment. Remain calm and report individuals to a supervisor and establishments to the Better Business Bureau for the region (the operator will provide local listings); contact the police in extreme situations. *Let's Go* always welcomes reader input regarding discriminating establishments. In larger cities, African-Americans can usually consult chapters of the **Urban League** and the **National Association for the Advancement of Colored People**, or **NAACP** (www.naacp.org), for info on events of interest to African-Americans.

TRAVELERS WITH CHILDREN

Family vacations often require more forethought and a slower pace. Consider the needs of children and pick establishments that are child-friendly. If you rent a car, ask about car seats. Be sure that your child carries some sort of ID in case he/she gets lost or in trouble, and arrange a meeting spot in case of separation.

Restaurants often have children's menus and discounts, and virtually all museums and tourist attractions have children's rates. Children under two generally fly for free or 10% of the adult airfare on domestic flights (this does not necessarily include a seat). Fares are usually discounted 25% for children from ages 2 to 11. For more information on traveling with children, consult the following books:

> *Adventuring with Children: An Inspirational Guide to World Travel and the Outdoors*, Nan Jeffrey. Avalon House Publishing (US$15).
>
> *Backpacking with Babies and Small Children*, Goldie Silverman. Wilderness Press ($10).
>
> *Gutsy Mamas: Travel Tips and Wisdom for Mothers on the Road*, Marybeth Bond. Travelers' Tales, Inc. (US$8).
>
> *Have Kid, Will Travel: 101 Survival Strategies for Vacationing With Babies and Young Children*, Claire and Lucille Tristram. Andrews McMeel Publishing ($9).
>
> *Trouble-Free Travel with Children*, Vicki Lansky. Book Peddlers ($9).

DIETARY CONCERNS

With its emphasis on beans, corn, squash, and chiles, Southwestern cuisine is perfect for vegetarians. *Let's Go* indicates vegetarian options in listings. You can also look for vegetarian and vegan cuisine at local health food stores and large natural food chains like **Trader Joe's** and **Wild Oats**. Vegan options are more difficult to find in smaller towns and inland; be prepared to make your own meals. The **North American Vegetarian Society**, P.O. Box 72, Dolgeville, NY 13329 (☎518-568-7970; www.navs-online.org), publishes info about vegetarian travel, including *Vegetarian Journal's Guide to Natural Food Restaurants in the US and Canada* ($12). Also try the Vegetarian Resource Group's website, www.vrg.org/travel, or Jed Civic's *The Vegetarian Traveler: Where to Stay If You're Vegetarian, Vegan, Environmentally Sensitive* (Larson Publishing; $16).

Travelers who keep **kosher** should contact synagogues in larger cities for information on kosher restaurants. Your own synagogue or college Hillel should have access to lists of Jewish institutions across the nation. You may also consult the kosher restaurant database at www.shamash.org/kosher. A good resource is the *Jewish Travel Guide*, edited by Michael Zaidner (Vallentine Mitchell; $17). If you are strict in your observance, you may have to prepare your own food on the road.

OTHER RESOURCES
TRAVEL PUBLISHERS & BOOKSTORES

> **Hunter Publishing,** 470 W. Broadway, fl. 2, South Boston, MA 02127 (☎617-269-0700; www.hunterpublishing.com). Has an extensive catalog of travel guides and diving and adventure travel books.
>
> **Rand McNally,** P.O. Box 7600, Chicago, IL 60680 (☎847-329-8100; www.randmcnally.com), publishes comprehensive road atlases.
>
> **Adventurous Traveler Bookstore,** P.O. Box 2221, Williston, VT 05495 (☎800-282-3963; www.adventuroustraveler.com).
>
> **Bon Voyage!,** 2069 W. Bullard Ave., Fresno, CA 93711 (☎800-995-9716, from abroad 559-447-8441; www.bon-voyage-travel.com). They specialize in Europe but have titles pertaining to other regions as well. Free newsletter.

WORLD WIDE WEB

 WWW.LETSGO.COM Our website now includes introductory chapters from all our guides and a wealth of information on a monthly featured destination. As always, our website also has info about our books, a travel forum buzzing with stories and tips, and additional links that will help you make the most of a trip to the Southwest USA.

How to See the World: www.artoftravel.com. A compendium of great travel tips, from cheap flights to self defense to interacting with local culture.

Rec. Travel Library: www.travel-library.com. A fantastic set of links for general information and personal travelogues.

Microsoft Expedia: www.expedia.msn.com. This site has everything you'd ever need to make travel plans on the web: compare flight fares, look at maps, make reservations. FareTracker (free) is a monthly mailing about the cheapest fares to any destination.

The CIA World Factbook: www.odci.gov/cia/publications/factbook/index.html. The CIA has tons of vital statistics on the US and the Southwest. Check it out for an overview of the American economy, and an explanation of the US system of government.

City Net: www.city.net. A site dispensing info on renting a car, restaurants, hotel rates, and weather for a wide array of cities and regions across the US.

ALTERNATIVES TO TOURISM

When we started out in 1961, about 1.7 million people in the world were traveling internationally each year; in 2002, travelers made nearly 700 million trips, a number projected to reach up to a billion by 2010. The dramatic rise in tourism has created an interdependence between the economy, environment, and culture of many destinations and the tourists they host. Within the US, this phenomenon has had perhaps the largest impact in the fragile wilderness areas and booming cities of the Southwest. Though the region claims some of the nation's most sparsely populated states, sunbelt communities are among the fastest growing. Nevada, 85% of which is public land, has been the fastest growing US state for the past 16 years according to Census Bureau estimates. Compounding this influx of residents is an equally dramatic escalation of tourism. The Southwest hosts tens of millions of visitors each year (over 35 million in Las Vegas alone), causing a strain on precious natural resources and native communities.

For the responsible traveler, the Southwest has unparalleled opportunities to enrich one's experience with community involvement. The primary issues affecting the region can generally be divided along the lines of the environment and the native cultures. Within the environmental realm, in particular, there exist countless ways for travelers to do their part for the region. The Southwest constantly needs willing volunteers and workers to help manage its magnificent lands. Wilderness preservation and maintenance, water conservation, wildfire management, support for independent farming, and environmental education will continue to be pressing issues in a region known for some of the country's most stunning and remote wilderness areas. At the same time, the Southwest is home to a number of communities—from Navajo to Hispanic to environmentalist to artist—struggling daily to preserve their way of life from the assimilationist whirlpool of mainstream culture. Conscientious travelers will find no shortage of ways to pitch in on either front, whether by joining a volunteer program at a park or reservation or by simply supporting local artists, tribes, and farmers whenever the chance arises.

Those looking to **volunteer** for these causes have many options. You can participate in projects from preserving adobe homes to building hiking trails either on an infrequent basis or as the main component of your trip. Later in this section, we recommend organizations that can help you find the opportunities that best suit your interests, whether you're looking to pitch in for a day or a year.

There are any number of other ways to integrate yourself with the communities you visit. **Studying** at a college or language program is one option. Many students seek a campus in the Southwest because their studies are directly related to the environment. Artist colonies draw inspiration from stark desert landscapes, while the Southwest's many nature-oriented schools follow curricula focused on protecting the environment. More and more, abundant and relatively untamed public lands act as the training ground of nature's stewards. Travelers also structure their trips by **work** they can do along the way, either working odd jobs as they go or doing full-time stints in cities. Though seasonal work in the US is often harder to come by than in foreign countries, farms, ranches, and camps often have opportunities for those interested. If you are not a US citizen, remember to navigate the proper government channels and obtain a **work visa** before setting off.

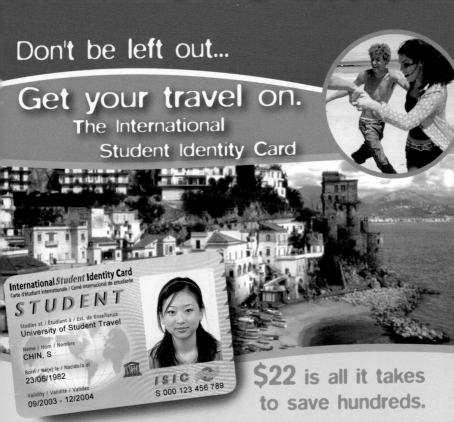

A NEW PHILOSOPHY OF TRAVEL

We at *Let's Go* have watched the growth of the 'ignorant tourist' stereotype with dismay, knowing that the majority of travelers care passionately about the state of the communities and environments they explore—but also knowing that even conscientious tourists can inadvertently damage natural wonders, rich cultures, and impoverished communities. We believe the philosophy of **sustainable travel** is among the most important travel tips we could impart to our readers, to help guide fellow backpackers and on-the-road philanthropists. By staying aware of the needs and troubles of local communities, today's travelers can be a powerful force in preserving and restoring this fragile world.

Working against the negative consequences of irresponsible tourism is much simpler than it might seem; it is often self-awareness, rather than self-sacrifice, that makes the biggest difference. Simply by trying to spend responsibly and conserve local resources, all travelers can positively impact the places they visit. Let's Go has partnered with **BEST** (**Business Enterprises for Sustainable Travel,** an affiliate of the Conference Board; see www.sustainabletravel.org), which recognizes businesses that operate based on the principles of sustainable travel. Below, they provide advice on how ordinary visitors can practice this philosophy in their daily travels, no matter where they are.

TIPS FOR CIVIC TRAVEL: HOW TO MAKE A DIFFERENCE

Travel by train when feasible. Rail travel requires only half the energy per passenger mile that planes do. On average, each of the 40,000 daily domestic air flights releases more than 1700 pounds of greenhouse gas emissions.

Use public mass transportation whenever possible; outside of cities, take advantage of group taxis or vans. Bicycles are an attractive way of seeing a community firsthand. And enjoy walking—purchase good maps of your destination and ask about on-foot touring opportunities.

When renting a car, ask whether fuel-efficient vehicles are available. Honda and Toyota produce cars that use hybrid engines powered by electricity and gasoline, thus reducing emissions of carbon dioxide. Ford Motor Company plans to introduce a hybrid fuel model by the end of 2004.

Reduce, reuse, recycle—use electronic tickets, recycle papers and bottles wherever possible, and avoid using containers made of styrofoam. Refillable water bottles and rechargable batteries both efficiently conserve expendable resources.

Be thoughtful in your purchases. Take care not to buy souvenir objects made from trees in old-growth or endangered forests, such as teak, or items made from endangered species, like ivory or tortoise jewelry. Ask whether products are made from renewable resources.

Buy from local enterprises, such as casual street vendors. In developing countries and low-income neighborhoods, many people depend on the "informal economy" to make a living.

Be on-the-road-philanthropists. If you are inspired by the natural environment of a destination or enriched by its culture, join in preserving their integrity by making a charitable contribution to a local organization.

Spread the word. Upon your return home, tell friends and colleagues about places to visit that will benefit greatly from their tourist dollars, and reward sustainable enterprises by recommending their services. Travelers can not only introduce friends to particular vendors but also to local causes and charities that they might choose to support when they travel.

Before handing your money over to any volunteer or study program, make sure you know exactly what you're getting into. It's a good idea to get the name of **previous participants** and ask them about their experience, as some programs sound much better on paper than in reality. The **questions** below are a good place to start:

–Will you be the only person in the program? If not, what are other participants like? How old are they? How much will you be expected to interact with them?

–Is room and board included? If so, what is the arrangement? Will you be expected to share a room? A bathroom? What are the meals like? Do they fit any dietary restrictions?

–Is transportation included? Are there any additional expenses?

–How much free time will you have? Will you be able to travel around?

–What kind of safety network is set up? Will you still be covered by your home insurance? Does the program have an emergency plan?

VOLUNTEERING

Though the Southwest, like rest of the US, is considered wealthy in worldwide terms, there is no shortage of aid organizations in need of volunteers. From understaffed public lands to underdeveloped Native communities, the hard work of volunteers makes a significant impact on the region's environmental and cultural health. And volunteering can be one of the most fulfilling experiences you have in life, especially if you combine it with the thrill of traveling in a new place.

Most people who volunteer in the Southwest do so on a short-term basis at organizations that take drop-in or once-a-week volunteers. These can be found in virtually every city and are referenced both in this section and in town and city sections themselves. The best way to find opportunities that match your interests and schedule may be to check the websites of local or national volunteer centers such as the **Points of Light Foundation** (www.pointsoflight.org) or **VolunteerMatch** (www.volunteermatch.org), which feature databases to link you with a particular program or volunteer center in the US. To search for a position that places you under the hot western sun, try the one- or two-week volunteer vacations offered at **www.americanhiking.org** or scan the **National Parks Service website** (www.nps.gov) for its litany of service opportunities. Most volunteers in the Southwest work to preserve the natural playgrounds that draw tourists to the region. Others commit time and energy to revitalizing the Native communities in the area. Intensive volunteer services may charge you a fee to participate. These costs can be surprisingly hefty, although they frequently cover airfare and most, if not all, living expenses. Most people choose to go through a parent organization that takes care of logistical details and provides a group environment and support system. There are two main types of organizations—religious and non-sectarian—although there are rarely restrictions on participation for either.

ENVIRONMENTAL ACTION

The millions of vacations spent in the Southwest come at a cost, as the strain of tourist droves takes its toll on the parks and recreation and wilderness areas. Dozens of programs welcome volunteer stewards to help maintain public lands, while others promote conservation and efficient use of natural resources.

The Student Conservation Association (SCA), 689 River Rd., P.O. Box 550, Charlestown, NH 03603-0550 (☎603-543-1700; www.thesca.org). SCA places high school and college students in outdoors settings throughout the Southwest and beyond, to tackle various important conservation projects. Joining the SCA is a tuition-free endeavor; special internships include stipends, while shorter summer positions grant educational awards.

Four Corners School of Outdoor Education, P.O. Box 1029, Monticello, UT 84535 (☎801-587-2156; www.fourcornersschool.org). Aiming to educate the keepers of the Southwest's outdoors areas, Four Corners School takes on volunteers to take part in wilderness excursions and archeological surveys throughout the Colorado plateau region. The $700-1700 fee includes camping accommodations and food for the entirety of their week-long programs.

Earthwatch, 3 Clocktower Pl. Suite 100, Box 75, Maynard, MA 01754 (☎978-461-0081 or 800-776-0188; www.earthwatch.org). Arranges 1- to 3-week programs in the United States and around the world to promote conservation of natural resources by assisting scientific field research. Fees vary based on program location and duration; costs average $1500 plus airfare for Southwest expeditions.

Utah State Parks, P.O. Box 146001, Salt Lake City, UT 84114-6001 (☎801-538-7220). The state park service seeks volunteers for numerous outdoor functions, including trail construction and maintenance, campground supervision, and wilderness interpretation for the public.

BTCV, 163 Balby Rd., Doncaster DN4 0RH, UK (☎+44 014 9182 1618; www.btcv.org/international/Holidays/index.htm). This international conservation organization is based in England, but organizes week-long to two-month volunteer "holidays" at locales around the world, including the Southwest. The 54-day river restoration project near Lake Tahoe costs $480.

New Mexico Volunteers for the Outdoors, P.O. Box 36246, Albuquerque, NM 87176 (☎505-884-1991; www.nmvfo.org.) Scores of projects involving restoring hiking and biking trails and maintaining park land. Camping accommodations provided.

The Trail Center, 3921 East Bayshore Rd., Palo Alto, CA 94303 (☎650-968-7065; www.trailcenter.org). This organization links willing workers to organizations in California and the Southwest. Volunteers build and maintain hiking trails in conjunction with regional organizations.

WORKING WITH WILDLIFE

The transformation of wilderness areas into recreation areas and suburbs has forced countless species out of their homes all over the United States, but particularly in the Southwest. Several programs realize the need to protect wildlife from ever-expanding tourist areas.

US Fish and Wildlife Service (Southwest Region), 500 Gold Ave. SW, Albuquerque, NM 87102 (☎505-248-6911; http://southwest.fws.gov/volunteer/index.html). Offers training for wildlife volunteer opportunities in Arizona, New Mexico, and Texas.

Texas Parks and Wildlife, 4200 Smith School Rd., Austin, TX 78744 (☎800-792-1112 ext. 7062; http://www.tpwd.state.tx.us/edu/enved/endang/tntflyer.htm). The Texas Nature Trackers program links volunteers with endangered plant and animal species. Data-gathering equipment provided.

Colorado Division of Wildlife, Grand Junction: 711 Independent Ave., Grand Junction, CO 81505 (☎970-255-6145; www.wildlife.state.co.us.) From helping bats to bluebirds, wildlife volunteers contribute to the protection of Colorado's wildlife. Flexible commitment schedule.

ALTERNATIVES TO TOURISM

NAVAJO NATION

The checkered history of US-Navajo relations has produced a unique political relationship between the two. The Navajo Nation, a sovereign tribal government operating out of Window Rock, AZ, spans 27,000 sq. mi. and three state borders while remaining within the territorial US. The Nation, or *Dine Bikeyah* (Land of the People), is run by executive, legislative, and judicial branches that create and execute laws for its 180,000 citizens. While this independence has helped preserve an ancient way of life and protect sacred lands from further US encroachment, it has also isolated Navajo citizens from the benefits of federal assistance programs. Navajo suffer from a poverty rate of over 50% and an unemployment rate nearly as high. Some residents live without complete plumbing, kitchen equipment, or phone service. Little revenue comes into the Nation, as the lack of commercial development and tourist infrastructure forces residents and visitors to spend money off the reservation. Education falters, and public works projects are sorely underfunded and understaffed. This stagnation has bred alcoholism and a high incidence of drunk driving, among other problems. There are many programs that allow you to work within the Navajo Nation assisting construction projects while learning more about the Navajo way of life.

Global Volunteers, 375 East Little Canada Rd., St. Paul, MN 55117-1628 (☎800-487-1074; www.globalvolunteers.org). Offers numerous opportunities to work with underdeveloped Navajo communities. Volunteers live, work, and dorm on reservations during one-week stays ($550-750).

Amizade, 367 South Graham St., PA 15260 (☎888-973-4443; www.amizade.org). Amizade runs programs out of Tuba City, AZ, and focuses on revitalization of the Navajo Nation through teaching and small construction projects. Accommodations range from hotels to dorms; meals provided.

Volunteers for Peace, 1034 Tiffany Rd., Belmont, VT 05730 (☎802-259-2759; www.vfp.org). International Workcamps place volunteers in areas of the Navajo Nation in need of upkeep or rebuilding. Workers sleep in tents and all food is cooked at the site. $200-400 for 2-week camps.

Breakthroughs Abroad, 1160-B Woodstock, Estes Park, CO 80517 (☎970-577-1908; www.breakthroughsabroad.org/navajo). Volunteers get to experience the Southwestern outdoors and Navajo culture before pitching in with projects on the reservation. Fifteen-day programs include meals and accommodations, but not airfare ($2100).

CULTURAL PRESERVATION

The Southwest nurtures a range of cultures whose artifacts and traditions need preservation. Increased tourism creates a pressure to steer resources and energy away from less profitable preservation programs. The programs below grant opportunities to impact the survival of the Southwest's cultural heritage.

Heritage Conservation Network, 1557 North St., Boulder, CO 80304 (☎303-444-0128; www.heritageconservation.net). Dedicated to conserving archaeological sites throughout the world, the Heritage Conservation Network takes on volunteers in the Southwest for their one- and two-week workshops ($875).

National Hispanic Cultural Center of New Mexico, 1701 4th St. SW, Santa Fe, NM 87102 (☎505-246-2261, ext. 142; www.nhccnm.org). Offers unpaid volunteer opportunities in all facets of the preservation, presentation, and research of Hispanic culture.

Bureau of Land Management (www.blm.gov/volunteer). Through widespread field offices, administers public lands all over the Southwest. The online volunteer opportunities database includes various historical and archaeological preservation projects.

STUDYING

Study programs range from basic language and culture courses to college-level classes, often for credit. To choose a program that best fits your needs, you will want to research all you can before making your decision—determine costs and duration, as well as what kind of students participate in the program and what sort of accommodations are provided.

UNIVERSITIES

To sample the life of an American college student, consider a visiting student program lasting either a semester or a full year. The best method by far is to contact colleges and universities in your home country to see what kind of exchanges they have with those in the Southwest. A more complicated option for advanced English speakers is to enroll full-time in an American institution. The Southwest hosts a number of reputable universities, among them the Universities of Utah, Nevada, Arizona, and New Mexico. Each state maintains a public state university system, and there are innumerable community, professional and technical colleges. Unfortunately, tuition costs are high in the US, and a full course of undergraduate study entails a four-year commitment.

Most university-level exchange programs are meant as language and culture enrichment opportunities, and therefore are conducted in English. Those relatively fluent in English may find it cheaper to enroll directly in a university, although getting college credit may be more difficult. The website **www.studyabroad.com** is a good resource for finding programs catering to your particular interests and has links to various semester abroad programs based on a variety of criteria, including desired location and focus of study.

LANGUAGE SCHOOLS

Unlike American universities, language schools are frequently independently-run organizations or divisions of foreign universities that rarely offer college credit. They are a good alternative to university study if you desire a deeper focus on the language or a slightly less-rigorous courseload.

Odyssey Language Institute, 641 E. Cobblestone Dr., Salt Lake City, UT 84047 (☎810-352-2737; www.odyssey-lang.com). English tutelage combined with outdoor adventure. Based in Salt Lake City, summer programs offer daily and weekend treks to the Uintas, while winter students enjoy time on the ski slopes. 16hr. of class per week during 2-4 week programs ($1700-2500).

Nomen Global Language Center, 384 West Center St., Provo, UT 84601 (☎801-375-7878; www.nomenglobal.com). $2090 for a 16-week course, $325 for a 2-week short course, with corresponding costs for shorter and longer programs. Housing can also be arranged; homestays $150 per week, accommodation rentals $225-1000.

American Language Programs, 56 Hobbs Brook Rd., Weston, MA 02493 (☎781-888-1515; www.alp-online.com). ALP runs programs in Phoenix that include homestay, meals, and intensive English training. $900-1080 per week (15-25hr.) for 1 person, $1600-1960 for 2 people.

ARCHITECTURAL & ARTS COLONIES

Attracted by the cheap land, the laid-back lifestyle, and the relative isolation, a number of art and architectural colonies flourish in the Southwest. Few generalizations can be made about them as a group; they vary greatly in size, in field, and in organization. Some are *de facto* colleges, offering specialized training at the graduate level and beyond, while others are more informal affairs. Inquire about the possibility of earning college credit.

Arcosanti, HC 74 BOX 4136, Mayer, AZ 86333 (☎928-632-7135; tminus@arcosanti.org; www.arcosanti.org.) Founded by Frank Lloyd Wright disciple Paolo Soleri, who still lives here part-time, Arcosanti is an experimental community based on Soleri's theory of arcology (a blend of architecture and ecology). It hosts 5-week workshops ($1050) in which participants help expand the settlement while learning about Soleri's project and developing their skills at construction and planning. For those with some background in construction or architecture and who complete the introductory workshop, an expense-paid internship is available for a 3-month commitment. See p. 126.

Taliesin West, 12621 N. Frank Lloyd Wright Blvd., Scottsdale, AZ 852610-4430 (☎480-860-2700; www.taliesin.edu). The Phoenix branch of the elite architectural school founded by Frank Lloyd Wright, Taliesin West offers a full course load of work leading to a Bachelor of Architectural Science or Master of Architecture degree. There are a small number of non-degree positions available. All slots are highly competitive. See p. 105

Santa Fe Art Institute, 1600 St. Michael's Drive, NM 87505 (☎505-424-5050; www.sfai.org). A world-class artistic center, the Santa Fe Art Institute offers one- and two-week workshops ($1000-1800) giving participants the opportunity to work with professional resident artists in Santa Fe.

Taos Institute of Arts, 108 Civic Plaza Dr., Taos, NM 87571 (☎505-758-2793, 800-822-7183; www.tiataos.com). 2-day to week-long intensive workshops in all kinds of media, from clay to photography to writing. Lodging discounts with nearby sponsor establishments. Most workshops cost around $420, materials not included.

OUTDOOR LEARNING

The Southwest's vast outdoors often acts as an interactive campus for students interested in preservation and recreation. Several programs grant the opportunity to explore the wilds of the Southwest while studying environmental stewardship.

National Outdoor Leadership School (NOLS), 284 Lincoln St., Landing, WY 82520-2848 (☎800-710-6657; www.nols.edu). From its Tucson location, NOLS trains leaders in outdoors excursions. Students use the Sonoran desert as a classroom for rock climbing, hiking, and canoeing lessons that enable them to pass this knowledge on to others. Courses range from a 3-week basic instruction in one skill ($3000) to a 3-month long semester of outdoor education ($9000).

Outward Bound, 100 Mystery Point Rd., Garrison, NY 10524 (☎866-467-7651; www.outwardbound.com), offers expeditional courses in outdoor education in the Southwest and throughout the US and overseas. Courses range from several days to over 40, and include special focuses, such as life & career renewal and couples.

Columbia University's Biospehere 2 Center, 32540 S. Biosphere Rd., Oracle, AZ 85623 (☎520-838-6100; http://www.bio2.columbia.edu/education). Students live near Biosphere 2 (see p. 147), an enclosed research site sustaining diverse ecosystems. Summer and semester-long astronomy and earth science courses are open to international students, after the submission of TOEFL scores. A student village outside Tucson provides dorms. Summer programs $3000-5000; semester $16,590-16,765.

Zion Canyon Field Institute, Zion National Park, Springdale, UT 84767 (☎435-772-3264: www.zionpark.org). From filming Zion to lessons about edible plants, students at the institute can experience a range of the park's attractions. Led by visiting instructors from various fields, classes last from one to three days ($25-100 per day).

VISA INFORMATION. Since the events of Sept. 11, 2001, the process for obtaining a US visa has become more involved, and applicants can expect to be subjected to more scrutiny. If you plan on visiting the US during the summer, be sure to set the visa application process in motion early. Embassies and consulates will often accept applications early and hold them for you until the earliest date they can be processed. Whether you are applying for a student visa or a work visa, there a various classifications and intricacies within each of these visa types depending on your education/skills and what exactly you intend to do in the US (e.g., seasonal agricultural vs. seasonal non-agricultural work). For info on student visas, the state department website (http://travel.state.gov/visa;foreignstuden.html) explains how to obtain an I-20 form and other required documents. If you are traveling to the US primarily for tourism but wish to undertake a course of study for less than 18hr. per week, you may need only a tourist visa. Those applying for work visas need a DS-156E form and should refer to http://travel.state.gov/visa;tempwkr.html. Citizens of Canada and Mexico are eligible for the TN visa under the NAFTA agreement and can refer to http://travel.state.gov/tn_visas.html for the TN visa's requirements.

WORKING

As with volunteering, work opportunities tend to fall into two categories. Some travelers want long-term jobs that allow them to get to know another part of the world as a member of the community, while other travelers seek out short-term jobs to finance the next leg of their travels. In the Southwest, travelers usually seek employment in the service sector or in agriculture, working for a few weeks at a time to finance their journey. This section discusses both short- and long-term opportunities for working in the Southwest. Make sure you understand the United States' **visa requirements** for foreign workers (see **Visa Information**).

Job seekers should look in the classified sections of major daily newspapers such as the *Arizona Republic* or the *Salt Lake Tribune*. Another option is temp agencies. It may be possible to work in exchange for room and board in parts of the Southwest; such instances are noted in the guide.

LONG-TERM WORK

If you're planning on spending a substantial amount of time (more than three months) working in the Southwest, search for a job well in advance. International placement agencies are often the easiest way to find employment abroad, especially for teaching English. **Internships,** usually for college students, are a good way to segue into working abroad, although they are often unpaid or poorly paid (many say the experience, however, is well worth it). The online database at **www.councilexchanges.org** is one place to start.

AU PAIR WORK

Au pairs are typically women, ages 18-27, who work as live-in nannies, caring for children and doing light housework in exchange for room, board, and a small spending allowance. Most former au pairs speak favorably of their experience and of how it allowed them to really get to know the Southwest without the high expenses of traveling. Drawbacks, however, often include long hours of constantly being on-duty, and the somewhat mediocre pay. In the US, weekly salaries typically fall well below $200, with at least 45hr. of work expected, and au pairs are expected to speak English and have at least 200 hours of childcare experience. Much of the au pair experience depends on the family with whom you're placed. The agencies below are a good starting point for looking for work as an au pair.

Accord Cultural Exchange, 750 La Playa, San Francisco, CA 94121, USA (☎415-386-6203; www.cognitext.com/accord).

Childcare International, Ltd., Trafalgar House, Grenville Pl., London NW7 3SA (☎+44 020 8906 3116; www.childint.co.uk).

InterExchange, 161 Sixth Ave., New York, NY 10013, USA (☎212-924-0446; www.interexchange.org).

SHORT-TERM WORK

ALTERNATIVES TO TOURISM

Traveling for long periods of time gets expensive, so many travelers work odd jobs for a few weeks at a time to make the cash to carry them another month or two. While this is a popular tactic, there are particular difficulties with it in the Southwest. The proximity of Mexico depresses wages, and competition for work is heightened, although educated travelers will have an advantage over most professional migrant workers.

One common way to make extra cash in the Southwest is agricultural work. Those who try agricultural labor should be prepared for a difficult and "character-building" experience. The harvest season runs May to October. Hungry for seasonal workers, ski resorts—especially those around Salt Lake City (see p. 246)—are a better bet because they offer benefits like free access to the mountain and discounted food and accommodations. Most mountains in Utah hire staff during their peak winter months. Another popular option is to work several hours a day at a hostel in exchange for free or discounted room and board. Most often, these short-term jobs are found by word of mouth, or simply by talking to the owner of a hostel or restaurant. Many places, especially due to the high turnover in the tourism industry, are always eager for help, even if only temporary. Random jobs (moving, working in cafes) can usually be found in bigger cities, like Phoenix and Albuquerque. Additionally, temp agencies can arrange for relatively short-term white-collar work (**www.net-temps.com** is a good place to start). *Let's Go* tries to list temporary jobs like these whenever possible; check the Practical Information sections in larger cities, or check out the list below for some of the available short-term jobs in popular destinations.

Willing Workers on Organic Farms (WWOOF), P.O. Box 2675, Lewes BN7 1RB, UK (www.wwoofusa.org; $20 to join). Organization features a large database of work on Southwestern organic farms, many of which rely heavily on short-term workers. Compensation is room and board.

Camp Counselors USA, Green Dragon House, Unit 4CC, 64-70 High Street, Croydon CR0 9XN, UK (☎+44 020 8668 9051; www.ccusa/CCUSA/why_do_ccusa.html), places people aged 18-30 as counselors in summer camps in the US.

Kelly Services, 999 West Big Beaver Rd., Troy, MI 48084. **Southwest branches:** 3030 N. 3rd St., Suite 1040, Phoenix, AZ 85012 (☎602-264-0717); 480 East 400 S, Salt Lake City, UT 84111 (☎801-363-4460); 6000 Uptown Blvd. NE, Suite 120, Albuquerque, NM 87110 (☎505-883-6873). International temp service.

The Canyons, 4000 The Canyons Resort Drive, Park City, UT 84098 (☎435-649-5400; www.thecanyons.com/jobs). Utah ski resort hosts annual job fairs to fill dozens of winter positions. Staffers receive discounted housing, food, and day care privileges, as well as free skiing and snowboarding.

Alliances Abroad, 702 West Ave., Austin TX (☎512-457-8062). Guarantees a position in the US seasonal workforce. Often in the unskilled or service areas, placements are not usually accompanied by a fat check. Program accommodates stays as long as 10 months, and provides a support network to help with immigration specifics.

FURTHER READING ON ALTERNATIVES TO TOURISM

Alternatives to the Peace Corps: A directory of third world and U.S. Volunteer Opportunities, by Joan Powell. Food First Books, 2000 ($10).

Invest Yourself: The Catalogue of Volunteer Opportunities, published by the Commission on Voluntary Service and Action (☎718-638-8487).

The Back Door Guide to Short-term Job Adventures: Internships, Extraordinary Experiences, Seasonal Jobs, Volunteering, Working Abroad, by Michael Landes. Ten Speed Press, 2000 ($16).

ALTERNATIVES TO TOURISM

THE GREAT OUTDOORS

This is what you came for. The scenery in the Southwest is unmatched and by far the single biggest attraction in the region. From Grand Canyon to Chaco Canyon, from the High Uinta Wilderness to the Gila Wilderness, the Southwest has vast tracts of public lands and innumerable recreation opportunities. However, enjoying your experience to the fullest requires forethought, preparation, and a little bit of knowledge about US public lands.

PUBLIC LANDS IN THE SOUTHWEST

The different agendas of farmers, ranchers, miners, tourists, and environmental activists form clear battle lines on the issues of land use and conservation, and as a result, the very concept of public land in the Southwest is a controversial issue. The Department of the Interior and the Department of Agriculture administer an intricate and sometimes confusing system of public land management. The National Park System gets all of the glory and tourists, but lands managed by the National Forest Service, the Bureau of Land Management, and the Department of Fish and Wildlife are abundant in the Southwest and in many cases offer similar recreational opportunities. Although the traveler might not care much about the structure of these federal and state landholdings, the classifications are important in determining which organization to contact for more info on specific activities, permits, and restrictions.

NATIONAL PARKS & MONUMENTS

National parks protect some of the most spectacular and heavily touristed scenery in the Southwest. Though their primary stated purpose is preservation, the parks also host a variety of recreational activities, including ranger talks, guided hikes, marked trails, bus tours, and snowshoe expeditions. For info, contact individual parks or the **National Park Service,** Office of Public Inquiries, 1849 C St. NW #1013, Washington, D.C. 20240 (☎202-208-4747). The slick and informative webpage (www.nps.gov) lists info on all the parks, detailed maps, and fee and reservation data. The **National Park Foundation's** *Complete Guide to America's National Parks* is available at any major bookstore or on amazon.com; a guide to national parks is available online at www.nationalparks.org.

Entrance fees vary widely. The larger and more popular parks charge a $4-20 entry fee for cars and occasionally a $2-7 fee for pedestrians and cyclists. The **National Parks Pass** ($50), available at park entrances or on the National Parks Service web site, allows the pass-holder's party entry into all national parks for one year. For an additional $15, the Parks Service will affix a **Golden Eagle Passport** hologram to your card, which will allow you access to sites managed by the US Fish and Wildlife Service, the US Forest Service, and the Bureau of Land Management. US citizens or residents 62 and over qualify for the lifetime **Golden Age Passport** ($10 one-time fee), which entitles the holder's party to free park entry, a 50% discount on camping, and 50% reductions on various recreational fees. Persons eligible for federal disability benefits can enjoy the same privileges with the **Golden Access Passport** (free). Golden Age and Golden Access Passports must be purchased at a park entrance with proof of age or federal eligibility. All passports (not the Parks Pass) are also valid at national monuments, forests, wildlife preserves, and other national recreation sites.

Most parks in the Southwest offer opportunities for both backcountry and developed **camping**; some welcome RVs, and a few even offer grand lodges. At more popular parks, reservations are essential.

DAMN, THIS PARK IS CROWDED! (2002 FIGURES FOR RECREATIONAL VISITORS)		
Lake Mead National Recreation Area	Nevada	7,550,284
Grand Canyon National Park	Arizona	4,001,974
Zion National Park	Utah	2,592,545
Glen Canyon National Recreation Area	Utah	2,106,896
Joshua Tree National Park	California	1,178,376
Death Valley National Park	California	897,596
Bryce Canyon National Park	Utah	886,436
Canyon de Chelly National Monument	Arizona	772,620
Canyonlands National Park	Utah	367,078
Big Bend National Park	Texas	327,747
Great Basin National Park	Nevada	87,057

NATIONAL FORESTS

Often less accessible and less crowded than National Parks, the lands that make up the system of **US National Forests** (www.fs.fed.us) are a purist's alternative to parks. While some forests have recreation facilities, most are equipped for only primitive camping—pit toilets and no water are the norm. Entrance fees are rare; camping is generally free or under $10. If you are interested in visiting and exploring a national forest, pick up *The Guide to Your National Forests* at any Forest Service branch, or call or write the main office (USDA Forest Service, P.O. Box 96090, Washington, D.C. 20090-6090; ☎202-205-8333). This booklet includes a list of all national forest addresses; request maps and other info directly from the forest(s) you plan to visit. (See **Reservations Please!,** p. 4)

BUREAU OF LAND MANAGEMENT

The US Department of the Interior's **Bureau of Land Management (BLM)** oversees 270 million acres of land in the western US, with an especially strong presence in Nevada, Utah, and the rest of the desert Southwest. The Bureau's pride and joy is Grand Staircase-Escalante National Monument, a hybrid park holding national monument status, yet managed entirely by the BLM. The BLM differs from the Forest Service and the Park Service in that it generally aims for sustainable land use rather than conservation. In keeping with this goal, BLM lands offer a variety of recreation opportunities, including hiking, mountain biking, rock climbing, river running, and often ATV and snowmobile use. Unless otherwise posted, all public lands are open for recreational use. BLM campgrounds charge up to $10, but dispersed primitive camping on BLM land is generally permitted and always free. For more info, contact individual state offices:

Arizona State BLM Office, 222 N. Central Ave., Phoenix, AZ 85004 (☎602-417-9200; www.az.blm.gov).

California State BLM Office, 2800 Cottage Way, Suite W1834, Sacramento, CA 95825 (☎916-978-4400; www.ca.blm.gov).

Colorado State BLM Office, 2850 Youngfield St., Lakewood, CO 80215 (☎303-239-3600; www.co.blm.gov).

GREAT OUTDOORS

Nevada State BLM Office, 1340 Financial Blvd., Reno, NV 89502 (☎775-861-6400; www.nv.blm.gov).

New Mexico State BLM Office, 1474 Rodeo Rd., Santa Fe, NM 87505 (☎505-438-7400; www.nm.blm.gov).

Texas BLM Office, 801 S. Fillmore St., Ste. 500, Amarillo, TX 79101-3545 (☎806-356-1000; fax 806-356-1041).

Utah State BLM Office, P.O. Box 45155, 324 South State St., Salt Lake City, UT 84145-0155 (☎801-539-4001; www.ut.blm.gov).

WILDERNESS AREAS

The **Wilderness Act of 1964** established a federal system to provide the maximum level of preservation to incorporated parcels of land. As it stands now, there are over 105 million acres of protected wilderness in the US. These areas are administered by several different agencies, including the Park Service, the Forest Service, the Bureau of Land Management, and the US Fish and Wildlife Service. Though exceptions exist, mining, vehicles (including bicycles), and permanent, man-made structures are generally prohibited. For more info on restrictions and permits in specific regions, contact the agency responsible for managing the area that interests you. Consult http://nwps.wilderness.net/map.cfm to locate wilderness areas in specific states.

STATE PARKS

Though much of the spectacular scenery and recreational opportunities in the Southwest reside on federal land, **state parks** hold their own; some are as worthy of a visit as nationally controled parks and forests. State parks are usually used for motorized recreation, which often means **all-terrain vehicles (ATV)** and **boats.** A large percentage of state parks in the Southwest feature lakes and other bodies of water. Prices for camping at public sites are usually better than those at private campgrounds. Some parks may limit your stay and/or the number of people in your group. Crowds are rarely a problem, except at the most popular parks. For general info, contact:

Arizona State Parks, 1300 W. Washington St., Phoenix, AZ 85007 (☎602-542-4174; www.pr.state.az.us).

California State Parks, P.O. Box 942896, Sacramento, CA 94296 (☎800-777-0369; www.cal-parks.ca.gov).

Colorado State Parks, 1313 Sherman St., #618, Denver, CO 80203 (☎303-866-3437; www.parks.state.co.us).

Nevada Division of State Parks, 1300 S. Curry St., Carson City, NV 89703 (☎775-687-4384; www.parks.nv.gov).

New Mexico State Parks Division, P.O. Box 1147, Santa Fe, NM 87504 (☎888-667-2757; www.emnrd.state.nm.us/nmparks).

Texas Parks and Wildlife, 4200 Smith School Rd., Austin, TX 78744 (☎800-792-1112 or 512-389-4800; www.tpwd.state.tx.us).

Utah Division of Parks and Recreation, P.O. Box 146001, 1594 W. North Temple, #116, Salt Lake City, UT 84114 (☎801-538-7220; www.stateparks.utah.gov).

CAMPING

Camping is probably the most rewarding way to slash travel costs. Considering the sheer amount of public land available for camping in the southwestern United States, it may also be the most convenient option. Well-equipped campsites (usu-

RESERVATIONS PLEASE! Though many campgrounds, both in national forests and national parks, are first-come, first-served, reservations can make travel much more relaxed and enjoyable. The **National Forest Service** takes reservations through the **National Recreation Reservation Center,** P.O. Box 140, Ballston Spa, NY 12020 (☎518-885-3639 or 877-444-6777; www.reserve-usa.com). Camping reservations require a $9 service fee for National Forest Service sites and are available for most forests, though they are often unnecessary except during high season at the more popular sites. You may write or call up to 240 days in advance to reserve individual campsites. The **National Park Reservation Service** (☎800-365-2267 or 301-722-1257; http://reservations.nps.gov) takes reservations for campgrounds in Grand Canyon, Zion, Death Valley, Carlsbad Caverns, and Joshua Tree National Parks. Campgrounds are reservable starting five months in advance. There is no additional fee for this service. Many **state park** campsites are also available for reservation. Check with individual state offices for more info.

ally including prepared tent sites, toilets, and potable water) go for $5-20 per night. In general, the more popular the park or forest, the better equipped and the more expensive the established campgrounds. Most campsites are first-come, first-served, though a few accept reservations, usually for a small fee (see below for more info). **Backcountry camping,** which lacks all amenities, is often free, but permits may be required in some national parks and may cost up to $20. Dispersed backcountry camping is usually inconvenient for those traveling by car, because it requires a long hike. For those sticking to the highways, the ubiquitous **Kampgrounds of America (KOA)** offer a ritzy kamping experience at a premium. All of the komforts of home add up to about $20-30 a night for a tent site. It is not legal or safe to camp on the side of the road, even on public lands; *Let's Go* lists areas where dispersed roadside camping is permitted.

EQUIPMENT

WHAT TO BUY...

The best camping equipment is both sturdy and light. High-quality gear is also definitely worth the investment, as such hazards as a leaky tent or poorly fitting boots can be annoying, painful, and downright dangerous. Equipment is generally more expensive in Australia, New Zealand, and the UK than it is in North America, so if you're coming to the US from abroad, you might wait to buy your gear until you've arrived in the Southwest.

Sleeping Bag: Most good sleeping bags are rated by "season," or the lowest outdoor temperature at which they will keep you warm ("summer" means 30-40°F at night and "four-season" or "winter" often means below 0°F). Sleeping bags are filled either with down (warmer, more packable and lighter, but more expensive and miserable when wet) or with synthetic material (heavier, more durable, and warmer when wet). Prices range from $80-210 for a summer synthetic to $250-500 for a good down winter bag. Because the climate of the Southwest is highly variable, do some research in order to buy exactly what you will need; many find that a 20°F bag is most versatile. **Sleeping bag pads,** including foam pads ($10-20) and air mattresses ($15-50), cushion your back and neck and insulate you from the ground. Self-inflating **Therm-A-Rest** sleeping pads are part foam and part air-mattress and partially inflate when you unroll them. Some can be converted into a comfortable camp chairs; all are worth the $45-80. Bring a **stuff sack** lined with a plastic bag to store your sleeping bag.

GREAT OUTDOORS

Tent: The most sturdy tents are free-standing, with their own frames and suspension systems. They set up quickly but require staking in high winds. Low-profile dome tents are the best all-around; nearly all their internal space is usable, which means little unnecessary bulk. Tent sizes can be somewhat misleading: two people *can* fit in a 2-person tent, but will be happier in a 4-person. If you're traveling by car, go for the bigger tent, but if you're hiking, stick with a smaller tent that weighs no more than 4-6 lbs. (2-3kg). Good 2-person tents start at $90, 4-person tents at $150. Seal the seams of your tent with waterproofer, and make sure it has a **rain fly** that can hold off a downpour. Other accessories include a **plastic groundcloth** and, for the luxurious, a **battery-operated lantern.**

Backpack: If you intend to do a lot of hiking, you should have a frame backpack. The widely popular **internal-frame packs** mold better to your back, keep a lower center of gravity, and can flex adequately to allow you to hike difficult trails that require a lot of bending and maneuvering. Make sure you stuff them tightly, since an internal-frame pack gets its rigidity and structure from what it holds. If your trip involves a significant number of flights, consider an "adventure travel" pack, which is designed to weather baggage handling systems as well as wilderness. NorthFace and Lowe-Alpine make durable models. Some find **external-frame packs** more comfortable for hikes over even terrain, since they keep the weight higher and distribute it more evenly. Whichever you choose, make sure your pack has a strong, padded hip belt, which transfers pressure from your back to your legs. Any serious backpacking requires a pack of at least 4000 cubic inches (65 liters). Allow an additional 500 cubic inches for your sleeping bag in internal-frame packs. Sturdy backpacks cost anywhere from $125-400. This is one area where it doesn't pay to economize—cheaper packs may be less comfortable, and the straps are more likely to fray or rip. Before you buy any pack, try filling it with something heavy and walking around the store to get a sense of how it distributes weight. A **waterproof backpack cover** or plastic garbage bags will prove invaluable if it rains, and it is always a good idea to store your belongings in plastic bags within your pack.

Boots: Be sure to wear hiking boots with good **ankle support** that are appropriate for the terrain you plan to hike. **Gore-Tex** fabric and part-leather boots are appropriate for day hikes or 2-3 day overnight trips over moderate terrain, but for longer trips or trips in mountainous terrain, stiffer **leather** boots are highly preferable. Your boots should fit snugly and comfortably over 1-2 wool socks and a thin liner sock. Breaking in boots properly means wearing them for several weeks; doing so will spare you painful and debilitating blisters. Apply wax or waterproofing treatment to your boots before heading out. If they get wet, dry them slowly. Resist the temptation to rest them near the campfire: intense heat cracks the leather and damages the adhesive bonding of the soles.

Water Purification and Transport: When venturing away from developed campgrounds that have potable water, you will need to carry water and purify any that you might find along the trail. Because giardia can wreak havoc on one's digestive system (see p. 29), even water taken from the Southwest's cleanest backcountry spring must be purified. Though iodine- and chlorine-containing tablets are the cheapest method of purification, they will not rid water of its muck or its characteristic taste. It can also be unhealthy to consume iodine tablets over a long period of time. Portable **water filters** pump out a crystal clear product but often require careful maintenance and extra disposable filters. Do not ever pump dirty water unless you want to repeatedly clean or replace clogged filter cartridges. For transport, plastic **canteens** or water bottles keep water cooler than metal ones do, and are virtually shatter- and leak-proof. Large plastic **water bags** or **bladders** can hold up to several gallons and are perfect for travel in the desert. Bladders weigh practically nothing when empty, though they are bulky and heavy when full.

Other Necessities: Raingear in two pieces, a top and pants, is far superior to a poncho. **Gore-Tex** is the best material if you are doing aerobic activity and need breathable raingear; **rubber** raingear will keep you completely dry but will get clammy if you sweat. For warm layers, **synthetics,** like polypropylene tops, socks, and long underwear, along with a fleece or pile jacket, keep you warm even when wet, and dry quickly. **Wool** also stays warm when wet, but is much heavier. Never rely on **cotton** for warmth (unless it's the inner warmth that comes from wearing "the fabric of our lives"). This "death cloth" will be absolutely useless if it's wet. When camping in autumn, winter, or spring, bring along a **"space blanket,"** which helps you to retain your body heat and doubles as a ground-cloth ($5-15). Though many campgrounds provide campfire sites, you will probably want to bring a **camp stove,** especially for places that forbid fires or wood gathering. Propane-powered Coleman stoves start at about $40; the more expensive **Whisperlite** stoves ($60-100), which run on cleaner-burning white gas, are lighter and more versatile. You'll need to purchase a **fuel bottle** and fill it with fuel to operate stoves. Other essential supplies include a **first aid kit, Swiss army knife, insect repellent, calamine lotion, waterproof matches** or a **lighter, duct tape,** and **large plastic garbage bags.**

...AND WHERE TO BUY IT

The mail-order/online companies listed below offer lower prices than many retail stores, but a visit to a local camping or outdoors store will give you a good sense of items' look and weight. Many local outdoor stores also have message boards where used equipment can be found.

Campmor, P.O. Box 700, 28 Parkway, Upper Saddle River, NJ 07458 (☎888-226-7667, outside US call 201-825-8300; www.campmor.com).

Discount Camping, 880 Main North Rd., Pooraka, SA 5095, Australia (☎08 8262 3399; info@discountcamping.com.au; www.discountcamping.com.au).

Eastern Mountain Sports (EMS), 1 Vose Farm Rd., Peterborough, NH 03458 (☎888-463-6367 or 603-924-7231; customerservice@ems.com; www.ems.com). Call to locate the branch nearest you.

L.L. Bean, Freeport, ME 04033-0001 (US/Canada ☎800-441-5713; U.K. ☎0800 891 297; elsewhere ☎207-552-3028; www.llbean.com). They refund/replace products that don't meet your expectations. The main store and 800 number are both open 24hr.

Mountain Designs, 51 Bishop St., Kelvin Grove QLD 4059, Australia (☎61 7 3856 2344; www.mountaindesigns.com).

Recreational Equipment, Inc. (REI), Sumner, WA 98352-0001 (☎800-426-4840 or 253-891-2500; www.rei.com).

YHA Adventure Shop, 19 High St., Staines Middlesex, TW18, UK (☎020 7085 1900; www.yhaadventure.com), is one of Britain's largest equipment suppliers.

LEAVE NO TRACE

The idea behind environmentally responsible tourism is to leave no trace of human presence behind while traveling in nature. There are many practical ways to reduce the impact you leave on the wilderness. A portable **stove** is a safer (and more efficient) way to cook than using vegetation to build a campfire, but if you must make a fire, keep it small and use only dead branches or brush rather than cutting live vegetation. Make sure your **campsite** is at least 150 ft. (70m) from the nearest water source, be it a spring, a stream, or a lake. If there are no toilet facilities, bury **human waste** (but not paper, which should be packed out if used) at least 6 in. (15cm) deep, above the water level, and 200ft. or more from any water source or campsite. To wash yourself or your dishes, carry water 200ft. away from water sources and use small amounts of biodegradable soap. Always pack your **trash,** including toilet paper and hygiene products, in a plastic bag and carry it with you until you reach a trash receptacle. Don't feed wildlife, and leave rocks, plants, and other natural objects as you found them. For more info on these issues, contact one of the following organizations:

GREAT OUTDOORS

MY KINGDOM FOR A MAP. One of the most neglected tenets of wilderness safety is carrying maps wherever you go. When hiking, biking, climbing, or camping, you should ALWAYS carry a compass and use a set of detailed topographical maps. The **United States Geological Survey,** 1400 Independence Rd., Rolla, MO 65401 (☎573-308-3500; http://edc.usgs.gov/products/map.html), sells indispensable 7½min. and 15min. topo maps. **Trails Illustrated,** affiliated with National Geographic (☎800-962-1643; www.trailsillustrated.com), sells larger topo maps of the Southwest's parks and other public lands.

Earthwatch, 3 Clock Tower Place, Box 75, Maynard, MA 01754, US (☎800-776-0188 or 978-461-0081; info@earthwatch.org; www.earthwatch.org).

Ecotourism Society, 733 15th St. NW, Ste. 1000, Washington DC 20005-2112, US (☎202-347-9203; ecomail@ecotourism.org; www.ecotourism.org).

Leave No Trace, P.O. Box 997, Boulder, CO 80306, US (☎303-442-8222 or 800-332-4100; www.lnt.org).

National Audubon Society, 700 Broadway, New York, NY 10003, US (☎212-979-3000; www.audubon.org).

Tourism Concern, Stapleton House, 277-281 Holloway Rd., London N7 8HN, UK (☎020 7753 3330; info@tourismconcern.org.uk; www.tourismconcern.org.uk).

WILDERNESS & DESERT SAFETY

GENERAL WISDOM

Stay warm, dry, and hydrated. The vast majority of life-threatening wilderness situations result from a breach of this simple dictum. On any hike, however brief, you should pack enough equipment to keep you alive should disaster befall you. This includes **raingear, hat** and **mittens, a first-aid kit, a reflector, a whistle, high energy food,** and **extra water.** On any trip of significant length, you should always carry a **compass** and a detailed **topographical map** of the area in which you are hiking, preferably an official map from the US Geological Survey. Dress warmly and in layers (see p. 64). Weather can change suddenly anywhere in the region, and in the higher peaks it can snow any time of the year. Check **weather forecasts** and pay attention to the skies when hiking. Whenever possible, hike in groups or with a partner. Hiking alone greatly magnifies the risks of traveling in the wilderness. Always be sure to let someone know when and where you are hiking.

THE DESERT & YOU

The body loses at least a gallon of liquid per day in the desert (two or more gallons during strenuous activity), so *always* keep drinking. Drinking huge quantities of water to quench your thirst after physical exertion is not as effective as taking preventative measures to stay hydrated. Whether you are driving or hiking, tote **two gallons of water per person per day.** Designate at least one container as an emergency supply. Always have water at your side. In the car, keep backup containers in a cooler. Drink the water you have; taking a few sips every 10min. as opposed to gulping it down on the hour allows your body to absorb it more effectively. People have died in the desert with water they were "saving." Dilute sweet beverages with water to avoid an over-reaction to high sugar content. Avoid alcohol and coffee, which cause dehydration. For long-term stays, a high-quality beverage with potassium compounds and glucose, such as **ERG** (an industrial-strength Gatorade available from camping suppliers), will help keep your strength up.

Most people need a few days to adjust to the heat, especially before difficult hikes. Sunglasses with 100% UV protection, sunscreen, and a hat are essential **sun protection,** but proper clothing is the most effective shield. Light-colored clothing helps reflect the sun's rays. If water is at a premium, wearing a sweaty shirt, though uncomfortable, prevents dehydration more effectively than going shirtless. If water is plentiful, performance synthetic fabrics such as CoolMax can quicken sweat evaporation, aid thermo-regulation, and increase overall comfort (for more on **heat exhaustion** and **heatstroke,** see **Essentials,** p. 28).

Heat is not the desert's only climatic extreme. At high elevations, temperatures during winter nights can drop well **below freezing**—a sweater is often necessary even in summer (see **Essentials,** p. 28). The desert is characterized by its lack of precipitation, but when it rains, it pours. **Flash floods,** especially in the spring and late summer into the fall, cause water to come down from rain-drenched higher elevations and wreak biblical devastation upon lands below, turning dry gulches into raging rivers. Canyons, streambeds, washes, and drainages of any sort can become death traps. When you are hiking in low-lying areas, be alert—check the weather forecast and don't assume that clear skies mean you are safe. Rain from hundreds of miles away can flood a canyon where you are hiking. Try not to walk in washes you can't scramble out of, beware of thunderstorms on the horizon, and never camp in washes or gullies.

FURTHER READING: WILDERNESS SAFETY

How to Stay Alive in the Woods, Bradford Angier. Macmillan ($9).

Everyday Wisdom: 1001 Expert Tips for Hikers, Karen Berger. Mountaineer ($17).

Making Camp, Steve Howe, et al. Mountaineer ($17).

THE DESERT & YOUR CAR

Desert conditions are as grueling on cars as they are on bodies; only recently serviced cars in good condition can take the heat. Prevention and preparation are crucial, so if you are planning a high-mileage roadtrip in the Southwest, a pre-trip check-up for your vehicle is a must. It is particularly important to inspect your cooling system, electrical system, and tires.

The Southwest's summer heat puts tremendous stress on an automotive **cooling system**. Driving in the evening, at night, or in the early morning may be preferable than overheating or being uncomfortably hot at midday. Bring with you **a gallon of extra coolant, extra quarts of oil, and at least five gallons of clean water**, which can serve as drinking or radiator water. Turn off the **air-conditioning** immediately if your car's temperature gauge climbs too high; air from open windows should be sufficiently comfortable at highway speeds. If your car overheats, pull over and try turning the heater on at full blast. If you hear radiator fluid steaming or bubbling, turn off the car for 30 min. If the car is overheating noiselessly, run it in neutral at about 1500 r.p.m. for a few minutes to allow the coolant to circulate. Never pour water onto the engine or try to lift a searingly hot hood, and if you decide to open your radiator cap to top it off, wait at least 45 min. for the coolant in it to cool off (lest you be spattered with boiling radiator fluid). **Desert water bags** are available at hardware or automotive stores for $5-10. When strapped onto the front of the car and filled with water, these large canvas bags prevent overheating by speeding up evaporation. During your pre-trip planning, you might also consider using a **motor oil** of higher viscosity, which will perform better in the Southwestern heat than the normal 10W-30 grade.

The best defense against tire problems is good maintenance. Most importantly, make sure your **tires** are inflated to the pressure recommended on their sidewalls. Overinflation and underinflation are both dangerous and can contribute to tire failure. It is a good idea to practice changing a flat before you start your trip, since some roads in the Southwest are just as removed from cellular phone reception as they are from civilization. First, bring your car to a level surface and apply the parking brake. Align your jack on the vehicle near the blown tire and begin to loosen the wheel's lugnuts with your tire iron. Loosen them gradually, working from the first nut to the one diagonal from it, then from one next to the first one to the one opposite it. Repeat the pattern until all are loose. Next, use the jack to slowly raise up the vehicle; once it is up, treat it as though it could fall at any moment. Remove the tire carefully and replace it with your spare, tightening the lugnuts with only your fingers. Lower the vehicle with the jack, then use the tire iron to re-tighten the lugnuts. Drive slowly for the first few yards to make sure the tire is on correctly. If possible, bring a **full-sized spare** rather than a miniature limited-mileage tire, which is good only for about 50 miles.

Though **dead batteries** are most common in cold weather, they are a mishap that can befall you anytime. If your battery dies, you need to **jump start** your vehicle. First, hail another vehicle and position the two cars' engines close to one another. With both engines off, open the hoods, identify the positive posts on both batteries, and attach the red jumper cable to both posts. Never let the red clips touch the black clips. Attach one black clip on the black cable to the negative post on the working battery, then attach the other clip to the bare metal on the disabled vehicle's engine frame (far from the battery). Start the working vehicle, revving it for a moment before starting the disabled vehicle. With both vehicles running, disconnect the cables in reverse order, beginning with the black cable attached to the bare metal. Drive the newly jumped vehicle for at least half an hour before turning it off to allow its battery to recharge.

Avoid running out of gas in the middle of nowhere by always keeping your tank above half full, and consider bringing **extra gas** with you in a **metal safety can.** A board, a shovel, and a tow rope may prove indispensable if your car gets stuck in sand, which can appear suddenly on rural gravel roads. In addition to these items, a **basic car maintenance/emergency kit** should include a wrench, a flashlight, a screwdriver or two, a tire pressure gauge, duct tape, flares, a knife, emergency blankets and food (in case you get stuck in winter or at night), a compass, and a car manual. Although towns are often sparse, major roads usually have enough traffic to ensure that breakdowns will be noticed. *Stay with your vehicle if it breaks down*; it is easier to spot than a person and provides crucial shade (see **Automobile Clubs,** p. 43).

FLORA & FAUNA

INSECTS

One of the distinctive features of the Southwest desert is the abundance of scurrying, hairy, and occasionally venomous critters. Knowing potential threats and keeping your distance will make your life less swollen and painful.

Though **spiders** have inspired many phobias and scary movies, the spiders present in the Southwest rarely pose a threat to human life. **Black Widows** are the most venomous, and are found throughout the Southwest (however, only adult females, characterized by a red hourglass shape on their abdomen, actually have venom). Though the venom of the Black Widow is 15 times as potent as that of a Prairie rattlesnake, the small amount injected with each bite means that bites rarely result in death. The **tarantula,** a large, hairy species of arachnid prevalent in the warm, dry desert regions of the Southwest, looks much scarier than it is. When provoked, the tarantula will bite, but for humans the bite is usually merely an annoyance. Some people even keep and train them as pets. Though the **brown**

GREAT OUTDOORS

recluse spider is not widespread in the region, a few desert species of recluse spider do make their home in the deserts of California, Arizona, southern New Mexico, and western Texas. These spiders, as their name suggests, are shy and reclusive. However, their bites are capable of producing a nasty, festering wound.

Scorpions populate many different climates worldwide, but are a particularly notable resident of the Southwest. The characteristic features of the scorpion are two pincers (called "pedipalps") and a long barbed tail that curves skyward in aggressive or defensive situations. Only one of the nearly 100 species of scorpion indigenous to the Southwest—the brown Arizona Bark Scorpion (Centruroides exilicauda)—poses any real threat to human life, and this singular species causes fatalities only in the elderly, infirm, or strongly allergic.

The best way to avoid contact with both spiders and scorpions is to always look where you are placing your hands and feet. **Turn down sheets** before bed and **shake out clothing and boots** before putting them on; these are the ways arachnids most often come into contact with humans. Both spiders and scorpions are nocturnal insects, so precautions are especially important at night and in the early morning. Be careful of holes in the ground or shaded areas under rocks or wood, places where spiders and scorpions hide out during the heat of the day.

An increasing concern in the Southwest is the gradual arrival of **Africanized honey bees** (popularly known as **killer bees**) from south of the Mexican border. In 1956, a Brazilian scientist trying to breed a honey bee that was better suited to a South American habitat imported southern African bees. Some of them escaped from captivity in 1957 and bred with local bees, creating an aggressive new breed that seems to spread rapidly. Though attacks are rare, six people in the United States have perished at the stingers of these insects, and all in the Southwest. Killer bees overwhelm their victims by sheer numbers, leaving hundreds of stings, especially on the head and face. If you encounter a swarm of aggressive bees, cover your head and seek sealed shelter in a house, shed, or car. DO NOT jump into water; the bees will wait for you to surface. Seek medical attention in cases of allergic reaction or numerous stings. To prevent attack, wear light-colored clothing and be alert to prevent attack.

SNAKES & OTHER REPTILES

The deserts of the Southwestern United States are home to a multitude of serpents; however, the only venomous species are the coral snake and the different types of rattlesnake. The neurotoxic **Coral Snake** is characterized by alternating red, black, and yellow bands. It's small in size relative to full-grown rattlesnakes but delivers its potent venom by chewing on its victim. The innocuous **King Snake** is often mistaken for its evil twin because of similar red, black, and yellow stripes. The difference is the order of colors, captured in the adage, "red on yellow, kill a fellow; red on black, friend of Jack."

The **Western Diamondback Rattlesnake** is the most common and feared member of the pit viper family found in the Southwest, mainly because of its mean temper and strong venom. It is the feistiest of desert snakes and causes more fatalities than any other reptile in the United States. Its close cousins, the **Red Diamondback** and **Speckled Rattlesnakes,** are also venomous and are prevalent around the Southwest, while the **Sidewinder** and the **Mojave Rattlesnake** are generally found only in and around the Mojave Desert.

Along with a variety of geckos, lizards, toads, tortoises, and other reptiles, the **Gila Monster** lives in the deserts of southern Utah and Nevada, southeastern California, Arizona, and New Mexico. Some fear the Gila Monster, whose teeth have grooves that deliver a neurotoxin as it chews its prey; but, ominous name notwithstanding, this 1.5-2ft. lizard is a minimal threat to humans who leave it alone.

GREAT OUTDOORS

SNAKES! Every year, around 8,000 people are bitten by poisonous snakes in the US, and many of these bites occur in the snake-friendly Southwest. Both in wilderness and suburban areas, travelers should keep in mind that they are interlopers in the snakes' natural habitat. Any snake will avoid an encounter with humans if given the chance, and most bites occur when someone has provoked, surprised, or cornered the offender. To prevent being bitten, stay on the trail, wear tough pants and boots if possible, watch where you place your hands and feet while hiking and climbing, and beware of the types of places snakes frequent, such as under rocks and logs. If you surprise a snake, stand still until it slithers away. If it bites you, here's what to do:

1. Try to relax and remain calm. Panicking will only help the venom spread. Remove any jewelry or restrictive clothing in case of swelling.
2. Allow the bite to bleed freely for 30 seconds, then clean and disinfect the area if possible.
3. Immobilize a bitten limb with bandages and/or a splint, and keep it at (to prevent swelling) or below (to prevent venom spread) heart-level.
4. If you have a pump suction device such as the Sawyer Extractor, apply it, following its directions carefully.
5. If you are without an extractor, place gauze over the wound and wrap it in an ACE-type bandage about as tight as you would wrap a sprain. You should be able to fit a finger under the bandage and/or detect a pulse. You may also want to place light restricting bandages above and below the bite to prevent swelling and venom spread. DO NOT apply a tourniquet.
6. Get the victim professional medical care as soon as possible. The antivenin that doctors administer is the only effective antidote for snake venom.
7. Identify the offending snake and inform the doctors. If you cannot, the snake should be killed and sent with the victim to the hospital, but ONLY if it can be killed safely, without risking another bite.

MOUNTAIN LIONS

These solitary animals are the feline regents of the Southwest. Inhabiting climates ranging from low desert to alpine forest, mountain lions (also called cougars) keep to themselves and thus seldom come into contact with humans. Most altercations result from lions protecting their young. If you happen to stumble upon a mountain lion, freeze, stand your ground, and then back away slowly to give the animal its space. There are several documented cases of mountain lions attacking young children who wandered off alone, so always make sure to keep children and pets nearby when you are on the trail.

BEARS

If you are hiking in an area that bears might also frequent, ask local rangers for information on bear behavior before entering any park or wilderness area, and obey posted warnings. No matter how irresistibly cute a bear appears, don't be fooled—they're powerful and unpredictable animals who are not intimidated by humans. No matter how much you may be hankering for a wild bear photo-op, it is wise to avoid encountering bears entirely when in the wilderness.

Fortunately, bears make avoidance relatively easy—they are uninterested in humans and tend to avoid groups of hikers they might come across. So make it easy on the bears—don't sneak up on them. Travel in groups, make lots of noise by singing, whistling or tying bells to your packs, and stay on marked trails. Never leave food or other scented items (trash, toiletries, the clothes that you cooked in) near your tent. Putting these objects into canisters is now mandatory in some national parks of the Southwest and the West. **Bear-bagging** involves bagging and hanging edibles and other odiferous items out of the reach of hungry paws, and it is the best way to keep your toothpaste from becoming a condiment (and yourself the main course). Try to hang the bag from a tree at least 100m away from your tent, ideally 10ft. off the ground and 5-10ft. away from anything climbable (namely the tree trunk). A bear's keen sense of smell will lead him to everything from scented soap and perfume to used feminine hygiene products. Non-essential conveniences like cologne, deodorant, and hairspray should stay home; anything else with a scent must go in the bearbag at night.

If you run into a bear by surprise, proceed with extreme caution. Speak to it in low, calming tones and back away slowly. Do not run, tempting as it may be—the bear will identify you as prey and give chase. If you will be traveling extensively in bear-infested areas, consider taking **bear pepper spray**—only slightly less effective against bears than muggers. Deployed from a hand-held aerosol can, bear spray is effective at a range up to 15 ft. and will temporarily blind and disorient the bear if sprayed in his face and eyes. Familiarize yourself with how to aim the sprayer, and remember that if the wind is blowing towards you, it may prove useless or even dangerous. Without bear pepper spray, different strategies should be used with different bear species. Black bears (black coloration, tall ears, no shoulder hump) are carrion eaters; if you play dead, you are giving them a free meal. The best course of action is to fight back, since resistance may actually deter a black bear. Try to appear as big and fierce as possible, make loud noises, and use rocks or sticks to defend yourself. If you're standing toe to toe with a grizzly bear, a natural predator, fighting back will get you killed; play dead, dropping to the ground and shielding your face and chest with your arms or backpack.

CACTI & OTHER FLORA

More than almost any other feature, cacti give the desert its forbidding and stoic image. From the **Joshua Tree** in California to the **Yucca** in Texas, from the common **Barrel Cactus** to the rare **Organ Pipe Cactus,** these occasionally large, succulent plants lend the Southwest its characteristic stateliness and flair. In bloom from late March to May, cacti have shallow root systems that collect and store the desert's scarce rainwater with great efficiency; the trade-off is the cacti's slow rate of growth. As you marvel at the striking landscapes they help create, keep your distance at all times or prepare to face unpleasant consequences. Even harmless-looking cacti can turn out to have thousands of tiny, skin-piercing spines that take hours to find and remove. Show respect for these magnificent succulents; damaging or removing cacti from public lands is illegal and results in hefty fines.

Like anywhere else, the Southwest has native toxic plants, but awareness and common sense should protect you from their ill effects. While **poison ivy/oak** find the arid climate inhospitable, they still exist in select parts of the Southwest and should be actively avoided, including and especially as fuel for campfires. These can be identified in part by their three-leaflet clusters and slightly oily appearance upon close examination. The noxious urushiol oil they produce causes a nasty allergic rash in most people. Obey the old adage, "leaves of three, let them be."

Native to all four major Southwestern deserts, **Jimson Weed** is a stout, green-leafed perennial that grows up to 2ft. high and blooms with white, trumpet-shaped flowers from March to November. Because of its hallucinogenic alkaloids, all parts of it are toxic and can be fatal if ingested. **Dogbane,** or Indian Hemp, is another plant species to avoid. The milky sap of this reddish-stemmed, green-leafed perennial causes skin to blister on contact. If you're not familiar enough with these plants to identify them in the wild, ask an expert or a ranger to point them out.

GREAT OUTDOORS

ORGANIZED TRIPS & OUTFITTERS

Organized adventure tours offer another way of exploring the wild. Stores and organizations specializing in camping and outdoors equipment can often provide good info on trips (see p. 65). Sales reps at REI, EMS, or Sierra often know of a range of cheap, convenient trips. They may also offer training programs for travelers.

When choosing an **outfitter** for a day or multi-day trip, check their credentials and qualifications. Local **Visitors Centers** have lists of established, experienced, and credentialed guide services; weigh your options before trusting life and limb to a person you have never met before. The organizations below offer guided trips all over the Southwest and the entire US. Contact them for specific trips and prices.

The National Outdoor Leadership School (NOLS), 284 Lincoln St., Lander, WY 82520-2848 (☎800-710-6657; admissions@nols.edu; www.nols.edu), offers educational wilderness trips all over the world, including many to the desert Southwest. They also offer courses in wilderness medicine training and leave no trace ethics.

Outward Bound, 100 Mystery Point Rd., Garrison, NY 10524 (☎866-467-7651; www.outwardbound.com), offers expeditionary courses in outdoor education in the Southwest and throughout the US and overseas. Courses range from several days to over 40 days, and include special focuses, such as life & career renewal and couples.

The Sierra Club, 85 Second St., 2nd fl. San Francisco, CA 94105 (☎415-977-5500; national.outings@sierraclub.org; www.sierraclub.org/outings), plans many adventure outings at all of its branches throughout the US, including the Southwest.

Specialty Travel Index, 305 San Anselmo Ave., Ste. 309, San Anselmo, CA 94960 (☎888-624-4030, 415-455-1643; info@specialtytravel.com; www.specialtytravel.com), is a directory listing tour operators worldwide.

TrekAmerica, P.O. Box 189, Rockaway, NJ 07866 (☎800-221-0596; www.trekamerica.com), recently merged with AmeriCan Adventures, operates small group active adventure tours throughout the US, including Alaska and Hawaii, and Canada. These tours are for 18- to 38-year-olds, and run 1-9 weeks.

OUTDOOR TRAVEL PUBLICATIONS

A variety of publishing companies offer outdoors guidebooks to meet the educational needs of novice or expert. For **books** about camping, hiking, biking, and climbing, write or call the publishers listed below to receive a free catalog.

Falcon Guides, Globe Pequot Press, P.O. Box 480, Guilford, CT 06437 (☎888-249-7586; www.falcon.com). Over 1000 guides to different outdoor-related activities. Books are mostly organized by activity and state, so they are best for the focused traveler.

The Mountaineers Books, 300 Third Ave W. Seattle, WA 98119 (☎206-284-8484; www.mountaineers.org). Over 400 titles on hiking (the *100 Hikes* series), biking, mountaineering, natural history, and conservation.

Sierra Club Books, 85 Second St., 2nd fl., San Francisco, CA 94105-3441 (☎415-977-5500; www.sierraclub.org/books). Books on the national parks and several series on different areas of the Southwest, all with an adventurous bent.

Wilderness Press, 1200 Fifth St., Berkeley, CA 94710 (☎800-443-7227 or 510-558-1696; www.wildernesspress.com). Over 100 hiking guides and maps for the western US, including *Backpacking Basics* ($10).

GRAND CANYON

The single biggest attraction in the southwest, the Grand Canyon extends from Lee's Ferry, AZ all the way to Lake Mead, NV. In the north, the Glen Canyon Dam backs up the Colorado into mammoth Lake Powell. To the west, the Hoover Dam traps the remaining outflow from Glen Canyon to form Lake Mead, a haven for water sports enthusiasts. Grand Canyon National Park is divided into three sections: the most popular South Rim, the more serene North Rim, and the canyon gorge itself. Traveling between rims takes approximately five hours by car with a long drive to the bridge in Lee's Ferry, or two days by a marathon hike via a descent to and ascent from the ancient canyon floor (21 mi. one-way). Sandwiched between the national park and Lake Mead, the Hualapai and Havasupai Reservations rest on the banks of the Colorado river. The remote Havasupai tribe protects several of the canyon's most spectacular waterfalls and welcomes thousands of tourists each year who make the ten-mile trek to their village.

AT A GLANCE: GRAND CANYON NATIONAL PARK

AREA: 1,218,376 acres.

FEATURES: The Canyon, Colorado River, North Rim, South Rim, West Rim, Kaibab Plateau, Tonto Platform.

HIGHLIGHTS: Taking a mule ride to Phantom Ranch, rafting down the Canyon, backpacking from rim to rim on the South and North Kaibab Trails, standing in awe at the edge of either rim.

GATEWAY TOWNS: Flagstaff (p. 111), Williams, Page, AZ (p. 87).

CAMPING: Mather Campground on the South Rim and the North Rim Campground require reservations (1-800-365-CAMP; $15). Backcountry camping requires a permit ($10 for permit, plus $5 per person per night, $10 per group).

FEES: Weekly pass $20 per car, $10 for other modes of transportation; covers both South and North Rim.

SOUTH RIM ☎ 928

During the summer, everything on two legs or four wheels converges on this side of the Grand Canyon. If you plan to visit at this time, make reservations well in advance for lodging, campsites, and/or mules, and prepare to battle the crowds. Still, it's much better than Disney World. A friendly Park Service staff, well-run facilities, and beautiful scenery help ease crowd-anxiety. Fewer tourists brave the canyon's winter weather; many hotels and facilities close during the off season. Leading up to the Park entrance, Rte. 64 is surrounded by Kaibab National Forest and encompasses the North Rim.

▐▀ TRANSPORTATION

There are two park entrances: the main **south entrance** is 58 mi. north of I-40, while the eastern **Desert View** entrance is 27 mi. away off Hwy. 89. Both are accessed via Rte. 64. From Las Vegas, the fastest route to the South Rim is U.S. 93 S to I-40 E, then Rte. 64 N at Williams. From Flagstaff, head north on U.S. 180 to Rte. 64. If the haul to the canyon is too much for your car, the **Grand Canyon Garage,** east of the Visitors Center on the main road, just before the rim lodges, is a good place to take a look. (☎638-2631. Open daily 8am-5pm. 24hr. emergency service.)

The **Grand Canyon Railway** (☎800-843-8724) runs a restored train from Williams, AZ to the Grand Canyon (2¼hr.; leaves 10am, returns 3:30pm; $68, children $27). **North Arizona Shuttle and Tours** (☎866-870-8687) departs its Flagstaff depot, 1300 S. Milton St., for the Grand Canyon daily (2hr.; leaves 7:30am, 2:30pm, returns to Flagstaff 10am, 4:30pm; $20 each way). Fares don't include the $6 entrance fee. Shuttles also head to Sedona twice a day ($25). **Free shuttle buses** run the West Rim Loop (daily 1hr. before sunrise to sunset) and the Village Loop (daily 1hr. before sunrise to 11pm) every 10-30min. A free **hiker's shuttle** runs every 30min. between the info center and the South Kaibab Trailhead, on the East Rim near Yaki Point. (Early buses run at 4, 5, and 6am.) For **taxi** service, call ☎638-2822.

ORIENTATION

Maps and signs in the park make it easy to orient yourself, though the size of the park can be overwhelming. Lodges and services concentrate in **Grand Canyon Village,** at the end of Park Entrance Rd. The east half of the village contains the Visitors Center and the general store, while most of the rim lodges and the challenging **Bright Angel Trail** lie in the west section. The shorter but more difficult **South Kaibab Trail** is off **East Rim Drive,** east of the village. Free shuttle buses to eight rim overlooks run along **West Rim Drive** (closed to private vehicles during the summer). Avoid walking on the drive; the rim trails are safer and more scenic. For most services in the park, call the **main switchboard** (☎638-2631).

WHEN TO GO. The South Rim, open year-round, is jam-packed in the spring, summer, and fall, and only the winter offers some measure of solitude, though services are closed and temperatures are chilly (lows in the 10s and 20s, highs in the 30s and 40s). Colder and less visited than its southern counterpart, the North Rim is open for day use only from October 15 to December 1, and from December 1 to May 15, the Rim closes entirely due to snow and ice. Summer temperatures rise with visitation figures but are highly variable from rim to rim—average summer highs are about 85°F on the South Rim, 75°F on the North Rim (due to higher elevation), and 110°F in the Inner Canyon.

PRACTICAL INFORMATION

Visitor Info: The first installment in the Park Service's plan to reshape visitor flow in the crowded park, the new **Canyon View Information Plaza,** across from Mather Point and just after the entrance to the park, is the one-stop center for Grand Canyon info. The Plaza houses the Visitors Center (open daily 8am-6pm), a bookstore (open daily 8am-7pm), restrooms, and helpful kiosks answering frequently asked questions. The Visitors Center stocks copies of *The Guide* (an essential given also at the park entrance), and assorted other pamphlets, including information on the Havasupai Reservation, access for those with disabilities, and hidden backcountry secrets and ranger projects. To get there, park at Mather Pt., then get out and hoof it for ½ mi. to the info plaza. For those looking for pre-trip info, the Park Service, through the Grand Canyon Association, sells a variety of informational books and packets (☎800-858-2808; www.grandcanyon.com or www.nps.gov/grca). The **transportation info desks** in **Bright Angel Lodge** and **Maswik Lodge** (☎638-2631) handle reservations for mule rides, bus tours, plane tours, Phantom Ranch, taxis, and more. Open daily 6am-8pm. Also, wheelchair accessible tours are available by prior arrangement (☎638-2631.)

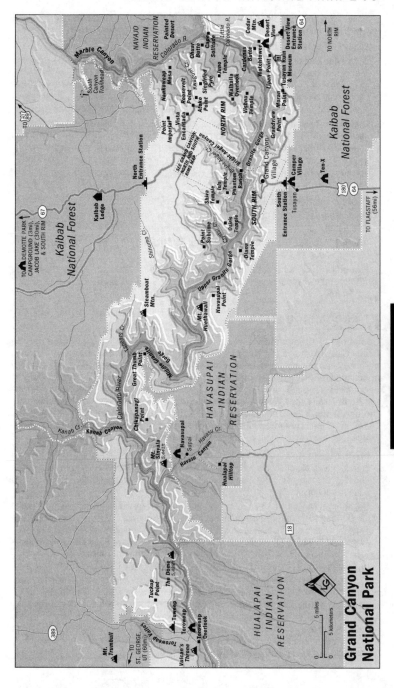

Grand Canyon
National Park

GRAND CANYON

Bank: Bank One (☎638-2437), in Market Plaza. Full-service branch with **ATM. Currency exchange** on traveler's checks, but not cash. Open M-Th 10am-3pm, F 10am-5pm.

Luggage Storage: In **Bright Angel Lodge** (see **Accommodations**). 6:30am-9pm.

Equipment Rental: General Store next to the Yavapai Lodge Cafeteria. Comfy hiking boots, socks included ($8 first day, $5 per additional day); sleeping bags ($9 first day, $5 per additional day); tents ($15 first day for a 2-person, $16 first day for 4-person, $9 per additional day for both); day packs ($6 for a large, $4 for a small), and other gear (stoves $5). Deposits required; major credit cards accepted. Open daily 7am-8:30pm.

Groceries: Canyon Village Marketplace (☎638-2262), a general store at the Yavapai Lodge complex. Offers 1hr. photo processing. Open daily in summer 7am-9pm. Near the east entrance, **Desert View General Store** stocks food. Open daily 7am-8:30pm.

Showers and Laundry: Available at concession-run **Camper Services,** adjacent to the Mather Campground in Canyon Village. Showers $1 per 5min. Laundry open daily 6am-9:45pm; showers 6am-11pm.

Weather and Road Conditions: ☎638-7888.

Medical Services: Grand Canyon Clinic (☎638-2551), take a left at the first stoplight after the South Rim entrance. Open M-F 7am-7pm, Sa 10am-4pm. 24hr. emergency first aid.

Internet Access: Grand Canyon National Park Library, (☎638-7768). Open M-Th 8:30am-noon and 1-4pm, except holidays.

Post Office: 100 Mather Business Ctr. (☎638-2512), in market plaza, next to the General Store at the Yavapai Lodge Complex. Open M-F 9am-4:30pm, Sa 10am-5pm. **Postal code:** 86023.

ACCOMMODATIONS

Compared to the six million years it took the Colorado River to carve out the Grand Canyon, the year it will take you to get indoor lodging near the South Rim is nothing. Summer rooms should be reserved **11 months in advance.** Even so, there are cancellations every day; you can check for vacancies or call the Grand Canyon operator (☎638-2631) and ask to be connected with the proper lodge. Reservations for **Bright Angel Lodge, Maswik Lodge, Trailer Village,** and **Phantom Ranch** can be made through **Xanterra Parks and Resorts,** 14001 E. Iliff, Ste. 600, Aurora, CO 80014 (☎303-297-2757). Most accommodations on the South Rim are very pricey, but Yavapai Lodge may have remaining rooms when all other lodges are full.

Maswik Lodge (☎638-2631), in Grand Canyon Village near the rim and several restaurants. Small, clean cabins with showers but no heat are $66. Motel rooms with queen beds and ceiling fans are also available. Singles $79; doubles $121. $7-9 for each additional person. ❹

Bright Angel Lodge (☎638-2631), in Grand Canyon Village. The cheapest indoor lodging in the park, located in a historic building right on the rim. Very convenient to Bright Angel Trail and shuttle buses. "Rustic" lodge singles and doubles with shared bath $53, with private bath $71. "Historic" cabins, some of which have fireplaces, are available for 1 or 2 people $84-107. $7 per additional person in rooms and cabins. ❸

Phantom Ranch (☎638-2631), on the canyon floor, a day's hike down the Kaibab Trail or Bright Angel Trail. Male and female dorms $28; seldom-available cabins for 1 or 2 people $71.50; $10.50 per additional person. Don't show up without reservations, which can be made up to 23 months in advance. Breakfast $17; box lunch $8.50; stew dinner $20; steak dinner $29, prepared the same way for over 50 years; vegetarian option $20. If you're dying to sleep on the canyon floor but don't have a reservation, show up at the Bright Angel transportation desk at 6am on the day prior to your planned stay and take a shot on the waiting list. ❷

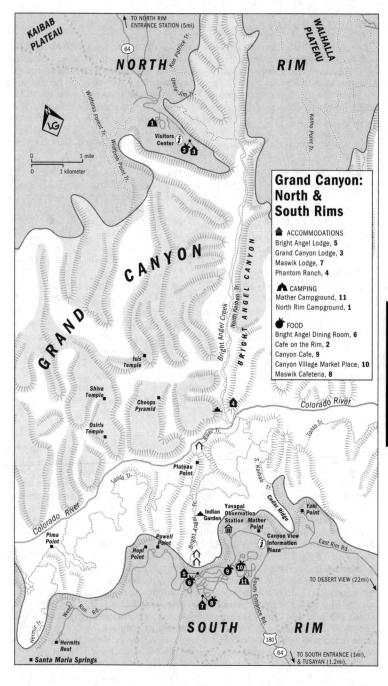

**Grand Canyon:
North &
South Rims**

🏠 **ACCOMMODATIONS**
Bright Angel Lodge, **5**
Grand Canyon Lodge, **3**
Maswik Lodge, **7**
Phantom Ranch, **4**

⛺ **CAMPING**
Mather Campground, **11**
North Rim Campground, **1**

🍴 **FOOD**
Bright Angel Dining Room, **6**
Cafe on the Rim, **2**
Canyon Cafe, **9**
Canyon Village Market Place, **10**
Maswik Cafeteria, **8**

CAMPGROUNDS

The campsites listed here usually fill up early in the day. In the **Kaibab National Forest,** along the south border of the park, you can pull off a dirt road and camp for free. No camping is allowed within ¼ mile of U.S. 64. **Dispersed camping** sits conveniently along the oft-traveled N. Long Jim Loop Rd.—turn right about one mile south of the south entrance station. For quieter and more remote sites, follow signs for the Arizona Trail into the national forest between miles 252 and 253 on U.S. 64. Sleeping in cars is not permitted within the park, but it is allowed in the Kaibab Forest. For more info, contact the **Tusayan Ranger Station,** Kaibab National Forest, P.O. Box 3088, Tusayan, AZ 86023 (☎638-2443). Reservations for some campgrounds can be made through **SPHERICS** (☎800-365-2267).

Mather Campground (call SPHERICS, ☎800-365-2267) in Grand Canyon Village, 1 mi. south of the Canyon Village Marketplace; follow signs from Yavapai Lodge. 320 shady, relatively isolated sites with no hookups. Check at the office even if the sign says the campground is full. 7-night max. stay. For Mar.-Nov., reserve up to 3 months in advance; Dec.-Feb. first come, first served. Sept.-May $12; June-Aug. $15. ❶

Ten-X Campground (☎638-2443), in Kaibab National Forest, 10 mi. south of Grand Canyon Village off Rte. 64. Removed from the highway, offers shady sites surrounded by pine trees. Toilets, water, no hookups, no showers. Open May-Sept. First come, first served; sites $10. ❶

Desert View Campground (☎638-7888), 25 mi. east of Grand Canyon Village. Short on shade and far from the hub of the South Rim, but a perfect place to avoid the crowd. 50 sites with phone and restroom access, but no hookups or campfires. Sites $10. Open mid-May to Oct. No reservations; usually full by early afternoon. ❶

Camper Village (☎638-2887), in Tusayan, 1 mi. south of the park entrance behind the general store. Two-person hookups and tent sites $18-26; showers and flush toilets; $2 per additional adult. First come, first served tent sites; reservations required for RVs. ❷

Trailer Village (☎638-2631), next to Mather Campground. 84 sites designed for the RV. Showers, laundry, and groceries nearby. Office open daily 8am-noon and 1-5pm. 2-person hookups $24; $2 per additional person. Reserve 6-9 months in advance. ❷

FOOD

Fast food has yet to sink its greasy talons into the South Rim (the closest McDonald's is 7 mi. south in Tusayan), but you can find meals at fast-food prices and get a slightly better return for your money. The **Canyon Village Market Place ❶,** at the Market Plaza 1 mi. west of Mather Point on the main road, has a deli counter with the cheapest eats in the park, a wide selection of groceries, a camping supplies department, and enough Grand Canyon apparel to clothe each member of your extended family. (☎638-2262. Open daily in summer 7am-8:30pm; deli open 7am-6pm. Sandwiches $2-4.) The well-stocked **Canyon Cafe ❶,** across from the General Store inside the Yavapai Lodge, offers a wider variety of food than the deli. (Open daily 6:30am-9pm. Hamburgers $3, pizza $3.50-5, dinners $5-7.) **Maswik Cafeteria ❶,** in Maswik Lodge, serves a variety of grilled food, country favorites, and Mexican specialties (including veggie options and healthy alternatives) in a wood-paneled cafeteria atmosphere. (Open daily 6am-10pm. Hot entrees $6-7, sandwiches $3-5.) **Bright Angel Dining Room ❷,** in Bright Angel Lodge, serves hot sandwiches for $7-9. Breakfasts run $6-7 and pricey dinner entrees range $10-15. (☎638-2631. Open daily 6:30am-10pm.) Just out the door of the dining room, the **Soda Fountain ❶** at Bright Angel Lodge chills eight flavors of ice cream and stocks a variety of snack-bar sandwiches. (Open daily 8am-8pm. 1 scoop $2.)

CANYON CAUTION. From your first glimpse, you may feel a compelling desire to see the canyon from the inside—an enterprise harder than it looks. Even the young at heart and in body should remember that an easy downhill hike can become a nightmarish 50° incline on the return journey: plan on taking twice as long to ascend as you took descending. Also keep in mind that the lower you go, the hotter it gets; when it's 85°F on the rim, it's around 100°F at Indian Gardens and around 115°F at Phantom Ranch. Heat stroke, the greatest threat to any hiker, is signaled by a monstrous headache and red, sweatless skin. For a day hike, take at least a gallon of water per person; drink at least a liter per hr. hiking upwards under the hot sun. Wearing a cotton t-shirt that is soaking wet is a good way to hike in extreme temperatures. Apply sunscreen regularly. Hiking boots or sneakers with excellent tread are also necessary—the trails are steep, and every year several careless hikers take what locals morbidly call "the 12-second tour." Poor preparation and over-exertion greatly magnify the risks of Canyon hiking. A list of safety tips can be found in *The Guide.* Speak with a ranger before embarking on a hike—they may have important info about the trail. Hiking down to the river and back to the rim in the same day is discouraged by rangers, though it seems these discouragements are often ineffective as most Helivac rescues are the result of these attempts. Resting at a campground is also recommended (see **backcountry permits,** p. 79). Parents should think twice about bringing children more than 1 mi. down any trail.

HIKING & BACKPACKING

Although the Grand Canyon experience for the majority of park visitors involves stepping out of the air-conditioned tour bus, walking eagerly to the rim with camera in hand, enjoying the views, snapping a few keepsake shots, and then retreating to the bus before beads of sweat begin to form, there are many more invigorating and exciting ways to enjoy the Canyon's grandeur. Outdoor recreation in the park focuses mainly on hiking and backpacking, though commercial outfits provide services like mule rides, rafting, and "flightseeing."

In determining what is an appropriate day hike, remember that the Canyon does not have any loops. Be prepared to retrace every single footstep uphill on the way back. For longer day hikes, it is strongly recommended that you begin before 7am. Because walking and climbing in the summer heat requires exceptional effort, the Park Service recommends not hiking between the hours of 10am and 4pm to escape the worst of the heat. Rangers present a variety of free informative **talks** and **guided hikes;** details are listed in *The Guide.* Rangers will also gladly offer advice regarding trail guides and maps; the *Official Guide to Hiking the Grand Canyon*, published by the Grand Canyon Association, is the preferred choice. The so-called corridor trails, which include the **Rim, Bright Angel, South Kaibab,** and **River Trails,** are the only trails on the South Rim of the Canyon that are regularly maintained and patrolled by the Park Service.

Stifling heat, scarce water, and drastic elevation changes, all under the weight of a heavy pack, make **backpacking** around the Grand Canyon a grueling experience. Still, applications for **backcountry permits** far outnumber availability, especially during the summer. If you get there late in the day, you can forget about getting a permit, and plan to start earlier the next day. The most popular backpacking routes connect the rim-to-river trails listed below and demand little in the way of navigational skills. Camping along such popular corridor routes is limited to **designated areas.** The Park Service divides the park into use areas, each with restrictions on camping and recreation. Much of the park remains inaccessible to trekkers because of cliffs and other impassable terrain. The footbridge spanning the Colorado River near Phantom Ranch is the only **river crossing**, making the ranch a necessary stop when traveling rim to rim. **Through-hiking** from the South to the North Rim generally connects either the Bright Angel or South Kaibab Trail with the North Kaibab Trail, covering 21-23 mi. and 10,000 ft. of elevation change. All overnight trips require a **backcountry permit** ($10 per group, $5 per person per day, plus a $10 permit fee), obtainable at the Backcountry Information Center next to the Maswik Lodge (P.O. Box 129, Grand Canyon, AZ 86023; www.nps.gov/ grca). Permits are available on the 1st of the month, four months before the proposed hike (e.g., July permits available March 1). Requests should include the proposed route, campsites, license plate numbers, group size, and contact info.

Rim Trail (12 mi. one way, 4-6hr.). With only a mild elevation change (about 200 ft.) and the constant security of the nearby shuttle, the Rim Trail is excellent for hikers seeking a tame way to see the Canyon. The handicap accessible trail follows the shuttle bus routes along Hermit Rd. past the Grand Canyon Village to Mather Point. The Rim Trail covers both paved and unpaved ground, with 8 viewpoints along Hermit Rd. and 3 east of it. Near the Grand Canyon Village, the Rim Trail resembles a crowded city street that runs behind the lodges, but toward the eastern and western ends, hikers have a bit more elbow room. Hopi Point is a great place to watch the sun set with its panoramic canyon views—The Guide lists times for sunsets and sunrises, and the "Choose your view" kiosk at the Visitors Center allows photographers to preview typical scenery at different locations and times of day. Bring lots of water, as little is available along the trail.

Bright Angel Trail (up to 18 mi. round-trip, 1-2 days). Bright Angel's frequent switchbacks and refreshing water stations make it the into-the-canyon choice of moderate hikers. Depending on distance, the trail can make either a day or overnight hike. The trail departs from the Rim Trail near the western edge of the Grand Canyon Village, and the first 1-2 mi. of the trail generally attract droves of day hikers eager to try just a taste of canyon descent. Rest houses are strategically stationed 1½ and 3 mi. from the rim, each with water between May and Sept. **Indian Gardens,** 4½ mi. down, offers restrooms, picnic tables, 15 backcountry campsites open year-round, and blessed shade. From rim to river, the trail drops 4420 ft. Although spread over 9 mi., the round-trip is too strenuous for a day hike. With the compulsory permit, overnighters can camp at Indian Gardens or on the canyon floor at Bright Angel Campground, while day hikers are advised to go no farther than Plateau Point (12.2 mi. round-trip) or Indian Gardens (9.2 mi. round-trip). Yield and wave bitterly to tourists descending by mule train. The **River Trail** (1.7 mi.) runs along the river, linking the Bright Angel with South Kaibab.

South Kaibab Trail (7 mi. one way to Phantom Ranch, 4-5 hr. descent). Those seeking a more challenging hike down might consider this route. Beginning at Yaki Pt. (7260 ft.), Kaibab is trickier, steeper, and lacks shade or water, but it rewards the intrepid with a better view of the canyon. Unlike most canyon-descending trails, the South Kaibab avoids the safety and obstructed views of a side-canyon route and instead winds directly down the ridge, offering panoramic views across the expanse of the canyon. Day hikes to Cedar Ridge (3 mi. round-trip; toilet facilities available) and Skeleton Point (6 mi. round-trip) are reasonable only for experienced, well-conditioned hikers due to the trail's steep grade. For overnight hikes, Kaibab meets up with Bright Angel at the Colorado River. Fewer switchbacks and a more rapid descent make the South Kaibab Trail 1.7 mi. shorter than the Bright Angel to this point. Guests staying at the Phantom Ranch or Bright Angel Campground (the only permitted camping area on the trail) use either the Bright Angel or South Kaibab to reach the ranch. Many hikers believe that the best route is to descend the South Kaibab Trail (4-5hr.) and come back up the Bright Angel (7-8hr.) the following day, though this is very strenuous. 4880 ft. elevation change.

Grandview Trail (6.4 mi. round-trip to the Mesa). The costs of hauling ore up to Grandview Point (7400 ft.) from Horseshoe Mesa (4800 ft.) along the Hopi Indian-built Grandview Trail proved too great for turn-of-the-century miners. Eventually, they gave up on mining and starting leading tourists down this harrowing descent. After hiking halfway down this wilderness trail today, however, you won't have the option of giving up—there's no water available without either descending past Horseshoe Mesa or returning to the Rim. The steep and strenuous hike requires route-finding and delicate footing on loose rocks, so hiking boots are a must. Backpackers can continue a steep 1.8 mi. to the Tonto Trail junction and follow the Tonto to canyon-floor destinations like Bright Angel Campground or Phantom Ranch. There is a reliable water source, Miners Spring, at the base of the Red Wall, 400 ft. below the eastern rim of the Horseshoe Mesa. Expect a full day of hiking to Horseshoe Mesa and back.

Hermit Trail (9.3 mi. one-way to the river). Embarking from the Hermit Trailhead at Hermit's Rest (6640 ft.), this strenuous route descends the Supai cliffs, switching back and forth frequently on loose rocks. The Hermit Trail offers panoramic views of the West Rim, less frequently seen than the rim surrounding the Grand Canyon Village because during the summer, the West Rim is accessible only by the red shuttle line. The trail ends at the base, near the Hermit Creek rapids, and water must be treated before drinking. Hikers planning to begin a multi-day trip from Hermit's Rest who have the required backcountry permit may drive their vehicles to the trailhead for parking. Following the trail all the way to the Colorado River covers 9.3 mi. and hikers are advised to allow at least 7hr. to reach the first overnight camping area, Hermit Creek (7.8 mi.), because of the slow pace mandated by a rocky, steep trail. Occasional rock slides and floods may obscure the trail, making route-finding skills necessary. Day hikers should not hike beyond the Santa Maria Springs, 2.5 mi. down the trail (5-6hr. each way).

Tonto Trail (up to 95 mi.). Threading its way along the entire length of the Tonto Platform, the solid sandstone Tonto Trail travels a total of 95 mi. and connects all of the other routes traveling from rim to river. The Tonto Platform, a jutting esplanade that appears table-flat from the rim actually contains many washes and gullies. The trail itself is a rugged, wilderness path and requires route-finding skills. Near Red Canyon the platform lies at 3600 ft.; by Garnet Canyon it drops to 2800 ft. Most hikers use the trail to connect other popular routes. There are 4.5 mi. of the trail between the Bright Angel and South Kaibab Trails, 21.3 mi. between S. Kaibab and Grandview Trails, and 12 mi. between the Hermit Trail and Indian Gardens on the Bright Angel Trail. Traveling west past the Hermit Trail, Tonto gradually becomes less and less trafficked and route-finding grows more important. Creeks cutting through the platform provide year-round water.

🏔 OTHER OUTDOOR ACTIVITIES

Beyond using your feet, there are other ways to conquer the canyon. **Mule trips** from the South Rim are expensive and booked up to one year in advance, although some do cancel. (☎303-297-2757. Daytrip to Plateau Point 6 mi. down the Bright Angel Trail $127, overnight including lodging at Phantom Ranch and all meals at $343 per person.) Mule trips from the North Rim (☎435-679-8665) are cheaper and more readily available, such as the 8hr. day trip to Roaring Springs waterfall ($95). Looking up at the Grand Canyon from a **whitewater raft** is also both popular and pricey. Trips into the Grand Canyon proper vary in length from a week to 18 days and are booked far in advance. The *Trip Planner* (available by request at the info center) lists several commercial guides licensed to offer trips in the canyon; check the park web site for info in advance of your visit. The only company permitted to guide one-day trips on the Colorado, **Wilderness River Adventures** (p. 92), operates out of Page, AZ. If the views from the rim fail to dazzle and astound you, try the higher vantages provided by one of the park's many **flightseeing** companies, all

GRAND CANYON

located at the Grand Canyon Airport outside of Tuyasan. **Grand Canyon Airlines** flies 45min. canyon tours hourly during the summer. (☎866-235-9422. $75, children $45. Reservations recommended, but walk-ins generally available. Discount for lunchtime tours, 11am-2pm.) Flying smaller planes on a wider range of trips, **Air Grand Canyon** offers 30-90min. flights. (☎800-247-4726. $74-174.) Both airlines team up with Wilderness River Adventures to offer one-day combination flightseeing/rafting tours. For a rapid vertical thrill, check out the popular helicopter flights from **Papillon Grand Canyon Helicopters.** Tours of the Canyon depart as frequently as every 30min. between 8am and 5pm. (☎800-528-2418. 30min. tours $105, children $95. 50min tours $175, kids $155.) Both **Scenic Airlines** (☎800-634-6801) and **Air Vegas Airlines** (☎800-255-7474) offer flight/hotel/canyon tour packages out of Las Vegas's northern airport. For a list of flight companies in the park, write the Grand Canyon Chamber of Commerce, Box 3007, Grand Canyon, AZ 86023.

HAVASUPAI RESERVATION   ☎928

West of the South Rim lies the tranquility of the Havasupai Reservation. Meaning "people of the blue-green waters," the Havasupai live on the canyon floor and seasonally on the rim in a protected enclave bordered by the national park. Ringed by dramatic sandstone faces, their village, Supai, rests on the verdant shores of the Havasu River. Just beyond town, this rushing wonder of crystal-clear water cascades over a series of spectacular falls. The grandest of them, Havasu Falls, plummets more than 100 ft. into a mist-enshrouded blue-green lagoon. Beneath the falls, ecstatic visitors frolic in the waters, gleefully soaking in the idyllic surroundings. Such beauty attracts thousands of visitors yearly, but luckily, a gruelling tenmile hike separates the falls from any paved surface and prevents the Disneyfication of the reservation. For most, blistered feet or a saddle-sore rump make bathing in the cool waters beneath the falls even sweeter.

▐ TRANSPORTATION. Supai and the campground can only be reached by a trail that originates on the rim at the Hualapai Hilltop. To reach the trailhead, take I-40 E from Flagstaff or Williams until Rte. 66 at Seligman (40 mi. from Williams). Follow Rte. 66 for 30 mi. until it meets with Indian Rd. 18, which ends at the Hilltop after 60 mi. No roads lead to Supai, although mules and helicopters can be hired to carry bags or people. For mule reservations, contact the **Havasupai Tourist Enterprise.** (☎448-2141. $75 one-way, half of which is required as a deposit. Includes 4 pieces of luggage not exceeding 130 lb. total. Groups leave at 10am.) **Skydance Helicopter** flies between the hilltop and village four days per week. (☎800-882-1651. Flights every 15-20min. on M, Th, F, and Su 9am-3pm. $70 one-way; first come, first served.) The hike down to Supai and on to the campground is not to be underestimated. The well-marked trail is a grueling, exposed 8 mi. to Supai and then an additional 2 mi. to the campground. Bring at least a gallon of water per hiker. It is also best to start hiking at dawn, whether entering or leaving the Canyon. Hiking during midday is dangerous. Even day visitors have to pay the $20 entrance fee. If you anticipate staying, do not hike down without a reservation—you may have to turn right around and walk back to the trailhead.

◼ ⁊ ORIENTATION & PRACTICAL INFORMATION. The trail to Supai begins at Haulapai Hilltop, 191 mi. from Grand Canyon Village, or 66 mi. from Peach Springs, AZ. Peach Springs has the nearest services—gas, food, and water. No services are available at Hualapai Hilltop. Approximate driving time from the Grand Canyon South Rim is four hours. Reservations for the campground, lodge, and mules can be made by contacting **Havasupai Tourist Enterprise.** (☎448-2141; www.havasupaitribe.com. Credit cards accepted and deposit required.) No **gas** or

water is available past Rte. 66; stock up beforehand. Visitors must first check in at the **Tourist Office** in Supai (open M-F 7am-7pm; Sa-Su 8am-5pm) before heading onto the campground. If the office is closed, proceed to the campground and pay the ranger in the morning. In the village, there's a post office, general store, and cafe. The village **cafe** serves American breakfasts ($4-5) and fast-food items ranging from the $3 plate of fries to the $5 burger. (Open daily in summer 6am-7pm; Sept.-Feb. 8am-5pm.) Across the sand street, the **General Store** stocks a surprising variety of camp foods, in addition to produce and fresh dairy. Prices are high, but not exorbitant. (Open daily 6:30am-7pm; in winter 8am-5pm.) All **trash** must be packed out of the Reservation.

▨ ▨ CAMPING & HIKING. The Havasupai tribe operates the two accommodations: the ▨**Havasupai Campground ❷** and the **Havasupai Lodge ❷**, both on the canyon floor. The friendly campground, 2 mi. beyond Supai, lies between Havasu and Mooney Falls. Campers will be hard-pressed to find fault with the grounds; they border the blue-green water of the Havasu River and are near the swimmer-friendly lagoons. The tribe charges a one-time entry fee ($20 per visitor and $10 per night) at the campground. Facilities are sparse: non-flush toilets whose smell can seep into the campground and no showers (though the falls are a quick jaunt away). No fires are allowed, so tote your own stove or munch on dry and canned food for a few days. A spring provides fresh water. The Havasupai Lodge, in Supai, offers basic accommodations ($75-96 for up to four people, plus the entrance fee).

The trail from Supai to the campground extends to **Mooney Falls** (1 mi. from campground), where visitors can maneuver down a slippery 200 ft. descent to splash around. Next, **Navajo Falls** (1½ mi. from campground) and **Havasu Falls** (2 mi. from campground) surge over cliffs and into warm, frothy pools. Swimming and frolicking are encouraged in the falls' lagoons.

NORTH RIM ☎928

If you're coming from Utah or Nevada or want to avoid the crowds at the South Rim, the park's North Rim is a bit wilder, a bit colder, and much more serene—all with a view almost as sublime as that from the South Rim. The real difference in view has to do with the position of the sun, whose southerly rays don't light the canyons as vividly for eyes and camera lenses gazing from the north. Any visit to the North Rim centers on the North Rim Lodge, an elegant structure in stone and exposed timber complete with a spacious lounge and dining room that look out into the canyon. The "other" rim entertains only a fraction of the number of visitors the South Rim sees, as over 400,000 people per year flood its observation decks. Sandwiched between canyons to the east and west, the park is most accessible along the lush Kaibab Plateau. Because of this remoteness, the North Rim tends to attract a slightly more upscale clientele, willing to shell out a few extra dollars to avoid the tiring tourist droves; expect to pay more for everything from lodging to groceries to showers. The North Rim's removed location also makes it hard to reach by public transportation, and by car it's a long four- to five-hour drive from the South Rim.

▨ ▨ ORIENTATION & PRACTICAL INFORMATION

To reach the North Rim from the South Rim, take Rte. 64 E to U.S. 89 N, which runs into Alt. 89; from Alt. 89, follow Rte. 67 S to the edge. Altogether, the beautiful drive is over 220 mi. From Utah, take Alt. 89 S from Fredonia. From Page, take U.S.

GRAND CANYON

89 S to Alt. 89 to Rte. 67 S. Snow closes Rte. 67 from early December to mid-May and park facilities (including the lodge) close between mid-October and mid-May. The visitor **parking** lot lies near the end of Rte. 67, strategically close to both the Visitors Center and lodge, about 13 mi. south of the park entrance. Trailhead parking is also available at North Kaibab and Widforss Trails and at scenic points along the road to Cape Royal.

Visitor Information: North Rim Visitors Center (☎ 638-7864), on Rte. 67 just before the Lodge. Open daily 8am-6pm. **Kaibab Plateau Visitors Center** (☎ 643-7298), at Jacob Lake, next to the Inn. Interpretive displays provide details on the creation of the canyon and its ecosystem, and backcountry permits are issued here. Open daily 8am-5pm.

Buses: Transcanyon, P.O. Box 348, Grand Canyon 86023 (☎ 638-2820). Buses run to the South Rim (5hr.; late May to Oct. leaving 7am from the North Rim Lodge; 1:30pm from the Bright Angel Lodge, South Rim; $65, round-trip $110). Reservations required.

Public Transit: A **hikers' shuttle** runs from the Lodge to the North Kaibab Trailhead (late May to Oct. 5:20 and 7:20am; $5, $2 per additional person). Tickets must be purchased in advance at the Lodge.

Gas and Car Repairs: Chevron, on the campground road just off Rte. 67. The station does not service cars, but can arrange a tow to Kanab for repairs. Open daily 7am-7pm.

Equipment and Groceries: The **General Store** is located next to North Rim Campground. Open daily 8am-8pm.

Showers and Laundromat: on the road leading to the Campground. Showers $1.25 per 5min. 7am-9pm daily.

Weather Conditions: (☎ 638-7888). Updated at 7am daily.

Post Office: Grand Canyon Lodge (☎ 638-2611). Open M-F 8-11am and 11:30am-4pm, Sa 8am-1pm. **Postal code:** 86052.

♠ ♥ ACCOMMODATIONS & CAMPING

The North Rim has only one campground, **North Rim Campground ❶**, and it generally fills entirely by reservation in summer. The kiosk opens at 8am, and people line up at 7am to vie for the few $15 spots remaining daily; calling ahead is the safest bet. **SPHERICS** (☎ 800-365-2267) handles reservations. If you can't get in-park lodgings, head for the **Kaibab National Forest ❶**, which runs from north of Jacob Lake to the park entrance. Here you can camp for free, as long as you're ½ mi. from the road, water, or official campgrounds, and 1 mi. from any commercial facility. There are popular undeveloped sites off Forest Road 611, at Saddle Mountain. As always with dispersed camping, facilities are absent and "Leave No Trace" ethics (see **Great Outdoors,** p. 65) are a must. Less expensive accommodations may be found in Kanab, UT, 80 mi. north, where motels hover around $40 and where the new **USA Hostels Grand Canyon ❶**, 143 E 100 South, Kanab, UT features renovated 6-bed dorm rooms, a full kitchen with free pancakes and waffles for breakfast, **Internet access,** laundry facilities, bonfire area, and beach-volleyball court. A shuttle connecting the North Rim to the hostel and Las Vegas is in the works; inquire with the friendly staff. (☎ 435-644-5554; www.usahostels.com. 40 beds. Reception 8am-midnight, check-out 10am. 6-bed dorms $15; private suite $32.)

Grand Canyon Lodge (☎ 638-2611; reservations ☎ 1-888-29-PARKS), on the edge of the rim. This swank rustic lodge is the only indoor rim lodging in the park. Reserve as early as six months in advance, or two years in advance for one of the four rim-view cabins. Check out the overlook near the reception area, providing comfy seats and a truly stunning look at the chasm. No TVs. Reception 24hr. Open mid-May to Oct. Singles or doubles in frontier cabins and hotel rooms $91, 4-person pioneer cabins $91-116. ❺

Jacob Lake Inn (☎643-7232), 32 mi. north of the North Rim entrance at Jacob Lake. Charming lodge and gift shop, cafe, and bakery. Reception daily 6am-9pm. Nicely furnished cabins for 2 $72-83; triples $86-88; quads $90-92; motel units $91-106. ❸

Kaibab Lodge (☎638-2389), 6 mi. north of the entrance gate, is rustic yet sophisticated. Two-person basic cabin $80, modern spaces with satellite TV $110-130 makes this place a somewhat pricey but comfortable alternative outside the park. ❸

North Rim Campground (call SPHERICS ☎800-365-2267), on Rte. 67 near the rim, the only park campground on this side of the chasm. Well-spaced pine- and aspen-shaded sites. Groceries, laundry, and showers nearby. 83 sites; no hookups. Open mid-May to mid-Oct. 7-night max. stay. Sites $15; 4 "premier sites" with canyon views $20. ❶

DeMotte Park Campground, about 16 mi. north of North Rim in Kaibab National Forest. Be an early bird to avoid disappointment; 23 woodsy sites are first-come, first-served, and generally fill by noon. $10 per vehicle per night. No hookups. ❶

Kaibab Camper Village (☎643-7804), 1 mi. south of Jacob Lake Inn on Rte. 67. Open May to mid-Oct. 50 tent sites, $12; 2-person hookup $22; $2 per additional person. ❶

Tuweep/Toroweap Campground, the national park's most remote and least crowded campground, is accessible only by 60 mi. of wash-boarded dirt road (not passable without high-clearance vehicle). To find Toroweap, turn left onto BLM Road 109, 7 mi. west of Fredonia, AZ and follow it south 61 mi. Peering over the frightening 3000 ft. drop from Toroweap Point to the roaring Colorado River makes the 2hr. drive from the Rte. 389 turnoff worthwhile. Arrive early to snag 1 of the 2 amazing spots on the point. 11 primitive sites available on a first come, first served basis. Sites free. ❶

◪ FOOD

The **Grand Canyon Lodge** ❸ monopolizes in-park eating options, which tend toward the pricey side. The solution is to buy groceries at the General Store and prepare your own canyon-side picnic. The lodge's dining room, treating guests to sweeping canyon views and haute cuisine, serves breakfast for $5-8, lunch for $6.50-8.50, and dinner for $13 and up. (☎638-2612, ext. 160. Open daily 6:30-10am, 11:30am-2:30pm, and 5-9:30pm. Reservations required for dinner.) Standard salads at the **Cafe on the Rim** ❶ range from $4-6, and cheese pizza by the slice goes for $2.50. (Breakfasts range $3-5. Open daily 7am-9pm.) The lodge also houses the **Rough Rider Saloon** ❷, which serves delicate baked goods, such as homemade scones ($2.45), and coffee in the morning and more conventional bar offerings in the afternoon. (Open daily 5:30am-10:30am and 11:30am-10:45pm. Beer $3.75-4.50.) A superb alternative to the North Rim establishments is **Jacob Lake Inn** ❸. The intimate diner counter, a fine-dining restaurant, and amiable bakery staff combine to offer a pleasing variety of options. Pick up a gravity-defying milkshake to make the remaining miles to the rim a bit more enjoyable. (Sandwiches $6, milkshakes $3, breakfasts $5-6, dinners $12-15.) **The Kaibab Lodge** ❸ presents the last dining option before North Rim eateries corner the market. (Breakfast 6am-9pm; dinner 6pm-8pm, featuring $6-8 burgers and $15-17 fish or steak.)

◪ HIKING & BACKPACKING

Hiking in the leafy North Rim feels like a trip to an alpine mountain. The trek, however, is the reverse of conventional outings—the hike back up comes after the legs are already a little weary from hiking down. All precautions for hiking at the South Rim are even more important at the North Rim, where the elevations are higher and the air is thinner. In-depth info on trails fills the pages of the North Rim's version of *The Guide*. Several day hikes of variable lengths beckon the active North Rim visitor. Trails offer views rivaling those of the South Rim without the hassle of elbowing through the crowd. For an indispensable resource on North Rim Trails, pick up a copy of the *Official Guide to Hiking the Grand Canyon*, published by the Grand Canyon Association and available in all Visitors Centers and gift shops. Or make sure you find a copy of *The Backcountry Guide*, complete with information about hiking and camping in the North Rim's more secluded spots.

Bright Angel Point Trail (½ mi. round-trip, 30min.-1hr.). Trail access begins both near the Visitors Center and from the Lodge veranda. This short, paved, and relatively flat trail travels along a narrow ridge to a viewpoint offering a panorama that includes Roaring Spring Canyon, the Transept, and the South Rim. A perfect choice for visitors looking for a quick glimpse of the Canyon's grandeur.

Cape Royal Trail (½ mi. round-trip, 30min.-1hr.). A short, paved jaunt to a point acclaimed by many to be the North Rim's best scenic vantage, and accessible to handicapped visitors. The trail departs from the parking lot at the end of the Cape Royal Rd. and travels to the edge of the Walhalla plateau (7865 ft.) for wondrous views of the Canyon. Also near the Cape Royal Rd. parking lot, the **Cliff Springs Trail** (1 mi. round-trip, 1-1½hr.) descends a narrow canyon, passing the Walhalla Glade ruins (the structural remains left by a culture inhabiting the area 3-4 thousand years ago) en route to a bubbling spring protected by towering cliffs. Resist the urge to sip from the natural spring; rangers do not recommend drinking it.

Uncle Jim Trail (5 mi. round-trip, 2-3hr.). This loop trail begins at North Kaibab Trailhead parking lot and follows the **Ken Patrick Trail** along the northernmost reaches of Roaring Spring Canyon. Just past the canyon, the trail diverges from Ken Patrick and completes a circle on a plateau that juts out in between the Roaring Springs and Bright Angel Canyons, granting breathtaking views of both. The trail and the lookout that it approaches bear the name of early-20th-century guide and hunter, Jim Owens, who led big shots like Teddy Roosevelt and Zane Grey on mountain lion hunts. Owens claimed to have killed more than 500 of these secretive beasts himself. Mule trains dot the trail.

Widforss Trail (9.8mi. round-trip, 6hr.). Named for landscape painter Gunnar M. Widforss, who chose these vistas as his subjects. Combining canyon views with alpine forest greenery, this less-traveled trail is perfect for a casual, if long, day's saunter. The trail begins at the Widforss Trailhead, clearly marked on Rte. 67 (8100 ft.) After tracing the edge of The Transept, a wide branch canyon of Bright Angel Canyon, the trail winds through the spruce fir forest characteristic of the Kaibab Plateau before arriving at splendid canyon views from Widforss Point (7900 ft.). There is no water available on the trail, so be sure to carry enough for the journey.

North Kaibab Trail (14.2 mi. one-way to the Colorado River, 3-4 days). The North Rim's half of the Kaibab Trail, this popular and well-maintained trail descends the Roaring Spring Canyon to the Bright Angel Canyon and eventually to the Colorado River, furnishing scenes that will not disappoint. Trailhead parking is in a designated lot off Rte. 67. The trail begins with a steep, 3000 ft. drop over 4.7 mi. to Roaring Spring. Day hikers are advised not to proceed beyond the spring because of the effort required in climbing back up to the rim. Moving past the Spring, the trail travels another 2.1 mi. to the Cottonwood Campground and then another 7.4 mi. to the river. Just before reaching the Colorado, the trail meets the Bright Angel and South Kaibab Trails, allowing options for a cross-canyon hike. Hikers must yield to mule trains using the trail's upper portions.

Thunder River/Deer Creek Trails (15 mi. one-way to the Colorado River). Perhaps some of the most scenic, strenuous, and least-traveled backpacking in the park, this trail combination promises dramatic waterfalls and sculpted narrows. The trail begins on Forest Road 232, accessible by turning off Rte. 67 onto Forest Service Road 422 W, then following 422 W to Forest Service Road 245, and finally turning onto Forest Service Road 232. The trail begins at 6400 ft. and, after descending steep cliffs, follows the Esplanade to Surprise Valley. The main trail then picks up the Thunder River, following it past a spectacular 100 ft. waterfall and eventually to the Colorado. The alternative Deer Creek Route leaves the Thunder River Trail in Surprise Valley, traveling west to the beautiful narrows of Deer Creek Valley and the falls where Deer Creek pours into the Colorado. For both the North Kaibab and Thunder River/Deer Creek Trails a backcountry permit is required. Helicopter rescues occur more on this trail than on any other.

▲ OTHER OUTDOOR ACTIVITIES

Park Rangers also host nature walks, lectures, and evening programs at the North Rim Campground and Grand Canyon Lodge. Check the info desk or campground bulletin boards for schedules. If the long drive has left you too sapped for a day hike, let someone else do the work. Rim-side **mule trips** go for $20, while half day options ($45) and all-day jaunts to Roaring Springs ($96) are also available through **Canyon Trail Rides.** These prices are often better than those at the South Rim. (☎435-679-8665. Open daily 7am-5pm. No credit cards.) Reservations are recommended, but because of smaller crowds, walk-ins can be accommodated more frequently than on the South Rim. To tour the Canyon along the culprit that created it, pick up a Grand Canyon River Trip Operators brochure and select from among the 20 companies offering multi-day trips down the Colorado.

LAKE POWELL & PAGE   ☎428

The decision to curb the Colorado River's steady procession to the Pacific was made in 1956, and ten years and ten million tons of concrete later, Glen Canyon Dam, the second-largest dam in the country, was completed. Stopped in its tracks in northern Arizona, the mighty river backed up into the once remote Glen Canyon. The monolith manages the water output for the lower basin of the Colorado River as far as the northern regions of Mexico, contains hydroelectric machinery that creates energy for much of the region, and has spawned a vacation destination that draws visitors to the crown jewel of a national recreation area. Lake Powell, the titanic oasis formed by the dam, has 1960 mi. of shoreline, exceeding the amount of beach lining continental America's Pacific coast. Darting around the lake on a personal watercraft or swimming in a narrow canyon, it's hard to imagine what the area looked like when John Welsey Powell, the lake's namesake, first led his crew down the Colorado in 1869.

Page (pop. 6800) lies just southeast of the dam and brims with businesses in competition for the summertime dollar. The town originally housed workers during the dam's construction. As a launchpad from which visitors can explore the "Grand Circle" of lakes, cliffs, and canyons, Page has a healthy tourist infrastructure of motels and cheap food, but little else. Besides the brilliant blue spread of Lake Powell, other natural wonders surround the area. Just east of Page, narrow Antelope Canyon wows visitors with sculpted sandstone and spectacular lighting. Farther east lies the Rainbow Bridge National Monument, the world's tallest natural bridge. Across the lake stretch the wild reaches of Grand Staircase-Escalante National Monument, and to top it off, Bryce Canyon National Park beckons with its unique pinnacles of red rock formations known as hoodoos.

✦ ORIENTATION

All tourist services available inside the recreation area operate under **ARAMARK,** the concessionaire contracted by the Park Service. The company operates four major marinas: **Wahweap** lies on U.S. 89 in the south near the dam; **Bullfrog** and **Halls Crossing** sit across the reservoir from each other, connected by Rte. 276 and daily ferry service; and **Hite** hides in Lake Powell's northernmost reaches on Rte.

GRAND CANYON

95. A single info line (☎800-528-6154) handles all questions and reservations for ARAMARK facilities. Although Park Service monitoring keeps the monopoly mostly in check, services inside the recreation area are pricier than those outside.

Page continues to serve a transient crowd and has much better bargains than those found inside the recreation area. Motels, unspectacular restaurants, and a litany of churches line Lake Powell Blvd., a wide, U-shaped road connecting with **U.S. 89** both north and south of town. Page's economy relies almost entirely on the tourist industry, and, as such, is highly seasonal. Expect price mark-downs at those few businesses that remain open through the winter.

🛈 PRACTICAL INFORMATION

Visitor Information: Carl Hayden Visitors Center (☎608-6404), just across the bridge from Page on U.S. 89N. Open May-Sept. daily 8am-6pm; Oct.-Apr. 8am-5pm. At the **Bullfrog Marina,** 45 mi. northeast of the dam by water and more than 300 mi. by land, a Visitors Center welcomes tourists entering the recreation area from Rte. 276 in Utah. Open Apr.-Oct. daily 8am-5pm. In Page, the **Chamber of Commerce,** 644 N. Navajo Dr. (☎888-261-7243) in the Dam Plaza, carries info on local services and rentals for watersports. Open daily 9am-6pm; in winter M-F 9am-5pm. In a pinch, kiosks at several corners of Lake Powell Blvd. have helpful info to get you through the night.

Bike Rentals: Lakeside Bicycles, 118 6th Ave. (☎645-2266). Front suspension bikes with helmet $25 per day. Open M-F 9am-6pm, Sa 8am-noon.

Showers: At Wahweap Campground. Guests free, campers and walk-ins $2. Free outdoor beach-type showers at Lone Rock Campground (see **Accommodations and Camping**).

Laundromat: Sunshine Laundry and Dry Cleaners, 131 S. Lake Powell Blvd. (☎645-9703). Open daily 7am-9pm. Wahweap and Bullfrog Marinas also offer machines. At Wahweap, atop the hill at the RV park.

Police: 808 Coppermine Rd. (☎645-4355). **Emergency:** ☎911.

Medical Care: Page Hospital, 501 N. Navajo Dr. (☎645-2424). 24hr. emergency care.

Internet Access: Free at the stylish **Page Public Library,** 479 S. Lake Powell Blvd. (☎645-4270). Open M-Th 10am-8pm, F-Sa 10am-5pm.

Post Office: 44 6th Ave. (☎645-2571). Open 8:30am-5pm M-F. **Postal code:** 86040.

🛏 ACCOMMODATIONS & CAMPING

Although the main drag through Page grows increasingly populated with high-end chain hotels, a few gems from an earlier, more affordable era remain. A cluster of quality budget accommodations resides on 8th Ave. between S. Navajo and Elm St. (from either direction on Lake Powell Blvd., head north on S. Navajo and make a left onto 8th Ave.). Pegged as "Page's Old Quarter," this "Avenue of Little Motels" shelters an idiosyncratic bunch of converted dam worker apartments. Or, for the price of one night in the **Wahweap Lodge,** you could buy yourself a decent tent, and camping on the lake is beautiful and inexpensive. Visitors with boats can camp nearly anywhere along the endless lakeshore, so long as they have a **portable toilet,** available for rent at the lake's marinas. Don't get caught without one—the rangers are vigilant, and besides, no one wants to swim in your sewage. Away from the dam area, tent sites and hookups are available at the **Bullfrog ❷, Halls Crossing ❶,** and **Hite Marinas ❶.** Call ARAMARK (☎800-528-6154) for camping info. Sites $6 at Halls Crossing and Hite Marina, $18 at Bullfrog.

▨ **Lake Powell International Hostel & Pension,** 141 8th Ave. (☎645-3898). This comfortable hostel with a European and young American clientele serves as a respite from the apartment-like motels lining the avenue. Sand volleyball, basketball hoop, free shuttles to lake and airport. Free clean and comfy bedding. Friendly owners grant various rooming options. Bunks $13; private bedrooms with shared bathrooms $18 per person, $25-28 for two; full apartments with kitchen, cable TV, VCR, and living room $40+. ❶

K.C.'s Motel, 126 8th Ave. (☎645-2947; www.kcmotel.com). Named for the owner's affectionate Yorkie, K.C.'s offers spacious, recently renovated suites with cable TV and multiple bedrooms for discount prices. Rooms start at $29, but rates drop in winter. ❷

Glen Canyon Motel, 800 Bureau St., behind the Page Boy Motel (☎645-9508). Clean and comfortable rooms with cable TV and good closet space set on a quiet side street. Under new management, the young and friendly owners happily welcome visitors to Page and make recommendations on all sightseeing questions. Singles start at $35 in summer, doubles $37.50; winter rates lower. ❷

Uncle Bill's Place, 117 8th Ave. (☎645-1224, www.canyoncountry.com/unclebill). Here the former mayoral candidate for the city of Page, Uncle Bill, has created along with his wife, a French chef, a homey atmosphere of 12 spacious and well-appointed rooms, most with cable TV and shared bathroom. There is a garden in the yard with a barbecue grill available for guest use. Singles $39; doubles begin around $45. ❸

Wahweap Campground/RV Park (☎800-528-6154), at Wahweap Marina. Near swimming areas, a beautiful stretch of lake known as the Coves, boat rentals, and ramps. Ask for a shady site. Shuttles to the lodge, showers, laundry, and general store keep campers happy. Tent sites $15, hookups $29. ❶

Lone Rock Campground, on Lone Rock Rd. just on the Utah side of the border. Camp anywhere on the beach to enjoy the water, the sunsets, the constant purring of RV generators, and the drone of ATVs operated by campers too lazy to walk 200 yards to the pit toilets. Water, showers, and boat ramp available. Sites $6. ❶

FOOD

Despite the fact that Page transforms into a bustling, cosmopolitan center for half the year, dining options in town barely escape the hum-drum steak, potatoes, and Mexican cuisine so pervasive in the area. Most eateries lie on Lake Powell Blvd., though some gather along N. Navajo Dr. There are two important bonuses to the over-abundance of Western cooking: hearty "cowboy appetite" portions and their bargain "ranch-hand" prices. If the meager choices have got you down, plan your own meal at **Safeway,** 650 Elm St. (☎645-8155).

Ranch House Grill, 819 N. Navajo Dr. (☎645-1420). Come for the breakfasts. The owner picked the name to evoke generous helpings of food, and his restaurant delivers. Bulging 3-egg omelettes ($4-6) come with hash browns and toast, biscuits and gravy, or two pancakes. Open daily 6am-3pm; breakfast served all day. ❶

The Sandwich Place, 662 Elm St. (☎645-5267) in Page plaza. "Fast food fit for grown-ups," including the standard regimen of deli subs and sandwiches ($4-5). The cheese steak is a filling option and not to be missed ($6). Open M-Sa 11am-9pm. ❶

Dos Amigos Restaurant and Cantina, 287 N. Lake Powell Blvd. (☎645-9394), in the Quality Inn. Prepares delectable Mexican fare and furnishes a stunning view and patio. Deals include a bargain list of lunch specials ($5-6) and an à la carte menu (tacos begin at $2.50) that fits even the tightest of budgets. Dinners start at $11, but include a soup/salad bar. Restaurant open 7am-11pm; cantina 10am-midnight. ❸

SIGHTS

Perhaps less intrigued by the thrills of cigarette boats and jet skis, many visitors to Lake Powell elect to pursue slightly more sedate but equally enthralling ways to spend a day. Both the **Rainbow Bridge National Monument** and **Antelope Canyon** draw countless visitors, who revel in the exquisite artistry of water at work on a sandstone canvas. **Antelope Canyon Adventures Guide Service,** 104 S. Lake Powell Blvd., located in the Safeway Plaza, is a Page-based authorized sight-seeing tour service that transports slot canyon enthusiasts in huge 4x4 trucks into the canyons for 1½hr. photo extravaganzas. (☎866-645-5501 or 645-5501; www.jeeptour.com. Tours leave 8, 10am, noon, 2, and 4pm. $20, ages 7-12 $10. Rates do not include Navajo entrance fee.)

RAINBOW BRIDGE NATIONAL MONUMENT. The damming of Lake Powell created easy access to Rainbow Bridge (an arcking rock structure spanning the water) originally a remote wonder of the natural world. Prior to the dam, visiting the world's tallest natural bridge (290 ft.) required a journey of at least three days. Now, tourists are whisked there and back in under 5hr. on snazzy cruise ships. Despite its current tourist-attraction status, the arch remains sacred to area Native cultures, as it has over centuries. Out of respect, visitors are asked not to approach, climb on, or pass through this breathtaking lesson in erosional art. *Nonnezoshi,* or "rainbow turned to stone" in Navajo, is said to bring trouble to those who pass under it without due prayer and reverence.

Hiking to Rainbow Bridge on Navajo land requires a **hiking permit,** obtainable by writing Navajo Nation Parks and Recreation Department *(Box 9000, Window Rock, AZ 86515)* a few weeks in advance or by calling ☎871-6647 on the day of your visit. Most visitors, however, come by boat. A courtesy dock floats about ½ mile from the bridge and is reachable after 4hr. ride from either the Wahweap, Halls Crossing, or Bullfrog Marinas. Only the park concessionaire, ARAMARK, has permission to offer guided tours, which are expensive but informative. *(☎800-528-6154. 7hr. full-day tours with lunch $105, children $69; 5hr. half-day tours $79, children $55.)*

ANTELOPE CANYON. Every visit to Antelope Canyon is unique because the precise angle of the sunrays that stream through the narrow opening creates a gallery of light and shadow that constanty changes. Photographers, both professional and amateur, delight in this natural studio. The canyon was rediscovered in 1931 by a 12-year-old girl tending sheep, which ushered in its era as a tourist attraction. For ages, Native Americans have approached this canyon, called *Tse bighanilini* ("the place where water runs through rocks") in Navajo, with profound respect and spiritual reverence. Although the English "Antelope Canyon" lacks the Navajo's poetic undertones, visitors to the canyon are inevitably filled with the same reverence.

Antelope Canyon is divided by Rte. 98 into two parts: upper and lower. **Upper Antelope,** the more accessible and frequently visited, is arguably the easier to appreciate. The best times to go are in the middle of the day between 11am and 2pm when the sun is shining straight over head, and in the early morning when the light lends the red sandstone a purplish hue. At dusk the light is not always sufficient for full appreciation of the slot canyon. Descending **lower Antelope** requires climbing ladders and slipping through extremely narrow gaps. *($6 Navajo use fee; shuttle to upper canyon or mandatory guide services in lower canyon $12.50.)* For info on Antelope Canyon, stop by the Navajo Nation's **kiosk** on Rte. 98 just west of the Navajo power plant. Private tour rates are pricier than driving up to the kiosk and making arrangements directly through Navajo Nation. If you need to kill a few hours waiting for the best time to enter the site, head to Antelope Point for a swim.

OTHER (DAM) SIGHTS. For a low-key and highly informational afternoon, visit the **John Wesley Powell Museum,** where friendly staff extend the legacy of the one-armed explorer, war-hero, professor, and bureaucrat. Visitors Center inside, long-boat outside. *(6 N. Lake Powell Blvd. ☎645-9496. Open in summer M-Sa 9am-5pm. $2.)* The **Carl Hayden Visitors Center** at the Glen Canyon Dam guides visitors into the guts of

Damming Motorized Recreation in the Southwest

Some take their nature with paddle, camera, and silence; others prefer fiberglass, gasoline, and the noise of churning pistons. America's National Parks have, in recent years, become a battleground for competing visions of the outdoor recreationalist's place in nature. The conflict generally pits kayakers, hikers, bikers, and climbers against dirt-bikers, ATVers, snowmobilers, and 4x4-drivers. The former outdoors ethic insists that man most enjoys nature when feeling small within it. The latter claims that man's love of the wild grows from his dominion over it. Neither side shows much appreciation for the other's chosen creed, raising a series of seemingly intractable concerns: Do parks and recreational areas demand a particular kind of use? Are certain forms of outdoor recreation inimical to the purpose of the National Parks Service? And, more importantly, who has the right to tell me what I can and cannot do on public lands?

As the result of a lawsuit brought against the National Parks Service (NPS) by a San Francisco environmental activist group, the Bluewater Network, jet skis and all other personal watercraft (PWC) will soon disappear from Utah's Glen Canyon National Recreation area. Bluewater Network alleges that the presence of PWC in National Parks compromises the Parks Service's chartered responsibility to protect park resources for future generations. PWC manufacturers have responded to charges that a single day's ride on a PWC produces as much smog-forming air pollution as 100,000 miles of passenger car driving. However, there's little they can do to combat Bluewater Network's second complaint, namely, that "the aggravating, high-pitched noise of jetskis destroys the experience for other recreational users."

Glen Canyon National Recreation Area is currently studying the effects of PWC use on Lake Powell recreation. During an ordinary summer season, jetskis crowd the enormous reservoir. As part of the settlement with Bluewater Network, the over-arching Parks Service policy states that PWC will be banned form all NPS areas unless that area's "enabling legislation, resources, values, other visitor uses, and overall management objectives" deem PWC use appropriate. Starting September 15, 2002, PWC were no longer allowed in National Recreation Areas until the completion of analysis regarding their use. Glen Canyon won't finish its study until 2003. If the study finds that PWC are compatible with Lake Powell recreation, the craft will be allowed back on the lake; if not, they could be banished indefinitely.

PWC enthusiasts have mobilized to counter the threatened ban. The Blue Ribbon Coalition, the national lobbying group for outdoor recreation rights, joined the fight in June 2002, promising to help ensure continued PWC access on the lake. The group's motto reads: "Preserving our natural resources *for* the public instead of *from* the public." This vision of "preservation" opposes the hands-off environmentalist position that values nature intrinsically; the case for the PWC side centers on recreationalist rights and choice. Despite ample rhetoric from both sides, the question of whose ideal nature the National Parks should protect remains unresolved.

Lake Powell appears representative of the battle in which low-tech environmentalists face off with mechanized thrill-seekers. In many ways it is, but a rich irony mocks the battle over a "natural" experience on Lake Powell: there's little natural about the lake (reservoir?) to begin with. The hordes of RVs and houseboats parading the recreation area and the fact that it is, after all, a dam seem to place it firmly in the grips of the nature-dominators. Fighting for a PWC ban on the lake seems an almost absurd position in such an unnatural setting. Perhaps the nature-preservers would be better off waiting until gas and oil leaks contaminate the reservoir, afflicting agriculture and poisoning urban populations in Las Vegas and Los Angeles. Maybe then they could get what they really want: the chance to paddle in silence through the revived ghost of a drowned Glen Canyon, a chance that would be made possible only by draining the whole "dam" thing.

Mark Kirby attended Deep Springs, one of the few colleges in the US that includes mending fences in their curricula. His cowboy training gave him the skills to cover the Grand Canyon and Utah for the inaugural edition of Let's Go: Southwest USA. Although he's gone on to write for the Let's Go guides to New Zealand and Alaska, he remains a dedicated Southwesterner, taking a balanced approach to the issues of the region. In fall 2003 he will join National Geographic's Adventure magazine.

the concrete behemoth, though in scaled-back fashion due to security measures. In addition to the guided tours, the films detailing the history of the dam and its construction are exceptional. *(Adjacent to the dam on U.S. 89.* ☎ *608-6404. Tours in summer every 30min. 8:30am-4pm; off-season every hr. Visitors Center open May-Sept. daily 8am-6pm; Oct.-Apr. 8am-5pm. Free.)*

🏔 OUTDOOR ACTIVITIES

Water cowboys' dreams have come true at Lake Powell, one of the last places where jet skis rule the scene. Even though their ubiquity has been threatened by proposed bans, attempts to curb the use of PWC's (personal watercrafts or jet skis) have failed. Jet skis are permitted everywhere on the lake except for the Escalante arm, the San Juan arm, and the Dirty Devil, where their use is restricted due to environmental concerns. Navajo Canyon and Labyrinthe Canyon near Antelope Point are both hidden gems for jet skiers who can navigate the slender side canyons. Recreation opportunities span all budgets: the affluent call as early as six months in advance for coveted week-long rentals of houseboats while the thrifty enjoy inflatable rafts, snorkeling, and beaches. Anglers have plenty of nooks to explore but must do so with an Arizona or Utah fishing license. Page sells Arizona licences, which are acknowledged in Utah after being stamped ($8). Fishing is year-round. There's also plenty of hiking in narrow slot canyons near the dam and in areas like Escalante Canyons (p. 314) on the lake's northwest shores. Tight budget or not, each vehicle must pay $10 to enter Glen Canyon Recreation Area.

BOATING & WATER SPORTS

Remember, your leisure pleasure is measured in horsepower. Rentals from ARA-MARK, although convenient, tend to be pricier than renting from vendors in Page. Boats and PWC's are rented at each marina, with rates varying little. For a pricier but more intimate option, houseboats are welcome on the lake. A 36 ft. boat, sleeping six, can be your home for three days and two nights if you're willing to fork over some serious cash.

Doo Powell, 130 6th Ave. (☎645-1230; www.doopowell.com). This boat and watercraft rental warehouse has all the top equipment for the best prices in town. Polaris and Kawasaki watercraft start at $99 for a full day, and speed boats are around $200 per day. Renters must slap down a hefty $500 deposit. Open daily 9am-5pm.

Wahweap Marina Boat Rentals, at the Wahweap Marina (☎800-528-6154 ext. 8109 or 645-1111). You name it, they have it, on the water and ready to go, albeit for a good chunk of dough. Renters must be 18+ with valid ID. Prices are comparable with other ARAMARK marinas. 14-23 ft. power boats $26 per hr., half-day $87, full-day $130, $575 per day for the "big dog"; personal watercraft $69 per hr., half-day $170, full-day $255; kayaks $10 per hour, half-day $20, full day $29. Reservations recommended.

Twin Finn Dive Center, 811 Vista Ave. (☎645-3114). PADI master trainer leads dives for all levels in Lake Powell, including PADI certification courses. Snorkel packages $9 per day, scuba packages $45, kayaks $35, canoes $60. Open M-Sa 7:30am-5:30pm.

Wilderness River Adventures, 50 S. Lake Powell Blvd. (☎645-3279). Features the only day-long float trips on the Colorado below the dam. The trips, conducted on motorized rafts, take visitors down the Colorado between towering cliffs and past the spectacular Horseshoe Bend. Half-day $59; child $49.

DAY HIKING

Horseshoebend Overlook (1 mi. round-trip, 30min.). 5 mi. south of the dam on U.S. 89. Look for turnoff just south of Mile 545, where a dirt road ascends a small hill just west of the highway. After parking on the shoulder and following the sandy trail from the hilltop, hikers behold the magnificent Horseshoe Bend. Traveling south, the river diverges around a tall sandstone spire, prompting a dramatic bend in the canyon. Sunsets create the scene for a dramatic natural light show. The conditions at Horseshoe Bend will likely mirror those that created Rainbow Bridge in a few million years.

Wiregrass Canyon (6 mi. round-trip, 3-5hr.). Natural bridges, precariously perched boulders, and colorful escarpments reward the hiker willing to travel this strenuous trail. The route begins west of Lake Powell, near Big Water, UT, and descends a wash to the shores of the lake. To reach the trailhead, follow U.S. 89 west to the sign for "Big Water City" between Miles 7 and 8. Follow signs for the Glen Canyon Recreation Area and park in the Wiregrass Canyon Backcountry Use Area parking lot. The roads are passable to all vehicles when dry and completely impassable when wet. There is no actual trail to the lake—hikers scramble and follow cairns through the wash. Hiking in the wash leads past two natural bridges and several drop-offs that become waterfalls during rainstorms. After heavy rain, don't make the mistake of getting caught in a flash flood while attempting to see one of these cataracts. Since the hike ends at the lake, avoiding an out-and-back means a strategically parked car on U.S. 89 or a tiring swim to Lone Rock.

Water Holes Canyon (variable distances and times). For another variation on the slot-canyon theme, visit the accessible narrows of Water Holes Canyon. The entrance to the canyon lies at Mile 542 on U.S. 89. Off the highway and up the canyon, the walls close in to form a dazzling section of narrows. In the other direction, hikers can go all the way to the Colorado, though that route requires a rope. The narrows of the canyon lie within the boundaries of the Navajo Reservation, and hiking the canyon requires a $6 permit. The best spot to get one is the Antelope Canyon kiosk on Rte. 98 (see **Sights,** p. 89).

GRAND CANYON

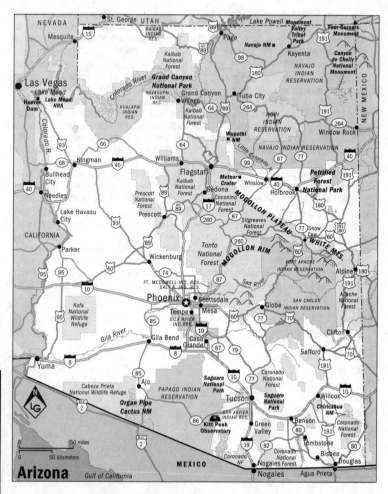

ARIZONA

Home to the Grand Canyon, the majority of the Navajo Reservation, seven national forests, and two large cities, the state of Arizona constantly defies its image as a land of endless uninhabited desert highway. The dry scrub of the Sonoran desert, spotted with cacti and the occasional dusty, pit-stop town, makes for a starkly beautiful landscape, while Arizona's cities, temperate sky-island forests, and northern mountain biking country provide enough variety for hours, days, or weeks of captivating exploration.

Hosting business jets more often than tumbleweeds, Phoenix and its more manageable and cosmopolitan little sister Tucson offer world-class museums, architectural curiosities, college nightlife, and metropolitan amenities. Yet their existence is barely felt by the small towns that dot the legendary Route 66 and hug the Mexican border. The Navajo Nation, occupying the northeastern corner of the state, greets travelers with boundless vistas, a deep sense of culture and history, and a poverty that serves as reminder Native Americans' experience in the US.

From the Red Rock spires and buttes of Sedona to the spiny Sonoran Desert and the vast expanse of the Grand Canyon, Arizona is a playground for the nature lover. Adrenaline junkies can get their fix biking Flagstaff's single track, summiting the 12,633 ft. Mt. Humphrey in the Coconino National Forest, or rock climbing in Sedona's red rock country. Must-see drives expose travelers to the crayola-box wonders of the Painted Desert and Petrified Forest, the metamorphosis of terrain along the Mt. Lemmon Drive, and the cliff dwellings of the Apache Trail. Bring your hiking boots, mountain bike, climbing rope, riding chaps, and kayak paddle; Arizona's vast wilderness will let you use it all and still throw you more adventure.

GREATER PHOENIX   ☎ 602

The name Phoenix was chosen for a small farming community in the Sonoran desert by Anglo settlers who believed that their oasis had risen from the ashes—like the fabled phoenix of Egyptian mythology—of ancient Native American settlements. The 20th century has seen this unlikely metropolis live up to its name; the expansion of water resources, the proliferation of railroad transportation, and the introduction of air-conditioning have fueled Phoenix's ascent to the ranks of one of America's leading cities. Shiny high-rises now crowd the business district, while a vast web of six-lane highways and strip malls surrounds the downtown area. Phoenix's rise has not been without turmoil, though: its greatest asset, the sun, is also its greatest nemesis. The scorching heat and arid landscape may put a damper on expansion, as H_2O is constantly in short supply. For the traveler, the Phoenix sun can be both friend and foe. During the balmy winter months, tourists, golfers, and business travelers flock to the resort-perfect temperatures. In the summer, the city crawls into its air-conditioned shell as temperatures climb to an average of 100°F and lodging prices plummet.

◥ INTERCITY TRANSPORTATION

Flights: Sky Harbor International (☎273-3300; www.phxskyharbor.com), just southeast of downtown. Take the Valley Metro Red Line bus into the city (3:15am-11:45pm, $1.25). The largest city in the Southwest, Phoenix is a major airline hub and tends to be an affordable and convenient destination. **America West** (☎800-235-9292) and **Southwest** (☎800-435-9792) are the busiest airlines.

Buses: Greyhound, 2115 E. Buckeye Rd. (☎389-4200; www.greyhound.com). To: **El Paso** (8hr., 14 per day, $37); **Los Angeles** (7hr., 14 per day, $37); **San Diego** (8hr.; 4 per day; M-Th $52, F-Su $56); **Tucson** (2hr., 11 per day, $16). Open 24hr. Without direct rail service to

AREA CODES. Phoenix's explosive expansion has caused it to outgrow its original 602 area code. The city is split into three area codes, with **602** limited to Phoenix proper, **623** for western greater Phoenix, and **480** for the East Valley (including Scottsdale, Tempe, and Mesa). As a consequence, all calls in Phoenix require 10-digit dialing—meaning local calls made within the city still require the area code. *Unless otherwise noted, all listings are in the 602 area code.*

Phoenix, **Amtrak** (☎800-USA-RAIL; www.amtrak.com) operates connector buses to and from rail stations in Tucson and Flagstaff for those interested in train travel. The Greyhound bus station is their busiest connecting Thruway motorcoach service location.

⊞ ORIENTATION

The intersection of **Central Avenue** (north-south) and **Washington Street** (east-west) marks the heart of downtown. One of Phoenix's peculiarities is that numbered avenues and streets both run north-south; avenues are numbered sequentially west from Central, while streets are numbered east. Think of Central Ave. as the heart of town; facing north, the first road to your right is **1st Street**, the first to your left is **1st Avenue**. Large north-south thoroughfares include **7th Street, 16th Street, 7th Avenue,** and **19th Avenue. McDowell Road, Van Buren Street, Indian School Road,** and **Camelback Road** are major east-west arteries.

Greater Phoenix includes a number of smaller, independent municipalities that sometimes have different street-naming schemes. The area's sprawl means you'll need a car to see many of the sights that are located outside of downtown.

NEIGHBORHOODS

Fed by dirt-cheap desert land and flat landscape, suburban sprawl has gotten out of control in Phoenix much the way Los Angeles went 30 years ago (but without beaches to limit the spread). Once a series of independent communities, the numerous townships of "the Valley of the Sun" (as metropolitan Phoenix is known) now bleed into one another in a continuous chain of strip malls, office parks, slums, and super-resorts. The *de facto* unification of all the disparate communities has not, however, resulted in homogenization or equalization—some are magnets for tourists and money, others for illegal immigrants and crime. Since many of the most intriguing and happening locales are located outside of downtown proper, it's useful to get acquainted with some of Phoenix's outer townships.

Just to the east of downtown Phoenix and south of the Salt River lies **Tempe,** the town that lays claim to both the third-largest university in the US (Arizona State University) and the nightlife to prove it. Don't leave town without experiencing at least one night as a Sun Devil (i.e., party!). East of Tempe, the suburban paradise of **Mesa** stretches out along Rte. 202. Tamer than its collegiate neighbor, Mesa is home to one of the largest Mormon colonies outside of Utah, as well as a host of cheap eats and chain motels in a family-friendly environment. **Scottsdale,** north of Mesa and northeast of downtown, is the playground of the (sometimes idle) rich. The very sound of the word conjures up images of expensive cars, immaculate homes, and world-renowned resorts. With pricey accommodations but engaging architectural sights, Scottsdale is a great place to visit (from Tempe or Mesa).

⊡ LOCAL TRANSPORTATION

Public Transportation, Downtown Phoenix: The free **DASH** (Downtown Area Shuttle) loops around downtown to the state capitol. (Runs M-F 6:30am-5:30pm, look for copper-black buses.) **Valley Metro** (☎253-5000) runs to and from Central Station, at Central and Van Buren St. Routes tend to operate M-F 5am-8pm, reduced service on Sa. Fare $1.25; disabled, seniors, and children $0.60. All-day pass $3.60, 10-ride pass $12. Bus passes and system maps at Terminal. In Tempe, **City of Tempe Transit Store,** 502 S. College Ave., Ste. 101, is a public transit headquarters. Red line runs to and from Phoenix and extends beyond Tempe to service Mesa. The last few stops of the yellow line are in Tempe. Bus passes and system maps at Terminal. Loloma Station, just south of Indian School and Scottsdale Rd., is Scottsdale's hub for local traffic. Green line runs along Thomas St. to Phoenix.

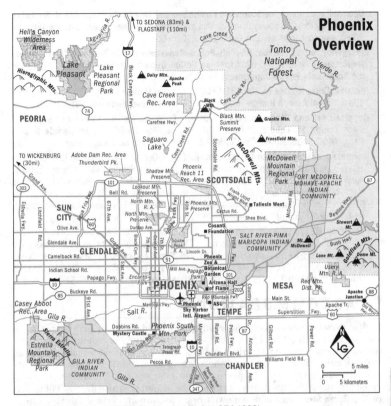

Phoenix Overview

Taxis: Yellow Cab (☎252-5252). **Discount Taxi** (☎254-1999).

Car Rental: Enterprise Rent-a-Car, 1402 N. Central St. (☎257-4177; www.enterprise.com), with other offices throughout the city. Compact cars at around $45 per day, with lower weekly and monthly rates. No surcharge for drivers over 21 (call ahead if under 21, as there are different requirements). A valid credit card and driver's license are required. N. Central St. office open M-F 8am-6pm, Sa 9am-noon; other offices' hours vary.

⁊ PRACTICAL INFORMATION

GREATER PHOENIX

Visitor Info: Greater Phoenix Convention and Visitors Center (☎254-6500 or 877-225-5749, recorded info and events calendar ☎252-5588; www.phoenixcvb.com). Several locations throughout the area. Downtown location: 2nd and Adams St. Open M-F 8am-5pm. Free **Internet access** (5min. limit). Biltmore Fashion Park location: 24th St. and East Camelback. Open daily 8am-5pm. Camping and outdoors information for the area is available at the **Bureau of Land Management Office,** 222 N. Central (☎417-9200). In Tempe, try the **Tempe Convention and Business Center,** 51 W. 3rd St., #105. (☎480-894-8158; www.tempecvb.com. Open M-F 8:30am-5pm.) The **Mesa Convention and Visitors Bureau,** 120 N. Center St., provides info about that neighborhood. (☎480-827-4700; www.visitmesa.com.

Open M-F 8am-5pm.) The **Scottsdale Convention and Visitors Bureau,** 4343 N. Scottsdale Rd. treats visitors to a bounty of info on that section of the Greater Phoenix area. (☎480-421-1004; www.scottsdalecvb.com. Open daily 8:30am-6pm.)

Emergency: ☎911. **Police: Phoenix Police Department** (☎262-6151); **Tempe Police Department** (☎480-966-6211); **Mesa Police Department** (☎480-644-2211); and the **Scottsdale Police Department** (☎480-312-5000).

Hotlines: Crisis Hotline (☎800-631-1314). 24hr. **Gay Hotline** (☎234-2752). Daily 10am-10pm. **Sexual Assault Hotline** (☎254-9000). **Suicide Prevention** (☎480-784-1500).

Hospital: Arizona State Hospital, 2500 E. Van Buren (☎244-1331). In Tempe and Mesa **Tempe St. Luke's,** 1500 S. Mill Ave. (☎480-784-5500). **Scottsdale Health Care,** 7400 E. Osborn Rd. (☎480-860-3000), serves the Scottsdale area.

Internet Access: Burton Barr Central Library, 1221 N. Central Ave. (☎262-4636). Open M-Th 10am-9pm, F-Sa 10am-6pm, Su noon-6pm. In Tempe, try **Tempe Public Library,** 3500 S. Rural Rd. (☎480-350-5555. Open M-Th 9am-9pm, F-Sa 9am-5:30pm, Su noon-5:30pm.) In Mesa, **Mesa Public Library,** 64 E. 1st St. (☎480-644-3100. Open M-Th 9:30am-9pm, F-Sa 9:30am-6pm, Su noon-9pm.) **Civic Center Library,** 3839 N. Drinkwater Rd., in Scottsdale. (☎480-312-2476. Open M-Th 9am-9pm, F-Sa 10am-6pm, Su 1pm-5pm.)

Post Office: 522 N. Central Ave. (☎800-275-8777). Open M-F 8:30am-5pm. General delivery: 1441 E. Buckeye Rd. Open M-F 8:30am-5pm. **Postal code:** 85034. **Tempe:** 233 E. Southern Ave. (☎800-275-8777). Open M-F 8:30am-5pm. **Postal code:** 85281. **Mesa:** 135 N. Center St. (☎800-275-8777). Open M-F 8:30am-5pm. **Postal code:** 85201. **Scottsdale:** 7242 E. Osborne Rd. (☎800-275-8777). Open M-F 8:30am-5pm. **Postal Code:** 85351.

▐ ACCOMMODATIONS

Budget travelers should consider visiting Phoenix during July and August when motels slash their prices by as much as 70%. In the winter, when temperatures drop and vacancies are few, prices go up; make reservations if possible. Although they are more distant, the areas around Papago Fwy. and Black Canyon Hwy. are loaded with motels and may present some safer options. The reservation-less should try the under-used Metcalf Hostel (see below) or cruise the rows of motels on **Van Buren Street** east of downtown toward the airport. Parts of this area can be unsafe; *examine a motel thoroughly before checking in.*

Catering to those whose money folds rather than jingles, greater Phoenix contains some of the nation's best luxury and high-end resort hotels. Peak-season prices soar, but usually dive a bit in the summer months.

Alternatively, **Mi Casa Su Casa/Old Pueblo Homestays Bed and Breakfast,** P.O. Box 950, Tempe 85280, arranges stays in B&Bs throughout Arizona, New Mexico, southern Utah, southern Nevada, and southern California. (☎800-456-0682. Open M-F 9am-5pm, Sa 9am-noon. $45 to $350.)

DOWNTOWN PHOENIX

▨ **Metcalf Hostel (HI-AYH),** 1026 N. 9th St. between Roosevelt and Portland (☎258-9830, phx-hostel@earthlink.net), a few blocks northeast of downtown. Look for the house with lots of foliage out front. From Central Station, take bus #10 down to Roosevelt St.—the hostel is half a block north. Last bus leaves at 8:30pm. The neighborhood has seen better days, so the coin lockers available in the dorms are probably a good idea, or bring your own lock. The ebullient owner, gushing helpful advice about the area, fosters a lively community in this decoratively renovated house. Dorm-style rooms with wooden bunks adjoin a kitchen and common room. Bikes for rent, and discounts to some city sights included in the price. Check-in 7-10am and 5-10pm. Light cleaning or other chores required. $15. ❶

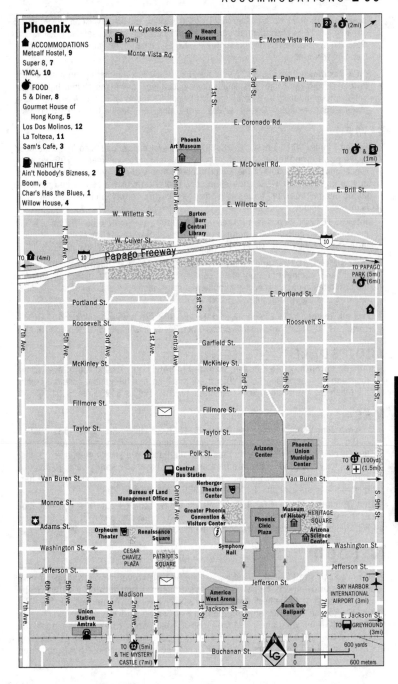

Phoenix

🏠 **ACCOMMODATIONS**
Metcalf Hostel, **9**
Super 8, **7**
YMCA, **10**

🍅 **FOOD**
5 & Diner, **8**
Gourmet House of
   Hong Kong, **5**
Los Dos Molinos, **12**
La Tolteca, **11**
Sam's Cafe, **3**

🍸 **NIGHTLIFE**
Ain't Nobody's Bizness, **2**
Boom, **6**
Char's Has the Blues, **1**
Willow House, **4**

ARIZONA

Super 8 Motel, 4021 N. 27th Ave. (☎248-8880; www.super8.com), west on Indian School Rd. from the 17 Fwy. just north of downtown. Straightforward service, safe and well lit, and close enough to a freeway and downtown to serve as a base for the Phoenix area. $39 summer, $49 winter. ❸

YMCA Downtown Phoenix, 350 N. 1st Ave. (☎253-6181). Another option in the downtown area, the YMCA provides small, single-occupancy rooms and shared bathrooms. Various athletic facilities. A small supply of women's rooms available. Ask at the desk about storing valuables. Open everyday 9am-10pm. 18+. Daily $30; weekly $119. ❷

TEMPE

Mission Palms, 60 E. 5th St. (☎480-894-1400; www.missionpalms.com). At the base of Tempe's Hayden Butte, this deluxe hotel is a steal in the summer for $99 per night (prices more than double in the winter). Choose among the smorgasbord of amenities at your fingertips (to wit: 2 hot tubs, a pool, health club, tennis center, and standard laptop Internet hookups) to pass the time, all the while knowing that raucous Mill Ave. is merely a minute's walk away. ❺

Motel 6, 1612 N. Scottsdale Rd (☎480-945-9506, www.motel6.com). Tempe's Mill Ave. becomes Scottsdale Rd. north of town. Vies with Super 8 for title of cheapest place in Tempe. Summer $36, winter $46. Online reservations yield $3 discount. ❷

Super 8 Motel, 1020 E. Apache Blvd. (☎480-967-8891; www.super8.com). Chain with digital cable standard in every room; continental breakfast, too. Consistently some of the best rates in town, especially with Internet reservation discount. Apr.-Aug. daily $39; weekly $190. Sept.-Mar. $49/$250. ❸

Days Inn Tempe, 1221 E. Apache Blvd. (☎480-968-7793; www.daysinn.com). A chain combining tidy rooms with no-frills prices. Pool. Rooms in summer $49; winter $79. ❸

SCOTTSDALE

Ramada on Fifth, 6935 5th Ave. (☎480-994-9461), just east of downtown. Clean rooms and low prices for the location make this branch of the national chain a deal in the otherwise resort-ridden Scottsdale area. Summer singles $42, winter $130. ❸

MESA

Best Western Dobson Ranch Inn & Resort, 1666 S. Dobson Rd. (☎480-831-7000 or 800-528-1356; www.dobsonranchinn.com). South of Hwy. 60 on Isabella Ave. Submitting its claim as the best resort in the area, the Ranch is a great alternative for those looking for exceptional value at a low cost. During baseball's spring training, don't be surprised to run into Chicago Cubs players. Two pools, a restaurant and massive banquet facilities are available for as little as $55 in the summer. ❹

Lost Dutchman Motel, 560 S. Country Club Dr. (☎480-969-2200). A good location near many restaurants and clean rooms are the best reasons to stay at the Dutchman. Full kitchenettes. Summer rates hover around $35, winter $50 and up. ❸

◘ FOOD

While much of the Phoenix food scene seems to revolve around shopping-mall food courts and expensive restaurants, rest assured that hidden jewels can be found. **McDowell** or **Camelback Road** offer a small variety of Asian restaurants. The **Arizona Center,** an open-air shopping gallery at 3rd St. and Van Buren St., boasts food venues, fountains, and palm trees. Sports bars and grilles hover around the America West Arena and Bank One Ballpark. Tempe's residents fill up on bar food in the many hybrid resto-bars that cater to college kids, while both Scottsdale and

Mesa have affordable and delicious options under their bourgeois swank and Mormon sobriety, respectively. The *New Times Weekly* (☎271-4000), available free at any newsstand or magazine rack, makes extensive restaurant recommendations.

DOWNTOWN PHOENIX

Los Dos Molinos, 8646 S. Central Ave. (☎243-9113). From downtown, head south on Central Ave quite a ways. Once you leave the *barrio*, it comes up suddenly on your right, between South Mountain and Euclid. Lively, colorful, and fun, Los Dos Molinos is worth the trip. Locals throng here on weekends, filling the restaurant and the colorful courtyard and spilling onto the street. Come early, as they don't take reservations, or try its sister establishment on 260 S. Alma School Dr. in Mesa. Enchiladas $3.50, burritos $3-7. Open Tu-F 11am-2:30pm and 5-9pm, Sa 11am-9pm. ❶

5 & Diner, 5220 N. 16th St. (☎264-5220), with branches in the greater metro area. 24hr. service and all the sock-hop music that one can stand. Vinyl booths, smiley service, and innumerable juke boxes convey what the 50s might have been like. Burgers go for $6-7.50 and sandwiches are $5-8. Best milkshakes in town run only $4. Afternoon blue-plate specials (M-F 11am-7pm, $3-6) change daily but are always worth the money. Open 24hr. ❷

Gourmet House of Hong Kong, 1438 E. McDowell Rd. (☎253-4859). Praised by local food critics despite its no-frills exterior, the Gourmet House serves so many dishes that the menu comes with a table of contents. 40 kinds of soup, noodle dishes, and rare Hong Kong specialities (such as chicken feet) are unceremoniously dished out. No non-smoking section. Entrees $5-7. Lunch specials $3-5. Take-out available. Open M-Th 11am-9:30pm, F-Sa 11am-10pm, Su 11am-9pm. ❷

Sam's Cafe, 2566 E. Camelback Rd. (☎954-7100), located in the Biltmore Fashion Plaza with 24th St. in Ste. #201. A casual bar and restaurant with s good Southwestern food ($7-13). The television is often tuned to tennis or golf, and the clientele tote bags from Nordstrom's, Bombay, and the other high-end chains in the mall. ❷

La Tolteca, 1205 E. Van Buren St. (☎253-1511). A local favorite, this unassuming cafeteria-style restaurant/Mexican grocery serves up uncommercialized Mexican fare in *grande* portions. Familiar dishes are offered alongside specialities like *cocido* soup ($5) and refreshing *horchata*, a sweet milk and rice drink ($1-2). Big burritos $3-4, dinner plates $5-6. Open daily 6:30am-9pm. ❶

TEMPE

▨ **Dos Gringos Trailer Park,** 216 E. University (☎480-968-7879). The best atmosphere in Tempe, bar-none. Dos, as it's affectionately known, draws people of all walks of life with its open, laid-back feel and its inexpensive yet tasty Mexican food. Contribute to the tally that makes Dos the #1 national consumer of Coronas, and chase your drinks with one of countless meals for under $6. Open M-Sa 10am-1am, Su 11-1am. ❶

▨ **Long Wong's,** 701 S. Mill Ave. (☎480-966-3147). A local musician hangout and venue, with the feel of an oversized garage serving beer and wings in six different flavors—the best wings in town. A hybrid bar/restaurant run by a young staff with an animated spirit. $5.25 for a dozen wings. $0.15 wings happy hour M-F 4-8pm and Sa-Su 11am-2pm. 21+. Cover $1-5, depending on the act in the bar. Take-out available. Open Su-Th 10:30am-11pm, F-Sa 10:30am-12:30pm; bar open daily until 1am. ❷

SCOTTSDALE

Sugar Bowl Ice Cream Parlor & Restaurant, 4005 N. Scottsdale Rd. (☎480-946-0051). Beat the heat in this fun and flavorsome ice cream parlor, where sundaes are piled high and thick ($3-5). Sometimes featured in the *Family Circus* comic strip. Open M-Sa 11am-11pm, F 11am-midnight, Su 11am-10pm. ❶

Ibiza Cafe, 4400 N. Scottsdale (☎480-421-2492, www.ibizacafe.com), one block south of Camelback. Billing itself as a "Western Mediterranean-inspired" fusion of Spanish, North African, and Italian foods, Ibiza delivers healthy, clean-feeling food ($9-19), *tapas* ($7-9), and *sangria* ($6). Happy hour daily from 4:30-6:30pm with $1 *sangria*, $5 *tapas* all day Tu, and half-price wine bottles W. Open Tu-Sa 11am-11pm. ❸

The Pink Pony, 3831 N. Scottsdale Rd. (☎480-945-6697). Opportunities to further dehydrate your sun-scorched self exist at the bar here. When you're ready, they also serve steak ($21-25) and other American food ($14-16). Open M-F 10am-10:30pm, Sa-Su 4-10:30pm; lunch served 11am-3pm, dinner starting at 5pm. ❺

MESA

Ripe Tomato Cafe, 745 W. Baseline Rd. (☎480-892-4340). The biggest, fluffiest omelettes ($6.50) this side of the desert fill up your entire plate for breakfast or lunch. Eat inside or out, but bring your appetite. Open 6am-2pm daily. ❶

Bill Johnson's Big Apple, 950 E. Main St. (☎480-969-6504). A sawdust-floored, country-western restaurant where the food is almost as good as the Old West decor. Pick from one of the largest selections of steak around and sample the homemade BBQ sauce. Kids eat free W, Su. Open M-Th and Su 6:30am-10pm, F-Sa 6:30am-11pm. ❷

🎭 🎵 NIGHTLIFE & ENTERTAINMENT

BARS & CLUBS

The free *New Times Weekly*, available on local magazine racks, lists club schedules for Phoenix's after-hours scene. The *Cultural Calendar of Events* covers area entertainment in three-month intervals. *The Source*, found in bars and clubs, covers gay and lesbian nightlife. As with other aspects of Phoenix, the nightlife and entertainment prospects are better in the cooler months, but there is always something going on no matter when you visit. The scene downtown is mixed—quality clubs spread too far to walk between compete with topless cabarets and seedy bars. Those of college age (literally or in spirit) may find Tempe's nightlife offerings more attractive (p. 103), and those with shinier credit cards might enjoy Scottsdale's growing celeb nightclub scene.

DOWNTOWN PHOENIX

🏆 **Char's Has the Blues,** 4631 N. 7th Ave. (☎230-0205). Char's houses local jazz acts, with crowds as enthusiastic as the bands. Dim red light hangs in the smoky air, and everyone knows the doorman and barkeep. One of Phoenix's best for live music. 21+. Cover Tu-Sa $3-6. Open F-Sa 7:30pm-1am, Su-Th 8pm-1am, music starting at 9pm.

The Willow House, 149 W. McDowell Rd. (☎252-0272). A self-proclaimed "artist's cove," it combines the best aspects of chic coffee house, New York deli, and quirky musicians' hangout. No alcohol. Coffee Happy Hour (half-price) M-F 4-6 pm. M is open mic for musicians, Th open mic for poetry. Almost-nightly live music starts at 8pm, 9pm weekends. Open M-Th 6am-midnight, F 6am-1am, Sa 7am-1am, Su 7am-midnight.

Ain't Nobody's Bizness, 3031 E. Indian School Rd. #7 (☎224-9977), in the east end of the mall. This large lesbian bar is the big sister of the Tucson club of the same name. Top 40 hits play regularly, while pool tables provide respite from the welcoming dance floor. On F and Sa, the bar attracts both men and women for a hot time. 2-for-1 happy hour Tu-F 4-7pm. 21+. Occasionally a cover charge when the Biz hosts guest vocalists. Open M-F 4pm-1am, Sa-Su 2pm-1am. No credit cards, but ATM on premises.

Boom, 1724 E. McDowell Rd. (☎254-0231; www.boomnightclub.com). The place for young gay men in Phoenix to see and be seen, this combined bar and dance club is popular with throngs of gyrating Adonis-featured youth who like to party until the wee hours of the morning. Find anonymity on the dance floor or intimacy in the couch lounges. 18+ after 1am. Open Th-F 4pm-1am, Sa 4pm-4am.

TEMPE

Bandersnatch Brew Pub, 125 E. 5th St. (☎480-966-4438). One of the last real taverns in the greater metro area, Bandersnatch has a huge patio and a dimly lit, but amusing, inside. Food like mom used to make it and a non-embellished atmosphere are the major draws, and now you can use the **Internet**, too. If you're game, be sure to ask about the "Beer in Your Face Club." Happy Hour M-F 3pm-7pm. 21+ after 9pm. Open M-Sa 11am-1am, Su noon-1am.

Library Bar and Grill, 501 S. Mill Ave. (480-929-9002). The bookshelves are for background decoration. The real ornaments here are the college-age female bartenders who make more money dancing on the bar, *à la Coyote Ugly*, than they do tending it. The sprawling floor has several nooks of couches with their own televisions, a stage, a patio, and, on Tu Ladies Night, a masculine ice sculpture. Sa live music, Su karaoke, Happy Hour M-F 4-7pm. Open daily 11am-1am termtime, otherwise Su hours are 4pm-1am.

Mill Cue Club, 607 S. Mill Ave. (☎480-858-9017). Those looking to mingle in style, welcome home. The leather sofas in the corner compliment the dark-paneled walls and the pool tables in the back, while the 20 oz. Long Island iced teas ($3.50) are sure to liven up your night in a hurry. Happy Hour 2pm-7pm daily. DJ spins hits Tu-Sa. 21+. No cover. Open daily 2pm-1am.

Mill Ave. Beer Company, 605 S. Mill Ave. (☎480-829-6775). The closest thing to a neighborhood bar in Tempe, the Beer Co. welcomes everyone with a smile and over 160 types of beer. Happy Hour M-F 4pm-8pm. Live music F-Su. 21+ after 7pm. Open M-F 11am-1am, Sa-Su noon-1am.

SCOTTSDALE

Mickey's Hangover, 4312 N. Brown Ave. (☎480-425-0111), off E. Drinkwater near 5th Ave. Trendy, retro late 70s/early 80s decor livens up the bar and couches, while ubiquitous lounge chairs and small tables encourage patrons to take a load off with a beer ($4). The outdoor patio, where guests lean against palm trees and drape over couches, flaunts Phoenix's elysian weather. Live music Su and soul on W. Open M-W 5pm-2am, Th-F 5pm-3am, Sa 7pm-3am, Su 8pm-2am.

SPORTS

Phoenix offers many options for the sports lover. NBA basketball action rises with the **Phoenix Suns** (☎379-7867) at the **America West Arena**, while the Ari-

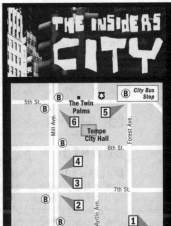

TEMPE PUB CRAWL

Even the most angelic abandon their inhibitions and become Sun Devils for a night at the watering holes in Tempe. Catch a green line bus when your liver gives up.

1 Start at **Dos Gringos Trailer Park,** munching tasty Mexican food as you sip on a seemingly bottomless $4 margarita.

2 Dig into some of Arizona's finest chicken wings at **Long Wong's.** Try the "suicide" variety—if you dare.

3 Rack 'em up at the **Mill Cue Club** and prepare to get schooled by the ASU kids.

4 Nurse your bruised ego back to health on sweet, sweet microbrews at the **Mill Ave. Beer Co.**

5 Stagger down to the last real tavern in Tempe, the **Bandersnatch Brew Pub.** If you love beer, try it topically and join the "Beer in your Face Club."

6 Stumble onto one of the broken couches at **Library's Bar & Grill** to end the night with live music and gyrating bartenders.

zona Cardinals (☎379-0101) provide American football excitement. The winter sees the NHL's **Phoenix Coyotes** (☎563-7825) take to the ice, while in the summer, the women's basketball team **Phoenix Mercury** takes it to the hoop at the America West Arena. The **Arizona Diamondbacks** (☎514-8400) play at **Bank One Ballpark,** an architectural wonder complete with a retractable roof, an outfield swimming pool, and "beer gardens." (☎462-6799. Tickets start at $6. Special $1 tickets available at Gate K 2hr. before games; first come, first served. Tours of the stadium offered throughout the year, proceeds benefitting local charities.)

◉ SIGHTS

DOWNTOWN

▩ **HEARD MUSEUM.** An internationally famous museum that underwent expansion in 1999, the Heard's ten galleries and various outdoor spaces make it the place to learn about Southwestern and Native American history. Renowned for its presentation of ancient Indian art, this museum also features exhibits focusing on contemporary Native Americans, with many interactive and traveling exhibits and some geared toward children. In addition, the museum occasionally sponsors lectures and Native American dances. *(2301 N. Central Ave., 3 blocks north of McDowell Rd. ☎ 252-8840, recorded info ☎ 252-8848. Open daily 9:30am-5pm. Free tours at noon, 1:30, and 3pm. $7, seniors $6, ages 4-12 $3, Native Americans with status cards free.)*

PHOENIX ART MUSEUM. This museum exhibits art of the American West, including paintings from the Taos and Santa Fe art colonies. The permanent collection houses pieces by the *Tres Grandes* of Mexican art (Orozco, Siquiros, and Riviera), as well as works by noted American artists including Jackson Pollock and Georgia O'Keeffe. Every major European and American period has representatives on display; the Renaissance, Spanish Catholic, and early American periods, along with Latin American art, are the most complete. *(1625 N. Central Ave., at McDowell Rd. ☎ 257-1880. Open Tu-Su 10am-5pm, Th 10am-9pm. $7, students and seniors $5, ages 6-17 $2. Free on Th and after 4:15pm.)*

ARIZONA SCIENCE CENTER. The Center offers playful, interactive science exhibits, demonstration labs for children, an IMAX theater, and a planetarium. Budget half a day if you're going with children, and an 1½hr. plus movie or planetarium time for adults. *(600 E. Washington St. in Heritage Sq., ☎ 716-2000. Open W-F 10am-5pm, Sa-Tu 10am-9pm. $9, ages 4-12 and seniors $7. IMAX or planetarium ticket $5.)*

PHOENIX MUSEUM OF HISTORY. Interactive exhibits document Phoenicians's ability to contend with the desert climate. Case in point: saloon keeper Jim Cotton in 1880 settled the dust problem in front of his saloon by upending hundreds of empty beer bottles into the sand and using their bottoms to create a level, solid walking surface. *(105 N. 5th St. in Heritage Sq. ☎ 253-2734. Open Tu-Sa 10am-5pm, free W 2-5pm. $5; seniors, students, AAA $3.50; ages 6-12 $2.50; under 6 free.)*

PAPAGO PARK & ENVIRONS

DESERT BOTANICAL GARDEN. Five miles east of downtown in Papago Park, a colorful collection of cacti, succulents, and other desert plants awaits. The park's trails make for a pleasant stroll, and many of its desert flowers are hard to find in the wild. *(1201 N. Galvin Pkwy. Take bus #3 east to Papago Park, on the outskirts of the city. ☎480-941-1225, recorded info ☎ 481-8134. Open daily May-Sept. 7am-8pm; Oct.-Apr. 8am-8pm. $7.50, students with ID $4, seniors $6.50, ages 5-12 $3.50.)*

PHOENIX ZOO. If you spot an orangutan along the park's hiking, biking, or driving trails, it's either a mirage or you've entered the Phoenix Zoo, located within the park and boasting a formidable collection of critters. *(455 N. Galvin Pkwy. ☎ 273-1341. Open Sept.-May daily 9am-5pm. $12, seniors $9, children $5; June-Aug. 7am-4pm; $9/$7/$5.)*

SOUTH PHOENIX SIGHTS

For those interested in astounding Southwestern architecture, the striking **Mystery Castle** is worth the 5 mi. trip south of downtown. Built in small increments over 15 years (ca. 1930), this home is a spectacle of creative use of space. Laugh along with the knowledgeable tour guides as they expound an endless supply of tidbits about the peculiarities of this masterpiece. (800 E. Mineral Rd. Go south on Central Ave., and turn left on Mineral Rd. before the South Mountain Park entrance. ☎ 268-1581. Open Oct.-June Th-Su 11am-4pm. $6, seniors $4, ages 6-15 $3.)

SCOTTSDALE

COSANTI. One of Frank Lloyd Wright's students liked Scottsdale so much he decided to stay after studying at Taliesin West. Cosanti is a working studio and bell foundry designed by the revolutionary "eco-architect" and sculptor Paolo Soleri. The buildings here fuse with the natural landscape even more strikingly than those at Taliesin West, and visitors can wander the grounds freely. Arrive early in the day, between 9am and noon, and watch the casting of the bronze wind bells for which Cosanti is famous. *(6433 Doubletree Rd. Traveling north on Scottsdale Rd., turn left on Doubletree Rd.. Open M-Sa 9am-5pm, Su 11am-5pm. $1 donation.)*

TALIESIN WEST. Taliesin West was built as the winter camp of Frank Lloyd Wright's Taliesin architectural collective. Now it serves as a campus for an architectural college run by his foundation. The beautiful compound, entirely designed by the master, seems to blend naturally into the surrounding desert and includes a studio, a cinema, and a performance hall. *(12621 Frank Lloyd Wright Blvd. Head east on the Cactus St. exit from the 101. ☎ 480-860-2700. Open Sept.-June daily 9am-4pm, closed Tu-W during July-Aug. 1hr. or 1½hr. guided tours required. See www.franklloydwright.org for specific tour info. $12.50-16, students and seniors $10-14, ages 4-12 $4.50.)* One of the last buildings Wright designed, the **Gammage Memorial Auditorium** stands in the Arizona State University campus in Tempe, its pink-and-beige earth tones blending with the surrounding environment. *(Take bus #60, or 22 on weekends. Mill Ave. and Apache Blvd. ☎ 480-965-3434. 20min. tours daily in winter.)*

◪ OUTDOORS

CITY & REGIONAL PARKS

The parks of Greater Phoenix (☎ 262-6801, www.ci.phoenix.az.us/prl/index.html; ☎ 506-2930, www.maricopa.gov/parks) offer Phoenicians and visitors alike a breathtaking escape from the urban sprawl that has come to define the greater metro area. Miles of hiking, biking, and even some equestrian trails traverse the sun-baked recreation areas. In all parks, be sure to use due caution and go prepared; don't forget it's the barren desert! Start early, bring lots of water, keep an eye out for wildlife, and never go alone. A quick stop by the ranger's station can helps to orient a newcomer to the park and provides an abundant source of reliable advice. There is no entrance fee to city parks, but no camping either. For regional parks, camping fees are $18 per night for sites with electricity and water and $10 for sites with no hookups. If not staying over night, park entrance fees are $5 per vehicle at all but Lake Pleasant, where there's also a $2 charge per watercraft. In all regional parks, camping is limited to 14 consecutive nights.

| **TIME:** 2hr. one-way |
| **DISTANCE:** 50 mi. |
| **SEASON:** year-round |

Rte. 88, a.k.a. the **Apache Trail,** winds from **Apache Junction,** a small mining town 40 mi. east of Phoenix, through the mountains along stunning stretches of forest, desert, and lake. The trail proper is approximately 50 mi. long, starting in Apache Junction and ending at Roosevelt Lake, with a 32 mi. unpaved stretch from Tortilla Flat to the end. From there, retrace your steps to get back to Apache Junction or follow Rte. 88 eastward toward **Globe** (32 mi.) and then take U.S. 60 west. It's wise to start early in the day; darkness falls early, and sights close. The route is well-traveled, but be sure to fill up the gas tank before setting out—past Apache Junction, the nearest gas is 61 mi. away on U.S. 188 heading toward Globe.

A few touristy sites greet you before the drive enters the State Park. Turn right off the trail onto Mining Camp Rd.; 1 mi. up you'll find the popular **Mining Camp Restaurant ❸.** Meal tickets may not be cheap, but it's all-you-can-eat. ($16, seniors $14.35, children $9. Open Oct.-June M-Sa 4-9pm, Su noon-9pm.) Back on the trail, **Goldfield Ghost Town Mine Tours,** 5 mi. north of the U.S. 60 junction on Rte. 88, offers tours of the nearby mines and gold-panning in a resurrected ghost town. (☎480-983-0333. Open daily 10am-5pm. Mine tours $5, ages 6-12 $3; gold-panning $4.50.) Perhaps more exciting are the hiking and jeep tours led from Goldfield by **Apache Trail Tours** (☎480-982-7661). Those who prefer horses can call either the **OK Corral Stables** (☎480-982-4040) or the **Apache Lake Ranch** (☎928-467-3168) for trail rides. The **Bluebird Mine Curio Shop,** a mile farther down, is a great resource for area history and mining lore. (Open summer daily 6am-6pm; winter 7:30am-5pm.) The first sign of crossing the invisible line into protected land is the lack of billboard advertising, which is strictly prohibited. Electricity, unfortunately, is not; power lines will be constant companions throughout the route.

❶ LOST DUTCHMAN STATE PARK. Steep, red, and haunting, the Superstition Mountains derive their name from Pima Native American legends, but they could have just as easily been named for the strange lore surrounding the legendary gold mine hidden in the hills. In the 1840s, a Mexican explorer found gold in the area but was killed before he could reveal the location of the mine. More famous is the case of Jacob Waltz, the "Dutchman" for whom the park is named (despite his being German), who produced about $250,000 worth of high-quality gold ore from somewhere in the mountains during the 1880s. Upon his mysterious disappearance in 1891, there were few clues to the whereabouts of the mine. Many who have come looking for it have died violent deaths—one prospector burned to death in his own campfire, while another was found decapitated in an arroyo. The mine has never been found. If you're feeling lucky, do some exploring of your own—there are innumerable roads and trails in the park, as well as a campsite. The view from Siphon Draw Trail (2.5 mi. one-way) is well worth the demanding hike. (☎480-982-4485. Water available. Day-use parking $6, $12 for campsite.)

❷ TONTO NATIONAL FOREST. After Lost Dutchman State Park begins Tonto National Forest. Your first right as you enter the camp is First Water Rd., which leads to a wealth of well-marked trailheads into the mountains. Keep in mind that the summer sun can be scorching and water scarce. Those who want to stick to driving have much to look forward to. The Trail's dramatic views of the arid landscape make it one of the most gorgeous driving routes in the nation. Buttes and canyons—rust-red, desert rose, and a dozen other shades—speckle the way. Most of the rocks are composed of basalt and volcanic ash; their spectacular beauty makes this region second only to the Grand Canyon as Arizona's most photographed landmark. Look for **camping ❶** along the Trail's lakes. (☎928-467-3200. Sites $4-10. National Forest Mesa office ☎480-610-3300.)

❸ TORTILLA FLAT. Originally a stage coach stop, Tortilla Flat now boasts a population of six and serves as a watering hole for tourists. The town keeps its spirits up and travelers nourished with a restaurant (meals $6-8), ice cream shop, and saloon. The restaurant is famous for its chili and hamburgers, as evidenced by the thousands of bills stuck to every imaginable surface of the interior by pleased visitors. (☎480-984-1776. Open M-F 9am-6pm, Sa-Su 8am-7pm.)

ROAD TRIP

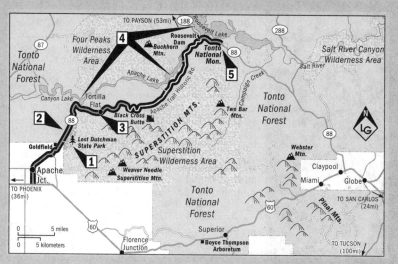

4 ARTIFICIAL LAKES: CANYON, APACHE, & ROOSEVELT LAKES. The blue waters of these man-made lakes contrast sharply with the red- and beige-hued rock formations surrounding them. Formed early this century, partly as a result of Franklin Roosevelt's Depression-busting efforts, the dams that produced these azure jewels in the desert also supply Phoenix with power. **Canyon Lake** sees the most traffic, with enough tourist visits to justify a marina, campground, restaurant, and dinner steamship (camping sites $10-12). The scene at **Apache Lake** is much the same; on the dirt stretch between the two it's not uncommon to see trailer-pulling trucks muscling each other for road space. **Roosevelt Lake** is more low-key and is the site of the **Theodore Roosevelt Dam,** the last dam constructed by hand in the US. On the far side of the dam you'll find the graceful Roosevelt Lake Bridge, spanning over 1000 ft. of canyon across the lake. **Inspiration Point,** a pull-out interpretive vista, commands an excellent view of the area. On your left in the direction of Globe is the Tonto National Forest **Visitors Center,** open daily 7:45am-4:30pm (☎928-467-3200).

5 TONTO NATIONAL MONUMENT. Five miles east of Roosevelt Dam on Rte. I-88, Tonto National Monument is the last sight on the trail proper, preserving 750-year-old ruins of Salado cliff dwellings accessed by a short trail. Some locals invoke the name of the Ancestral Puebloans, although "Tonto" was originally a derisive name given to the natives by the Spaniards. (Cliffs open daily 8am-4pm. $3 per person, under 17 free.)

Tonto National Monument marks the end of the Apache Trail proper, but the return route along Rte. 88/U.S. 60 could also prove interesting. Innumerable campgrounds flank the first stretch of Rte. 88, and gas stations and convenience stores regularly sprout to service motorists. Rte. 88 junctions into U.S. 60 5 mi. west of the tiny hamlet of **Miami, AZ.** A more promising sight is the **Boyce Thompson Arboretum** just outside the town of Superior. A desert botanical garden, the Arboretum brings together plants from every desert in the world. The grounds feature a seasonal creek, a man-made, lake and a cactus garden. (☎520-689-2723; http://ag.arizona.edu/bta/. Open year-round daily 8am-5pm. Admission $6, ages 5-12 $3.)

THE BIG SPLURGE

HUMMING IN THE DESERT

Plenty of macho outfitters around Arizona run off-road jeep or Hummer tours driven by former combat soldiers and specializing in bone-rattling rides across washboard roads and eroded gullies. The first company to offer Hummer tours, however, has developed an environmental conscience, maturing from all mean to all green. Not to say that **Desert Storm Hummer Tours** employees are any less macho: supplying all the grit you can handle are a former Navy SEAL and three ex-Marines, some with combat experience. The difference now is that Desert Storm employs a biologist and an archaeologist, offers nighttime astronomy tours, and organizes the Sonoran Quest program, in which chain gangs work in conjunction with the US Forest Service to clear the desert of debris.

Daytime tours (8am and 1pm) include commentary on the history, geology, and archaeology of the desert while the twilight tour (5:30pm) is the best bet for spotting wildlife. Night tours include a choice of trying out third-generation military nightvision goggles or a guided sky tour using the company's 11 in. telescope on their private, 4000 ft. mountain.

15525 N.83rd Way Suite 8 Scottsdale, AZ ☎ 922-0020; www.dshummer.com. Open daily 8am-8pm. Tours 8am, 1, 5:30, and 7pm. $95, children $75, night tours $125.

WITHIN THE CITY LIMITS

SOUTH MOUNTAIN PARK. The trails in South Mountain Park on Central Ave. south of downtown offer an array of beautiful views of the city and routes accessible by foot, bike, horse, or car. Petroglyphs may surprise visitors picnicking on boulders higher up. For a demanding outing, try the **National Trail** *(14½ mi. one-way)*; for something more subdued but still difficult, the **Desert Classic** *(11 mi. one-way)* will do, and is very popular with beginner and intermediate mountain bikers. Both begin past the ranger's kiosk at 48th St. and Guadalupe. *(☎ 602-495-0222. Open daily 5am-10:30pm; Summit Rd. gate closes at 9pm.)* **Equestrians** without their own steeds can join trail rides at either **All Western Stables,** 10220 Central Ave. *(☎ 276-5862),* for trail rides *($20 per hr.)* or a 4hr. summit ride *($70),* or next door at **South Mountain Stables,** 10001 Central Ave. *(☎ 276-8131)* for similar prices.

PIESTEWA PEAK. In the middle of the Phoenix Valley and offering a steep ascent is Piestewa Peak (formerly Squaw Peak) City Park and Preserve. A 1200 ft. elevation gain in 1.2 mi. demands at least 1hr. for a comfortable climb. The view up **Summit Trail** is worth the grueling ascent, but note that almost weekly, someone (unprepared, inept, or both) is airlifted or evacuated from the trail. Get to the park early; parking fills up quickly and summer weather 9am-8pm is inhospitable. *(☎ 602-262-7901. Open daily 5am-11pm.)*

TEMPE

TEMPE TOWN LAKE. The mostly dry riverbed of the Salt River in Tempe has been filled in to form a man-made lake, hence the apparently contradictory name **Rio Lago Cruises** (River Lake Cruises). The gleaming river is now home to an unlikely crew team and offers the public a chance to pedal a boat ($12 per hour) or paddle a kayak ($10 per hour). Take exit 6 from the 202 Loop Fwy. to Rio Salado Parkway and look for Tempe Beach Park. (Call ☎ 480-517-4050 for hours.) Alongside the riverbank is a grassy park with barbecue grills, ramadas, and ice cream stands.

MESA

Still farther east of the city flows the Salt River, one of the last remaining desert rivers in the US. **Salt River Recreation** arranges tubing trips. *(☎ 480-984-3305. Open daily May-Sept. 9am-4pm. Tube rental $12.)*

NEAR CENTRAL PHOENIX

MCDOWELL MOUNTAIN REGIONAL PARK. McDowell Mountain Regional Park is worth the 40min. drive from downtown Phoenix. With 76 campsites and a roaring **competitive track** built specifically for trail runners, mountain bikers, and horseback riders looking to scratch gravel, McDowell eschews the myth that the desert is no place for sport. Showers are included in the $18 camping fee. (*From Scottsdale Rd. take Shea Blvd. east; turn left on Palisades Blvd., which will take you into the town of Fountain Hills, and follow the signs to the park. ☎480-471-0173. Open 24hr.*)

LAKE HAVASU CITY   ☎928

Created by the damming of the Colorado River in 1938, Lake Havasu embodies a new West, fueled by tourist dollars and an urge to kick back. Entrepreneur Robert McCulloch willed the city (now 50,000-strong) to life in 1963 as a place to test boat engines. He drew up a community plan, brought the London Bridge from England, and people arrived with boats in tow. Motorboats and jet skis ceaselessly churn the green waters into a roiling froth. When not thundering along, the boats float down the channel with well-oiled, bikini-clad gals reclining languidly on the bow. Spring break is prime time in this party town, while high temperatures keep the adrenaline to a minimum in the summer.

■ ⁊ ORIENTATION & PRACTICAL INFORMATION. The lake is on the California-Arizona border; the city is on Arizona's Rte. 95, 21 mi. south of I-40. Tiny town Parker is 40 mi. to the south; the gambling halls of Laughlin are 70 mi. north. **Route 95** runs north-south through the city, intersected downtown by the east-west **McCulloch Boulevard.** East of Rte. 95 is **Lake Havasu Avenue,** home to stucco installations of fast-food spots. McCulloch runs west over a channel, spanned by the actual London Bridge, and connects to The Island, where beach resorts flourish. The **Visitors Center** is in English Village, a mock British square with a brewery and food stands at the corner of Rte. 95 and London Bridge Rd. (☎855-4115. Open daily 9am-4pm.) **City Transit Services** is on call with curb-to-curb shuttle services throughout Lake Havasu City. (☎453-7600. Operates M-F 6am-9pm, Sa-Su 6am-6pm. $3, under 10 $2, under 5 free.) Bike rental is available at **MBK Bikes,** 151 Swanson Ave. (☎453-7474. Open M-F 9am-6pm, Sa 10am-5pm, Su 11am-4pm. Mountain bikes $20 per day, cruisers $13.) For those not interested in motorboats (a decided minority here), **Crawdaddy's Kayak Rental and Tours** rents kayaks ($24 per day) and other small watercraft and provides maps of the waterways. Services include: **police,** 2360 McCulloch Blvd. (☎855-1171); **emergency** (☎911); **laundry** at **Sundance Country,** 121 N. Lake Havasu Ave. (☎855-2700); **Havasu Regional Medical Center,** 101 Civic Center Ln. (☎855-8185); and the **post office,** 1750 McCulloch Blvd. (☎855-2361. Open M 7:45am-5pm, Tu-F 8:30am-5pm, Sa 10am-1pm.) **Postal code:** 86403.

⁊ ACCOMMODATIONS. There is an abundance of affordable motels along London Bridge Rd., though rates tend to be higher on summer weekends. The shiny **Windsor Inn ❷,** 451 London Bridge Rd., offers inexpensive rooms and all the desert amenities. Since you pay by the bed, two people can get the single price if they're willing to share a bed or one crashes on the couch. (☎855-4135, 800-245-4135. Singles Su-Th $36, F-Sa $49; doubles $42/$59.) The budget chain **Super 8 Motel ❸,** 305 London Bridge Rd., offers predictable accommodations at predictable prices. (☎855-8844. Singles Su-Th $41, F-Sa $51; doubles $45/$56.) Campers should visit **Lake Havasu State Park ❶,** west off Rte. 95 on Industrial Rd., where there's a main camp (☎855-2784; 43 sites; showers, toilets, boat-launch; $14 per site) and **Cattail Cove ❶** (61 sites; showers, toilets, RV hookups; $19), with a beach and boat docks.

◧◪ FOOD & NIGHTLIFE. In addition to Lake Havasu Ave., there is also a tremendous concentration of fast food along Rte. 95, particularly where it intersects London Bridge Rd. For a less generic taste, try the Irish-inspired **Slainee's ❷,** 1519

ARIZONA

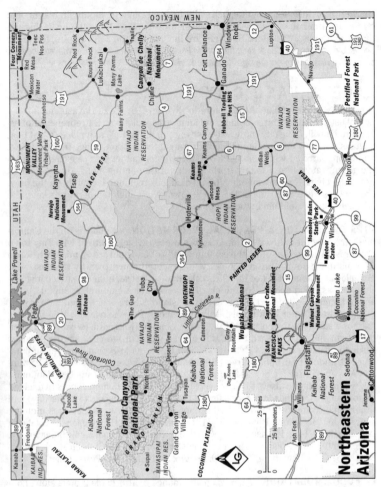

Queens Bay Rd., which has hearty entrees ($7 and up, with soup/salad), a slew of pool tables, and live tunes on weekends. (☎505-8900. Open daily 10am-1am.) At the **Barley Brothers Brewery and Grill ❷**, 1425 McCulloch Blvd. on The Island, knowledgeable bartenders serve inventive local brews (pint $4) as well as more refined cuisine. (☎505-7837. Open Su-Th 11am-10pm, F-Sa 11am-11pm. Sandwiches $8.) A short but dark walk over London Bridge from the Brewery, the colossal **Kokomo's on the Channel**, 1477 Queens Bay Rd., is the London Bridge Resort's open-air superclub where you can shake your sun-burned tailfeathers. Expect the action to pick up after 11pm. (☎855-0888. Weekend cover $5-15. Mixed drinks $4, DJ-announced specials $1. Open daily 11am-1am.)

⬛⚠ **SIGHTS & ACTIVITIES.** Lake Havasu's most unusual claim to fame is the **London Bridge**. Originally built in London, England in 1824, it was painstakingly dismantled and reconstructed under the sponsorship of Robert McCulloch. The reconstructed bridge was dedicated in October 1971. See the bridge and associated tourist "attractions" at the intersection of Rte. 95 and London Bridge Rd. Without a doubt, the place to be in Lake Havasu is on the water. Any number of tourist publications can direct you to a reputable boat rental. Loungers should try **Windsor Beach,** west on Industrial Rd. from Rte. 95, in Lake Havasu State Park (day-use $8). Free beaches line the eastern shore of The Island, but swimmers can avoid boat traffic by sticking to the southern end. Take Smoketree from Rte. 95 to get to **Rotary Beach,** where sand, volleyball, and picnic areas await.

FLAGSTAFF ☎928

Born on the 4th of July, the city of Flagstaff began as a rest stop along the transcontinental railroad, its mountain springs providing precious aqueous refreshment on the long haul across the continent to the Pacific Ocean. In the past 100 years, Flag has seen the logging industry come and go, claimed as one of its own a Boston-Brahmin-turned-astronomer in search of canal-digging Martians, and felt the unrelenting onslaught of tourists—backpackers and fannypackers alike. Now Flagstaff's numerous outdoors shops point adventure-seekers of all kinds to their many outdoor resources. But one thing definitely hasn't changed after all this time: Flagstaff is still a major rest stop on the way to Southwestern must-sees. More sedate travelers pass through on their way to the Grand Canyon, Sedona, and the Petrified Forest—all within day-trip distance by car or shuttle. The energetic citizens welcome all to their unusual rock formations by day and to their hopping breweries by night; many of them wandered into town with camera in hand and ended up settling down themselves. Retired cowboys, earthy Volvo owners, New Agers, and mountain bikers comprise much of the young-spirited population.

▄▀ TRANSPORTATION

Trains: Amtrak, 1 E. Rte. 66 (☎774-8679). Two trains leave daily. Eastbound train leaves at 5:28am, heading to **Kansas City** and **Chicago** via **Winslow** (1hr., $14-23), **Gallup, NM** (2½hr., $35-61), and **Albuquerque** (5hr., $63-110). Westbound train leaves at 9:23pm, heading to **Los Angeles** (12hr., $68-119). Amtrak has occasional discount offers and specials that may reduce their rather steep rates considerably. Station open daily 4:45pm-7:30am.

Buses: Two bus lines provide service to regional destinations. Check at the Grand Canyon International Hostel and Debau International Hostel for their special private Grand Canyon and Sedona shuttles.

Greyhound: 399 S. Malpais Ln. (☎774-4573), across from Northern Arizona University (NAU) campus, 3 blocks southwest of the train station on U.S. 89A. Turn off 89A by Dairy Queen. To: **Albuquerque** (6½hr., 5 per day, $41); **Las Vegas** (5-6hr., 3 per day, $47); **Los Angeles** (10-12hr., 8 per day, $49); **Phoenix,** including airport (3hr., 5 per day, $22). Terminal open 24hr.

Sedona Shuttle Service: Coconino/Yavapai Shuttle Service (☎775-8929 or 888-440-8929) offers daily trips from Flagstaff to **Sedona.** The 1hr. trip leaves from Flagstaff M-F at 8am and 4pm and returns from Sedona at 2:30pm. On Sa, the Flagstaff-Sedona leg leaves at 10am with no return trip. No Su service. One-way $18.

Public Transit: Mountain Line (☎779-6624). Routes cover most of town. Buses run once per hr.; route map and schedule available at Visitors Center in Amtrak station. One-way $0.75, seniors and disabled $0.35, children $0.60; book of 20 passes $13.

Taxis: Friendly Cab (☎774-4444).

Car Rental: Enterprise Rent-A-Car (☎526-1377), 3420 E. Rte. 66. Starting at $39 per day. 21+. Must have license and credit card. Open M-F 7:30am-6pm, Sa 9am-noon.

FLAGSTAFF TWIN HOSTELS

🏠 **Grand Canyon Int'l Hostel,** 19 S. San Francisco St. (☎888-442-2696; www.grandcanyonhostel.com), near the train station. Sunny, clean, and classy, and friendly despite its size (32 beds). Free parking, showers, linen, tea, and coffee. Access to kitchens, TV room with cable, Internet ($2 per 30min.), free breakfast (7-10am), and laundry facilities ($1 wash, $0.25 per dry). Free pick-up from Greyhound station. Offers tours to the Grand Canyon ($50) and to Sedona ($25). Reception 7am-midnight. No curfew. Sometimes travelers work for lodging—inquire with the manager. Reservations with credit card. 4-bed dorms Oct.-May $15, June-Sep. $17; private rooms without bath Oct.-May $30/33 week/weekend and June-Sept. $34/37. ❶

🏠 **Du Beau Int'l. Hostel,** 19 W. Phoenix St. (☎800-398-7112; www.dubeau.com), also just behind the train station. The Du Beau lives up to its ritzy name with recently renovated dorm rooms (most with 8 beds), private bathrooms, and a lively, well-equipped common room. Reception 7am-midnight. Under the same ownership as the Grand Canyon Hostel, Du Beau offers all the same services. 8-bed dorms Oct.-May $15, June-Aug. $17. Private rooms with bath Oct.-May $32/35 and June-Sep. $36/39. ❶

⚡ ORIENTATION

Flagstaff sits 138 mi. north of Phoenix (take I-17), 26 mi. north of Sedona (take U.S. 89A), and 81 mi. south of the Grand Canyon's south rim (take U.S. 180). The downtown area revolves around the intersection of **Leroux Street** and **Route 66** (formerly Santa Fe Ave.). The Visitors Center, bus station, both hostels, and a number of inexpensive restaurants lie within a half mile of this spot. **South San Francisco Street,** a block east of Leroux St., hosts many outdoors shops. Split by Rte. 66, the northern area of Flagstaff is slightly more touristed and upscale while the area south of the tracks is down to earth, housing hostels and vegetarian eateries.

🔢 PRACTICAL INFORMATION

Visitor Info: Flagstaff Visitors Center, 1 E. Rte. 66 (☎774-9541 or 800-842-7293), in the Amtrak train station. Open Memorial Day-Labor Day daily 7am-7pm; rest of year 8am-5pm.

Equipment Rental and Outfitting: Peace Surplus, 14 W. Rte. 66 (☎779-4521), 1 block from Grand Canyon Hostel. Rents tents ($7-9 per day), packs ($5-6 per day), sleeping bags ($6 per day), and stoves ($3 per day), as well as alpine, nordic, and snowshoe packages in winter. 3-day min. rental; hefty $100-200 credit card or cash deposits are required. Open M-F 8am-9pm, Sa 8am-8pm, Su 8am-6pm. **Summit Divers and Watersports,** 103 S. Milton (the western part of Rte. 66 in town) rents kayaks for $35 per day, $45 for two days, and $65 for a weekend. (☎556-8780. Open M-Sa 10am-5pm.) **Four Season Outfitters and Guides,** 107 W. Phoenix Ave. (☎226-8798; www.fsoutfitters.com), offers guided backcountry hikes and canyoneering in Escalante or the Grand Canyon. Reflecting Flagstaff's love affair with its natural surroundings, **Goshawk Ecotours** (☎773-1198) guides nature trips of all kinds for $18 per hr. ($50 minimum).

Laundromat: White Flag Coin-op, 16 S. Beaver St. (☎774-7614). Coin-op, with attendant. Drop service also available. Open M-Sa 7am-9pm, Su 7am-7pm.

Emergency: ☎911. **Police:** Sawmill Rd. (general info ☎556-2316, non-emergencies ☎774-1414).

Pharmacy/Grocery: Fry's Food and Drug Store, 201 Switzer Canyon (☎774-2719), 1 mi. east of San Francisco St. on Rte. 66. Open daily 6am-midnight.

Medical Services: Flagstaff Medical Center, 1200 North Beaver St. (☎779-3366), provides medical services in the area, including 24hr. emergency service.

Internet Access: Free access at NAU's **Cline Library** (☎523-2171). Take Riordan Rd. east from Rte. 66. Open M-Th 7:30am-10pm, F 7:30am-6pm, Sa 10:30am-5pm, Su noon-10pm. $3 per ½hr., $5 per hr. at the **Flagstaff Public Library**, 300 W. Aspen Ave. (☎779-7670). Open M-Th 10am-9pm, F 10am-7pm, Sa 10am-6pm.

Post Office: 2400 N. Postal Blvd., on Rte. 66, for general delivery. (☎714-9302. Open M-F 9am-5pm, Sa 9am-noon). **Postal code: 86004. Downtown,** 104 N. Agassiz St. (☎779-3559. Open M-F 9am-5pm, Sa 9am-1pm. **Postal Code:** 86001.

ACCOMMODATIONS

When swarms of summer tourists from southern Arizona descend on Flagstaff, hotel prices shoot up. Historic **Route 66** is home to many cheap motels, although the private rooms at the hotels below rival them in price and quality. *The Flagstaff Accommodations Guide*, available at the Visitors Center, lists all area beds. If you're here to see the Grand Canyon, check the hostel notice board; some travelers leave their still-valid passes behind, and you might find a ride to the next town as well. Also see **The Hidden Deal: Flagstaff Twin Hostels,** p. 112.

The Weatherford Hotel, 23 N. Leroux St. (☎779-1919). The oldest hotel in Flagstaff, dating to 1898, the Weatherford has 8 spacious rooms with amazing balconies and bay windows. Equipped with elegant furnishings and located in the middle of downtown, but lacks TV and in-room phones. Reservations recommended. Rooms $55. ❸

Hotel Monte Vista, 100 N. San Francisco St. (☎779-6971 or 800-545-3068; www.hotel-montevista.com), downtown. Feels like a classy hotel, with quirky decor and a faux peeling-brick lounge that was used in the filming of *Casablanca* (see **Nightlife,** p. 114). Chock-full of colorful history; staff swears the hotel is chock-full of ghosts too. Private rooms named after movie stars they once slept start at $60 on weekdays. ❹

CAMPING

Free backcountry camping is available around Flagstaff in designated wilderness areas. Pick up a map from the **Peaks Ranger Station,** 5075 N. 89A (☎526-0866), to find out where. All backcountry campsites must be located at least 200 ft. away from trails, waterways, wet meadows, and lakes. There is a 14-night limit for stays in the Coconino National Forest. For info on camping, call the **Coconino National Forest Line** (☎527-3600; open M-F 7:30am-4:30pm).

Lakeview Campground, on the east side of Upper Lake Mary, 11½ mi. south on Lake Mary Road (off I-17 south of Flagstaff), is surrounded by a pine forest that supports an alpine ecosystem. Drinking water, pit toilets, no reservations. Open May-Oct. $10 per vehicle per night. ❶

Pinegrove Campground (☎877-444-6777; reservations www.reserveamerica.com), sits 5 mi. south of Lakeview at the other end of Upper Lake Mary. Set in a similarly charming locale, offers drinking water and flush toilets. $12 per vehicle. ❶

Ashurst/Forked Pine Campground, flanks both sides of Ashurst lake (a smaller, secluded lake on Forest Rd. 82E). Turn left off Lake Mary Rd., across from Pine Grove Campground. Water and flush toilets are on-site, and the fishing is stupendous. 64 sites are available on a first come, first served basis. $10 per vehicle. ❶

FOOD

All the deep-fat-frying chains are readily available outside of downtown, but near the heart of Flagstaff, the creative and off-beat joints rule. The downtown core brims with pubs, restaurants, and cafes that suit all tastes.

Macy's European Coffee House and Bakery, 14 S. Beaver St. (☎774-2243), behind Motel Du Beau. Macy's is a cheery and earthy hangout serving only vegetarian food and a number of excellent vegan selections. $4-7 specials change daily. Get there early and start the day with a bowl of granola ($4) and one of their fresh-roasted coffees ($1-3.50). Open Su-Th 6am-8pm, F-Sa 6am-10pm. Food served until 1hr. before close. Cash or check only. ❶

Mountain Oasis Global Cuisine and Juice Bar, 11 E. Aspen St. (☎214-9270). Mountain Oasis offers a pleasant, softly lit eating area with live classical guitar on F during the summer. A wide variety of food from around the world, including vegetarian, vegan, and organic options. Open Su-Th 11am-9pm, F-Sa 11am-10pm, but may close early if business is slow. ❷

Alpine Pizza Company, 7 Leroux St. (☎779-4109). Comfortably worn-in wood panelling sets the mountain-town tone of Alpine Pizza Company, one of Flagstaff's top pizza joints. Pool tables, foosball, and neon beer ads are pretty standard decoration for a place like this; newspapers with scrawled public commentary used as wallpaper in the men's room are anything but. Small single-topping pizza $8. Happy Hour Tu-Th 4-8pm. Open daily 11am-10pm. ❷

Mountain Harvest Deli, 2 S. Beaver St. (☎779-9456), across from the Du Beau International Hostel, Mountain Harvest crafts organic ingredients into tasty sandwiches, some vegetarian ($5-6). Also has grocery section and juice bar. Wheatgrass anyone? Open M-Sa 8am-8pm, Su 9am-7pm. ❶

◤ NIGHTLIFE

The students of Northern Arizona University are the clientele for Flagstaff's fleet of pubs, bars, and nightspots. The student body is as diverse as it is energetic, gravitating toward a variety of social and musical scenes. Youth, families, and travellers all gather at Heritage Square on Aspen between San Francisco and Leroux. Watch out for firedancers and listen for traditional drummers, folk guitarists, and more on summer weekends.

Charly's, 23 N. Leroux St. (☎779-1919), plays live jazz and blues in one of Flagstaff's classiest buildings. Live music nightly, including local rock and reggae bands. Pub fare entrees $13-17. Upstairs Zane Grey Ballroom picks up the overflow of beautiful people with nightly drink specials ($2.75) and a bar brought in by train from Tombstone. Happy hour 5-7pm. Open Su-Th 11am-10pm, F-Sa 11am-11pm. Bar open daily 11am-1am.

Joe's Place, 700 E. Rte. 66 (☎774-6281), on the corner with Agassiz. Hosts bands of all descriptions weekend nights. Lively everyday, features open mic M and Su, pool tournaments Tu. Happy Hour 4-7pm with $2.25 mixed drinks and $1.75 domestic bottles. Open daily 11am-1am.

Pay 'n Take Market, 12 W. Aspen between Leroux and Beaver (☎226-8595). With the feel and retro decor of a convenience store, alcohol might well be the last thing you'd expect to buy. For a glass of wine or an imported beer, order drinks at the bar or pull out your own from the glassed refrigerator lining the east wall. Open M-W 7am-10pm, Th-Sa 7am-1am, Su 9am-9pm.

Monte Vista Lounge, 100 N. San Francisco St. (☎774-2403), where bank robbers used to go to celebrate after a heist. At least one is known to have died here, contributing to the many Monte Vista ghost stories. Crowd is eclectic, mostly local. Live music (punk, rockabilly) F-Sa, DJs Tu-Sa. Happy hour 5-9pm. Open daily noon-1am.

The Museum Club (a.k.a. the **Zoo**), 3404 E. Rte. 66 (☎526-9434). The premier spot for honky-tonk action, built during the Depression as a roadhouse to liven spirits. Now, cowboy gusto is revived with liquor and top-notch country music. Watch out for a big name country star in June 2004. Cover $3-5. Open daily 11am-3am.

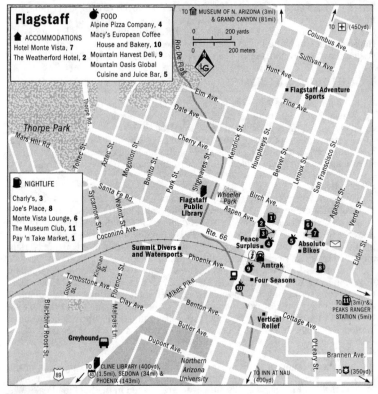

Flagstaff

FOOD
Alpine Pizza Company, 4
Macy's European Coffee
House and Bakery, 10
Mountain Harvest Deli, 9
Mountain Oasis Global
Cuisine and Juice Bar, 5

ACCOMMODATIONS
Hotel Monte Vista, 7
The Weatherford Hotel, 2

NIGHTLIFE
Charly's, 3
Joe's Place, 8
Monte Vista Lounge, 6
The Museum Club, 11
Pay 'n Take Market, 1

TO MUSEUM OF N. ARIZONA (3mi) & GRAND CANYON (81mi)
TO (450yd)

Columbus Ave.
Sullivan Ave.
Hunt Ave.
Rio De Flag
Elm Ave.
Dale Ave.
Cherry Ave.
Fine Ave.
■ Flagstaff Adventure Sports
Thorpe Park
Mars Hill Rd
Thorpe Rd.
Toltec St.
Aztec St.
Mogollon St.
Bonito St.
Park St.
Sitgreaves St.
Kendrick St.
Humphreys St.
Beaver St.
Leroux St.
San Francisco St.
Agassiz St.
Verde St.
Santa Fe Rd.
Sycamore St.
Walnut St.
Coconino Ave.
Flagstaff Public Library
Wheeler Park
Birch Ave.
Aspen Ave.
Rte. 66
Peace Surplus
Summit Divers and Watersports ■
Phoenix Ave.
Amtrak
■ Four Seasons
Kingman St.
Florence St.
Tombstone Ave.
Clay Ave.
Mikes Pike
Benton Ave.
Butler Ave.
Absolute ■ Bikes
Elden St.
TO (3mi) & PEAKS RANGER STATION (5mi)
Cottage Ave.
Vertical Relief
O'Leary St.
Greyhound
Dupont Ave.
Brannen Ave.
Blackbird Roost St.
Gilo St.
Malpais Ln.
TO CLINE LIBRARY (400yd), (1.5mi), SEDONA (34mi) & PHOENIX (143mi)
Northern Arizona University
TO INN AT NAU (400yd)
TO (350yd)

SIGHTS

LOWELL OBSERVATORY. In 1894, Boston mathematician Percival Lowell chose Flagstaff as the site for an astronomical observatory and spent the rest of his life here studying heavenly bodies and culling data to support his theory that life exists on Mars. The Lowell Observatory, where an assistant discovered the planet Pluto, doubles as a tribute to his genius and a high-powered research center sporting five professional, optical telescopes. During the daytime, admission includes tours of the telescopes, as well as a museum with hands-on astronomy exhibits. If you want stars in your eyes, come back at night for an introductory program about the night sky and the chance to look through a telescope. *(1400 W. Mars Hill Rd., 1 mi. west of downtown off Rte. 66. ☎774-3358; www.lowell.edu. Open daily Nov.-Mar. noon-5pm, Apr.-Oct. 9am-5pm. Evening programs Nov.-Mar. F-Sa 7:30pm; Apr.-May and Sept.-Oct. W, F, Sa 7:30pm; June-Aug. M-Sa 8:00pm. $4, students, seniors, and AAA $3.50, ages 5-17 $2.)*

OTHER SIGHTS & EVENTS. North of town near the museum, the **Coconino Center for the Arts** houses exhibits, festivals, performers, and even a children's museum *(☎779-2300)*. In the second weekend of June, the annual **Flagstaff Rodeo** comes to town with competitions, barn dances, a carnival, and a cocktail waitress race. Competitions and events go on from Friday to Sunday at the Coconino County Fair Grounds. *(On Hwy. 89A just south of town, ask at the Flagstaff Visitors Center for*

details.) On the **4th of July,** the town celebrates its birthday with street fairs, live music, outdoor barbecues, a parade, and, of course, fireworks. At the tail-end of the summer (Labor Day), the **Coconino County Fair** digs its heels into Flagstaff with rides, animal competitions, and carnival games. **Theatrikos,** a local theater group, stages plays year-round. *(11 W. Cherry Ave. ☎ 774-1662; www.theatrikos.com.)*`

⚡ OUTDOOR ACTIVITIES

With the northern **San Francisco Peaks** and the surrounding **Coconino National Forest,** Flagstaff presents options for the rugged outdoorsman or those simply interested in walking off last night's indiscretion. Due to 7000 ft. altitudes, bring plenty of water, regardless of the season or activity. In late spring and summer, National and State Park Rangers may close trails if the fire danger gets too high; winter snow can also shut down routes. Check with rangers for current conditions.

SPELUNKING

Unlike the slow-forming limestone caves of southern Arizona, the caves surrounding Flagstaff formed in only a few hours during volcanic eruptions. Large rivers of lava flowed across the countryside and cooled on the outside, creating hollow tunnels. Some (like the one in Sunset Crater National Monument) are closed to the public, and visitors are cautioned against exploring any unmarked openings. Happily, the Forest Service maintains safe access to the longest such flow in Arizona, the ¾ mi. **Lava River Cave.** Inside are features unique to lava flow caves, including flow ripples on the floor, cracks formed as cooling lava shrank, and "lavasicles" hanging from the ceiling. It's possible to see ice not far from the entrance much of the year. Bring water, sturdy footwear, and three flashlights. To get there, take U.S. 180 14 mi. north from Flagstaff, turn left on unpaved FS Rd. 245 near mile marker 230, proceed 3 mi., and turn left on FS Rd. 171 and follow the signs.

HIKING

It's important to note that many trails are multipurpose; the hiking trails of the Mary's Lakes regions also make fantastic singletrack for mountain bikers. The trails in the San Francisco Peaks, however, are located in the Kachina Peaks Wilderness area and are off limits to mechanized vehicles. The Coconino National Forest has trails for hikers of all abilities. Consult the **Peaks Ranger Station,** 5075 N. 89A (☎ 526-0866), for trail descriptions and possible closures. Be sure to carry plenty of water when you hike—most hikes do not have reliable water sources.

Humphrey's Peak (9 mi. round-trip, 6-7hr.). This strenuous but popular hike ascends Arizona's highest mountain. The trailhead is at the Snow Bowl Ski Area in the first parking lot to the left. From the parking lot, the trail winds in and out of alpine forest, and eventually above tree line. The summit of Humphrey's Peak affords a 360° panoramic view of northern Arizona, including the mesas of the Hopi reservation, Oak Creek Canyon, and the Grand Canyon. Watch the weather during summer; it's better to turn back than risk being caught at such elevations in a lightning storm. 3400 ft. elevation gain.

Elden Lookout Trail (6 mi. round-trip, 7-9hr.). This hard trail begins ¼ mi. past the Peaks Ranger Station, north of town on U.S. 89. Leading to the peak of Mt. Elden, it crosses over petrified lava flows and through conifer forests, as well as an aspen grove that represents the first regrowth from a 1977 forest fire. 2400 ft. elevation gain.

Weatherford Trail (17½ mi. round-trip, 9-12hr.). Originally a car track for pleasure rides by the owners of Model-T Fords, the trail has since been narrowed and refashioned as a long route for hikers and horseback riders. Drive 2 mi. north of Flagstaff on Rte. 180, then turn left on Forest Rd. 420 (Schultz Pass Rd.). The road forks soon after; take the left fork and continue on 5 mi. to Schultz Tank; the trailhead is next to the tank. This moderate-to-strenuous trail is excellent for wildlife spotting. 3200 ft. elevation gain.

ARIZONA

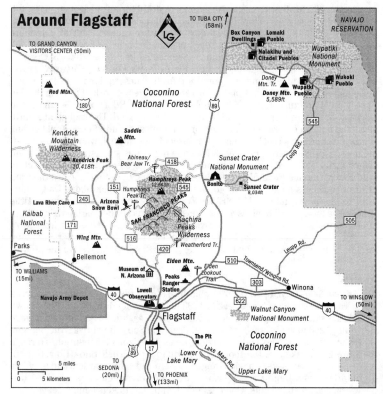

Around Flagstaff

Abineau/Bear Jaw Trail (6 mi. round-trip, 4-5hr.). Head north of town along U.S. 180; turn right on Forest Rd. 151 and follow it until it intersects Forest Rd. 418. Turn right and drive past the Potato Tank; 2 mi. later, the road will intersect Forest Rd. 9123J. Turn right; the trailhead is less than 1 mi. away. The steep trail is remote and one of the least traveled in the wilderness. 1900 ft. elevation gain.

ROCK CLIMBING

The volcanic tumult of the Flagstaff area makes for an endless variety of climbing opportunities. **Vertical Relief,** 205 S. San Francisco St. in downtown Flagstaff, offers equipment, guides, and an extensive indoor climbing gym. They also sell *Flying on the Cheap*, a local climbing guidebook. (☎556-9909 or 877-265-5984; www.verticalrelief.com. Guided outdoor climbs: half-day one person $160, each additional person $85; full-day $225/$125. Indoor climbing: day pass $14, students $12, monthly pass $59; F after 7pm is teen night, $9 day pass and $3 shoe rental with high school ID. Open M-F 10am-11pm, Sa-Su noon-8pm.) **West Elden** offers beginner bouldering and top-roped crack options starting at 5.5 in the Yosemite rating system. Ask at Vertical Relief for directions.

MOUNTAIN BIKING

Flagstaff promises excellent mountain biking and attracts enough mountain bikers to keep a thriving outfitting industry going. **Absolute Bikes,** 18 N. San Francisco St., fixes any vehicle on two wheels and runs a rental operation. (☎779-5969. Front suspension $25 for first day, $20 for second, and $10 for all subsequent days; full suspension $35/$25/$15.) They also lead free road rides Tuesday at 6am and mountain rides Fridays at 3pm. For hard-core adventure racers, **Flagstaff Adventure Sports,** 612 N. Humphreys St., will baby your mangled ride back to health and sell you ultralight racing gear to ease your trail-impacted knees. (☎779-5393. Open M-Sa 10am-6pm.) Leaf through a copy of *Cosmic Ray's Fat Tire Takes & Trails* mountain biking guide at any outdoors shop for trail descriptions.

The **Schultz Creek Trail** leads bikers into an extensive network of trails in the San Francisco Mountains. Take 180 north to Schultz Pass Rd. (Forest Service Road 420) and park in the dirt lot as the road becomes unpaved. The trail climbs north along the bottom of a ravine and after almost 4 mi. splits into **Sunset Trail** heading south and **Little Elden Trail** heading east. Sunset climbs through woods before cresting and descending along **Brookbank Trail** down glorious singletrack dropoffs and switchbacks. This 4 mi. stretch spits out riders bearing sloppy grins of satisfaction onto Forest Service Road 557. Ride this road safely either 4 mi. back to the trailhead or to access locally renowned and more technical **Rocky Ridge Trail,** which leads to the same trailhead. Little Elden Trail affords access to the bottom of **Little Bear Trail,** a moderate 3.5 mi. ascent to Sunset Trail; return by bearing right at both intersections. An easier route is the **Fisher Point** ride, a gentle descent from town towards Walnut Canyon. Take Beaver St. south and turn left on Butler Ave., then right on Lone Tree; pick up the Urban Bike Route (9 mi., 2-3hr.) left to the point.

SKIING

The **Arizona Snow Bowl,** operates four chairlifts (and a tow rope) and maintains 32 trails. The majestic **Humphrey's Peak** (12,633 ft.) is the backdrop for the Snowbowl, though the skiing takes place from 11,500 ft. off of **Agassiz Peak.** With an average snowfall of 260 in. and 2300 ft. of vertical drop, the Snow Bowl rivals the big time ski resorts of the Rockies and easily outclasses its Arizona competition. To reach the Snow Bowl, take U.S. 180 about 7 mi. north to the Fairfield Snow Bowl turnoff.

The Snow Bowl caters to a wide range of skiers and snowboarders and is evenly divided between beginner, intermediate, and advanced runs. (☎779-1951; www.arizonasnowbowl.com. Open daily 9am-4pm. Lift tickets adult weekend full-day $40, half-day $32; midweek $40/$25; ages 8-12 $22/$17.) **Equipment rental** is available on the mountain. (Half-day ski package $15, full-day $20; extreme performance package $30/$20; snowboards $27/$20.)

◈ DAYTRIPS FROM FLAGSTAFF

WUPATKI NATIONAL MONUMENT. Situated 18 mi. northeast of Sunset Crater, Wupatki possesses some of the Southwest's most scenic Pueblo sites along a stunning road with jaw-dropping views of the Painted Desert and the Navajo Reservation. The Sinagua moved here in the 11th century after the Sunset Crater eruption's ash left a fertile plain to the north. Archaeologists posit that in less than 200 years, droughts, disease, and over-farming forced the Sinagua to abandon these stone houses on the sides of *arroyos* in view of the San Francisco Peaks. Seven empty pueblos face the 14 mi. road from the Visitors Center to where it meets U.S. 89. The largest and most accessible, Wupatki, on a ½ mi., round-trip loop trail from the Visitors Center, rises three stories. About 4 mi. northwest of the Visitors Center, the spectacular Doney Mountain Trail climbs a ½ mi. from the picnic area to the summit. Backcountry hiking is not permitted. ☎679-2365. *Open June-Aug. daily 8am-6pm; Sept.-May 8am-5pm. Monument open daily sunrise to sunset. $5, under 16 free; includes admission to Sunset Crater Volcano National Monument.*

SUNSET CRATER VOLCANO NATIONAL MONUMENT. The crater encompassed by Sunset Crater Volcano National Monument appeared in 1065. Over the next few decades, a 1000 ft. high cinder cone took shape as a result of periodic eruptions. The self-guided **Lava Flow Nature Trail** wanders 1 mi. through the surreal landscape surrounding the cone, 1½ mi. east of the **Visitors Center,** where gnarled trees lie uprooted amid the rocky black terrain. Lava tube tours have been permanently discontinued due to falling lava, and hiking up Sunset Crater itself is not permitted. Those intent on peering into a volcano can hike the 1 mi. round-trip trail into Lenox Crater (250 ft. elevation gain), departing the road 1 mi. east of the Visitors Center. Particularly beautiful is the 18 mi. drive north through the Coconino National Forest to Wupatki National Monument. *12 mi. north of Flagstaff on U.S. 89.* ☎ *526-0502. Open June-Aug. daily 8am-6pm; Sept.-Nov. and Mar.-May 8am-5pm; Dec.-Feb. 9am-5pm. $5, under 16 free; includes admission to Wupatki.* The **Bonito Campground ❶,** in the Coconino National Forest at the entrance to Sunset Crater, provides tent sites. *Drinking water, flush toilets. $12.*

WALNUT CANYON NATIONAL MONUMENT. The remnants of more than 300 rooms in 12th-century Sinaguan dwellings make up Walnut Canyon National Monument, constructed in a 400 ft. deep canyon. A glassed-in observation deck in the **Visitors Center** overlooks the canyon, while the steep, self-guided 1 mi. round-trip **Island Trail** snakes down 185 ft. on pavement and stairs from the Visitors Center, passing 25 cliff dwellings. The 0.8 mi. **Rim Trail** offers views of the canyon and passes rim-top sites. Every Saturday morning 10am-1pm, rangers lead groups of five on two mile hikes into Walnut Canyon to the original ranger cabin and more remote cliff dwellings. Hiking boots, long pants, and reservations are required for these challenging 2½hr. hikes. There's also a trailhead for the Mexico-to-Utah **Arizona Trail** 1.7 mi. west of the entrance road. *10 mi. east of Flagstaff, off I-40, at exit 204.* ☎ *526-3367. Open June-Aug. daily 8am-6pm; Sept.-Nov. 8am-5pm; Dec.-Feb. 9am-5pm; Mar.-May 8am-5pm. Island Trail closes one hour before park. $5, under 16 free.*

METEOR CRATER. Originally thought to be a volcanic cone, the crater is now understood to be the impact site of a giant iron-nickel meteorite that fell to earth and 50,000 years ago. Visitors are not allowed to hike down into the crater, which measures 4100 ft. across, so they must fight the hordes for an unspectacular view over the guard-railed edge. (Hint: turn around. The view of the desolate, lunar countryside is every bit as bracing as the mining debris-filled crater). The site was used to train Apollo astronauts in the 1960s, and a **museum** documents the history of the crater's role in the space program and early mining attempts. Also included is the hourly, hour-long rim walk. Conspicuously missing in action is the meteor itself; scientists believe that most of it was vaporized at the moment of impact, since it was traveling at an impressive 110 mi. per second. *35 mi. east of Flagstaff at exit 233 on I-40.* ☎ *289-2362 or 289-5898 for groups. Open daily 6am-6pm; off-season 8am-5pm. Rim walk 9:15am-2:15pm, closed-shoe footwear required.$12, seniors $11, ages 6-17 $6. Museum free with crater admission.*

JEROME. Precariously perched on the side of Mingus Mountain, Jerome once attracted miners, speculators, saloon owners, and madams who came to the city following the copper boom of the late 1800s. By 1920, the city ranked as Arizona's third largest. However, the 1929 stock market crash threw Jerome's economy into a downward spiral, and by mid-century Jerome was a ghost town. More recently, bikers, hippies, ex-cowboys, and artists have arrived, drawn by the charm and spectacular scenery of the town. Jerome's current incarnation is, in one respect, drastically different from its start—tourist mining has replaced copper mining as the main industry. The **Jerome State Historic Park,** ½ mi. off U.S. 89A just as you enter town, provides a worthwhile panoramic view of the town and a small museum with a fascinating 3-D model of a mine. If Jerome's bountiful hills tempt you to stay the night, try **The View Motel ❷**, 818 U.S. 89A, lives up to its name, and also features fridges, microwaves, countertops for cooking, and a heated pool. *Take US 89A 60 mi. south of Flagstaff. View Motel: ☎634-7581. Rooms $30-60 depending on season and number of guests.*

BEYOND FLAGSTAFF

Within two hour's drive of Flagstaff, a stunning range of Southwestern scenery and activities presents itself. To the south, a drive through beautiful red-rock country will lead you to new-agey Sedona or the town of Prescott and its wealth of outdoors fun. East of the city, Rte. 66 leads to the Petrified Forest and Painted Desert, and to the northeast, the Navajo Nation spans the rest of the state. With this in mind, don't let the Grand Canyon be your only daytrip from Flagstaff.

SEDONA   ☎928

Considering Sedona is a UFO-sighting hotspot, one wonders if Martians are simply mistaking its striking red rock towers for home. The scores of tourists who descend upon the town year-round (Sedona and nearby Oak Creek Canyon rival the Grand Canyon for tourist mass) certainly aren't. They come for sights that would make Newton question gravity, or at least consider its implications more seriously. Dramatic copper-toned behemoths dotted with pines tower over Sedona, rising from the earth with such flair that they feel like a perfectly manufactured tourist attraction. Some of the more imaginative folks in town will tell you that they were man-made, perhaps by the Egyptians. Also the New Age capital of the US, Sedona has enough spiritual healers and vortices to alleviate any crisis, mid-life or otherwise. Though the downtown is overrun with overpriced boutiques and cafes, the trails through the rocks are simply spectacular.

◼ 🛈 ORIENTATION & PRACTICAL INFORMATION

Sedona lies 120 mi. north of Phoenix (take I-17 north to Rte. 179) and 30 mi. south of Flagstaff (take 89A south). The airport is tiny, with no regular flights, and neither Greyhound nor Amtrak provides service here. For the car-less, the **Sedona-Phoenix Shuttle** (☎282-2066) is one of few options, running six trips daily between the two cities ($65 round-trip). The **Sedona Chamber of Commerce**, at Forest Rd. and U.S. 89A, provides info on accommodations, camping, and local attractions. (☎282-7722. Open M-Sa 8:30am-5pm, Su 9am-3pm.) The **police** department is on the main drag, **U.S. 89A** (emergency ☎911; non-emergency ☎282-3102). At the western edge of town, the **Sedona Medical Center,** 3700 W. U.S. 89A (☎204-3000), provides medical services in the area. The **Sedona Public Library,** 3250 White Bear Rd., has free **Internet access.** (☎282-7714. One block north of U.S. 89A on Dry Creek Rd. at the west end of town. Open M 10am-8pm, Tu and Th 10am-6pm, W 10am-8pm, F-Sa 10am-5pm.) **Post office:** 190 W. U.S. 89A. (☎282-3511. Open M-F 8:45am-5pm.) **Postal code:** 86336. **Temporary employment:** Sedona's tourist businesses furnish a wealth of opportunities for short-term work in the summer season. Look for help-wanted signs in shops and restaurants, or ask directly inside.

🏠 🏕 ACCOMMODATIONS & CAMPING

Lodging in the city gets a bit pricey, so it's not a bad idea to make Sedona a daytrip from Flagstaff or Cottonwood. For those set on staying the night, there is a hostel, but prices at most other accommodations easily break the bank. Most of the camp-

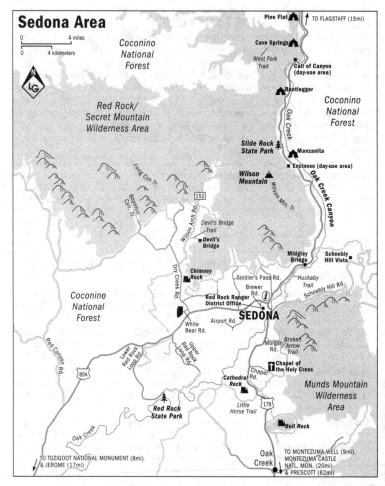

Sedona Area

0   4 miles
0   4 kilometers

Coconino National Forest

Pine Flat
TO FLAGSTAFF (15mi)

Cave Springs

West Fork Trail

Call of Canyon (day-use area)

Bootlegger

Coconino National Forest

Red Rock/ Secret Mountain Wilderness Area

Slide Rock State Park

Manzanita

Encinoso (day-use area)

Oak Creek

Wilson Mountain

Wilson Mtn. Tr.

Oak Creek Canyon

152

Long Cyn. Tr.

Boynton Cyn. Tr.

Wilson Arch Rd.

Devil's Bridge Trail

Devil's Bridge

Midgley Bridge

Schnebly Hill Vista

Chimney Rock

Soldier's Pass Rd.

Huckaby Trail

Dry Creek Rd.

Brewer Rd.

Red Rock Ranger District Office

Schnebly Hill Rd.

SEDONA

Coconino National Forest

White Bear Rd.

Airport Rd.

Broken Arrow Trail

Morgan Rd.

Lower Red Rock Loop Rd.

Upper Red Rock Loop Rd.

89A

Chapel of the Holy Cross

Chapel Rd.

Cathedral Rock

Munds Mountain Wilderness Area

Red Canyon Rd.

Red Rock State Park

Little Horse Trail

179

Oak Creek

Bell Rock

TO TUZIGOOT NATIONAL MONUMENT (8mi) & JEROME (17mi)

Oak Creek

TO MONTEZUMA-WELL (9mi), MONTEZUMA CASTLE NATL. MON. (20mi) & PRESCOTT (62mi)

sites in the area cluster around U.S. 89A as it heads north along Oak Creek Canyon en route to Flagstaff. There are private campgrounds aplenty, but most cater to the RVs rather than backpackers.

Hostel Sedona, 5 E. Soldier Wash Dr. (☎282-2772). The cheapest place to stay in town and possibly the only establishment without a trace of pretension. Set in green surroundings and featuring a full kitchen, common room with TV, and hammock, the Hostel Sedona is the best bet for budget travelers staying the night. $15, cash only. ❶

White House Inn, 2986 W. U.S. 89A (☎282-6680). One of the cheapest options in Sedona. Some singles and doubles come equipped with kitchenettes, while others have resort-like views. $47 and up. ❸

Los Abrigados Lodge, 270 N. Hwy. 89A (☎282-7125, 800-521-3131). Boasts an incredible view of surrounding carmine monoliths and has a pool and spa. Shares a location with some of Sedona's best shopping and food. Rooms from $139. ❺

IS THE FORCE WITH YOU? Could a powerful force be lurking near the Sedona airport and parks? Psychic **Page Bryant** thought so in 1980, when he divined several vortices, areas of supposed psychic and spiritual energy, around town. People who enter the vortices have claimed to have experienced episodes of extreme psychic and emotional alertness, and sometimes **spiritual healing** in the long term. Vortices have become a sensation among the New Age crowd since Bryant's discovery, and much conjecturing and scientific study on the subject has been conducted. **Extra-terrestrial meddling**, spiritual presences, high magnetism from Sedona's metal-rich rocks, and **parallel universe cross-over** have all been cited as causes. Perhaps you can unlock the mystery: the main vortices are at the airport, Bell Rock, Cathedral Rock, and Boynton Canyon.

Manzanita, Bootlegger, Cave Springs, and **Pine Flat** (☎527-360, reservations ☎877-444-6777). Four US Forest Service campgrounds between 9 and 20 mi. north of Sedona along 89A. All have similar facilities, including picnic tables, drinking water (except Bootlegger), toilets, and trash containers. 7-night max. stay. Sites $16. ❶

FOOD

Like many things in Sedona, restaurants can be expensive. But there are a few good deals to be had.

The Coffee Pot Restaurant, 2050 W. U.S. 89A (☎282-6626), a local favorite, this is the place to stop for breakfast. Serves 101 varieties of omelettes ($4-8) and Mexican lunch starting at $4. Open daily 6am-2:30pm. ❶

The Red Planet Diner, 1665 W. U.S. 89A (☎282-6070). This standard diner beams patrons in with its flying saucer and extraterrestrial allure. Martian milkshakes ($4) and Universal noodle bowls ($6-13) taste "out-of-this-world." Open daily 11am-11pm. ❷

India Palace, 1910 W. U.S. 89A (☎204-2300), in the Basha's shopping center, has a $6.50 lunch buffet with curried vegetables, tandoori chicken, and a variety of dairy-based deserts. The menu has vegetarian options and entrees under $10. Open daily 11am-2:30pm and 5-10pm. ❷

Casa Rincon, 2620 W. U.S. 89A (☎282-4849). Boasting some of the best dining in town, Rincon attracts patrons with a daily Happy Hour (3-6pm, $3 margaritas), mouthwatering combination platters ($10-13), and almost daily live entertainment. DJs, *mariachi* bands, and local entertainers fill the dance hall. Open daily 11:30am-9pm. ❷

◎ SIGHTS

RED ROCK STATE PARK. Fifteen miles west of Sedona on the well-marked Red Rock Loop Rd. on U.S. 89A, Red Rock State Park serves as a nature preserve and recreation area along a woody, secluded area of Oak Creek. Numerous trails crisscross the park and are great for wildlife watching. None of the trails is particularly challenging or steep, and no single trail is longer than 2 mi. round-trip. The Visitors Center has a brochure with detailed trail listings. In addition to the plethora of self-guided trails, rangers lead occasional interpretive hikes—bird hikes take place on Wednesday and Saturday mornings, hikes up Eagle's Nest Loop to the House of Apache Fire (a ruined chalet) on Saturday, and full moon hikes twice per cycle. No swimming or wading allowed in the park. (☎282-6907. *Visitors Center open May-Aug. daily 9am-6pm, Sept.-Apr. daily 9am-5pm. Park open Apr.-Nov. daily 8am-6pm; Oct.-Mar. 8am-5pm. $6 per car, $1 per pedestrian or cyclist.*)

CHAPEL OF THE HOLY CROSS. Lying just outside a 1000 ft. rock wall, the Chapel of the Holy Cross rests in the middle of red sandstone rock formations outside of Sedona and represents a feat of inspired architecture on the part of the Catholic community that funded its construction. A winding, paved path leads to the Chapel, where candles burn around a modern icon of Jesus. While the view from the parking lot is a religious experience itself, a look from inside is nothing short of divine. *(780 Chapel Rd. ☎ 282-4069. Open M-Sa 9am-5pm, Su 10am-5pm.)*

MONTEZUMA CASTLE NATIONAL MONUMENT. Built by the Sinagua tribe in the 12th century, this 20-room cliff dwelling was originally assumed to be an Aztec construction, and a local myth claims the Castle as Montezuma's last refuge. While it's now known that the Sinagua were unrelated to the Columbian-era Aztecs, let not the misnomer keep you from this fascinating site. Unfortunately, you can't get very close to the castle, but the view from the 0.3 mi. paved path below is excellent and wheelchair-accessible. *(10 mi. south of Sedona at exit 289 on I-17. ☎ 567-3322. Open Memorial Day to Labor Day daily 8am-7pm, otherwise 8am-5pm. $3, under 17 free.)*

TUZIGOOT NATIONAL MONUMENT. Built between 1125 and 1400, this dramatic Sinaguan building stands on a ridge and overlooks the Verde Valley. Take a break inside the reconstructed pueblo building at the top of the hill and experience the cooling effects of the architecture. *(Take U.S. 89A to Rte. 279 and continue through Cottonwood to the monument, 20 mi. southwest of Sedona. ☎ 634-5564. Open Memorial Day to Labor Day daily 8am-7pm; otherwise 8am-5pm. $3, under 17 free.)*

◪ HIKING

It's nearly impossible to go wrong with any of the well-maintained and well-marked trails in and around Sedona. Most trailheads are located on the forest service roads that snake from the highways into the hills and canyons around Sedona. Always bring water, sun protection, and appropriate clothing and food. For gear and advice, stop in at **Canyon Outfitters** (see **Rock Climbing,** p. 125).

West Fork Trail (7 mi. round-trip, 3hr.). The best way to experience the crowded Oak Creek Canyon alongside 89A between Sedona and Flagstaff is to park at Call of Canyon day-use area ($7) and hike up the west fork of the canyon. The trail begins at the canyon bottom, exposing hikers to neck-craning views early on. At times, it seems the canyon walls block every exit, but a crook in the stream always leads farther into the wilderness. Bring hiking sandals or watersocks for wading through pools and swimming holes after the trail peters out at 3.5 mi. The canyon leads another 7.5 mi. to a Forest Service road, and camping is allowed after 6 mi. (about 1½hr. past the end of the trail). Always check with a ranger before you go, since water level and weather affect safety.

FS #161—Huckaby Trail (5.2 mi. round-trip, 4hr.). This moderate trail runs between Schnebly Rd. and Midgley Bridge, crossing Oak Creek. It switchbacks down the canyon, ending under Midgley Bridge. Take Schnebly Hill Rd. from 89A; parking is on the left.

Long Canyon Trail (7.4 mi. round-trip, 4hr.). A gentle canyon hike though some stunning red-rock country. Take Dry Creek Rd. north from the 89A, turn right onto Long Canyon Rd., and park on the left at the trailhead.

Devil's Bridge Trail (1.6 mi. round-trip, 1.5hr.). Leads to a spectacular example of a Southwestern arch; not at all far from the road, but crowded. Take Dry Creek Rd. north from 89A, and turn right on Forest Service Rd. 152; park on the right at the trailhead.

Wilson Mountain Trail (10.4 mi. round-trip, 5 hr.). Park at Midgely Bridge on 89A in Oak Creek Canyon and hike up a steep canyon to the alpine meadow, offering gorgeous views of Oak Creek Canyon, the Sedona rock formations, the San Francisco Peaks, and even the Mogollon Rim. From there, continue on the Wilson Mountain Trail to the summit, and return the same way. 2300 ft. elevation gain one-way.

ARIZONA

⚡ OTHER OUTDOOR ACTIVITIES

The singular beauty of the rock formations around Sedona makes it a formidable tourist magnet. The influx of tourists means prosperity and development, but it has also resulted in intense use of all trails, roads, and facilities. Thus, the area around Sedona has been specially organized within Coconino National Forest as **Red Rock Country.** Within this area, the **Red Rock Pass** is required for parking on any of the Forest Service roads. Passes cost $5/$15/$20 for daily/weekly/annual coverage and are available at the ranger station, the tourist info office, and various local businesses. Rangers ticket vehicles parked on the forest roads that fail to display passes. For the best info about the area, visit the **Red Rock Ranger District Office,** 250 Brewer Rd. Heading north on U.S. 89A, it's the first right before Burger King. They have detailed topographical and trail maps and camping and hiking advice. (☎282-4119. Open M-F 8am-4:30pm.) Those coming up from the south might stop at the **South Gateway Visitors Center,** 7000 N. U.S. 179. (Open daily 8:30am-5pm.)

Much of Sedona's environs fall into the areas of the **Red Rock Secret Mountain Wilderness** and the **Munds Mountain Wilderness.** Be sure to pay attention to the well-marked borders between the undeveloped parts of Sedona and these wilderness areas; inside the wilderness, in addition to the Red Rock Pass requirement, strict rules protect the natural habitat. In the Red Rock Secret Mountain Wilderness Area, no backcountry camping is allowed, and mountain bikes and motorized vehicles are banned from both wilderness areas.

MOUNTAIN BIKING. In the words of one Sedona biker, Sedona singletrack unfurls like a ribbon beneath you. The red on it isn't from your blood—yet. Be humble, confer with local riders for advice, and you may even ride the heady slickrock without contributing a crimson hue of your own. **Mountain Bike Heaven,** 1695 W. U.S. 89A, is the outfitter of choice. Rentals start at $25 (front suspension; full-suspension $35) per day, and MBH leads occasional free bike trips. (☎282-1312. Open M-F 8am-6pm, Sa 8am-5pm, Su 8am-4pm.) *Cosmic Ray's* guide acts as a primer for those interested in serious biking in the area and lists a few "must do" routes. For the already toothless (or looking for cheap front-tooth removal) the rollicking Huckaby trail (see **Hiking,** p. 123) makes for an exciting, fast ride.

Along the **Broken Arrow Trail** (8 mi. round-trip, 2hr.), barrels full of rocks serve as posts. A twisty singletrack leads uphill for about 1 mi., after which several trails branch to the left, leading to a deep sinkhole and Submarine Rock along a variety of paths. Go right to continue along the trail for another several miles. At about the third mile, the trail intersects with a jeep road at a jeep loop. Two bike routes radiate from the jeep loop: the one on the right leads up to Chicken Point; the one on the left is the continuation of the trail (dubbed Little Horse), which meanders for a while to a gate. Past the gate, the trail twists around again, crossing a broader wash and sharply turning every which way. It splits off several times; stay to the left. The Little Horse trailhead comes up soon, and you've rejoined Rte. 179. An informal trail parallels 179 back to Morgan Rd. To get to the trailhead, head south on Rte. 179 for 1.3 mi. to where a broken arrow sign clearly marks the turnoff to Morgan Rd. (left from the Y-intersection). The trailhead is just down that very road, past a cattleguard.

Soldier's Pass (2.3 mi. round-trip, 1hr.) is an entire area rather than a single ride, so the maze of tracks around the trail can be very confusing. Hit the trails with one of the local bike clubs until you're familiar with the myriad tracks that criss-cross the area. The loop, however, is straight forward enough, if a bit short. From Sedona, take Soldier's Pass north until its junction with Rim Shadow Dr. Turn right and follow the main road to the parking lot (open 6am-8pm). From the parking lot, go north on a jeep road that dead-ends. A singletrack begins where the road leaves off; follow it as it winds past a scattering of pools, eventually reaching the Devil's Kitchen sinkhole. From here, the trail bears left, back to the parking lot.

ROCK CLIMBING. The rock formations that punctuate the Sedona landscape provide ample opportunities for aspiring spider-men. Finding some of the more out-of-the-way places (and making the most of the obvious ones) may require some expert advice. **Canyon Outfitters,** 2701 W. U.S. 89A, can provide just that. (☎282-5294. Open M-F 9am-6pm, Sa 9am-5pm, Su 11am-4pm.) David, the climbing expert there, self-publishes the *Red Lizard Guide Book,* giving exact details and directions to the climbing areas around Sedona. Bouldering is best at **Anvil Wall** (5.6-5.11) in the **Uptown Crags** area, reachable via Schnebly Hill Rd. Park at the Huckaby Trailhead and follow the trail for less than a mile before a turnoff leads left to the large climbing area. On their own, Uptown Crags make for good sport climbing, with pitches from 5.8 and up.

Traditional leading and top-roping is found in massive overload (literally hundreds of problems from 5.3-5.13 concentrated in a few hundred yards) at **Overlook,** a long cliff band in Oak Creek Canyon. Take 89A north of town to parking at the Oak Creek Vista pull-off and follow the access trail from there. Excellent traditional problems also await at **Coffeepot Crags.** To reach the crags and their highlight, **Dr. Rubo's Wild Ride** (5.9), take Soldier's Pass Rd. to the terminus, park your ride, and go left on foot. Perhaps the most dramatic pinnacles are the ruddy, topheavy formations of **Cathedral Rock,** which, while intimidating, are surprisingly doable for the intermediate traditional climber. **The Mace** at Cathedral Rock is rated 5.9+ and includes a leap-across that takes the climber from one pinnacle down 12 ft. and across 6 ft. to another, landing on a ledge over 400 ft. in the air.

DRIVING. Scenic driving is nearly as plentiful as the red rocks, and the Chamber of Commerce is helpful in suggesting routes. The Red Rock Loop (20 mi., 1hr.) provides views of mind-blowing rock formations and some dirt road adventure. Dry Creek and Airport Rd. are also good drives. For those hoping to see Sedona's wild off-road side, jeep tours are available from several of companies. **Pink Jeep Tours,** 276 N. U.S. 89A, offers rides in their ubiquitous pink jeeps modified for off-roading. *(☎ 282-3500. Trips run about $35-75, and last 2-4hr.)*

PRESCOTT
☎928

Prescott has been known to call itself "Everyone's Hometown." It lives up to its claim—from the town green to the town hall, Prescott radiates American small-town charm. At the same time, it revels in its "westerness:" ten-gallon hats are common fashion accessories, and the main drag is nicknamed "Whiskey Row." Perhaps the most appealing attraction is the nearby Prescott National Forest, with its wealth of hiking, mountain biking, climbing, and camping opportunities, all within easy reach of Prescott's services and inexpensive accommodations.

■ ⁊ **ORIENTATION & PRACTICAL INFORMATION.** The junction of Rte. 69 and U.S. 89 form the basis for Prescott's street system. Upon its entry into town, Rte. 69 is dubbed Gurley Street, while U.S. 89 carries the names **Montezuma Street** and **White Spar Road.** The city's green, Courthouse Plaza, the concentration of its older, more stately buildings, and the popular Whiskey Row center on the intersection of these major streets. Tourist information can be found at Prescott's **Chamber of Commerce** along Whiskey Row. (☎445-2000, 800-266-7534. Open M-F 9am-5pm, Sa-Su 10am-2pm). Wilderness info and trail maps are available at the **Forest Service Office,** 344 S. Cortez St., the street just before Montezuma inbound from Phoenix.

(Open M-F 8am-4:30pm.) Other services include: the **police** on S. Marina St. (☎778-1444), close to downtown; **emergency** (☎911); the **Yavapai Regional Medical Center**, 1003 Willow Creek Rd. (☎445-2700); the **library**, 215 E. Goodwin St. (☎777-1500), with free **Internet access;** and the post office, next to the Chamber of Commerce on Whiskey Row. (Open 8:30am-5pm.) **Postal code:** 86302.

⌐⌐ ACCOMMODATIONS & FOOD. The only inexpensive accommodations available in town are the hotels around Gurley St. All motels have lower prices Monday through Thursday, while weekend prices rise considerably, especially on holiday weekends. Call ahead to determine weekend prices, which can vary tremendously. **The Colony Inn ❷**, 1225 E. Gurley St., is affordable and comfortable. (☎800-350-3782. M-Th singles $33, doubles $38. Continental breakfast.) **The Heritage House ❷**, 819 E. Gurley St., presents another reasonably inexpensive option. (☎445-9091. Singles $35, doubles $40.) Make Granite Basin your base of operations and you can enjoy great camping at the **Yavapai Campground ❶**. Take Montezuma north past where it becomes Iron Springs, then right on Granite Basin Rd. (25 sites. Max. stay 14 days. $10. Water and toilets.)

El Charro ❷, 120 N. Montezuma St., is an unpretentious Mexican eatery with hearty meals and $6 lunch specials. (☎445-7130. Open daily 11am-9pm, lunch specials 11am-2pm.) A community lunch spot, the **Prescott Pantry ❶**, 1201 Iron Springs Rd., serves delicious salads, sandwiches, and juicy local gossip. (☎778-4280. Open M-F 8am-5:30pm, Sa 8am-4:30pm.) The **Gurley Street Grill ❷**, 230 W. Gurley St., is a popular spot with tourists and locals alike, featuring delicious breadsticks, several vegetarian options, and yuppie favorites. (☎445-3388. Open daily 11am-midnight.)

◙ SIGHTS. The **Sharlot Hall Museum,** 415 W. Gurley St., preserves the history of Prescott, which was once upon a time the capital of the entire Arizona Territory. The museum was founded by Sharlot Mabridth Hall, a local historian, one-time member of the Electoral College (her vote went to Calvin Coolidge), and inductee into the Arizona Women's Hall of Fame. Fascinating exhibits on local Native American peoples and frontier life are housed in 19th- and early 20th-century log cabins set in a garden. (☎520-445-3122. Open Apr.-Oct. M-Sa 10am-5pm, Su 1-5pm; Nov.-Mar. M-Sa 10am-4pm, Su 1-5pm. $5 suggested donation.) **Arcosanti,** an experimental city sitting 35 mi. west of Prescott off of I-17, invites architects, environmentalists, and curious explorers to Paolo Soleri's inventive project. The goal of the city is to create a living environment that optimally fuses with the surrounding natural environment. Under construction since 1970, Arcosanti employs revolutionary architecture to reach its ends. The building materials are modern materials—concrete, steel and insulation—but are used in a more artful way than at many of the expensive modern showcase buildings in L.A. and New York. Come for a visit, or stay to volunteer. (☎632-7135; www.arcosanti.org. Visitors Center open daily 9am-5pm. Tours daily every hr. 10am-4pm. $8 donation requested.)

⫶ OUTDOOR ACTIVITIES. Set in the higher ground of mountainous northern Arizona, the **Prescott National Forest** is the main attraction, providing a remarkable climatic change from the hotter and drier country to the south and plenty of opportunities for hiking, biking, climbing, and camping. Laura and Mike at **Granite Mountain Outfitters,** 320 W. Gurley St., sell gear and know where to go for hiking and climbing. (☎776-4949. Open M-F 9am-5:30pm, Sa 1:30-4pm.) Bikers should stop in at **High Gear,** 505 E. Sheldon, for last-minute gear and helpful trail tips. (☎445-8417. Open M-Sa 9am-5:30pm.) Visit the Forest Service Office (see **Orientation and Practical Information,** p. 125) for info, maps, and to find out about the $2 parking fee most Prescott outdoor recreation areas charge (Wednesdays are free).

A popular **hike** with a view is the **Spruce Mountain Lookout** (8.7 mi. round-trip, 1200 ft. gain, 5hr.). Take Mt. Vernon south from Gurley St.; after it turns into Senator Highway, look for the Spruce Mountain Loop Trailhead. The other notable mountain trail in the area ascends **Granite Mountain** (7 mi. round-trip, 1600 ft. gain, 4hr.). Take Montezuma north from town; after it becomes Iron Springs, and turn right on Granite Basin Rd. A short but impressive hike is the **Thumb Butte Trail,** a steep, paved path up the town's landmark rock formation (1.4 mi. round-trip, 1.5hr.). Gurley St. going west becomes Thumb Butte Rd., and a large Forest Service recreation area marks the trailhead.

A good intermediate **mountain biking** area is the **Granite Basin Loop** system, about 12 mi. of trail providing 3hr. of good riding. Any rider will enjoy the fast, easy trail system surrounding **Thumb Butte,** and any number of short combos are possible. **Spruce Mountain Lookout** is a more serious ride; alot about 2hr.

Bouldering awaits in abundance at the **Groom Creek** climbing area south of town. Follow directions to **Spruce Mountain Loop,** then take Forest Service Road 307 north to the boulders. The beautiful, rounded rocks surrounding Watson Lake form the eminently sport-climbable **Watson Lake Dells,** with a wide range of difficulties. Take U.S. 89 north and turn right on Willow Lake Rd.; park at its end ($2). **Thumb Butte,** noted for its easy hiking and riding, also offers sport and traditional routes, but only outside of the February to mid-July Peregrine Falcon nesting season. Call rangers or the outfitters listed above for details. World-class traditional climbing (which regularly attracts European climbers) on **Granite Mountain** is also subject to the peregrinations of local falcons, but it's worth the wait.

PETRIFIED FOREST NATIONAL PARK ☎928

Sixty thousand acres of technicolor formations, chiseled stone ramparts, and countless stands of glistening, petrified trees draw countless visitors to the park annually, and for good reason—this geological peculiarity feels like a fantasyland. Some 225 million years ago, when Arizona's desert was a swampland, volcanic ash covered the logs, slowing their decay. When silica-rich water seeped through the wood, the silica crystallized into quartz, producing rainbow hues. Layers of colorful sediment were also laid down in this floodplain, creating the stunning colors that stripe its rock formations.

When a route for the transcontinental railroad was being scouted in the mid-1800s, surveyors stumbled across this incredible region. Within a few years of the building of the railroad, the "forest" became a prime attraction for sightseers and collectors. In the decades that followed, thousands of tons of rock were removed to accommodate visitors. Local residents recognized that the supply of petrified wood was not limitless. In 1906, the area was designated a national monument, and in 1962, it was made a national park. A unique attraction in the Southwest, the park welcomes over half a million visitors per year. Still, much of the solitude of this magical world is preserved just out of sight of the park drive and waits to be explored by those willing to get off the beaten track.

■ ⑦ ORIENTATION & PRACTICAL INFORMATION. Roughly speaking, the **Painted Desert National Park** can be divided into two parts: the northern **Painted Desert** and the southern **Rainbow Desert.** An entrance station and Visitors Center welcomes guests at each end, and a 28 mi. road connects the two sections. With lookout points and trails at intervals along the road, driving from one end of the park to the other is a good way to absorb the spectrum of colors and landscapes.

You can enter the park either from the north or the south. (Open summer 7am-7pm, call for off-season hours. Entrance fee $10 per vehicle, $5 per pedestrian; $5 motorcycle.) **Amtrak** and **Greyhound** both run through **Winslow** and **Gallup, NM;** buses also stop at the Circle K in **Holbrook.** To access the southern section of the park, take U.S. 180 from St. Johns 36 mi. west or from Holbrook 19 mi. east. Holbrook is a major stopover town on I-40 and offers travelers a full range of services. The **Rainbow Forest Museum** provides a look at petrified logs up close and serves as a **Visitors Center.** (☎524-6822. Open daily 7am-7pm. Free.) To reach the northern section of the park, take I-40 to exit 311, 107 mi. east of Flagstaff and 65 mi. west of Gallup, NM. The **Painted Desert Visitors Center** is less than 1 mi. from the exit and shows a video overview of the park every 30 min. (☎524-6228. Open summers daily 7am-7pm; call for off-season hours.) **Water** is available at both the Visitors Centers and the Painted Desert Inn. There's **gas** at the Painted Desert Visitors Center. In case of **emergency,** call the ranger dispatch (☎524-9726).

⚑⛶ ACCOMMODATIONS & FOOD. There are no established campgrounds in the park, but **backcountry camping** is allowed in the fantastical Painted Desert Wilderness with a free permit. Backpackers must park their cars at Kachina Point and enter the wilderness via the 1 mi. access trail. No fires are allowed. For the less mobile, **free camping** is also allowed at the **Crystal Forest Museum and Gifts,** a private trading post just outside the park boundaries at the junction of U.S. 180 and the park road. (☎524-3500. Bathrooms and payphones.)

From Gallup to the park, Rte. 66 ambiance and services essentially disappear beneath the ever-encroaching desert, but the road rises again at full strength in Holbrook, 26 mi. west of the park, where budget accommodations and roadside diners abound. Visitors and journalists from around the world fight to stay at the **Wigwam Motel ❸,** 811 W. Hopi Dr., where 15 concrete tepees have awaited travelers for half a century. Take exit 286 from I-40 south on Navajo Blvd. and turn right at Hopi Dr. (☎524-3048; clewis97@apartrails.com. Reception 4-9pm. Check-out 11am. Singles $42; doubles $48. Reservations highly recommended.)

You can experience another Rte. 66 fixture by hitchin' your horse (or, for that matter, your fuel-efficient hatchback) at **Joe and Aggie's Cafe ❷,** 120 W. Hopi Dr., where the Mexican specialties ($4-9) are hard to beat. (☎524-6540. Open M-Sa 7am-8pm.) **Gallup,** NM (p. 418), and **Flagstaff,** AZ (p. 111), offer more plentiful lodging and eating options.

◰⛰ SIGHTS & OUTDOORS. Most travelers opt to drive the 28 mi. park road from north to south, since the northern Visitors Center offers an explanatory video, but the trip is magnificent in either direction. While it isn't necessary to park and get out at every one, visiting a couple of the many viewpoints gives a good impression of the colorful expanse in the north. The **Painted Desert Inn** (open daily 9am-5pm) at **Kachina Point** is a National Historic Landmark that houses a small, interesting museum but no longer lodges guests. The panoramas from Kachina Point are among the best in the park, and the point provides access for travel into the **Painted Desert Wilderness,** the park's designated region for backcountry hiking and camping. There are **no trails** in the wilderness, and no permits are required for day hikes. The half-day **Black Forest** hiking route exposes hikers to petroglyphs; **Alpha Stump,** one of the few intact tree stumps in the park; and **Onyx Bridge,** a petrified tree bridging a ravine. Begin at Kachina Point and take the 1 mi. trail to the wilderness, then simply bear north through the washes for another 2 mi. When to turn around is strictly up to the hiker, since trails don't last long in the shifting sands of the northern wilderness. For an overnighter to remote **Pilot Rock** (6234 ft.), take the Kachina Point wilderness access trail, but bear northwest instead, skirting the badlands. Head west for a couple of miles, then straight north through the badlands another few miles to the rock. The round-trip runs about 16 mi. As with all off-trail wilderness travel, bring a topographic map (available at both Visitors Centers), a compass, and learn to use them before trying either of these hikes.

As the road crosses I-40, it enters the Petrified Forest portion of the park. The next stop is the 100-room **Puerco Pueblo,** which was built by ancient pueblo peoples sometime before AD 1400. A short trail through the pueblo offers viewpoints of nearby petroglyphs. Many more petroglyphs may be seen at **Newspaper Rock,** but from a greater distance. Be sure to notice the incredible petrified tree cross-section encased in rock above and to the left of the glyphs.

The road then wanders through the eerie moonscape of **The Tepees** before arriving at the 3 mi. **Blue Mesa** vehicle loop. This area exhibits some of the park's wildest geology. Brilliant blue clay hills are mixed with tree fragments in a sort of impressionist's daydream. The moderate **Blue Mesa Trail** (1 mi.) loops through the belly of the badlands and offers respite from the cars and crowds. Farther south is the **Crystal Forest Trail** (.8 mi.), which survived early looters' scavenging relatively unscathed, while the overlook at **Jasper Forest** provides views of an area that saw heavy looting by souvenir seekers around the turn of the 19th century. **Giant Logs Trail,** right out of the southern Visitors Center, features **Old Faithful,** which at over 9 ft. in diameter is the largest tree in the park. Picking up fragments of the wood is illegal and traditionally unlucky; if the cops don't get you, the demons will. Those who *must* have a piece can buy one at any of the myriad kitschy stores along I-40. The wood proffered here comes from private land containing petrified remains.

NAVAJO RESERVATION   ☎928

Although anthropologists believe the Navajo are descended from groups of Athabascan people who migrated to the Southwest from Northern Canada in the 14th and 15th centuries, the Navajo themselves view their existence as the culmination of a journey through three other worlds to this life, the "Glittering World." Four sacred mountains bound Navajoland—Mt. Blanca to the east, Mt. Taylor to the south, San Francisco Peak to the west, and Mt. Hesperus to the north. The largest reservation in the United States, Navajoland extends from the northeast corner of Arizona into Utah and Arizona and borders the San Juan River's south side. All of it is considered holy.

During the second half of the 19th century, Indian reservations evolved out of the US government's *ad hoc* attempts to prevent fighting between Native Americans and Anglos while facilitating white settlement of native lands. Initially, the reservation system imposed a kind of wardship over the Native Americans, which lasted for over a century until a series of Supreme Court decisions beginning in the

ARIZONA

RESERVATION RULES. For visitors to the reservation, cultural sensitivity takes on a new importance; despite the many state and interstate roads that traverse the reservation, the land is legally and culturally distinct. Superficially, much of the Navajo Nation and other reservations resemble the rest of the US. In reality, Native Americans prefer that Anglos—the term used to refer to the non-reservation US society— consider themselves guests on the reservation and act accordingly. The reservation, a blend of modern and traditional life, has its own police force and laws. Driving or hiking off designated trails and established routes is considered trespassing unless done with a guide. Possession and consumption of alcohol are prohibited on the reservation. General photography is allowed unless otherwise stated, but photographing the Navajo people requires their permission (a gratuity is usually expected). Tourist photography is not permitted among the Hopi. As always, the best remedy for cultural friction is simple respect, since no hard and fast rules are clearly stated.

1960s reasserted the tribes' legal standing as semi-sovereign nations. Today, the **Navajo Nation** is the largest reservation in America and covers more than 27,000 square miles of northeastern Arizona, southeastern Utah, and northwestern New Mexico. Home to over 250,000 Navajo, or Dineh ("the People") as they call themselves, the reservation comprises one-tenth of the US Native American population. Within the Navajo borders, the smaller **Hopi Reservation** is home to around 10,000 Hopi ("Peaceable People").

Local news and events are written up in the Navajo Times. For a taste of the Navajo language and Native American ritual songs, tune your **radio** to 660AM, "The Voice of the Navajo." Remember to advance your watch 1hr. during the summer; the Navajo Nation runs on **Mountain Daylight Time,** while the rest of Arizona, including the Hopi Reservation, does not observe daylight savings and thus operates on Pacific Time during the warmer months and Mountain Standard Time during the cooler months. The **area codes** for the reservation are ☎ 928 in Arizona, 505 in New Mexico, 435 in Utah.

Monument Valley, Canyon de Chelly, Navajo National Monument, Rainbow Bridge, Antelope Canyon, and the roads and trails that access these sights all lie on Navajo land. Those planning to hike through Navajo territory should head to the parks and recreation department for a backcountry permit or mail a request along with a money order or certified check to Navajo Parks and Recreation Department, P.O. Box 9000, Window Rock, AZ 86515 (☎ 928-871-6647. $5 per person). The "border towns" of Gallup, NM (p. 418), and Flagstaff, AZ (p. 111) are good gateways to the reservations, with car rental agencies, inexpensive accommodations, and frequent Greyhound service on I-40. Budget travelers can camp at the National Monuments or Navajo campgrounds, or stay in one of the student-run motels in high schools around the reservation.

CANYON DE CHELLY ☎928

The red-hued cliffs of Canyon de Chelly ("D'SHAY") national monument and the explorable surrounding canyons have a remarkable history, having served as a home to native peoples for almost five millennia. The Archaic, Basketmaker, Ancestral Puebloan, Hopi, and, finally, the Navajo have all utilized the protection offered by the cliffs and the rich soil of the canyon floor. However, like much of the region, Canyon de Chelly's history has been spotted with repeated conflicts between Native Americans and Anglos. In 1805, in what is now called Massacre Cave, 115 women and children were shot by Spanish soldiers. In the 1860s, the famed Kit Carson starved the Navajo out of the canyon in order to displace them to central New Mexico.

■ ▞ **ORIENTATION & PRACTICAL INFORMATION.** The most common route to the park is from **Chambers,** 80 mi. south, at the intersection of I-40 and U.S. 191; you can also come from the north via U.S. 191. The monument sits 3 mi. east of **Chinle** on Navajo Rte. 7. One of the larger towns on the reservation, Chinle, at the intersection of Navajo Rte. 7 and U.S. 191, has ATMs, gas stations, grocery stores, laundromats, restaurants, a hospital, and a post office. A number of **Navajo Transit System** (☎ 729-4002) buses run daily from there with limited service to Flagstaff, AZ, Farmington, NM, and Gallup, NM. The monument is also accessible via Navajo Rte. 64 out of **Tsaile,** 28 mi. northeast of the Visitors Center. The monument's **Visitors Center** is a good resource and provides sign-up sheets for the guided tours; it's also the place to fill up on water (☎ 674-5500. Open daily 8am-5pm). In an **emergency,** contact the park ranger (☎ 674-5500, after hours 674-5523).

▛ ▞ **ACCOMMODATIONS & CAMPING.** Camp for free in the monument's **Cottonwood Campground ❶,** a half a mile from the Visitors Center. This giant camp-

Native peoples in modern times

Even today tourists harbor images of the American Indians (also appropriately referred to as "Indians" or "Native Americans") of the Southwest frozen in time, typically locked somewhere in the 1880s. Rife with pottery, rug weaving, and jingle dancing, this romanticized portrait is largely the product of Hollywood films of 30s-50s. These movies portrayed Indians either as skilled artisans practicing ancient art forms in serene teepee villages, or as ruthless "savages" fighting the "white man" and his family. This is not to say that traditional arts and crafts are no longer important in Indian Country. Any traveler who visits the Santa Fe Indian Market and Albuquerque's Gathering of Nations Powwow can experience firsthand the immense value of artistic expression in the Southwest's Indian culture. But these public forums, not to mention the celluloid stereotype, do not begin to capture the complete story of the Southwest's Indians.

Without question, clashes between the US and the Indian nations throughout history have left the tribes in tremendously disadvantaged conditions. For the Indians, the legacy of this struggle includes a litany of social and economic ills, including higher rates of poverty, alcohol addiction, and unemployment; lower rates of homeownership, home quality, and educational attainment; and lower life expectancies than those of virtually all their non-Indian neighbors. Despite these obstacles, Indian people are building sovereign nations that are increasingly exercising real decision-making power over their natural resources, social agendas, and governmental bodies. Indians are constructing efficient governments, diversifying their economic and social enterprises, and drawing upon unique cultural resources, both traditional (such as arts and crafts) and contemporary.

For anyone seeking to understand and appreciate the Indians of the Southwest, the land itself of Indian Country offers much to be uncovered. Through treaties, acts of war, the division of tribal lands, and the subsequent fragmentation of individual landholdings, the land under Indian control has in many cases shrunk to the point that it is no longer an asset for any kind of socioeconomic development. Of course, to many Indians, their connection with the land goes far deeper than economic concerns. According to

noted author Keith Basso, "the people's sense of place, their sense of their tribal past, and their vibrant sense of themselves are inseparably intertwined." Though greatly diminished, there are still significant tribal landholdings in the Southwest, and taking time to see the lands—whether by foot, bike, horseback, or car—is the first critical step toward understanding Indian culture. Experiencing the harsh and rugged beauty of Indian Country is a first step to seeing life through the eyes of those who live there.

There are no better teachers of modern Indian culture than the people living in, the individuals you meet at the markets, coffee shops, and roadside stands. Many travelers unused to conditions of poverty find the abject privation of some Indian communities unsettling; be prepared to adjust your expectations in anticipation of reservation poverty. Once acclimated, spend an afternoon shooting hoops with the future of the Native Nations, the basketball-crazed youth who hone their skills upon hardwood courts bearing tribal insignia. Talk to the elders, who, when outsiders are willing to listen, are often open to sharing their triumphs and struggles. While some legends and histories are withheld strictly for members of the Indian community, there is still much to learn from those with the knowledge.

Gaining a more complete picture of Indian life in today's Southwest is a demanding undertaking, and it is unlikely that any traveler could amass, even in a lifetime, a thorough understanding of the region's disparate groups of Indians. But there is a picture more complete than that of simple artisans or "savage, bloodthirsty heathens" trapped in the images of the 1950s silver screen, and more complete than that of people endlessly trapped in destitution, to be discovered on the Southwest's tribal lands, if one only knows how to look. An understanding of the complex, resilient, and modern people that comprise the Southwestern Indians requires the time to look and listen, a desire to diverge from the beaten path, and, most importantly, the courage to potentially find oneself lost far from the nearest paved road. Your reward awaits you both in the unique landscape of the Southwest and in the folkways of the Indian people who, despite seeing much of their land and way of life disappear, remain deeply connected to what remains.

Eric Henson is a member of the Chickasaw Nation and a Research Fellow at the Harvard Project on American Indian Economic Development. He currently works as a senior consultant at Lexecon, Inc.

WHAT LANGUAGE IS THIS? After the release of the Nicholas Cage vehicle *Windtalkers* (2002), an odd sort of fame emerged for the **Navajo Code Talkers** of the US Marine Corps. With the bombing of Pearl Harbor in December 1941 and subsequent outbreak of hostilities, the skill and implications of Japanese code-breaking were readily apparent. In looking for a code that would stymie Japanese efforts, the US military turned to a number of young men from the Navajo Reservation. Initially, 29 Navajos were enlisted into the elite ranks of the code talkers, and by the end of the war over 400 men had entered the US Marines to make up this vital communications web in the Pacific. The code was critical to the success of a number of US engagements, including the victory at Iwo Jima, and was never broken by the Japanese. You can visit an exhibit commemorating the actions of these courageous men at the **Burger King**, of all places, along Rte. 160 in **Kayenta.**

ground rests in a lovely cottonwood grove and benefits from strong breezes. (☎674-5500. 96 sites. Restrooms, picnic tables, water except in winter, and dump station. 5-night max. stay. First come, first served; no reservations.) If Cottonwood is full, **Spider Rock Campground ❶**, 8 mi. southeast of the Visitors Center near the Spider Rock turnoff, is quieter and at a higher elevation (over 6,000 ft.), offering 40 primitive sites near the canyon rim. (☎674-8261. Sites $10, reservations accepted.) The **Many Farms Inn ❷**, 16 mi. north of Chinle and a quarter of a mile north of the intersection of Navajo Rte. 59 and U.S. 191, serves as a stopover from Canyon de Chelly to Monument Valley or Navajo National Monument. Housed in the local high school, the rooms are a bit institutional and have shared bathrooms, but you won't find a better deal in Navajo Nation. (☎781-6362. Open June-Aug. daily, Sept.-May M-F. Reception 7am-10pm. Check-out noon. Doubles $30.) **Gallup**, NM (p. 418), **Farmington**, NM, and **Cortez, CO** (p. 354) also provide cheap lodgings.

⚠ RIM DRIVES. The paved Rim Drives that skirt the edges of the canyon's precipitous cliffs are the easiest way to see the canyon. Although the drives are less intense than plunging into the canyon on foot, in a four-wheel-drive vehicle, or on the back of a trusty steed (through any of the many horseback riding companies catering to the monument), they still capture the panoramic glory of the monument. The **North Rim** (34 mi. round-trip) and the **South Rim** (37 mi. round-trip), both open year-round, take a few hours to appreciate fully. Booklets on the drives ($1) are available at the Visitors Center. Make sure to lock your car and take valuables with you, as thefts have been reported at the overlooks.

The first stops on the North Rim Drive are the two viewpoints that comprise **Ledge Ruin Overlook.** While the ruins are not as spectacular as some of the others in the canyon, the spot provides excellent views of the fields of corn, pumpkin, melon, and squash that the Navajo have cultivated over hundreds of years. The next turnoff leads to the **Antelope House Overlook** and its two viewpoints. To the west, the impressive Antelope House Ruin is tucked underneath an overhang on the canyon floor, and to the east at the junction between Canyon del Muerto and Black Rock Canyon stands the **Navajo Fortress,** a buttress where Navajo warriors held off Kit Carson and his troops for several months in the 1860s. The last turnoff on the North Rim Drive heads out to the **Mummy Cave,** the monument's best introduction to the archaeological significance of the canyons, and **Massacre Cave Overlooks.** The large dwellings in Mummy Cave Ruin done in the mesa verde style are a testament to the architectural know-how of the Ancestral Puebloans. Two mummified bodies were found here in the central tower. From the overlook it is easy to see the predicament of the Navajo trapped in Massacre Cave. Fifteen miles north of this last overlook turnoff is the small town of Tsaile.

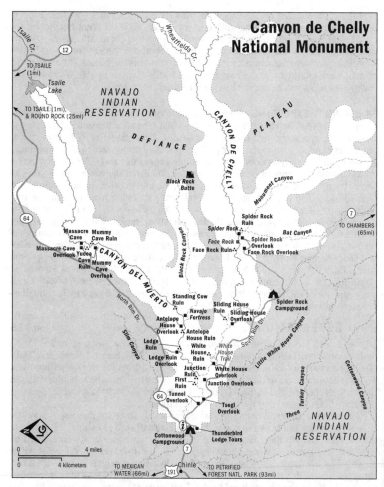

Canyon de Chelly National Monument

The South Rim Drive first passes the **Tunnel Overlook,** which is the starting point of many guided hikes into the canyon but offers only a narrow view of the inner canyon. Entry is not permitted through the Tunnel Overlook trailhead without an authorized guide. The next turn-out is the **Tsegi Overlook,** which gives an impression of the immense space inside the canyon. The views of the confluence of Canyon del Muerto and Canyon de Chelly from **Junction Overlook** are among the most spectacular in the entire monument. The next stop is the **White House Overlook,** which serves as trailhead for the fantastic **White House Trail** and is a great viewpoint in its own right. The moderate 3 mi. round-trip trail is the only way to enter the canyon without a guide and is well worth the couple of hours it takes to descend five switchbacks (600 ft.) to the ancient dwellings and grunt your way back up. Bring water, and save the overlook until afterwards to preserve the suspense of the hike. At **Sliding House Overlook,** you can see a cliff dwelling losing its battle against gravity as it actually slides off its ledge. A bit farther along the South

Rim Drive, the inconspicuous **Face Rock Overlook** is difficult to see without binoculars but provides views of four different dwellings, all at different heights on the cliff. **Spider Rock Overlook,** the last stop on the South Rim Drive, affords great views of a narrow sandstone monolith towering 800 ft. above the canyon floor. Native American lore says the whitish rock at the top contains the bleached bones of victims of what is known as the kachina spirit to the Hopi or Spider Woman to the Navajo, who has a taste for the blood of disobedient children.

■ **HIKING & EXPLORING.** To explore the floor of the canyon beyond the White House Trail (see The Rim Drives), visitors must hire an **authorized guide**; reservations can be made through the Visitors Center. Two hikes led by Navajo guides enter the canyon. (4 mi. round-trip. 4hr. June-Aug. daily 9am. $15 per person.) Traveling on the canyon floor is an incredible experience and offers a perspective on the terrain that cannot be matched on the rim. From the canyon floor you can see petroglyphs, pictographs, hanging gardens and greater detail in the ruins. Guided tours also provide access to dwellings not visible from the canyon rim, including a better view of Massacre Cave. Guides for hikes and vehicle tours of the canyon can be hired through **Tsegi Guide Association.** (☎ 674-5500. 3hr. min. $15 per hr. You provide the four-wheel-drive vehicle. Required permit free at Visitors Center.) If you don't have four-wheel-drive, **De Chelly Tours** (☎ 674-3772) and **Thunderbird Lodge Canyon Tours** (☎ 674-5841 or 800-679-2473) offer tours for $43 per person per half day in trucks which hold up to 24 people. **Justin's Horse Rental,** located on South Rim Dr. at the canyon's mouth, offers horseback tours. (☎ 674-5678. Open daily 9am-sundown. Horses $10 per hr., mandatory guide $15 per hr. 2hr. min. Reservations advised.)

HOPI RESERVATION   ☎ 928

Like an island mountain on a Navajo nation ocean, Black Mesa, so-called for its dark-colored vegetation and its three spurs (First Mesa, Second Mesa, and Third Mesa), has harbored the Hopi people and its traditions for over a millennium. Today inhabitants of the Hopi Reservation continue to live in the mesa-top villages their ancestors founded in the AD 900s and practice the techniques of dry farming that have been passed down from generation to generation.

Exploring the reservation requires a car, especially since the nearest transportation is the trains and buses that run through **Flagstaff** (p. 111) about 100 mi. from the villages, and **Winslow,** about 60 mi. away. The three mesas are connected by Rte. 264, which runs east-west between Rts. 160 and 191, and rely on the services provided by the modern towns of **Polacca** and **Kykotsmovi,** which lie beneath them. From the south, Rts. 2, 87, and 77 are all stunning scenic drives to the reservation. On Second Mesa, the **Hopi Cultural Center,** 7 mi. west of the intersection of Rte. 264 and 87, serves as a Visitors Center and contains the reservation's only **museum,** displaying Hopi baskets, jewelry, pottery, and info about the tribe's history. (☎ 734-2401. Open M-F 8am-5pm, Sa-Su 9am-3pm. $3, under 14 $1.) **Free camping** is allowed at ten primitive sites, some with picnic tables, next to the Cultural Center. The Hopi Reservation, like the rest of Arizona, stays on **Mountain Standard Time** throughout the year. **No cameras** are allowed on the reservation.

The villages on **First Mesa** are the only places in the reservation geared toward visitors. To reach the mesa top, take Rte. 264 into Polacca and follow the signs. The **Ponsi Hall Community Center** serves as a general info center and a starting point for **guided tours.** The 30-60min. tours depart throughout the day and venture to the precarious **Walpi,** perched on the southern tip of the mesa. (☎ 737-2262. Open June-Aug. daily 9am-6pm; Sept.-May 9:30am-5pm. Tours $5.) The villages on the **Second** and **Third Mesas** are even less developed for tourism. They each feature shops and stalls hawking beautiful Hopi art, including elaborately detailed kachina dolls which sell for hundreds of dollars. On the Third Mesa, **Old Oraibi** has been home to the Hopi since the early AD 1100s and challenges a few New Mexican pueblos for the title of oldest continuously inhabited village in the US.

Visitors are welcome to attend a few Hopi **village dances** throughout the year. Often announced only a few days in advance, these religious ceremonies usually occur on weekends and last from sunrise to sundown. The dances are formal occasions; do not wear shorts, tank tops, or other casual wear. Photos, recordings, and sketches are strictly forbidden. Often several villages will hold dances on the same day, giving tourists the opportunity to village-hop. The **Social** and **Butterfly Dances,** held in the fall around Labor Day, are a good bet for tourists. The spectacular **Harvest Dance** of mid-September at the Second Mesa Village brings together tribes from all over the US; admission is free. Inquire at the cultural center.

NAVAJO NATIONAL MONUMENT ☎928

This small portion of the vast Tsegi Canyon system packs a big punch with two of the best-preserved Ancestral Puebloan cliff dwellings in the Southwest: Betatakin and Keet Seel. In the second half of the 13th century, a small population of the ancestors of the modern Hopi inhabited these intricate dwellings and farmed the fertile canyon floors. Despite all the work put into their construction, drought left the villages vacant by AD 1300. In the hundreds of years that followed, these architectural wonders were left undisturbed. Around the turn of the 19th century, the dwellings were "discovered" by white fortune-hunters and looted to fulfill the growing demand for prehistoric Southwestern artifacts. In the face of this threat, President Warren G. Harding designated the area a national monument in 1909, effectively sealing the sites from further destruction. The remoteness of these dwellings, which had preserved their integrity for hundreds of years, today has a similar effect, making the Navajo National Monument a fantastic place to escape into the quieter regions of Navajoland while viewing the full extent of Ancestral Puebloan architecture.

🚩 PRACTICAL INFORMATION. From U.S. 160, 20 mi. southwest of **Kayenta** and 50 mi. northeast of **Tuba City**, Rte. 564 travels 9 mi. north to the monument entrance and Visitors Center, which provides helpful info and houses a number of exhibits. (☎672-2700. Open daily 8am-5pm.) The **Black Mesa general store,** (☎677-3322. Open daily 9am-5pm.) at the junction of Rts. 564 and 160, has groceries but no ATM. The Visitors Center and the campground have **water**. The monument broadcasts **weather** and **road conditions** on 1610AM. No ground fires are allowed. In case of **emergency**, call ☎697-5600.

The free **Navajo Campground ❶** next to the Visitors Center is a forested refuge and a welcome relief in the summer from the heat of the flatlands. It has only 31 sites, but there's an additional overflow campground nearby. (First come, first served. 7-day max. stay. No hookups or running water.) A quick 50 mi. east in Tuba City, the **Grey Hills Inn ❸**, less than 1 mi. east on Rte. 160 from the intersection of Rts. 264 and 160, offers motel rooms with shared bathrooms. (☎283-4450. Reception 24hr. Singles $49, doubles $54. Rates somewhat negotiable.) Finally, the new **Anasazi Inn ❸** is a clean, well-appointed option for those looking to visit Monument Valley or hike in the national monument. (☎697-3793. Singles approximately $50. Reception 24hr. Located within eyesight of the monument entrance.)

◙ SIGHTS. The monument contains three cliff dwellings: **Inscription House** has been closed since the 1960s due to its fragile condition but may reopen in the next few years; the other two sites, **Betatakin** and **Keet Seel**, admit a limited number of visitors. The stunning Keet Seel (open late May to early Sept.) can be reached only

ARIZONA

via a challenging 17 mi. round-trip **hike**. The trail drops 1200 ft. from the canyon rim to the floor and follows the streambed to the site. Hikers can make this trip in a long day or stay overnight in a **free campground** nearby. Total access is limited to 20 people per day, so to ensure a permit on a specific date, contact the Visitors Center in advance. For those winging it, the permits are generally not all taken.

Ranger-led tours to Betatakin, a 135-room complex, are limited to 25 people and generally take 5hr. The 5 mi. hike descends 700 ft. and follows a heavily forested canyon to the site. (Late May to early Sept. 1 per day at 8:15am. First come, first served on the morning of the tour.) If you're not up for a long hike, the wheelchair accessible yet steep 1 mi. round-trip **Sandal Trail** lets you gaze down on Betatakin from the canyon rim and includes plaques detailing the native use of flora for such tasks as making arrow shafts. **The Aspen Forest Overlook Trail**, another 1 mi. hike, winds through a canyon of aspens and firs (rarities in these parts) to a great view, albeit with no ruins. Write to Navajo National Monument, HC 71 Box 3, Tonales 86044, for more info.

MONUMENT VALLEY   ☎ 435

The red sandstone towers of Monument Valley are one of the Southwest's most otherworldly sights. Paradoxically, they're also one of the most familiar, since countless Western films have used the butte-laden plains as a backdrop. For hundreds of millions of years, sediment from the Rocky Mountains was deposited in the lowland basin where these 400-1000 ft. monoliths now tower. Deep internal pressures then lifted these newly formed layers of rock some 3 mi. above sea level to create an enormous plateau. Over the last 50 million years the forces of erosion have worked their magic by wearing down the layers of rock and creating the geological wonders we see today. Some years before John Wayne and his coterie of Hollywood luminaries arrived, Ancestral Puebloans managed to sustain small communities here, despite the hot, arid climate. Today the valley is the crown jewel of Navajo Nation Parks and Recreation.

The park entrance lies off U.S. 163, just across the Utah border, 24 mi. north of **Kayenta** and 25 mi. south of Mexican Hat. The **Visitors Center** has info on the park drive and road conditions; they can also arrange vehicle, horse, and hiking tours. (☎801-727-3353. Park and Visitors Center open May-Sept. daily 7am-7pm; Oct.-Apr. 8am-5pm. The drive closes at 6:30pm in summer and 4:30pm in winter. $3, under 7 free.) In winter, snow laces the rocky towers, and the majority of tourists flee.

Mitten View Campground ❶, a quarter of a mile southwest of the Visitors Center, offers 99 sites, showers, restrooms, and panoramic views, but no hookups. (Sites $10; in winter $5. 14-day max. stay. Register at the Visitors Center; no reservations.) **Goulding's Monument Valley Campground ❶**, 3 mi. west of Rte. 163 on the road opposite the tribal park, promises more protected camping but without the scenery. (☎727-3231. Laundry, showers, pool. Reception 7am-10pm. Sites $15.)

MOGOLLON RIM COUNTRY

The Mogollon Rim represents the divide between two climatic and ecological zones, producing a stretch of the state that spans from sweltering desert to more elevated woodlands. This chunk of Arizona, east of Phoenix between Navajo Nation and Tucson, goes relatively untrodden. Mogollon Rim Country is largely remote and undeveloped, offering a beautiful wilderness to travelers yearning for a little less civilization. The easiest way to access it is to drive north from Payson (a hub of sorts in Mogollon Rim country) on Rte. 260 and turn left on Forest Service Rd. 300, from which several viewpoints overlook the southern lowlands. Lakeside campgrounds offer fishing and a large network of trails along the rim make for good hiking. The adventurous should ask a ranger about the mountain bike trails that plummet down the face of the rim, offering dramatic views in return for steep, technical singletrack.

TONTO NATURAL BRIDGE STATE PARK   ☎928

Located 10 mi. north of the town of Payson on Rte. 87, the fantastic **Tonto Natural Bridge** is the longest natural travertine arch in the world and widest natural water crossing in North America. It is large and strong enough to support the road leading to its parking area, and tourists often pass over without even realizing it. Four viewpoints give the observer an eyeful of the cavernous, cathedral-like passage. For further exploring, a path leads down to water level, and scrambling is permitted in order to pass beneath the bridge. Thrill-seekers may try to find the cave where David Gowan hid from Apaches in 1877 before homesteading the flat area now occupied by the state park. Water dripping down from the expansive natural domes that support the crossing has smoothed out the rocks inside; even the dry ones can be slippery, so bring trusty shoes and a healthy dose of common sense.

In addition to the bridge, the park is home to a colony of bats, a herd of javelinas (porcine herbivores native to the Southwest), and a pride of feral cats. Be careful around the feral cats; although they make for cute pictures and physically resemble their domesticated cousins, these kitties are wild and unaccustomed to humans. (☎476-4202. Visitors Center open daily 10am-5pm. Park open Memorial Day to Labor Day daily 8am-7pm; Sept.-Oct. 8am-6pm; Nov.-Mar. 9am-5pm; Apr. 8am-6pm. $6 per vehicle.)

MOGOLLON RIM

The single most important geographic and ecological divide in Arizona, the Mogollon Rim marks the southern edge of the central woodlands climatic and ecological zones and the northern frontier of what turns into the Saguaro desert farther south. At parts, the Rim itself looms 2000 ft. over the countryside to its south. The area is a favorite haunt of local campers and outdoors types and has seen a certain amount of isolated recreational development, mainly around the eastern paved area and the lakes. Most of the area around the rim falls in the **Sitgreaves National Forest,** and the **ranger station** in Payson has maps of the region. (Located on Rte. 260. ☎474-7900. Open winter M-F 8am-5pm, summer M-Sa 8am-5pm.) From Memorial Day to Labor Day a better bet is the **Mogollon Rim Visitors Center,** just off of Rte. 260 at the junction with Forest Rd. 300 (to contact the Visitors Center, call the Black Mesa Ranger District office at ☎535-4481).

The best way to experience the Rim is to travel down unpaved and rugged **Forest Road 300,** which follows the Rim for almost 50 mi. between Rts. 87 and 260. The road takes 2½hr. to drive without stopping, but visitors should take breaks to look over the edge and to hike or bike any of the innumerable trails. It can be accessed from either end—the western side of Forest Rd. 300 junctions with Rte. 87 near Strawberry, some 25 mi. north of Payson. The eastern part of the road junctions with Rte. 260 some 36 mi. to the east of Payson at the Visitors Center. Less than 4 mi. into the drive heading east, other forest roads will begin branching to the north; these lead to Rte. 87 and after 10 mi. constitute the quickest means of returning to a major paved highway. Note that not all northbound roads necessarily lead to highway; some lead to lakes and recreation sites. All roads are well marked with mileages. It is just under 50 mi. in length, offers no fuel, and is paved for less than 2 mi. at the eastern end. The road can be choppy and rocky, and is exceptionally dusty in dry weather. Due to the relative proximity of gas stations to the western end of the road in and around Strawberry, it may be much wiser to travel the road west to east.

ARIZONA

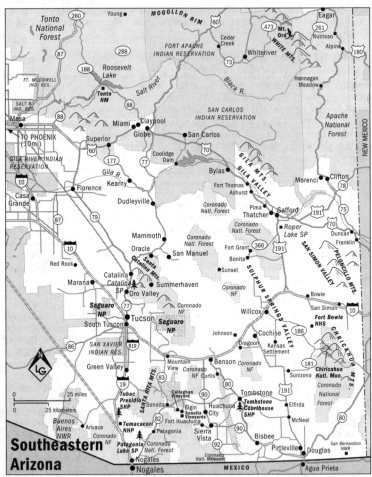

Southeastern Arizona

The appeal of the Rim lies mainly in the gorgeous views it affords of Southern Arizona, but there are other perks as well. The entire Rim features a number of free **dispersed campgrounds ❶.** Before the end of the pavement in the eastern portion is the turn off to **Woods Canyon Lake,** the largest of the Rim lakes and well-frequented by fishermen. **Potato Lake,** on a spur road 4 mi. in from Rte. 87 is another popular fishing hole, while 12 mi. past the end of the eastern pavement lies **Bear Canyon Lake,** recommended by travelers and locals alike. The road passes historical markers, cabin ruins, and trailheads while granting its famous mile-high view.

TUCSON   ☎ 520

Part of Mexico until the Gadsden Purchase, Tucson (TOO-sahn) may now be the next big thing in Arizona. Its scientists and astronomers are at the cutting edges of their fields, its downtown thrives with artists and hipsters from the University of

Arizona, and the surrounding historic districts are undergoing renovation and gentrification. Families and retirees populate the sprawling suburbs, where backyards approach mountains that cradle the newest and most pristine public cavern in the country, as well as a ring of national parks, forests, and recreation areas. The wilderness around Tucson arguably harbors more hiking, biking, and equestrian trails and more Sonoran wildlife and saguaro cacti than any one town deserves. This city offers the conveniences of a metropolis without the nasty aftertaste, and arguably better tourist attractions than almost any other Southwestern city.

▐ TRANSPORTATION

Flights: Tucson International Airport, (☎573-8000; www.tucsonairport.org), on Valencia Rd., south of downtown. Bus #6 goes downtown from the terminal drop-off area. Round-trip to: **Dallas** (2hr., 4 per day, $230); **L.A.** (1hr., 7 per day, $99); **Phoenix** (25min., 4 per day, $165). **Arizona Stagecoach** (☎889-1000) goes downtown for around $14 per person, $3 each additional person. Reservations recommended. 24hr.

Buses: Greyhound, 2 S. 4th Ave. (☎792-3475), between Congress St. and Broadway. To: **Albuquerque** (12-14hr., 7 per day, $90); **El Paso** (6hr., 9 per day, $37); **Los Angeles** (9-10hr., 7 per day, $48); and **Phoenix** (2hr., 7 per day, $16). Open 24hr.

Trains: Amtrak, 400 E. Toole Ave. (☎623-4442) on 5th Ave., 1 block north of the Greyhound station. To: **Albuquerque** via El Paso (4 per week, $99); **Las Vegas** via LA (3 per week, $124); **Los Angeles** (3 per week, $72); **San Francisco** via LA (3 per week, $130). Book 2 weeks ahead or rates are substantially higher. Open Sa-M 6:15am-1:45pm and 4:15-11:30pm, Tu-W 6:15am-1:45pm, Th-F 4:15-11:30pm.

Public Transit: Sun-Tran, (☎792-9222). Buses run from Tucson's Ronstadt terminal downtown, at the corner of Congress and 6th St. Fares $1.00, seniors, disabled, and students $0.40, day pass $2. Service roughly M-F 5:30am-10pm, Sa-Su 8am-7pm; times vary by route.

Taxis: Yellow Cab, ☎624-6611.

Car Rental: American Car Rental, 3150 E. Grant Rd. (☎320-1495). Rates start at $20 per day. No surcharge 21-25. Credit card deposit required on most cars. Open M-F 8am-6pm, Sa 8am-4pm, and Su 11am-4pm.

Outdoor Outfitters: Summit Hut has two locations, 504 E. Speedway Ave. and 605 E. Wetmore Rd., offering outdoor gear, rentals, books, and advice on area adventures. (☎800-499-8696. Open M-F 9am-8pm, Sa 9am-6pm, Su 10am-5pm.) **Fairwheel Bicycles,** 1110 E. 6th St. (☎884-9018) at Fremont. $20 first day, $10 each additional day for mountain bikes; $30 and $20 for road bikes. Also offers repair and sales. Credit card deposit required. Open M-F 9am-6pm, Sa 9am-5:30pm, Su noon-4pm.

▐▋ ORIENTATION & PRACTICAL INFORMATION

Just east of I-10, Tucson's downtown surrounds the intersection of **Broadway Boulevard** and **Stone Avenue,** two blocks from the train and bus terminals. The **University of Arizona** is 1 mi. northeast of downtown at the intersection of **Park** and **Speedway Boulevard.** "Avenues" run north-south, "streets" east-west; because some of each are numbered, intersections such as "6th and 6th" are possible. Speedway, Broadway, and **Grant Road** are the quickest east-west routes through town. To go north-south, follow **Oracle Road** through the heart of the city, **Campbell Avenue** east of downtown, or **Swan Road** farther east. The hip, young crowd swings on busy **4th Avenue, University Boulevard,** and **Congress Street,** all with small shops, quirky restaurants, and a slew of bars.

ARIZONA

Visitor Information: Tucson Convention and Visitors Bureau, 100 S. Church Ave. off Congress St. (☎770-2142 or 800-638-8350 ext. 142; www.visittucson.org), in the shopping plaza. The bureau offers a Tucson Attractions Passport for $10 that earns many discounts around town, as well as 2-for-1 entries to popular attractions like the Arizona-Sonora Desert Museum. Open M-F 8am-5pm, Sa-Su 9am-4pm.

Bi-Gay-Lesbian Organization: Gay, Lesbian, Bisexual and Transgendered Community Center, 300 E. 6th St. (☎624-1779). Open M-F 10am-7pm; Sa 10am-5pm.

Emergency ☎911.**Police:** non-emergency ☎791-4444.

Hotlines: Rape Crisis, ☎327-7273. **Suicide Prevention,** ☎323-9373. Both 24hr.

Medical Services: University Medical Center, 1501 N. Campbell Ave (☎694-0111).

Internet Access: Free at the **University of Arizona main library,** 1510 E. University Blvd. Open Sept.-May M-Th 7:30am-1am, F 7:30am-9pm, Sa 10am-9pm, Su 11am-1am; June-Aug. M-Th 7:30am-11pm, F 7:30am-6pm, Sa 9am-6pm, Su 11am-11pm. Also free at the **Tucson-Pima Public Library,** 101 N. Stone, where the first 2 hours of **parking** are also free during library hours. (☎791-4393. Open M-W 9am-8pm, Th 9am-6pm, F 9am-5pm, Sa 10am-5pm, Su 1-5pm.)

Post Office: 1501 S. Cherry Bell (☎388-5129). Open M-F 8:30am-8pm, Sa 9am-1pm. **Postal code:** 85726.

 # ACCOMMODATIONS

There's a direct correlation between the temperature in Tucson and the warmth of its lodging industry to budget travelers: expect the best deals in summer, when rain-cooled evenings and summer bargains are consolation for the midday scorch. **The Tucson Gem and Mineral Show,** the largest of its kind in North America, is an added hazard for budget travelers. Falling at the end of January and beginning of February, the mammoth show fills up most of the city's accommodations for its two-week run and drives prices up considerably. Unless you've made arrangements in advance, this is a bad time to drop in on Tucson.

Hotel Congress and Hostel, 311 E. Congress (☎800-722-8848 or 622-8848). Conveniently located across from the bus and train stations, this hostel offers superb lodging to night-owl hostelers. In the afternoon lucky guests might catch a local singing and playing the piano in the lobby, and the hotel arranges live music W-F from 7-9pm. The cafe downstairs serves great salads and omelettes. Club Congress, which adjoins the lobby, booms until 1am on weekends, making it rough on early birds. Private rooms come with bath, phone, vintage radio, and ceiling fans. Dorms $18 with hostel card, $24 without. Singles start at $40 and doubles can run up to $90, depending on the season. 10% discount for students, military, and local artists. ❶

The Flamingo Hotel, 1300 N. Stone Ave. (☎800-300-3533 or 770-1910). Houses not only guests but Arizona's largest collection of Western movie posters. There are dozens of rooms available, from the Kevin Costner room to the Burt Lancaster suite (both with A/C, cable TV, telephones, and pool access). Laundry facilities are on-site; breakfast, pool, and AAA and AARP discounts. Singles and doubles May-Aug. $29; Sept.-Nov. all rooms $49; Dec.-Apr. up to $85. ❹

Loews Ventana Canyon Resort, 7000 N. Resort Dr. (☎299-2020). A quintessential five-star hotel located 5 mi. north of downtown. Take Pima St. east from the University of Arizona to Sabino Canyon Rd., turn left, and then turn left immediately again at Sunrise Dr. Resort Dr. is on your right. At the base of an 80 ft. automated waterfall, the incredible Ventana Canyon Resort delivers on every level—from its relaxing spa to its championship golf course to the beautiful surrounding Catalina Mountain foothills. Rooms start at $80 and surpass $160. ❺

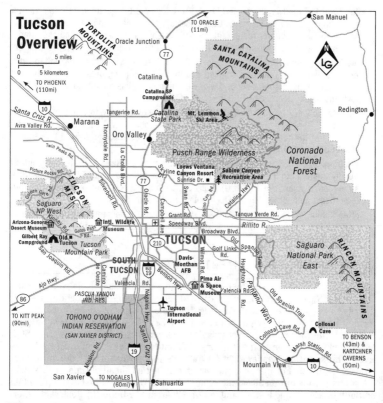

Tucson Overview

TORTOLITA MOUNTAINS

Oracle Junction

TO ORACLE (11mi)

San Manuel

SANTA CATALINA MOUNTAINS

0 — 5 miles
0 — 5 kilometers

TO PHOENIX (110mi)

Catalina

Catalina SP Campgrounds

Santa Cruz R.

Marana

Tangerine Rd.

Catalina State Park

Mt. Lemmon Ski Area

Redington

Avra Valley Rd.

Oro Valley

Pusch Range Wilderness

Coronado National Forest

Twin Peaks Rd.

Picture Rocks Rd.

Golden Gate Rd.

Saguaro NP West

Thornydale Rd.

La Cholla Blvd.

Silverbell Rd.

Loews Ventana Canyon Resort

Sabino Canyon Recreation Area

Skyline

Sunrise Dr. ■

Catalina Hwy.

Arizona-Sonora Desert Museum

Gilbert Ray Campground

Old Tucson

Tucson Mountain Park

Intl. Wildlife Museum

Gates Pass Rd.

Grant Rd.

Speedway Blvd.

Tanque Verde Rd.

Rillito R.

Broadway Blvd.

TUCSON

Saguaro National Park East

RINCON MOUNTAINS

San Joaquin Rd.

SOUTH TUCSON

Camino de Oeste

Davis-Monthan AFB

Golf Links Rd.

Old Spanish Trail

Ajo Hwy.

Valencia Rd.

Pima Air & Space Museum

Houghton Rd.

Valencia Rd.

Old Spanish Trail

TO KITT PEAK (90mi)

PASCUA YANQUI IND. RES.

TOHONO O'ODHAM INDIAN RESERVATION (SAN XAVIER DISTRICT)

Tucson International Airport

Nogales Hwy.

Santa Cruz R.

Mission Rd.

Pantano Wash

Collosal Cave Rd.

Collosal Cave

TO BENSON (43mi) & KARTCHNER CAVERNS (50mi)

Marsh Station Rd.

San Xavier

TO NOGALES (60mi)

Sahuarita

Mountain View

CAMPING

Gilbert Ray Campground (☎883-4200). Gilbert Ray is the best bet for those wanting to access Saguaro West. Located along the McCain Loop Rd., the campground offers sites with toilets and drinking water within easy reach of the city as well as all the various Speedway sights. $7. ❶

Catalina State Park (☎628-5798), north of Tucson on Oracle Rd. Catalina State Park features tent sites fully equipped with hot showers, water, and toilets. Picnic sites are available. $12. ❶

Spencer Canyon (☎576-1477), on Catalina Hwy. between miles 21 and 22, northeast of Tucson. Sites have potable water and toilets. $12, day use $3 per vehicle. This site was closed at the time of publication due to fire. ❶

FOOD

Like any good college town in the US, Tucson brims with inexpensive but tasty eateries to suit meager student budgets. Although every style of cooking is represented in the city's many restaurants, south-of-the-border fare reigns. Good, cheap Mexican spots are everywhere.

elle, 3048 E. Broadway Blvd. (☎327-0500), brings out the gastronome in all who are lucky enough to sample its menu. Cool classical jazz resonates through this stylish, self-described "wine country restaurant" as guests enjoy mouth-watering chicken penne ($12) in an elegant, inviting milieu. Open M-F 11:30am-10pm, Sa 4:30pm-10pm. ❸

Time Market, 444 E. University Blvd. (☎622-0761), serves $2 pizza slices, enhanced by toppings like piñon nuts and smoked gouda. Calzones ($7), organic groceries, and, most importantly, a good beer and wine selection make this the ultimate college shop-down-the-block. Open daily 7:30am-10pm. ❶

La Indita, 622 N. 4th Ave. (☎792-0523), delights customers with traditional Mexican cuisine ($3-9) served on delicious tortillas. The operation is still supervised by *la indita* herself, and the food takes on an added kick as a result. Open M-Th 11am-9pm, F 11am-6pm, Sa 6-9pm, Su 9am-9pm. ❶

India Oven, 2727 N. Campbell Ave. (☎326-8635), between Grant and Glenn, provides a friendly shelter from the torrent of Mexican food. The garlic *naan* ($2.35) is exquisite, as is the mango yogurt drink ($2.50). Daily $6 lunch buffet. Vegetarian dishes $6-7, tandoori meats and curries $7-11. Open daily 11am-10pm. ❶

Coffee Xchange, 2443 N. Campbell Ave. (☎409-9433), caters to the bookish crowd living north of the university. Sells bagels, sandwiches, and salads ($2-6) in addition to hot joe. Open 24hrs. ❶

🎭 🎵 NIGHTLIFE & ENTERTAINMENT

The free *Tucson Weekly* is the local authority on nightlife, but the weekend sections of the *Star* or the *Citizen* also provide good coverage. Throughout the year, the city of the sun presents **Music Under the Stars,** a series of sunset concerts performed by the **Tucson Symphony Orchestra** (☎882-8585). For **Downtown Saturday Nights,** on the first and third Saturday of each temperate month, Congress St. is blockaded for a celebration of the arts with outdoor singers, crafts, and galleries. Every Thursday the **Thursday Night Art Walk** lets you mosey through downtown galleries and studios. For info, call the **Tucson Arts District** ahead of time (☎624-9977). UA students rock out on **Speedway Boulevard,** while others do the two-step in clubs on **North Oracle.** Young locals hang out on **4th Avenue** or **University Boulevard,** where most bars have live music and low cover charges.

Club Congress, 311 E. Congress St. (☎622-8848), has DJs during the week and live bands on weekends. The friendly hotel staff and a cast of regulars make it an especially good time. Congress is the venue for most of the indie music coming through town. M is 80s night with 80¢ vodkas. Open daily 9pm-1am. Cover $3-5.

IBT's, 616 4th Ave. north of 6th St. (☎882-3053), the single most popular gay venue in Tucson, can be hard to spot—no sign hangs on the unmarked door. Inside is another story. Dance music pumps through a classic club environment to a capacity crowd on weekends. Attention-grabbing dancers may find themselves on the large-screen video display before heading out to the second bar in an enclosed, open-air courtyard. W and Su drag shows wow audiences. Parking and rear entrance available on Hoff St. No cover. Open daily 9am-1am.

Che's Lounge, 350 4th Ave. (☎623-2088), has lines early in the night on weekends and crowds during the week. Live music Sa. Open daily 4pm-1am.

Ain't Nobody's Bizness, 2900 E. Broadway Blvd. (☎318-4838), in a shopping plaza, is the little sister of its Phoenix namesake and the big mama of the Tucson lesbian scene. With a large bar, themed contests, and pool tournaments, "Biz" attracts crowds of all backgrounds and has some of the best dancing in Tucson. Open daily 2pm-1am.

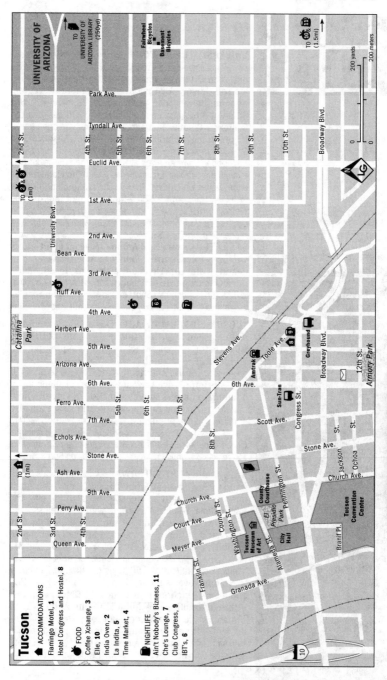

Tucson

▲ ACCOMMODATIONS
Flamingo Motel, **1**
Hotel Congress and Hostel, **8**

🍴 FOOD
Coffee Xchange, **3**
Elle, **10**
India Oven, **2**
La Indita, **5**
Time Market, **4**

🌙 NIGHTLIFE
Ain't Nobody's Bizness, **11**
Che's Lounge, **7**
Club Congress, **9**
IBT's, **6**

UNIVERSITY OF ARIZONA

TO UNIVERSITY OF ARIZONA LIBRARY (250yd)

Fairwheel Bicycles
Basement Bicycles

TO (1.5mi)

Park Ave.
Tyndall Ave.
Euclid Ave.
1st Ave.
2nd Ave.
Bean Ave.
3rd Ave.
Huff Ave.
Herbert Ave.
5th Ave.
Arizona Ave.
6th Ave.
Ferro Ave.
7th Ave.
Echols Ave.
Stone Ave.
Ash Ave.
9th Ave.
Perry Ave.
Queen Ave.

2nd St.
3rd St.
4th St.

University Blvd.

Catalina Park

TO 2 & 3 (1mi)
TO 1 (1mi)

4th St.
5th St.
6th St.
7th St.
8th St.
9th St.
10th St.

Broadway Blvd.

5th St.
6th St.
7th St.
8th St.

Stevens Ave.
Toole Ave.
Amtrak
Greyhound
Sun-Tran

6th Ave.
Scott Ave.
Congress St.
Stone Ave.
St.
St.

Broadway Blvd.
12th St.
Armory Park

Church Ave.

County Courthouse
El Presidio Park
Pennington St.
Tucson Museum of Art
City Hall
Washington St.
Council St.
Court Ave.
Meyer Ave.
Franklin St.
Alameda St.
Jackson
Ochoa
Church Ave.
Branif Pl.
Tucson Convention Center
Granada Ave.

200 yards
200 meters
0
0

N

ARIZONA

HISTORIC
DOWNTOWN TUCSON

Start your tour early in the day; the sights below operate 9am-5pm.

1 Lunch early at **El Charro**, Tucson's oldest Mexican restaurant, housed in a 1900s-era family home.

2 Walk down Court to Telles, where **La Casa Cordova**, Tucson's oldest home, houses a Presidio exhibit on the area.

3 Through the courtyard, the **Tucson Museum of Art** exhibits one of the finest collections of art in the state.

4 Stop by the **Edward Nye Fish House**, through the passageway by the museum cafe. Built in 1867 on the site of the Presidio Barracks, it now houses the **Campbell Collection of Western American Art**.

Down Church Ave., the brightly colored adobe of the Barrio Histórico beckons. Head to "El Tiradito," a Catholic shrine to a youth killed in a love triangle, where you can light a candle and make a wish.

◉ SIGHTS

UNIVERSITY OF ARIZONA. Lined with cafes, restaurants, galleries, and vintage clothing shops, 4th Avenue is an alternative magnet and a great place to take a stroll. Lovely for its varied and elaborate vegetation, the **University of Arizona's** mall sits where E. 3rd St. should be, just east of Park Ave. On campus the **Center for Creative Photography** houses various changing exhibits, including the archives of Ansel Adams and Richard Avedon. (☎621-7968. *Open M-F 9am-5pm, Sa-Su noon-5pm. Archives available to the public, but only through print-viewing appointments. Free.*) The **Flandrau Science Center** on Cherry Ave. at the campus mall offers an open telescope W-Sa 7-9pm by night and dazzles visitors with a laser light show by day. (☎621-7827. *Open M-Tu 9am-5pm, W-Sa 9am-5pm and 7-9pm for telescope, Su noon-5pm. $3, under 14 $2. Shows $5/$4, seniors $4.50.*) The **University of Arizona Museum of Art** offers visitors a free glimpse of modern American and 18th-century Latin American art, as well as the singularly muscular sculpture of Jacques Lipchitz. (*1031 N. Olive.* ☎621-7567. *Open mid-Sept. to mid-May M-F 9am-5pm, Su 12-4pm; M-F 10am-3:30pm, Su noon-4pm otherwise.*)

TUCSON MUSEUM OF ART. This major attraction is distinguished by its location in the center of the Presidio Historic Block, which boasts an impressive collection of Pre-Columbian and Mexican folk art, as well as art of the American West. The museum itself presents impressive traveling exhibits in all media, in addition to its permanent collection of varied American, Mexican, and European art. Art classes are also available to the public at the Museum School. (*140 N. Main Ave.* ☎624-2333. *Open M-Sa 10am-4pm, Su noon-4pm. Closed M between Memorial Day and Labor Day. $5, students $2, seniors $4, under 13 free. Everyone free on Su.*)

SIGHTS ON WEST SPEEDWAY. As Speedway Blvd. winds its way west from Tucson's city center, it passes by a variety of sights. Closest to the city, the **International Wildlife Museum** is wild but lifeless—the creatures were stuffed long ago. As a natural history museum it is first-rate, with child-friendly touchable exhibits. (*4800 W. Gates Pass Rd.* ☎617-1439. *Open M-F 9am-5pm, Sa-Su 9am-6pm, last entrance at 4:15pm. $7, seniors and students $5.50, ages 6-12 $2.50.*) Farther west, Speedway's name changes to Gates Pass Rd., and it later junctions into Kinney Rd. **Gates Pass,** west of the International Wildlife Museum on the way to Kinney Rd., is an excellent spot for watching the rising and setting of the sun. The left fork leads to **Old Tucson Studios,** an elaborate Old West-style town constructed for the movie *Arizona* (1938) and used as a backdrop for Westerns ever since, including many John Wayne films and the 1986 classic, *The Three Amigos*. It's open year-round to tourists, who can stroll around in the Old West mock up, view gun fight re-enactments and other tourist shows and, if lucky, watch the filming of a current Western. (☎ *883-0100. Open Oct.-May daily 10am-6pm, June-Sept. 10am-3pm, sometimes closed on M in winter. Call ahead as occasionally Old Tucson is closed for group functions. $14.95, seniors $13.45, ages 4-11 $9.45, cash only.*) Those opting to take the right fork eschew the Wild Wild West for the natural, wild West; less than 2 mi. from the fork lies the **Arizona-Sonora Desert Museum**, a first-rate zoo and nature preserve. The living museum re-creates a range of desert habitats and features over 300 kinds of animals. A visit requires at least 2hr., preferably in the early morning before the animals take their afternoon siestas. (*2021 N. Kinney Rd. ☎ 883-2702. Follow Speedway Blvd. west of the city as it becomes Gates Pass Rd., then Kinney Rd. Open Mar.-Sept. daily 7:30am-5pm; Oct.-Feb. 8:30am-5pm, June-Sept. Sa 7:30am-10pm. $9, Oct.-May. $12, ages 6-12 $2.*)

CAVES. Kartchner Caverns State Park, filled with magnificent rock formations and home to over 1000 bats, enjoys enormous popularity. This is a "living" cave that contains water and is still experiencing the growth of its formations, so while conditions may be damp, the formations shine and glisten in the light. Taking a tour is the only way to enter the cave. The entrance fee also covers the museum, nearby hiking, and the under-used county campground. (*Located 8 mi. off I-10 at exit 302. ☎ 586-4100. Open daily 7:30am-6pm. 1hr. tours run every 20min. 8:40am-4:40pm. Entrance fee $10 per vehicle, tour $14, ages 7-13 $6. Reservations strongly recommended.*)

Near Saguaro National Park East (p. 146), **Colossal Cave** is one of the only dormant (no water or new formations) caves in the United States. It offers horseback rides (☎ 647-3450), hiking, camping on county land, and 1hr. guided tours of the cave. After the no-touch policies of Kartchner Caverns, the Saturday night ladder tours offered here—running through otherwise sealed-off tunnels, crawlspaces, and corridors—will come as a treat. (☎ *647-7275. Open mid-Mar. to mid-Sept. M-Sa 8am-6pm, Su 8am-7pm; mid-Sept. to mid-Mar. M-Sa 9am-5pm, Su 9am-6pm. $7.50, ages 6-12 $4. Ladder tour: Sept.-Mar. Sa 5:30-8pm, Mar.-Sept. Sa 6:30-9pm; $35, includes meal and equipment rental, reservations required.*)

▚ OUTDOOR ACTIVITIES

SAGUARO NATIONAL PARK WEST

North of the desert museum, the western half of Saguaro National Park (Tucson Mountain District) has limited hiking trails and an auto loop. The **Bajada Loop Drive** runs less than 9 mi. but passes through some of the most striking desert scenery the park has to offer. The paved nature walk near the **Visitors Center** passes some of the best specimens of Saguaro cactus in the Tucson area. The towering cacti take decades to reach maturity and don't start sprouting their trademark raised arms until around age 75. There is no camping available in the park, and mountain biking is allowed only on vehicle roads and not on the hiking trails. (☎ 733-5158. Park open 24hr.; Visitors Center daily 8:30am-5pm; auto loop 7am-sunset. Free.)

There are a variety of hiking trails through Saguaro West; **Sendero Esperanza Trail,** beginning at the Ez-kim-in-zin picnic area, is the mildest approach to the summit of **Wasson Peak,** the highest in the Tucson Mountain Range (4687 ft.). The moderate trail to the peak winds 4 mi. one-way. No reliable water is available along the trail—be sure to carry plenty. The **Hugh Norris Trail** is a slightly longer, slightly more strenuous climb to the top of Wasson Peak, and it offers gorgeous desert views the whole way. Five miles one-way, the round-trip hike will take most of the day. The trailhead is clearly marked, off the Bajada Loop Drive.

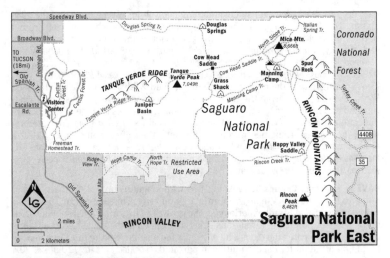

Saguaro National Park East

SAGUARO NATIONAL PARK EAST

Also known as the Rincon Mountain District, the eastern portion of Saguaro National Park lies just east of the city of Tucson on **Old Spanish Trail;** take I-10 E to exit 279 and follow Vail Rd. to Old Spanish Trail. **Backcountry camping** is allowed in this portion of the park; free mandatory permits for backcountry camping may be picked up at the **Visitors Center** any time until noon on the day you intend to go camping. Mountain biking is permitted inside the park, but only around the **Cactus Forest Loop Drive** and **Cactus Forest Trail,** at the western end of the park near the Visitors Center. (☎733-5153. Visitors Center open daily 8:30am-5pm. $6 per vehicle, $3 per pedestrian.)

The trails in Saguaro East are longer than those in the western part of the park. With over 128 mi. of trails, many hikes here must be done over the course of two days (trailside camp sites are available for this). One of the only trails that can easily in the park that can be completed in a single day hike is the **Cactus Forest**. Smaller trails and trail systems branch off of the main Cactus Forest trail. In the Rincon Valley area, the **Hope Camp Trail** is less than 3 mi. one-way, but must be shared with horses.

TUCSON MOUNTAIN COUNTY PARK

Located west of Tucson along Speedway/Gates Pass/Kinney, Tucson Mountain County Park includes Gates Pass itself as well as many of the Tucson mountains. A variety of trailheads, picnic areas, and a campsite radiate from Kinney Rd. before it reaches the Saguaro National Park West. For drivers, the **McCain Loop Road** loops around the Arizona-Sonora Desert Museum and passes through some of the most rugged and wild stretches of desert. Entrance to the park is free, and mountain biking is popular along its many trails.

The **Golden Gate Loop** is one of the longer trails in the park. An easy 8 mi. loop with little elevation change, the trail circles Golden Gate Mountain. To reach the trailhead, park on one of the lots on eastern Gates Pass Rd. and follow David Yetman Trail ½ mi. The loop crosses several washes that can present hazards during summer thunderstorms. From the same trailhead, the **David Yetman Trail** presents a more difficult, 11.6 mi. round-trip loop, though it may be shortened by exiting at various trailheads.

🔲 DAYTRIPS FROM TUCSON

BIOSPHERE 2

Biosphere is 30min. north of Tucson; take I-10 west to the "Miracle Mile" exit, follow the miracles to Oracle Rd., then travel north until it becomes Rte. 77 N. From Phoenix, take I-10 to exit 185, follow Rte. 387 to Rte. 79 (Florence Hwy.), and proceed to Oracle Junction and Rte. 77. ☎ 800-838-2462. Call for daily tour info. Open daily 8:30am-5:30pm, last admission at 5pm. $13, seniors and students $11.50, ages 13-17 $9, ages 6-12 $6.

Ninety-one feet high, with an area of more than three acres, Biosphere 2 is sealed off from Earth ("Biosphere 1") by 500 tons of stainless steel. In 1991, eight research scientists locked themselves inside this giant greenhouse to cultivate their own food and knit their own socks as they monitored the behavior of five man-made ecosystems: savanna, rainforest, marsh, ocean, and desert. After two years, they began having oxygen problems and difficulty with food production. No one lives in Biosphere 2 now, but it's still used as a research facility. The Guided 2hr. tours include two short films, a walk through the laboratory's research and development models for the Biosphere 2 ecosystems, and a stroll around Biosphere 2 itself, including the crew's living quarters. Walking around unchaperoned is also permitted.

MISSION SAN XAVIER DE BAC

South of Tucson off of I-19 to Nogales, take the San Xavier exit and follow the signs. ☎ 294-2624. Open for viewing 7am-5pm; masses held daily. Admission is free both to the church and to small adjoining museum, although donations are accepted.

Built by the Franciscan brothers in the late 1700s, the Mission San Xavier de Bac is the northernmost Spanish Baroque church in the Americas, and the only such church in the US. Located on the Tohono O'odham Indian Reservation, there were few opportunities and fewer funds to restore it until the late 20th century. In the early 90s, a local group gathered money in order to preserve and protect this singular church; since then, the mortar has been restored, the frescoes have been retouched and preserved, and the statuary cleaned of centuries of soot and desert sand. The result is a dazzling house of God, well-deserving of its nickname "the white dove of the desert."

SABINO CANYON

Take Speedway Blvd. to Swan Rd. to Sunrise Dr. The entrance is at the intersection of Sunrise Dr. and Sabino Canyon Rd. ☎ 749-2327. Runs July-Nov. every hr. 9am-4pm, Dec.-June every 30min. 9am-4:30pm; $6, ages 3-12 $3. Visitors Center: ☎ 749-8700. Open M-F 8am-4:30pm, Sa-Su 8:30am-4:30pm.

Northeast of downtown Tucson, the cliffs and desert pools of **Sabino Canyon** provide an ideal backdrop for scenic picnics and day hikes. Locals beat the Tucson heat by frolicking in the area's water holes throughout the summer. No cars are permitted in the canyon, but a shuttle makes trips through the area. The National Forest's **Visitors Center** lies at the canyon's entrance. The forest area outside the canyon is the **Pusch Ridge Wilderness,** which is located within the **Coronado National Forest.** The northern and eastern border of the wilderness is the Mt. Lemmon Hwy., and the wilderness here stretches to the south and west sides of the Coronado National Forest. Hiking trails criss-cross through the Forest, Wilderness, and Sabino Canyon in multitudes. **Biking** within the park is only permitted from 5pm to 9am when the shuttle is inoperative, and not on Wednesday or Saturday. In the Pusch Wilderness Area, biking is forbidden, while in the rest of the Coronado forest it is freely permitted.

SOUTHERN ARIZONA

South of Tucson, Arizona boasts some of the most fascinating and idiosyncratic geology, wildlife, and towns that the state has to offer. From the border town of Nogales to the Disneyland-esque Tombstone to the artist colony of Bisbee, life in southern Arizona cannot easily be categorized. The inimitable volcanic rock of Chiricahua National Monument provides a spectacle for the eyes, and if you're willing to make a trek, the extremely remote and untouristed Organ Pipe Cactus National Monument will not disappoint.

ORGAN PIPE CACTUS NATIONAL MONUMENT ☎ 520

Cozying up to the Mexican border, the lonely dirt roads of Organ Pipe Cactus National Monument encircle an extraordinary collection of the flora and fauna of the Sonoran. Foremost among them is the Organ Pipe Cactus itself, common in Mexico but found only in this region of the US. Its texture and color are similar to a Saguaro, but while the Saguaro is commonly shaped like a body with two or more arms, the Organ Pipe is only arms, which sprout tentacle-like from the soil.

■ ░ **ORIENTATION & ACCOMMODATIONS.** Located on U.S. 85 5 mi. south of the tiny hamlet of **Why,** Organ Pipe Cactus National Monument is one of the most isolated national parks in the US. It's nearly empty during the summer, but in the cooler winter months the campground grows busy on weekends. The **Visitors Center,** 5 mi. north of the Mexican border on Rte. 85, distributes maps and provides hiking recommendations. (☎387-6849. Open daily 8am-5pm.)

The adjacent **Twin Peaks Campground ❶** offers water, restrooms, and grills, but no hookups (tent sites $10). Primitive camping is available at **Alamo Canyon ❶,** 3 mi. east of Rte. 85 on a dirt turnoff (just north of a bridged wash) for $6, but is free on land administered by the **BLM** at mile marker 55 on the west side of Rte. 85. **Backcountry camping** requires a permit and fee from the Visitors Center, which is good for 14 days of camping. For further information, write to the Superintendent, Organ Pipe Cactus National Monument, 10 Organ Pipe Rd., Ajo AZ 85321-9626 or check www.nps.gov/orpi. The closest indoor accommodation is in **Lukeville,** a border town with a gas station, hotel, and border crossing. The **Gringo Pass Campground and Motel ❸** has several typical rooms in addition to a glut of RV and tent sites. (☎602-254-9284. Singles and doubles $56-65; quads $76-99. Hookups $15 and tent sites $11. RV lots closed in summer.) **Ajo,** 14 mi. north of the park boundary, has a greater array of lodging and services.

▟ **OUTDOOR ACTIVITIES.** Two scenic loop-drives penetrate the park's desert landscape and lead to a few trailheads. Both are winding and unpaved, *so keep your speed low.* No water is available along either drive. The popular **Ajo Mountain Drive** (21 mi. round-trip; 2hr. one-way.) circles along the foothills of the steep, rocky Ajo Mountains, the highest range in the area. On the other side of the park, the sometimes closed **Puerto Blanco Drive** (53 mi. round-trip; 4-5hr.) winds through the colorful Puerto Blanco Mountains, passing oases, cacti, and abandoned mines along the way. An exceptional feature along the drive is **Quitobaquito,** a spring, creek, and marshland in the area where the drive meets the Mexican border. In stark contrast to the baking heat and relative silence of the desert, the oasis is at least 10°F cooler and hums with insects, song birds, and other animals. The road leads to within ¼ mi. of the pond and marsh; walk the last stretch. In the midst of your cool respite, however, be aware that the busy Mexican Rte. 2 zips by merely 100 yards away from the spring, and with large breaks in the fencing. Thefts do occur in the parking lot. Lock your doors, and don't leave your CD player, video camera, digital camera, laptop, or Fabergé egg in plain sight.

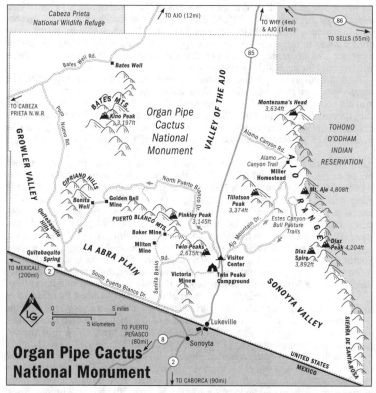

Cabeza Prieta
National Wildlife Refuge

TO AJO (12mi)

TO WHY (4mi)
& AJO (14mi)

86

TO SELLS (55mi)

Bates Well Rd.

Bates Well

85

TO CABEZA
PRIETA N.W.R

BATES MTS.

Kino Peak
3,197ft

Organ Pipe
Cactus
National
Monument

VALLEY OF THE AJO

Montezuma's Head
3,634ft

Alamo Canyon Rd.

TOHONO
O'ODHAM
INDIAN
RESERVATION

Alamo
Canyon Trail

Miller
Homestead

CIPRIANO HILLS

North Puerto Blanco Dr.

AJO RANGE

Mt. Ajo 4,808ft

GROWLER VALLEY

Pozo Nuevo Rd.

Bonita
Well

Golden Bell
Mine

PUERTO BLANCO MTS.

Pinkley Peak
3,145ft

Baker Mine

Tillotson
Peak
3,374ft

Estes Canyon-
Bull Pasture
Trails

Quitobaquito Hills

Milton
Mine

Twin Peaks
2,615ft

Ajo Mountain Dr.

Diaz
Peak 4,204ft

Quitobaquito
Spring

LA ABRA PLAIN

Rd.

Senita Basin

Visitor
Center

Diaz
Spire
3,892ft

TO MEXICALI
(200mi)

2

South Puerto Blanco Dr.

Victoria
Mine

Twin Peaks
Campground

SONOYTA VALLEY

N
LG

0   5 miles
0   5 kilometers

TO PUERTO
PEÑASCO
(80mi)

8

Lukeville

Sonoyta

SIERRA DE SANTA ROSA

**Organ Pipe Cactus
National Monument**

2

UNITED STATES
MEXICO

TO CABORCA (90mi)

Several hikes offer a quieter, more engaging means of experiencing the park, but
sure to bring plenty of water. About halfway around the loop of the Ajo Mountain
Drive lies the beginning of the **Estes Canyon-Bull Pasture Trail.** This strenuous 4½ mi.
round-trip hike climbs through the mountains to a plateau that affords an astounding view from all sides. An easier trek leads from the end of Twin Peaks campground to **Victoria Mine,** the oldest lead and silver mine in the area (4½ mi. round-
trip). Ruddy-walled **Alamo Canyon** and an abandoned cattle ranch are accessible by
a half a mile walk from the campsite (see above), and backcountry options in the
Ajo Range are innumerable. See the rangers for further ideas. For those who prefer two wheels, most roads in the park double as biking trails, but be sure to exercise caution on the busy thoroughfares in the park.

CORONADO NATL. FOREST (NOGALES DISTRICT)

If it seems like every green space on the map of southern Arizona is part of the
Coronado National Forest, it's because the forest consists of a dozen mountainous
"sky islands" separated by tracts of desert, city, and highway. Between Tucson and
Nogales and split by I-19, two giant chunks of the **Nogales Ranger District** of the
Coronado National Forest fill up most of Santa Cruz County. The alpine climate in
the mountains provides a cooler, wetter contrast to the desert that surrounds Tucson. The **Nogales District Ranger Station,** 303 Old Tucson Rd., just north of Nogales

ARIZONA

on I-19 at the Ruby Rd. exit, dispenses maps of the area, including detailed trail descriptions on request. (☎520-281-2296. Open daily 8am-4:30pm.) The Tucson-based **Southern Arizona Hiking Club** (☎520-751-4513; www.sahcinfo.org) leads guided hikes in the area—call or pick up their bulletin at the ranger station for more info. No mountain bikes are permitted in designated wilderness areas; check with rangers for details about restrictions.

There are surprisingly few maintained campgrounds in the Nogales district. The **Bog Springs Campground ❶**, with 13 sites, and water, grants access to several hikes (sites $10). Another campground sits to the west of Nogales along Ruby Rd., accessible from the Ruby Rd. exit off of I-19. **White Rock Campground ❶**, on Pena Blanca Lake, offers fishing, a boat launch, and drinking water ($3 day-use or $7 overnight). **Backcountry camping** is free, but parking areas may charge a fee.

❷ OUTDOOR ACTIVITIES. There are plenty of **hiking** opportunities in the forest, but all of the hikes listed here are off-limits to mountain bikes and closed in the winter. The strenuous **Old Baldy Trail** (#372) is the most direct way of reaching the summit of Mt. Wrightson (9450 ft.), the highest peak in the Santa Rita range (elevation gain 4050 ft.). To access the trailhead, take I-19 N from Nogales to the Continental Rd. exit. From there, take Madera Canyon Rd. (Forest Road 62) until Forest Road 70, then take a left to the Roundup Picnic area. Turn left, and there is a parking lot for the trailhead. This 4.5 mi. round-trip trail ascends to gorgeous views of Southern Arizona's mountain ranges. The **Super Trail** (#134) is the easier and longer (8.1 mi.) ascent up Mt. Wrightson, sharing a trailhead and the same views with Old Baldy. The **Bog Springs/Kent Springs Loop** (#156/157) meanders through stands of sycamore, juniper, and walnut, in addition to the Arizona bamboo that flourishes in this surprisingly green and moist area. To access the 4.3 mi. loop trail, use the directions to Madera Canyon Rd., but instead of driving to Roundup picnic area, drive to Bog Springs Campground, park in the parking area, and follow the old roadbed past campground #13. (1800 ft. elevation gain.)

Although the above trails are all off-limits to bikes, the area does presents some opportunities for two-wheel excursions. The rigorous 13 mi. **Elephant Head Mountain Bike Route** (#930/930A) follows a variety of single-track trails and forest roads between its northern end on Proctor Rd. (Forest Road 70) and the Whipple Observatory Visitors Center, its southern terminus (1000 ft. elevation gain). To reach the northern end, take I-19 to Madera Canyon Rd. After 11 mi., turn onto Prescott Rd. (Forest Road 70), and follow it for 2 mi. until the route begins at the road's junction with Forest Road 4074.

NOGALES   ☎520

The site of one of Arizona's largest border crossings, Nogales has grown into a touristy bottleneck of sorts, brimming on one side and quiet on the other. The Mexican side of the city boasts over 200,000 people, while the American district is home to one-tenth that number. Store signs all over Nogales are either bilingual or entirely in Spanish, about half of the local TV stations show Mexican programming, and even the highway mileage signs are done Mexican-style; between here and Tucson, all distances are given on signs in kilometers. Welcome to Mexico's northern-most city.

Nogales lies at the southern terminus of I-19, which continues onward into Mexico as Hwy. 15, and splits with its commercial doppelganger, "Business I-19", a.k.a. Grand Ave., for the length of the town. The two roads merge north of town and are linked by the shopping-mall-lined Mariposa Rd. Rte. 82 connects Nogales to the smaller communities in Arizona's southeastern pocket, branching off of Grand Ave. at the northern end of downtown and leading onward to the towns of Patagonia, Tombstone, and Bisbee.

CROSSING THE BORDER There are border checkpoints on Grand Ave. in the middle of Nogales and on I-19 west of the city. The Grand Ave. crossing sees heavy local traffic while the I-19 crossing is where larger commercial vehicles and long-distance travelers cross. Crossing into Mexico in Nogales is easy for American or Canadian citizens; no visas are required for entry if you stay for less than 72 hours and travel less than 21km. For residents of another country, consult the Mexican Consulate for specifics. Although only proof of citizenship is necessary for these daytrips (a valid or expired passport, birth certificate, or naturalization forms), in most cases these documents aren't even checked. Longer excursions into Mexico are more complicated. Citizens of the United States, Australia, Japan, and most larger European countries do not have to get a visa as long as they do not engage in profitable activities or intend to study. For more information, visit the Mexican consulate (☎287-2521, or www.mexonline.com/consulate.htm) on Grand Ave. If you plan on driving your car in Mexico, you must purchase Mexican car insurance before you cross the border, as American insurance does not always transfer. Consult your individual agency. A host of stores along Grand Ave. sell Mexican insurance. Getting back into the United States is not always quite so simple; American customs and immigration officials keep a close eye on the traffic that passes this border. Hour-long delays at the Nogales crossing are not uncommon. American citizens have to worry most about customs rather than immigration; the inspectors will ask about contraband. They may also inspect obvious hiding places for illegal immigrants. Tourists to the US crossing the border should be aware of their visa status to ensure that there will be no problem with readmittance; visitors from nations qualifying them for visa exemption needn't worry—you will be asked to fill out a form, but that's all. Students, legal immigrants, and aliens on work visas should be more wary; there are usually restrictions on readmittance in those circumstances. *Border Patrol, Tucson Office ☎670-6871. Border open daily 6am-10pm.*

The **Greyhound** bus terminal, 26 N. Terrace Ave. (☎287-5628), is close to the border, west of Grand Ave., and sells tickets to Phoenix (3½-5hr., 7 per day, $22) and Tucson (1½hr., 7 per day, $8). Extensive **visitor info** is available at the **Chamber of Commerce,** 123 W. Kino Pkwy., in Kino Park at the northern end of town. (☎287-3785. Open M-F 8am-5pm.) Services include: **police,** 777 N. Grand Ave. (☎287-9111); **Carondelet Holy Cross Hospital,** 1171 W. Target Range Rd. (☎287-2771), off of I-19 at the last exit before the Mexican border; free **Internet access** at the **library,** 518 N. Grand St. (☎287-3343; open winter M and W 10am-6pm, T and Th 10am-8pm, F 9am-5pm, Sa 9am-4pm, summer hours vary); and **post office,** 300 N. Morley Ave., a block east of Grand Ave. (☎287-9246. Open M-F 8:30am-5pm, Sa 10am-12pm.) **Postal code:** 85621.

Unfortunately, budget accommodations in Nogales are a bit dodgy. The chain motels along Mariposa and Grand are inexpensive and reliable, though fairly colorless. Under new management, the **Time Motel** ❷, 921 Grand Ave., provides guests with TV, A/C, phones, fridges, microwaves, and a pool at budget prices. (☎287-0702. In summer singles $32, doubles $36; in winter $36/$40.) You'll find a larger pool and interior hallways at the **Americana Motor Hotel** ❷, 639 N. Grand Ave., but fridges or microwaves are not included. (☎800-874-8079. $40 singles, $50 doubles.) If it's cheap Mexican food you crave, head south of the border; if it's great Mexican food you crave, **El Tapatio de Nogales** ❷, 557 N. Grand Ave., is a friendly joint across from the library offering the exotic tastes of Mexican horchata, jasmine, and tamarindo drinks. (☎287-4400. Open M-F 9am-6pm Sa 10am-6pm.)

ROUTE 82/80: NOGALES TO TOMBSTONE

The stretch of state highway linking the towns of Nogales and Tombstone passes through wide swaths of wilderness punctuated by nothing but small, picturesque townships. The 71 mi. between the two towns are some of the most pleasant you'll ever drive in this region, if not the country. With towns like Patagonia and Sonoita along the way, there is no shortage of gas stations en route, but prices and hours tend to be best in Nogales.

Immediately outside Nogales, the road crosses the **Santa Cruz River.** Past the river, the highway is flanked on either side by the **Coronado National Forest,** a woodsy backdrop to the rugged landscape, and then reaches **Patagonia Lake State Park.** Formed when Sonoita creek was dammed in the late 60s, the lake is used by locals for all water sports, and the park offers a **campground ❶,** a beach, and excellent fishing (☎520-287-6965. 110 sites, showers. $5 per night, $22 for hookups, $7 day use. Entrance closed 10pm-5am.) Past the park, buttes and rock formations rise on either side of the road leading up to **Patagonia,** a pretty town that prospered from both the railroad and ranching and survived the fall of both. Patagonia tends to be cooler than Nogales, but summer nearly shuts the town down completely.

The highway continues past Patagonia along the Sonoita Creek before entering **Sonoita** itself. The rangeland surrounding the small town boasts some of Arizona's prized vineyards and eateries. The fresh, organic food at **Grasslands Restaurant & Bakery ❷,** 3119 Rte. 83, is well worth a stop for lunch. (☎455-4770. Baked goods $1-5. Open Th-Su 8am-3pm, winter W-Su.) Sonoita's surrounding vineyards are also worth the stop, with myriad wines to sample and buy. The farthest south, **Sonoita Vineyards** offers visitors breathtaking views of the valley and sprawling vineyards. It is the product of a University of Arizona professor's agricultural experiment and one of the first vineyards in the state. (☎455-5893. Open M-F 10am-4pm.)

North of Sonoita Vineyards and the town of Elgin is the **Callaghan Vineyard.** (☎455-5322. $3 tastings F-Su 11am-3pm.) Nine miles south of town in the village of **Elgin,** somehow located due south of Sonoita but north of Sonoita Vineyards, sits the large **Elgin Complex Winery,** whose house pride, "Tombstone Red," is also the best-selling wine in Arizona. (☎455-9309. Tours daily 10am-5pm.) The next 38 mi. pass through nearly barren wilderness, and only buttes and distant mountains break the lull of the arid Arizona desert. **Fairbank,** the sole town on this stretch of the road, is so small that it is barely noticeable. Approaching Tombstone, the scenery morphs into a Hollywood Western, buzzards circling and heat blasting. The only thing missing are the cattle skulls (and you can find those in the tourist-trap shops of Tombstone).

TOMBSTONE
☎520

Long past its glory days when Tombstone was the largest city between the Pacific and the Mississippi, the town has sanitized itself from an authentic, debauched and dangerous Western town into a Cowboy Disneyland. In Tombstone you can get anything you want—as long as it's a shot of rot-gut or a gunfight re-enactment.

By inviting visitors to view the barnyard where Wyatt Earp and his brothers kicked some serious butt, Tombstone has turned the **shootout at the O.K. Corral,** on Allen St. next to City Park, into a year-round tourist industry. The voice of Vincent Price narrates the town's history next door to the O.K. Corral in the **Tombstone Historama,** while a plastic mountain revolves onstage and a dramatization of the gunfight shows on a movie screen. (☎457-3456. Shootout open daily 9am-5pm, arrive before 2pm re-enactment. Historama shows daily 9am-4pm, every hr. $7.50 admission to both attractions.) For something a little different, the **Rose Tree Museum,** at 4th St. and Toughnut St., shelters over 8000 square feet of the largest rose tree in the world. (☎457-3326. Open daily 9am-5pm. $2, under 14 free.) Site of the longest poker game ever played in Western history (8 years, 5 months, and 3 days), the **Bird Cage Theater,** at 6th St. and Allen, was named for the suspended cages that once housed prostitutes. (☎457-3421. Self-guided tour. $6, $5.50 seniors.)

Staying in Bisbee to commute for half a day in Tombstone is not a bad idea. Those who would rather stay in town, the **Larian Motel ❷,** on the corner of Fremont and 5th St. in Tombstone, is exceptionally clean, roomy, nicely furnished, and within easy walking distance of all sights. (☎457-2272. Singles $40-45, doubles $45-59.) The many guest houses and bed and breakfasts in town represent a pricier but much cozier alternative.

For moonshine and country music, smell your way to **Big Nose Kate's Saloon,** on Allen St. and 5th St., named for "the girl who loved Doc Holliday and everyone else too." Bartenders serve drinks with names like "Sex in the Desert." (☎457-3107. Live music. Open daily 10am-midnight, depending on the crowd.) **Nellie Cashman's Restaurant ❶,** on 5th St. off of Allen, named after the "angel of the mining camps" who devoted her life to clean living and public service, is a little less Old West and a bit more down-home. (☎457-2212. Open daily 7:30am-9pm.)

To get to Tombstone, head to the Benson exit off I-10, then go south on Rte. 80. Turn off Hwy. 80 into the dirt parking lot on the east side between 3rd St. and 4th St., or turn west onto 3rd St., left on Allen, and free parking is ahead on your right. All the attractions are within a couple short blocks of these parking areas. The nearest **Greyhound** station is in **Benson.** The **Douglas Shuttle** (☎364-3761) has service to Tucson ($10), Bisbee ($5), and Benson ($5).

The **Tombstone Visitors Center,** a large, white building on 4th St. and Allen, provides brochures and maps, although Tombstone is so small that nothing takes long to find. (☎457-3929. Open M-F 9am-4pm, Sa-Su 10am-4pm.) The Tombstone **Marshal's office** (☎457-2244) is just behind City Hall. **Internet access** is available at **Gitt Wired,** 5th and Fremont. (☎457-3250. Open 7am-5pm. $0.15 per min.) The **post office** is at 100 N. Haskell Ave. **Postal code:** 85638.

BISBEE ☎520

One hundred miles southeast of Tucson (p. 138) and 20 mi. south of Tombstone (p. 152), mellow Bisbee, a former mining town, is known throughout the Southwest as a laid-back artists' colony and an excellent base for exploring the rest of southeastern Arizona. Once known for its mines and labor troubles (in 1918, at the end of WWI, 1200 striking miners were deported at gunpoint to the desert in New Mexico), now Bisbee's citizens are probably farther left than the agitators they once deported. Visitors can go spelunking in Coronado National Memorial, hike the adjoining stretch of Coronado National Forest, visit Sonoita wine country, or cross into Mexico, all within an hour's drive. The few sights in town are mine-related, but Bisbee's hippie population make it a terrific place to stroll, chat, and drink coffee in an artsy cafe.

▸ PRACTICAL INFORMATION. Greyhound does not serve Bisbee, but the local **Douglas Shuttle** (☎364-3761) links Bisbee with surrounding cities served by the major bus company, including both Tombstone ($5) and Tucson ($15). Maps, brochures, and advice on the area can be found at the **Chamber of Commerce,** 31 Subway St. (☎432-5421. Open M-F 9am-5pm, Sa-Su 10am-4pm.) Pick up one of their maps: the streets of Bisbee are labyrinthine, and without a map you will be lost. With a map you'll still be lost, but you'll feel better. For cheap groceries, head just outside of Old Bisbee on 80 East and look for the sign for the **Bisbee Food Co-op & Deli,** 72 Erie St., Lowell Plaza. (☎432-4011. Open M-Sa 9am-7pm, Su 10am-5pm.) **Canyon Wash Laundromat,** on 226 Tombstone Canyon Rd., is near the south end of town. (Open daily 8am-8pm. Washing and drying each $0.75.) The **post office** on Main St. is one block south of the highway exit. (☎432-2052. Open M-F 8:30am-4:30pm.) **Postal code:** 85603.

⚐ ☖ ACCOMMODATIONS & FOOD. For the traveler steeped in nostalgia, **The Shady Dell ❷**, 1 Douglas Rd., consists of a vintage 1950s trailer park with half a dozen lovingly restored campers. Play records on a 1950s gramophone in a trailer, or brave the seas of Bisbee in their most recent addition, a fully-restored yacht, drydock and all. For an even more authentic experience, eat at **Dot's Diner ❷** on the premises. (☎432-3567. Trailers $35-75, RVs $15, camping $10.) About a 10min. walk from downtown, the **Jonquil Motel ❷**, 317 Tombstone Canyon, offers clean, smoke-free rooms and a backyard perfect for barbecues or lounging. (☎432-7371. Singles $40-45, doubles $55-65; in winter about $10 more.) At the south end of town, the **School House Inn ❸**, 818 Tombstone Canyon Rd., houses guests in a remodeled 1918 school house. Rooms are all themed and vary in size; the Principal's Office is palatial indeed, while the numbered classrooms have a cozier sort of charm. (☎432-2996 or 800-537-4333. All rooms have private bath, full breakfast included, TV in common room. No children under 14. Single bed $60; double/queen/king $75-85; 2-bed suite $95.)

A number of cheap eateries line the main drags of Bisbee's downtown. Most restaurants feature classic, hearty American fixins' for around $5-9. Meat-a-tarians can get a fix at **Old Tymers ❷**, with steaks ($12) and hamburgers ($6-7) cooked any way they like, from bleeding to burnt. (☎432-7304. Open M-Th 11am-9pm, F-Sa 11am-10pm, Su 11am-8pm.)

◪ SIGHTS. Queen Mines, on the Rte. 80 interchange entering Old Bisbee, ceased mining in 1943 but continues to give educational 1¼hr. tours. (☎866-432-2071. Tours at 9, 10:30am, noon, 2, and 3:30pm. $12, ages 4-15 $5.) The Smithsonian-affiliated **Mining and Historical Museum,** 5 Copper Queen, highlights the discovery of Bisbee's copper surplus and the lives of the fortune-seekers who extracted it. (☎432-7071. Open daily 10am-4pm. $4, seniors $3.50, under 3 free.)

For a less earthly and more heavenly experience, visit the **Chihuahua Hill Shrines.** A 20 min. hike over rocky ground leads to two shrines, the first Buddhist and the second Mexican Catholic. To reach these shrines, head up Brewery Ave. to a grocery store on the right. Behind the store, two staircases head up the hill; take the left-most. After the climb up the stairway, turn left and follow a concrete driveway for a very short time. Right before the private property sign, turn right off of the paved road and start hiking through the rock. At the cross, bear up and follow the trail. The view alone of the town and desert is worth the ascent.

⚠ OUTDOOR ACTIVITIES. About 25 mi. west of Bisbee along Rte. 92 near the Mexican border, **Coronado National Memorial** marks the place where Francisco Coronado and his expedition first entered American territory. A small Visitors Center houses exhibits about the expedition and a video documenting the famous voyage. The park contains a few hiking trails, including the southernmost section of the **Arizona Trail,** and offers the chance to do some independent spelunking. **Coronado Cave,** unlike its cousins Kartchner and Colossal near Tucson, is a small, relatively dry cave and is safe to explore without a guide. Imagine yourself searching for Geronimo, who may have evaded US forces here, but give yourself the advantage by bringing two flashlights and water. Rangers require a flashlight anyway, in return for the free permit. The cave is 0.8 mi. from the Visitors Center along a short, steep path, so plan on 30min. for the trail and at least an hour in the cave. (☎366-5515. Park open daily dawn to dusk. Visitors Center open daily 9am-5pm.) Back on Rte. 92 and about 7 mi. past the Coronado turnoff is Ramsey Canyon Rd.,

DELUGE The concept of a monsoon is more evocative of Indochina than Arizona, but the seasonal storms that batter the southern part of the state are aptly named. June in Arizona brings with it stereotypical desert weather: heat, sun, more heat, and more sun. Perhaps only a lonely cloud mars the perfect blue sky in Tucson in late June, but come July 4, it's joined by a regular posse of precipitation. After the intense, dry heat of June, the monsoonal flow arrives in July and August. Though the temperature remains fairly high, daily thunderstorms pop up and pour down on the desert. These storms have a few peculiarities. Due to the lack of moisture in the desert, vast quantities of dust are taken up into the clouds, producing intense static electricity and some of the most spectacular lightning in the world. The storms are also extremely localized; it is possible to cross the street in Tucson and go from sunny weather into the teeth of driving rain. Apart from constituting a meteorological curiosity, these storms pose dangers to travelers. Hiking at high altitudes during stormy weather increases the risk of lightning strikes and exposure, especially in the afternoon; aim to head back from peaks around noon. The faint of heart, and those who faint in the heat, should consider visiting southern Arizona in the winter months, when the only extreme weather will be on the Weather Channel in your overpriced hotel room.

where lies **Ramsey Canyon Preserve,** attracting nearly as many bird-watchers as birds. In the middle of migratory routes for many North American birds, the preserve draws thousands of hummingbirds in the late summer. Other species, including the golden eagle and a number of bats, pass through en masse. A short 0.8 mi. trail meanders through the manicured grounds, passing by a hummingbird garden, a frog pond, and a butterfly park. (Open daily 8am-5pm. $5, under 16 free; first Sa of every month free.)

CHIRICAHUA NATIONAL MONUMENT ☎520

Over 25 million years ago, Chiricahua was a heap of volcanic ash extruded from the massive Turkey Creek Caldera. Fortunately, since then the powers of erosion have over time sculpted the hardened rock into spectacular formations with forbidding mountains looming in the background. Pillars of stacked stones cluster in groups all over the area, and tons of rock are perched precariously, appearing as though they'll fall immediately (though they've been like that for hundreds of years, so don't worry). A cross between Zion and Bryce Canyon, Chiricahua was aptly called the "Land of the Standing-Up Rocks" by Apaches and the "Wonderland of Rocks" by early pioneers. And while Chiricahua nearly equals the natural splendor of Utah's Bryce and Zion Canyons, it happily falls short of their popularity and tourism numbers, indulging visitors with peace and tranquility.

ORIENTATION & PRACTICAL INFORMATION. Chiricahua is 40 mi. from I-10 and 70 mi. from **Bisbee** (p. 153); from Bisbee, go east on Rte. 80 to Rte. 191 N, then to 181 N. The cheapest gas station in all of southeastern Arizona is on Rte. 191 coming from Douglas. The **Visitors Center** sits just beyond the entrance station to the park. (☎824-3560, ext. 104. Open daily 8am-5pm. Restrooms and payphone. Entrance fee $5.) The entirety of Chiricahua National Monument, except for a strip around the main road, is federally designated wilderness: as such, there is no biking, climbing, or backcountry camping allowed. On the positive side, rangers offer a one-way shuttle from the Visitors Center and campsite to Echo Canyon and Massai Point trailheads (8:30am daily).

⌐▐ ▐▀ ACCOMMODATIONS & CAMPING. Although no backcountry camping is permitted along the trails, there is an established campground inside the park. **Bonita Canyon ❶** features toilets, picnic grounds, water, and easy access to the park trails, but no showers. (24 sites. 14-day max. stay. $12.) Nearby indoor accommodations include the plush, ranch-style **Chiricahua Foothills Bed and Breakfast ❹**, with well-decorated rooms facing a green courtyard. Lunch and dinner are available on request at extra cost. (☎824-3632. Doubles $70.) Farther south between the 51- and 52-mile markers on Rte. 181, the **Dreamcatcher Bed and Breakfast ❹**, 13097 Hwy. 181, sprawls along 27 acres. (☎824-3334. Room with queen bed $70, suite with cable TV and kitchenette $90. National Forest access available.)

◪ HIKING. There is a bountiful selection of **day hikes** in the monument, and many combinations of the descriptions below are possible. From the parking lot, the ◪**Echo Canyon Trail** leads 1.6 mi. through an impressive cluster of formations before junctioning with the **Hailstone** and **Upper Rhyolite Trails**. For a longer loop, continue down the Upper Rhyolite Trail 1.1 mi. farther as the path wanders through pine forest. The trail junctions with the **Sarah Deming Trail**, which steeply ascends the opposite face of the canyon. The highest point of the hike comes after 1.6 mi., and you can either hike the **Heart of Rocks Scenic Loop,** which offers extraordinary views of and passage through the monument's incredible rock formations, or continue immediately along **Big Balanced Rock Trail,** which winds across ridge tops for 1 mi. Here there is also a half-mile spur leading to the aptly named **Inspiration Point,** which affords a commanding view of the formations and canyons below. The return trip follows the **Mushroom Rock Trail** and **Ed Riggs Trail,** with more forest and fewer views than the Echo Canyon beginning. Together, these trails are approximately 2 mi. in length. The whole loop clocks in at 7.4 mi. and takes 4-5hr.; add 1.1 mi. and 45min. for the Heart of Rocks Loop and 1 mi. and 35 min. for the Inspiration Point Trail. The trail is fairly strenuous and without reliable water. The trails are clearly marked both at the trailheads and junctions and on the free monument map provided, but for added peace of mind and safety 25¢ can buy you a more detailed **trail map** at the Visitors Center.

The central loops are the bread and butter of Chiricahua, leading through the most spectacular country and racking up the brunt of the monument's mileage, but a few side treks also merit attention. Separate from the loop complex of Echo Canyon is the 4.8 mi. round-trip **Natural Bridge Trail.** Beginning off the main road on a clearly marked trailhead 1.5 mi. past the Visitors Center, this trail gains and loses 500 ft. over 2.4 mi., ending at a point where the rocks form a small natural bridge. The trail takes 3hr. to complete. Another trail leads from a parking lot at the extreme end of the main road up to the top of **Sugarloaf Mountain,** affording gorgeous views of the mountain crags and valleys. There is an approximately 500 ft. gain over the steep, 0.8 mi. trail; allow 2hr. for the hike.

CALIFORNIA

California's desert divides roughly into the Low and High Deserts, names which indicate differences in both altitude and latitude. The Sonoran, or Low Desert (p. 172) occupies southeastern California from the Mexican border north to Needles and west to the Borrego Desert. The Mojave, or High Desert, averages elevations of 2000 ft., spanning the southern central part of the state, bounded by the Sonoran to the south, San Bernardino and the San Joaquin Valley to the west, the Sierra Nevadas to the north, and Death Valley to the east. Four major east-west highways cross the desert. In the Low Desert, I-8 hugs the California-Mexico border, while I-10 passes Joshua Tree and Palm Springs. I-15 cuts through the Mojave from Barstow, the Mojave's main pit stop, on to Las Vegas, while I-40 cuts southeast through Needles and on to the Nevada desert. West of the desert, Los Angeles is a major hub for Southwest travel, and Route 395 provides a major route up the east side of the Sierras to Reno.

⚲ HIGHLIGHTS OF CALIFORNIA

DEATH VALLEY. Visit the lowest point in the US at **Badwater** (p. 178), or hike to **Telescope Peak** (p. 179).

JOSHUA TREE. Take on the world-class boulders at the **Wonderland of Rocks** and **Hidden Valley** (p. 162).

GHOST TOWNS. Explore the ghost towns of the California Desert, including **Bodie** (p. 195) and **Skidoo** (p. 180).

HIGH DESERT

The High Desert is the picture of desolation. Atop a plateau, the desert unfolds at heights around 5000 ft. The Mojave conceals unlikely treasures for those patient and brave enough to explore it. Genuine summer attractions are rare, but temperate winters allow one to trudge across drifting dunes and creep through ghost towns. At Joshua Tree, some of the best bouldering in the US awaits climbers.

JOSHUA TREE NATIONAL PARK ☎ 760

When devout Mormon pioneers crossed this faith-testing desert in the 19th century, they named the enigmatic tree they encountered after the Biblical prophet Joshua. The tree's crooked limbs resembled the Hebrew general, and, with arms upraised, seemed to beckon these Latter-Day pioneers to the Promised Land. Even today, Joshua Tree National Park inspires reverent awe in those who happen upon it. Its piles of wind-sculpted boulders, guarded by legions of eerie Joshua Trees, continue to evoke the devastation of the walls of Jericho.

In recent years, climbers, campers, and daytrippers from Southern California have added to the mosaic of lonely rock piles in the park. The boulder formations strewn across the desert badlands have nearly limitless potential for first ascents. "Josh," as outdoor enthusiasts call it, has become a world-renowned mecca for both casual and elite climbers. History buffs will appreciate the vestiges of human occupation: ancient rock petroglyphs, 19th-century dams built to catch the meager rainfall for livestock, and gold mine ruins dotting the landscape. But the most attractive aspect of Joshua Tree is its remoteness and freedom from the commercial mayhem that has infested many national parks. Its natural beauty is interrupted only by a few paved roads and signs, with vast tracts left almost untouched since the days when miners coaxed precious metals out of the scarred terrain.

At the north entrance to the park lies Twentynine Palms, settled after World War I by veterans-turned-homesteaders looking for a hot, dry climate to soothe their battle-weary bodies. Today, the town also hosts the world's largest US Marine Corps base, as well as murals depicting people and events from the town's past.

AT A GLANCE: JOSHUA TREE NATIONAL PARK

AREA: 794,000 acres.

FEATURES: Pinto Mountains, Hexie Mountains, Eagle Mountains, Little Bernadino Mountains, High/Low Desert Transition Zone, and Lost Palms Oasis.

HIGHLIGHTS: Climbing virtually anyplace in the park, hiking to the top of Ryan Mountain or to the bottom of Lost Palms Oasis, camping at the more remote Belle Campground, driving the four-wheel-drive Geology Tour Rd.

GATEWAY TOWNS: Joshua Tree, Twentynine Palms, Yucca Valley.

CAMPING: Park campgrounds range from free to $35. Registration required for backcountry camping.

FEES: Weekly pass $10 per vehicle, $5 per pedestrian or bike.

▐ TRANSPORTATION

The park is ringed by three highways: **Interstate 10** to the south, **Route 62 (Twentynine Palms Highway)** to the west and north, and **Route 177** to the east. The northern entrances to the park are off Rte. 62 at the towns of **Joshua Tree** and **Twentynine Palms.** The south entrance is at **Cottonwood Spring,** off I-10 at **Route 195,** southeast of Palm Springs near the town of Indio. The **park entrance fee,** valid for seven days, is $5 per person or $10 per car.

 WHEN TO GO. Because of intense heat and aridity, it is best to avoid visiting Joshua Tree from June to September. The park's most temperate weather is in late fall (Oct.-Dec.) and early spring (Mar.-Apr.); temperatures in other months often span uncomfortable extremes (summer highs 95-115°F, winter lows 30-40°). For more advice on beating the heat, see **The Desert and You,** p. 66.

CALIFORNIA

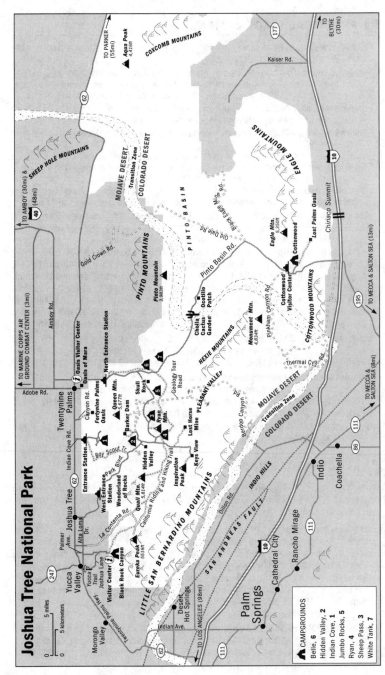

Joshua Tree National Park

CALIFORNIA

CAMPGROUNDS
Belle, **6**
Hidden Valley, **2**
Indian Cove, **1**
Jumbo Rocks, **5**
Ryan, **4**
Sheep Pass, **3**
White Tank, **7**

▼ PRACTICAL INFORMATION

Visitor Information: The best way to orient yourself at Joshua Tree is to stop at one of the many Visitors Centers that ring the park.

Headquarters and Oasis Visitor Center, 74485 National Park Dr. (☎367-5500; www.nps.gov/jotr), ¼ mi. off Rte. 62 in Twentynine Palms, is the best place to familiarize yourself with the park. Friendly rangers, plus displays, guidebooks, maps, restrooms, and water. Open daily 8am-5pm.

Cottonwood Visitor Center, at the southern gateway of the park, 7 mi. north of I-10 and 25 mi. east of Indio. Information, water, and picnic areas are available here. Open daily 8am-4pm.

Indian Cove Ranger Station, 7295 Indian Cove Rd. (☎362-4367). Open Oct.-May daily 8am-4pm; closed summers.

Park Center, 6554 Park Blvd. (☎366-3448; www.joshuatreeparkcenter.com), a private shop on the road from the Twentynine Palms Hwy. to the West Entrance in Joshua Tree that offers information and maps for purchase, as well as a gift shop. Open M-Sa 9am-6pm, Su 9am-4pm.

Twentynine Palms Chamber of Commerce, 6455 Mesquite Ave., Ste. A (☎367-3445), provides info on transportation, accommodations, and food. Open M-F 9am-5pm; may close for lunch.

Rock Climbing Gear and Guiding: Nomad Ventures, 61795 Twentynine Palms Hwy. (☎366-4684), in the town of Joshua Tree, has a ton of gear for sale or rent. Staff is well-qualified to give information and advice, especially for more experienced climbers. Open daily 9am-6pm. **Joshua Tree Rock Climbing School** (☎800-890-4745; www.rockclimbingschool.com), from Twentynine Palms Hwy., head south on Hillview, then turn right onto Desert Air Rd. will set you up with gear, guiding, and instruction, no matter what your level of experience. Inquire about their climber's cabins: 2-bed rooms with bath and kitchen ($125). Climbers can also pick up gear and experience the desert's grooviness at **Coyote Corner,** 6535 Park Blvd. (☎366-9683), where the gear smells of incense, and you can buy both. Showers available. Open daily 9am-6pm.

Emergency: 24hr. Dispatch (☎909-383-5651). Call collect. **Cellular phones** will probably not get reception anywhere in the park. **Hi-Desert Medical Center,** 6601 White Feather Rd. (☎366-3711), in Joshua Tree. Emergency care 24hr.

Internet Access: Twentynine Palms Branch Library, 6078 Adobe Rd. (☎367-9519), ¾ mi. north from the Twentynine Palms Hwy. in Twentynine Palms. Open M-T 12-8pm, W-F 10am-6pm, Sa 9am-5pm. In Joshua Tree, try the **Joshua Tree Branch Library,** 6465 Park Blvd. (☎366-8615), north from the Twentynine Palms Hwy. Open M-F 10am-6pm.

Post Office: 73839 Gorgonio Dr. (☎800-275-8777), in Twentynine Palms. Open M-F 8:30am-5pm. **Postal Code:** 92277.

▼ ACCOMMODATIONS

Those who are unwilling to stay at desert campgrounds but want to spend more than a day at the park can find inexpensive motels in Twentynine Palms, the self-proclaimed "Oasis of Murals."

29 Palms Inn, 73950 Inn Dr., is an attraction in its own right. Its 19 distinctly different rooms face the Mara Oasis, which has supported life for over 20,000 years. More recently, the life here has been of the celebrity genus, with guests like Michelle Pfeiffer and Nicholas Cage. Robert Plant gets the most attention; he composed his post-Zeppelin hit "29 Palms" here. Check out the garden, and enjoy its produce in the restaurant. (☎367-3505; www.29palmsinn.com. Reservations required Feb.-Apr. Doubles June-Sept. Su-Th $50-75, F-Sa $75-115; Oct.-May $10-20 extra. Cottages for 4-8 people also available for rent.) ❹

Motel 6, 72562 Twentynine Palms Hwy. (☎367-2833; www.motel6.com). Clean and reliable, and includes a pool, laundry, and free morning coffee. Make reservations online to save $3-4. Singles $40-44, doubles $46-50; each additional adult $3. ❸

Harmony Motel, 71161 Twentynine Palms Hwy. (☎367-3351; www.harmonymotel.com). While creating the album *Joshua Tree* in 1987, U2 stayed in one of the 10 units here. All rooms recently refurbished and have A/C. New communal cooking area. One-bed singles and doubles $60-70, negotiable in the summer low season. ❹

🏕 CAMPING

Camping is an enjoyable and inexpensive way to experience the beauty of the park—except in the scorching heat of summer. Even then, when the sun goes down the temperatures drop to comfortable levels. Pre-noon arrivals are the best way to guarantee a site, since most campgrounds in the park operate on a "first-come, first-camp" basis and accept no reservations (campgrounds that require separate fees do take reservations). Spring weekends and holidays are the busiest times. Reservations can be made for group sites only at Cottonwood, Sheep Pass, Indian Cove, and Black Rock Canyon via the Internet at www.nps.gov/jotr. Well-prepared and experienced campers can register for a backcountry permit at the Visitors Center or at self-service backcountry boards located throughout the park. Wilderness regulations require that backcountry campers camp at least 1 mi. from roads and 500 ft. from trails; rangers can provide maps of designated wilderness areas. All established campsites have tables, firepits, and pit toilets. There are no hookups for RVs, and only campgrounds that take reservations offer water or flush toilets—visitors who plan a longer stay should pack their own supplies. (14-day max. stay Oct.-May; 30-day camping limit each year.)

🏕 **Indian Cove,** 3200 ft., on the north edge of Wonderland of Rocks. Enter at the north entrance on Indian Cove Rd. off of Twentynine Palms Hwy. Popular spot for rock climbers. 101 sites. Sites $10; 13 group sites $20-35. ❶

🏕 **Jumbo Rocks,** 4400 ft., near Skull Rock Trail on the eastern edge of Queen Valley. Take Quail Springs Rd. 15 mi. south of the Visitors Center. The highest and coolest campground in the park, featuring many sites surrounded by—that's right—jumbo rocks. Front spots have shade and protection. Wheelchair accessible. 125 sites. Free. ❶

White Tank, 3800 ft. Few people, but watch for coyotes that may try to keep you company as you gaze at the Pinto Mountains. Cowboys built up White Tank as a reliable cattle watering hole. 15 sites amid huge boulder towers. Free. ❶

Hidden Valley, 4200 ft., in the center of Queen Valley off Quail Springs Rd. Secluded alcoves are perfect for pitching tents, and enormous shade-providing boulders serve as perches for viewing the sun at dawn and dusk. Its proximity to numerous popular climbing boulders makes it a rock climber's heaven. The 39 sites fill up quickly. Free. ❶

Sheep Pass, 4500 ft., on the trail to Ryan Mountain. Huge boulders and lots of Joshua trees make this site fairly cool and secluded. 6 group spots only, which can be reserved up to 3 months in advance. $20-35. ❷

Belle, 3800 ft., is an ideal place to stare at the starry heavens. Hold out for one of the sites on the road's second loop. 18 sites tucked in the crevices of big boulders. Free. ❶

Ryan, 4300 ft., has fewer rocks, less privacy, and less shade than nearby Hidden Valley. The 3 mi. round-trip trail ascends to Ryan Mountain, which served as the headquarters and water storage for the Lost Horse gold mine. The sunrise is spectacular from nearby Key's View (see p. 163). 31 sites. Free. ❶

🍴 FOOD

Although there are no food facilities within the park, Twentynine Palms offers both groceries and grub. If you are willing to cook, the **Stater Brothers** supermarket, 71727 Twentynine Palms Hwy., has a good selection and saves you a bundle.

(☎367-6535. Open M-Th and Su 6am-10pm, F-Sa 6am-11pm.) For healthy, natural, and organic food and supplements try **Joshua Tree Health Foods,** 61693 Twentynine Palms Hwy. (☎366-7489. Open M-Sa, 9am-6pm.)

Wonder Garden Cafe, 73511 Twentynine Palms Hwy. (☎367-2429). Locals recommend this spot, an organic juice pub, fresh sandwich deli, and smoothie joint all in one. Eat inside, in the garden, or take out. Adjoins a natural foods market next door. Open M-F 6:30am-6pm, Sa 8am-5pm, Su 8am-4pm. ❷

Rocky's New York Style Pizza, 73737 Twentynine Palms Hwy. (☎367-9525). No surprises here. This is where many locals go to satisfy their cravings. Pizzas and subs $7-15. Open M-Sa 11am-10pm. ❸

Andrea's Charbroiled Burgers, 73780 Twentynine Palms Hwy. (☎367-2008). Wise old men and others in the know dine anytime from breakfast ($3-6) to lunch and dinner ($2-7) for hearty eggs, pancakes, or burgers of various types. Open daily 6am-9pm. ❶

The Beatnik Cafe, 61597 Twentynine Palms Hwy. (☎366-2090). Serves hot coffee, but you may prefer to soothe your heat-addled brain with frosty beer or ice cream while you search the Internet for heat stroke treatments. Check the door for this week's live music schedule. Internet access $2 for the first 15 min., $3.50 for 30min., and $6 for 1hr. Open M-Th and Su 7am-midnight, F-Sa 7am-2am. ❶

▲ OUTDOOR ACTIVITIES

Over 80% of Joshua Tree is designated wilderness, safeguarding it against development and restricting paved roads, toilets, and campfires from encroaching into the park. As a result, it offers truly remote territory for backcountry desert hiking and camping. Hikers eager to reap the rewards of this primitiveness should pack plenty of water and keep alert for flash floods and changing weather conditions. Be sensitive to the extreme fragility of the desert and refrain from venturing off established trails. Do not enter abandoned mine shafts, as they are unstable and often filled with poisonous gases. For equestrians who bring their own horses, the **California Riding and Hiking Trail** provides 35 mi. of desert riding. Check with rangers for equestrian regulations, or stop in at **Joshua Tree Ranch,** 2 mi. south of the town of Joshua Tree on Park Blvd. (☎355-5357. $30 per hr.)

The tenacious wildflowers that struggle into colorful bloom each spring (mid-Mar. to mid-May) attract thousands of visitors. To avoid the social stigma accompanying floral ignorance, get updates on the status of yucca, verbena, cottonwood, mesquite, and dozens of other wildflowers via the **Wildflower Hotline** (☎367-5500)—the menu at this number is also useful for weather and guided tour information. The beds of wildflowers provide a habitat for Joshua Tree's many animal species, and the trees and reeds of the park's oases play host to ladybugs, bees, golden eagles, and bighorn sheep.

ROCK CLIMBING

The crack-split granite of Joshua provides some of the best rock climbing and bouldering on the planet, for experts and novices alike. The world-renowned boulders at **Wonderland of Rocks** and **Hidden Valley** are always swarming with hard-bodied climbers, making Joshua Tree the most climbed area in America. Because of the area's limitless potential, enumerating climbs is impossible; check with **Joshua Tree Climbing School** or **Nomad Ventures** (see p. 160) for advice, rentals, and guides. While hiring a guide is expensive for one person ($225 a day), it becomes more affordable if you arrange to go with several others ($100 per person for four people). Adventurous novices will find thrills at the **Skull Rock Interpretive Walk,** which runs between Jumbo Rocks and Skull Rock. The walk offers not only info on local plants and animals but also exciting yet non-technical scrambles on monstrous boulders. Before placing or replacing any bolts or other permanent protection, check with a ranger to see if your route is in designated wilderness. Bolts are not allowed within wilderness portions of the park.

HIKING

Despite the plethora of driving routes, hiking is perhaps the best way to experience Joshua Tree. The desert often appears monotonous through a car window, and it is only while walking slowly that one begins to appreciate the subtler beauties of the park. On foot, visitors can tread through sand, scramble over boulders, eye the occasional historical artifact, and walk among the park's stoic namesakes.

The Visitors Center has info on the park's many hikes, which range from a 15min. stroll to the **Oasis of Mara** to a three-day trek along the **California Riding and Hiking Trail** (35 mi.). The ranger-led **Desert Queen Ranch Walking Tour** covers the restored ranch of resourceful homesteader Bill Keys ($5; call for reservations). Anticipate slow progress even on short walks; the oppressive heat and the scarcity of shade can force even the heartiest of hikers to feel the strain. Drinking a liter of water an hour is not unreasonable on desert hikes.

Lost Horse Mine/Mountain (4.1-8.2 mi. round-trip, 2.5-5hr.). The trailhead is located near the end of the road to Key's View. The mine rests in peace at the end of a 2 mi. trail, commemorating the region's gold prospecting days with rusted machinery and abandoned mineshafts. If you don't want to return yet, keep following the trail up to the saddle of Lost Horse Mountain and beyond; the trail loops around back to the trailhead.

Ryan Mountain (3 mi. round-trip, 2hr.). From the top, the boulders in the encircling valley bear an uncanny resemblance to enormous beasts of burden toiling toward a distant destination. Bring lots of water for the strenuous, unshaded climb to the summit.

Lost Palms Oasis (7.5 mi. round-trip, 5hr.). Beginning at Cottonwood Springs, this trail rises onto a plateau before reaching a steep canyon filled with palm trees and a refreshing oasis at the bottom. Moving quickly until the canyon, the trail trades speed for the shade of the canyon walls. Lunch in the cool depths of the canyon, or take an overnight in the wilderness between Cottonwood and the oasis.

Inspiration Peak (2.2 mi. round-trip, 1hr.) A more solitary version of Keys View, originating from the same parking lot. It has the same great view, but fewer people. Arrive in time for sunrise to watch the morning alpenglow of Mts. San Jacinto and San Gorgonio.

Quail Mountain (15 mi. round-trip, 7hr.). The highest peak in the park, with excellent views of Mts. San Jacinto and San Gorgonio, the western half of the park, and the Mojave desert to the north. Park at the backcountry board where the Keys View Rd. crosses the California Riding and Hiking Trail and head west on the trail until the 24-mile marker (6 mi., 400 ft. elevation gain, 2hr.). Turn north on the dirt road until it ends and continue on the faint trail in the same direction. Aim for the easternmost of the two peaks before you ascend the rightmost gully. (1.5 mi., 1500 ft. elevation gain, 1½hr.)

DRIVING

The craggy mountains and boulders of Joshua Tree acquire a fresh poignancy at sunrise and sunset, when an earthy crimson washes across the desert. Daytrippers may miss out on these moments of quiet serenity for which the High Desert is justly renowned. A self-paced **driving tour** is an easy way to explore the park and linger until the sunset hours. The 34 mi. stretch through the park from Twentynine Palms to the town of Joshua Tree provides access to the park's most outstanding sights and hikes. An especially spectacular leg of the road is **Keys View** (5185 ft.), 6 mi. off the park road and just west of Ryan Campground. On a clear day, you can see forever—or at least to Palm Springs and the Salton Sea. It's also a great spot to watch the sunrise and take short hikes (see **Outdoor Activities: Hiking**, p. 163). The longer drive through the park from Twentynine Palms to I-10 traverses both High and Low Desert landscapes, also passing through the Pinto Basin with impressive views. The **Cholla Cactus Garden,** a grove of spiny succulents, lies just off the road.

YUCCA VALLEY ☎760

Yucca Valley, northwest of the park, is graced with a few unusual attractions and the genuinely helpful **California Welcome Center,** 56711 Twentynine Palms Hwy. (☎365-5464. Open daily 9am-6pm.) The **Hi-Desert Nature Museum,** in Yucca Valley's Community Complex, accessible by Damosa Rd., has several precious gemstones, as well as captive scorpions and snakes. Turn north on Damosa Rd. (☎369-7212. Open Tu-Su 10am-5pm. Free.) Alternatively, drive out to the infamous silver-domed "energy machine" officially known as the **Integratron.** Created by the eccentric George Van Tassel in the 1950s, the metallic and wood Integratron was supposed to create a "powerful vortex for physical and spiritual healing," but Van Tassel died mysteriously just before finishing it. Tours now lead visitors throughout the strange structure, and on the first three Sundays of the month the public can experience a rejuvenating "sound bath," where they are surrounded by resonating quartz crystal. Be sure to call ahead before you visit, and bring a blanket. To get to the Integratron from Yucca Valley, take Hwy. 62 to Old Woman Springs Rd. Turn north and continue 11 mi. farther to Landers. Once there, turn right at Reche Rd. and go 2 mi. to Belfield Rd. Turn left and go about 2 mi. more to 2477 Belfield. (☎364-3126; www.integratron.com. Tours F-Su noon-4pm. $5. Sound bath 4:30-5pm, $7.)

The **Big Morongo Canyon Preserve,** just west of Yucca Valley, is the temporary home for thousands of migratory birds in the spring and fall. In addition to providing the birds with a much-needed rest stop, the marsh's cool, moist habitat nurtures a grove of cottonwoods that shade early morning birdwatchers. With the help of friendly caretakers, visitors can easily identify over 50 species in the first two or so hours of sunlight on spring mornings. The short walks on boardwalks over the marsh are just long enough to enjoy the early morning hours before taking on the nearby desert. Horseback riding is allowed in the lower canyon. To get there, take East Dr. south from Hwy. 62 and turn left on Covington Dr.; the entrance is located at 11055 East Dr. (☎363-7190. Open daily 7:30am-sunset. Free.)

LOW DESERT

Withstanding a flat, dry, and barren environment, only a few resilient species have learned to flourish amidst the dust and broken rocks of California's Low Desert, also known as the Sonoran Desert. Despite its arid climate, irrigation has brought abundant life both to the region's miles of date groves as well as to the posh resorts of Palm Springs.

PALM SPRINGS ☎760

From the area's first known inhabitants—the Cahuilla Indians—to today's geriatric fun-lovers and rapidly growing numbers of gay tourists, the restorative oasis of Palm Springs (pop. 43,520) has attracted many visitors over the years. The medicinal waters of the city's natural hot springs ensure not only the vitality of its wealthy residents, but also its longevity as a resort town. While Palm Springs is home to gaggles of retirees, it is also a winter retreat for fat-cat golfers and a prime destination for gay and lesbian travelers. With warm winter temperatures, many celebrity residents, and more light pink and stucco than a Miami Vice episode, this desert city provides a sunny break from everyday life.

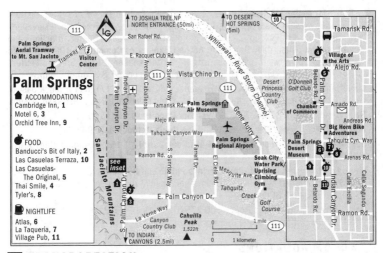

Palm Springs

▲ ACCOMMODATIONS
Cambridge Inn, **1**
Motel 6, **3**
Orchid Tree Inn, **9**

🍴 FOOD
Banducci's Bit of Italy, **2**
Las Casuelas Terraza, **10**
Las Casuelas-
The Original, **5**
Thai Smile, **4**
Tyler's, **8**

🍷 NIGHTLIFE
Atlas, **6**
La Taqueria, **7**
Village Pub, **11**

⌐ TRANSPORTATION

Airport: Palm Springs Regional, 3400 E. Tahquitz-Canyon Rd. (☎318-3800). Only has state and limited national service.

Buses: Greyhound, 311 N. Indian Canyon Dr. (☎325-2053 or 800-231-2222), near downtown. Open daily 8am-6pm. To: **L.A.** (7 per day, $19.50-21, round-trip $32-36); **San Diego** (7 per day, $23.50); **Las Vegas** (6 per day, weekdays $53, weekends $59).

Public Transportation: SunBus (☎343-3451). Local bus connecting all Coachella Valley cities (Info office open daily 5am-10pm). Lines #23, 24, and 111 cover downtown and surrounding locales. The *SunBus Book,* available at info centers and in most hotel lobbies, includes schedules and a system map. Fare $0.75, transfers $0.25.

Taxis: Yellow Cab (☎345-8398). **Ace Taxi** (☎321-6008).

Trains: Amtrak, at the corner of N. Indian Canyon Rd. and Train Station Dr., a few blocks south of I-10 (☎800-872-7245).

Car Rental: Starting at about $35 per day (excluding insurance); higher in winter. **Rent-A-Wreck,** 67555 Palm Canyon Dr. #A102, Cathedral City (☎324-1766 or 800-535-1391; www.rentawreck.com). Usually only rents to those 21 and older. $10 surcharge for those under 25. **Budget** (☎327-1404 or 800-221-1203), at Palm Springs Regional Airport. Must be 21 with major credit card; under 25 surcharge $20 per day.

Bike Rental: Bighorn Bicycles, 302 N. Palm Canyon Dr. (☎325-3367). Mountain bikes $8 per hr., $22 for 4hr., $29 per day. Tours available. Open Sept.-June Su-Tu and Th-Sa 8am-4pm. **Tri-A-Bike,** 44841 San Pablo Ave. (☎340-2840), in Palm Desert. Mountain bikes $7 per hr., $19 per day, $65 per wk. Open M-Sa 10am-6pm, Su noon-5pm.

✈ 🚲 ORIENTATION & PRACTICAL INFORMATION

Palm Springs is a 2-3 hr. drive from L.A. on **I-10.** Exit I-10 at Indian Ave., which becomes **Indian Canyon Drive,** the major north-south road through Palm Springs. Indian Canyon Dr. and the north-south stretch of **Palm Canyon Drive,** the city's two main drags, connect to I-10. East Palm Canyon Dr. (Rte. 111) abuts the southern edge of the city. There are two main east-west boulevards: **Tahquitz-Canyon Road** runs east to the airport, while **Ramon Road,** four blocks south, accesses I-10.

Visitor Information: Visitors Center, 2781 N. Palm Canyon Dr. (☎778-8415 or 800-347-7746; www.palm-springs.org), 1 block beyond Tramway Rd. Free hotel reservations and friendly advice. Pick up *The Official Visitor's Guide* or *Weekender* for attractions and entertainment. Open daily 9am-5pm. At the **Chamber of Commerce,** 190 W. Amado Rd. (☎325-1577; www.pschamber.org), grab the seasonal *Palm Springs Visitors Guide,* buy a map ($1), or make hotel reservations. Open M-F 8:30am-4:30pm.

Laundromat: Arenas Coin-Op, 220 E. Arenas Rd. (☎322-7717), half a block east of Indian Canyon Dr. Wash $2, dry 10min. 25¢. Open daily 7am–9pm. Last wash at 8pm.

Road Conditions: ☎800-427-7623. **Weather Conditions:** ☎345-3711.

Police: 200 S. Civic Dr. (☎323-8116). **Rape Crisis Hotline:** (☎568-9071).

Medical Services: Desert Regional Medical Center, 1150 N. Indian Canyon Dr. (☎323-6511).

Library and Internet Access: Palm Springs Public Library, 300 S. Sunrise Way (☎322-7323). Free Internet available in 30min. slots. Open M-Tu 9am-8pm, W-Th and Sa 9am-5:30pm, F 10am-5:30pm.

Post Office: 333 E. Amado Rd. (☎800-275-8777). Open M-F 9am-5pm, Sa 9am-1pm. **Postal Code:** 92262; General Delivery 92263.

ACCOMMODATIONS

Like most famous resort communities, Palm Springs caters mainly to those seeking a tax shelter, not a night's shelter. Nonetheless, affordable lodgings are fairly abundant. Motels cut prices 20-40% in the summer. Many offer discounts through the Visitors Center, and promotional publications often have terrific coupon deals, offering rooms for as little as $25. Reservations may be necessary in the winter. Prices listed don't include the county's **11.5% accommodation tax.**

Orchid Tree Inn, 251 S. Belardo Rd. (☎325-2791 or 800-733-3435). Large rooms with tasteful Spanish ambience overlook a courtyard with lush gardens and pool. Tucked behind the main downtown strip and near good shopping. 1- or 2-person rooms start at $79 in July and Aug., but increase to $110-175 during the winter. Weekend rates $15-20 more. Studios, suites, and bungalows also available. ❺

Miracle Springs Resort and Spa, 10625 Palm Dr. (☎251-6000 or 800-400-4414; www.miraclesprings.com), in Desert Hot Springs. The newer, classier, and more luxurious of the 2 hotels atop the famed hot springs. 110 spacious units with bedrooms and living areas, some of which overlook the 8 pools of "miracle" water. Spa, restaurants, and banquet facilities. Standard rooms from $99 in off-season; from $139 in winter. ❺

Cambridge Inn, 1277 S. Palm Canyon Dr. (☎325-5574 or 800-829-8099). Large rooms with refrigerators and phones. Laundry, continental breakfast, pool, and jacuzzi. Rooms July-Aug. Su-Th from $44, F-Sa from $60; Sept.-June $69-$125. ❹

Motel 6, 660 S. Palm Canyon Dr. (☎327-4200 or 800-466-8356), located south of city center. Other locations at 595 E. Palm Canyon Dr. (☎325-6129) and 63950 20th Ave. (☎251-1425), near the I-10 off-ramp. Pool and A/C. Sept.-June singles Su-Th $40, F-Sa $46; doubles Su-Th $46, F-Sa $52. July-Aug. $5 less. Additional person $3. ❸

FOOD

Palm Springs offers great, expensive food, from greasy-spoon to trendy fusions. Try **Ralph's,** 451 S. Sunrise Way, for groceries. (☎323-9799. Open daily 6am-1am.)

 Thai Smile, 651 N. Palm Canyon Dr. (☎320-5503). As friendly as the name implies, Thai Smile serves authentic and inexpensive Thai cuisine. Vegetarian options (tofu pad thai $8). Don't miss the $5 lunch specials. Open daily 11:30am-10pm. ❷

Banducci's Bit of Italy, 1260 S. Palm Canyon Dr. (☎325-2537). The promise of delicious Italian food draws an older crowd to this Palm Springs staple every night of the week. The rich fettucine alfredo comes with antipasto, minestrone soup, and buttery garlic bread ($13). Entrees $8-15. Open daily 5-10pm. ❸

Las Casuelas—The Original, 368 N. Palm Canyon Dr. (☎325-3213). Its success made chainhood inevitable, but locals insist The Original lives up to its name. Authentic Mexican entrees ($7-13), tight eating quarters, and colorful decor give it that south-of-the-border feel. (Open Su-Th 10am-10pm, F-Sa 10am-11pm.) For a much trendier, expanded version with live music, try **Las Casuelas Terraza,** 222 S. Palm Canyon Dr. (☎325-2794). Open M-F 11am-11pm, Sa-Su 10am-11pm. ❷

Tyler's, 149 S. Indian Canyon Dr. (☎325-2990). If Starbucks were a burger shack, it'd probably resemble this trendy lunch spot in the middle of La Plaza. Classic American fare—tasty burgers, malts, and root-beer floats. Don't let the unremarkable prices fool you; everything is a la carte, so it adds up. Burgers $4-6. Soda-fountain drinks $2.50-4. Open M-F 11am-4pm, Sa 11am-5pm; in summer Tu-Sa 11am-4pm. ❷

SIGHTS & ACTIVITIES

Most people come to Palm Springs's balmy winter climate to drink, party, golf, lounge poolside, and schmooze with celebs, but the city also has its share of sights. **Mt. San Jacinto State Park,** Palm Springs's primary landmark, offers a variety of outdoor recreation. Hiking trails in the park are accessible year-round via the aerial tram, and cross-country skiing is available in winter at higher elevations, though access is easier and cheaper from nearby Idyllwild. Despite its benign appearance in the crowded winter season, the desert surrounding Palm Springs is a summertime furnace, with highs consistently in the hundreds.

DESERT HOT SPRINGS SPA. A trip to Palm Springs would not be complete without a visit to the town's namesake. This spa features eight naturally heated mineral pools of different temperatures, as well as saunas, massages, and body wraps. *(10805 Palm Dr. in Desert Hot Springs. ☎800-808-7727. Open daily 8am-10pm. M and W $5; Tu $3; Th men $3, women $5; F men $5, women $3; Sa-Su $6. After 3pm weekdays $3, weekends $4, holidays $7. Rates include admission to pools, dry sauna, and locker rooms.)*

PALM SPRINGS DESERT MUSEUM. This remarkable museum features frequently changing exhibits centered on art, history, and culture. The museum sponsors performances in the 438-seat **Annenberg Theatre** (☎325-4490) as well as wintertime curator-led field trips into the canyons. *(101 Museum Dr. Take SunBus #111. ☎325-7186. Open Su noon-5pm, Tu-Sa 10am-5pm. $7.50; seniors $6.50; students, children ages 6-17, and military $3.50; free 1st F of each month. Field trips $5.)*

UPRISING ROCKCLIMBING CENTER. Prepare for nearby Joshua Tree National Park at this gigantic outdoor climbing structure, the only one of its kind in the United States. Whether you're a beginner or expert, you'll find a fun challenge in the shaded plastic rock. Instruction and supervision available. Excursions to Joshua Tree, Idyllwild, and Mission Gorge by arrangement. *(1500 Gene Autry Trail. ☎888-254-6266; www.uprising.com. Open Sept.-June M-F 10am-8pm, Sa-Su 10am-6pm; July-Aug. Tu-F 4-8pm, Sa-Su 10am-6pm. Day pass $15, equipment rental $7, lessons $45+ per day. Parking $6, in the Knotts lot.)*

PALM SPRINGS AERIAL TRAMWAY. If Mt. San Jacinto's 10,804 ft. peak is too much for your legs to take, this world-famous tram can whisk you to the top in 10min. At 8516 ft., the observation deck has great views of the Coachella Valley. Travelers planning to take one of the beautiful hikes from the upper tram station should note that temperatures are invariably 20-30°F cooler than the desert floor.

(On Tramway Rd. off N. Palm Canyon Drive. ☎325-1449 or 888-515-8726; www.pstramway.com. Trams run at least every 30min. Last tram down at 9:45pm. M-F 10am-8pm, Sa-Su 8am-8pm. Round-trip $21, seniors $19, ages 3-12 $14, ages 2 and under free.)

INDIAN CANYONS. These four canyons hold the city's only naturally cool water, as well as remnants of the Cahuilla Indian communities. Ranger-led tours demonstrate how the Cahuilla people once used the area's flora and fauna, including the world's densest patch of naturally occurring palm trees. In the cooler months, these canyons are beautiful places to hike, picnic, or horseback ride. *(Three of the canyons are located 5 mi. south of town at the end of S. Palm Canyon Dr. ☎325-3400 or 800-790-3398. Open daily 8am-5pm. Tours M-Th 10am-1pm, F-Su 9am-3pm. Admission $6; students, seniors, and military $4.50; ages 6-12 $2; 5 and under free. Tours $6; children $2. Tahquitz Canyon is located at the west end of Mesquite Rd. ☎416-7044. It has a separate Visitors Center, as well as a spectacular 60 ft. waterfall during the winter. Tours $12.50, children $6.)*

KNOTT'S SOAK CITY WATER PARK. Nothing spells excessive Palm Springs frivolity better than splashing around in thousands of gallons of the desert's most precious resource. Slip, slide, and soak in the large wave pool and lazy inner tube river, and on 18 different waterslides and attractions. *(Off I-10 S at Gene Autry Trail between Ramon and E. Palm Canyon Dr. ☎327-0499. Open Mar.-Aug. daily 11am-6pm; Sept.-Oct. Su and Sa 11am-6pm. $24, children under 5 ft. and seniors $14, ages 2 and under free. $14 after 3pm. Parking $6.)*

◐ NIGHTLIFE

The glitz of Palm Springs doesn't disappear with the setting sun; this city's nightlife is almost as heralded as its golf courses. Although a night of total indulgence here might cost a small fortune, several bars provide drink specials and lively people-watching. Relive college glory days at the popular **Village Pub,** 266 S. Palm Canyon Dr. Tourists and locals alike swap jokes, swill beer, and groove to the folksy live rock. The crowd is usually 25+, but it gets younger on the weekends. Under 21 restricted to the front eating area after 9pm. (☎323-3265. Open daily 11am-2am.) Those more interested in glow sticks, tight bodies, and techno beats can head to **Atlas,** 210 S. Palm Canyon Dr. This hip, ultra-modern **restaurant ❷** and dance club is in the heart of downtown. Its fusion specialties are as modern as its music. (☎325-8839. Entrees $15-25. Local DJs nightly. 21+ for dancing. Open daily 11am-2am.) **La Taquería,** 125 E. Tahquitz Way (☎778-5391), specializes in ultra-fresh and healthy Mexican cuisine; the mist-enshrouded tile patio is great for Moonlight Margaritas ($8.50) and some tipsy swaying in the conga lines.

Palm Springs is a major destination for gay and lesbian travelers. The gay scene sparkles with bars, spas, and clothing-optional resorts. The *Gay Guide to Palm Springs,* available at the Visitors Center, provides a wealth of pertinent info.

◖ SEASONAL EVENTS

Downtown, **Village Fest** (☎320-3781) takes over Palm Canyon Dr. every Thursday night from 6-10pm (in summer 7-10pm). Vendors market food, jewelry, and arts and crafts wares, while people of all ages sample the booths and enjoy live entertainment and cool evening air. This weekly event is a great time to bring the kids.

Attempting to fulfill his campaign promise to heighten Palm Springs's glamour quotient, former mayor Sonny Bono instituted the annual **Nortel Networks Palm Springs International Film Festival** (☎778-8979; Jan. 8-19 in 2004). The **Annual National Date Festival,** Rte. 111 in Indio (☎863-8247; Feb. 13-22 in 2004), is not a hook-up scene but a bash for dried fruit lovers. Palm Springs is also famous for its tennis tournaments and its professional golf tournaments, like the **45th Annual Bob Hope Chrysler Classic** (☎346-8184; Jan. 21-25 in 2004) and the LPGA's **33rd Annual Kraft Nabisco Championship** (☎324-4546; Mar. 22-28 in 2004).

NEAR PALM SPRINGS

Since the **Coachella Valley** is the self-proclaimed "Date Capital of the World," slick back your hair, suck down a breath mint, and head to the **Shields Date Gardens, 80225 Rte. 111,** in nearby Indio. This palm grove sets itself apart with its amusing free film titled *The Romance and Sex Life of the Date.* A date crystal milkshake ($3) shows how sweet a real good date can be. (☎347-0996 or 800-414-2555. Open Sept.-May daily 8am-6pm; June-Aug. daily 9am-5pm.) Northeast of Palm Springs in Thousand Palms, the **Coachella Valley Preserve's** Visitors Center can help you plan a hike through mesas, bluffs, or the **Thousand Palms Oasis,** a grove of palm trees which is home to the protected fringe-toed lizard. (☎343-2733 or 343-4031. Open Sept.-June sunrise-sunset.)

ROUTE 66 & INTERSTATE 40

Route 66 was designated as such in November 1926, replacing the National Old Trails Road as the principal road for commerce and migration between the Mississippi Valley and Southern California. Running from Chicago to Los Angeles and spanning seven states, the road was taken by Okies fleeing the Dust Bowl, by wide-eyed Easterners in the post-war boom, and now by tourists headed for the Grand Canyon and Disneyland. Scattered along the heat-buckled asphalt are the remnants of an earlier tourist culture. Greasy-spoons, gaudy motels, and odd towns—stripped of their former luster for most—testify to the American urge to embellish the harshest of places. Much of Rte. 66 has been swallowed up by interstate or left to languish as gravel or forlorn dirt. In other places, it forges on as a patchwork of state and county roads (businesses sell $4 maps tracing its modern-day route). A good portion of Rte. 66 is not worth traveling, particularly the vast desert stretches, where I-40 is invariably faster and more convenient.

BARSTOW
☎760

Sitting midway between L.A. and Las Vegas on I-15, Barstow (pop. 23,056) is replete with cheap eats and sheets, not to mention the beauty of the California desert for those willing to explore the hot, desolate area.

🛈 PRACTICAL INFORMATION. The **Amtrak train** station, 685 N. 1st St. (☎800-USA-RAIL/872-7245), lacks ticket counters, so buy tickets by phone. One northbound and one southbound train leave the station per day. One train per day departs for L.A. (4am, $26). **Greyhound buses,** 681 N. 1st St. (☎256-8757, 800-231-2222; open M-Sa 9am-2pm, 3:30-6pm), go to **L.A.** (6 per day, $23) and **Las Vegas** (7 per day, $25). The **Barstow Chamber of Commerce,** 409 E. Fredricks St., off Barstow Rd., has info on hotels, restaurants, and attractions. (☎256-8617. Open M-F 10am-4pm.) Other services include: **police,** 220 E. Mountain View Rd. (☎256-2211); **Barstow Community Hospital,** 555 S. 7th St. (☎256-1761); and the **post office,** 425 S. 2nd Ave. (☎256-9304. Open M-F 9am-5pm, Sa 10am-1pm.) **Postal Code:** 92311.

🛏🍴 ACCOMMODATIONS & FOOD. East Main St. offers an endless line of motels. Prices fluctuate depending on the season, day of the week, and whether Vegas accommodations are full. One of the best values is unsurprisingly found at

BRIGHT LIGHTS, BIG SHADOW

Las Vegas dominates the southern Nevada landscape, so it only seems fitting that its over-the-top spirit sends ripples into the desolation of the surrounding desert. Tiny Jean and Primm, both miles south of Vegas, boast thrill rides, cheap food, and gambling. Traveling farther into the Mojave, however, visitors detect more subtle Sin City influences. The pit-stop town of Baker is an unlikely suspect, but still demonstrates some of the showmanship of glittery Vegas. Baker's California zip code renders it unable to attract visitors with gambling, so it has made a name for itself by trumping up, electrifying, and shamelessly promoting the location's most palpable feature: the heat. Its 134 ft. thermometer, built in 1991, records temperatures on a scale larger than any other such instrument in the world. The mercury-filled obelisk can be seen from miles away, and neon lights make it a beacon in the desert night. Speeding past the town, my easily amused mind found it difficult to resist guessing the three-digit temperature and comparing my estimate to the actual one broadcast several stories in the air. Plucky, sweltering Baker proved it belongs on the same block as Las Vegas, flaunting its desert climate to attract the consumers who keep local cash registers jingling.

—Robert Cacace

the **Best Motel ❸**, 1281 E. Main St., which is fairly clean and quite friendly, with all the usual amenities you find at American roadside motels. (☎256-6836. Singles $34; doubles $38. Weekly rates available.)

Every restaurant chain this side of the Colorado has a branch on Main St. You'll find a more inviting variety in Barstow's local offerings. **Rosita's Mexican American Food ❷**, 540 W. Main St., has a festive dining room filled with the aromas of its tasty offerings. (☎256-9218. Lunch specials Tu-F under $5. Dinners $6-11. Open Tu-Sa 11am-9pm, Su 10am-9pm.) **DiNapoli's Firehouse Italian Eatery ❸**, 1358 E. Main St., serves traditional pizzeria fare in a recreated old-fashioned firehouse. (☎256-1094. Dinner entrees $8-15. Open Su-Th 11am-9pm, F-Sa 11am-10pm.)

EASTERN MOJAVE DESERT   ☎760

The land between I-15 and I-40 is among the most isolated in all of California. There are few towns here, and you can never assume that services will be available between Barstow and Baker along I-15 or Barstow and Needles along I-40. But travelers who only use these towns as pit stops miss out on the Mojave's stunning natural features. Many of the Eastern Mojave's attractions exist within the confines of the federally controlled Mojave National Preserve, whose 1.6 million acres of federally stewarded desert scenery boast dry lake beds, volcanic cinder cones, sweeping sand dunes, and the occasional splash of water. Dramatic geological formations rise from the seemingly infinite landscape, and resilient creatures crawl along the scorched terrain. Serene as the emptiness may be, most drivers press onward quickly from this area, praying that their cars up to the task (see **The Desert & Your Car**, p. 67).

Hunting and **fishing** are allowed in the preserve, but finding water may be an angler's toughest challenge. For those with the required California hunting license, deer and quail are popular targets in season. Watch out for protected desert tortoises sunning themselves on desert roads, and avoid disturbing them in the preserve, their last natural stronghold. **Afton Canyon Natural Area** (Barstow BLM, ☎252-6000) lies 36 mi. northeast of Barstow en route to Las Vegas. Follow I-15 to Afton Rd., and follow the dirt road east. The flowing water you see in this "Grand Canyon of the Mojave" is no mirage, but a rare above-ground appearance of the Mojave River. Canyon walls tower 300 ft. above the rushing water and its willow-lined shores. All manner of desert animals—including golden eagles, bighorn sheep, and desert tortoises—reside in and around the canyon. **Hikers** may explore the small side canyons tucked along

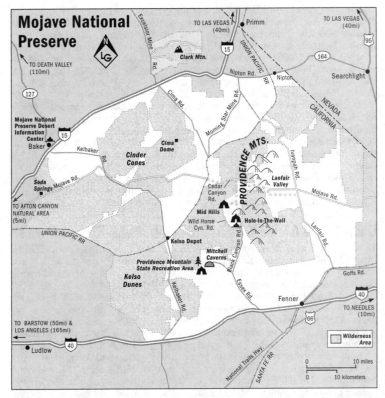

Mojave National Preserve

N LG

TO LAS VEGAS (40mi) Primm

TO LAS VEGAS (40mi)

Excelsior Mine Rd.

Clark Mtn.

TO DEATH VALLEY (110mi)

15

UNION PACIFIC RR

Nipton Rd.

Nipton

95

164

Searchlight

127

Cima Rd.

Morning Star Mine Rd.

NEVADA

CALIFORNIA

Mojave National Preserve Desert Information Center

Baker

15

Kelbaker Rd.

Cinder Cones

Cima Dome

PROVIDENCE MTS.

Lanfair Valley

Ivanpah Rd.

Mojave Rd.

Soda Springs

Mojave Rd.

Cedar Canyon Rd.

TO AFTON CANYON NATURAL AREA (5mi)

UNION PACIFIC RR

Mid Hills

Wild Horse Cyn. Rd.

Hole-In-The-Wall

Lanfair Rd.

Kelso Depot

Black Canyon Rd.

Providence Mountain State Recreation Area

Mitchell Caverns

Kelso Dunes

Kelbaker Rd.

Essex Rd.

Goffs Rd.

Fenner

40

TO BARSTOW (50mi) & LOS ANGELES (165mi)

Ludlow

40

66

National Trails Hwy.

SANTA FE RR

TO NEEDLES (10mi)

Wilderness Area

0   10 miles

0   10 kilometers

unmarked trails, but should bring a flashlight if they go. Visitors are free to camp at one of 22 developed sites with water, fire pits, shaded picnic tables, and restrooms ($6 per person).

The **Kelso Dunes** blanket a spectacular, barren landscape within the Mojave National Preserve. Stretching up to 4 mi. and 700 ft. high, the dunes are off-limits to off-road vehicles. It takes 2-3hr. one-way to hike from the trailhead to the dune summit, and bear in mind that the formation acts as a giant oven in the summer— don't get baked on the dunes. From the top you can hear the dune sands singing on a windy day—the cascading sand groans like bending metal. The dunes are about 30 mi. southeast of Baker via Kelbaker Rd. from Barstow; either take I-40 to the Kelbaker Rd. exit (80 mi. to the east) or I-15 to Baker. Kelbaker Rd. itself offers phenomenal views of every conceivable desert formation from the Kelso Dunes and crusty lava flows to glacier-hewn granite heaps. **Dune buggies** and **jeeps** are still permitted at the **Dumont Dunes,** just off Rte. 127 about 33 mi. north of Baker. Look for the 3.5 mi. road turning off of 127 just after Harry Wade Rd. There is no sign; keep your eyes peeled. The dunes are strewn with man-made striations—those from WWII training exercises are still visible in parts of the Mojave. Tracks remain in the sands for decades, so consider what legacy you want to leave behind.

Providence Mountains State Recreation Area is a popular, high-altitude (4000-5000 ft.) region with six **primitive campsites** (☎928-2586; sites $10) and a **Visitors Center,** both on Essex Rd., 17 mi. north of I-40. View the spectacular **Mitchell Caverns** on an informative 1.5 mi. tour through the stalactite-cluttered limestone chambers. (1½hr. June-Aug. Sa-Su 1:30pm; Sept.-May M-F 1:30pm, Sa-Su 10am, 1:30, 3pm. $4, 16 and under free. Tour reservations ☎928-2586, $2 surcharge.) There are 61 primitive but beautiful sites surrounded by piñon and juniper trees at the unseasonably cool **Mid Hills ❶** (5600 ft.), and **Hole-in-Wall ❶** (4200 ft.) in the East Mojave National Scenic Area. (Both $12; limited water, pit toilets, no hookups.) The road into Mid Hills is neither paved nor recommended for RVs. From Essex Rd., follow Black Canyon Rd. to Mid Hill or Wild Horse Canyon Rd. to Hole-in-Wall.

Stop in Baker to visit the **Mojave National Preserve Desert Information Center,** which supplies friendly suggestions about popular recreation spots, maps of the area, more detailed directions, and a modest exhibit on the area's geology. (☎733-4040. Open daily 9am-5pm, but call ahead.) Before leaving town, head across the street for a less than conventional meal, try **The Mad Greek ❷,** on the main drag in Baker. The $7.50 Kefte-k-Bob brings shades of Athens to the Mojave Desert. (☎733-4354. Open daily 6am-midnight.) The **Baker Bun Boy ❷** is a good place to stop for coffee and conversation. (☎733-4660. Open daily 6am-midnight.) And even if you tried, you couldn't miss Baker's claim to fame: **the world's tallest thermometer.**

DEATH VALLEY NATIONAL PARK ☎760

The devil owns a lot of real estate in Death Valley. Not only does he grow crops (at Devil's Cornfield) and hit the links (at Devil's Golf Course), but the park is also home to Hell's Gate itself. Unsurprisingly, the area's extreme heat and surreal landscape support just about anyone's idea of the Inferno. Visitors can stare into the abyss from the appropriately named Dante's View, one of several panoramic points approaching 6000 ft. in elevation, or gaze wistfully into the distant, cool heavens from Badwater, the lowest point (at 282 ft. below sea level) in the Western Hemisphere. Winter temperatures dip well below freezing in the mountains, and summer readings in the Valley average around 115°F. In fact, the second-highest temperature ever recorded in the world (134°F in the shade) was measured at the Valley's Furnace Creek Ranch on July 10, 1913. Fortunately, the potentially fatal threshold of 130°F is rarely crossed, and the region sustains a motley crew of rugged plants and animals. Many threatened and endangered species, including the desert tortoise and the desert bighorn sheep, inhabit Death Valley. Though the land seems desolate and barren, over 500 different plant species thrive.

Human inhabitants have a long history inside the Valley as well. The Shoshone Indians lived in the lower elevations during the winters and retreated into the cooler peaks during the summers. During the Gold Rush, travelers came into the Valley searching for a shortcut across the Sierras. They were unsuccessful, and skedaddled as soon as they could find a way out, though not before lives were lost. Looking back at the scene of their misery, someone said, "Goodbye, Death Valley!" and the name stuck. Later, miners looking for gold found borax (a type of salt used as a detergent and fire retardant) instead, and boom towns grew around the mines.

AT A GLANCE: DEATH VALLEY NATIONAL PARK

AREA: 3.3 million acres.	**GATEWAYS:** Beatty, NV (p. 180), Lone Pine (p. 183).
CLIMATE: Very arid and hot.	
FEATURES: Badwater, Mosaic Canyons, Telescope Peak, Scotty's Castle.	**CAMPING:** 30-day max. stay, 14-day max. stay in Furnace Creek. Backcountry camping is free.
HIGHLIGHTS: Take Dante's View, drive to the bottom of Ubehebe Crater, photograph the Death Valley Sand Dunes.	**FEES & RESERVATIONS:** $10 entrance fee per vehicle, $5 for non-vehicles.

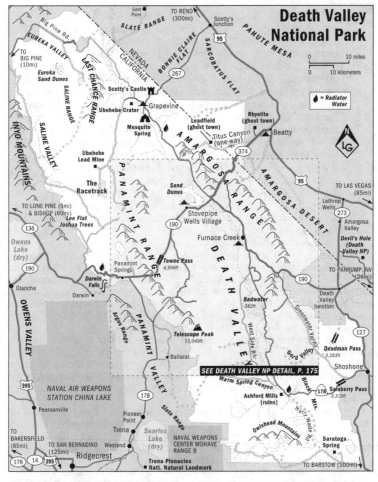

Death Valley National Park

Once the borax was depleted, the prospectors took off and left behind a medley of skeletal towns like Skidoo and Rhyolite. These ghost towns now lend Death Valley a deserted, post-apocalyptic atmosphere that suits the stark landscape. The desolate beauty gave rise to the tourism industry; in 1933 the US government set aside over 3 million acres as a national park.

☐ TRANSPORTATION

BY CAR. Cars are virtually the only way to get to and around Death Valley (3½hr. from Las Vegas; 5hr. from L.A.; 7hr. from Tahoe City; 10½hr. from San Francisco). If you plan on sharing gas costs, renting a car can be much cheaper and more flexible than any bus tour in the area. The nearest car rental agencies are in Las Vegas (p. 197), Barstow, and Bishop.

WHEN TO GO. Although the average high temperature in July is 115°F and the night-time low 88°F, even summer visits can be enjoyable with wise planning. The Furnace Creek Visitors Center distributes the free pamphlet, *Hot Weather Hints.* Some summer days are simply too hot to hike, even with abundant water. Severe heat exhaustion strikes even the fittest trekkers, so do not overestimate your tolerance. (See **The Desert & You,** p. 66.) You can drive through and admire the beauty of the valley in July and August, but to enjoy the many hiking and camping options, visit between November and April. Winter is the coolest time (temperatures average 39-65°F in the Valley, with freezing temperatures and snow in the mountains) and also the wettest, with infrequent but violent rainstorms that can flood canyons and obliterate roads, trails, and ill-placed tract housing. Call ahead to find out which areas, if any, are washed out before exploring the park. Desert wildflowers bloom everywhere in March and April, but the season is accompanied by tempestuous winds that whip sand and dust into a blinding frenzy for hours or even days. Over winter holidays and three-day weekends, and during Easter and Thanksgiving, congested trails and campsites, traffic jams, hour-long lines for gas, and 4hr. waits at Scotty's Castle plague the area.

Conditions in Death Valley are notoriously hard on cars, particularly passenger vehicles. Radiator water (*not* suitable for drinking) is available at critical points on Rte. 178 and 190 and Nevada Rte. 374. There are only four **gas stations** in the park, and though prices at these run as much as $0.50 higher per gallon than they do outside the Valley, be sure to keep the tank of your car at least half full at all times. Check ahead with park rangers for road closings and do not under any circumstances drive on wet and slippery backcountry roads.

Although **four-wheel-drive vehicles** and **high-clearance** trucks can be driven on narrow roads that lead to some of Death Valley's most spectacular scenery, these roads are intended for drivers with backcountry experience and are dangerous no matter what you're driving. Always travel with 2 gallons of water per person per day. In the case of a breakdown, stay in the shade of your vehicle. (For more tips, see **The Desert and Your Car,** p. 67.)

Of the seven entrances to Death Valley National Park, most visitors choose the one via Rte. 190 from the east. Although this is the steepest entrance, the road is well maintained and the Visitors Center is relatively close to here. Since most of the major sights adjoin the north-south road, though, the day-tripper can see more of the park by entering from the southeast (Rte. 178 W from Rte. 127 at Shoshone) or the north (direct to Scotty's Castle via Nevada Rte. 267). Unskilled mountain drivers in passenger cars should under no circumstances attempt to enter on the smaller Titus Canyon or Emigrant Canyon Dr.

 ORIENTATION

Death Valley is on the eastern edge of the state, next to Nevada and south of Inyo National Forest. Rte. 190 cuts east-west across the Valley. Many sites fall along Rte. 178, which runs north-south through the lower part of the park. Most of Death Valley is below sea level. Wildflowers, snow-capped peaks, and some of the hottest, driest land in the entire world can all be found in Death Valley. It rains very infrequently inside the park, but when it does, traffic is often impeded because the hard, compacted ground is prone to flash floods. In this harsh and overheated corner of California, even the topography runs into the extremes.

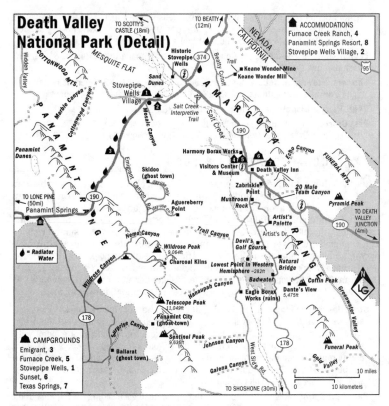

Death Valley National Park (Detail)

TO SCOTTY'S CASTLE (18mi)

TO BEATTY (12mi)

NEVADA
CALIFORNIA

ACCOMMODATIONS
Furnace Creek Ranch, **4**
Panamint Springs Resort, **8**
Stovepipe Wells Village, **2**

Hidden Valley
COTTONWOOD MTS.
MESQUITE FLAT
Marble Canyon
Cottonwood Canyon
PANAMINT
Historic Stovepipe Wells 374
Beatty Cutoff
Trail
Keane Wonder Mine
Keane Wonder Mill
95
Sand Dunes
Stovepipe Wells Village **1**
2
Mosaic Canyon
Salt Creek Interpretive Trail
Salt Creek
AMARGOSA
Panamint Dunes
3
Emigrant Canyon Rd.
Skidoo (ghost town)
day-use only
Harmony Borax Works
Visitors Center & Museum **4 5**
6
7
Death Valley Inn
190
Echo Canyon
FUNERAL MTS.
RANGE
TO LONE PINE (50mi)
190
Panamint Springs
8
▲ = Radiator Water
Aguereberry Point
Nemo Canyon
Trail Canyon
Wildrose Canyon
Wildrose Peak 9,064ft
Charcoal Kilns
Hanaupah Canyon
Zabriskie Point
Mushroom Rock
Artist's Palette
Artist's Dr.
Devil's Golf Course
Lowest Point in Western Hemisphere −282ft
Badwater
Eagle Borax Works (ruins)
20 Mule Team Canyon
Pyramid Peak
TO DEATH VALLEY JUNCTION (4mi)
190
Natural Bridge
Dante's View 5,475ft
Coffin Peak
Telescope Peak 11,049ft
Panamint City (ghost town)
178
Surprise Canyon
Sentinel Peak 9,636ft
Johnson Canyon
Ballarat (ghost town)
West Side Rd.
178
Funeral Peak
Greenwater Valley
Galena Canyon
Gold Valley
TO SHOSHONE (30mi)

N
LG

0   10 miles
0   10 kilometers

CAMPGROUNDS
Emigrant, **3**
Furnace Creek, **5**
Stovepipe Wells, **1**
Sunset, **6**
Texas Springs, **7**

▼ PRACTICAL INFORMATION

Furnace Creek Visitors Center (☎786-3244; www.nps.gov/deva), on Rte. 190 in the Valley's east-central section. For info, write: Superintendent, Death Valley National Park, Death Valley, CA 92328. Guides and topographical hiking maps ($4-8), schedules of activities and guided hikes, and weather forecasts. A 12min. slide show and nightly lectures in winter. Park entrance fee can be paid here. Open daily 8am-6pm.

Contact Stations: Weather reports, a small book selection, and park info at each station. Emergency help provided. **Grapevine** (☎786-2313), at Rte. 190 and 267 near Scotty's Castle; **Stovepipe Wells** (☎786-2342), on Rte. 190; **Shoshone** (☎832-4308), at Rte. 127 and 178 outside the valley's southeast border; and **Beatty, NV** (☎702-553-2200), on Nevada Rte. 374. All are technically open daily 8am-5pm but are staffed sporadically.

Hiking Information: The private website **www.deathvalley.com** has general information on Death Valley as well as message boards and detailed hiking resources. **Death Valley Hikers' Association** publishes the informative *Dustdevil;* write for info c/o Darrell Tomer, P.O. Box 123, Arcata, CA 95521.

Gas Stations: Fill up outside Death Valley at Lone Pine, Olancha, Shoshone, or Beatty, NV. Once in Death Valley, pay $0.15-0.50 more per gallon to maintain a high gas level. Don't play macho with the fuel gauge; fill up often. For gas in the Valley: Furnace Creek

Visitors Center (open 7am-7pm), Stovepipe Wells Village (open 7am-9pm), Panamint Springs (open 24hr.), or Scotty's Castle (open 9am-5:30pm). **AAA towing service, minor repairs, propane gas,** and **diesel fuel** available at the Furnace Creek Chevron.

Laundromat: (☎786-2345) On Roadrunner Ave. at Furnace Creek Ranch. $1 each for wash and dry. Open 24hr.

Showers: Stovepipe Wells Village (☎786-2387). Non-guests $2. Open daily 8am-midnight. **Furnace Creek Ranch** (☎786-2345) also $2. Open daily 7am-11pm.

24hr. Ranger Dispatch and Police: ☎911 or 786-2330.

Post Office: Furnace Creek Ranch (☎786-2223). Open Oct. 1-May 15 M-F 8:30am-5pm; May 16-Sept. 30 M, W, F 8:30am-3pm, Tu, Th 8:30am-5pm. **Postal Code:** 92328.

░░ ACCOMMODATIONS & FOOD

Affordable beds and inexpensive meals can be as elusive as the desert bighorn sheep. Motel rooms in surrounding towns are cheaper than those in Death Valley, but are over an hour away from top sights. Never assume that rooms will be available, but your chances (and the prices) will be better in the summer. In the winter, camping with a stock of groceries saves money and driving time, summer camping, especially at lower elevations, can be uncomfortable. (For more affordable accommodations outside the Valley, see **Life After Death Valley,** p. 180.) For groceries, **Furnace Creek Ranch Store** is well-stocked but expensive. (☎786-2381. Open daily 7am-9pm.) **Stovepipe Wells Village Store** is smaller and also expensive. (☎786-2578. ATM. Open daily 7am-9pm.) Both stores sell charcoal, firewood, and ice.

Stovepipe Wells Village (☎786-2387), 30 mi. northwest of Furnace Creek Visitors Center on Rte. 190, is at sea level, though nothing seems more remote than the ocean. When it's too hot to camp, the village offers comfortable rooms and a mineral water swimming pool. The rooms lack TVs and phones, but who cares—they've got A/C. The **dining room ❸** prepares plenty of food at stiff prices (breakfast buffet 7-10am, $8; dinner buffet 6-9pm, $17). Rooms for up to 2 people $50-92; each additional person $11. RV sites available. Full hookups $22. ❸

Panamint Springs Resort (☎775-482-7680; www.deathvalley.com), 23 mi. east of the park's western border on Rte. 190, is remote but comfortable at a higher elevation than other lodging options. The complex includes 18 rooms, RV hookups, campsites, a restaurant and bar, and gas. None of the rooms include TV or phones, but a pay phone is available for public use. The only other tie to civilization here is the overhead roar of naval fighter jets on maneuvers from China Lake Naval Weapons Station. Doubles from $65; RV sites $10-25; campsites $12. ❹

Furnace Creek Ranch (☎786-2345; www.furnacecreekresort.com), in Furnace Creek. A central location—a cafe, bar, resaurant, laundromat, and grocery store are all in the same complex—makes this place supremely convenient, though it is pricier than other options. Singles and doubles from $85 in the summer and $105 in the winter. ❺

▙ CAMPING

The National Park Service maintains nine campgrounds in Death Valley, all of which can provide an inexpensive and comfortable way of seeing the park. Some of the hottest sites are closed during the summer (Sunset, Texas Spring, and Stovepipe Wells) and Thorndike and Mahogany Flat are closed due to snow and ice in the winter. Pay attention to elevation: the higher up you are, the more comfortable your visit will be when the temperature climbs into the triple digits. The Visitors Center keeps records about site availability; be prepared to battle for a space if you come during peak periods. All campsites have toilets, but none have showers. All provide water except for Thorndike and Mahogany Flat, and the Visitors Center has unlimited free water (as warm as a bath), but never depend heavily upon any source of water except what you carry with you. Since fires are prohibited outside of firepits, a camping stove may prove extremely useful. Roadside camping is not permitted, but **backcountry camping** is free and legal, if you check in at the Visitors Center and pitch tents at least 2 mi. from your car and any road and a ¼ mi. from any water source. All sites limit stays to 30 days except Furnace Creek, which has a 14-day limit.

Furnace Creek (☎800-365-2267), 196 ft. below sea level, north of the Visitors Center. Furnace Creek is particularly uncomfortable in summer, even though many of the 136 sites are shaded. First site to fill in winter, especially with RVs. Near Furnace Creek Ranch's facilities ($2 shower access; laundry). 14-day limit. Reservations Oct.-Apr. Beginning on the fifth of each month, reservations can be made five months in advance. Sites $16 in winter; $10 in summer. ❶

Sunset, 196 ft. below sea level, and **Texas Springs,** at sea level, in the hills above the Furnace Creek Ranch Complex. These two sites are the best place for tents near Furnace Creek activities. Over 1000 sites available, some with shade. For wind protection, stick close to the base of the hills. Generators prohibited. Water, some firepits, and some tables. Flush toilets and dump station. Open Oct.-Apr. Sites $10-12. ❶

Stovepipe Wells, at sea level, near the airstrip, 4WD trails, and sand dunes. Reminiscent of a drive-in movie lot. Tents compete with RVs for 190 gravel sites. Spots near the trees offer better protection from sandstorms. Hotel and general store nearby. A few tables and fireplaces. Easy to confuse it with the trailer park. Open Oct.-Apr. Sites $10. ❶

Mesquite Spring, 1800 ft., near Scotty's Castle, 2 mi. south of Grapevine Ranger Station. Located in a small valley among dry brush, some of the 30 gravel sites offer shade and protection from wind. Listen for the howls and hoots of coyote and owls. Picnic tables, firepits, water, and flush toilets. Sites $10. ❶

Emigrant, 2100 ft., off Rte. 190, 9 mi. west of Stovepipe Wells Village across from the ranger station, on the way down from Towne Pass through Panamint Range. This is a tent-only site. Gorgeous view of Stovepipe Wells and the Valley's sand dunes, though sites are located directly next to Rte. 190. The 10 sites can be relatively comfortable even in the summer. Flush toilets and water. No fires. Free. ❶

🅖 SIGHTS

Plan your approach to Death Valley carefully. If exploring the Valley in one day, adopt a north-south or south-north route. You'll be able to see a lot of the park without backtracking. If you're going for a few days, it pays to first visit the Furnace Creek Visitors Center on Rte. 190 (which connects east-west). Camera-toters should keep in mind that the best photo opportunities are at sunrise and sunset.

SCOTTY'S CASTLE. Remarkably out of place in the desert, this castle's imaginative exterior rises from the sands, complete with minaret and Arabian-style colored tile. The saga of the Castle's construction began with the friendship between Chicago insurance millionaire Albert Johnson and infamous local con-man Walter Scott (a.k.a. "Death Valley Scotty"). Scott had conned wealthy Easterners (including Johnson) into investing in his non-existent gold mine; after Scott and Johnson became friends and then partners in crime, Johnson built this ridiculous vacation home and told people it was built on the gold fortune. The museum and "living" tour guides provide more details of the bizarre story. (*From Rte. 190, look for sign near mile marker 93 and take road junction to Park Rte. 5; follow Rte. 5 for 33 mi. to castle. ☎786-2392. Open daily 9am-5pm. Tours every hr. May-Sept.; more frequently Oct.-Apr. $8, seniors $6, ages 6-15 $4. Tickets can be purchased until 1hr. before closing, but there are often lines.*)

FROM BADWATER
TO WORSE

n 1977, Al Arnold inaugurated one of the world's most painful endurance races when he ran rom Badwater, the western hemisphere's lowest point, to the top of Mt. Whitney, the highest peak n the contiguous US. It took him 34 hours, and he shed 17 pounds. This brutal run is now the **Badwater Ultramarathon.**

Each July, in Death Valley's blazing heat, 70-80 runners embark on this grueling 135 mi. run to Mt. Whitney. There's no prize money, and no relief. But here are temperatures of 130°F, 13,000 ft. in cumulative elevation change, and 4700 ft. of joint-rattling descents. IVs are prohibited, and there are no official aid stations. Support crews have passed out from the heat while sitting in their cars. To the Associated Press, two-time finisher Greg Minter reported hallucinating: "I saw a dinosaur around mile 108."

Pam Reed, a 42-year-old mother from Arizona, has won the past two years, finishing in under 28 hours. She never ate or slept, sustaining herself on a liquid diet, including eight Red Bull energy drinks. Her support crew of two vans raced to spray her down with water every ¼ mi.

"People I meet there don't brag about it, they just do it," Al Arnold, now 75, told the *Contra-Costa Times.* Every year, when Arnold is done addressing the runners, he shouts "BANG!," and they're off.

BADWATER. A briny pool four times saltier than the ocean, this body of water is huge in the winter, but withers into a salt-crusted pond by summer. The surrounding flat is the lowest point (282 ft. below sea level) in the Western Hemisphere. The pools shelter extremely threatened Badwater snails, many of which are crushed by oblivious waders. The boardwalk provides a closer look at the strange orange floor, but getting in the water is prohibited. *(18 mi. south of the Visitors Center.)*

DEVIL'S GOLF COURSE. Lucifer himself probably couldn't stay below 100 strokes on this "golf course," actually a vast expanse of gnarled salt pillars formed by cyclical flooding and evaporation. This is Death Valley at its most surreal; the jagged crystaline deposits, some quite delicate and beautiful, stretch as far as you can see. In the summer you can occasionally hear tinkling sounds as hollow structures expand and shatter. *(15 mi. south of the Visitors Center.)*

⬛ HIKING & BACKPACKING

It is not an exaggeration to say that tourists die every year while foolishly hiking with too little water in the brutal heat. There are days too hot to hike even with abundant water. Severe heat exhaustion strikes even the fittest people, so do not overestimate your tolerance. Another danger is **flash flooding.** Especially when hiking in canyons, be aware of the weather forecast and always have an escape route out of the canyon should torrents of water come pouring down the canyon.

During the summer, most hikers escape to the high elevations of the Panamint and Amargosa Ranges. During winter, hiking in the valleys and badlands is tolerable, even pleasant. Rangers and the handouts they dispense give the distances and times of recommended hikes. Always bring a map with you—a few steps off the trail and you are in real wilderness.

AROUND FURNACE CREEK & BADWATER
This is the hottest region of the park. If you *must* hike here in the summer, carry a liter of water per hour and make sure that you are off the trail by 10-11am.

Natural Bridge Canyon (1 mi. round-trip, 1hr.). The trailhead is located at Natural Bridge parking area; take Badwater Rd. 13.25 mi. south of Rte. 190, take a left, and follow the unmarked, graded road 1.5 mi. to the parking area. A large, conglomerate natural bridge stands 0.3 mi. up the trail and a bit farther, the trail ends at a series of dry falls.

⚡ OTHER OUTDOOR ACTIVITIES

Ranger-led programs are generally unavailable in summer, but many popular programs, such as the **car caravan tours** and **interpretive talks,** are available in winter and spring. Astronomy buffs should speak to one of the rangers, who often set up telescopes at Zabriskie Point and offer freelance stargazing shows. During **wildflower season,** rangers offer tours of blooming sites. Wildflower-watching is best after a heavy rainfall.

Driving is a popular activity in the park, and is especially nice in the summer, when a car affords a tenuous climate control. (For more on park driving and its special hazards and necessary precautions, see **Transportation,** p. 173.) Here are some of the park's most beloved drives.

ZABRISKIE POINT. There is a reason Zabriskie Point crawls with shutterbugs, both tourists and professional photographers: it provides beautiful views of Death Valley's corrugated badlands, especially when the first or last rays of the sun soften the colors. For an intimate view of the Valley, take the short detour along **20-Mule-Team Road.** The well-maintained dirt road is named for the gigantic mule trains that used to haul borax 130 mi. south to the rail depot at Mojave. The view of the dry lakebeds and undulating yellow rock formations is particularly stunning late in the day. Before the sunset ends, scamper 2 mi. down Gower Gulch to see the glittering cliffs of **Golden Canyon.** *(3 mi. south of Furnace Creek by car. Take the turn-off from Rte. 190, 1 mi. east of the museum.)*

ARTIST'S DRIVE. This one-way loop contorts its way through brightly colored rock formations. The loop's early ochres and burnt siennas give way at **Artist's Palette** to sea green, lemon yellow, periwinkle blue, and salmon pink mineral deposits in the hillside. The scene is most dramatic in the late afternoon, when the setting sun causes rapid color changes in the deposits. The dizzying and intense 9 mi. drive turns back on itself again and again, ending up on the main road only 4 mi. north of the drive's entrance. *(On Rte. 178, 10 mi. south of the Visitors Center.)*

EMIGRANT CANYON ROAD. This winding road leads from the Emigrant Campground to Wildrose Canyon Dr. In between, there is a turn-off for the four-wheel-drive skedaddle to the ruins of **Skidoo,** a ghost town 5700 ft. up in the Panamint Range. Skidoo was the backdrop for the only full-length movie ever shot in Death Valley (Erich von Stroheim's *Greed,* 1923). A few miles down Emigrant Canyon Rd. is the turn-off for the dirt road to **Aguereberry Point** (may require four-wheel-drive), known for its fine sunset views. Turn left at Wildrose Canyon Dr. and then go 10 mi. (last 2 mi. unpaved gravel) to the 10 beehive-shaped furnaces known as the **Charcoal Kilns.** These huge ovens were built in 1876 and once fired 45 cords of wood at a time to process silver and lead ore. It boggles the mind to imagine ovens operating full-blast in Death Valley, in a time before air-conditioning existed.

LIFE AFTER DEATH VALLEY

BEATTY   ☎ 775

While some may consider **Beatty** (pop. 1,700) the armpit of Nevada, it is more fittingly described as the elbow. Situated 120 mi. northwest of Las Vegas, **Route 95,** the highway that stretches between Reno and Sin City, makes a peculiar right-angled turn in the center of town, and the community centers around this funny bone of sorts. Essentially, Beatty offers weary travelers A/C and low-key casinos, lulling them before or after the overwhelming experience of Death Valley, for

Desolation Canyon (2 mi. round-trip, 2hr.). To access this trail, go 3¾ mi. south
190 on Badwater Rd.; go left on Desolation Canyon Rd., and take the left for
end. The trail leads up a narrow slot canyon. Make a right at all forks in the car

Dante's Ridge (1-8 mi. round-trip). From this 5475 ft. summit, one can truly apr
the astonishing and primeval landscape of the Valley's floor. A palette of lig
washes over a 100 mi. stretch. Temperatures at the summit are around 20°F coo
in the Valley and the area is perfect for a breakfast picnic when the rising sun fills
ley with golden light. From the Visitors Center, drive 14 mi. east along Rte. 1!
right at the Dante's View turn-off. The 13 mi. climb is especially steep at the to

NEAR STOVEPIPE WELLS

Sand Dunes (2 mi. one-way). Two miles from Stovepipe Wells, these large dunes
extremely fine quartz sand may seem out of place in the Valley, but make for a §
hike that feels good between the toes. But be warned that perceived distance;
misleading; peaks that appear close may really be a 2hr. arduous climb. If you w
your hand at making like Ansel Adams and snapping some memorable picture:
the Visitors Center for the handout on photographing in the setting or rising sun
north of the Visitors Center.)

Mosaic Canyon (4 mi. round-trip, 2-3hr.). A ½ mile-long corridor of eroded marl
this site stands out as a true natural wonder. A simple and relatively flat 2 mi. ti
from the parking lot around the canyon to some awesome vistas. Occasiona
sheep sightings are a bonus. Take the turn-off from Rte. 190, 1 mi. west of S
Wells, to the 2½ mi. alluvial fan, accessible by foot, horse, or car.

PANAMINT MOUNTAINS

Telescope Peak Trail (7 mi., one-way) This trail through the **Panamint Mounta**
up to the summit of the park's highest peak (11,049 ft.). The strenuous hike
Mahogany Flat campground and winds 3000 ft. up past charcoal kilns and bi
pines, providing unique views of Badwater and Mt. Whitney. It is helpful to buy to
ical maps of the area at a ranger station. The trek becomes a technical mountair
winter, requiring axes and crampons, but is usually snow-free by June. Let a ran
when you will be climbing and when you expect to return.

Wildrose Peak Trail (8.4 mi round-trip, 4-6hr.). From the Charcoal Kilns park
this trail gains 2000 ft. as it winds north to Wildrose Peak. Less crowded t
scope, it's a good alternative in winter when snow does not usually affect this

NORTHERN DEATH VALLEY

Ubehebe Crater & Peak. This blackened volcanic blast site is nearly 1 mi. wide
ft. deep. It can be seen by car, but take the twisty gravel trail leading to the fl
crater to truly appreciate the hole's dimensions. The climb back out is gruelin§
unpaved road continues 23 mi. south of the crater to the vast **Racetrack Playa**
up lake basin providing access into Hidden Valley and up White Top Mountair
trails left by mysterious **moving rocks** on this lake basin. For an outstanding vi
Racetrack, follow the **Ubehebe Peak Trail** (6 mi. round-trip) from the Grandstar
area along a steep, twisting pathway 8 mi. west of Scotty's Castle.

Fall and Red Wall Canyons. Both canyons are accessible from the Titus Cany
parking area, 3 mi. east of Scotty's Canyon Rd. between the Visitors Center an
Canyon. There are no trails on either canyon, so the routes necessitate some r
ing and plenty of arduous hiking. Fall Canyon is the next canyon north of Titu;
and the mouth of the canyon lies only ½ mi. north of the parking area. Red
mouth is 1.5 mi. farther north of Fall Canyon and requires hiking up an alluvi
access to the canyon proper. While Red Wall is less frequented, both canyons
tacular and offer some of the most spectacular narrows in the park.

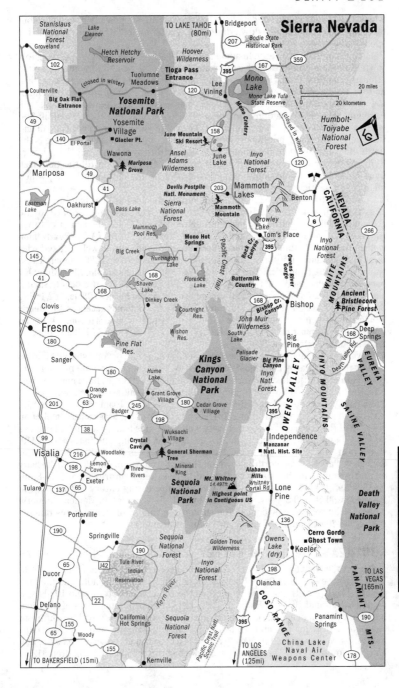

Sierra Nevada

CALIFORNIA

which it is the northeastern gateway. The casinos are supposedly open 24hr., but most nights the action dies down dramatically after midnight. At the end of a day spent in the desert, you will too.

4.5 miles outside of Beatty, heading toward Death Valley on Hwy. 374, the ghost town of **Rhyolite** crumbles under the watchful eye of the BLM. Rhyolite exploded after prospectors Shorty Harris and Ed Cross discovered gold in the area in 1904, and for several madcap years the town saw a frenetic rush of prospecting, building, and saloon hopping. At its height, it was home to an opera house, a stock exchange, at least 53 saloons, and nearly 10,000 people. In 1912, townsfolk fled when a financial panic struck, and by 1919 Rhyolite was a ghost town. The jail and train depot still stand, but the most infamous relic of Rhyolite's crazy prime is the **Bottle House,** constructed from 30,000 beer bottles by miner Tom "Iron Liver" Kelly. Newer constructions by Belgian artist Albert Szukalski fill the **Gold Well Open Air Museum,** a free public sculpture garden on the city's south side, which includes a gigantic cinder-block nude.

CoachUSA (☎800-559-9522) runs daily **buses** between Las Vegas and Reno that pass through Beatty in both directions. Buy a ticket and hop aboard at the Exchange Club, located at the junction of Hwys. 95 and 374 in the center of town. (☎553-2368. **Las Vegas,** 3hr., 2:45pm, $27; **Reno,** 7hr., 10:45am, $57.) The **Beatty Information Station of Death Valley National Park,** 3rd and Main Sts., is well stocked with books, maps, and safety info for desert-bound drivers. (☎553-2200. Open Tu-Sa 8am-4pm.) **Bank of America,** 101 N. 2nd St. (☎553-2268), has a **24hr. ATM.** Many RV parks have **laundry** service. Services include: **emergency** (☎911); **Nye County Sheriff,** 426 S. C Ave. (☎553-2345); **medical services** at the **Beatty Medical Clinic,** 702 Irving St. (☎553-2208; open M-F 8am-12pm and 1-5pm); free **Internet access** at the **Beatty Public Library,** 4th and Ward St. (☎553-2257; open M, W, and Th 10am-4pm; Tu noon-7pm); and **post office:** 600 E. Hwy. 95. (☎553-2343. Open M-F 8am-1pm and 2pm-4:30pm.) **Postal Code:** 89003.

Travelers looking to share stories from Death Valley and beyond should head no farther than the **Happy Burro Hostel ❸** at 100 W. Main St., a one-time brothel converted into comfortable dorm-style accommodations. All rooms have microwaves, refrigerators, TVs, and use of a communal kitchen. Breakfast is included. (☎553-9130; happyburro@pcweb.net. Reception 24hr. Check-out 10am. HI members $15, non-members $18; private rooms $35.) Sleep in peace at the **Stagecoach Hotel ❷** on Hwy. 95 at the north end of town. Beatty's nicest rooms feature amenities such as access to a pool and jacuzzi, as well as the adjoining casino and bar. (☎533-2419. Reception 24hr. Check-out 11am. Singles and doubles from $35.) **Bailey's Hot Springs RV Park ❶,** 5 mi. north of town on Hwy. 95, is ideal for campers, with shady sites, showers, and hot baths at three different temperatures from 8am-8pm. (☎553-2395. RVs $15, Tents $12.) The most interesting eatery in town is the **Ensenada Grill ❷,** 600 S. Hwy. 95, a funky hybrid of 50s diner and Mexican taqueria whose Bajan roots are evident in the shrimp specialities like camarones rancheros. (☎553-2600. Dinners $6-12. Open Tu-Su 11am-8pm.)

SOUTHEAST OF DEATH VALLEY ☎775

In **Death Valley Junction** at Hwys. 127 and 190 lives mime and ballet dancer Marta Becket, whose **Amargosa Opera House** is a lonely outpost of high culture in the high desert. The Opera House was opened as the Amargosa Hotel in the 1920s and named a National Historic Place in 1980. Becket incorporates parts of classical ballet, modern dance, and pantomime into a one-woman show with 47 different characters, drawing acclaim from the *Wall Street Journal* and the *New York Times,* as well as packed houses. (☎852-4441. Performances Oct., Dec.-Jan., and May Sa; Nov. and Feb.-Apr. M and Sa. Shows begin at 8:15pm. $15, children $12.)

The town of **Shoshone,** at Hwys. 127 and 178, acts as the southeastern gateway to Death Valley and a base for outdoor adventures. The **Shoshone Museum** displays several informative exhibits and answers general questions about the area. (☎852-4524. Open daily 10:30am-6pm.) The **Charles Brown General Store and Service Station** is the only place to stock up and fill up. (☎852-4242. Open daily 7am-8:30pm.)

Next door is the low-slung **Shoshone Inn ❹,** offering clean (if drab) rooms with kitchenettes, a hot spring-fed swimming pool, and cable TV. (☎852-4335. Singles starting at $53; doubles $63.) The nearby **Shoshone Trailer Park ❶** has RV hookups, showers, a pool, and even some shade. (☎852-4569. Sites for two $10; hookups $15; each additional person $5.) An oasis of French cuisine in the middle of the desert, **Cafe Si Bon ❶** offers crepes, espresso, and **Internet access.** (☎852-4307. Crepes $5-7. Internet $1 per 10min. Open M and W-Su 7am-5pm.)

Eight miles south of Shoshone off of Hwy. 127 is the small town of **Tecopa,** offering a kind of alternative desert experience. Follow the signs to the **Desertaire Hostel HI-AYH ❶,** 2000 Old Spanish Trail Hwy., 6 mi. from Hwy. 127, where friendly owner Adelaide and cheap sheets await. (☎877-907-1265 or 852-4580. Check-in 4-8pm. Dorms $15 for HI-AYH members, non-members $18; private rooms, members $25, non-members $28.) Run by Inyo country, **Tecopa Hot Springs Park & Campground ❶,** 3 mi. from Hwy. 127, is just what the doctor ordered for weary desert rats. (☎852-4264. Hot springs free. Camping sites $10, with electricity $14.)

You would swear the **China Ranch Date Farm,** off Furnace Creek Rd. 10 mi. from Hwy. 127, was a mirage if you couldn't taste the dates it produces. Tucked away in a lush valley surrounded by desert hills, Brian and Bonnie Brown harvest dates from their trees to create amazing shakes ($3), cookies, and breads. (☎852-4415; www.chinaranch.com. Open daily 9am-5pm.)

U.S. 395: LONE PINE TO RENO

Cutting through Owens Valley from arid desert in the south to alpine lakes in the north, U.S. 395 passes just to the east of the mountains surrounding Death Valley. Several towns along the way, including Lone Pine, Bishop, and Lee Vining, provide excellent stop-overs from which to explore the unlimited activities in the nearby White Mountains, Yosemite National Park, and Death Valley.

LONE PINE ☎ 760

It's no surprise that Hollywood opened a franchise in Lone Pine (pop. 2060), a town flanked to the east by the scorching depths of Death Valley and to the west by the rampart of the High Sierra, with its turrets of Mt. Whitney and the otherworldly Alabama Hills. For those who didn't grow up admiring Western heroes like Roy Rogers and The Lone Ranger, *Gladiator* and, regrettably, *Gone in 60 Seconds* are a few of the more than 300 films and TV shows shot in Lone Pine's striking landscape. The natural wonders surrounding the town stir up the same awe, reverence, and sense of possibility that the frequently glamorized Western frontier evoked throughout American folklore. Hikers, anglers, mountain bikers, rock climbers, and artists are drawn to this slice of the American West. Once in town, however, myth and legend take a back seat to travelers' real-life exploits in Lone Pine's outdoor environment.

■✈ 🛈 ORIENTATION & PRACTICAL INFORMATION

Straddling U.S. 395 near the intersection of Hwy. 136, Lone Pine is the first Sierra town northeast of Death Valley. Bishop is 60 mi. north, while L.A. is 4hr. and 210 mi. south. When Tioga Pass is open, Yosemite is a 3hr., 140 mi. drive north, while

CALIFORNIA

in the winter it's 5-6hr. and 210 mi. Upon reaching Lone Pine, U.S. 395 becomes Main St.; Washington St. is one block west. Whitney Portal Rd. serves as the dividing line between north and south in town.

Buses: Carson Ridgecrest Eastern Sierra Transit (CREST) (☎800-922-1930 or 872-1901) has bus service up and down 395. Buses run between Bishop and Ridgecrest and back M, W, F, stopping in Lone Pine on the way. To **Ridgecrest** (1½hr., 10:55am, $9.50), to **Bishop** (1hr., 4:20pm, $6). Buses run from Bishop to Reno and back on Tu, Th, and F. Buses leave from Statham Hall at the corner of Jackson and E. Bush Sts.

Shuttle Service: ☎888-313-0151 or 878-2119. "Anywhere, Anytime."

Visitor Information:

Interagency Visitors Center (☎876-6222). At U.S. 395 and Hwy. 136, about 1 mi. south of town. A joint venture between a number of agencies, including the Forest Service, the BLM, and National Park Service. Excellent maps and guidebooks, plus small exhibits. Informative handouts on hiking in the area. Open daily 8am-4:50pm.

Chamber of Commerce, 120 S. Main St. (☎876-4444, 877-253-8981; www.lonepinechamber.org). Cheerful, knowledgeable employees provide info on movies, special events, accommodations, and food in town. Open M-Sa 7:30am-5pm, Su 8am-1pm.

Mount Whitney/Inyo National Forest Ranger Station, 640 S. Main St. (☎876-6200; www.fs.fed.us/r5/inyo). Topographical and trail maps for backcountry travel. Issues **wilderness permits,** which are free and **required** in the backcountry. All trails within Eastern Sierra Wilderness areas have overnight usage quotas. Reserve permits up to 6 months in advance for the quota season, May 1-Nov. 1 ($5); self-register in the winter. 40% of trail quotas saved for walk-ins during the quota season. **Mt. Whitney** has 60 overnight and 115 day-use permits ($15), all of which must be reserved in advance (no walk-ins). A lottery is held every Feb. to grant permits. Consult the ranger station or the website for an application, which must be mailed or faxed. Some spots usually remain and can be claimed beginning in May. Station open daily 8am-6pm. **Wilderness Reservations,** 351 Pacu Ln., Ste. 200, Bishop, CA 93514 (☎873-2483; fax 873-2484).

Bank: El Dorado Savings Bank, 400 N. Main St. (☎876-5511). **24hr. ATM.** Open M-Th 9am-5pm, F 9am-6pm).

Laundromat: Lone Pine Laundromat, 105 W. Post St., just off Main St. Wash $1.50, dry $0.25 per 10min. Change machines. Open daily 7am-8pm.

Showers: Kirk's Sierra Barber, 114 N. Main St. (☎876-5700; call 876-4354 for showers after-hours). $4. Open Tu-F 8am-5pm. Ditch your shampoo and take a dip in the **public swimming pool,** at Lone Pine High School, 538 S. Main St. Open Jun.-Aug.

Emergency: ☎911. **Weather Info:** ☎800-427-7623.

Police: Inyo County Sheriff, Lone Pine Substation, 210 N. Washington St., at the corner of W. Bush and Washington (☎876-5606); County Headquarters (☎878-0383).

Hospital: Southern Inyo, 501 E. Locust St., at the corner of Mt. Whitney Dr. in the northeast part of town (☎876-5501).

Pharmacy: Lone Pine Drugs, 200 N. Main St. (☎876-5569). Open M-Sa 9am-9pm, Su 9am-7pm.

Internet Access: Inyo County Free Library, Lone Pine Branch (☎876-5031). On S. Washington St. Open M-Tu and Th-F 9am-noon and 1-5pm; W 9am-noon, 1-5pm, and 6-9pm; Sa 10am-1pm. Free ½hr. per day.

Post Office: 121 Bush St. (☎876-5681). Between Jackson and Main St. Open M-F 9am-5pm. **Postal Code:** 93545.

⚑ ACCOMMODATIONS

Lone Pine has a number of clean but relatively expensive motels. Weekdays in late fall, winter, and early spring are generally cheapest, but rates fluctuate by demand.

Dow Villa Motel, 310 S. Main St. (☎876-5521, reservations 800-824-9317; www.dowvillamotel.com). Built in 1923 during the early years of Lone Pine's Hollywood heyday to house pouty movie stars, the historical hotels' welcoming lobby has couches, a TV, fireplace and tea and coffee bar. Pool and jacuzzi open 24hr. Dow Villa has contemporary rooms and more amenities. Old hotel double rooms with shared bath start at $40, private baths $54. Modern villa rooms, some sleeping up to 6 people $82-125. ❸

Mt. Whitney Motel, 305 N. Main St. (☎800-845-2362 for reservations only, 876-4207). Rooms at this well-kept motel in the center of town are chock-full of amenities like fridges, microwaves, and coffee makers. Pool and cable TV. Mid-Oct. to Apr. singles $36-59, doubles $49-59; May to mid-Oct. singles $49-79, doubles $59-89. ❸

Lone Pine Budget Inn Motel, 138 Willow St. (☎876-5655). This small motel just off the main drag is perhaps the best deal in town. Rooms have refrigerators, microwaves, coffee makers, and cable TV. Continental breakfast included. Singles $30-69, doubles $44-99, triples (sleeping up to 6) $59-129, depending on time of year. ❷

CAMPING

Whitney Portal Campground (Mt. Whitney ranger ☎876-6200, reservations 877-444-6777), 8000 ft., on Whitney Portal Rd. 13 mi. west of town. Surrounding evergreens, a rushing stream, and phenomenal views make this an exceptional campground—just don't forget about the bears. Wood $5. 7-night max. stay. Some sites reserved for first-come, first-camp. Open Memorial Day-Columbus Day. Sites $14, additional vehicle $5; group sites $30. ❶ Served by the **Whitney Portal Store,** which carries light supplies, guidebooks, and some outerwear. Pay phone and a small restaurant. Open May 9am-6pm, June 8am-8pm, Jul. and Aug. 7am-9am, Sept. 8am-8pm, Oct. 9am-6pm.

Diaz Lake Campground (☎876-5656), 3700 ft., on U.S. 395 2 mi. south of downtown Lone Pine. 200 shaded sites overlooking Diaz Lake. The sites are situated on the lake's far shore with easy access to this wet playground. Grills, flush toilets, and showers. Open year-round. 15-day max. stay. Sites $10. ❶

Portagee Joe (☎876-5656), 3800 ft., ½ mi. from downtown Lone Pine, off Whitney Portal Rd. on Tuttle Creek Rd. Tree-lined camping by a small stream. 15 sites. Water and vault toilets. Open year-round. Sites $10. ❶

Tuttle Creek, 4,000 ft., head up Whitney Portal Rd. 3.5 mi., then turn left on Horseshoe Meadow Rd. and the campground will be on the right. In the no-mans-land between the Alabama Hills and the Sierra, this campground offers spectacular views on all sides. Facilities are spartan (no water, vault toilets), but, heck, they're free. 82 sites. 14-day max. stay. Open Mar.-Oct. ❶

FOOD

Lone Pine has its share of coffee shops and steakhouses, but not much else. Many are nondescript, but cheap, decent fare is offered. Grab groceries at **Joseph's Bi-Rite Market,** 119 S. Main St., or eat at its hearty, if heavy, hot deli. (☎876-4378. Open Nov.-May M-Sa 8am-8pm, June-Oct. M-Sa 8am-9pm, year-round Su 8:30-7pm.)

High Sierra Cafe, 446 S. Main St. (☎876-5796). Down-to-earth food and prices. The BBQ beef sandwich is a great post-climb treat. A favorite with the locals, High Sierra serves everything on the menu all the time. Sandwiches ($4-8); entrees ($8-17). ❷

Seasons Restaurant, 206 S. Main St., on the corner of Rte. 395 and Whitney Portal Rd. (☎876-8927). The most upscale restaurant in town, serving "continental" cuisine ($15-23) including some great steaks and pastas. Respectable selection of Californian and imported wines. Open daily 5-10pm; in winter M-Sa 5-9pm. ❹

Bonanza Mexican Restaurant, 104 N. Main St. (☎876-4768), dishes out fresh and fla-vorful favorites ($6.50-11) from south of the border. Try the specialty Enchiladas Cama-rones ($11) with a cold cerveza. Open M-Th 11am-9pm, F-Su 7am-9pm. ❷

Mt. Whitney Restaurant, 227 S. Main St. (☎876-5751). Walls in this down-home joint are papered with the stars of the silver screen (and the boob tube) and their memora-bilia. Chow down on "the best burgers in town" (including ostrich, venison, or buffalo burgers) and other tasty grub ($6-12) under the watchful eyes of Gene Autry and John Wayne. Open daily May-Oct. 6:30am-10pm, Nov.-Apr. 6:30am-9pm. ❷

🎦 SIGHTS

If **Mount Whitney** is the star of the show, the surrounding heights of the **Inyo National Forest** comprise a staggering supporting cast. Six of the 13 peaks in California over 14,000 ft. are located in the 13-mi. Whitney Escarpment west of Lone Pine.

Well before Whitney Portal on the way up Whitney Portal Rd. is **Movie Road,** which leads to the scenic **Alabama Hills.** A bouldered dreamscape of golden-brown granite formations, the hills were the stage set for Hollywood "cowboy 'n' Indian" tales like *How the West Was Won* (1962) and *Posse From Hell* (1961). In all, over 250 Westerns were filmed here, including such television shoot-'em-ups as *Bonanza* and *Rawhide*, and, more recently, countless SUV commercials. Recent flicks include *Maverick, Star Trek: Generations,* and *G.I. Jane.* The Chamber of Commerce dispenses **movie location map guides** that helps you find where a num-ber of films were shot. Lone Piners celebrate the Hills' glamorous career at the annual **Lone Pine Film Festival** (☎876-9103; www.lonepinefilmfestival.org) every Columbus Day weekend, where selections from the more than 400 films shot in the region are screened and stars, past and present, make appearances.

On U.S. 395, 11 mi. north of Lone Pine and 5 mi. south of Independence, is the **Manzanar National Historic Site** (☎878-2194; www.nps.gov/manz), a testament to one of the most shameful chapters in American history. Manzanar was the first of ten "relocation camps," or internment centers, the US established during WWII to contain Japanese Americans, whom the government saw as a potential threat to national security. From March 1942 to 1945, more than 11,000 people were held here. Aggressively and conspicuously ignored by the government, the camp was reduced to a few building foundations and some barbed wire before it was estab-lished as a National Historic Site in 1992. On the last Saturday of every April, an annual pilgrimage of former internees and their descendants is held at the camp's cemetery. The day of remembrance and education is open to the public.

Once a 75 sq. mi. lake used to transport bullion from nearby gold mines in the 1870s, **Owens Dry Lake,** 5 mi. south of town on Rte. 395, is today a mineral-rich, multi-colored, dry lakebed, thanks to the water diversion schemes of Los Angeles. In the 1920s, freshwater streams that fed the river were incorporated into the L.A. aqueduct, leaving the lake to dry up in the sun. Bacteria are responsible for the lake bed's pinkish hue. The dry salts that have been exposed since this massive evaporation caused a serious dust problem in the area; the Environmental Protec-tion Agency has deemed the air quality around Owens Lake the poorest in the US.

One of the best-preserved ghost towns in the state, **Cerro Gordo** (☎876-1860, 876-5030), or "Fat Hill," was once producing nearly 10,000 lb. of silver a day, all bound for L.A., where it accounted for one-third of all business transactions in the city's port in the late 1800s. All told, more than $17 million was extracted from the mine. Today, there are tours of the town, featuring old-time hotels, offices, a brothel, mining structures, and a museum. Cerro Gordo is 8 mi. up the steep, dirt Cerro Gordo Rd. (passable only with high-clearance vehicles) from Keeler, 13 mi. south of Lone Pine along Hwy. 136. Tours daily 9am-3pm (last tour at 2pm), $5.

◪ OUTDOORS

Climbing Mt. Whitney requires significant preparation, both in terms of physical endurance and logistics. Unlike other Inyo trails, the Mt. Whitney trail is on a reservation-only system for most of the year, meaning no first come, first served permits ($15) are issued during the quota season, May 1-Nov. 1. The trail is so popular that its permits are distributed by lottery. Throughout the month of February, lottery applications (available through Wilderness Reservations, 351 Pacu Lane, Suite 200, Bishop, CA 93514; ☎873-2483; www.fs.fed.us/r5/inyo.351) are accepted for both day (115) and overnight (60) use permits. The odds of getting a spot are highly dependent on dates and group size. A few permits go unissued during the lottery every year and can be reserved beginning May 1.

One of the nation's most popular trails, the **Mount Whitney Trail,** which peaks at the highest point in the lower 48 states, is full of adventurers, experienced and amateur, looking for bragging rights. While more a strenuous hike than mountain climb, a non-technical ascent is only feasible late spring to early fall when there is not much snow and ice. Even then the mountain can get quite cold, especially at night, so only attempt the journey with proper gear. The trailhead for **Mount Whitney** is at 8365 ft., and the route ascends over 6000 ft.; **hikers should be wary of the effects of altitude.** Hike slowly and allow extra time in your itinerary, but most importantly, spend time at high elevations before setting out. The 11 mi. trek to the top usually takes two days, though the very fit and acclimated can do it in one long day. **Lone Pine is bear country.** Ingenious bears are adept at breaking into cars and ripping apart backpacks (see **Bears,** p. 70). Rent a bear-proof food container at ranger stations in Lone Pine ($5 per week) or the Portal Store ($2 per day).

Rock climbs along the North Fork of Lone Pine Creek—many of which begin in the area around Iceberg Lake—head to the summits of Mt. Whitney, Mt. Russell, and Mt. Carillon. The **Mountaineers Route** on Mt. Whitney, which follows the couloir that separates the northeast ridge from the east buttress, can often be taken to the summit in the summer and fall months without any technical equipment but a good deal of outdoor savvy. Mt. Whitney's **East Face** (5.4) and **East Buttress** (5.6) present a year-round challenge to experienced rock climbers. Take a look at a climbing guidebook for more detailed information, or contact **Sky's the Limit** guides (☎800-733-7597; www.skysthelimit.com) if you don't want to go it alone.

A backcountry, multi-day route to the Mt. Whitney summit, the **Cottonwood Lakes Trail** (10,000 ft. at the trailhead) sets out within the Golden Trout Wilderness, passes over New Army Pass, and then joins the Pacific Crest Trail in Sequoia National Park. It leads through some of the Sierra's most pristine wilderness before approaching the peak from the west. In addition, there is camping (sites $6), equestrian facilities, and several day hikes in the Horseshoe Meadows area. **Cottonwood Pack Station** (☎878-2015; www.lone-pine.com/packstation) runs pack trips ranging from half-day rides to multi-day excursions out of Horseshoe Meadow ($360-450 per person per day). These trips explore terrain in the Inyo National Forest, Sequoia, and Kings Canyon National Parks.

The southern Owens Valley is known for its "Big Air" potential among **hang gliding** and **paragliding** aficionados. Walt's Point at 9000ft. on Horseshoe Meadow Rd. is a renowned launching spot. In 1991, Carrie Castle set a cross-country distance record from Walt's Point, flying 200 mi. to Austin, NV. Castle, a Bishop native, offers tandem flights and instruction to enthusiasts of all levels (☎872-2087).

To reach Horseshoe Meadows and the Cottonwood Lakes Trailhead, follow Whitney Portal Rd. for 4 mi. from Lone Pine and take Horseshoe Meadow Rd. 20 mi. to the trailhead. The trail is on the quota system from the end of June to Sept. 15. Stop by the Mt. Whitney Ranger Station in Lone Pine for permits (☎876-6200).

Many **day hikes** explore the Eastern Sierra out of the Whitney Portal. The **Meysan Lake Trail** is a strenuous 4.7 mi. haul from Whitney Portal to an exquisite high-altitude lake. The trail is infrequently maintained and difficult to follow in some places; the stretch from Camp Lake to Meysan Lake is nothing more than a faint path on a rocky slope. Meysan Lake provides access to climbing routes on a number of peaks including Lone Pine Peak, Mt. Mallory, and Candlelight Peak. The **Whitney Portal Trail** offers a challenging 4 mi. hike from the Lone Pine campground to Whitney Portal campground, or a more moderate trip if done downhill in the opposite direction. The trail follows Lone Pine Creek through densely forested higher altitudes and the more open terrain of the valley floor, offers incredible views of Mt. Whitney and the Sierras to the west, as well as the Alabama Hills and Inyo and White Mountains to the east.

While not as publicized as Bishop to the north, Lone Pine is a **rock climbing** hotspot in its own right. In addition to the multi-pitch climbs in the **Whitney Portal** area (above), the **Alabama Hills** are peppered with over 200 sport climbs and some great crack climbs. Most routes are in the 5.10 range, but recently visiting climbers have put up several 5.12s and 5.13s.

If you've got bulletproof muscles and high-octane willpower, you may want to dig into one of the toughest marathons in the country. Each year on the first weekend of May, Lone Pine stages the high elevation **Wild Wild West Marathon,** considered the seventh-most difficult in the nation. Interested athletes can enter by contacting the **Chamber of Commerce** (☎877-253-8981 or 876-4444).

BISHOP & OWENS VALLEY ☎760

Situated in the northern end of the Owens Valley just minutes from extensive world-class hiking, climbing, horsepacking, and fishing, Bishop is the place for visitors to stop and recharge en route to the surrounding rivers, mountains, and desert valleys. The largest city in the Eastern Sierras, this resort town has many of the things absent from the rest of the region, such as international cuisine, bookstores, and coffeehouses; and some of the things that aren't, like casinos, strip-malls, and fast food. As for in-town attractions, fishing in the clear blue lakes of Bishop Creek Canyon, bouldering in the Buttermilks, and enjoying one of the many seasonal festivals all make the town worth a visit. The Owens Valley is wedged between the snow-capped, knife-edged Sierras and the sloping yet towering White Mountains, making it "the deepest valley on Earth." In the early 20th century, Owens Valley's freshwater streams began providing water for the budding desert city of L.A., leading to the water scandal upon which the movie *Chinatown* (1974) was loosely based.

▐▀ TRANSPORTATION

Bus: Carson Ridgecrest Eastern Sierra Transit (CREST), 201 S. Warren St., one block west of Main St. (☎800-922-1930 or 872-1901). Provides bus service up and down Rte. 395. Buses run between Mammoth and Ridgecrest and back M, W, F, stopping in Bishop. To **Ridgecrest** (2½hr., 9:45am, $15.50) and **Mammoth** (1hr., 5:20pm, $5.50). Buses run between Bishop and Reno and back on Tu, Th, and F (4½hr., 7am, $23). Greyhound has canceled service to the Eastern Sierra, but you can take it to **Carson City,** where CREST (☎800-922-1930) runs Tu and Th-F at 2pm, arriving in Bishop at 6:30pm. One-way fare $20.

Public Transportation: Dial-A-Ride (☎872-1901 or 800-922-1930). Runs a fixed route around town ($0.50) and will travel up to 1 mi. off its route to pick up or drop off for an additional cost of $0.75. M-F 8am-5pm. Call ahead for flexible stops. In addition, door-to-door buses serve the greater Bishop area (including trailheads) with rates based on distance traveled. Twice daily shuttles (7am and 5:30pm) to **Mammoth** ($5.50) and **Crowley Lake** ($3). Open M-Th 8am-5pm, F-Sa 8am-midnight (last call 11:30pm).

Taxi/Trailhead Shuttle: Kountry Korners (☎877-656-0756 or 938-2650). Provides year-round shuttle service.

Rental Car: U-Save, 107 S. Main St. (☎800 207-2681 or 872-1070). Open daily 8am-6pm. **Eastern Sierra Motors,** 1440 N. Hwy. 6 (☎873-4291). Fords from $47-67 per day, $285-400 per week. 150 mi. per day. 21+. Open M-F 7:30am-6pm, Sa 8am-5pm.

✈️🅿️ ORIENTATION & PRACTICAL INFORMATION

Bishop is located on Rte. 395 in the northern end of Owens Valley. Lone Pine, at the base of Mt. Whitney, is 60 mi. south. Via the Tioga Pass, the town is 140 mi. from Yosemite. Death Valley is 165 mi. to the southeast, L.A. is 270 mi. south, and Reno is 205 mi. north via Rte. 395.

Visitor Information:

Bishop Area Chamber of Commerce and Visitors Bureau, 690 N. Main St. (☎888 395-3952 or 873-8405; www.bishopvisitor.com). At the City Park. Area maps and info. Get a free copy of the *Bishop, California Vacation Planner* for up-to-date listings of special events. Open Sa-Su 10am-4pm, mid-Apr. through mid-Oct. M-F 9am-5pm, mid-Oct. through mid-Apr. M-F 9am-4:30pm.

White Mountain Ranger Station, 798 N. Main St. (☎873-2500; www.fs.fed.us/r5/inyo). Excellent campground and trail info for all of Inyo National Forest. Weather report and message board. Wilderness permits reservable up to 6 months in advance; must be picked up by 10am on the day of departure. Walk-in permits are held open for all trails. Open daily mid-May to mid-Sept. 8am-5pm; mid-Sept. to mid-May M-F 8am-4:30pm.

Bank: Washington Mutual, 400 N. Main St. (☎873-5031). **24hr. ATM.** Open M-F 9am-6pm, Sa 9am-1pm.

Laundromat: Sierra Suds, 163 Academy St. (☎873-8338). Wash $1.25, dry $0.25 per 10min. Open daily 7am-9pm, last wash 8pm.

Fishing Licenses: Culver's Sporting Goods, 156 S. Main St. (☎872-8361). Annual non-resident $82.45, 10-day non-resident $30.70; annual resident $30.70. Open Apr-Oct. M-Th 6am-8pm, F-Sa 8am-9pm. Nov.-Feb. daily 7am-5pm, Mar. 7am-6pm.

Outdoor Gear: Wilson's Eastside Sports, 224 N. Main St. (☎873-7520). A hiking and climbing mecca that also rents bear canisters (1-2 days $8, $4 per day thereafter). Open daily May-Sept. 9am-9pm; Oct.-Apr. 9am-6pm.

AAA Emergency Road Service: ☎800-400-4222. Call ☎872-8241 for local branch.

Road Conditions: Caltrans, ☎800-427-7623.

Emergency: ☎911. **Police: Bishop Police Department,** 207 W. Line St. (☎873-5866).

Pharmacy: Rite Aid Pharmacy, 1375 Rocking West Dr. (☎873-7883). Along Hwy. 395 north of town. Open M-Sa 8am-9pm, Su 8am-7pm.

Hospital: Northern Inyo Hospital, 150 Pioneer Ln. (☎873-5811). 24hr. emergency care.

Library and Internet Access: Inyo County Free Library, 210 Academy St. (☎873-5115). 30min. free. Open M-Th 10am-8pm, F 10am-6pm, Sa 10am-1pm.

Post Office: 595 W. Line St. (☎873-3526 or 800-275-8777). Open M-F 7:30am-4pm, Sa 9am-1pm. **Postal Code:** 93514.

🏠 ACCOMMODATIONS

Hotels are plentiful in Bishop, but cheap hotels are not. Thrifty travelers are better off camping in or near Bishop. Those traveling in groups, especially those looking to fish, may find a cabin is the best option. **Cardinal Village Resort,** at the North Fork of Bishop Creek Canyon (☎873-4789; www.cardinalvillageresort.com), and **Bishop Creek Lodge**, 2100 South Lake Rd. at the South Fork of Bishop Creek Canyon (☎873-4484; www.bishopcreekresorts.com), both offer cabin accommodations. (2-3 night min. stay, $90-275.)

El Rancho Motel, 274 Lagoon St. (☎872-9251 or 888-872-9251). 2 blocks west of Main St. A quintessential motel; drive up to your door. 16 rooms with TV, A/C, coffeemakers, and refrigerators. Reception 7:30am-11:30pm. Kitchen $8 extra. Singles $40-55; doubles $45-67. Extra occupant $5. Prices lowest Nov. to mid-Apr. ❸

Bardini House, 515 Sierra St. (☎873-8036, 872-4413, or 872-1348). The Bardini House features dormitory beds in a small house in a residential neighborhood. Kitchen, grill, and back patio are at the disposal of guests. Maximum stay 10 nights. Reservations required. $10/night. ❶

Bishop Village Motel, 286 W. Elm St. (☎872-8155 or 888-668-5546). This comfortable motel caters to fishermen and other outdoors folk with a heated pool, grilling area, and fish-freezing facilities. Quiet rooms a block away from Main St. feature refrigerators and cable TV; some rooms have kitchens. Economy rooms $39-49, suites $69-79. ❸

Elms Motel, 233 E. Elm St. (☎873-8118 or 800-848-9226). The Elms Motel's two-room cottages are "dutch clean," pristinely quiet, and of a more relaxed era. All have A/C, coffeemakers, and cable TV. Flanks Bishop Park. Fish-cleaning facilities. Singles $37-42; doubles $43-48. ❸

▨ CAMPING

Most campgrounds around Bishop are well-kept and easily accessible. Sites host a consistent flow of campers throughout the summer but are especially crowded during the Mule Days celebration over Memorial Day weekend and the Tri-County Fair over Labor Day weekend (book a year in advance).

There are over 30 **Inyo National Forest** campgrounds in the Bishop Ranger District (most open May-Oct.). The closest campgrounds to town are private, however, and can be found on or near Rte. 395 just north and south of Bishop. **Millpond ❶**, 4500 ft., 6 mi. north of Bishop on Saw Mill Rd., has 70 cool and shady spots near Millpond County Park and McGee Creek. (☎873-5342. Open Mar.-Oct. Sites $16 and up.) Southwest of town on Rte. 168 are a whole slew of USFS campgrounds along Bishop. **Four Jeffrey ❶**, 8100 ft., is home to over 100 open sites on a hillside above the south fork of Bishop Creek. It's also wheelchair accessible. (14-day limit. Open late-Apr. to Oct. Sites $14. Extra vehicle $5.) For wilder camping, **North Lake ❶**, 9500 ft., and **Sabrina Lake ❶**, 9000 ft., both have stunning scenery, trail access to the John Muir Wilderness, and fishing, of course. These chilly sites feature vault toilets, water, and big helpings of nature. (7-day limit. North Lake open mid-June-Sept.; Sabrina Lake open mid-May-Sept. Sites $14. Extra vehicle $5.)

Pleasant Valley ❶, 4100ft., 6½ mi. north of town off of Hwy. 395, is home to 200 sites for year-round camping near the Happy and Sad Boulders and Owens River Gorge. Water and toilets. (14-day limit. Sites $10.) Nearby, on the west side of Hwy 395, free camping can be found 5 mi. west on Round Valley Rd. (off of Swamill Rd.) at **Horton Creek ❶**, 5000 ft. Fifty-three unshaded sites have vault toilets, but no potable water. (14-day limit. Open May-Oct.)

Some of the best camping in the area is found just north of town, between Bishop and Mammoth Lakes, on Rte. 395, along **Rock Creek ❶**, 7000-10,000 ft. Ten campgrounds with over 300 sites scatter the canyon, nearly all of which are secluded and shady. There are excellent fishing, mountain biking, climbing, and hiking opportunities in the area. Most sites have piped water and flush toilets. (Open May-Oct. Sites $15-16.)

FOOD

Stock up on groceries at **Manor Market,** 3100 W. Line St., which is locally-owned and offers lots of natural foods (☎873-4296. Open M-Sa 6am-9pm, Su 6am-8pm), or **Vons,** 1190 N. Main St. (☎872-9811. Open 24hr.)

Taqueria Las Palmas, 136 E. Line St. (☎873-4337). This authentic taqueria is popular with locals and climbing bums alike. The friendly waitstaff dishes out specialty flautas, buffalo burritos ($9), and a full range of Mexican beers. Open daily 11am-9pm. ❷

Western Kitchen, 930 N. Main St. (☎872-3246). Along with all the usual American fare, this Western kitchen also serves some delicious dishes from the East. Depending on your mood, go for an omelette ($5-7), steak ($7-9), or choose from an extensive list of Thai specialties (curries $7.50-$9.50). Open daily 6am-9pm. ❷

Erik Schat's Bakery, 763 N. Main St. (☎873-7156). Popular and savory since 1938. Breads and pastries ($3-5) baked fresh daily and served with excellent coffee. The hearty salads, soups, and sandwiches ($3.50-7) like the Mule Kick are especially rejuvenating after a day in the hills. Try the sheepherder's bread. Open May-Oct. M-Th and Sa 6am-6:30pm, F 6am-10pm, Su 6am-8pm; Nov-Apr. M-Th and Sa 6:30am-6:30pm, F 6am-10pm, Su 6:30am-7pm. ❶

Kava Coffeehouse, 206 N. Main St. (☎872-1010). A hip spot to scarf healthy eats like the Kava Quiche ($5) and slurp fresh smoothies ($4). Outstanding coffee. Local artisans' wares grace the cabinets. A favorite hang out for local climbers; chess night every Tu (5-8pm). Open M-F 6:30am-8:30pm, Sa 7am-8:30pm, Su 7am-3:30pm. ❶

▲ OUTDOOR ACTIVITIES

EAST OF BISHOP

The mountains forming the Owens Valley—some of the highest ranges on the continent—are a backpacker's Eden. In the eastern half of Inyo National Forest, which is split by Hwy. 395, the yellow sands of the **White Mountains** rise to heights rivaling the Sierras, but with much less fanfare. To escape the crowds gallivanting on the western slopes of the valley, head east; you'll undoubtedly see more cows than people. If it's elevation you're in search of, tackle the tough 7.5 mi. slog to the top of **White Mountain Peak** (14,246 ft.), the third-tallest mountain in California. The hike gains over 2500 ft. on the way to the summit from the locked Bancroft Gate at the White Mountain Research Station. Park your car at the station on White Mountain Rd., 26 mi. from Hwy. 168 and 38 mi. from Big Pine. Unlike Mt. Whitney, a day-use permit is not necessary, yet one can climb nearly as high.

Scattered across the face of the White Mountains are California's **bristlecone pines,** the oldest living organisms on the planet. Gnarled, twisted, and warped into fantastic shapes, the bristle-cone pine trees may grow only one inch every 100 years. The preservative qualities of these cold, dry, extreme altitudes (trees grow at elevations of up to 12,000 ft.) have allowed the "Methuselah" specimen in the Schulman Group to survive for nearly 4700 years; to prevent vandalism, visitors are not told which one of the trees is the "Methuselah." To reach the **Ancient Bristlecone Pine Forest** (☎873-2500 or 873-2573), follow Hwy. 168 off Hwy. 395 at Big Pine for 12 mi. Turn left at the sign to the Bristlecone Pine Forest and the White Mountains Research Station. The 11 mi. paved road climbs to **Schulman Grove,** at nearly 10,000 ft. Before the grove, 8 mi. down the road, you'll come to **Sierra View Overlook,** where you can see the great wall of the Sierras, including parts of Yosemite and Mt. Whitney on a clear day. Two short **hikes** head out from Schulman. The moderately strenuous 4.5 mi. Methuselah Walk and easy 1 mi. Discovery Trail lead through the hills and past these astonishing trees. The drive to the even-higher Patriarch Grove, home of some of the most striking specimens, is a beautiful but unpaved 12 mi. from Schulman.

A number of valleys are tucked beneath eastern slopes of the White and Inyos, including Fish Lake Valley, Deep Springs Valley (home of **Deep Springs College**), part of Death Valley National Park, and the uninhabited ◼**Eureka Valley,** the valley northwest of Death Valley. Its magnificent and haunting sand dunes create one of the region's more surreal landscapes. If the sand is cool, climb to the top of the dunes and roll down. Friction in the sand that you disturb resonates in a bizarre, deep hum. Local Native Americans called it "the singing of the sands." Death Valley Rd., off Hwy. 168 east of Big Pine, passes through Eureka Valley on its way to Scotty's Castle. The paved and gravel Death Valley Rd. runs 37 mi. southwest from the intersection with Hwy. 168 before turning off near Eureka Valley Rd., a 10 mi. gravel and dirt track that cuts across the valley floor to the dunes. Four-wheel-drive is preferable, especially if there's snow or if the road is washed out.

WEST OF BISHOP

A lot of fun can be had near Bishop in Big Pine and Bishop Creek Canyons, to the south and west, and in Buttermilk Country and Rock Creek, to the west and north-west. Wilderness permits are required year-round for overnight trips in the **John Muir Wilderness,** which includes most of the East Sierra from Mt. Whitney to Mammoth. All trailheads within the Wilderness have usage quotas, but 40% of permits are available on a walk-in basis. If you make a reservation for a permit (☎873-2483), there is a $5 fee. **Sierra Mountain Center,** 174 W. Line St. (☎873-8526; www.sierramountaincenter.com) and **Sierra Mountaineering International,** 236 N. Main St. (☎872-4929; www.sierramountaineering.com) offer guide services for any sort of outdoor adventure you can dream up.

Head south on Hwy. 395 to Big Pine, then head west on Crocker St. for 10 mi. to reach the mouth of **Big Pine Canyon,** which Big Pine Creek has cut through thick groves of Jeffery Pines. This area is home to the southernmost glaciers in the US, remnants from the last ice age that shaped much of the landscape. The largest of these glaciers is **Palisade Glacier,** about 2 mi. in length and many hundred feet thick. The **North Fork Trail** (or **Big Pine Lakes Trail**) is a popular route for hikers as well as rock and ice climbers looking to access the glacier or the rock pinnacles above them, the Palisades. The trail passes First, Second, and Third Lakes as well as the stone cabin of Hollywood legend Lon Chaney before reaching the foot of Palisade Glacier. It's an 18 mi. hike round-trip with a 4500 ft. elevation gain to the base of the glacier. The summit of North Palisade (14,242 ft.), one of the tallest peaks in the Sierras is nearly another 2000 ft. higher. Some of the best alpine climbing in the region can be found on the Celestial Aretes (5.6 to 5.9) at **Temple Crag,** which is part of the Palisades escarpment. **Fishing** enthusiasts favor Big Pine's seldom-traveled **South Fork Trail,** which leads to lakes laden with trout. The route becomes sketchy above Willow Lake (4 mi. from trailhead).

Six miles north of Big Pine and 7 mi. south of Bishop on Hwy. 395 are **Keough's Hot Springs.** The springs have been exploited as a full-fledged business venture during the day, complete with a 40 ft. by 100 ft. pool, lifeguards, and snack bar. (☎872-6911. $7.) Under the cloak of darkness, however, the water that is diverted into the pool by day continues down the hill and makes for some terrific hot tubbing in the creek. To reach these healing waters, turn onto Keough Hot Springs Rd. and about ½ mile in make a right-hand turn down to the creek.

Follow Line St. (Hwy. 168) west of Bishop to the lakes and campgrounds of **Bishop Creek Canyon.** Within the canyon walls, 15 mi. down the highway, the road splits. Turning left at the fork will take you to **South Lake** (9700ft., 9 mi.), while continuing straight will take you to **Lake Sabrina** (9125ft., 5 mi.); both stunning mountain reservoirs are teeming with fish and the trailheads granting access into the Sierras. The official angling season spans late Apr. through late Oct. Contact the Chamber of Commerce (☎ 873-8405) for general fishing and tournament info. From South Lake, hikers can pick up the **Bishop Pass Trail,** which connects with trails leading to Green, Treasure, and Chocolate Lakes and mountain meadows filled with wildflowers in the spring. More adventurous hikers can forge deeper into the wilderness and tackle some of the nearby 13,000 ft. peaks, including **Mount Goode** (13,085 ft.), whose **North Buttress** (5.9) is a classic alpine route. The Bishop Pass Trail eventually meets up with the John Muir Trail, which stretches between Yosemite and Mt. Whitney. **Mountain biking** along **Coyote Flat** offers some of the most spine-tingling downhills around. Just be sure you know how to get back up.

From the fork, Hwy. 168 continues west 4 mi. to **Sabrina Basin,** which offers secluded hiking and fishing opportunities. On the southern side of the road, **Cardinal Pinnacle** offers a number of multi-pitch routes on superb granite. Lake Sabrina is the trailhead for routes up to pristine alpine lakes including Blue, Hungry Packer, and Midnight Lakes. **North Lake** can be accessed by a single-lane dirt road heading north just before Lake Sabrina. From the campground here, the **Paiute Pass Trail** follows the north fork of Bishop Creek up to Paiute Pass (11,423 ft.), where it joins the **John Muir Trail.**

Nearly 8 mi. up Hwy. 168, the Buttermilk Rd. turnoff leads to some world-famous boulders in **Buttermilk Country.** Named for the dairy farms that once refreshed stagecoach parties passing the region, the area is marked by giant granite boulders great for climbing and mountain biking. About 4 mi. down the road, you'll come to the **Peabody Boulders,** the most celebrated of the outcroppings.

While the Buttermilks are the most famous, the possibilities for climbing around Bishop don't end there. Over 600 boulder problems tattoo the landscape at the **Happy and Sad Boulders,** along Chalk Bluff Rd. off of Hwy. 6 just north of downtown Bishop. Nearby, in the heart of the Volcanic Tableland, the **Owens River Gorge** is a sport climber's paradise. With hundreds of bolted climbs (5.6 to 5.13), you could climb here every day for a year and still have new routes waiting for you. The Gorge Rd. turnoff is 14 mi. north of Bishop along Hwy. 395 at the foot of Sherwin Grade. Turn left (north) on the Gorge Parallel Rd. and there are parking areas 3, 4½, and 6 mi. along from which you can drop into the gorge.

The forests and mountains along **Rock Creek Canyon** are frequented year-round. Hair-raising precipices, plunging canyons, and alpine wildflowers mesmerize photographers and casual onlookers alike. Take Hwy. 395 24 mi. north of Bishop, turn west on Rock Creek Rd., and continue up Rock Creek Canyon as far as you can go: Mosquito Flat (10 mi.) in the summer, the locked gate in the winter. **Little Lakes Valley** cradles a necklace of lakes full of trout in the shadow of 13,000 ft. peaks. The **Little Lakes Trail** sets out from Mosquito Flat and climbs gradually to explore the upper valley's lakes and meadows. **Mono Pass Trail,** which branches off from the Little Lakes trail about ¼ mile from the trailhead, leads to beautiful **Ruby Lake** and its staggering sheer granite walls. It continues to Mono Pass (12,040ft.), and connects with the John Muir Trail. Rock Creek also boasts some great mountain biking on the **Lower Rock Creek Trail,** which starts at Tom's Place, ranking among the top. There are numerous campgrounds on the way to Mosquito Flat (see above), and plenty of day-parking at each of the three trailheads. In winter, the evergreen forests and lake basins of this "range of light" (as Muir described the Eastern Sierra) make for spectacular **cross-country skiing.** Rock Creek is one of the best areas. **Rock Creek Lodge** (☎ 877 935-4170 or 935-4170; www.rockcreeklodge.com) maintains groomed trails and is home to a ski school.

Pine Creek Pack Train (☎ 800 962-0775 or 387-2797) and **Rainbow Pack Outfitters,** 600 S. Main St. (☎ 873-8877 or 872-8803) both run horsepacking operations out of the town of Bishop. These specialized rides explore the heights of the Sierras

CALIFORNIA

thanks to horsepower and tend to cost around $100 for a full day of riding and $50 for a half-day trip. Overnight trips run a couple hundred dollars per night; call for more information.

🎵 ENTERTAINMENT

There might not be a hopping bar scene in Bishop, but hog-riders and other free spirits manage to find excitement at the few watering holes that line Main St. (Hwy. 395). **Rusty's,** 112 N. Main St., is among the darkest and most popular. (☎873-9066. Open daily 8am-2am.) Although activity and excitement seem to permeate everyday life in Bishop, several annual events add more spice to this swinging metropolis. Haul your ass to town during Memorial Day weekend for the world's largest mule event, **Mule Days** (☎872-4263; www.muledays.org). View 110 mule sporting events, 430,000 mule-obsessed fans, 700 mules, and the famous Mule Days Parade, which is long enough to be listed in the Guinness Book of World Records. The **Hotrods, Hippies & Polyester 50s-70s Dance** (☎873-3588) grooves every February, and the **Air Show** flies by on Fourth of July weekend. The City Park (behind the Visitors Center) has hosted **evening concerts** in the gazebo for 40 consecutive summers. (June-Aug. M 8-9pm. Free.) Food, games, and fun characterize the massive **Tri-County Fair** (☎873-3588) over Labor Day weekend, which features rodeos, homemade salsa, beer and wine contests, and a demolition derby.

LEE VINING & MONO LAKE ☎760

One million years old, Mono Lake is the Western Hemisphere's oldest enclosed body of water. Today, Mono supports not only its own delicate and unique ecosystem but also the water needs of greater metropolitan L.A. Seventy miles north of Bishop on 395, Lee Vining provides stunning access to Yosemite via Inyo National Forest, as well as the best access to Mono Lake and the ghost town of Bodie.

■🗂 **ORIENTATION & PRACTICAL INFORMATION.** Lee Vining sits 70 mi. north of Bishop on U.S. 395 and 10 mi. west of the Tioga Pass entrance to Yosemite. Bodie lies 28 mi. northwest of Lee Vining off U.S. 395. Addresses in Lee Vining consist only of P.O. Box numbers, so general directions or cross-streets are provided instead. The **Mono Lake Committee and Lee Vining Chamber of Commerce,** at Main and 3rd St., dispenses info on activities in the area and lake preservation info. (☎647-6595; www.leevining.com or www.monolake.org. Open late June to Labor Day daily 9am-10pm; Labor Day to late June 9am-5pm.) **Mono Basin National Forest Scenic Area Visitors Center,** off U.S. 395, ½ mi. north of Lee Vining, has info on Mono County's wilderness areas. (☎873-2408. Open M-F 9am-5:30pm; winter F-Su 9am-4pm.) Rent kayaks at **Caldera Kayaks,** at Crowly Lake Marina, Mammoth Lakes. (☎935-4942. Half-day $25, full-day $35, tour $65.) The **post office** is in a big brown building on 4th St. (☎647-6371. Open M-F 9am-2pm and 3-5pm.) **Postal Code:** 93541.

🍴🛏 **ACCOMMODATIONS & FOOD.** Accommodations can be pretty pricey, but the cheapest options are on **Main Street,** or 10 mi. south of town on the 14 mi. **June Lake Loop.** The best options include ▨**El Mono Motel ❸,** at Main and 3rd St. (☎647-6310; singles $49), **Tioga Lodge ❺,** 2 mi. north of town on the western shore of Mono Lake. (☎647-6423; singles from $97), and **Gateway Motel ❺,** in the center of town (☎647-6467; summer from $89, winter from $49). Most campsites are clustered west of Lee Vining along Rte. 120. **Lundy** and **Lee Vining Canyons ❶** are the best spots for travelers headed for Mono Lake. (No water. Open May-Oct. $7.)

Lee Vining Market, on U.S. 395 at the southern end of town, is the closest thing to a grocery store. (☎647-1010. Open Su-Th 7am-9:30pm, F-Sa 7am-10pm.) **Nicely's ❶,**

on U.S. 395, just north of the Visitors Center, is a local favorite with the ambience of a diner. (☎647-6477. Open daily 6am-9pm; in winter closed W. Entrees $5-9.) **Mono Cone ❶,** on U.S. 395 at the northern end of town, is a local institution whose opening signals the beginning of summer. (☎647-6606. Open daily 11am-7pm.)

◙ ▲ SIGHTS & OUTDOORS. One of the area's best-preserved ghost towns, **Bodie** was "the most lawless, wildest, and toughest mining camp the West has ever known," though it looks pretty tame now. Off U.S. 395, 32 mi. north of Lee Vining and 13 mi. east of Rte. 270, the toughest town in the West survived until 1932, when the infamous Bodie Bill, a 2½-year-old child, incinerated 90% of the town with one match. The remaining 10%, however, is brimming with a haunting romantic appeal.

In 1984, Congress set aside 57,000 acres of land surrounding Mono Lake and named it the **Mono Basin National Forest Scenic Area** (☎873-2408). To get there, take U.S. 395 S to Rte. 120, then go 4 mi. east and take the Mono Lake South Tufa turn-off 1 mi. south to Tufa Grove. For a $3 fee (national parks passes accepted), travelers may investigate the **South Tufa Grove,** which harbors an awe-inspiring hoard of these calcium carbonate formations. The Mono Lake Committee offers **canoe tours** of the lake that include a crash course in conservation and Mono's natural history. (☎647-6595. 1hr. tours depart from South Tufa at Mono Lake mid-June to early Sept. Sa-Su at 8, 9:30, and 11am; bird-watching is better on earlier tours. Tours $17, ages 4-12 $7. Reservations required.)

The unique terrain of this geological playground makes it a great place for hikers of all abilities. Easy trails include the ¼ mi. **Old Marina Area Trail,** east of U.S. 395, 1 mi. north of Lee Vining, the 1 mi. **Lee Vining Creek Trail,** which begins behind the Mono Basin Visitors Center, and the **Panum Crater Trail,** 5 mi. south on U.S. 395 near the South Tufa turnoff. Those undaunted by the prospect of a punishing trek should head 10 mi. east of U.S. 395 on Rte. 120, where an exceptionally steep trail leads 1 mi. to the glistening **Gardisky Lake.** Another peaceful but tough hike starts at **Lundy Lake,** off U.S. 395, 7 mi. north of Lee Vining, and leads to **Crystal Lake** and the remains of an old mining town. The well-maintained hike gains 2000 ft. in its 3 mi. ascent, and grants little shade. Rangers lead a number of free hikes throughout the summer, including bird-watching excursions, a hike to Panum Volcano, and stargazing trips. Inquire at the Visitors Center (☎873-2408) about schedules.

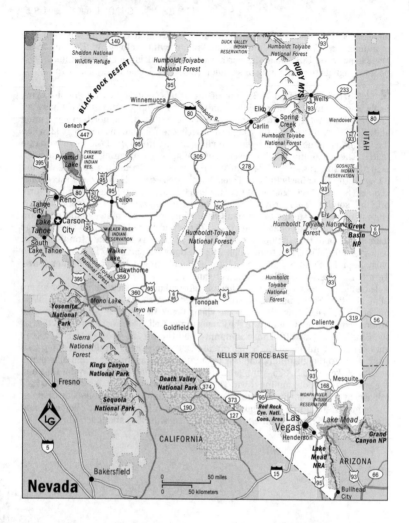

NEVADA

The mountains and deserts of Nevada's Great Basin stretch for hundreds of miles across land that rejects all but the most persistent traces of life. At the few outposts of human habitation, legalized prostitution and gambling mark the state as a purveyor of loose, Wild West morality. Yucca Mountain, north of Las Vegas, represents one of man's most ignominious projects: the embattled land around the site has been the territory of little more than cattle and fighter jets for so long that it's the proposed repository for US nuclear waste. Beyond patches of shimmering lights, sin, and showtunes, Nevada is barren, dusty, and unkind to flesh and bone.

Despite this widespread sense of desolation, the nation's fastest growing state shelters pockets of fecundity within its borders. Booming population growth in Las Vegas ranks this concrete oasis as of the West's largest residential communities, and it can be a hellishly good time. Similar growth marks Nevada's northern metropolitan center, Reno. The peaks of the Snake and Ruby ranges are aberrations in the desert, supporting a rich variety of unique ecosystems. Uncrowded and pristine, these lands afford the chance for real wilderness solitude. Three massive lakes—the man-made Lake Mead, the crystalline-blue Pyramid Lake, and the mountain-ringed Lake Tahoe—provide refreshing retreat from brutal desert heat.

Nevada is also home to an eclectic mishmash of backgrounds and traditions. The Basque people, European settlers from the early 19th century, still work the land in northern Nevada, infusing the area with a vibrant culture and unique cuisine. The modern boomtown of Elko preserves cowboy culture with its Western Folklife Center and annual Cowboy Poetry and Music Gatherings. The yearly performance art spectacle of Burning Man rises up out of the Black Rock Desert, sandwiched between the cross-road town of Winnemucca and tiny Gerlach. With more people arriving every day for their slice of the American Dream, suburban Las Vegas is a burgeoning bazaar of Latin American and Asian cultures. Nevada exemplifies America at its most excessive, barren, and thrilling extremes.

▨ HIGHLIGHTS OF NEVADA

GREAT BASIN NATIONAL PARK. Hike **Wheeler Peak** (p. 243), explore dazzling **Lehman Cave** (p. 242), and spy bristlecone pines, the earth's oldest organisms (p. 242).

LAKE TAHOE. The waters, winds, slopes, and trails of Tahoe (p. 223) create a gorgeous, year-round outdoor playground.

ELKO. Go for a morning hike in the **Ruby Mountains** (p. 235), and spend the afternoon soaking in the cowboy lifestyle (p. 234).

LAS VEGAS
☎ 702

Rising out of the barren Nevada desert, Las Vegas is a shimmering tribute to excess. Gambling, whoring, and mob-muscle built this city, and continue to add to its dark mystique. Mafia influence in Vegas has notably diminished in the last thirty years, however, having been replaced by the even more notorious, if family-friendly, corporate mob. In the new Las Vegas, malls full of boutique shops, multiple theme park casinos, and a perpetual carnival atmosphere allow access into the wallets of all ages and degrees of risk aversion. The recent residential boom around the city attests to the changing face of one of America's fastest growing cities, as block upon block of pastel cookie-cutter homes stretch toward the mountains. Rather than calming the Vegas scene, metropolitan growth has heightened tourism and taken excess to new levels. Nowhere else in America do so many cast off their inhibitions and indulge otherwise dormant appetites. More than willing to shed the family image it has tried to cultivate, Vegas remains all about money and sex (but mostly money). The opulent mega-casinos that dominate Vegas are unbelievably successful at maximizing profits, be it with over-the-top entertainment, fine dining, or by squeezing out billions from a 0.5% advantage in blackjack. For every winner, there's always a loser—a broken heart and a busted wallet for every twinkling light in Vegas.

NEVADA

▣ TRANSPORTATION

Flights: McCarran International (☎261-5743), at the southwestern end of the Strip. Main terminal on Paradise Rd. Shuttle buses run to the Strip ($4.25 one-way, $8 round-trip) and to downtown ($5.50 one-way, $10.50 round-trip); taxis $13-14.

Buses: Greyhound, 200 S. Main St. (☎384-9561, 800-231-2222), downtown at Carson Ave., near the Plaza Hotel/Casino. Tickets sold 24hr. to **LA** (5-7hr., 22 per day, $38) and **San Francisco** (13-16hr., 6 per day, $65).

Public Transportation: Citizens Area Transit (CAT; ☎228-7433). Bus #301 serves downtown and the Strip 24hr. Buses #108 and 109 serve the airport. All buses wheelchair accessible. Buses run daily 5:30am-1:30am (24hr. on the Strip). Routes on the Strip $2, residential routes $1.25, seniors and ages 6-17 $0.60. For schedules and maps, try the tourist office or the **Downtown Transportation Center,** 300 N. Casino Center Blvd. (☎228-7433), complete with poker machines and a cashier. **Las Vegas Strip Trolleys** (☎382-1404) are not strip joints; they cruise the Strip every 20min. daily 9:30am-1:30am. Trolley fare $1.65 in exact change.

Taxis: Yellow, Checker, and **Star** (☎873-2000). All Las Vegas taxis initially charge $2.70, with each additional mile $1.80. For pickup, call 30min. ahead of time. Handicap-accessible cabs available. McCarran Airport an additional $1.20 fee.

Car Rental: Sav-Mor Rent-A-Car, 5101 Rent-A-Car Rd. (☎736-1234, 800-634-6779), at the airport. From $30 per day, $130 per week; 150 mi. per day included, each additional mi. $0.20. Must be 21+, under-25 surcharge $12 per day. Discounts can be found in tourist publications. Open daily 5:30am-1am; airport window opens at 7am.

▣ ORIENTATION

Driving to Vegas from L.A. is a straight, 300 mi. shot on I-15 N (4½hr.). From Arizona, take I-40 W to Kingman and then U.S. 93 N. Las Vegas itself has two major casino areas. The **downtown** area, around 2nd and Fremont St., has been converted into a pedestrian promenade. Casinos cluster beneath a shimmering space-frame structure covering over five city blocks. The other main area is **the Strip,** a collection of mammoth hotel-casinos along **Las Vegas Boulevard.** Parallel to the east side of the Strip and in its shadow is **Paradise Road,** also strewn with casinos. Both areas are very busy; traffic can be frustrating. For faster travel north or south, use one of the major roads further east, such as Maryland Pkwy. As in any major city, some areas of Las Vegas are unsafe, so remain on well-lit pathways and don't wander too far from major casinos and hotels. **The neighborhoods just north of Stewart St. and west of Main St. in the downtown vicinity merit particular caution.**

Despite, or perhaps because of, its reputation for debauchery, **Las Vegas has a curfew.** Those under 18 are not allowed unaccompanied in most public places Sunday through Thursday from 10pm to 5am and Friday through Saturday from midnight to 5am. Laws are even harsher on the Strip, where no one under 18 is allowed unless accompanied by an adult from 9pm to 5am Monday through Friday and 6pm to 5am on the weekends. **The drinking and gambling age is 21.**

▣ PRACTICAL INFORMATION

Visitor Information: Las Vegas Convention and Visitor Authority, 3150 Paradise Rd. (☎892-0711), 4 blocks from the Strip in the big pink convention center by the Hilton. Info on headliners, conventions, shows, hotel bargains, and buffets. Open M-F 8am-5pm. To make reservations for tours, hotels, shows, try the **Las Vegas Tourist Bureau,** 5191 S. Las Vegas Blvd. (☎739-1482; www.lvtb.com). Open daily 7am-11pm.

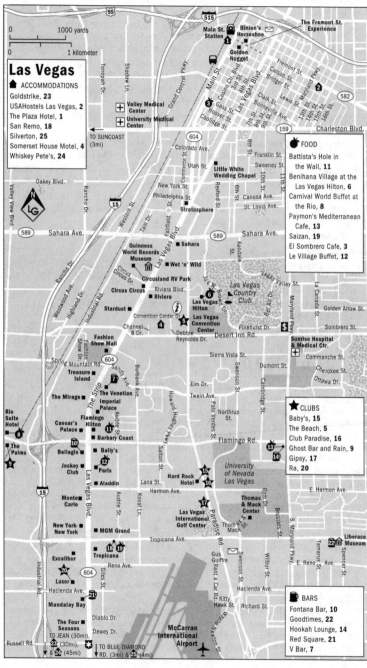

Las Vegas

▲ ACCOMMODATIONS
Goldstrike, **23**
USAHostels Las Vegas, **2**
The Plaza Hotel, **1**
San Remo, **18**
Silverton, **25**
Somerset House Motel, **4**
Whiskey Pete's, **24**

🍎 FOOD
Battista's Hole in
  the Wall, **11**
Benihana Village at the
  Las Vegas Hilton, **6**
Carnival World Buffet at
  the Rio, **8**
Paymon's Mediterranean
  Cafe, **13**
Saizan, **19**
El Sombrero Cafe, **3**
Le Village Buffet, **12**

★ CLUBS
Baby's, **15**
The Beach, **5**
Club Paradise, **16**
Ghost Bar and Rain, **9**
Gipsy, **17**
Ra, **20**

🍸 BARS
Fontana Bar, **10**
Goodtimes, **22**
Hookah Lounge, **14**
Red Square, **21**
V Bar, **7**

N E V A D A

Tours: Coach USA, 795 E. Tropicana Ave. (☎384-1234 or 800-634-6579). City tours (3½hr., 1 per day, $39). Bus tours from Las Vegas to **Hoover Dam/Lake Mead** (4hr., 2 per day, $39) and the **Grand Canyon's South Rim** (full-day, $149). Discounts for children ages 3-11 and with coupons from tourist publications. Reserve in advance.

Bank: Bank of America, 1140 E. Desert Inn Rd. (☎654-1000), at the corner of Maryland Pkwy. Open M-Th 9am-5pm, F 9am-6pm. Phone assistance 24hr.

ATMs: Plentiful in all major casinos, but there is at least a $2 charge for each use. Those at gas stations or banks often charge lower fees.

Bi-Gay-Lesbian Organization: Gay and Lesbian Community Center, 953 E. Sahara Ave. (☎733-9800). Open M-F 11am-8pm, Sa 10am-3pm.

Laundry: Cora's Coin Laundry, 1099 E. Tropicana Ave. (☎736-6181). Wash $1, dry 25¢ per 10min. Open daily 8am-8pm. Video poker while you wait for your socks to dry.

Marriage: Marriage License Bureau, 200 S. 3rd St. (☎455-4416), in the courthouse. 18+ or at least 16 with parental consent. Licenses $55; cash only. No waiting period or blood test required. Open Su-Th 8am-midnight, F-Sa 24hr.

Divorce: Must be a Nevada resident for at least 6 weeks. $150 service fee. Permits available at the courthouse M-F 8am-5pm.

Road Conditions: ☎877-687-6237. **Weather Conditions:** ☎263-9744.

Police: Corner of Russell Rd. and S. Las Vegas Blvd. ☎229-3111.

24-Hour Crisis Lines: Compulsive Gamblers Hotline (☎800-LOST-BET/567-8238). **Gamblers Anonymous** (☎385-7732). **Rape Crisis Center Hotline** (☎366-1640). **Suicide Prevention** (☎731-2990 or 800-885-4673).

Internet Access: Free Internet access is available at **Clark County Library,** 1401 E. Flamingo Rd. (☎507-3400), but expect a wait. Open M-Th 9am-9pm, F-Su 10am-6pm.

Post Offices: 4975 Swenson St. (☎736-7649). Open M-F 8:30am-5pm. **Postal Code:** 89119.

⚑ ACCOMMODATIONS

Despite having over 100,000 rooms, hotels fill on weekends. Rates fluctuate greatly; a $30 room during a slow period can cost hundreds during a convention weekend. Use the prices below as a general guide. Check free, readily available publications like *What's On In Las Vegas, Today in Las Vegas, 24/7, Vegas Visitor, Casino Player, Tour Guide Magazine, Best Read Guide,* and *Insider Viewpoint of Las Vegas* for discounts, info, and schedules of events. If you get stuck, call the **Room Reservations Hotline** (☎800-332-5333) or go to a tourist office.

Strip hotels are at the center of the action, but their inexpensive rooms sell out quickly. More hotels cluster around Sahara Rd. and S. Las Vegas Blvd. Motels line **Fremont Street,** though this area is a little rougher; it is best to stay in one of the casinos in the **Fremont Street Experience** (see **Casinos,** p. 203). Inexpensive motels are also along the southern stretch of the Strip, across from the ritzy **Mandalay Bay.** In the room rates listed below, the 9% state hotel tax is not included.

■ **San Remo,** 115 E. Tropicana Ave. (☎800-522-7366). Just off the Strip, this is a smaller, friendlier version of the major player casinos, without the gimmicks, crowds, and high prices. Live entertainment every night, featuring the "Showgirls of Magic" ($39). Rooms may go as low as $32 during slow periods, but are usually Su-Th $42, F-Sa $70. ❹

■ **Silverton,** 3333 Blue Diamond Rd. (800-588-7711; www.silverton-casino.com). Cheaper because it's off the Strip (4 miles south on I-15), this mining town-themed gambling den offers clean and updated accommodations, a relief from the tired and worn budget hotels in the area. Free Las Vegas Blvd. shuttle until 10pm. Singles Su-Th $35, F-Sa $69. Beyond 2 adults, additional person $10. RV hook-ups $24-28. ❸

■ **Whiskey Pete's** (☎800-367-7383), in Primm Valley, NV, 45 min. south of Vegas on I-15, just before the California stateline. Whiskey Pete's is the cheapest of 3 Western-themed casinos right in the middle of the desert. Cheap as fool's gold and across the street from Desperado, the wildest roller-coaster in Nevada ($6). Beware young guns; you must be 21 to rent a room. Su-Th $19, F-Sa $50; prices vary with availability. ❷

USAHostels Las Vegas, 1322 Fremont St. (☎800-550-8958 or 385-1150; www.usa-hostels.com). A funky, fun place to stay with friendly staff, but far from the Strip and in an unattractive neighborhood. Rooms are sparse but clean and the atmosphere caters to students and foreigners. Private and dorm rooms are available. Pool, jacuzzi, laundry, kitchen, and billiard room. Shared bathrooms. Offers free pickup from Greyhound station 10am-10pm. Su-Th dorms $14-19; suites $40-42. F-Sa dorms $17-23; suites $49-51. Must have international passport, proof of international travel, or student ID. ❷

Goldstrike, 1 Main St. (☎800-634-1359), in Jean, NV, 20min. from the Strip on I-15, exit 12. A genuine Vegas experience at cut-rate prices. Inexpensive restaurants (prime rib $7, dinner buffet $7.50), loose slots, and low-limit tables. Making a reservation may net cheaper prices. Rooms Su-Th $20-30, F $40, Sa $50. Additional person $3. ❸

Somerset House Motel, 294 Convention Center Dr. (☎888-336-4280; www.somerset-house.com). A no-frills establishment within short walking distance of the Strip. Many of the large and impeccably clean rooms feature kitchens. Dishes and cooking utensils provided upon request. Unbeatable weekend rates. Singles Su-Th $35, F-Sa $44; doubles Su-Th $44, F-Sa $55. Additional person $5. Senior discount available. ❸

Plaza Hotel/Casino, 1 Main St. (☎800-634-6575; www.plazahotelcasino.com), in the heart of downtown across from Fremont St.'s casinos. Includes tennis courts, barber-shop, salon, and pool. Singles Su-Th $32, F-Sa $79. ❸

⚑ CAMPING

Shockingly enough, there is camping in Vegas. With watersports rentals and camp-sites, **Lake Mead National Recreation Area ❶**, 25 mi. south on Rte. 93/95, is an artifi-cial lake on the NV-AZ border. Las Vegas Bay is closest. (☎293-8906. Showers at Calville and Overton Beach. Sites with flush toilets $10.) Named for its rock forma-tions that seem to bleed in the sun, **Valley of Fire State Park's ❶** Atlas Rock petro-glyph site is worth the drive. Take I-15 north to Rte. 169, a fun drive through desert foothills. (☎397-2088. No electricity or hookups. Sites $13.) **Circusland RV Park ❷,** 500 Circus Circus Dr., has a pool, jacuzzi, convenience store, showers, and laun-dry. (☎734-0410. Open 5am-midnight. Hookups Su-Th $18-28, F-Sa $2 extra.)

🍴 FOOD

Everyone comes to gorge at Vegas's gigantic buffets. For the really, really hungry, there is no better value. The trick to buffet bliss is to find places that are more than glorified cafeterias, which can be difficult. Beyond buffets, Vegas has some of the world's best restaurants, though few have prices palatable to the budget traveler.

■ **Le Village Buffet,** 3655 Las Vegas Blvd. (☎946-7000). French cooking without the French portions. Set in a recreated French Alps village, the Le Village buffet, crammed with crab legs, salmon, prime rib, veal, and crepes, is more than worth its higher price. Restrain yourself during the main course; the dessert will be worth it. Breakfast $13, lunch $17, dinner $22. Open daily 7am-10pm. Su brunch 11:30am-4:30pm. ❸

■ **Carnival World Buffet at the Rio,** 3700 W. Flamingo Rd. (☎252-7777). One of the great Vegas feasts. Perhaps the most well-known and highly-rated buffet in Vegas, the Rio boasts 12 uniquely themed food stations, from sushi to Mexican. Breakfast $10, lunch $12, dinner $17. Open daily 7am-10pm. ❷

Benihana Village at the Las Vegas Hilton, 3000 Paradise Rd. (☎ 732-5755). Indoor village with koi pond, rain, bonzais, and multi-level dining area. Charismatic hibachi chefs slice, sear, and serve your 5-course meal as you watch. Filling entrees are worth every penny of the $16-30 price tag. Open daily 5:30-10:30pm. ❹

El Sombrero Cafe, 807 S. Main St. (☎382-9234), is where the locals go for authentic Mexican food. The portions are huge and the staff is friendly. Their combination plates offer a lot of food for a little money ($8-11). Lunch $7. Open M-Sa 11am-10pm. ❷

Paymon's Mediterranean Cafe, 4147 S. Maryland Pkwy. (☎731-6030), serves fresh, delicious Greek and Mediterranean specialties. Try the delicious combo plate with couscous, tabouli, and stuffed grape leaves ($10) or a big falafel and hummus pita bread sandwich ($6). Attached to **The Hookah Lounge** (see **Nightlife,** p. 206). Open M-Th 11am-1am, F-Sa 11am-3am, Su 11am-4pm. ❷

Battista's Hole in the Wall, 4041 Audrie Ave. (☎ 732-1424), behind the Flamingo. 33 years' worth of celebrity photos, novelties from area brothels and the head of "Moosolini" (the fascist moose) adorn the walls. Pricey, but generous portions. Dinner $18-34, includes all-you-can-drink house wine. Open Su-Th 4:30-10:30pm, F-Sa 4:30-11pm. ❺

Saizan, 115 E. Tropicana Ave. (☎ 739-9000), in San Remo behind the first floor slots. The best sushi bar near the Strip, offering only the freshest sushi and sashimi. Combo platters ($14-19) provide an excellent sampling. Open daily 5:30pm-midnight. ❹

◎ SIGHTS

Before slot machines suck you dry of greenbacks, explore some of the city's simpler oddities. Fans of classical music and kitsch will be delighted by the renovated **Liberace Museum,** 1775 E. Tropicana Ave., and its exhibits of the showman's velvet, rhinestone, fur, and suede stage costumes. (☎798-5595; www.liberace.com. Open M-Sa 10am-5pm, Su noon-5pm. $12, students and seniors $8, under 12 free. Guided tours 11am and 2pm.) The **Auto Collection** on the 5th floor of the Imperial Palace Casino, 3535 S. Las Vegas Blvd., is a worthwhile destination. Visitors can feast their eyes on 300 classic cars and dream of how they're going to spend their jackpot. (☎794-3179. Open daily 9:30am-9:30pm. Admission $7; 65 and over, 11 and under, $3.) The **Tropicana,** 3801 S. Las Vegas Blvd., houses the **Casino Legends Hall of Fame,** the world's largest gaming museum. The collection boasts Nevada gambling memorabilia from more than 700 casinos, over 500 of which no longer exist, and a fairly comprehensive walk look at the origins of today's Las Vegas, reminding visitors that even in a place designed for escaping the past (and present), history still exists. (☎739-2222. Open daily 9am-9pm. Admission $6.95, seniors $5.95.)

It's been said that God made men and Sam Colt made 'em equal. Experience coltish justice at the **Gun Store,** 2900 E. Tropicana Ave. A small sum lets you try out an impressive array of pistols, including the enormous Magnum 44. For a bit more, let off 50 machine gun rounds at the on-site range. (☎454-1110. Open daily 9am-6:30pm.) Offering services ranging from 3min. drive-through whirlwinds to elaborate fantasy-themed extravaganzas, the **Little White Wedding Chapel,** 1301 Las Vegas Blvd., is a mainstay of the city's matrimonial traditions. Luminaries like Frank Sinatra, Michael Jordan, and Demi Moore and Bruce Willis have been hitched here. A life-changing drive through the *Tunnel of Vows* begins at a romantic $40 (plus a donation to the minister), and possibilities expand with the imagination. (☎382-5943, 800-545-8111; www.alittlewhitechapel.com. No reservations required for drive-through services. Have a marriage license ready. Open 24hr.)

Way out in Primm Valley, along I-15 at **Buffalo Bill's Casino** on the Cali border, the **Desperado Roller Coaster** is the tallest and fastest bad-boy in the Vegas area and one of the best coasters on the West Coast. (☎386-7867. Open M-Th 11am-9pm, F 11am-midnight, Sa 10am-midnight, Su 10am-10pm. $7.)

🏛 CAINO

Casinos spend millions to attract tourists by fooling guests into thinking they're somewhere else and luring them with jackpots, liquor, and food—in that order. As if Las Vegas wasn't escapist enough, spitting images of Venice, New York, Monte Carlo, Paris (complete with the Eiffel Tower), and ancient Egypt (complete with the Pyramids) thrive on the Strip. Efforts to bring families to Sin City are evident in the arcades and thrill rides on every corner. Still, Vegas is no Disney World. The plethora of steamy nightclubs and topless revues, not to mention scantily clad waitresses and free liquor, prove that profits are the casinos' priority.

Casinos, bars, and some wedding chapels are open 24hr., so whatever your itch, Vegas can usually scratch it. Look for casino "funbooks" that feature deals on chips and entertainment. Cash goes in a blink when you're gambling, so it pays to have a budget. Gambling is illegal for those under 21. There are far more casinos harboring far more attractions than can be listed here; use the following as a compendium of the best, but explore Vegas for yourself—there are ways to fulfill fantasies where you'd least expect it.

THE STRIP

The undisputed locus of Vegas's surging regeneration, the Strip is a fantasyland of neon, teeming with people, casinos, and restaurants. The nation's 10 largest hotels line the legendary 3.5 mi. stretch of Las Vegas Blvd., named an "All-American Road" and a "National Scenic Byway." Despite the sparkling facade, the Strip's seedy underbelly still shows; porn is peddled behind family fun centers, and night denizens sporting open alcohol containers wander in search of elusive jackpots.

Mandalay Bay, 3950 S. Las Vegas Blvd. (☎632-7777; www.mandalaybay.com). Undoubtedly Vegas's hippest casino, Mandalay Bay does its best to convince New York and LA fashionistas they haven't left home. Swank restaurants and chi-chi clubs make gambling seem an afterthought. Shark Reef features 15 species of shark. (Open daily 10am-11pm; last admission 10pm. $15, 5-12 $10, 4 and under free.) Afterwards you may or may not want to check out the surf and sand beach, complete with 6 ft. waves.

Bellagio, 3600 S. Las Vegas Blvd. (☎693-7444; www.bellagio.com). The world's largest five-star hotel, the Bellagio houses a gallery of fine art (open daily 9am-8pm; $15, students and seniors $12) and carefully maintained botanical gardens (free). The Via Bel-

THE INSIDERS CITY

BUDGET CASINO CRAWL

Sin City doesn't have to be expensive. Try this route for a dazzling night in Vegas for under $20.

1 Lunch endlessly at **Paradise Buffet at the Flamingo** ($10).

2 Stroll through the opulent **Grand Canal Shops at the Venetian,** where gondoliers sing along the indoor canal.

3 At the **Forum Shops at Caesar's Palace,** day turns to night on the sky-like ceiling. An animatronics show welcomes guests to Caesar's world hourly.

4 Gaze in awe from atop the **Eiffel Tower at the Paris** ($9).

5 Catch the spectacular aqua ballet of the **Water Show at the Bellagio**—for free.

6 Starting at 8pm, you can see the roaring, foaming **Volcano at the Mirage** erupt every 15min.

7 For a true pyrotechnics treat, watch the **Pirate Battle at Treasure Island.** Swashbuckling happens every 1½hr.

lagio Shops, home to Prada and Tiffany's, offer Las Vegas's finest shopping. (☎693-7111. Open daily 10am-midnight.) At the fountains on the lakefront, water jets shoot several stories into the air during a spectacular aquatic ballet. (Shows M-F 3-8pm every ½hr. and 8pm-midnight every 15min., Sa-Su and holidays noon-8pm every ½hr. Free.)

Venetian, 3355 S. Las Vegas Blvd. (☎414-1000; www.venetian.com). This palatial casino features the upscale Grand Canal Shoppes, named for its chlorinated "canal." Singing gondoliers push tourists in small boats while everyone takes pictures. (☎414-4500. Open Su-Th 10am-11pm, F-Sa 10am-midnight.) The **Guggenheim Hermitage Museum** represents the apotheosis of the new Vegas, with artwork from Russian and Austrian collections, as well as from the Guggenheim Foundation. (☎866-484-4849. Open daily 9:30am-8:30pm. $15, students $11, children 6-12 $7, under 6 free.) Elaborate architectural replicas of Venetian plazas, bridges, and towers adorn the exterior.

Caesar's Palace, 3570 S. Las Vegas Blvd. (☎731-7110; www.caesars.com). At Caesar's, busts abound: some are plaster, others barely concealed by cocktail waitress's low-cut get-ups. None are real. The pricey Forum Shops led the high-end shopping craze at Strip casinos and continue to lure consumers with fine eateries and animatronic shows. (☎893-4800. Open M-F 10am-11pm, Sa-Su 10am-midnight.) With ever-changing attractions, Caesar's continues to be a trendsetter on the Strip.

Monte Carlo, 3770 S. Las Vegas Blvd. (☎730-7000; www.monte-carlo.com). The elegant Monte Carlo takes after its namesake in providing a sophisticated gaming experience where players bet enormous amounts of money—in style. Blackjack, baccarat, craps, single-O roulette, as well as a state-of-the-art race and sports book and Back Street Arcade for younger gamers (or those just young-at-heart).

Luxor, 3900 S. Las Vegas Blvd. (☎262-4000; www.luxor.com). This iconoclastic casino and architectural marvel recreates the majestic pyramids of ancient Egypt in opaque glass and steel. When gambling loses its appeal, the IMAX Theater offers a slew of movies. (☎262-4400. Shows daily 9am-11pm. $9-14.) Wander into the past at a full-scale replica of King Tut's Tomb. (Open Su-Th 9am-11pm, F-Sa 9-1am. Admission $5.)

Paris, 3655 S. Las Vegas Blvd. (☎946-7000; www.parislasvegas.com). The smallest of the "theme" casinos, with enough "real" Parisian attractions, including mimes and tasty crêpes, to please any French post-modernist who visits. Half-scale Eiffel Tower boasts a view of the Strip and near-scale Arc de Triomphe. (Open Su-Th 10am-midnight, F-Sa 10-1am. Ride to the top $9-12, seniors and kids 6-12 $7-9, under 5 free.)

The Mirage, 3400 S. Las Vegas Blvd. (☎791-7111; www.mirage.com). Arguably the casino that began Vegas's regeneration in the early 90s. Its Dolphin Habitat shelters 8 bottlenose dolphins (open M-F 11am-7pm, Sa-Su 10am-7pm) and is free with admission to Siegfried and Roy's Secret Garden, featuring white tigers and lions. (Open M-Tu and Th-F 11am-5pm and 10am-5pm. Admission $12, 10 and under free). Outside, a volcano erupts in fountains of fire every 15min. 6pm-midnight daily.

MGM Grand, 3799 S. Las Vegas Blvd. (☎891-1111; www.mgmgrand.com). A huge bronze lion guards Las Vegas's largest hotel and casino, and a few live felines can be seen inside at the Lion Habitat. (Open daily 11am-1pm. Free.) In addition to more than 5000 rooms, the MGM hosts world-class sporting events and concerts, packing the essence of Sin City's offerings under one roof.

New York, New York, 3790 S. Las Vegas Blvd. (☎740-6969; www.nynyhotelcasino). Towers mimic the Manhattan skyline, re-creating the glory of the Big Apple at this tacky casino. Traverse the sidewalk under a replica of the Brooklyn Bridge or check out Coyote Ugly, where bartenders strut their stuff on the countertops. Manhattan Express Roller Coaster, the wildest thrill ride on the Strip, is open daily 11am-11pm ($12).

Treasure Island, 3300 S. Las Vegas Blvd. (☎894-7111; www.treasureisland.com). Newly refurbished and fully embracing the recent wave of pirate chic, Treasure Island is fervently reinventing itself for a younger crowd. Buccaneer Bay Sea Battle, long deemed one of the best free shows in Las Vegas, was undergoing an extensive overhaul by Emmy Award-winning director Kenny Ortega at the time of publication. The new spectacle will debut in fall of 2003.

Circus Circus, 2880 S. Las Vegas Blvd. (☎734-0410; www.circuscircus.com). While parents run to card tables downstairs, children spend their quarters upstairs on the souped-up carnival midway and in the titanic game arcade. (Open 24hr. Free shows daily, every ½hr. 11am-midnight.) In the hotel complex, Adventuredome is the world's largest indoor theme park. Canyon Blaster ($5), a double-loop, double-screw roller coaster, is first among dome rides. (☎794-3939. Open M-F 10am-midnight, Sa-Su 9am-midnight. $3-5.) **A.J. Hackett Bungy,** 810 Circus Circus Dr. (☎385-4321), drops you from a tower high above the Strip for $54. Open Su-F 11am-8:30pm, Sa 11am-10pm.

Aladdin, 3667 S. Las Vegas Blvd. (☎785-5555; www.aladdincasino.com.). More a sight than casino, the sleazy decor is overwhelming. The Desert Passage (☎866-0710) retail area is a garish replica of a North African town, complete with "weather patterns," ambient noise, and 140 shops. Open Su-Th 10am-11pm, F-Sa 10am-midnight.

Stratosphere, 2000 S. Las Vegas Blvd. (☎380-7777; www.stratospherehotel.com). The tallest structure west of the Mississippi River, the 1149 ft. free-standing tower can be seen from anywhere in the city and affords postcard-like photo opportunities. The world's two highest thrill rides rumble atop its observation deck. (Open Su-Th 10-1am, F-Sa 10-2am. $8 to head up to top; rides $5-8.) The casino itself is no great shakes—as they say, size isn't everything.

Flamingo Hilton, 3555 S. Las Vegas Blvd. (☎733-3111; www.flamingolasvegas.com). Mobster Bugsy Siegel bucked the cowboy casino trend with this resort-style Strip casino in 1946, thereby setting Vegas's trajectory for decades to come. Sprawling pool area plays home to penguins, flamingos, and fish.

DOWNTOWN & OFF-STRIP

The tourist frenzy that grips the Strip is less noticeable in "old" Downtown Vegas. Glitter Gulch offers smaller hotels, cheaper alcohol and food, and some serious gambling. Accordingly, the family atmosphere of the Strip is substantially lacking. Years of decline were reversed with Las Vegas's city-wide rebound and the 1995 opening of the Fremont Street Experience. The open desert sky above that thoroughfare is but a memory, and in its place, a canopy of neon has arisen, playing laser light shows at night. Construction of a pedestrian promenade furthered the area's renaissance. **Despite the renewal, don't stray far from Fremont at night.**

Golden Nugget, 129 Fremont St. (☎385-7111; www.goldennugget.com). A vein of Strip-like class downtown, this four-star hotel charms with marble floors, elegant chandeliers, and high-end gambling. Without the distractions of rollercoasters and replicas, the Golden Nugget is a tribute to what Vegas used to be.

Binion's Horseshoe Hotel and Casino, 128 Fremont St. (☎382-1600). The Binion family brought their love of high-stakes gaming from Texas. A place to learn the tricks of the trade by watching rather than playing, this casino is the site of the World Series of Poker, and a serious gambler's paradise. High craps odds, single-deck blackjack, and a willingness to honor almost any bet are Horseshoe hallmarks.

The Plaza, 1 Main St. (☎386-2110). Grandiosely stands guard at the western end of the Fremont Street Experience. Center Stage Restaurant furnishes a great view of the nightly light shows and the 1- and 2-cent slots make it tough to go for broke.

Hard Rock Hotel, 4455 Paradise Rd. (☎693-5000; www.hardrockhotel.com). The largest night scene in Vegas, the Hard Rock is furbished with all sorts of music memorabilia and often the stars to go along with it. Feels more like a giant lounge than a casino, especially thanks to The Joint, a tiny venue that attracts rockers for intimate concerts.

The Palms, 4321 W. Flamingo Rd. (☎942-7777; www.palms.com). This trendy spot does a crazy job of bridging the gap between local casino and tourist destination. Known especially for its wild clubs and lounges, the Palms is the place to be if you're young and single in Las Vegas. Just ask Brittany Spears.

Río, 3700 W. Flamingo Rd. (☎777-7777). Just across I-15 on Flamingo Rd., the all-suite Río features clubs, restaurants, and a casino floor wrapped up in a Brazilian carnival. Popular with locals, caters to folks who want the Strip's offerings without being there.

Las Vegas Hilton, 3000 Paradise Rd. (☎732-5111). You won't miss it thanks to the enormous "Las Vegas Hilton" sign. Its $70 million Star Trek: The Experience immerses you in the Trekkie universe with slot machines on "the bridge." Entrance includes admission to the Star Trek Museum, which presents the cultural phenomenon with astonishing intricacy. (☎888-GO-BOLDLY/462-6535. Open daily 11am-11pm, $25.)

ENTERTAINMENT

Vegas entertainment revolves around the casino axis. Big bucks will buy you a seat at a made-in-the-USA phenomenon: the **Vegas spectacular.** These stunning, casino-sponsored productions feature marvels such as waterfalls, explosions, fireworks, and casts of hundreds (including animals). You can also see Broadway plays and musicals, ice revues, and individual entertainers in concert. All hotels have city-wide ticket booths in their lobbies. Check out some of the free show guides—*Showbiz, Today in Las Vegas, What's On*—for listings. For a more opinionated perspective, check out one of the independents—*Las Vegas Mercury, City Life, Las Vegas Weekly*—or the *Las Vegas Review-Journal's* weekly entertainment supplement, *Neon.* Some "production shows" are topless; many are tasteless, but there are a few exceptions: the **Cirque de Soleil's** creative shows—*O, Mystere* and the brand-new, racy *Zumanity*—are bank-busting ($88-150) yet awe-inspiring displays of human agility and physical strength channeled as artistic expression at the Bellagio, Treasure Island, and New York, New York. "Limited view" tickets are discounted, and the view isn't that limited. **Blue Man Group** at the Luxor, a production that pushes the limits of stage entertainment with unique percussion sets and audience participation, is darn cool ($79-90).

For a show by one of the musical stars who haunt the city, e.g. **Celine Dion** (Caesar's Palace), **Gladys Knight** (Flamingo), or **Wayne Newton** (Stardust), you'll have to fork over at least $50. "Magicians of the Century" **Siegfried and Roy** go for $105.50 at the Mirage. Incredible impersonator/singer/dancer **Danny Gans** also entertains there (about $100). The tricks of **Lance Burton's** (a mainstay at the Monte Carlo) are good, old magic ($55-60), while **Penn and Teller** at the Río are far darker. With some of everything, former street performer **The Amazing Jonathan** stages one of Vegas's edgiest productions ($47-58). Chicago's classic comedic institution **The Second City** also graces the stage at the Flamingo for a reasonable $36.

NIGHTLIFE

Nightlife in Vegas gets rolling around midnight and runs until everyone drops—or runs out of money. In a city that never sleeps, inebriated clubhoppers bounce from one happening joint to the next to the next to the next...

CLUBS

Ghost Bar and **Rain,** 4231 W. Flamingo Rd. (☎938-BOOO/2666 and 940-RAIN/7246), at the Palms. Indisputably the hottest nightspot, drawing partyers in droves. You may wait in line for hours, but once you're in, groove with Vegas' hottest bodies while DJs throw down on the 1s and 2s. Ghost Bar is on the 55th fl., with a deck and 360° view of Vegas. Open M-Sa 8pm-"late." Rain has over 25,000 sq. ft. of dance floor and really intense displays of fire, fog, and, of course, rain. Cover $10-20. Open Th-Sa 11pm-5am.

Baby's, 4455 Paradise Rd. (☎693-5555), inside of the Hard Rock Hotel. With multiple levels and bars (one floats in a pool), this eye-catching club offers the chillest scene in Vegas. World-class DJs spin progressive house, trance, and hip-hop. If you're looking for a night on the town, Baby's is not to be missed. Cover $10-20. Open W-Sa 11pm.

Gipsy, 4605 Paradise Rd. (☎731-1919). This enormous GLBT club heats up every night of the week with drag queens (M), go-go dancers (W), lip sync contests (Th), cabaret shows (Su), and wild dance parties to create one of the town's most swinging scenes. Happy Hour daily 9pm-2am $2 mixed drinks. Cover $5-7. Open daily 9pm.

Ra, 3900 S. Las Vegas Blvd. (☎262-4949). Egyptian-themed nightclub at the Luxor, where famous DJs spin a variety of sounds with trance/break beats (W), hip-hop and R&B (Th, Sa), and house (F). Vegas's trendiest club, it's the place to see and be seen. Dress code (not casual) strictly enforced. Cover men $20, women $10. Open W-Sa 10pm.

The Beach, 365 Convention Center Dr. (☎731-1925). At this tropical-themed club, DJs spin Top 40 and hip-hop on 2 levels, creating as close to a frat party scene as you can get in Las Vegas. Ladies drink free Su-M, W 9pm-11pm. Jeans are cool; dress code strictly enforced. Cover men $10. Open Su-Th 10pm-4am, F-Sa 10pm-6am; sports bar open 24hr.

Club Paradise, 4416 Paradise Rd. (☎734-7990), opposite Hard Rock Casino. Repeatedly voted best gentleman's cabaret (read: strip joint) in the US. It's safe, and the g-strings stay on. As sophisticated as a topless bar gets. Beer $6, cocktails $6-8. Cover $10 before 9pm, $20 after. Open M-F 4pm-6am, Sa-Su 6pm-6am.

BARS

Red Square, 2950 Las Vegas Blvd. (☎632-7407), in Mandalay Bay. Probably the sweetest bar on the Strip, this Miami Beach import pulls off post-Communist chic with ease. Serving amazing martinis and frozen vodkas, Red Square is the hippest way to enjoy the fall of the Soviet Union. Cocktails $9.50. Open Su-Th 5pm-1am, F-Sa 5pm-5:30-am.

V Bar, 3355 Las Vegas Blvd. (☎414-3200). This elegant bar in the Venetian deftly recreates the New York lounge scene. A minimalist design and mellow beats make V Bar equally suitable for hanging low or dancing. Open daily 6pm-4am.

FACING A LIQUID ASSETS SHORTAGE

Asked to support faux Venetian canals, ubiquitous gushing fountains, elaborate water ballets, and more than 1.5 million residents, all amid the southern Nevada desert, Las Vegas' water supply is, not surprisingly, perpetually in short supply. Despite its underground springs, Las Vegas (Spanish for "the meadows") has not seen heavy natural irrigation since prehistoric times. Explosive urban sprawl, coupled with borderline irresponsible use of water at big-name casinos, is rapidly outstripping the supply of water allotted to Nevada by the states sharing rights to Colorado River. Las Vegas's share, which is the lowest of the cities sharing the river, is a meager 300,000 acre-feet of water. With more than 5000 people moving to the area each month, the only conceivable solution may be to cut the ceaseless influx of residents. Southern Nevada is rapidly exhausting its stores of conserved water, forcing it to dip into reserves that neighboring Arizona does not yet need to rely on. Expanding Arizona urban areas make this solution less viable with each passing year. Experts are fearful that water restrictions may not solve the growing problem, and it is far from clear that a population accustomed to gluttonous water use is willing to change its ways.

Hookah Lounge, 4147 S. Maryland Pkwy. (☎732-3203). Features nearly 20 flavored tobaccos (no alcohol, though) and a funky, intimate vibe that attracts pre-club crowds. Full bar and flavored teas. Open M-Th 5pm-1am; F-Sa 5pm-3am.

Fontana Bar, 3600 S. Las Vegas Blvd. (☎693-7111). The talented crooners who perform nightly at this flawless bar in the Bellagio conjure up images of the Las Vegas of yore. Sit back and enjoy the lakefront view. Open Su-Th 5pm-1am, F-Sa 5pm-2am.

Goodtimes, 1775 E. Tropicana Ave. (☎736-9494). A gay bar in the renovated Liberace plaza with a $10 all-you-can-drink special on M. W karaoke. Draft beers $2-3. Open 24hr.

▣ LEAVING LAS VEGAS

Outside Vegas, outdoor excitement runs high. Roadtrippers gawk at the monumental engineering of the Hoover Dam; boaters bask in the Lake Mead shoreline; hikers and climbers test the canyons and crags of Red Rocks. Las Vegas swelters, but higher elevations nearby are much cooler. There's even skiing in the winter.

MT. CHARLESTON

Take Hwy. 95 north out of Las Vegas and watch for the left turn onto Hwy. 157 about 20 mi. out of town, which leads to a couple of campgrounds and numerous trailheads. Located in the Spring Mountain National Recreation Area. ☎515-5400.

North of Las Vegas sits 11,918 ft. Mt. Charleston, located within the Toiyabe National Forest and offering temperate alpine climates when Vegas sweats in 110°F heat. Should the urge to lace up some hiking or climbing shoes strike you, Mt. Charleston and Kyle Canyon can accommodate your intentions. In early spring, the **Mary Jane Falls Trail** reveals awesome vistas of sublime Kyle Canyon and cascading waterfalls. The trailhead (off Hwy. 157) welcomes hikers to the 2.5 mi. trek with a 1000 ft. incline up the slopes of Mt. Charleston. The **South Loop** (8.5 mi.) ascends to the summit of Mt. Charleston and is for more experienced hikers. **Cathedral Rock's** limestone faces are a winter hotspot for Yosemite climbers, with its great sport routes at **The Hood, The Glass House,** and nearby **Robbers Roost.** For a shot of snow and sun, head to the **Lee Canyon Ski Area,** just north of Mt. Charleston at the end of Hwy. 156.

RED ROCK CANYON

From Vegas, take Charleston Blvd./Hwy. 159 west and continue for 18 mi. until you reach the signs indicating the turn for the 197,000-acre park. Open June-Aug. 6am-8pm; Mar.-May and Sept.-Nov. 6am-7pm; Dec.-Feb. 6am-5pm. $5. Visitors Center: ☎515-5350. Open daily Nov.-Mar. 8am-4:30pm; Apr.-Oct. 8am-5:30pm. In case of emergency call ☎911 or 293-8998.

Less than 20 mi. west of the Strip, the Red Rock Canyon National Conservation Area escarpment is a stupendous network of crimson sandstone bluffs and washes. Stick to the 13 mi. **scenic auto route** or hike into the desert itself. Red Rocks is also one of America's premier **rock climbing** destinations. An excellent **Visitors Center** introduces the myriad wonders of this flourishing desert ecosystem with interactive exhibits and guided walking tours. The **campground ❶** sits off Hwy. 159, 2 mi. east of the Visitors Center, with picnic tables, grills, water, and toilets ($10). For group site reservations, call ☎515-5352. Backcountry camping and overnight climbing require permits. (☎515-5050. Free.)

The most popular **hikes** run through the washes of **Calico Hills** and **Calico Tanks,** accessible from the first few pullouts along the scenic road. These hikes vary in length (2-6 mi.) and Calico Tanks in particular affords spectacular views of the Strip. For a more difficult trek, head to the summit of **Turtlehead Peak** from the Sandstone Quarry parking lot on a trail that climbs 1700 ft. in 2.5 mi. If you're looking to cool off, **Ice Box Canyon** lives up to its name, and the shady trail climbs 300 ft.

Las Vegas Area

Desert National Wildlife Refuge

0   5 miles
0   5 kilometers

TO MESQUITE (65mi)

Valley of Fire State Park

Overton

Virgin R.

Overton Beach

Gold Butte Rd.

TO TONOPAH (196mi)

LAS VEGAS RANGE

Las Vegas Valley

Garnet

MUDDY MOUNTAINS

Hwy. 167

Overton Arm

Echo Bay

Gold Butte

Scanson Ferry Rd.

TO MT. CHARLESTON PK. (2mi)

Northshore Scenic Dr. (167)

Black Mountains

NEVADA

Lake Mead National Rec. Area

Red Rock Canyon National Conservation Area

Las Vegas

Las Vegas Bay

Lake Mead

ARIZONA

Rainbow Blvd.

Sunset Rd.

Lakeshore Scenic Dr.

Bonelli Landing

Las Vegas Blvd.

Henderson

Boulder Beach

Hoover Dam

Colorado R. Black Dam

White Hills

Temple Bar

Greggs Hideout

Arden

TO JEAN (25mi), PRIMM VALLEY (40mi), & L.A. (275mi)

TO LAUGHLIN (90mi)

Boulder City

TO KINGMAN AZ (65mi)

in a little more than a mile to pools and waterfalls after rainfall. As for climbing, the Red Rocks **climbing rangers** offer a wealth of information (☎ 515-5138 or 515-5042); or, stop by **Desert Rock Sports,** 8201 W. Charleston, which offers a comprehensive selection of climbing gear and guidebooks to the region and beyond. (☎ 254-1143. Open M-F 9am-7pm, Sa 9am-6pm, Su 10am-6pm.) There are several crags accessible from the first and second pullouts of the scenic drive; they include **Dog Wall, Tuna and Chips Wall, Black Corridor, The Gallery,** and **Sweet Pain Wall,** this last offering the most popular climbs in all of Red Rocks. Classic multipitch routes lie along Pine Creek and Juniper Canyon.

HOOVER DAM

Take I-15, Hwy. 93/95, south 26 mi. from Las Vegas to Boulder City. From Boulder City head east 5 mi. on Hwy. 93 to the Nevada side of the dam. ☎ 291-8687. Open daily 9am-5pm. Tours, including an elevator trip down to the generators, every 15min. daily 9:30am-4:30pm. Parking on the Nevada side costs $5; free on the Arizona side. $10, seniors $8, ages 7-16 $4, 6 and under free.

Built to subdue the flood-prone Colorado River and provide water and energy to the entire Southwest, this looming ivory monolith, also known (by Democrats, as least) as the Boulder Dam, took 5000 men five years of seven-day weeks to construct. By its completion in 1935, 96 workers had died. Their labor rendered a 726.4 ft. colossus that now shelters precious agricultural land, pumps more than 4 billion kilowatt-hours of power to Vegas and L.A., and furnishes the liquid playground of Lake Mead. Though it altered the local environment, the spectacular engineering feat weighs 6,600,000 tons and measures 660 ft. thick at its base and 1244 ft. across the canyon at its crest. Tours and an interpretive center explore the dam's history and future.

LAKE MEAD

There are a few ways to access the lake. Take Lake Mead Blvd./Hwy. 147 off I-15 east 16 mi. to Northshore Rd., which provides access to the lake all the way up to Overton at the north end and reaches south toward Las Vegas Bay. Alternatively, Lakeshore Dr. departs Hwy. 93, 4 mi. east of Boulder City, and 30 mi. south of Vegas, at the Visitors Center and follows the southeast shore of the lake. $5 fee to enter the recreation area. Visitors Center: ☎ 293-8990; www.nps.gov/lame. Open daily 8:30am-4:30pm.

When the Colorado River met the Hoover Dam, Lake Mead was formed. This 100 mi. long behemoth is the largest reservoir in the US and the country's first national recreation area. First-time visitors to the lake will benefit from a trip to the **Alan Bible Visitors Center,** 4 mi. east of Boulder City, for its helpful staff and informative brochures and maps. For maps and abundant information about area services, pick up *Desert Lake View* at one of the several ranger stations dotting Lake Mead's shores. In case of an **emergency** call ☎ 800-680-5851 or 293-8932. **Backcountry hiking** and camping is permitted in most areas. **Hunters** can target deer and bighorn sheep in season, and Lake Mead offers some of the best sport **fishing** in the country, as large-mouth and striped bass are prevalent throughout the lake. Contact the **Nevada Division of Wildlife** (NDOW; ☎ 486-5127) for information on obtaining licenses and hunting and fishing restrictions. Despite these other diversions, Lake Mead seems to be the domain of armies of weekend adventurers driving white pickup trucks with **jet skis** in tow. For the unprepared, boats and other watercraft rentals are at the various concessionaires along the shores. The most popular **Boulder Beach** is the departure point for many water-based activities, is accessible from Lakeshore Dr. at the south end of the lake, about 2 mi. north of the Visitor Center. (☎ 800-752-9669 or 293-3484. Jet skis $55 per hr., $285 per day; fishing boats $60 for 4hr., $110 per day. Hefty security deposit required on all vessels.) Alongside the Park Service **campsites** ($10), concessionaires often operate RV parks (most of which have become mobile home villages), marinas, restaurants, and motels.

VALLEY OF FIRE

The most direct route to the park from Las Vegas carries you north along I-15 for 45 mi. Head east on Hwy. 169 and enter the park for a $5 fee. Visitors Center: ☎ 397-2088. Open daily 8:30am-4:30pm.

Northwest of Lake Mead, brilliantly colored rocks come alive in striking formations at the **Valley of Fire,** Nevada's first state park. The robust crimson sandstone evokes landscapes usually associated with southwestern Utah but sits just a short drive from the casinos of the Strip. Hwy. 169 bisects the park and leads to the extensive exhibits and short films on display at the **Visitors Center.** There are **hiking** trails throughout the park, many leading to petroglyph sites. Campgrounds at the western end of the park near **Atlatl Rock ❶** and **Arch Rock ❶** offer 51 sites. (Showers, water, and toilets; no hookups. $13.)

RENO-TAHOE TERRITORY

Edging toward the High Sierra along California's eastern border, the Reno-Tahoe area is the state of Nevada's second-most visited region, thanks in part to Las Vegas's seedier younger brother to the north, Reno. Nearby, the harsh, flat desert gives way to Tahoe's shimmering alpine lakes and horizon-breaking mountains, the mind-blowing desolation of Black Rock Desert, and the elegant rock formations of mammoth Pyramid Lake.

RENO ☎ 775

Its decadent casinos only a dice throw away from snowcapped mountains, Reno captures both the capitalist frenzy and the natural splendor of the West. The hub of northern Nevada's tourist cluster (including nearby Lake Tahoe), Reno, the self-proclaimed "biggest little city in the world" compresses the gambling, entertainment, and dining experience of Las Vegas into a few city blocks. While visitors today are likely to arrive with skis in hand, in the early 1900s many travelers came with divorce papers, as it was a celebrity break-up destination, where getting a

Reno

▲ ▲ ACCOMMODATIONS

Davis Creek Campground, **13**
Eldorado, **5**
Harrah's Reno, **6**
Hilton KOA, **10**
Reno Hilton, **9**
Silver Legacy, **3**
Sundowner Casino Hotel, **2**
Truckee River Lodge, **8**

🍴 FOOD
Bangkok Cuisine, **12**
Miguel's Mexican Food, **11**
Pneumatic Diner, **7**
La Strada, **4**

🍸 NIGHTLIFE
Circus Circus, **1**

divorce was easier than making a hard eight on the craps table. Whatever your reason for visiting, Reno continues to be the Sierra's answer to Vegas, attracting risk-takers who crave the rush of hitting it big without theme-park distractions.

▐ TRANSPORTATION

Flights: Reno-Tahoe International Airport, 2001 E. Plumb Ln. (☎328-6499, 888-766-4685), off of Hwy. 395 at Terminal Way, 3 mi. southeast of downtown. Served by Alaska, America West, American, Continental, Frontier, Northwest, Skywest, Southwest, and United. Most major hotels have free shuttles for guests; otherwise, take **Citifare** bus #13 (daily 6:15am-1:30am). Taxis from downtown to airport $10-12.

Trains: Amtrak, 135 E. Commercial Row (☎329-8638, 800-872-7245), at E. Commercial Row and Lake. Ticket office open daily 8:30am-5pm. Arrive at least 30min. in advance to purchase tickets. One train per day headed westbound to **Sacramento** (5hr., $65), continuing on to **San Francisco** (via Emeryville, 7.5hr., $71). One train per day headed eastbound to **Salt Lake City** (11hr., $88).

Buses: Greyhound, 155 Stevenson St. (☎322-2970, 800-231-2222), between W. 1st and W. 2nd St. Open 24hr. To: **Las Vegas** (1 per day, 10hr., $72 one-way express); **San Francisco** (12 per day, 5-6hr., $30-32 one-way); **Salt Lake City** (4 per day, 9hr., $57-61 one-way).

Public Transportation: Reno Citifare (☎348-7433) serves the Reno-Sparks area. Main terminal between Plaza St. and E. 4th on Center St. Major routes operate 24hr. $1.50, ages 6-18 $1.25, seniors and disabled $0.75. **Sierra Spirit** (☎348-RIDE) circles downtown Reno, hitting stops along Sierra and Center Sts. between 9th and Liberty Sts. every 10min. (Su-W 10am-8pm, Th-Sa 10am-midnight. $0.50). **PRIDE** (☎866-NV-PRIDE) runs buses between Reno city center and Carson City (M-F 4:50am-7pm, Sa-Su 8:40am-10:20pm; $3, under 18 $2, seniors and disabled $1.50).

Taxis: Whittlesea Checker Taxi, ☎322-2222. **Reno-Sparks Cab,** ☎333-3333.

Car Rental: Alamo (☎323-7940 or 888-426-3296), **Avis** (☎785-2727 or 800-831-2847), and **Budget** (☎800-527-7000 or 800-527-0700) are in the airport. **Enterprise,** 809 W. 4th St. (☎328-1671 or 800-736-8222). **Rent-A-Wreck,** 295 Gentry Way (☎322-7787 or 877-880-5603).

☀ ORIENTATION

Fifteen miles from the California border and a 445 mi. desert sprint north from Las Vegas (p. 197), Reno sits at the intersection of **I-80,** which stretches between Chicago and San Francisco, and **Highway 395,** which runs along the eastern slope of the Sierra Nevada from Southern California to Washington.

Most major casinos are "downtown" between West and Center St. and 2nd and 6th St. The neon-lit streets are heavily patrolled, but don't stray far east of the city center at night. Virginia St. is indisputably Reno's main drag; South of the Truckee River has cheaper accommodations, outlying casinos, and strip mall after strip mall. The #1 bus runs between downtown and the Meadowood Mall. Sparks, a few miles northeast along I-80, has several casinos where the locals go. The *Reno/ Tahoe Visitor Planner*, available at information kiosks throughout the city, has a local map and is a helpful city guide. The legal drinking and gambling age is 21.

🛈 PRACTICAL INFORMATION

Visitor Information: Reno-Sparks Convention and Visitors Authority, 1 E. 1st St. (☎800-FOR-RENO; www.renolaketahoe.com), on the 2nd fl. of the Cal-Neva Building. Open M-F 8am-5pm.

Bank: US Bank, 300 S. Virginia (☎688-6620), at the corner of Liberty and Virginia. Open M-Th 9am-5pm, Sa 9am-6pm. **24hr. ATM.** Reno thrives on fast money, so there are ATMs on almost every corner.

Library: Washoe County Library-Downtown Reno Branch, 301 S. Center St. (☎327-8300), between Ryland and Liberty Sts. Free **Internet access** against the backdrop of an indoor fountain. Open M 10am-8pm; Tu-Th 10am-6pm; F and Su 10am-5pm.

Marriage: Men and women over 18 (and those 16-17 with a parental OK) can pick up a marriage license at the **Washoe County Recorder's Office,** 75 Court St. (☎328-3275), for $55 (cash, V, MC)—all you need is a partner and an ID. Open daily 8am-midnight, including holidays. Numerous chapels in Reno are eager to help you tie the knot, but two of the most well-known are the **Park Wedding Chapel,** 136 S. Virginia (☎323-1170), across from the Courthouse, and the **Heart of Reno Wedding Chapel,** 243 S. Sierra St. (☎786-6882).

Divorce: To obtain a divorce permit, you must be a resident of NV for at least 6 weeks and pay a $265 fee. Call ☎329-4101 (M-F 9am-4pm) to arrange a lawyer referral. Both parties can immediately remarry.

Market: Sparks Hometowne Farmer's Market (☎353-2291) runs every Th evening June-Aug. at Victorian Square in downtown Sparks.

Laundromat: LaunderLand Coin-op Laundry, 680 E. 2nd St. (☎329-3733), corner of 2nd and Wells. Wash $1.75, drying free. Open daily 7am-10:30pm; last load 9:30pm.

Equipment Rental: Reno Mountain Sports, 155 E. Moana Ln. (☎825-2855). Rents packs ($9-12 per day), tents ($15 per day), sleeping bags ($15 per day), bear canisters ($7 per day), climbing shoes ($8 per day), and kayaks ($35-45 per day). Open M-F 9am-7pm, Sa 9am-6pm, Su 10am-5pm.

Weather Info: ☎673-8100. **Road Conditions:** ☎877-687-6237.

Emergency: ☎911. **Police:** 455 E. 2nd St. (☎334-2121, 334-COPS).

24hr. Crisis Lines: General Counseling and Rape Crisis, ☎800-992-5757. **Compulsive Gamblers Hotline,** ☎800-522-4700.

24hr. Pharmacy: Walgreen's, 750 N. Virginia (☎337-8700).

Medical Services: St. Mary's Hospital, 235 W. 6th St. (☎770-3000; emergency ☎770-3188), between West St. and Arlington Ave. 24hr.

Post Office: 50 S. Virginia St. (☎786-5936), at the corner of Mill and Virginia Sts. Open M-F 8:30am-5pm. **Postal code:** 89501.

ACCOMMODATIONS

While weekend casino prices are usually high, weekday and off-season discounts mean great deals. **Eldorado ❸,** 345 N. Virginia (☎800-648-5966 or 786-5700) and **Silver Legacy ❸,** 407 N. Virginia St. (☎800-687-7733 or 325-7401), offer good deals with central locations and massive facilities. (Rates can drop to $35, but hover around $60 for a single.) Heterosexual prostitution is legal in most of Nevada (though not in Reno), which may be reflected in some motels' low rates and consequent lack of wholesomeness. Rates below don't include Reno's **12% hotel tax.**

Harrah's Reno, 219 N. Center St. (☎800-427-7247 or 786-5700), between E. 2nd St. and Commercial Row. Harrah's central location, two towers of 964 luxurious rooms, seven restaurants, pool, and health club leave little to be desired. 65,000 sq. ft. casino draws large crowds with Reno's highest table limits. Sammy's Showroom and the Plaza host top performers. Free valet parking. Singles/doubles M-Th start at $49; F-Su $89. ❸

Reno Hilton, 2500 E. 2nd St. (☎800 648-5080 or 789-2000), off Hwy. 395 at the Glendale exit—you can't miss it. More than 2000 elegant rooms, a 9000-seat outdoor amphitheater, driving range, 50-lane bowling center, health club and spa, and shopping mall make the Hilton Reno's biggest hotel/casino. Press your luck in the 115,000 sq. ft. casino, or for something even more stomach-churning (depending on how you wager), check out the Ultimate Rush reverse bungee. Rooms $35-149. ❸

Sundowner, 450 N. Arlington Ave. (☎800-648-5490 or 786-7050), between W. 4th and W. 5th Sts. This working man's casino represents the meat and potatoes of Reno's gambling industry. No frills, but the rooms are clean and come with everything you'd expect, such as A/C and telephones. Pool, hot tub, and jacuzzi on premises. Rates are some of the lowest in town. Rooms Su-Th starting at $26, F $50, Sa $70. ❷

Truckee River Lodge, 501 W. 1st St. (☎800 635-8950 or 786-8888), corner of Ralston and 1st St., a short walk from the slots. A non-smoking joint, it is against everything typically Reno. Functional rooms, from twins to a 2-bedroom suite, all with kitchenettes and cable TV. Rents bikes and arranges all kinds of outdoor adventures. Weekly rates available. Twins Su-F $48, Sa $70; 2-bedroom suite Su-F $120, Sa $160. ❸

CAMPGROUNDS

Campers can drive to the woodland campsites of **Davis Creek Park ❶,** 18 mi. south on Hwy. 395 to Hwy. 429, then follow the signs ½ mi. west. (☎721-4901. Volleyball courts and trout-packed Ophir Creek Lake. Showers and toilets on site. Sites $15, additional car $5; pets $1.) The challenging Ophir Trail (6 mi. one-way), which ascends over 4000 ft. to meet the Tahoe Rim Trail, is for the adventurous. To be closer to the action, bunk down in the urban jungle at the **Hilton KOA ❷**, 2500 E. 2nd St. (☎ 888-562-5698 or 789-2147), next to the Hilton. There's no grass, but campers have access to the Hilton's pool, tennis courts, and fitness center. (Hookups $27-38). Farther afield, many camp at **Pyramid Lake** (p. 231), 35 mi. northeast of Reno.

🌓 FOOD

The cost of eating out in Reno is low, but the food quality doesn't have to be. Casinos do a lot of business, offering a wide range of all-you-can-eat buffets and next-to-free breakfasts. Escaping the clutches of these giants is worthwhile, as inexpensive eateries outside of the mainstream abound. Still, if you want to do it yourself, there are 24hr. supermarkets aplenty. Go natural at **Wild Oats Market**, 5695 S. Virginia St. (☎ 829-8666), between McCarran and Meadwood Mall Way. Open daily Sept.-May 7am-10pm, June-Aug. 7am-11pm.

🏆 **Pneumatic Diner**, 501 W. 1st St. (☎ 786-8888 ext. 106), at the corner of Ralston and W. 1st St. in the Truckee River Lodge. This funky diner is a subversive melting pot fighting against the hegemony of Reno's homogenous casinos. All-natural ingredients make up a menu with nods to Italian, Mexican, French, and Middle Eastern food. Beverage concoctions (try the Snoopy, $1.50-4), breakfast ($1.50-6.50), sandwiches like the ratatouille baguette ($5.50), and other American food ($4-7.50). Open M-F 11am-11pm, Sa 9am-11pm, Su 7am-11pm. ❷

Bangkok Cuisine, 55 Mt. Rose St. (☎ 322-0299), near the corner of S. Virginia and Mt. Rose. With delicious Thai food served and an elegant setting, this restaurant makes a welcome haven from Reno's ubiquitous steaks and burritos. A huge menu with all sorts of soups ($4-7), noodles ($8-12), fried rices ($8-12) and curries ($8-10), as well as house specialities like the stuffed Thai omelette ($8). Open M-Sa 11am-10pm. ❷

La Strada, 345 N. Virginia St. (☎ 348-9297), in the Eldorado Hotel. Serving northern Italian cuisine in the heart of the Eldorado, La Strada has won numerous accolades for its dazzling food. Pastas made fresh daily ($10-20) as well as beef and fish entrees ($13-24). Even on a budget you can enjoy a bit of elegance. Open daily 5pm-10pm. ❸

Miguel's Mexican Food, 1415 S. Virginia St. (☎ 322-2722). Miguel's is a Reno classic, praised by both locals and critics alike. The substantial lunch menu ($6-9) offers delicious fare in generous servings. Don't miss the outstanding guacamole ($7) and *sopapillas* (3 for $1). Dinner entrees $5-14. Open Su noon-8pm; Tu-Th 11am-9pm; F-Sa 11am-10pm. ❷

👁 🎵 SIGHTS & ENTERTAINMENT

There's far more to Reno culture, however, than its nightlife. The newly reopened **Nevada Museum of Art**, 160 W. Liberty St., is housed in an architectural delight that's even more post-modern than the city's casinos and was inspired by the Black Rock Desert. The museum is now home to several art galleries as well as a sculpture plaza, and also hosts visiting shows by the likes of such artists as Diego Rivera, Edward Hopper, and Dennis Oppenheim. (☎ 329-3333. Open Tu-W and F-Su 11am-6pm, Th 11am-8pm. Admission $7, students and seniors $5, children 6-12 $1, children 5 and under free.) Cultural events in Reno heat up in the summer: try the popular **Artown** festival (☎ 322-1538; www.renoisartown.com), held every July for the entire month. The event features dance, jazz, painting, and theater, and almost everything is free. August roars in with the chrome-covered, hot-rod splendor of **Hot August Nights** (☎ 356-1956; www.hotaugustnights.com), a celebration of classic cars and rock 'n' roll.

For the more athletically inclined, the **Reno Rodeo** (☎329-3877; www.renoro-deo.com), one of the richest in the West, gallops in for eight days every June. In September, the **Great Reno Balloon Race** (☎826-1181), in Rancho San Rafael Park, and the **National Championship Air Races** (☎972-6663; www.airrace.org), at Reno/Stead Airport, draw an international group of contestants who take to the sky as spectators look on. If you prefer more old-fashioned modes of transportation, nearby Virginia City hosts **Camel Races** (☎847-0311) during the weekend after Labor Day, in which both camels and ostriches scoot about town.

■ NIGHTLIFE

Reno is like a giant adult amusement park, its casinos serving as the main attractions. Knowing what's good for business, casinos offer free gaming lessons. The most popular games and minimum bets vary between establishments, but slots are ubiquitous. Drinks are usually free if you're gambling, but alcohol's inhibition-dropping effects can make betting a bad experience. If you're under 21, you cannot collect big winnings, so consider your jackpot a donation to the casino's coffers.

Almost all casinos offer live nighttime entertainment, but most shows are not worth the steep admission prices. **Harrah's**, 219 N. Center St. (☎786-3232), is an exception, carrying on a dying tradition with its **Night on the Town** in Sammy's Showroom. Starting at $39, Harrah's offers dinner at one of its restaurants and a performance by one of its cadre of critically acclaimed performers. At **Circus Circus**, 500 N. Sierra (☎329-0711), a small circus on the midway above the casino floor performs "big top" shows approx. every half an hour (M-Th 11:30am-11:30pm; F-Su 11:15am-11:45pm). For more entertainment listings and info on casino happenings, check out the free *This Week* or *Best Bets* magazines. *The Reno News & Review*, published every Th, provides an alternative look at weekly happenings and events off the casino path.

NEAR RENO

Leaving Reno to the east, Nevada's Basin and Range country dominate vistas in every direction. Yet the crest and trough pattern that covers much of Nevada and parts of Utah, Oregon, and California is not as homogenous a landscape as may first appear while clipping along I-80. A bit of exploration reveals the diversity of the terrain, and two of the Great Basin's most striking features, Pyramid Lake and the Black Rock Desert, make ideal daytrips to escape Reno's lights and slots.

PYRAMID LAKE   ☎775

When John Fremont "discovered" Pyramid Lake in 1844, he saw a rock structure near its shore that looked enough like a pyramid to earn the lake its name. A playground to local boating and fishing enthusiasts, a scenic wonder to tourists, and a financial and cultural lifeblood to the Paiute people, the lake's significance bridges cultures. Despite its popularity, travelers who venture off the beaten path can experience one of the West's most breathtaking desert lakes in solitude.

Highway 445 traces the lake's western shore, and numerous dirt tracks drop down to sandy beaches. While most of the many turn-offs are well compacted, others require four-wheel-drive. More adventurous (or rash) travelers get stuck all the time; call **Smith-Tobey Towing** (☎575-7320) or **Hanneman Towing** (☎575-2345) to be rescued. After **Warrior Point**, the road turns to gravel, so be prepared to share the road with thrill-seeking dirt-bikers and ATVers. Highway 447 parallels the lake to the east on the way to Gerlach (60 mi. north of Nixon), but a view of the water is quickly obscured by one of the Great Basin's ubiquitous ranges.

FISH OR FAMINE During the first half of the 20th century, Pyramid Lake attracted celebrity anglers ranging from Herbert Hoover to Clark Gable, all striving to snag a big Lahontan Cutthroat trout. In 1925, an angler pulled a world-record 41 lb. trout out of the lake. Anglers were reeling in such enormous fish because, thanks to the 1902 Newlands Reclamation Act, farmers near Fallon, NV diverted much of the Truckee's flow for agriculture. The construction of the Derby Dam in 1905 continued to decrease water levels in the Truckee, eventually destroying the Cutthroat's spawning grounds and leaving only the oldest, biggest fish in the lake. By the mid-1940s, however, the Cutthroat was extinct in Pyramid Lake, and by 1968, the lake's level had dropped over 80 ft. Recent litigation by tribal authorities has resulted in a settlement agreement among all the parties claiming water rights in the Truckee Basin. Since 1997, thanks to this agreement and above-average rainfall, the lake level has risen nearly 20 ft. This change in habitat along with aggressive fishery work by the Paiute tribe has enabled the successful re-introduction of the Cutthroat, making the Lake once again an angler's paradise. The trout fishing season runs Oct.-June, when it is not uncommon for fishermen to catch Lahontan Cutthoarts weighing upwards of 10lbs.

The small town of Nixon at the southern end of the lake hosts the **Pyramid Lake Visitors Center,** a quarter mile west of the junction of Hwys. 446 and 447 and adjacent to the high school. The Visitor Center is distinguished by its unconventional architecture; the building is rooted in the surrounding landscape and designed to be accessible to "native people of many nations." Rotating exhibits showcase historic and contemporary Paiute culture. (☎574-1088. M-F 8am-4:30pm. Free.) Next door is the **Pyramid Lake Health Center,** 705 Sutcliffe Hwy. (☎574-1018, 574-1020; Open M-Tu and Th-F 8am-noon and 1-4:30pm, W 8am-noon). The **Pyramid Lake Police Station** (☎574-1014) is located on S. Hollywood Rd. in the center of Nixon. In case of **emergency,** dial ☎911. The **Nixon Post Office,** 199 Hwy. 447 (☎574-1033. Open M-F 8:45am-noon and 12:30-4:45pm). The **Nixon Store,** 50 Hwy. 447 (☎574-0122), at the junction of Hwys. 446 and 447, sells gas and permits and offers a supplies and a small snack bar. (Open daily 7am-9pm; kitchen M-F 9am-3:30pm.)

Whether boating, fishing, or camping, a permit is required. The **Ranger Station,** 2500 Sutcliffe Dr. (☎476-1155) in Sutcliffe, on the western shore of the lake, sells permits for different activities. (Day use $6, boating or fishing $7, camping $9, jet skiing $12. Open daily 7am-5pm.) The ranger station looks over an **RV park** with full hookup sites and showers ($18). For those without an RV who are not prepared to brave camping on the beach, **Crosby Lodge ❷,** 700 Sutcliffe Dr. (☎476-0400) has spotless cabins with microwaves and refrigerators, and converted RVs that sleep up to seven and have full kitchens. Cabins start at $37, and RVs run from $90-105. Crosby's is home to a bar, restaurant, convenience store (which sells permits and gas), and grille to meet most immediate needs. (Open M-Th 7am-8pm, F 7am-9pm, Sa 6:30am-9pm, Su 6:30am-8pm.)

BLACK ROCK DESERT

This insufferably harsh desert in Nevada's northwest corner is one of the wildest places in the contiguous United States. Much of Black Rock is pristine terrain untouched by modern travelers, and recent legislation in the form of the Black Rock Desert-High Rock Canyon-Emigrant Trails National Conversation Area Act, passed by President Clinton in December of 2000, strives to ensure that 1.2 million acres of this landscape will remain virgin wilderness. It is by design, then, that much of this undisturbed terrain does not welcome exploration. The inhospitable Black Rock Desert is virtually devoid of potable water, often impassable in any type of vehicle, and full of hot springs that can boil flesh. Despite these dangers—

or perhaps because of them—parts of the Black Rock have recently become a playground for a variety of limit-pushing recreationalists. Extreme pursuits in the area include land sailing, no-limits golf, amateur rocketry, mountain biking, pick-up truck croquet with a 7 ft. ball, and the Burning Man Festival. Thanks to government protection, the otherworldly expanse of desert and mountains will continue to inspire and entice artists, outdoorsmen, and thrill-seekers for years to come.

▐ ORIENTATION. The Black Rock Desert lies in northwest Nevada, the barren basin of ancient Lake Lahontan. Extensive block-faulting is responsible for the several mountain ranges (4800-8000 ft.) jutting out of the desert floor, the high water table, and the hot springs. The desert is about 110 mi. northeast of Reno via **I-80** and **Highway 447,** continuing on 75 mi. northwest to Cedarville, CA and extending north from Gerlach, NV with an area of over 2000 sq. mi. The Black Rock is dominated by an immense playa (a dry lake bed, once submerged under 500 ft. of water) that is one of the flattest places on earth, with only 5 ft. in elevation change over a 25 mi. stretch. Beyond the playa, the desert then splits into two wings, with one wing jutting northwest towards Oregon and bound on the west by the **Calico Mountains** and **High Rock Lake Wilderness Areas.** The second wing extends towards the **Jackson Mountains** in the northeast and includes the Quinn River Valley. The **Black Rock Range** divides the two wings. Exploring much of the desert requires a four-wheel-drive vehicle with high-clearance and durable tires. From Gerlach, Hwy. 34 ventures north along the western edge of the playa, providing travelers with 20 mi. of paved road and numerous offshoots onto the lake bed.

▟ OUTDOOR ACTIVITIES. Off-roading is the area's primary form of recreation, but the inexperienced should heed the words on the wall of a restaurant in Gerlach: "Black Rock, where the pavement ends and the West begins." **Highway 34,** headed north between the Granite and Calico Ranges, is a reliable gravel road passable to most vehicles. Sheer and spectacular cliffs in High Rock Canyon dazzle hikers and drivers alike, although reaching the canyon by road past High Rock Lake (15 mi. north of the intersection with Hwy. 34) requires high-clearance and four-wheel-drive. High Rock Canyon also offers the Black Rock's only **rock climbing.** The **Jungo Road** travels 100 mi. between Gerlach and Winnemucca, and although the road is flat and well-compacted, jagged rocks between Gerlach and Sulphur make heavy-duty tires a necessity.

Most visitors to the Black Rock Desert venture no farther than the playa northeast of Gerlach. The spacious and undisturbed lake-bed welcomes all varieties of eccentric pursuits, but come prepared with your own equipment: there are no out-

BLACK ROCK SAFETY. Safety concerns are serious business in the Black Rock Desert. Outside Gerlach paved roads disappear. **Off-road tires are highly recommended, and a full-size spare is a must.** The playa is composed of silt and clay, so mucky conditions arise without warning. Extreme caution should be exercised when driving off-road. Many people who become stuck in the winter and spring must wait until the dry season to retrieve their cars. If you get stuck, wait with the vehicle rather than braving the desert environment. Check playa conditions at the **Texaco** in Gerlach or the **BLM** offices in **Winnemucca** (p. 231) before heading out. When in the desert, always carry abundant water, food, and sunscreen. Be sure to give someone your itinerary. Finally, several accidents have occurred when visitors have attempted to cross the train tracks at the playa's eastern edge. Despite its remoteness, the playa sees heavy train traffic from the Union-Pacific line; be cautious near the tracks.

BURNING MAN Every year during the week of Labor Day, volunteers transform a swath of the Black Rock Playa near Gerlach, NV, into Black Rock City, a city-as-art-installation that hosts Burning Man, a communal celebration of self-expression nearly 30,000 people strong and the largest single event in the country practicing Leave-No-Trace ethics. Organizers tout its non-commercial virtue: there's no money in Black Rock City, and gift-giving reigns. More importantly, Burning Man admits no spectators; everyone must contribute their own creativity. Participants express themselves by doing everything from donning alien suits to offering free shaves to performing daring pyrotechnic displays. The week-long celebration culminates when an enormous wooden human sculpture bursts into flames. To find out more about this ephemeral event, peruse the web site (www.burningman.com) or call ☎415-865-3800. If you happen to be in Gerlach in the weeks preceding or following Labor Day, stop by the Burning Man offices, 390 Main St., to get a taste of the event's culture.

fitters to supply gear for playa adventures like land sailing or turbine-engine racing. The historic **Applegate Pioneer Trail** runs through the desert, darting between the Black Rock's many hot springs. The BLM discourages hot spring use because even cooler springs can occasionally produce plumes of deadly heat. That said, **Trego** hot springs, northeast of Gerlach, is generally cool enough to permit soaking. To reach the hot springs, head 3 mi. south of Gerlach across the playa on Hwy. 447 to the turn off on the left hand (east) side of the road. The hot springs (and shade) are just under 14 mi. ahead in a little oasis just north of the road.

GERLACH   ☎775

Although the Black Rock is administered from Winnemucca's Bureau of Land Management, Gerlach, the town nearest the playa, is a staging ground for Black Rock enthusiasts. The tiny hamlet 60 mi. north of Pyramid Lake is a mixture of traditional, blue-collar mining folks combined with a small, avant-garde population of artists. The railroad is the biggest presence in Gerlach; the Burning Man offices are the second biggest; the third is a man named Bruno.

Heading to the playa, detour down **Dooby Lane** to see the "world's only drive-through folk art experience." Created by local artist DeWayne Williams, this 2 mi. drive showcases an eccentric collection of aphorisms, affirmations, memorials (most prominently to Elvis, complete with cape), marriage commemorations, Christian revelations, and advertising. Bear right at the Hwy. 447/34 junction (onto Hwy. 34) and travel 2 mi. to Guru St. Gerlach is also a staging ground for the **Burning Man** festival (see above). Organizers maintain a small field office and museum of artifacts from previous festivals at 390 Main St. (☎557-2200), as well as a ranch off Hwy. 34 a little more than 20 mi. out of town.

There's an unmanned kiosk beside the water tower in the center of town that provides travelers with all sorts of info on the area. Basic medical service is available at the **Gerlach Medical Clinic,** 350 Short St. (☎557-2312), off Diablo Dr. north of downtown (open M-F 8am-noon and 1-5pm), while the **Washoe County Sheriff** (☎557-2284) is on W. Sunset Blvd. The **Gerlach Post Office** sits at 345 E. Sunset Blvd. (☎800-275-8777. Open M-F 9am-1pm and 1:30-5pm.) In case of **emergency,** dial ☎911. Gerlach has its own gas station, **Bruno's Texaco,** 565 Main St., at the southern entrance to town, that also has BLM pamphlets and reports of playa conditions. (☎557-2272. Open daily 6:30am-9pm.) **Bruno's Country Club ❷,** on Main St., offers Gerlach's only accommodations, a saloon where Bruno bartends at night, and the best place to eat. Its diner-esque **restaurant ❶** serves up delicious and hearty homemade ravioli for $11 and thick $3 milk shakes. (☎557-2220. Restaurant open daily 5am-9pm. Small singles with a black-and-white TV start at $31, doubles $36.)

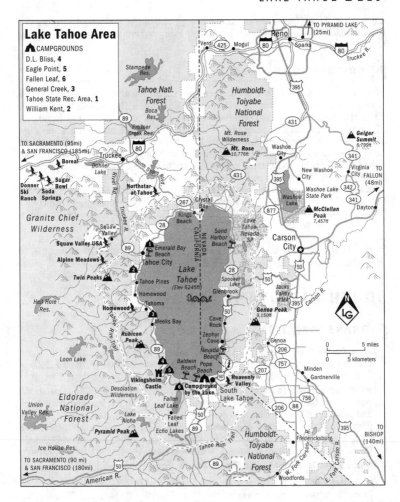

Lake Tahoe Area

▲CAMPGROUNDS
D.L. Bliss, **4**
Eagle Point, **5**
Fallen Leaf, **6**
General Creek, **3**
Tahoe State Rec. Area, **1**
William Kent, **2**

LAKE TAHOE

☎ 530/775

The Tahoe area's natural beauty attracts outdoor fanatics from across the globe, and its burgeoning entertainment and hotel industries eagerly support their excursions. In a town without an off-season, visitors can try their luck at almost everything you can imagine, from keno to kayaking. No matter the reason for visiting, the centerpiece and the one constant in every experience remains Lake Tahoe, the highest alpine lake in all of North America.

After the Bonanza Road was cut to reach California mines during the 19th-century Gold Rush, money started to pour into the Tahoe Basin. By the turn of the century, the lake was a haven for San Francisco's rich and famous. Now, everyone can enjoy Tahoe's pure blue waters, tall pines, and high-rise casinos breathtakingly silhouetted by the glow of the setting sun. An outdoor adventurer's dream in

NEVADA

any season, Tahoe has miles of biking, hiking, and skiing trails, long stretches of golden beaches, and possibilities for almost every watersport imaginable to man, from canoeing to parasailing.

ORIENTATION

In the northern Sierra on the border between California and Nevada, Lake Tahoe is just over a 3hr. drive from San Francisco, California. The lake rests about 100 mi. northeast of Sacramento (via **Highway 50**) and 35 mi. southwest of Reno (via **Highways 395** and **431**). Coming from the south **Highway 395** runs 20 mi. east of the lake. Road conditions in Tahoe can be treacherous from September-May, when tire chains may be required and four-wheel-drive is often recommended. Lake Tahoe is divided into two main regions, **North Shore** and **South Shore.** The North Shore includes Tahoe City in California and Incline Village in Nevada, while the South Shore comprises South Lake Tahoe in California and Stateline in Nevada. Proclaimed "The Most Beautiful Drive in America," Hwy. 50 combines with Hwys. 28 and 89 to form a 75 mi. asphalt ring around the lake; the entire winding loop takes nearly 3hr. to drive.

> **TAHOE AREA CODES.** The area code for Lake Tahoe is **530** unless otherwise specified. The Nevada side of the lake is **775.**

SOUTH LAKE TAHOE, CA

◻ TRANSPORTATION

Tahoe Casino Express (☎775-785-2424, 800-446-6128). Provides shuttle service between the Reno airport and South Shore Tahoe casinos. (Daily 6:15am-12:30am; $19, round-trip $34, children under 12 free.)

Public Transit: South Tahoe Area Ground Express or **STAGE** (☎542-6077). Operates in both NV and CA on the South Shore. It runs routes between the Stateline, NV casinos and the Hwy. 89/50 intersection. (6:40am-12:40pm. $1.25, day pass $2, 10-ride pass $10.) Casinos operate free shuttles on Hwy. 50 to ski resorts and motels. **Bus Plus,** ☎542-6077, has door-to-door service in the city (24hr., $3) and in El Dorado County (7am-7pm, $5). In summer, STAGE meets North Shore's TART at Emerald Bay.

Taxis: Domino Taxi, ☎544-6666. **Yellow Cab Co.,** ☎544-5555, 775 588-1234.

Car Rental: Many have branches in Nevada casinos. **Avis** (☎775-588-3361) in Caesar's Tahoe, Stateline, NV. **Enterprise** (☎775-586-1077) in the Horizon lobby, Stateline, NV. **Hertz** (☎775-586-0041) in Harvey's, Stateline, NV.

24hr. Road Service: ☎587-6000 or 800-937-4757.

■ ORIENTATION

Though located in California, **South Lake Tahoe** is just 48 mi. from Reno along Hwys. 395 and 50, 33 mi. from Tahoe City via. Hwys. 50 and 89, 45 mi. from Truckee on Hwys. 50 and 89. Within California, the city is 110 mi. from Sacramento via Hwy. 50, and 200 mi. from San Francisco via Hwy. 50 and I-80. **Hwy. 50 (Lake Tahoe Boulevard)** is the main drag of both South Lake Tahoe and the neighboring town of Stateline, NV. At the western end of town, Hwy. 89 heads up the western shore of Lake Tahoe. The major cross streets in town are **Ski Run Boulevard, Wildwood Avenue,** and **Park Avenue.**

▼ PRACTICAL INFORMATION

Visitor Information:

Lake Tahoe Visitors Authority, 1156 Ski Run Blvd. (☎544-5050 or 800 288-2463; www.virtualtahoe.com). An information clearinghouse for the entire lake with a particular focus on the South Shore. Open M-F 8:30am-5pm.

Tahoe-Douglas Chamber of Commerce and Visitors Center, 195 Hwy. 50 (☎775-588-4591; www.tahoechamber.org). In Stateline, NV. Open daily May-Oct. 9am-6pm, Nov.-Apr. 9am-5pm.

Taylor Creek Visitors Center (USFS), (☎543-2674; www.fs.fed.us/r5/ltbmu). 3 mi. north of South Lake Tahoe on Hwy. 89. A good resource for planning outdoor excursions, with detailed maps of the area. Issues permits for the Desolation Wilderness. Camping fee $5 per person per night, $10 per person for 2 or more nights, $20 for 1-year pass. Under 12 free. Reservations (☎644-6048, $5) are available for overnight permits mid-June through Labor Day. Open daily Memorial Day weekend through mid-June and Oct. 8am-4pm, mid-June through Sept. 8am-5:30pm.

Lake Tahoe Basin Management Unit, 35 College Dr. (☎543-2600; www.fs.fed.us/r5/ltbmu). Off Al Tahoe Blvd. A year-round information and permit source. Open daily 8am-4:30pm.

Bank: Bank of the West, 2161 Lake Tahoe Blvd. (☎531-3390). Open M-Th 9am-5pm, F 9am-6pm, Sa 9am-1pm. **24hr. ATM.**

Laundromat: Uncle Bob's Laundromat, 2180 Lake Tahoe Blvd. (☎542-1910). Wash $1.25, dry $0.25 per 8min. Open daily 7am-10pm.

Weather: ☎541-0200, enter category number 5050.

Road Conditions: California ☎800-427-7623 or 546-LAKE(5253), ext. 43 outside of CA; Nevada, ☎877-687-6237 or 775-793-1313.

Emergency: ☎911. **Police: South Lake Tahoe Police,** 1352 Johnson Blvd. (☎542-6100). Off Al Tahoe Blvd.

Crisis Hotlines: General, ☎800-992-5757. **Gamblers Anonymous,** ☎573-2423. **Tahoe Women's Services,** ☎546-3241.

Pharmacy: Longs Drugs, 2358 Lake Tahoe Blvd. (☎544-1500). Open M-Sa 7am-9pm, Su 8am-8pm.

Medical Services: Barton Memorial Hospital, 2170 South Ave. (☎541-3420). At 3rd St. and South Ave. off Lake Tahoe Blvd.

Library: El Dorado County Library-South Lake Tahoe Branch, 1000 Rufus Allen Blvd. (☎573-3185). Free **Internet access.** Open Tu-W 10am-8pm, Th-Sa 10am-5pm.

Post Office: South Lake Tahoe, 1046 Al Tahoe Blvd. (☎800-275-8777). Open M-F 8:30am-5pm, Sa noon-2pm. **Postal code:** 96151.

▼ ACCOMMODATIONS

On the South Shore, the blocks bordering Hwy. 50 on the California side support the bulk of the area's motels. Particularly glitzy and cheap in South Lake Tahoe, motels cost next to nothing mid-week. The North Shore is much more polished. Fall and spring represent the most economical times to visit Tahoe because, while not a true off-season, things do slow down. Look for discount coupons in newspapers. Whatever your budget, nearby campgrounds are a good option in warmer months. For camping options around the lake, see **Camping,** p. 224.

▨ **Tahoe Valley Lodge,** 2214 Lake Tahoe Blvd. (☎800-669-7544 or 541-0353; www.tahoevalleylodge.com). The immaculately kept rooms in this sparkling establishment take the mountain motif to an extreme, juxtaposing rough-hewn logs with mile-high comforters. There's no shortage of amenities, however; all rooms feature queen-size beds, cable TV, coffeemakers and many have microwaves, refrigerators, and in-room spas. Put yourself into the lap of luxury. Reception 24hr. Singles $95, Doubles $125. ❺

NEVADA

Royal Inn, 3520 Lake Tahoe Blvd. (☎544-1177). Get the royal treatment with beds queen and rooms clean, along with a ton of cable TV channels. Heated pool and laundry facilities. Singles Su-Th $28-35; doubles $39-49. Weekends and holidays see greatly inflated rates, but don't be bashful about mentioning that *Let's Go* brought you here—you may be handsomely rewarded. ❷

Doug's Mellow Mountain Retreat, 3787 Forest Ave. (☎544-8065). From the north turn left onto Wildwood Rd. west of downtown Stateline, and after 3 blocks take a left on Forest Ave.; it's the 6th house on the left. Easygoing Doug supplies a modern kitchen, BBQ, and fireplace in a woodsy house amidst a residential neighborhood. **Internet access** $5 per hr. Bedding included. No curfew, flexible check-in and check-out times. Dorms $15 per person; private rooms $25. Discounts for stays over a week. ❶

Best Tahoe West Inn, 4107 Pine Blvd. (☎800-700-8246/3 or 544-6455), off Park Ave. on the shore side of downtown. Within walking distance of the casinos but closer to the beach and away from the hubbub, the Tahoe West is a great base for exploring the lake and its surroundings. The modern rooms are chock full of amenities, and there is a pool, jacuzzi, and sauna on the premises. Reception open 7am-11pm. Rooms June-Aug. $54-99 (and sometimes lower), Sept.-May $34-89. ❸

▌ FOOD

If you want to forage, try **Safeway,** 1020 Johnson Blvd., at Lake Tahoe Blvd. and Johnson Blvd. (☎542-7740. Open 24hr.) **Grassroots Natural Food Market,** 2040 Dunlap St. (☎541-7788), off Lake Tahoe Blvd. near the Hwy. 89/50 intersection (open M-Sa 9am-8pm, Su 10am-6pm).

Sprouts Natural Foods Cafe, 3123 Harrison Ave. (☎541-6969), at the intersection of Lake Tahoe Blvd. and Alameda Ave. Natural foods in unnaturally large portions, this place keeps everyone satisfied. Try the breakfast burrito with avocados ($5), the tasty smoothies ($3-3.75), or a shot of wheat grass ($2). Open daily 8am-10pm. ❶

The Red Hut Cafe, 2723 Lake Tahoe Blvd. (☎541-9024), and 22 Kingsbury Grade (☎588-7488). A Tahoe original since 1959, the friendly staff dishes out homestyle cooking. Waffles piled with fruit and whipped cream $5.75, avacado burgers $6.50. Open daily 6am-2pm. No credit cards. ❶

Lakeside Beach Grill, 4081 Lakeshore Blvd. (☎544-4050), on the water between Park and Stateline Ave. Located right on the beach, the tasty menu compliments the spectacular views. Try inventive entrees ($7-11), like the calamari burger, in a relaxed setting. Open daily June-Sept. 11am-7pm. ❷

Orchid Thai, 2180 Lake Tahoe Blvd. (☎544-5541). The only Thai restaurant in town serves terrific fare that doesn't cost a ton. Options for vegetarian diners include the Pad Basil Garden ($7) or crispy tofu ($4). Carnivores are sated with Pottery Shrimp ($11) and a wide range of curries ($7-13). Open M-Sa 11am-10pm, Su 3pm-10pm. ❷

▌▐ NIGHTLIFE & ENTERTAINMENT

Nightlife in South Lake Tahoe centers around the casinos, which are busy 24/7. To get in you have to be 21 and have a government-issued form of picture ID.

Caesar's Palace, 55 Hwy. 50 (☎888-829-7630 or 775-588-3515). Roman theme extends through large casino, sportsbook, restaurants, and clubs. Within Caesar's, the popular **Club Nero** (☎775-586-2000) is a hotspot for dancing and drinking, with $1 drinks on M, Latino night on Tu, wet t-shirt contests and free admission for ladies on W, ladies night with free admission and well drinks until midnight on Th, F, and Sa, and $1 drafts on Su. Cover $5-25. Open daily 9pm.

Harrah's, Hwy. 50 (☎800 427-7247 or 775-588-6611). Casino glamour and glitz taken to the max in this slot machine heaven replete with restaurants, bars, and cocktail lounges. Home to **Altitude Nightclub** (☎775-586-6705), which hosts its fair share of foam parties. Cover $5-25. Open M-Tu and Th-Sa from 9pm.

The Brewery, 3542 Lake Tahoe Blvd. (☎544-BREW/2739). Stop in and try one of the 7 microbrews on tap. The sassy Bad Ass Ale packs a fruity punch, and pizzas (starting at $10) come crammed with as many toppings as you want. Laid-back atmosphere makes this spot a favorite for locals. Open Su-Th 11am-10pm, F-Sa 11am-2am.

TAHOE CITY

▐ TRANSPORTATION

Trains: Amtrak (☎800-USA-RAIL/872-7245). Runs trains between Chicago and San Francisco that stop at the Truckee Depot in downtown Truckee. One west-bound train daily to **Sacramento** (4½hr., $22-40) and **Oakland/San Francisco** (6½hr., $45-93), and one east-bound train to **Reno** (1hr., $10-21).

Buses: Greyhound (☎800-231-2222). At the Truckee Depot. To: **Sacramento** (3hr.) **San Francisco** (5½hr., 5 per day, $37-39) and for **Reno** (1hr., 3 per day, $10-12).

Public Transit: Tahoe Area Regional Transport or **TART** (☎550-1212 or 800-736-6365; www.laketahoetransit.com). Connects the western and northern shores from Incline Village through Tahoe City to Meeks Bay, where it joins with South Lake Tahoe (STAGE) buses in the summer. Stops daily every hour or half hour 6:30am-6pm, depending on the route. Buses also run out to Truckee and Squaw Valley and back 5 times per day (7:30am-4:45pm). $1.25, day pass $3. Exact fare required.

Taxis: Alpine Taxi, ☎546-3232. **Checker North Tahoe,** ☎866-420-8294 or 546-8844.

24hr. Road Service: ☎587-6000 or 800-937-4757.

✦ ORIENTATION

Tahoe City sits 16 mi. southeast of Truckee, CA via Hwy. 89, 33 mi. from South Lake Tahoe via Hwys. 89 and 50, 48 mi. from Reno via Hwy. 89 and I-80, and 208 mi. from San Francisco via I-80. The town centers around the intersection of **Highway 89,** which is called **West Lake Boulevard** and heads south to the beaches and parks of the west shore, and **Highway 28,** which goes by **North Lake Boulevard** in central Tahoe City and is the main commercial drag.

▐ PRACTICAL INFORMATION

Visitor Information: North Lake Tahoe North Visitors Bureau, 380 North Lake Blvd. (☎583-3494; www.mytahoevacation.com). A helpful office with tons of info on the area. Open M-F 9am-5pm, Sa-Su 9am-4pm.

Bank: US Bank, 705 North Lake Blvd. (☎583-2346). Open M-Th 9am-5pm, F 9am-6pm. **24hr. ATM.**

Market: Foothill Farmer's Market, on Hwy. 28 east of town. Th 8am-1pm late May-Oct.

Laundromat: Big Tree Cleaners, 531 North Lake Blvd. (☎583-2802). Wash $1.50, dry $0.25 per 10min. Open daily 7am-10pm.

Road and Weather Conditions: ☎800-427-7623, 530-546-LAKE/5253, ext. 43.

Emergency: ☎911. **Police: Placer County Sheriff,** 2501 North Lake Blvd. (☎581-6330), east of town on Hwy. 28.

Pharmacy: Tahoe City Pharmacy, 599 North Lake Blvd. (☎583-3888). Open M-F 9am-6pm, Sa 9am-5pm.

Medical Services: Incline Village Community Hospital, 880 Alder Ave. (☎775-833-4100). Off Hwy. 28 in Incline Village. **Tahoe Forest Hospital,** 10121 Pine Ave. (☎587-6011). At Donner Pass Rd. and Pine Ave. in Truckee.

Library: Tahoe City Library, 740 North Lake Blvd. (☎583-3382). Free **Internet access.** Open Tu and Th-F 10am-5pm; W noon-7pm; Sa noon-4pm.

Post Office: Tahoe City, 950 North Lake Blvd. (☎800-275-8777). In the Lighthouse Shopping Center. Open M-F 8:30am-5pm. **Postal code:** 96145.

ACCOMMODATIONS

The North Shore offers more refined accommodations along Hwy. 28, but rates are relatively high, especially in Tahoe City and Incline Village, where lodgings tend to be booked solid, and well in advance, for weekends and holidays. Camping options abound in the North Shore (see **Camping,** below).

Firelite Lodge, 7035 North Lake Blvd. (☎800-934-7222 or 546-7222), in Tahoe Vista 8 mi. east of Tahoe City. Sleek, modern quarters complete with amenities like micro-waves, refrigerators, coffee makers, patios overlooking the pool, and spas that create a European feel. Guest laundry service and continental breakfast. Open daily 8am-11pm. Singles in summer and winter from $59; off-season singles begin at $49. ❸

Tahoe City Inn, 790 North Lake Blvd. (☎581-3333 or 800-800-8246; www.tahoecity-inn.com), in downtown Tahoe City. Deluxe rooms sport kitchenettes, jacuzzis, and VCRs, with access to an extensive video library. Comfy queen beds, coffeemakers, mini-fridges, and cable TV are standard. Peak season Su-Th $85-160, F-Sa $105-160; late Apr. to mid-June and late Sept.-late Nov. Su-Th $59-140, F-Sa $79-140. ❹

Tamarack Lodge, 2311 North Lake Blvd. (☎583-3350 or 888-824-6323), 3 mi. north of Tahoe City, across from Lake Forest Beach. Clean lodge in the woods. Outdoor BBQ and fireplace, phones, cable TV, and friendly management. Some rooms with kitchen-ettes and cabins with full kitchens. Rooms from $54, cabins (sleeping 4) $125 in high season; rooms from $44, cabins $105 in low season. ❸

Cedar Glen Lodge, 6589 North Lake Blvd. (☎546-4281 or 800-500-8246; www.cedar-glenlodge.com), in the town of Tahoe Vista, 8 mi. east of Tahoe City. Cedar Glen fea-tures basic rooms complimented by numerous amenities, including private beach access, heated pool, and a hot tub and sauna. BBQ pits, playground, hammock, and, in the spring and summer, lots of flowers also add to the allure. Morning newspaper and breakfast coupons included in nightly rate. The facility also has cottages with eat-in kitchens available for a higher price. Open Su-Th 8am-7pm, F-Sa 8am-9pm. Singles from $75; doubles from $85. ❹

CAMPING

The Taylor Creek Visitor Center provides up-to-date information on camping around Tahoe City (see **Tourist and Information Services,** p. 221). Campgrounds ring the entire lake, but **Route 89** is particularly inundated with sites between Tahoe City and South Lake Tahoe. Sites can be booked on weekends in July and August, so it pays to reserve a spot in advance; call the **California State Parks Reservation Center** (☎800-444-7275) for California State Parks, or the **National Recreation Reser-vation System** (☎877-444-6777; www.reserveusa.com) for California Land Manage-ment. Backcountry camping is allowed in designated wilderness areas only for those who have obtained a permit for doing so from the Forest Service (see **Tourist and Information Services,** p. 221). The listings below run from north to south.

Tahoe State Recreation Area (☎583-3074), on the eastern edge of Tahoe City off Hwy. 28. A thin strip of land along the lake with a long pier. Water, flush toilets, showers ($0.50). Open May-Nov. 39 sites, $15; $4 per additional vehicle. ❶

William Kent (☎583-3642), on Hwy. 89, 2 mi. south of Tahoe City, with shady spots tucked away in the trees, is one of the most popular campgrounds on the west shore. Beach access across Hwy. 89. Clean flush toilets and water. Open June-Labor Day. 95 sites, $16. $5 per additional vehicle. ❷

General Creek (☎525-7982), in Sugar Pine Point State Park. 1 mi. south of Tahoma, off Hwy. 89, just a few miles north of Meeks Bay. This popular campground features tennis courts, cross-country ski trails, bike trails, a nature center, the historic Ehrman mansion, and a lakeside dock. Water, BBQ pits, and flush toilets. Hot showers $0.50. Open year-round. 175 sites, $15; additional vehicle $4. ❷

D.L. Bliss (☎525-7277), 11 mi. south of Homewood off Hwy. 89. One of the most scenic campgrounds on the lake with access to Lester Beach and trailheads for the Rubicon and Lighthouse Trails. Grills, water, flush toilets, and showers. Open late-May through Sept. 168 sites, $15-19. $5 additional vehicle. ❷

Eagle Point (☎541-3030), in Emerald Bay State Park. 12 mi. north South Lake Tahoe off Hwy. 89. On the slopes above spectacular Emerald Bay, this campground boasts some of Lake Tahoe's best views. Grills, water, flush toilets, and showers. Open late-May through September. 100 sites, $15. Additional vehicles $5. ❷

Fallen Leaf (☎544-0426), 2 mi. north of South Lake Tahoe off Hwy. 89. With 206 shady sites beside Fallen Leaf Lake and access to Baldwin and Pope Beaches, a good option for those looking to mix the action of South Lake Tahoe with the call of the wild. Water, flush toilets, but no showers. Open late-May-Sept. $18. ❷

⬛ FOOD

If you're a bit of a chef yourself head to **Safeway**, 850 North Lake Blvd. (☎583-2772. Open daily Sept.-June 6am-10pm, July-Aug. 6am-1am.) Alternatively, you can go *au naturel* at **New Moon Natural Foods** 505 West Lake Blvd., just south of Tahoe City. (☎583-7426. Open M-Sa 9am-7pm, Su 10am-6pm.)

Jake's on the Lake, (☎583-0188), in the Boatworks Shopping Mall. Tahoe City's big kahuna brings a taste of the South Seas to the shores of the lake in a relaxed wood-paneled dining room. Hawaiian-inspired creations dominate the lengthy menu, but there are plenty of options for landlubbers as well, like the New Rack of Lamb ($22). Come here to immerse yourself in a little aloha. Open daily 11:30am-2:30pm, M-F 5:30-9:30pm, Sa-Su 5-9:30pm. ❹

Syd's, 550 North Lake Blvd. (☎583-2666). This chill joint in the center of town serves up caffeine fixes ($2-3) and smoothies ($3.75) as well as deliciously fresh sandwiches like the Hummus Humongous ($4.50) and The Gobler ($5) on bagels or other breads. Open daily 6:30-5pm, July-Aug. 6am-7pm. ❶

Sancho's, 7019 North Lake Blvd. (☎546-7744), in the town of Tahoe Vista, located 8 mi. east of Tahoe City. The simple Mexican fare at this little hole-in-the-wall is a local favorite—at these low prices, Sancho's will sure to be your favorite as well. Tacos ($1.50), burritos ($4.50), and tostadas ($3.75), with all sorts of filling choices like carne asada, carnitas, and chorizo. Try the terrific Tostada ceviche with shrimp and mahi-mahi ($4.50). Open daily 11am-9pm. ❶

Yama, 950 North Lake Blvd. (☎583-9262), in the Lighthouse Shopping Center. This sushi bar and robata grill is a slice of sophistication tucked away in an otherwise uninspiring strip mall. They skewer anything from eggplant to salmon. Off the stick, Philly Roll ($5.75) or the more hardcore Punk Rock Roll ($8) are worth a try. Open Su-Th 5:30-9pm, F-Sa 5:30-10pm. ❶

NEVADA

🔊 🎵 NIGHTLIFE & ENTERTAINMENT

The **Pierce Street Annex,** 850 North Lake Blvd., in the Lighthouse Shopping Center, is the most popular bar in town with crowds almost every night. The sole source of sustenance comes in liquid form. Free pool on Su, DJ W-Sa, locals night Th, so try to blend. (☎583-5800. Open daily 2pm-2am.) Down the beach a ways, **Sierra Vista,** 700 North Lake Blvd. (☎583-0233), is the place to head for live music on the weekends. Bands generally start rocking at 10pm, and tickets ($5-10) are available at the door. The **Naughty Dawg,** 255 North Lake Blvd., across from the fire station, sizzles on M when beers start at $0.50 at 8pm and increase by $0.50 every half hour until 10pm. Afterwards cool off with a mixed drink in your own dawgy bowl. (☎581-3294. Open daily 11:30am-2am, kitchen 11:30am-11pm.)

🥾 HIKING

Hiking is a great way to explore the Tahoe Basin. Visitors Centers and ranger stations provide detailed info and maps for all types of hikes. Backcountry users must obtain a wilderness permit from the US Forest Service (see **Tourist and Information Services,** p. 221) for any hike into the Desolation Wilderness; 700 hikers are allowed in this area on any given day. Due to erratic weather conditions in the Sierra, hikers should always bring a jacket as well as drinking water. Ask where the snow has (or has not) melted—it's not usually all gone until July. **Alpenglow Sports,** 415 North Lake Blvd., in Tahoe City, offers an wide array of outdoor gear. *(☎583-6917. Open M-F 10am-6pm, Sa-Su 9am-6pm.)*

After decades of work, the 165 mi. **Tahoe Rim Trail** has been completed. The route encircles the lake, following the ridge tops of the Lake Tahoe Basin. The trail welcomes hikers, equestrians, and, in most areas, mountain bikers. Camping is allowed on most parts of a trail although backcountry permits are required in the Desolation Wilderness. Hiking is moderate to difficult. On the western shore, its routes comprise part of the Pacific Crest Trail. There are eight trailheads around the lake, so consult one of the ranger stations in the region for those best suited to your interests. Popular trailheads include **Spooner Summit** at the Hwy. 50/28 junction and **Tahoe City** off Hwy. 89 on Fairway Dr.

SOUTH SHORE. The southern region of the basin offers many moderate to strenuous hiking trails. The picturesque **Emerald Bay,** on Hwy. 89 between South Lake Tahoe and Tahoe City, is best explored on foot. This crystal-clear lake finger embraces Tahoe's only island, Fannette, while alpine lakes and dramatic waterfalls make the area a mini-paradise. ◪**Emerald Bay State Park,** which abuts the Desolation Wilderness, offers hiking and biking trails of varying difficulty, as well as camping. One of the best hikes in Tahoe is the **Rubicon Trail,** which wraps 6 mi. around the beach and granite cliffs of Emerald Bay. There are trailheads at D.L. Bliss Park and Vikingsholm. The challenging **Eagle Falls Trail** heads into the heat of the Desolation Wilderness and offers spectacular views of the High Sierra. The trail starts from the Eagle Lake parking lot and ascends to Eagle Lake (1 mi.) and into the Desolation Wilderness. *(Permits required for this hike.)*

The 63,960 acres of **Desolation Wilderness** make up an amazing expanse for extended backcountry travel. The **Pacific Crest** and **Tahoe Rim Trails** converge while in the wilderness. Desolation boasts glacial lakes and valleys, granite peaks, and sub-alpine forests that betray some of the region's most breathtaking vistas. All visitors to the area must have a wilderness permit. Day hikers can self-issue free permits from any of the eastern trailheads. Overnight hikers must register for a backcountry camping permit *($5 per night, $10 for 2 or more nights, $20 per year)* at one

NEVADA

of the ranger stations, and the Forest Service imposes overnight-use quotas from mid-June through Labor Day. To reserve a permit ahead of time. (☎644-6048. *$5 fee. Half of all permits during quota season are kept for walk-ins.*)

Those looking for a more leisurely excursion can enjoy the nature trails around the Taylor Creek Visitors Center, 3 mi. north of South Lake Tahoe on Hwy. 89. The **Lake of the Sky Trail** (½ mi. round-trip) is dotted with informative signs about the lake's origins, its early inhabitants, and current wildlife. The centerpiece of the Visitors Center, however, is the **River Profile Chamber,** which features a cross-section of a Tahoe creek. *(The chamber is accessed by the ½ mi. round-trip Rainbow Trail.)*

Lower and **Upper Echo Lakes,** off Hwy. 50 south of Tahoe, are much smaller, wilder versions of Tahoe; granite tablets and pine trees tower over the lakes, stretching on for miles within pristine backcountry perfect for exploring. **Echo Chalet,** 2 mi. west of Hwy. 50 on the near shore of Lower Echo operates **boat** service across the lake. (☎659-7207. *Runs M-Th 8am-6pm, F-Su 8am-7pm in-season. No reservations. One way $7 with at least 2 people; pets $3.)* From the drop-off point, a well-maintained path (part of the Pacific Crest Trail) skirts the north shore of the lakes to the Upper Echo boat landing and into the Desolation Wilderness. Day hiking wilderness permits are available at the chalet; mandatory overnight permits are issued at the forest service (see **Lake Tahoe Basin Management Unit,** p. 221). Another 2 mi. along Hwy. 50, just before Twin Bridges, is the **Horsetail Falls** trailhead. These impressive falls, dropping toward the Pacific, are unlike anything running into Lake Tahoe. To access them, you'll have to make the short (1.3 mi.) but tough hike through the slippery canyon. Inexperienced hikers should beware—each year, sight-seekers have to be rescued by Forest Service helicopters.

NORTH SHORE. At 10,778 ft., **Mount Rose,** in the Mount Rose Wilderness, is one of the nation's newest and part of the Toiyabe National Forest. It is one of the tallest mountains in the region as well as one of the best climbs. The panoramic view from the summit offers views of the lake, Reno, and the Sierras. The 6 mi. (12 mi. round-trip) trek starts out as an easy dirt road hike but ascends switchbacks for the last couple of miles. *(Take Hwy. 431 north from Incline Village to the trailhead.)*

The **Granite Chief Wilderness,** west of Squaw Valley, is a spectacular outdoor destination; its rugged hiking trails and mountain streams wind through secluded forests in 5000 ft. valleys to the summits of 9000 ft. peaks. The **Alpine Meadows Trailhead,** at the end of Alpine Meadows Rd. off Hwy. 89 between Truckee and Tahoe City, and the **Pacific Crest Trailhead,** at the end of Barker Pass Rd. (a.k.a. Blackwood Canyon Rd.) grant access to the wilderness. *(Permits are not required.)*

EAST SHORE. The **Marlette Lake Trail** begins at Spooner State Park, NV, at the junction of Hwys. 50 and 28. The hike climbs 5 mi. through the moderately difficult terrain of the aspen-lined North Canyon to Marlette Lake. During the mining boom water from the lake was diverted to Incline Village and used to shoot logs through a tunnel into Washoe Valley. They were then used in Virginia City mines.

⛷ SKIING

With its world-class alpine slopes, knee-deep powder, and luxuriant (or notorious) California sun, Tahoe is a skier's mecca. There are 15 ski resorts in the Tahoe area. Visitors Centers provide info, maps, free publications like *Ski Tahoe* and *Sunny Day,* and coupons (see **Practical Information,** p. 221). For daily ski info updates, use www.visitortips.com/tig/skitahoe. All the major resorts offer lessons and rent equipment. Look for multi-day packages that offer significant discounts over single-day rates. Lifts at most resorts operate daily 9am-4pm; arrive early for the best skiing and shortest lines. Prices do not include ski rental, which generally costs

CREST TO CREST: THE TRAIL OF THE WEST

As the longest hiking route in America, the **Pacific Crest Trail (PCT)** snakes, swerves, and scales up 2650 mountainous miles from Mexico to Canada, passing through all sorts of climates—from deserts to sub-Arctic regions—along the way. True to its name, the PCT always keeps to the crest—the trail maintains an average elevation of over 5000 ft. It dishes out quality as well as quantity, passing through some of the most pristine wilderness on the West Coast while topping out at the summit of **Mount Whitney** (14,494 ft.), the highest peak in the contiguous United States. Although the PCT was begun in 1968, the trailblazing task was so immense that it was not officially completed until 1993. No matter how much of the trail you choose to bite off, proper supplies and conditioning are vital. The **Pacific Crest Trail Association** (☎916-349-2109 or 888-728-7245; www.pcta.org) gives tips on how to prepare for the journey. Contact them at 5325 Elkhorn Blvd., Box 256, Sacramento 95842.

$20-30 for a full day. Numerous smaller ski resorts offer cheaper tickets and shorter lines. **Granlibakken** (☎583-4242 or 800-543-3221), is the oldest ski resort at Lake Tahoe and sports the cheapest lift tickets ($18); **Homewood Mountain Resort** (☎525-2992) has great views of the lake on more than 1260 acres and top-notch tree skiing. Skiing weather ranges from bikini to frost-bitten, and snow (artificial or otherwise) typically covers the slopes into early summer. Off-season skiing may not compete with winter powder, but it's generally much cheaper. For ski and snowboard rentals in Tahoe City stop by **Tahoe Dave's**, 620 North Lake Blvd. (☎583-6415 for skis or 583-0400 for boards. Skis, boots, and poles $20-36; board, boots, and bindings $25-36. Open in-season Sa-Th 7:45am-8pm, F 7:45am-midnight.) In South Lake Tahoe, **Trinity Mountain Sports**, 1060 Ski Run Blvd. (☎544-1621. Skis and boards $17-28. Open in season Su-Th 8am-6pm, F-Sa 8am-7pm.) Rates listed below are for peak season.

Squaw Valley (☎583-6985, 583-5585 or 888-SNOW-321/766-9321; www.squaw.com), 5 mi. north of Tahoe City off Hwy. 89. The site of the 1960 Olympic Winter Games, and with good reason: the groomed bowls make for some of the West's best skiing. Squaw boasts 4000 acres of terrain across 6 Sierra peaks. The 33 ski lifts, including the 110-passenger cable car and high speed gondola, access high-elevation runs for all levels. Open late Nov.-May. Full-day lift ticket $58, half-day $42, seniors and 13-15 $29, under 12 $15, over 76 free. Night skiing mid-Dec. through mid-Apr. daily 4-9pm $20. Non-skiing cable car ride $17.

Heavenly (☎775-586-7000), on Ski Run Blvd. off South Lake Tahoe Blvd. The largest and most popular resort in the area, with over 4800 skiable acres, 29 lifts, and 84 trails. Upwards of 10,000ft., its vertical drop is 3500 ft., Tahoe's biggest. Few shoots or ridges. Its lifts and slopes straddle the California-Nevada border and offer dizzying views of both. Full-day lift ticket $57, ages 13-18 $47, seniors and ages 6-12 $29.

Mt. Rose (☎800-SKI-ROSE/754-7673 or 775-849-0704), 11 mi. from Incline Village on Rte. 431. A local favorite because of its long season, short lines, and advanced focus. Full-day lift ticket $48, seniors $28, ages 13-17 $38, ages 6-12 $12, over 70 (mid-week) and under 6 free; half-day $38, ages 13-17 $33. Tu 2 for 1 tickets, W students $19, Th women $19.

Alpine Meadows (☎583-4232 or 800-441-4423), on Hwy. 89, 3 mi. north of Tahoe City. An excellent, accessible family vacation spot and local hangout with more than 2000 skiable acres. Not as commercial as Squaw, it has long expert bowls with good powder skiing. Full-day lift ticket $56, ages 13-18 $42, ages 7-12 $10, ages 65-69 $30, over 70 $8, under 6 $6. Basic ski rental $27, under 13 $18.

Northstar-at-Tahoe (☎ 562-1010; www.skinorthstar.com), on Hwy. 267 13 mi. north of Tahoe City. Family-oriented ski area emphasizes beginning and intermediate trails. 200 new acres on Lookout Mountain cater to advanced skiers, and its 2420 total acres are the most on the North Shore. Full-day lift ticket $57, ages 13-22 $44, under 13 $19.

⚑ OTHER OUTDOOR ACTIVITIES

BIKING. Miles of excellent trials and killer views make Tahoe a mountain biking hotspot. The lake's premier ride is the **Flume Trail,** in Nevada State Park ($5 entrance fee). The trail begins near the picnic area at Spooner Lake. This 23 mi. singletrack loop has magnificent views of the lake from 1500 ft. off the deck. **Flume Trail Mountain Biking,** at Spooner Lake, rents bikes and runs bike shuttles to favorite trails. (☎ 775-749-5349. Bikes $34-49 per day, bike shuttles $10-15. Open May-June 9am-6pm, July-Aug. 9am-7pm, Sept.-Oct. 9am-5pm.) Other smoking tire trails include **Mr. Toad's Wild Ride,** a 3 mi., 2200 ft. descent south of South Lake Tahoe off Hwy. 89, and **McKinney/Rubicon Road,** a loop ride to difficult peaks that climbs off Hwy. 89 north of Tahoma. For rentals in South Lake Tahoe check out **South Shore Bike & Skate** 1056 Ski Run Blvd. (☎ 541-7272. Mountain bikes $25-45 per day.) In Tahoe City head to **The Backcountry,** 690 North Lake Blvd. (☎ 581-5861. Mountain $30-40 per day, road $40 per day. Open May-Oct. 8:30am-6pm), or **Olympic Bike Shop,** 620 North Lake Blvd. (☎ 581-2500. Mountain bikes $25-45 per day, road $30 per day. Open May-Oct. 9am-6pm.)

Cyclists can cover parts of the Lake Tahoe loop on their steeds. The **Pope-Baldwin Bike Path** on the South Shore runs parallel to Hwy. 89 for over 3 mi. past evergreen forests until the path links up with the **South Lake Tahoe Bike Path** (via bike lanes on Hwy. 50), which goes through South Lake Tahoe and into Nevada. On the North Shore, the **Tahoe Trailways Bike Path** extends from Tahoe City for over 15 mi. in three directions, providing excellent access to beaches and hiking trails.

ROCK CLIMBING. Alpenglow Sports, 415 North Lake Blvd., in Tahoe City, provides rock and ice climbing literature, supplemented by a whole lot of know-how. The shop rents climbing shoes for $8 a day. (☎ 583-6917. Open M-F 10am-6pm, Sa-Su 9am-6pm.) There are many popular climbs in Lake Tahoe, but climbing shouldn't be undertaken without knowing the ropes—proper safety precautions and equipment are a must. Inexperienced climbers can try their hand (or hands) at bouldering in **D.L. Bliss State Park.** A host of popular climbing spots are scattered along the South Shore. The super-popular **Ninety-Foot Wall** at Emerald Bay, **Twin Crags** at Tahoe City, and **Big Chief** near Squaw Valley, are some of the more famous area climbs. **Lover's Leap,** in South Lake Tahoe, is an incredible (and an incredibly crowded) route spanning two giant cliffs. East of South Lake Tahoe off Hwy. 50, **Phantom Spires** have amazing ridge views, while **Pie Shop** offers serious exposure.

CROSS-COUNTRY SKIING & SNOWSHOEING. One of the best ways to enjoy the solitude of Tahoe's pristine snow-covered forests is to cross-country ski. Strap on your skis and venture onto the thick braid of trails around the lake. **Porters,** 501 North Lake Blvd., in Tahoe City, rents cross-country skis for $10-15. (☎ 583-2314. Open daily Oct.-Apr. 8am-6pm, May-Sept. 9am-6pm.)

Another option is to visit one of region's renowned cross-country ski resorts. **Spooner Lake,** at the junction of Hwys. 50 and 28, offers 57 mi. of machine-groomed trails and incredible views. (☎ 775-749-5349. $19, children $3.) **Tahoe X-C** maintains 40 mi. of trails for all abilities winding through North Shore forests. (2 mi. northeast of downtum Tahoe City on Dollar Hill off of Hwy. 28. ☎ 583-5475. $18; mid-week $13; children $6.) Snowshoeing is easier to pick up than cross-country skiing. Follow hiking or cross-country trails, or trudge off into the woods. Equipment rentals are available

NEVADA

at many sporting goods stores for about $15 per day. Check local ranger stations for ranger-guided winter snowshoe hikes.

◪ **BEACHES.** Many beaches dot Lake Tahoe, providing the perfect setting for a day of sunning and people-watching. *(Parking generally costs $3-7; bargain hunters should leave cars in turnouts on the main road and walk to the beaches.)*

On the North Shore, **Sand Harbor Beach,** 2 mi. south of Incline Village on Hwy. 28, has gorgeous granite boulders and clear waters that attract swimmers, sunners, snorklers, and boaters to its marina. The parking lot *($5)* often fills by late morning. **Tahoe City Commons Beach,** in the heart of Tahoe City just off North Lake Blvd., contains a playground for kids, sandy beach for sunbathing, and pristine lake waters for swimming. Boats, jet-skis, wakeboards, and waterskis can be rented at **Tahoe Water Adventures,** 120 Grove St. (☎583-3225), next to the beach. For kayak rentals, instruction, and tours, head to **Tahoe City Kayak,** 1355 North Lake Blvd., east of town. (☎581-4336. *Singles $50 per day, tandem $60 per day. Open daily May-Sept. 10am-6pm.)* For a rush, try **Lake Tahoe Parasailing,** 700 North Lake Blvd. (☎583-7245.)

The West Shore offers **Meeks Bay,** 10 mi. south of Tahoe City, a family-oriented, social, and equipped with picnic tables, volleyball courts, BBQ pits, campsites, and a store. **D.L. Bliss State Park,** 17 mi. south of Tahoe City on Hwy. 89, is home to **Lester Beach** and **Calawee Cove Beach** on striking Rubicon Bay. It's also the trailhead for the Rubicon Trail, which leads to the Vikingsholm mansion (see **Outdoors Sights,** p. 230). *(Parking here is $5 and limited, so check at the Visitors Center at the entrance or look to park on the road and walk in.)*

Baldwin Beach, on the South Shore, and neighboring **Pope Beach,** near the southernmost point of the lake off Hwy. 89, are shaded expanses of shoreline popular with the South Lake Tahoe crowds. It's easy to find a parking spot on the highway and avoid the fee. Quiet spots on both beaches can be found on their edges. For kayak tours, lessons, and rentals check out **Kayak Tahoe,** 3411 Lake Tahoe Blvd., near the intersection of Johnson Blvd. and Lake Tahoe Blvd. (☎544-2011. *Singles $50 per day, tandems $75 per day; tours $45-75; lessons $32-155.)* **Nevada Beach,** on the east shore, 3 mi. north of South Lake Tahoe off Hwy. 50, is close to the casinos and offers a sandy sanctuary from the jangling slot machines. **Zephyr Cove Beach,** 5 mi. north of South Lake Tahoe, has renovated its facility, hosting a youthful crowd keen on beer and bikinis. You can rent any sort of water craft you're interested in from power boats *($119 per hr.)* to jet-skis *($99 per hr.)* to kayaks *($18 per hr.)*, and even a parasail *($49-59 per person)* at **Zephyr Cove Marina.** (☎775 589-4908.) Zephyr Cove is also the launch site for the famous **M.S. Dixie II** paddlewheel, which cruises the lake regularly. (☎775-589-4906, 800-23-TAHOE/82463. *Adults $25, children $8.)*

◙ **OUTDOORS SIGHTS.** Much of what Lake Tahoe has to offer is spectacular, but ▨**Emerald Bay,** between South Lake Tahoe (10 mi.) and Tahoe City (23 mi.) on Hwy. 89, is simply jaw-dropping. The highway towers hundreds of feet above this finger of the lake, and rock faces and evergreen forests spring from the lakeshore to create one of the most photographed panoramas in the world. The remains of a stone teahouse sit at the summit of **Fanette Island,** a tiny isle in the middle of the bay, while on the shore rests **Vikingsholm,** a 38-room precise replica of a Scandinavian castle. The house is about a mile walk from a parking lot on the highway above and is open for tours daily from Memorial Day to Labor Day 11am-4pm ($2).

Heavenly Mountain Gondola (see **Skiing,** p. 227), in the heart of the new village in downtown South Lake Tahoe, whisks visitors along at 13 ft. per sec. to an elevation of 9136 ft. for breath-taking views of the Lake Tahoe Basin and hair-rasing possibilities for getting down. (☎775-586-7000. Runs daily 10am-sunset. $20, ages 6-12 $12.) **Squaw Valley** (see **Skiing,** p. 227), on Hwy. 89 between Tahoe City and Truckee, also offers a scenic cable car ride that climbs to the mountaintop High

Camp (8200 ft.), with a year-round ice-skating rink, tennis club, pool, spa, as well as trailheads for mountain bike and hiking trails. Restaurants and shops at the top are pricey. (☎583-6955. Runs daily late-June through Aug. 9:40am-10pm; Sept. through mid-Oct. 9:40am-4pm. $17, under 12 $5; after 5pm $8.)

INTERSTATE 80

Running through Nevada's wild northern reaches, I-80 shuttles locals, tourists, and commercial traffic past desert scrub, sand dunes, and snow-capped mountains. East of Lake Tahoe's alpine heights, plucky Winnemucca is a quaint stopover for slots, cheap rooms, and a unique taste of Basque culture. Speeding east, I-80 meets the mining town of Elko, whose rugged Ruby Mountains serve as Mother Nature's natural aphrodisiac, drawing outdoors nuts from all over the place. On the Utah border, the nearby Bonneville Salt Flats give humdrum Wendover a nitro boost of excitement. Amtrak runs one train per day along this route, making stops in Winnemucca, Elko and Reno.

WINNEMUCCA   ☎775

Before Winnemucca assemblyman Phil Tobin's 1931 gambling bill was approved in Nevada, his town existed as a sleepy wagon crossing and mining site. After the meteoric ascent of gaming, Tobin's prophecy—"Nevada would be a place today where people hurry through if the [gambling] bill had not been passed"—seems to have come true. The growing town of Winnemucca features casinos, some recreational activities, and a distinctive Old West charm that inspired its most recent wave of reinvention. Today, the buckaroo crowd is older: Winnemucca tourism is all about the AARP, the retirement lifestyle, and nickel slots.

Although Winnemucca is not a noted outdoors destination, nearby mountains host a wide range of activities. The **BLM**, 5100 E. Winnemucca, provides info about local recreational activities and administers the awesome **Black Rock Desert.** (☎623-1500. Open M-F 7:30am-4:30pm.) A few miles north of town and west of U.S. 95 are sizeable sand dunes, offering a pristine pallet for outdoor pursuits from off-roading to dune skiing. Closer to home, **Water Canyon** provides ample opportunity for leisurely day hikes. Local bikers from **Bikes and More,** 423 Bridge St. have, along with the BLM, established the exhilarating **Bloody Shins Trail,** a 12 mi. single-track ride that climbs about 1000 ft. Visit the shop for info about biking and other outdoor pursuits. (☎625-2453. Open Tu-Sa 10am-5:30pm).

Originally a simple crossing of the Humboldt River, Winnemucca now rests at the crossroads of I-80, running between Salt Lake City, Reno, and U.S. 95. **Winnemucca Boulevard** is the main strip in town, lined with motels and casinos. **Amtrak** (☎800-872-7245) stops on Railroad St. between Aiken and Lay St., bound for **Reno** (1 per day, 3hr., $31, locals warn that it often runs late) and **Salt Lake City** (1 per day, 8hr., $55). **Greyhound** (☎800-231-2222) sends buses to **Salt Lake** (3 per day, $59-63) and **Reno** (3 per day, $30-32). Pick up in town is at the **Winner's Corner** service station, 240 W. Winnemucca Blvd. (☎623-4464). The **Humboldt County Chamber of Commerce and Visitors Center** sits in a vacated casino at 30 W. Winnemucca Blvd. (☎623-2225; www.winnemucca-nv.org. Open M-F 8am-noon and 1-5pm; Sa 9am-noon and 1-4pm; Su 11am-4pm.) **Citibank**, 311 S. Bridge St., has a **24hr. ATM**. (☎625-8560. Open M-Th 9am-5pm, F 9am-6pm.) Services include: the **Winnemucca Police Department,** 25 W. 5th St. (☎623-6396); **Humboldt General Hospital,** 118 E. Haskill St. (☎623-5222), at the corner of E. Haskill and Mizpah St.; **Fourth Street Laundromat,** 547 4th St. (☎623-6790; open daily 7:30am-10:30pm); a **pharmacy** at **Raley's,** 1125 W. Winnemucca Blvd. (☎623-2548; pharmacy M-F 9am-7pm, Sa 9am-6pm; store daily

7am-11pm); free **Internet access** at the **Humboldt County Library,** 85 E. Fifth St. (☎623-6388; open M and Th-Sa 9am-5pm, Tu and W 9am-9pm); and the **post office,** 850 Hanson St. (☎623-2456. Open M-F 8:30am-5pm.) **Postal code:** 89445.

With a slew of motels competing for the almighty dollar, singles often hover near $30. The **Pyrennes Motel ❷,** 714 W. Winnemucca Blvd. (☎623-1116), in the center of town, features spacious and spotless rooms, with microwaves and fridges, starting at $38 and climbing $10 June-Aug. At the eastern end of downtown, **Budget Inn ❷,** 251 E. Winnemucca Blvd. (☎623-2394), offers a lot of bang for your buck in rooms with microwaves, refrigerators, and cable TV, starting at $25. Outside of town, **Hi-Desert RV Park ❶,** 5575 E. Winnemucca Blvd. (☎623-4513), touts grassy, full hookups for $22.50 and tent sites for $16, along with a ton of amenities. For campers, the BLM's **Water Creek Recreation Area ❶,** up Water Canyon Rd., has free, aspen-shaded sites, but no facilities. (Take Hanson St. south 4.5 mi. 3-night limit.)

At **Las Margaritas ❷,** 47 E. Winnemucca Blvd., tasty margaritas complement mountainous Mexican dishes. The extensive menu ranges from single tacos ($1.75) to massive, $9 super burritos. (☎625-2262. Open M-Sa 11am-9pm, Su 11am-8pm.) **DJ's Flyin' Pig Bar-B-Q ❷,** 1100 W. Winnemucca Blvd., smokes some of the best pork around. The BBQ Pig Sandwich ($6.95) feeds one, but the Ribs, Ribs, Ribs platter ($28) fills 4-6 people. (☎623-4104. Open Su-Th 6am-11pm, F-Sa 6am-12am.) The **Winnemucca Hotel and Bar ❷,** 95 Bridge St., has served up Basque food family-style since 1863. The town's oldest building houses an classic bar and a family kitchen that cooks epic meals. The six-course lunch is a steal at $7, while dinner runs $14. (☎623-2908. Open daily for lunch 12-1pm, dinner 6:15-9pm.)

ELKO & THE RUBY MOUNTAINS   ☎775

While countless other Nevadan towns have decayed, Elko (pop. 34,047) has charted a different course. Three of the West's most prosperous industries—mining, ranching, and gaming—have nurtured Elko's sharp ascent. Now, 1993's "Best Small Town in America," proudly serves as the commercial and governmental heart of northern Nevada, welcoming visitors from across the country thanks to its new airport. The Ruby Mountains, which got their name when early settlers mistook the garnets they found in Lamoille Creek for rubies, are Elko's big draw for adventurers, and these jewels in the region's crown are the real deal. In the 21st century Elko looks set to continue to thrive, at least until the costs of extracting microscopic gold particles from the Carlin Trend begin to exceed the profits. The town's prosperity has set the stage for modernity's clash with tradition, a conflict visible as boot repair shops and taxidermists brush up against yoga centers and cellular phone suppliers. It's still unclear who will win this showdown.

▌▀ TRANSPORTATION

Flights: Elko Regional Airport, 775 Terminal Way (☎777-7190), off Mountain City Hwy. **Skywest** (☎738-5138, 800-221-1212) flies to **Reno** (1-3 times daily) and **Salt Lake City** (3-5 times daily), while **Casino Express** (☎738-1826, 800-258-8800; www.casinoexpressairlines.com) flies charter flights to many smaller West and Midwest destinations for about $150.

Trains: Amtrak (☎800-872-7245). South of town, the westbound stop is on Water St. off of 11th St.; the eastbound stop is on Sharps Access off of 12th St. Runs trains to **Reno** (6hr., 1 per day, $50) and **Salt Lake City** (6hr., 1 per day, $38).

Buses: Greyhound, 1950 E. Idaho St. (☎738-3210, 800 231-2222), in the Tesoro service station next to Chuck's Oil City, runs 6 buses daily along I-80. To: **Reno** (5hr., 3 per day, $49-52) and **Salt Lake City** (5hr., 4 per day, $48-51).

Public Transit: Northeastern Area Transit (NEAT; ☎ 777-1428), operates city buses up and down Idaho St. ($1) and to Spring Creek ($2). M-F 9am-3pm.

Taxi: Elko Taxi (☎ 738-1400).

Car Rental: Avis, at the airport (☎ 738-4426). Open M-F 7am-10:30pm, Sa 8am-5:30pm, Su 8am-10:30pm. **Enterprise,** also at the airport (☎ 738-2899). Open Su-Th 7:30am-8pm, F 7:30am-7pm, Sa 8am-1pm.

■ 🛈 ORIENTATION & PRACTICAL INFORMATION

Located on I-80 near the Idaho and Utah borders, Elko is 230 mi. from Salt Lake City (p. 246) and 295 mi. from Reno (p. 210). Hwy. 225 heads north from town toward Boise (255 mi.). Elko spreads out along **Idaho Street,** with the center of downtown at the intersection of 5th St. and Idaho. Fast food and chain motels cluster near the I-80 interchanges at both ends of town. Heading southeast on Lamoille Hwy. (Hwy. 227), the suburban community of Spring Creek is sandwiched between Elko and the verdant Ruby Mountains. To reach the Lamoille Canyon and the Rubies, take either 12th St. or 5th St. south to Lamoille Highway, and continue for 20 mi. With a mountain backdrop, Lamoille is a ranching community with a small-town feel.

Visitor Information: Elko Chamber of Commerce, 1405 Idaho St. (☎ 738-7135, 800-428-7143; www.elkonevada.com), at Sherman Station. Home to pamphlets upon pamphlets of Elko info and a large staff to answer any questions. The Visitors Center stands in an exhibit of transplanted log cabins from frontier Nevada. Ask about the town's 5 brothels—the most of any town in the state.

Bank: Bank of America, 605 Idaho St. (☎ 738-7203.) Open M-Th 9am-5pm, F 9am-6pm, Sa 9am-1pm. **24hr. ATM.**

Laundromat: Jet Coin OP, 332 6th St. (☎ 738-7802). Open daily 7am-9pm.

Road Conditions: ☎ 877-NV-ROADS/687-6237.

Emergency: ☎ 911. **Crisis Line:** ☎ 738-9454.

Police: 1401 College Ave. (☎ 777-7300), at the corner of 14th St. and College Ave.

Pharmacy: Smith's, 1740 Mountain City Hwy. (☎ 777-1333). Open 24hr. Pharmacy open M-F 9am-9pm, Sa 9am-7pm, Su 10am-6pm.)

Hospital: Northeastern Nevada Regional Hospital, 2001 Errecart Blvd. (☎ 738-5151), off Lamoille Hwy. 2 mi. south of town.

Library: Elko Public Library, 720 Court St. (☎ 738-3066), offers **free Internet access.** Open M-Tu 9am-8pm, W-Th 9am-6pm, and F-Sa 9am-5pm.

Post office: 275 3rd St. (☎ 777-9803). Open M-Sa 8:30am-5pm. **Postal code:** 89801.

🏠 🏕 ACCOMMODATIONS & CAMPING

Inexpensive rooms abound in Elko, nearly all of them along Idaho St. During summer months, excellent camping attracts many to Lamoille Canyon, about 20 mi. south of town. Take Lamoille Hwy. (Hwy. 227) southeast to Lamoille Canyon Rd., which climbs 12 mi. into the Rubies' wilds. For free **dispersed camping,** take the dirt road to the private **Camp Lamoille,** 5 mi. from the intersection of Lamoille Canyon Rd. and Hwy. 227, and camp at one of the established sites along the creekbed.

▧ **Lamoille Hotel,** on Hwy. 227 in Lamoille, (☎ 753-6363), 20 mi. south of Elko. Small, cozy, and family-owned. 3 rooms for $65 each, double/triple occupancy with living room, A/C, and satellite TV; kids stay free. Great food at the adjacent **Pine Lodge** (dinner Tu-Su 5-9pm). Call ahead to reserve rooms, especially on May-Sept. weekends. ❹

Thunderbird Motel, 345 Idaho St. (☎ 738-7115). This upscale motel in the center of town features spacious, modern rooms with a pool on the premises and complimentary breakfast buffet at the Red Lion Inn down the street. Singles start at $49, doubles $59. Prices drop about $10 in slow periods. ❸

Towne House Motel, 500 W. Oak St. (☎ 738-7269), off Idaho St. Clean rooms with microwaves, fridges, cable TV, A/C. Singles $32-36; doubles $36-48. ❷

Thomas Canyon Campground, 8 mi. into the Lamoille Canyon Scenic Byway. There are developed campsites, potable water, and vault toilets. Tent sites $14. ❶

◖ FOOD

Despite Elko's role as epicenter of northeastern Nevada, its range of dining options generally includes steak, steak, and steak. Still, there are a couple spots that break the mold. For those who want to do it themselves, **Roy's Grocery,** 560 Idaho St., carries an extensive selection of Mexican items in addition to the standard line up. (☎ 738-3173. Open M-Sa 6am-10pm, Su 8am-9pm.)

Just Pastries, 382 5th St. (☎ 753-7816). Despite the name, this Italian restaurant dishes out homemade pastas like spaghetti *aglio-olio* (garlic and oil), fresh breads, and delectable deserts in a stylishly simple setting. Sandwiches go for $4-5 while pasta dishes run $7-9. Open Su 5-9pm, M 11am-2pm, and Tu-Sa 11am-2pm and 5-9pm. ❷

Star Hotel & Restaurant, 246 Silver St. (☎ 738-9925, 753-8696). Folks flock from miles around to dine at Elko's oldest Basque eatery. Sidle up to the bar for a drink while you wait for a spot at a table and a family-style dinner ($13-23). Lamb and steaks are the specialties. Open M-F 11:30am-2pm and 5-9:30pm, Sa 5-9:30pm. ❸

Sergio's, 739 Idaho St. (☎ 777-7736). This Sonoran-style Mexican joint feels as though it could have been transplanted straight from Juarez. Ruby-red booths and bare walls allow diners to focus on the biggest burritos ($4) in town at the lowest prices. Open M-Th 9am-9pm, F-Sa 8am-10pm. ❸

The Grill at O'Carroll's Bar, on Hwy. 227 in Lamoille (☎ 753-6451). Delicious breakfasts ($3.50-7) are perfect before a trek into the Rubies, but the lunch (sandwiches $4.50-7.50) and dinner menu could leave you too full for a backcountry trip. Juicy ribeye steak on a slice of sourdough runs only $7. M-Th 8am-4pm, F-Su 8am-8pm. ❷

◉ ◘ SIGHTS & FESTIVALS

Elko celebrates cowboy culture with museums, exhibits, and annual events. The **Western Folklife Center,** 501 Railroad St., in the historic Pioneer Hotel, is perhaps the premier national institution devoted to the subject. (☎ 738-7508; www.westernfolklife.org. Open M, W-F 10am-5:30pm, Tu 10:30am-5:30pm, Sa 10am-5pm. Free.) The exhibit gallery features Native American arts and examples of cowboy craftsmanship, among other treasures. The center's annual **National Cowboy Poetry Gathering,** held in late January, draws sagebrush bards and crowds of thousands from throughout the West. (☎ 738-7508, 888-880-5885.) To see how cowboys do it these days, walk across the street to **J.M. Capriola Company,** 500 Commercial St., where 70 years of experience in leather crafting is brought to bear in creating some of the West's best saddles. (☎ 738-5816; www.capriola.com. Open M-F 8am-5:30pm, Sa 9am-5:30pm.) Elko boasts the highly informative **Northeastern Nevada Museum.** With galleries featuring contemporary art by the likes of Ansel Adams and Edward Weston, exhibits of local history, mining, and ranching practices, Nevada's largest gun collection, and over 200 hunting-trophy taxidermies with animals from seven continents, the museum has something for everyone. (1515 Idaho St. ☎ 738-3418. Open M-Sa 9am-5pm, Su 1-5pm. Adults $5, 13-18 and 65+ $3, 3-12 $1, under 3 free.)

Other popular town events are the **National Basque Festival** (☎738-1240), held in early July to celebrate the Basque heritage of many Elko natives, and the enormous **Elko Mining Expo** (☎738-4091), held in mid-June, which boasts the mind-boggling "heavy equipment games." One of the most exciting events is the **Silver State Stampede,** which draws rodeo fans to the county fairgrounds in July. (☎738-3616.)

Just a short drive from Elko, visitors can tour the working ranches and beautiful vistas of cowboy country. The expansive grazing lands of Elko County offer a glimpse into the West's past. A slew of ranches package this experience into commercial opportunities, granting outsiders a chance to live the cowboy life, if they have credit cards in tow. Contact **Eagle's Nest Station** (☎744-4370), **Jazz Ranch** (☎777-3277), **Reds Ranch** (☎753-6281), **Ruby Crest Ranch** (☎744-2277) or the Visitors Center for more info.

🎵 🎭 ENTERTAINMENT & NIGHTLIFE

Elko is home to four casinos, each of which run booming 24hr. business. The **Red Lion Inn and Casino,** 2065 Idaho St. (☎738-2111, 800-545-0044), and the **Gold Country Inn and Casino,** 2050 Idaho St. (☎738-8421, 800-621-1332), are affiliated and located across the street from each other at the eastern end of town. Downtown, the **Stockmen's Casino,** 340 Commercial St. (☎738-5141), and its sister property, the **Commercial Casino,** 345 4th St. (7☎38-3181), capitalize on Elko's cowboy culture. Each casino tries to pry your money from your pocket with familiar games like blackjack and roulette. The Red Lion and Gold Country run 24hr. restaurants. The recently remodeled Commercial is over 100 years old, its main entrance guarded by a 10 ft. polar bear called "White King."

Despite the dominance of the casinos, some of Elko's best nightlife centers on a few downtown bars. The **Stray Dog Pub,** 374 5th St., has 15 beers on tap, including local microbrews, and serves up great appetizers (Asiago cheese dip, $4) and sandwiches (grilled eggplant, $6) in a hip setting. (☎753-4888. Cafe open daily 3pm-9pm, pub 3pm-last customer.) The **Silver Dollar Club,** 400 Commercial St., is a converted bank with parking reserved for Harleys. A trough beneath the bar marks the place where miners used to relieve themselves when nature called. More modern amenities include bathrooms and a pool table. (☎777-1475. Open daily 24hr.)

🏔 OUTDOOR ACTIVITIES

Elko is tucked between two glaciated ranges, the Jarbidge, which includes some of the state's wildest mountains, and the Rubies, which present almost unlimited opportunities for wilderness adventures. For info on outdoor activities, stop by the **Forest Service Ranger Station,** 2035 Last Chance Rd., and be sure to grab a copy of the guide to the Rubies. (☎738-5171. Open M-F 7:30am-4:30pm.) The **Elko BLM,** 3900 E. Idaho St., is another good resource for backcountry exploration. (☎753-0200. Open M-F 7:30am-4:30pm). Elko's one true outdoors store, the **Cedar Creek Clothing Company,** 453 Idaho St., offers backcountry essentials, advice on hiking and rock climbing in the Rubies, and ski and snowshoe rentals. (☎738-3950. Open Tu-Sa 9am-5:30pm. Alpine skis $20-25, cross-country $15, snowshoes $10.) It also carries local Larry Hyslop's helpful compendium of hikes in the Rubies. Visit **T-Rix Bicycles,** 717 W. Idaho St., at the intersection of Idaho and Mountain City Hwy., to discuss the area's growing riding opportunities, rent a steed for $20-25 per day, or take part in Thursday night group rides. (☎777-8804. Open M-Sa 9am-6pm.)

The **Ruby Mountains** are the primary playground for Elko's wilderness junkies. The most easily accessible area in the Rubies is stunning Lamoille Canyon, dubbed "Nevada's Yosemite" by locals. The Rubies are characterized by rocky peaks, cirque basins, high glacial lakes, and steep, narrow canyons. The mountains offer excellent hiking, mountaineering, and skiing, among other outdoor opportunities. Bird enthusiasts keep a look out for the exotic Himalayan snowcocks who inhabit perches in glacial-cirques. This rare species thrived in the Rubies after being introduced in the 1960s. Lamoille Lake and Lamoille Creek are great spots for brook and rainbow trout **fishing**. Much of the land surrounding the National Forest is private, making Lamoille Canyon the main jumping-off point for range exploration. This sort of concentrated access means that by going off-trail from Lamoille, experienced backcountry explorers can spend days in trailless, infrequently-traveled wilderness. Heavy snow generally remains in the Rubies until mid-June (sometimes into July) and returns again by November.

DAY HIKES

The **Lamoille Lake/Liberty Pass** (4-6 mi. round-trip, 3-5hr.) trail sets out from the end of Lamoille Canyon Rd. Following the first 3 mi. of the Ruby Crest trail, this day hike begins at 8800 ft. and climbs to Liberty Pass at 10,450 ft., passing several small pools and the larger Lamoille Lake. Keep your eyes peeled for mountain goats and bighorn sheep. Many day hikers turn around after 2 mi. at Lamoille Lake, but the views are spectacular from the pass. Snow lingers at higher elevations well into summer. **Island Lake's** (4 mi. round-trip, 3-4 hr.) trailhead lies just before the parking lot at the end of Lamoille Canyon Rd. This relatively untrodden hike switches back and forth along the canyon's western wall and climbs to lovely Island Lake, surrounded by huge peaks. **Thomas Canyon Trail** (4 mi. round-trip, 2-3hr.) begins from the trailhead at the rear of the Thomas Canyon Campground. This moderate trail climbs gradually along the canyon floor, follows the creek, and tops out at a glacial cirque with two cascading waterfalls.

BACKPACKING

The **Ruby Crest National Recreation Trail** begins at the end of Lamoille Canyon Rd. and winds 43 mi. through the Ruby Wilderness to Harrison Pass. This remote route begins at 8800 ft., averages 9500 ft., and finishes at Harrison around 7500 ft. The trail passes above striking glacial valleys and near spectacular alpine lakes surrounded by jagged peaks. Expect to see few other hikers and plenty of wildlife, including mountain goats and bighorn sheep. There is limited water during the middle section of the hike from North Furlong Lake to Overland Lake (10 mi.); budget four to five days for the complete route.

OTHER OUTDOOR ACTIVITIES

The Rubies offer some great **rock climbing** on its glaciated granite formations, with a number of top-roped routes on western faces near the canyon entrance. There's more climbing in the **Abode Range** a few miles north of Elko. Both trad and sport routes have been established on faces here. To reach the crags take 5th St. north from town until the pavement ends and go on about 5 mi. to the Sno Bowl turnoff, where the left fork leads to climbing areas.

Elko also boasts northeastern Nevada's only **backcountry alpine skiing**. **Ruby Mountains Heli-Skiing** (☎ 753-7628, 753-6867), runs trips into the backcountry of the Ruby and Independence Ranges each winter via helicopter and snow cat, taking advantage of the exquisite powder in the Great Basin's wettest range. **Cedar Creek Clothing Company** (p. 235) is a good resource for do-it-yourself backcountry skiing info. Downhill skiing at **Elko's Sno-Bowl** (☎ 738-4431), 5 mi. north of downtown, gains more fans each season. The ski area is community-run, so lift tickets are cheap ($125 per season). Ski and snowboard rentals are also available at the lift ($15). In the summer, several good **mountain bike** routes cruise the slopes.

Southeast of the range, about 60 mi. from Elko, the **Ruby Lake Wildlife Refuge** is a 17,000-acre landing strip and motor lodge for more than 220 species of migrating waterfowl in spring and fall. Reach the refuge and its campground by following Hwy. 228 out of Spring Creek over the recently paved Harrison Pass. For more info about hunting and fishing in the area, contact the **Nevada Division of Wildlife,** 60 Youth Center Rd., east of town off of Idaho St. (☎777-2300. Open M-F 8am-5pm.)

WENDOVER & BONNEVILLE SALT FLATS   ☎775

Straddling the Utah-Nevada border, Wendover presents a dual personality to travelers and a much-needed respite from miles of desolate desert expanses. On the Nevada side of the border (West Wendover), a modern-day boomtown glitters in the scorching sun, built around thriving casinos and little else. In Utah a tiny community with a small-town feel bakes on the salt flats—both sides operate on **Mountain Time.** This dialectic creates a synthetic strip of casinos, gas stations, motels, and fast food joints. Just east of Wendover, UT, at exit 4 of I-80, the barren salt flats of the **Bonneville Speedway** have hosted land speed record racing since 1914. The speedway, 80 ft. wide and 10 mi. long, is part of 44,000 acres of public lands administered by the BLM. Speed trials like **Bonneville Speed Week** (mid-Aug.) and the **Bonneville World Finals** (mid-Oct.) are held throughout late summer and fall. During the rest of the year the flats are often underwater. Call **Mr. Tow** (☎435-665-2525) if you get stuck. Southeast of town on the flats around the **Wendover Army Air Field,** the Enola Gay pilots used dummy bombs during the months leading up to August 11, 1945 to drill the procedures involved in atomic deployment. The field is now the **Wendover Airport,** 345 S. Airport Apron (☎435-665-2308), off 1st St. in Wendover, UT, which caters to small private planes and is home to a great small museum that chronicles the US Army's presence in Wendover.

Visit the **West Wendover Tourism & Convention Bureau's Nevada Welcome Center,** 735 Wendover Blvd., for info on Wendover's historic sites and current attractions. (☎664-3138, 866-299-2489. Open daily 9am-5pm, sometimes earlier.) If stranded in Wendover and desperate for relief, **Greyhound** bus (☎800-231-2222) runs out of the **Pilot Travel Center,** 1200 W. Wendover Blvd. (☎664-3400), heading to **Reno** (2 per day, 6hr., $66-68) and **Salt Lake** (3 per day, 2hr., $29-31). **Wendover Area Transit** zips down Wendover Blvd. in both states daily from 7am-1am ($0.50). Services include: **24hr. ATM** at **Keybank,** 245 E. Wendover Blvd. (☎435-665-2283; open M-F 9am-5pm); **emergency** (☎911); **West Wendover Police,** 801 Florence Way (☎664-2930); a **pharmacy** at **Smith's,** 1855 W. Wendover Blvd. (☎664-3197; open M-F 10am-7pm, Sa 9am-1pm); **Wendover Community Health Center,** 925 Wells Ave. (☎664-2220; open M-Sa 8am-5pm.); **Fred's Laundromat,** 215 E. Wendover Blvd. (☎435-665-2322; open 24hr.); **Wendover Library,** 590 Camper Dr. (☎664-2510), with **Internet access;** and the **post office,** 810 Alpine St. (☎664-2929. Open M-F 8:30am-4:30pm.) **Postal Code:** 89883.

Wendover is a weekend getaway town for gambling folk, so rates for accommodations at the casinos fluctuate wildly depending on the day of the week and season. On the Nevada side of Wendover Blvd., five casinos nearly monopolize the lodging market. Weekday rates plummet, but on busy weekends, prices soar and rooms book rapidly. At the far western end of Wendover Blvd., **The Red Garter Casino ❷** seduces guests with low promotional rates. (☎982-2111. Rooms Su-Th $22, F $40 and up, Sa $50 and up.) Right on the Nevada-Utah line are Wendover's least tacky hotel/casinos, the **Montego Bay ❷** (☎877-666-8346) and the **State Line Nugget ❷** (☎800-848-7300). The newly renovated rooms at the Montego Bay are the best in town (rooms Su-Th $35, F $70, Sa $80), while the casino at the State Line, the oldest casino in town and home of the giant "Cowboy Bill", has recently been elegantly remodeled (rooms Su-Th $35, as high as $99 on weekends). Motel prices on the Utah side don't tend to fluctuate so much, making them the best deal in town on the weekends. One of the nicest is the made-over **Bonneville Inn ❸,** 375 E. Wendover Blvd., which has a pool and spacious rooms (☎435-665-2500. $40). Wendover also boasts a **KOA Campground ❶**, 651 N. Camper Dr., that accommodates RVs and tent-campers alike with a pool and laundry facilities. (☎664-3221. Tent sites $19, hookups $21.) If you've had enough of casino fare, head to **La Cabana ❷**, 1930 Plateau Way, in the mall above Smith's at the west end of town, for Mexican combo platters ($5-8) and the $2 ceviche. (☎664-3931. Open daily 10am-10pm.)

EAST CENTRAL NEVADA

Nearly 200 mi. south of Interstate 80 and 250 mi. north of Las Vegas, amid desert vegetation, the Snake Range, containing the highest peaks of the Basin and Range province, rises from the scrub. Due to the area's continued obscurity, the mining town of Ely and the backcountry of Great Basin National Park remain relatively undisturbed by the West's droves of summer tourists.

ELY   ☎ 775

With a lonely 70 mi. of U.S. 6 separating Ely (rhymes with "really") and the entrance to Great Basin National Park, this mining and gaming town hardly fits the profile of a typical "gateway" city, but its barren surroundings and the convergence of Hwys. 6, 50, and 93 make Ely the locus of much trans-Nevadan traffic. In the beginning of the century, development of the area's copper resources brought the county seat, an influx of residents, and a railroad system, but, with its natural wealth significantly depleted, today's Ely is a shadow of its old self. Remnants of past glory—like the stately Nevada Hotel and Casino, once the tallest building in the state—still line Ely's main drag, but the dilapidated storefronts and run-down motels give the impression of a town striving to reinvent itself as a crossroads for travelers in search of the West's many treasures.

Highways 6, 50, and **93** meet in Ely and radiate towards Reno (320 mi.), Vegas (245 mi.), Utah, Idaho, and California. **Gas** stations line the arteries as they approach town. Restaurants, shops, casinos, and budget motels crowd Ely's Autland St., a segment of Hwy. 50. **Nevada Express**, 430 Campton St., across from Sacred Heart Catholic Church on Murray St. (an extension of W. 4th St.), sends buses to Vegas. (☎289-2188, 289-2877; M-F 7am-5:30pm; every other week on Tu and F; one-way $47.) For tourist info, try the **White Pine County Chamber of Commerce**, at 636 Autland St. (☎289-8877. Open M-F 9am-5pm.)

Ely Ranger District, 350 E. 8th St., east of town off Hwy. 93, provides info on the Humboldt National Forest near Ely and Great Basin. (☎289-3031. Open M-F 7:30am-4:30pm.) Other services include: **Bank of America,** 1689 E. 7th St. (☎289-7900), in Gorman's Market on Great Basin Blvd., south of downtown, with a **24hr. ATM; Sportsworld,** 1500 Aultman St., for outdoor gear (☎289-8886; open M-Sa 8am-5:30pm, Sa 8:30am-4pm); **Great Basin Laundry Center,** 1230 Aultman St. (☎289-4012; open daily 7am-9pm, last wash 8pm); **road conditions** (☎877 NV-ROADS); **emergency** (☎911); **White County Sheriff,** 1785 Great Basin Blvd. (☎289-8808, 289-4833); **William Bee Ririe Hospital,** 1500 Ave. H (☎289-3001); free **Internet access** at **White Pine County Library,** 900 Campton St. (☎289-3737; open M-Th 9am-6pm, F 9am-5pm, 1st and 3rd Sa of each month 10am-2pm); and the **post office,** 2600 Bristlecone Ave. (☎289-9276. Open M-F 8:30am-5pm, Sa 10am-2pm.) **Postal code:** 89301.

Many of Ely's 17 hotels and motels are located on Aultman St. Far and away the best is the grand **Hotel Nevada ❷**, 501 Aultman St., a relic from another era. Many rooms are shrines to celebrities who have stayed here, like Mickey Rooney and Wayne Newton. (☎289-6665, 888-406-3055. Singles $30-38; doubles $40-48.) The **Rustic Inn ❷**, 1555 Aultman St., is one of the cheapest in town, with clean rooms kept by friendly owners. (☎289-6797. Singles from $25; doubles from $35.)

Aultman St. has several steak-and-potatoes chop houses, including restaurants in the downtown casinos. **Gorman's Market,** 1689 E. 7th St., fulfills supermarket needs. (☎289-3444. Open daily 7am-10pm.) When it comes to meals, **La Fiesta ❶** prepares lunch specials ($6.25-6.75) and the $10 Taquitos La Fiesta. (☎289-4112. Open daily 11am-9:30pm, lunch specials 11am-3pm.) For a change of pace, **Twin Wok ❷,** 700 Great Basin Blvd., bridges oceans with both Chinese and Japanese cuisine. Try Mandarin entrees ($8-10) or slightly pricier ($11-15) hibachi selections. (☎289-3699. Open daily 11am-10pm.)

GREAT BASIN NATIONAL PARK   ☎775

Great Basin, for many years a National Monument, was established as a National Park in 1986 on account of its many astounding offerings for outdoors enthusiasts: awe-inspiring glaciers, prehistoric pine trees, and miles of ornamented sauterne chambers and unrefined trails. As the only national park situated entirely within Nevada's borders, Great Basin National Park borrows its name from the geological region whose basin and range topography extends through much of the state. Wave upon wave of towering peaks and sandy valleys make up the entire Great Basin region, which earned its name because the region's water supplies can never escape to the ocean.

The park represents the area's geography at its wildest extremes. The Snake Range forms the north-south spine of the park; the park's various creeks, lakes, and forests sit in the shadow of its jagged peaks. Despite the apparent desolation of the Great Basin's vast desert stretches, each range's alpine environment supports a surprisingly diverse biological community. Nowhere in the region is this more true than in Great Basin National Park itself, which shelters several rare species of flora and fauna, including everything from the ancient bristlecone pine to the Golden Eagle. Far removed from the crowds and amenities of some of the West's other protected lands, Great Basin affords visitors the opportunity to explore its natural riches in peace.

AT A GLANCE: GREAT BASIN NATIONAL PARK	
AREA: 77,100 acres.	**GATEWAY TOWNS:** Ely (p. 238), Baker.
FEATURES: Wheeler Peak, Lehman Caves, Bristlecone pine groves.	**CAMPING:** Park campgrounds $10; backcountry camping free, no permit required.
HIGHLIGHTS: Touring the Grand Palace Room in Lehman Caves, hiking to the summit of Wheeler Peak, standing beneath the massive Lexington Arch.	**FEES:** No entrance fee, admission to Lehman Caves $2-8.

■ ORIENTATION

Tucked quietly away in eastern Nevada, Great Basin National Park lies 285 mi. from Las Vegas (p. 197), 235 mi. from Salt Lake City (p. 246), and 70 mi. from Ely (p. 238), its nearest Nevada neighbor of any size. The park lies south of Hwy. 6/50, and Hwy. 487 parallels the park to the east. Only one paved road, Highway 488, enters the park, from the east at the northern end, and it leads to the Visitors Center, providing access to all four of the park's developed campgrounds along the way. Improved gravel roads grant access to the park's northern reaches and central drainage, while a high-clearance dirt road ventures into the park's wild southern mountains. Ely bills itself as a gateway to the park and offers most comforts, but the small town of Baker (5 mi. from the Visitors Center) and the Border Inn (13 mi. from the park on U.S. 6/50) also provide basic services.

WHEN TO GO. Because of its elevation (the Visitors Center is at 6825 ft.), Great Basin remains tolerably cool, even in the thick of the summer. In July and August, the two most popular months to visit, highs hover in the mid-80s. Winter highs average in the low 40s, lows in the 10s and 20s. October may be the best time to visit the park as visitation drops off and the leaves change color, but temperatures remain in the 50s and 60s. Only Lower Lehman Campground remains open year-round. Although the park rarely experiences significant crowding, visitors in the off-season may have the entire park to themselves.

⚡ PRACTICAL INFORMATION

As any trip to a national park should, a visit to Great Basin begins with an informational foray to the Visitors Center. The **Great Basin National Park Visitors Center** greets travelers at the end of Hwy. 488 with a bookstore, theater, and park info desk. (☎234-7331; www.nps.gov/grba. Open May-Oct. daily 7:30am-5:30pm, Nov.-Apr. 8am-4:30pm.) ATV use, hunting, and possession of firearms and fireworks are prohibited in the park. **Backcountry camping** does not require a permit, but the park recommends completing a backcountry registration form at the Visitors Center before beginning your trek. The Forest Service permits horses, mules, burros, and llamas on trails and in the backcountry, but pets are prohibited there and must be leashed while in campgrounds. Mountain bikers can pedal any of the park's roads but are excluded from the trail system.

Most services lie in Baker or at the Border Inn (p. 240), which offers rooms, an **ATM**, a **convenience store**, a bar and greasy-spoon diner, **laundry facilities**, **showers** ($3; $4.50 with towels, soap, and shampoo), and the only **gas** on Hwy. 6/50 between Ely and Delta, UT. Other services include: **road conditions** (☎877 NV ROADS/687-6237); **emergency** (☎911); **medical facilities** 70 mi. away in Ely (although the Park Service is prepared to conduct emergency rescues); and the **post office**, at Baker Ave. and Carson St., in Baker. (☎234-7231. Open M-F 8:30am-noon and 1-4:30pm, Sa 8:30-11:30am.) **Postal code:** 89311.

🏠 🏕 ACCOMMODATIONS & CAMPING

Four developed campgrounds (not including the site near Baker Creek) accommodate Great Basin visitors, in addition to several primitive sites along Snake and Strawberry Creeks and nearly unlimited backcountry camping. Scenic **primitive camping ❶**, with fire grates, picnic tables, and pit toilets at some sites, rewards the visitor willing to travel gravel roads off the beaten path. **Snake Creek Road,** a little more than 5 mi. south of Baker off of Hwy. 487, travels through the lush Snake Creek drainage and allows easy access to six primitive sites. **Strawberry Creek Road,** 3.5 mi. north of the Hwy. 50/6 and Hwy. 487 junction, leads to four primitive sites along Strawberry Creek.

Silver Jack Motel, 14 Main St. (☎234-7323), in Baker. Cheery rooms adorned with antiques and quilts, and cabins complete with kitchens. Singles $39; doubles $44. ❸

Border Inn (☎234-7300), straddling the UT/NV border along Hwy. 50/6. Caters to the trucker crowd (non-smokers pay more), with sizeable rooms featuring TVs and VCRs. Movies are available for a $5 deposit. Singles $31-36; doubles $37-42. ❷

Wheeler Peak Campground (9890 ft.). Offers the most scenic sites, nestled among aspen groves and pine forests in the shadow of 13,063 ft. Wheeler Peak. Access to the campground comes at the end of the serpentine Wheeler Peak Scenic Drive (not recommended for vehicles over 24 ft.), 12 mi. from the Visitors Center. Open June-Sept. Pit toilets and potable water. 37 sites, 1 wheelchair accessible. $10. ❶

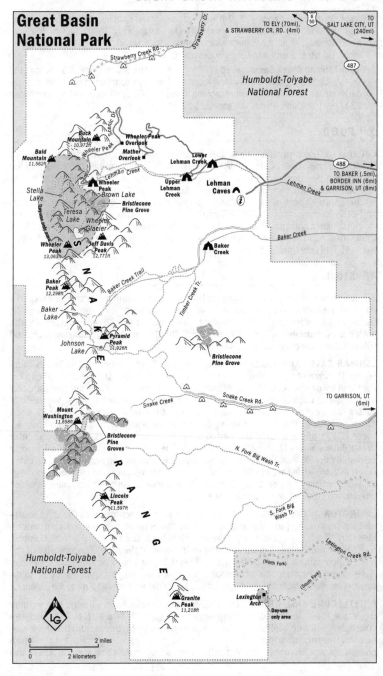

Great Basin National Park

TO ELY (70mi)
& STRAWBERRY CR. RD. (4mi)

TO
SALT LAKE CITY, UT
(240mi)

6
50

487

Humboldt-Toiyabe
National Forest

Strawberry Cr.

Strawberry Creek Rd.

Buck
Mountain
10,972ft

Wheeler Peak
Overlook

Mather
Overlook

Scenic Dr.

Wheeler Peak Scenic Dr.

Lower
Lehman Creek

Bald
Mountain
11,562ft

Lehman Creek

Wheeler
Peak

Upper
Lehman
Creek

Lehman
Caves

488

TO BAKER (.5mi),
BORDER INN (6mi)
& GARRISON, UT (8mi)

Lehman Creek

Stella
Lake

Brown Lake

Bristlecone
Pine Grove

Teresa
Lake

Wheeler
Glacier

Baker Creek

Wheeler
Peak
13,063ft

Jeff Davis
Peak
12,771ft

Baker
Creek

Baker
Peak
12,298ft

Baker Creek Trail

Timber Creek Tr.

Baker
Lake

S N A K E

Johnson
Lake

Pyramid
Peak
11,926ft

Bristlecone
Pine Grove

Snake Creek

Snake Creek Rd.

TO GARRISON, UT
(6mi)

Mount
Washington
11,658ft

Bristlecone
Pine
Groves

N. Fork Big Wash Tr.

R A N G E

Lincoln
Peak
11,597ft

S. Fork Big
Wash Tr.

Lexington Creek Rd.

Humboldt-Toiyabe
National Forest

(North Fork)

(South Fork)

Granite
Peak
11,218ft

Lexington
Arch

Day-use
only area

N
LG

0   2 miles
0   2 kilometers

NEVADA

Baker Creek Campground (7530 ft.). The graded gravel road headed south off of Hwy. 488 just within the park boundary passes by this serene spot. Perched on the banks of Baker Creek, 3.5 mi. from the Visitors Center. Open May-Oct. Pit toilets and potable water. 34 sites, 2 with wheelchair access. $10. ❶

Upper Lehman Creek Campground (7800 ft.). Along the Scenic Drive, 3.5 mi. from the Visitors Center. Try sites 17-24 for a more removed and spacious stay. Hosts informational ranger talks during summer months. Open May-Oct. Pit toilets and potable water. 23 sites, 1 site with wheelchair access. $10. ❶

🍴 FOOD

Catering to those unwilling to trek to Baker or pack their own grub, the Visitors Center's **Lehman Caves Cafe ❶** serves breakfast ($5), deli sandwiches ($5), and ice cream, and peddles all manner of national park memorabilia. (☎234-7221. Open Apr.-May and Sept.-Oct. daily 8am-4pm, kitchen until 2:30pm; June-Aug. 8am-5pm, kitchen 4pm.) For a more substantial menu, check out **T&D's ❶** restaurant, bar, and convenience store in the center of Baker. The store (open daily 8am-7pm) stocks grocery and camping essentials, and the restaurant serves breakfasts ($3-4, F-Su), deli sandwiches and burgers ($4-7), and Mexican favorites. (☎234-7264. Open M-Th 11am-9pm, F-Su 7am-9pm.)

👁 SIGHTS

Because much of the park remains undeveloped, exploring its far reaches requires good hiking boots, plenty of water, several days of food, and strong legs. Luckily, for those not enthusiastic about hauling a burly pack through the backcountry, the park's most notable features, **Wheeler Peak, Bristlecone Groves, Lexington Arch,** and **Lehman Cave,** are accessible via shorter excursions.

LEHMAN CAVE. Absalom Lehman came across these splendid caves in 1885, and before the turn of the century he was charging visitors for the pleasure of exploring them by candlelight. They continue to delight travelers with their fantastic formations. The Park Service prohibits self-guided tours, offering three varieties of **guided tours:** entrance into the first room only, the Gothic Palace *(30min.; $2, under 12 free)*; a tour of the Gothic Palace, Lodge Room, and Inscription Room *(1hr.; $6; under 12 $3)*; and a tour of the entire accessible cave including the spectacular **Grand Palace Room** *(1½hr.; $8, under 12 $4)*. The cave remains at 50°F all year, a refreshing break from the sun in the summer months; just be sure to bring an extra layer. *Advance tickets ☎234-7331, ext. 242. Tours every half hour from mid-June to mid-Aug. 8am-4:30pm; every 2 hr. Sept.-May 9am-3pm. Reservations recommended in summer. No children under 5 permitted on the Grand Palace tour.*

LEXINGTON ARCH. A mammoth, six-story limestone sculpture in the wild southeast section of the park, Lexington Arch is evidence of nature's powerful craftsmanship. The 3.4 mi. round-trip hike switches back and forth up several hundred feet before paralleling a drainage back to the base of the arch. The majority of the trail, which gains a total 820 ft., sits on Forest Service land, so dogs are welcome. *(Drive south 12.2 mi. from the intersection of Hwys. 487 and 488 through Garrison, UT, to the sign for Lexington Arch. Follow the rough, high-clearance dirt road nearly 12 mi. to the trailhead.)*

BRISTLECONE PINE GROVE. The Great Basin Bristlecones, gnarled but striking trees, are the world's oldest living organisms (see **Oh $#&%!!!,** p. 243). Bristlecones demonstrate biological adaptation to extreme environments; the trees sustain on mountain slopes where few other trees can by growing only when conditions are favorable and virtually hibernating when they are not. There are

OH $#&%!!! The dendrochronologist's worst nightmare: meticulously counting the rings on a tree you've just cut down, only to discover that you've killed the world's oldest living organism. Such a disaster occurred in 1964 when a researcher cut and sectioned a Great Basin bristlecone pine that had been growing on the side of Mt. Wheeler for over 4900 years. These gnarled trees thrive in incredibly adverse growing conditions and often look as though they're on death's door. In fact, it is those trees that grow in the harshest environments and appear to be closest to the abyss that live the longest. Larger, more robust bristlecones livin' the fat life in less extreme conditions only reach the tender age of 300 or 400 years. The reason these trees are so rugged comes from their ability to adapt to the ever-changing environment. During wet, warm, favorable years, the bristlecone develops as any other tree would, thickening its girth and sending out new branches. Unlike other trees, however, the bristlecone dies back during dry, cold years so that its living foliage can sustain given its available resources. Hence, large parts of these ancient trees are no longer living, while a minimal portion perseveres. Over the thousands of years, fierce winds and winter ice sculpt and polish the dense, resinous dead wood, giving the bristlecones their austere appearance. Understanding this growth/stasis cycle and measuring the width of bristlecone rings has provided vital climatological data about the past 4500 years. Scientists continue to study the trees to learn about ancient climates, but, learning from their colleague's folly, they now use core-sampling as an alternative to cutting and sectioning.

several bristlecone groves throughout the park, but the grove below Wheeler Peak is the easiest to access. Follow the Wheeler Peak Scenic Drive to the end and take the trail (600 ft. elevation gain, 2.8 mi. round-trip) from **Bristlecone Trailhead** to the famous trees. Ranger-guided tours depart from the trailhead at 10am a few days a week during July and Aug. Check at the Visitors Center for more information.

⚑ OUTDOOR ACTIVITIES

For the experienced **spelunker,** the park contains extensive limestone caverns. Exploring them requires a permit from the Park Service, acquired two weeks in advance and with proof of significant prior caving experience. Although cycling in the park is limited to roads, **mountain bikers** will relish excellent riding at the BLM's Sacramento Pass Recreation Site, east of the park along Hwy. 50/6. Some of the best trails in the area explore Black Horse Canyon, northeast of the park, accessible off of Hwy. 6/50 via the marked forest road, ¾ mi. south of Sacramento Pass.

DAY HIKING

Several trails along the Wheeler Peak Scenic Drive grant ample opportunities to peel off the car seat and stretch weary legs. For a less crowded jaunt, try the longer trails departing from the Baker Creek Trailhead.

Mountain View Nature Trail (0.3 mi. round-trip; 30min.). Beginning at Rhodes Cabin next to the Visitors Center, this trail provides a brief glimpse into park ecology and geology for those pressed for time. Stop by the Visitors Center for an informative trail guide.

Alpine Lakes Loop Trail (2.7 mi. round-trip; 1½-2½hr.). This gradual climb (600 ft. elevation gain) on a heavily used trail allows quick access to 2 scenic lakes, Stella and Teresa, carved out by glaciers in the last Ice Age, as well as good views of Wheeler Peak, which looms overhead. Trailhead located at the end of Wheeler Peak Scenic Drive.

Lehman Creek Trail (7 mi. round-trip; 4-6hr.). This is the only day hike in Great Basin National Park that is flagged for winter use by hikers. The Lehman Creek Trail is a

NEVADA

steeply pitched jaunt that hugs the babbling creek that gives it its name for much of its course, with over 2000 ft. in elevation change through a range of Great Basin habitats. The trail departs from either the end of Wheeler Peak Scenic Drive or either of the Lehman Creek campgrounds.

Wheeler Peak Trail (8.2 mi. round-trip; 5-8hr.). From the trailhead parking lot near the top of the Wheeler Peak Scenic Drive, this strenuous trek (elevation gain 2900 ft.) follows the precipitous ridgeline, affording endless views east and west, to the summit of Wheeler Peak (13,063 ft.). Because of the afternoon thunderstorm potential, hikers should start early and bring warm clothing and raingear. Altitude sickness and extreme weather conditions are constant threats at these elevations.

Baker Lake Trail (12 mi. round-trip; 6-9hr.). A trek to pristine Baker Lake for the ambitious day-hiker. The trail begins at the Baker Lake Trailhead (8000 ft.) and climbs gradually past great vistas to the lovely alpine lake surrounded by cliffs (10,620 ft.). Few attempt the long haul, creating potential backcountry solitude along a well-marked trail. The route can also be a 2-day, up-and-back overnight hike.

BACKPACKING
Southern stretches of the park offer a slew of potential wilderness routes for the experienced hiker. There are no maintained trails in the park south of Snake Creek; proficient map and compass skills are vital. Much of the backcountry rises above 9000 ft., and snow cover prevents pedestrian passage for most of the year. Even at lower elevations, travel is not much easier, as bushwacking through mountain mahogany can be nearly impossible. One of the park's most popular excursions is the **Baker Lake/Johnson Lake Loop** (13.1 mi. round-trip; 2-3 days). Beginning at the Baker Lake trailhead (8000 ft.), this hike travels to Baker Lake (10,620 ft.) and over a high ridge (11,290 ft.) offering spectacular panoramic views, then down to Johnson Lake. Both lakes afford well-deserved solitude and scenic camping. The trail is well-marked for most of the way, with the exception of the steep climb between Baker and Johnson Lakes, where it's everyone for himself over the ridge. A variant of this loop travels from Baker Lake up the south face of Baker Peak (12,298 ft.) and along the knife-like ridgeline to Wheeler Peak.

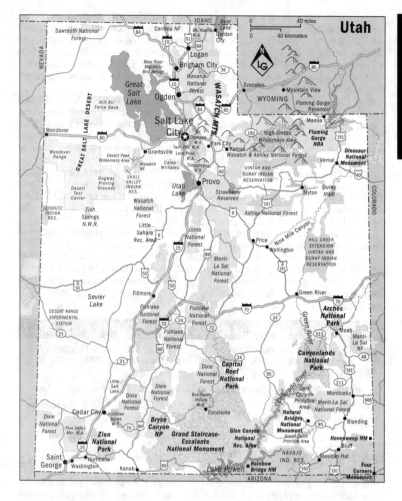

UTAH

From the majestic peaks of the Wasatch Mountains to the sculpted slickrock of its southern deserts, Utah is a land of contrasts, surprises, and profound beauty. Whether hiking deep within the cathedral walls of a slot canyon, floating weightlessly atop the Great Salt Lake, or traversing a knifeblade ridge in Zion, a visitor can't help but wonder at the power and enormity of nature and geologic time.

Anglo settlement of this ancient land began in 1847, when Brigham Young arrived in the Salt Lake Valley with his flock of Mormon pioneers. Currently, over 60% of the state's population belongs to the Church of Jesus Christ of Latter Day Saints, and the Mormon lifestyle defines Utah's modern culture. Still, the state is not nearly as homogeneous as stereotypes and statistics might suggest. Bolstered by the 2002 Olympic Games, flourishing Salt Lake City hosts an array of increasingly diverse communities.

Most Utahns live in the 100 mi. corridor that runs between Salt Lake City and Provo, leaving the rest of the state sparsely populated and often well preserved. The so-called Grand Circle of five unbelievably spectacular national parks (Zion, Bryce, Capitol Reef, Canyonlands, and Arches), along with the rugged Grand Staircase-Escalante National Monument, stretch across the southern desert, offering countless opportunities for outdoors enthusiasts, including technicolor canyons, bizarre rock formations, and unlimited hiking. Throughout the state, remote alpine forests and high-altitude wilderness areas provide for solitude, adventure, and infinite awe. In the winter, the Wasatch Mountains, as well as Big and Little Cottonwood Canyons, rise as a backdrop to Salt Lake City and draw seas of skiers with the world's best powder and top-notch resort facilities.

Utah attracts thrill-seekers of all kinds, both from the formidable under-18 demographic that resides within its borders as well as from various communities of adventurers outside of Utah. In particular, the capital, Salt Lake City, has become an international gateway of sorts to the West, primarily on account of its many expert linguists, themselves former Mormon missionaries who have returned home to raise families and enjoy the splendor of the vast landscapes unfolding in every direction.

■ HIGHLIGHTS OF UTAH

MOAB. Though the area has quickly become a mecca for outdoors enthusiasts, hiking in the **Needles** (p. 286), exploring the remote **La Sal Mountains** (p. 279), and climbing the **Fisher Towers** (p. 278) will get you away from the crowd.

HIGHWAYS. Route 95 (p. 5) and **Route 12** (p. 318) have the best roadside vistas.

WILDERNESS. The high peaks of the **Uintas** (p. 269), and the narrows of **Escalante** (p. 314) encompass boundless acres of pristine wilderness.

SALT LAKE CITY   ☎ 801

Tired from five grueling months of travel, Brigham Young looked out across the Great Salt Lake and proclaimed: "This is the place." In this desolate valley where few trees grew, he ordered them planted and hoped that his small band of Mormon pioneers had finally found a haven where they could practice their religion freely, safe from the persecution they had faced in the East. To this day, Salt Lake City is still dominated by the influence of Mormons. The Church of Jesus Christ of Latter-Day Saints (LDS) owns the tallest office building downtown and welcomes visitors to Temple Square, the spiritual epicenter of the Mormon religion.

Yet despite its commitment to preserving tradition, Salt Lake is rapidly attracting high-tech firms (Utah has more computers per household than any other state in the United States), as well as droves of outdoor enthusiasts drawn by world-class ski resorts, rock climbing, and mountain trails. Though the state's population demographics reflect homogeneity—a mere 15% of its residents are members of ethnic minorities—its capital city supports a quite surprising variety of culturally diverse communities.

Salt Lake City

🏠 **ACCOMMODATIONS**
The Avenues Hostel, **4**
City Creek Inn, **2**
Ute Hostel, **12**

🍴 **FOOD**
Orbit, **7**
Red Iguana, **1**
Ruth's Diner, **9**
Sage's Cafe, **11**
Tibet Cafe Shambala, **3**

NIGHTLIFE
Bricks, **6**
Club Axis, **5**
DV8, **8**
Zipperz, **10**

TRAX Light Rail

▤ TRANSPORTATION

Flights: Salt Lake City International, 776 N. Terminal Dr. (☎575-2400), 6 mi. west of Temple Sq. UTA buses #50 and 150 run between the terminal and downtown ($1.25). Service ends at 6pm on Su and buses leave only hourly M-Sa 7-11pm. Taxi to Temple Sq. costs about $15. **Southwest Airlines** (☎800-435-9792) flies to: **Oakland** ($135); **Las Vegas** ($110); **Los Angeles** ($135); **Baltimore** ($323); and **Phoenix** ($142).

Trains: Amtrak, 340 S. 600 W (☎322-3510). *Be advised: the area around the station can be dangerous at night.* To **Denver** (15hr., 1 per day, $75-112) and **San Francisco** (19hr., 1 per day, $77-115). Station open daily 10:30pm-6am.

Buses: Greyhound, 160 W. South Temple (☎355-9579), near Temple Sq. To: **Denver** (7-10hr., 5 per day, $54); **Las Vegas** (12-13hr., 2 per day, $49); and **Los Angeles** (15-18hr., 2 per day, $93). Open daily 6:30am-11:30pm, summer 6:30am-2:30am, ticket window until 10:30pm.

Public Transit: Utah Transit Authority (UTA, ☎743-3882). Frequent service to University of Utah campus; buses suburbs, airport, mountain canyons, and the #11 express runs to Provo ($2.25). New TRAX light rail follows Main St. from downtown to Sandy and to the University of Utah. Buses every 20min.-1hr. M-Sa 6am-11pm. Fare $1-2, senior discounts, under 5 free. Maps available at libraries and the Visitors Center. UTA Buses and TRAX trains traveling downtown near the major sites are free.

Taxis: Ute Cab, ☎359-7788. Yellow Cab, ☎521-2100. City Cab, ☎363-5550.

Car Rental: Enterprise, 1148 S. Main St. (☎534-1622). Cars start at $40 per day. 21+ rentals require a license and credit card. Open M-F 7:30am-6pm, Sa 9am-noon.

■ ORIENTATION

The city's grid system may seem confusing at first but makes navigation easy once you get used to it. Brigham Young designated **Temple Square** as the heart of downtown. Street names increase in increments of 100 and indicate how many blocks east, west, north, or south they lie from Temple Sq.; the "0" points are **Main Street** (north-south) and **South Temple** (east-west). State St., West Temple, and North Temple are 100 level streets. Occasionally, streets are referred to as 13th S or 17th N, meaning 1300 S or 1700 N. Local address listings often include two numerical cross streets, acting as a type of coordinate system (no maps needed!). A building on 13th S (1300 S) might be listed as 825 E. 1300 S, meaning the cross street is 800 E (8th E). Smaller streets and those not in the grid may have non-numeric names.

■ PRACTICAL INFORMATION

Visitor info: Salt Palace Convention Center and Salt Lake City Visitors Bureau, 90 S. West Temple (☎534-4902). Located in Salt Palace Convention Center, 1 block south of Temple Sq. Open daily 9am-5pm.

Hotlines: Rape Crisis, ☎467-7273. **Suicide Prevention,** ☎483-5444. Both 24hr.

Gay/Lesbian Information: The Little Lavender Book (☎323-0727; www.lavenderbook.com), a directory of gay-friendly Salt Lake City services. Distributed twice yearly.

Laundry: McFarlands Cleaning Centers, 154 S. 400 E. (☎531-6684). Open daily 7am-9:30pm. Self- service machines and professional dry cleaning available.

Emergency: ☎911. **Police:** 315 E. 200 S (☎799-3000).

Medical services: University Hospital, 50 N. Medical Dr. (emergency ☎581-2291).

Library and Internet access: Salt Lake Public Library, 209 E. 500 S (☎524-8200). Free Internet access. M-Th 9am-9pm, F-Sa 9am-6pm, Su 1-5pm. Free Internet access is also available at the **Family Search Center** on Temple Sq. Open M-Sa 9am-9pm.

Post Office: 230 W. 200 S, 1 block south and 1 block west of Visitors Center. Open M-F 8am-5pm, Sa 9am-2pm. **Postal code:** 84101.

Employment: The ski hills around Salt Lake city employ literally thousands of workers over both the ski season and the summer months. Positions include everything from lift operator to ski medic to cook. Most hiring is now done through the individual resorts' websites, although **Snowbird** (p. 254) also has a job hotline (☎947-8240). Work at ski hills typically entails a commitment for most of the season. However, the restaurants in the Park City resort are usually willing to hire short-term staff during the high season. The procedure is fairly informal; show up with a resume and ask if they need anyone.

■ ACCOMMODATIONS

Affordable chain motels cluster at the southern end of downtown, around 200 W and 600 S, as well as on North Temple.

■ **Base Camp Park City,** 268 Historic Main St. (☎655-7244, 888-980-7244; www.parkcitybasecamp.com), 30 mi. east of Salt Lake City on I-80 and south on Rte. 224. This dazzling, state-of-the-art hostel offers 70 affordable beds in the heart of expensive Park City, a beautiful and historic mining town located high in the mountains (over 7,000 ft.). Free **Internet**, free parking, discounts on selected Main St. restaurants, spectacular movie/DVD theater, and free transportation to Deer Valley, The Canyons, and Park City ski areas. Taxis/shuttles from Salt Lake City airport available. Summer dorms $25, winter $35; private room (sleeps up to 4) $80/$120. Make reservations by phone or online as far in advance as possible during ski season. ❷

City Creek Inn, 230 W. North Temple (☎533-9100; citycreekinn.com), a stone's throw from Temple Sq. Offers 33 tastefully decorated, immaculate ranch-style rooms for cheaper rates than any of its downtown competitors. The incredibly friendly owners keep two handicap-ready rooms and give AAA discounts. Singles $53, doubles $64. ❸

Ute Hostel (AAIH/Rucksackers), 21 E. Kelsey Ave. (☎595-1645, 888-255-1192), near the intersection of 1300 S and Main. Located 2 blocks from TRAX line for downtown/ski-shuttle access. Young international crowd. Free pickup can be arranged from airport, Amtrak, Greyhound, or the Visitors Center. Kitchen, no curfew, free tea and coffee, parking, linen. Check-in 24hr. 14 dorm beds, $15 each. 2 private rooms; singles $25, doubles $35. Reservations accepted in advance only with pre-payment, recommended from July-Sept. and Jan.-Mar. Cash only. ❶

The Avenues Hostel (HI-AYH), 107 F St. (☎359-3855). 15min. walk from Temple Sq. in a residential area. Features free parking, a new entertainment system, 2 kitchens, and mountain bikes rentals ($10 per day, $100 deposit). Reception 7:30am-noon, 4-10:30pm. Dorms $17 (non-members), doubles $36 (non-members), $5 key deposit. Reservations recommended July-Aug. and Jan.-Mar. ❶

🏕 CAMPING

Big Cottonwood Canyon and rocky **Little Cottonwood Canyon** provide camping in the mountains rising to the east of Salt Lake City. To find the campgrounds, take I-215 to exit 7 (6200 S) and follow the signs to Big or Little Cottonwood Canyon. Brown recreation signs point the way to the campsites, which lie roughly 30 mi. from downtown Salt Lake. Arrive early on weekends; for summer weekends, call in advance. The **Salt Lake Ranger District** (☎943-1794) fields calls for camping reservations and more info.

Tanners Flat, in Little Cottonwood Canyon. Hosts 39 tent sites that include water faucets and flush toilets. Open early May to late Oct. $12. ❶

Albion Basin, in Little Cottonwood Canyon. At a higher altitude than Tanners, provides 25 sites, water faucets, and pit toilets. Open early July to late Sept. $12. ❶

Spruces, in Big Cottonwood Canyon. Its 97 sites feature water faucets and flush toilets. Open late May to early Oct. $14. ❶

Redman, in Big Cottonwood Canyon. Water faucets and pit toilets accompany each of the 43 sites at this campground. Open mid-June to late Sept. $12. ❶

Antelope Island State Park, in the middle of the Great Salt Lake (☎800-322-3770, reservations recommended). Beaches, hiking trails, picnic spots, and the occasional buffalo form an idyllic camping location. $10 per vehicle; $8 each additional night; additional day-use fee. ❶

🍴 MORAL FIBER

Good, cheap restaurants are sprinkled around the city and its suburbs, and despite its white-bread reputation, Salt Lake hosts a number of ethnic cuisines. Cheap Mexican eateries have proliferated, as have brewpubs in the downtown area. If you're in a hurry downtown, **ZCMI Mall** and **Crossroads Mall,** both across from Temple Sq., have food courts. For groceries, large franchise stores serve the Salt Lake area, found mostly outside downtown on major roads like State St. or N. Temple.

MORMON HISTORY

In 1827, in an obscure town in upstate New York, the angel Moroni delivered to Joseph Smith a set of golden tablets inscribed with a prophetic record in mystical language. Aided by divine guidance and stone spectacles, Smith translated the plates into English and published the Book of Mormon in 1830, the date traditionally marking the founding of the Mormon Church.

Though the tablets vanished soon afterwards, Smith's church grew rapidly. Facing persecution, they were forced farther and farther west. In 1846, 30,000 Mormon pioneers were expelled from Nauvoo, IL, prompting the Great Trek that would ultimately lead to the founding of Salt Lake City.

Mormons believe their faith to be the restoration of true Christianity, and just as the Bible tells the story of the eastern half of the world, the Book of Mormon is both a history of the ancient Americas and a record of Christ's coming to the New World.

Some 113 temples worldwide serve as venues for unique and often misunderstood ceremonies. Sunday services are deemed too mundane for these sacred spaces, and only the worthy—church members certified by their bishop to have paid their dues and not cheated on their spouses—may enter. Inside, members engage in the rituals of "sealing" and perform "work for the dead."

(Continued on next page)

Sage's Cafe, 473 E. 300 S (☎322-3790). This organic, vegan cafe is a hotbed of culinary innovation. Describing themselves as "culinary astronauts," talented chefs produce a variety of delectable dishes. Try the basil and macadamia nut pesto pasta dish for $13. Sugar- and oil-free meals available. Smoothies, milkshakes (both $4), and iced house chai ($3) are sure to please. Weekday lunch buffet $6.75. Open W-Th 5pm-9:30pm, F 5pm-10pm, Sa 9am-10pm, Su 9am-9pm. ❷

Ruth's Diner, 2100 Emigration Canyon Rd. (☎582-5807; www.ruthsdiner.com.) Vending the best breakfasts in SLC and a full bar with live music at night. Originally run out of a trolley car, Ruth's is the second-oldest restaurant in Utah and has been a Salt Lake City landmark for 70 years. Huge portions, delicious omelettes like the "Rutherino" ($6-7), and brownie sundaes ($6) help it outlast rivals. Open daily 8am-10pm. ❶

Red Iguana, 736 W. North Temple (☎322-4834), across the bridge from downtown in the bright orange building. This immensely popular eatery serves up authentic pre-Colombian Mexican food. *À la carte* burritos, enchiladas, tacos ($5-7), and combo plates ($10-12). Open M-Th 11am-10pm, F-Sa 11am-11pm, Su noon-9pm. ❷

Orbit, 540 W. 200 S (☎322-3808; www.orbitslc.com), close to the dance clubs in the old industrial district. With a sports bar and patio seating, Orbit boasts sleek decor and a diverse crowd. Sandwiches ($7-10), dinner entrees ($10-16), and pizzas ($8-10). Open M-W 11am-11pm, Th-F 11am-1am, Sa 10am-1am, Su 10am-10pm. ❸

Tibet Cafe Shambala, 382 4th Ave. (☎364-8558), in a quiet residential neighborhood just northeast of Temple Sq. Enjoy the bountiful Tibetan food lunch buffet ($6) under the benevolent gaze of the Dalai Lama. Entrees $5-7. Open M-Sa 11am-3pm and 4-9:30pm. ❶

◉ SIGHTS

LATTER-DAY SIGHTS. The majority of Salt Lake City's sights are sacred to the Church of Jesus Christ of Latter-Day Saints, and free. The seat of the highest Mormon authority and the central temple, **Temple Square** is the symbolic center of the Mormon religion. The square has two **Visitors Centers,** north and south. Visitors can wander around the flowery 10-acre square, but the sacred temple is off-limits to non-Mormons. An automated visitor info line (☎800-537-9703) provides up-to-date hours and tour info. Forty-five-minute tours leave from the flagpole every 10min., showing off the highlights of Temple Sq. *The Testaments,* a film detailing the coming of Jesus

Christ to the Americas (as related by the Book of Mormon), is screened at the **Joseph Smith Memorial Building.** ☎ *240-4383 for film show times, 240-1266 to arrange a tour. Open M-Sa 9am-9pm. Free.*

Temple Sq. is also home to the **Mormon Tabernacle** and its famed choir. Weekly rehearsals and performances are free. *(Organ recitals M-Sa noon-12:30pm, Su 2-2:30pm; in summer also M-Sa 2-2:30pm; Choir rehearsals Th 8-9:30pm; choir broadcasts Su 9:30-10am, must be seated by 9:15am.)* In the summer, there are frequent free concerts at **Assembly Hall** next door. ☎ *800-537-9703.*

The **Church of Jesus Christ of Latter Day Saints Office Building** is the tallest skyscraper in Salt Lake City. The elevator to the 26th floor grants a view of the Great Salt Lake in the west opposite the Wasatch Range. *(40 E. North Temple. ☎ 240-3789. Observation deck open M-F 9am-4:30pm.)* The LDS church's collection of genealogical materials is accessible and free at the **Family Search Center,** 15 E. South Temple St., in the Joseph Smith Memorial Building. The Center has computers and staff to aid in your search. The actual collection is housed in the **Family History Library.** *35 N. West Temple. ☎ 240-2331. Center open M-Sa 9am-9pm. Library open M 7:30am-5pm, Tu-Sa 7:30am-10pm.*

MUSEUMS. Visiting exhibits and a permanent collection of world art wow enthusiasts at the newly expanded **Utah Museum of Fine Arts,** on the University of Utah campus. *(☎ 581-7332. Open M-F 10am-5pm, Sa-Su noon-5pm. Free.)* Also on campus, the **Museum of Natural History** focuses its display space on the history of the Wasatch Front. *(☎ 581-6927. M-Sa 9:30am-5:30pm, Su noon-5pm. $4, ages 3-12 $2.50, under 3 free.)* The **Salt Lake Art Center** displays an impressive array of contemporary art and documentary films. *20 S. West Temple. ☎ 328-4201. Open Tu-Th and Sa 10am-5pm, F 10am-9pm, Su 1-5pm. Suggested donation $2.*

GREAT SALT LAKE. Administered by the Great Salt Lake State Marina, the Great Salt Lake is a remnant of primordial Lake Bonneville and is so salty that only blue-green algae and brine shrimp can survive in it. The salt content varies from 5-27%, providing unusual buoyancy. No one has ever drowned in the Great Salt Lake—a fact attributable to the Lake's chemical make-up. Decaying organic material on the lake shore gives the lake its pungent odor, which locals prefer not to discuss. **Antelope Island State Park**, in the middle of the lake, is a favorite for visitors. *(Bus #37, Magna, will take you within 4 mi., but no closer. To get to the south shore of the lake, take I-80 17 mi. west of Salt Lake City to exit 104. To get to the island, take exit 335 from I-15 and follow signs to the causeway. ☎ 625-1630. Open daily 7am-10pm; in winter dawn to dusk. Day use: vehicles $8, bicycles and pedestrians $4.*

(Continued from previous page)

"Sealing" binds spouses and family members together for eternity, while "work for the dead" allows non-Mormon ancestors the privilege of higher degrees of Mormon salvation. Church members can "stand in" for their deceased relatives by being baptized again (twice per dead ancestor). Spirits can choose to accept or reject Mormon blessings.

To pay for elaborate temples and maintain the church welfare network, members are required to tithe 10% of their annual income. In addition, most Mormon men, and a growing number of women, serve two-year missions in far-flung corners of the world. As a result, the Mormonism is the world's fastest growing religion.

While many still associate Mormonism with polygamy, the practice of having multiple wives was officially overturned by a prophetic revelation in 1890. Similarly, a policy barring blacks from holding church offices was overturned in 1978.

And just as its missions have attracted millions of converts, the Mormon Church has proven highly adept at managing its worldly affairs. Church assets eclipse $30 billion, and its annual revenue of roughly $6 billion, $5 billion of which derives from tithing, places it midway up the Fortune 500 between Paine Webber and Nike. Holdings range from America's largest beef ranch to the Beneficial Life Insurance Corp.

For more information, visit www.mormon.org. Those curious about the purpose of life may wish to click on the "Purpose of Life" heading, which explains things in detail.

🎵 🔊 ENTERTAINMENT & NIGHTLIFE

At the **Delta Center,** 301 W. South Temple, NBA Western Conference powerhouse Utah Jazz take on their rivals, now without city icon and perennial all-star Karl Malone. (☎325-7328. Season Oct.-Apr. Tickets $10-38), For those who would rather listen to jazz than watch them dribble and dunk, Salt Lake City's sweltering summer months jam with frequent evening concerts. Every Tuesday and Friday at 7:30pm, the **Temple Square Concert Series** presents a free outdoor concert in Brigham Young Historic Park, with music ranging from string quartet to unplugged guitar (☎240-2534; call for a schedule). The **Utah Symphony Orchestra** performs in **Abravanel Hall,** 123 W. South Temple. (☎533-6683. Office open M-F 10am-6pm. Tickets Sept. to early May $15-40. Limited summer season; call 1 week in advance.) The University of Utah's **Red Butte Garden,** 300 Wakara Way (☎587-9939; www.redbuttegarden.org), offers an outdoor summer concert series with reputable national acts.

The free *City Weekly* lists events and is available at bars, clubs, and restaurants. Famous for teetotaling, the early Mormon theocrats instated laws making it illegal to serve alcohol in a public place. Hence, all liquor-serving institutions fall under the "private club" designation, serving only members and their "sponsored" guests. In order to get around this cumbersome law, most bars and clubs charge a "temporary membership fee"—essentially a cover charge. Despite the Mormons' contempt for the bottle, a surprisingly active nightlife centers on S. West Temple and the run-down blocks near the railroad tracks.

Bricks, 200 S. 600 W (☎238-0255), Salt Lake's oldest and largest dance club, featuring 2 floors of thumping house, multiple bars, an outdoor patio, pool tables, and the city's best sound system. Bricks also hosts national acts that span the musical spectrum. Separate 18+ and 21+ areas. Cover $5-7. Open nightly 9:30pm-2am.

Club Axis, 100 S. 500 W (☎519-2947; clubaxis.com). Salt Lake's version of a pretentious super-club, with VIP lounges, DJ's, jungle-themed bar, and multiple dance floors. F gay/alt. lifestyle night, W and Sa dress to impress. Separate 18+ and 21+ areas. Cover $5-7. Open W-Sa 10pm-2am.

DV8, 115 S. West Temple (☎539-8400). Salt Lake's 2nd-largest club features dance music on F and Sa and live acts M-Th. Lounges, bars, pool tables, and 2 dance floors fill 6 stories. Live shows all ages. Club nights 21+. Cover $5-7. Open F-Sa club nights 9pm-2am; live acts, from gutter punk to space rock, begin near 6:30pm.

Zipperz, 155 W. 200 S (☎521-8300), across from Salt Palace Convention Center. A diverse mix of the Salt Lake gay and lesbian crowd flocks to this classy bar/dance club. Sip martinis ($4.75) in the wingchairs or groove on the 2nd-story dance floor. W 80s night, Sa dance party. 21+. Cover $5-6. Open nightly Su-Th 2pm-2am, F-Sa 5pm-2am.

⛷ PARK CITY & SKI RESORTS

Utah sells itself to tourists with pictures of intrepid skiers on pristine powder, hailed by many as "the greatest snow on earth." Seven major ski areas lie within 45min. of downtown Salt Lake City. With three mountains, nearby **Park City** is the quintessential ski town, featuring the excellent but lonely ⛺**Base Camp Park City** (see p. 248) as its only budget option. Rates at local resorts can climb as high as the snow-capped peaks, so call or check mountain websites for deals before purchasing lift tickets or rooms. Utah's ski hills also offer excellent employment opportunities. If you are interested in working while you ski, check the employment section on each hill's website or call Snowbird's job hotline (☎947-8240), a good source for positions in the Cottonwood Canyons.

Alta (☎359-1078; www.alta.com), 25 mi. southeast of Salt Lake City in Little Cottonwood Canyon. Cheap tickets; magnificent skiing. Open since 1938, this no-frills resort continues to eschew opulence and reject snowboarders. 8 lifts, including 1 high-speed, and 5 tows serve 54 trails (25% beginner; 40% intermediate; 35% advanced) on 2200 skiable acres. 500 in. of champagne powder annually. Season mid-Nov. to mid-Apr. with skiing daily from 9:15am-4:30pm. Lift tickets: full day $38, half-day $29, day pass for beginner lifts only $22. Joint ticket with nearby Snowbird $68. Rentals: 4 rental shops in Alta ski village offer competitive rates.

Solitude (☎800-748-4754; www.skisolitude.com), in Big Cottonwood Canyon 30 min. south of Salt Lake. Budget prices for luxurious runs at a beautiful resort. Uncrowded slopes and 20km of nordic trails at Silver Lake (8700 ft.) promise tranquility. 7 lifts, including 1 high-speed, serve 63 trails (20% beginner; 50% intermediate; 30% advanced) on 1200 skiable acres. Vertical drop 2050 ft. from a summit of 10,035 ft. Annual snowfall 500 in. Season Nov. to late Apr. Skiing and snowboarding daily 9am-4pm. Lift tickets: full-day $44, half-day $37, seniors (60-69) $37, over 70 $10, children $24. Nordic Center full-day $10, half-day $7. Rentals: adult ski package $24 per day, snowboards $28, high performance ski package $38. There are summertime hiking and biking trails in Big Cottonwood Canyon and Mill Creek Canyon. Lake Blanche trail (3.2 mi.) takes about 3hrs. after an elevation gain of 2600 ft., passing around three beautiful lakes with views of Sundial Peak; its highest elevation point is 8920 ft. For a special trek-in restaurant and a night to remember, make reservations for a 5-course meal at the Yurt. In the winter, this Mongolian style hut awaits visitors ¼ mi. into the wilderness near Solitude. (☎615-9878. $80 per person. Call for reservations.)

Brighton (☎800-873-5512; www.skibrighton.com), just south of Salt Lake in Big Cottonwood Canyon, Brighton offers bargain skiing and snowboarding in a down-to-earth atmosphere. Brighton is especially family- and beginner-friendly, but features a snowboarding terrain park and a great deal of backcountry skiing for the virtuoso. 10 lifts, including 3 high-speed quads, serve 66 trails (21% beginner; 40% intermediate; 39% advanced) on 850 skiable acres. More than 500 in. of snow falls annually on the mountain, which has a base of 8750 ft. and a summit of 10,500 ft., creating a vertical drop of 1750 ft. Open early Nov. to late Apr. daily 9am-4pm and M-Sa until 9pm for night skiing. Lift tickets: full-day $39, half-day $34, night $24, children under 10 free. Rentals: adult ski/board package $26 per day, child ski/board package $18, high performance ski/board package $32.

THE BIG SPLURGE

OLYMPIAN FOR A DAY

With a range of camps that take place at the same facilities that hosted the 2002 Winter Olympics, summer at **Olympic Park** has its own highs for the adrenaline junky. Ski jumper wannabes can take a literal crash course in freestyle aerial thanks to the park's **Flight School and aerial jumping arena,** which includes multiple bungee jumping stations and a 750,000 gal. splash pool. The steepest ramp launches wetsuit-clad skiers and snow boarders some 60 ft. into the thin mountain air before they cannon-ball into the water below. 1988 Olympian Chris "Hatch" Haslock is on hand to teach you the tricks that qualify you as totally fearless and just shy of insane. *(Jun.-Sept. Tu-Su beginning at 12:30pm. $40 per session.)*

If soaring and flipping aren't your thing, the **Comet** awaits on solid ground. One of only two **Olympic bobsled** courses in the US, this ride can hurtle you in summer months through 15 curves over 0.8 mi. at a screaming 70 mph top speed. Special rolling bobsleds and professional pilots let passengers experience up to 4 Gs of force. Paying $200 in the wintertime may seem too pricey, but making a $65 advance reservation during the summer is well worth it. *(☎435-658-4206; www.olyparks.com. Late May-late Aug. Tu-Sa 1-4pm.)*

The Canyons (☎ 435-649-5400; www.thecanyons.com), in Park City. With lodges, shops, and restaurants styled in chic Southwestern motifs and an abundance of territory, The Canyons is quickly becoming a world-class destination. 16 lifts, including 7 high-speed, serve 146 trails (14% beginner; 44% intermediate; 42% advanced) on 8 mountain peaks and over 3500 skiable acres. The Dreamscape lift provides access to more intermediate terrain. Skiers and snowboarders enjoy 3190 ft. of vertical thrill, with a summit of 9990 ft. Annual snowfall 355 in. Open Nov.-Apr. daily M-F 9am-4pm, Sa-Su 8:30am-4pm. Lift tickets: full day $62, half-day $45; children and seniors $31/$24. Rentals: adult ski/board package $34 per day, child ski package $24, child board package $27, high performance ski package $40. Free season pass in exchange for one day of work at the resort per week. Call ahead for more info. A newly constructed park welcomes snowboarders to some of the best terrain in the country. A year-round resort, The Canyons offers hiking, horseback riding, and mountain biking in the summer.

Deer Valley (☎ 435-649-1000; www.deervalley.com), in Park City. Host of the slalom, moguls, and aerial events of the 2002 Winter Olympics and a genuine world-class ski area. With the area's most expensive lift tickets, Deer Valley attracts primarily the affluent, leaving the slopes sparse for pristine bowl skiing. 19 lifts, including 6 high-speed, serve 88 trails (15% beginner; 50% intermediate; 35% advanced) on 1750 acres. Featuring a 9570 ft. summit and a 3000 ft. vertical drop, the mountain receives 300 in. of annual snowfall. No snowboards. Skiing Dec.-Apr. daily 9am-4:15pm. Lift tickets: full-day $67, half-day $46; children $36/$28; senior $46/$30. Rentals: adult ski package $39 per day, child ski package $28, high performance ski package $49. In the summer months, Deer Valley has hiking, mountain biking, horseback riding, and a camp for kids.

Park City (☎ 435-649-8111; www.parkcitymountain.com). Its exceptional facilities earned it the Olympic snowboarding events in 2002. With terrific skiing terrain, luxurious lodging, and a lift connecting the mountain to the town's posh stores, Park City is the total experience. 15 lifts, including 5 high-speed, whisk skiers to 100 trails (18% beginner; 44% intermediate; 38% advanced) on 3300 skiable acres. 350 in. annual snowfall. Vertical drop 3100 ft. Season mid-Nov. to mid-Apr. Open daily 9am-4pm, night skiing until 9pm after Dec. 25. Lift tickets vary by season: high season full-day $60+, half-day $42; ages 65-69 $30; 70+ free. Rentals: adult ski package $20 per day, child ski package $17, snowboard packages $32, high performance ski package $37. Hiking, mountain biking, climbing, and horseback riding activities in the summer.

Snowbird (☎ 742-2222 or 800-640-2002; www.snowbird.com) sprawls up Little Cottonwood, a canyon world-renowned for its powder. Now in its 31st year, Snowbird has skiing for all levels and resort amenities for those who prefer days off the slopes. 13 lifts, including the 125-passenger aerial tram ($14 in summer) service 85 trails (27% beginner; 38% intermediate; 35% advanced) on 2500 skiable acres. A lift connects the resort with Alta. Annual snowfall 500 in. Vertical drop 2900 ft. from a summit of 11,000 ft. Skiing and snowboarding mid-Nov. to mid-May. Open daily 9am-4:30pm; night skiing W and F until 8:30pm. Tickets: full-day including tram $56, lifts only $47; half-day $48/$40; 2 children under 12 free with adult. Joint ticket with Alta $68. Rentals: adult ski packages from $19, child ski packages $16, snowboard packages $29, high performance ski package $40. Also hosts backcountry skiing and mountaineering courses. Offers extensive summer hiking and biking trails, along with an Adventure Park ropes course. Bikes allowed only on the upper trails on even numbered dates.

◪ OTHER OUTDOOR ACTIVITIES

Salt Lake area outdoor enthusiasts cherish the easy access to trailheads, fishing, skiing, and climbing of the Wasatch Front Range. Most popular points of access fall within a 30min. drive from downtown Salt Lake, but lie within closer proximity to Park City (20 mi.) and Alta (less than 10 mi.). **Mill Creek Canyon, Big Cottonwood**

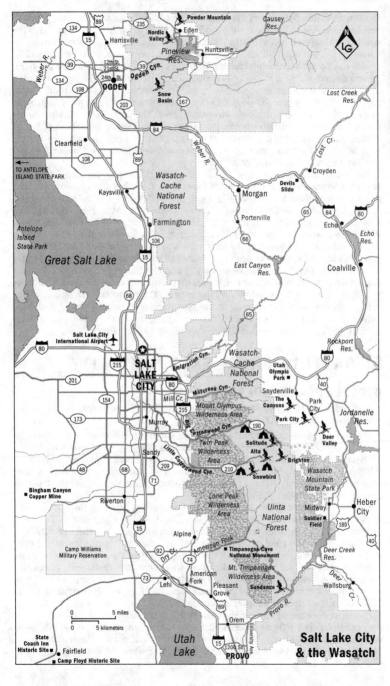

Salt Lake City & the Wasatch

UTAH

Canyon, and **Little Cottonwood Canyon** all cut into the Wasatch immediately east of Salt Lake. Access to these canyons is off Wasatch Blvd., which runs parallel to the southbound stretch of I-215. **UTA** shuttles serve all three canyons regularly. The easiest place to obtain info on the canyons and other area recreational possibilities is the **Forest Service Information Station** in **REI**, 3285 E. 3300 S. (☎466-6411; camping reservations ☎877-444-6777. Open Tu-Sa 10:30am-7pm.) Dispersed camping is allowed in all three canyons but prohibited within ½ mi. of the road. Forest service regulations prohibit dogs from the Cottonwood Canyons, as both provide drinking water to the Salt Lake metropolitan area. The **Great Western Trail**, a developing long route that will eventually connect Canada and New Mexico, winds through the area, with a trailhead at the top of Mill Creek Canyon. Most trails remain within their canyon, making for excellent day hikes. The **Pipeline Trail** and the **Donut Falls Trail** are highlights.

The mountains rising west of the city shelter a range of **biking** trails. **Wild Rose Mountain Sports,** 702 Third Ave., rents full-suspension bikes from $25 per day and gives expert trail advice. (☎533-8671. Open M-Th 9:30am-7pm, F-Sa 9:30am-6pm.)

Both Big and Little Cottonwood Canyons feature extensive **rock climbing.** The rock is mostly granite, with the exceptions of the limestone Hellgate Cliffs and Albion Basin areas. A mixed bag of climbing styles comes into play in the Cottonwood Canyons, but no matter the style rock quality is well above average in most places. Difficult bouldering problems vex climbers along the first 5 mi. of Little Cottonwood. The Secret Garden (V0-V3) and the Cabbage Patch (V1-V5) are known to be outstanding, and deliver on their reputation. **Ice climbers** pick their way up ice falls on the south side of the canyon. **Exum Mountain Adventures** offers private guiding services as well as courses in basic mountaineering and rock climbing for all levels. (☎550-3986. One-day group rock course $90 per person, $215 for private lesson, weekend winter ice climb $90 per person.)

⚡ DAYTRIP FROM SALT LAKE CITY

DESERET PEAK WILDERNESS

To reach Deseret Peak, take I-80 west from Salt Lake about 20 mi. to Rte. 36 south. Follow signs for Rte. 138 west and Grantsville.

Forty-seven miles west of Salt Lake lies an imposing wilderness area providing relief from the Wasatch Front weekend crowds. The Deseret Peak Wilderness, designated in 1984, includes 25,508 acres with elevations ranging 5500-11,000 ft. Wildlife is abundant, including deer, coyotes, mountain lions, wild horses, and bald and golden eagles. Higher elevations feature jagged escarpments, tranquil basins, and all varieties of alpine flora.

Once in the town of Grantsville, stock up on supplies and travel through town to the brown Forest Service sign for North and South Willow Canyon Rds. The most popular access to the area is from the Loop Campground at the end of South Willow Canyon Rd. The road lies 6 mi. south of Grantsville. The less-traveled North Willow Canyon Rd. is spotted with campsites, many of them trash-littered. For summer hiking, be sure to bring plenty of water and sunscreen. Also, check the forecast before embarking on a hike, as violent thunderstorms frequently ravage the wilderness area. For further information contact the local **BLM office** at ☎801-977-4300 or the **Salt Lake Ranger District** at ☎801-733-2660.

The most popular, and arguably most spectacular, hike in the region summits the peak itself via the **Deseret Peak Trail.** Expect to encounter a few other hikers on summer weekends, but you'll climb in solitude most of the time. The trail begins at 7440 ft. at the end of the South Willow Canyon Rd. Follow the **Mill Fork Trail** to the

Deseret Peak-Vickory Trail. Vibrant aspen grove foliage awaits fall hikers along the Mill Fork. Once on the Deseret Peak Trail, the final part of the climb winds through rugged terrain, but the views are well worth the extra exertion. Trailhead to summit (11,031 ft.), the route stretches 4 mi. Coming down from the peak, follow the Deseret Peak-Vickory Trail north along the ridge to the **Dry Lake Fork Trail,** which intersects the Mill Fork Trail about 1.1 mi. from South Willow Canyon Rd. The Dry Lake descent route is also about 4 mi., making for a round-trip of 8 mi. Expect to spend about 8hr. on the trail: though popular with locals, the Forest Service classifies it as very difficult.

LOGAN & BEAR LAKE ☎ 435

In 1824, when Ephraim Logan descended into the beautiful Cache Valley (French for "hidden treasures"), he encountered a hardy group of fur trappers. Solitary by nature and by trade, these rugged outdoorsmen gathered infrequently to barter and exchange stories. Ever since, Logan (pop. 50,000) has been a gathering place for adventurers seeking out its many canyons and secretly untrammeled wilderness. The valley itself has evolved from a location for grazing, fur trapping, lumbering, and agriculture to include cultural events like the Logan Summer Fest, held during the second week in June every year. Utah State students represent almost half of Logan's residents and take advantage of this small town's cheap restaurants while avoiding its expensive lodging.

⬛🛈 ORIENTATION & PRACTICAL INFORMATION. About 1hr. north of the town of Ogden, Logan spreads out along **Route 89** (called **Main** in town), extending toward the mountains through a charming downtown stretch. 500 N leads to the Utah State Campus, whereas 1400 N accesses a growing infestation of strip malls. Following Rte. 89 through town leads to Logan Canyon, and offers stunning views along the way. After winding through the canyon to the northeast, Logan Canyon Rd. terminates at Garden City on the impossibly turquoise Bear Lake, a popular watersports haven, half of which is classified as Idaho waters. **Greyhound,** 754 W. 600 N (☎752-2877. Open M-F 9:30am-noon and 2-7:30pm), runs two buses daily to Salt Lake City (2hr., 3:35am and 6:40pm, $16.25 one-way). For more info about Logan and surrounding environs, stop first at the **Cache Chamber of Commerce,** 160 N. Main, for helpful literature. (☎752-2161. Open summer M-F 8am-5pm, winter M-F 8am-5pm.) In Garden City, the **Bear Lake Visitors Center,** on Logan Canyon Hwy., has information on activities at Bear Lake. (☎946-2760. Open summer M-Sa 10am-6pm, Su 11am-5pm.) **IHC Logan Regional Hospital** (☎716-1000) provides full medical care at the intersection of 1400 N and 500 E in Logan. For medical assistance in Garden City, go to **Bear Lake Memorial Hospital's Fast Aid Medical Clinic** (☎208-847-1630), a small 24hr. clinic on Logan Canyon Hwy. Free **Internet access** is available at Logan's Cache County Library, 255 N. Main (open M-Th 10am-9pm, F-Sa 10am-6pm). The **post office** is at 151 N. 100 W. (☎752-7246. Open M-F 8:30am-5:30pm, Sa 8:30am-12:30pm.) **Postal code:** 84321.

🛌🍴 ACCOMMODATIONS & FOOD. Logan lodging is steep and dominated by national chains. **Days Inn ❸,** 364 S. Main, has the lowest rates in town and spotless rooms with microwaves and minifridges. (☎753-5623. Singles start at $40 in winter, $50 in summer; doubles $50/$60.) On the glamorous, resort-dominated Bear Lake, the **Bear Lake Motor Lodge ❸,** 50 S. Bear Lake Blvd., rents bright, clean rooms, some with kitchenettes. (☎946-3333 or 946-2791. Singles $59 in summer, $39 in winter; $10 per extra person. Reservations needed summer weekends.) The Forest Service-operated **Sunrise Campground ❶,** above Garden City along Logan Canyon Hwy., perches over Bear Lake in an aspen forest. (Open mid-June to mid-Oct. Toi-

UTAH

lets and running water. Tent sites $12.) Eight miles south of Garden City on Rte. 30, **Rendezvous Beach State Park** ❶ has 186 sites along the shoreline. (☎946-3343. Running water, toilets, and showers. Tent sites $14, full hookups $20.)

Logan offers an uncommon variety of reasonably priced restaurants, representing many types of ethnic fare. Most restaurants lie along Main, although the shopping plazas north of downtown also contain Logan eateries. Don't miss the 1920s era soda fountain at the town classic **☒Bluebird Cafe** ❷, 19 N. Main. Drawing praise since 1914, its tasty and inexpensive traditional American grub (lunches $4-7, dinners $8-10) is famous as far away as Ogden. For $6, try the Bluebird Chicken. (☎752-3155. Open M-Th 11am-9:30pm, F-Sa 11am-10pm.) Built in an old railway station at the corner of 600 W and Center St., **Cafe Sabor** ❸ serves up good hot tamale and traditional Mexican fare. (☎752-8088. Open F-Sa 11am-10pm.)

⚠ OUTDOOR ACTIVITIES. Rte. 89 between Logan and Bear Lake has "scenic byway" designation, and the helpful **Forest Service Information Center** welcomes visitors at the canyon's entrance. (☎755-3620. Open M-F 8am-4:30pm, Sa 10am-4pm.) Stop for the useful brochure guide to the canyon and for the historical kiosk, as well as for info on other worthwhile area routes. Mile markers along the byway correspond to descriptions in the brochure, making for a comprehensive tour of the canyon. Along the road, pull-outs allow parking for activities such as backcountry skiing near Beaver Mtn., day hiking, fly fishing, and rock climbing . Located in Raspberry Sq. at the end of Rte. 89 is **Pugstone's Ripples & Waves Sporting,** 20 North Bear Lake Blvd. (☎946-2855, call for hours of operation.) Pugstone's is a custom outfitter for fly fishing and water sports on Bear Lake. Canoe, kayak, ski, and hiking gear rental, as well as books, maps, and advice, are available at **Trailhead,** 117 N. Main in Logan. (☎753-1541. Open M-Sa 10am-6pm. Backpacks $5 per day; cross-country skis $10; snowshoes $8; canoes $20; kayaks $15.) A Trailhead favorite is the **Jardine Juniper Hike** in Logan Canyon, a one-way, 5.5 mi. route with a 2000 ft. elevation gain. For mountain bikes and snowboards, **Norda's Mountain Outfitters** is less than a block away at 77 N. Main. (☎752-2934. Open M-Sa 10am-7pm. Full-suspension bikes $25 per day; snowboards $20; basic skis $16, high end $25.) **Bitter Sweet,** located within Trailhead offers three-day climbing lesson packages ($85), rents climbing shoes ($4), and sells other climbing equipment.

NORTHEASTERN UTAH

Centered on the small town of Vernal, this portion of Utah lies in the northern reaches of the Colorado Plateau, bounded by the high peaks of the Uintas. Tracts of land composing the Uintah and Ouray Indian Reservation dot the landscape. The cooler climate of the Uintas and the waters of Flaming Gorge and the Green River provide visitors with a pleasant break from the parching summer heat.

VERNAL   ☎435

Historically an important mining and cattle center, Vernal has shifted to a Dinosaurland tourism economy. Vernal's geographic location allows speedy access to the lush, high Uintas, the ancient canyons of Dinosaur National Monument, and the blazing red walls of Flaming Gorge. Though not a destination itself, Vernal prides itself on being a friendly base for regional exploration.

▣ ◪ ORIENTATION & PRACTICAL INFORMATION. To see virtually all there is to see in Vernal, drive down U.S. 40. A stopover town for nearly a century, Vernal has evolved to meet the needs of vacationers just passing through. Strip malls

TIME: 6hr. driving time

DISTANCE: 78 mi.

SEASON: year-round

Nicknamed "the world's longest art gallery," the sandstone cliffs of **Nine-Mile Canyon** have served as a canvas for Native American artists through the ages. Though people such as the Fremonts have inhabited the canyon for 12,000 years, the majority of the petroglyphs, held to be some of the best in the world, date roughly from AD 1000. The Scenic Backcountry Byway travels a full 78 mi. from Myton to Wellington, but the majority of the petroglyphs appear along a shorter 50 mi. corridor toward the southern end of the route. The name "Nine-Mile Canyon" is actualy derived from a map produced by John Wesley Powell's expedition through Utah in 1869: Powell's mapmaker found a creek at the ninth mile marker, dubbing it "Nine-Mile Creek."

A roadtrip through the canyon can begin from either the north or south. From Rte. 40 in the north, a sign points the way to Nine-Mile Canyon 1.5 mi. west of Myton. Take a right at the first fork in the road. The 32 mi. gravel road leading from Myton to the canyon is not especially scenic and is without rock art. From the south, the main access route is 8 mi. east of Price in the town of Wellington. Turn north on 2200 E (Soldier Creek Rd.) at the Chevron Station. The first 12 mi. of the road up to the Soldier Creek Mine are paved.

Dedicate a full day to driving through the canyon, allowing 6hr. for driving and time for walks to and from the petroglyphs. The rough road is impassible when wet, and washboard ruts, punctuated by axle-breaking potholes, reduce speed to 20 m.p.h. Sandy patches and blind corners mandate caution.

As there are no services, stock up on water, food, and gas beforehand, and bring a spare tire and emergency kit. Binoculars and a canyon guide will help locate petroglyphs. **Nine-Mile Canyon Ranch Bunk and Breakfast ❷**, 25 mi. north of Wellington, offers the only accommodations in the canyon, complete with home-cooked meals. Camping is allowed even if the owners are away. (☎ 435-637-2572; www.ninemilecanyon.com. Bunk rooms $60, cabins $40; camping with water, toilets, and picnic tables $10.)

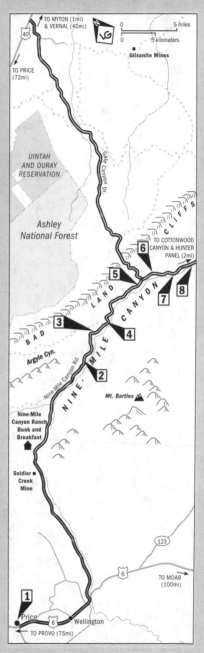

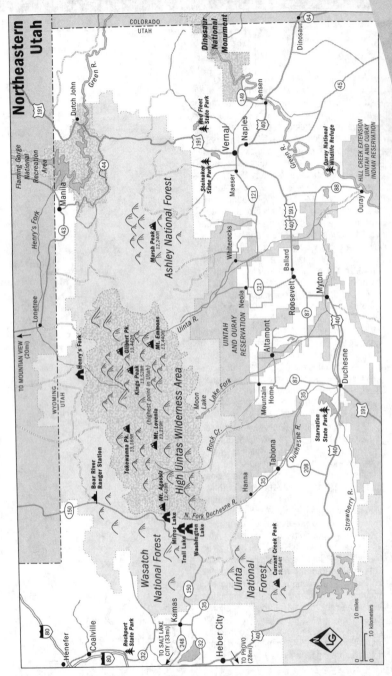

Northeastern Utah

COLORADO
UTAH

Dinosaur National Monument

Flaming Gorge National Recreation Area

Green R.

Dutch John

Red Fleet State Park

Jensen

Dinosaur

Manila

Henry's Fork

TO MOUNTAIN VIEW
(20mi)

Lonetree

Marsh Peak
12,240ft

Ashley National Forest

Vernal

Naples

Steinaker State Park

Maeser

Ouray National Wildlife Refuge

HILL CREEK EXTENSION
UINTAH AND OURAY
INDIAN RESERVATION

Henry's Fork

Gilbert Pk.
13,422ft

Kings Peak
13,528ft
(highest point in Utah)

Mt. Emmons
13,440ft

Whiterocks

Ouray

WYOMING
UTAH

Tokewanna Pk.
13,165ft

Mt. Lovenia
13,219ft

High Uintas Wilderness Area

Uinta R.

Neola

Ballard

Roosevelt

Myton

Bear River Ranger Station

Mt. Agassiz
12,428ft

Moon Lake

Lake Fork

UINTAH AND OURAY
RESERVATION

Altamont

Henefer

Coalville

Minor Lake

Trail Lake

Washington Lake

N. Fork Duchesne R.

Rock Cr.

Mountain Home

Duchesne

Wasatch National Forest

Tabiona

Hanna

Duchesne R.

Starvation State Park

Rockport State Park

Kamas

TO SALT LAKE
CITY (33mi)

Heber City

TO PROVO
(28mi)

Uinta National Forest

Currant Creek Peak
10,584ft

Strawberry R.

N
LG

0   10 miles
0   10 kilometers

Summer temperatures can soar to 100°F. Despite the heat, proper viewing of much of the art requires leaving the car. Although most of the land along Nine-Mile Canyon belongs to private ranchers, primitive camping lies 13 mi. up **Gate Canyon**. Mountain bikers frequently ride the canyon and side loops in tributary canyons. Note that the mile markers along the canyon start from Wellington but are equally useful to southbound travelers as navigational aids.

1 PREPARATION. Starting in Price, a quick stop at **Eastern Utah College's Prehistoric Museum,** 153 E. Main St., provides enriching background knowledge, but a visit is not required to appreciate the drive. (☎637-5060. Open summer daily 9am-6pm. $3 suggested donation.) In Vernal, the **Northeast Utah Visitors Center,** 235 E. Main, stocks a variety of helpful pamphlets on the canyon. (☎789-7894. Open daily 8am-9pm.) For general info and info on biking, contact the **Price BLM Office,** 125 S. 600 W. (☎636-3600. Open M-F 7:45am-4:30pm.)

2 MILE 26: THE FIRST PETROGLYPHS. A rocky outcropping protected by a squat wooden fence appears 26 mi. north of Wellington. The rocks just inside the fence display a number of petroglyphs. This extensive collection serves as an excellent way to train the eye on what to look for when driving up the canyon; most other panels are more difficult to spot. Before leaving, look up to spot an impressive panel carved into the rock just above a narrow ledge.

3 MILE 30: HARPER. 30 mi. past Wellington rests an assemblage of battered structures that have the look of an old homestead site. These abandoned buildings were part of the once-bustling town of Harper, which used to spread nearly 1 mi. along the canyon. Able to flourish while the road served as the principal link between Price and the Uintah Basin, Harper went bust when the railroad diverted freighters away from the canyon.

4 MILE 31.5: PIG HEAD ROCK. Rounding a corner brings into view a gigantic and looming boulder, perched perilously close to the road. Don't worry, it won't fall—it's been there since pioneer days. Some say it looks like Porky Pig; pre-cartoon pioneers called it "Giant's Chew of Gum." About 20 ft. farther up the road, a well-trodden foot path leads to a smattering of petroglyphs. After examining the main panel, follow the outcropping left and right for more viewing.

5 MILE 34: GATE CANYON. After passing several ranch buildings, Nine-Mile Canyon Rd. meets a junction with Gate Canyon and the road to Myton. Gate Canyon earned its name for a stone arch that once spanned the canyon over the road. Stagecoach employees destroyed the decaying arch at the turn of the century to protect travelers.

6 MILE 38.7: THE GRANARY. A cattle-guard crosses the road just before it bends around a towering, sheer rock face. Spotting the intact granary high on the cliff requires either very careful eyes or binoculars, since it hides against a background of light-colored rock, perched on a ledge about 300 ft. above the canyon floor. The Prehistoric Museum exhibit (see **Preparation**) contains a photograph of the granary useful in helping to pick it out against the cliff face. The Fremont people used granaries to store and protect surpluses of corn, beans, and squash.

7 MILE 42.7: RASSMUSSEN'S CAVE. Rassmussen's cave, really an alcove, was used heavily by the Fremont culture, as evidenced by the numerous petroglyphs and the depressions worn into the rock by corn grinding. Earlier excavations at the cave unearthed mummified bodies and native artifacts. Today, the alcove suffers from visitor negligence: trash and graffiti mar the once-beautiful site.

8 MILE 45: THE HUNTER PANEL. 1½ mi. up Cottonwood Canyon, which lies roughly 44 mi. from Wellington, is the drive's most celebrated petroglyph, the hunter panel. This complex scene seems to depict a herd of antelope-like prey and a native hunter poised for the kill, though some have argued that it could also portray a medicine man and his spiritual connection to the animals. This remarkable glyph tops off a visit to the canyon.

ROAD TRIP

vie for highway-front real estate. **Greyhound** runs buses to **Denver** (8hr., 2 per day, $56) and **Salt Lake City** (4½hr., 2 per day, $35) from Frontier Travel, 72 S. 100 W (☎789-0404. Open M-F 8:30am-5:30pm). **The Northeast Utah Visitors Center,** 235 E. Main (☎789-7894. Open daily 8am-7pm), provides info on Vernal, Dinosaur National Monument, and other regional recreational activities. Pick up info and maps of hiking and biking trails here. For cash, head to **Wells Fargo Bank,** at the corner of Main St. and Rte. 191 N (M-F 9am-5pm, Sa 9am-12pm). The **Ashley Valley Medical Center,** 151 W. 200 N (☎789-3342), treats rafting injuries and all other ailments. For free **Internet access** in Vernal, visit the Ashley County Public Library, 155 E. Main St., down the road from the Visitors Center. (☎789-0091. Open M-Th 10am-9pm, F-Sa 10am-6pm.) **Laundry** facilities are available at West End Laundromat 933 Main St. (open M-Sa 7:30am-6pm). Mail kitschy dinosaur postcards from the **post office,** 67 N. 800 W (open M-F 9am-5pm, Sa 10am-1pm). **Postal code:** 84078.

⌂ ♜ ACCOMMODATIONS & CAMPING. Although camping near Vernal is optimal, the town does support several motels. In high-demand summer months, be aware that prices may not match quality. The comfortable **Sage Motel ❸,** 54 W. Main, has standard rooms, A/C, satellite TV, and free local calls. (☎789-1442 or 800-760-1442. Singles $45 in winter, $50 in summer; doubles $55/$60.) On the outskirts of town toward the National Monument, **Split Mountain Motel ❷,** 1015 E. U.S. 40, has clean rooms with A/C, microwave, and minifridge. (☎789-9020. Singles $40 in winter, $45 in summer; doubles $50/$55.)

There's plenty of camping in and around Vernal for those who prefer the convenience of remaining close to civilization and avoiding the scorching heat of the national monument. Just north of town on Rte. 191, **Steinnaker State Park ❶** has 29 well-developed sites with water spigots and flush toilets on a gorgeous beach and reservoir. (☎789-4432. Open Apr. to mid-Oct. Tent sites $11.) For the camping amenities that only a KOA can provide, head to **Campground Dina RV Park ❶,** 930 N. Vernal Ave., about 1 mi. north of Main on U.S. 191 in Vernal. (☎789-2148 or 800-562-7574 for reservations. Heated pool, showers, laundry, mini golf, and a convenience store. Grassy tent sites for up to two people $18, full hookups $22, each additional person $2. Call ahead for summer weekends.)

▯ FOOD. Betty's Cafe ❶, 416 W. Main in Vernal, piles breakfast favorites on your plate ($5-7), but save $1.50 for a cinnamon roll. (☎781-2728. Open M-Sa 6am-4pm, Su 6am-noon. Cash only.) Imported to the Weston Inn from nearby LaPointe, **Stockman's ❶,** 1684 W. U.S. 40, lures hordes of hungry Vernalites for an exciting menu of Southwest cuisine, steak, and seafood. Burgers ($5-7), all you can eat sirloin steak ($11), and gargantuan, decadent desserts ($5-6) are highlights. (☎781-3030. Open Tu-F 10am-11pm, Sa 11:30am-11pm.) Stock up for a camping excursion at **Jubilee Foods,** 575 W. Main. (☎789-2001. Open until midnight.)

◙ ⚑ SIGHTS AND OUTDOORS. For Western history buffs, the **Western Heritage Museum,** 328 E. 200 S, offers revealing info about Josie Basset and the Wild Bunch. (☎789-7399. Open M-F 9am-6pm, Sa-Su 10am-5pm. Free.) The **Western Park** (☎789-1352), at the same address, hosts the National Rodeo every July and other competitions weekly. For another perspective on Western culture, the **Northern Ute Indian Pow Wow,** held on the Fourth of July in Ft. Duchesne, 26 mi. west of Vernal, draws large crowds from around northeast Utah.

As a gateway, Vernal is surrounded by outdoor destinations but has no real attraction or park of its own. However, enterprising outfitters offer products and services to accommodate a variety of outdoor sports in the region. **Basin Sports,** 551 W. Main (☎789-2199; open M-F 9am-7:30pm, Sa 9am-7pm), sells budget outdoor gear for camping, hunting, and rafting. **Altitude Cycle,** 580 E. Main, rents Cannondale bikes in the off-season and provides free advice on area riding year-round. The **Can you Moo? Trail** (11.5 mi.; 600 ft. of climbing), 10.5 mi. out of Vernal at Rte. 40W, and **Retail Sale Trail** (7.8 mi., 300 ft.), 6.2 mi. out of Vernal on McCoy Flat, are particular favorites. (☎781-2595. Open M-F 10am-6pm, Sa 9am-5pm. Bike rentals Sept.-May $10 per hr., $25 per half-day, $35 per full-day. Coed group rides W.) **River Runners,** 417 E. Main, is Vernal's do-it-yourself river-running contractor, a great alternative to the town's rafting outfits. They offer boat rentals and shuttling services for those brave enough to run the rivers on their own; they will coordinate entire rafting vacations. (☎800-930-7238. Open M-Sa 8am-5pm. Rafts from $85 per day, kayaks $25 per day, canoe package $35 per day. Call well in advance for reservations.) In business for more than a decade, **Atlantis Divers,** 206 W. Main, offers beginner open-water certification ($280). A dive shop? In the desert? Enthusiasts can tote their gear to Flaming Gorge for a dive, or try out more extreme river, nitrox, and ice diving in the area. (☎789-3616. Open M-F 9am-6pm, Sa 8am-1pm.)

DINOSAUR NATIONAL MONUMENT ☎435

Situated at the confluence of the Green and Yampa Rivers, the 330 sq. mi. Dinosaur National Monument is a natural historian's promised land. These rapidly flowing tributaries of the Colorado have sliced through the eons recorded in sedimentary stratigraphy, creating an informative geology lesson amidst vast desert expanses. Of course, there are the fossils too: Dinosaur contains the world's most concentrated collection of Jurassic Era dinosaur bones. On top of these large fossilized remains, the monument's sandstone cliffs served as a canvas upon which Archaic and Fremont Native Americans carved a dazzling array of petroglyphs. Filled with these natural and man-made wonders, the monument provides a superb arena for outdoor recreation, be it hiking, biking, backpacking, or river running.

AT A GLANCE: DINOSAUR NATIONAL MONUMENT

AREA: 210,277 acres.

FEATURES: Green River, Yampa River, Echo Park, Dinosaur Quarry, Split Mountain.

HIGHLIGHTS: Running the rapids of the Green or Yampa Rivers on a one-day trip, camping out in Echo Park (accessible only to high-clearance vehicles), hiking the Sound of Silence Trail.

GATEWAY TOWNS: Vernal, UT (p. 258), Rangely, CO.

CAMPING: Park campgrounds $6-12; free permit required for backcountry camping.

FEES AND PERMITS: Weekly park pass for vehicles $10, pedestrian or bike $5; yearly pass $20. Permits required for river running (one-day $35, multi-day$140) and fishing (state-issued license $8.)

■ ♉ ORIENTATION & PRACTICAL INFORMATION

The national monument's western and main entrance lies 20 mi. east of Vernal, on Hwy. 149, which splits from U.S. 40 southwest of the monument in Jensen, Utah. Several other roads access the park: Jones Hole Rd. in the northwest; Rte. 318 and a 10 mi. unpaved road in the north; Harper's Corner Rd. in the south; and Deerlodge Rd. in the east from U.S. 40, west of Elk Springs, Colorado. Once inside the park, pay a visit to the **Dinosaur Quarry Visitors Center,** a remarkable Bauhaus building that houses exhibits, a bookstore, and an exposed river bank brimming with dinosaur bones. During the summer, a **shuttle** whisks passengers up the half a mile to the Visitors Center every 15min. (☎781-7700. Wheelchair accessible. Open June-

Aug. 8am-7pm, Sept.-May 8am-4:30pm.) A second Visitors Center at **Monument Headquarters,** 45 mi. along Hwy. 40 from the Rte. 149 turnoff in Dinosaur, CO, has info on scenic canyons and river running, but no fossils. (☎970-374-3000. Open June-Aug. daily 8am-4:30pm, Sept.-May M-F 8am-4:30pm.) There are no **services** within the national monument. **Gas** is available in Vernal and Jensen, UT (15 mi. from Dinosaur) and in Dinosaur, CO. Multi-day campers should stock up on food in Vernal, which also provides the closest restaurants and indoor lodging.

Wise travelers avoid the scorching summer sun by visiting in the spring and fall, but most come in the summer, primed to fight the heat and other curious tourists. To protect the monument's resources, the Park Service has instated a series of **regulations.** Vehicles must stay on designated roads, campfires should be built only in firepits, and pets must be leashed at all times and are not allowed on trails or in the backcountry. The monument's greatest hazard is the sun: drink plenty of water and apply sunscreen frequently.

■ CAMPING

The monument contains six designated camping areas. The most easily accessible site during summer months, **Green River ❶,** lies along Cub Creek Rd. about 5 mi. from the entrance fee station. (88 sites. Flush toilets and water. $12.) Nearby **Split Mountain ❶** hosts only groups during the summer, but is open to all during winter months. For both campgrounds, water is turned off in the winter and tent sites are free. **Echo Park Campground ❶,** 13 mi. along Echo Park Rd. off the Harper's Corner Drive, is perched on a high-clearance, four-wheel-drive road above the confluence of the Green and Yampa Rivers. Views of the rivers and canyons at Echo Park rank among the monument's best. (9 sites. Pit toilets and water in summer only, free when water is turned off. $6.) The northern- and easternmost corners of the monument also have campsites, at **Gates of Lodore ❶** (17 sites; pit toilets and water in summer only, free when water is turned off; $6) and **Deerlodge Park ❶** (8 sites; pit toilets, no water; free). Gates of Lodore lies 10 mi. east of Rte. 318, and Deerlodge Park is 17 mi. off U.S. 40 in Colorado. Both sites are convenient for river runners.

■ OUTDOOR ACTIVITIES

The national monument offers a variety of informative and recreational activities, catered to suit all lengths of stay. For those passing through, a stop at the Dinosaur Quarry Visitors Center provides an overview of the monument's features, as well as the chance to see dinosaur bones in the riverbank quarry. For travelers with time to see more, there are miles of road, trail, and river to explore.

ON THE RIVER

Perhaps the best way to see Dinosaur National Monument is as the early explorers did: by boat. A day or multi-day float down the Green or Yampa River funnels travelers through roaring rapids (some Class III) and magnificent canyons. Numerous rafting outfits operate in the area, but only two have permits to run daily rafting trips. Daily trips float from Rainbow Park to the take-out near Split Mountain Campground. **Don Hatch River Expeditions,** 221 N. 400 E. in Vernal, is descended from one of the nation's earliest commercial rafting enterprises, dating to 1929. Well-respected Hatch Expeditions floats through the monument and the nearby Flaming Gorge. Be sure to request a paddle trip if you're interested in helping steer the raft. (☎789-4316 or 800-342-8243; www.hatchriver.com. Open M-F 9am-5pm. One-day trip $66, age 6-12 $56; seniors 10% off. Advance reservations recommended.) **Adrift Adventures,** at the corner of Rte. 149 and U.S. 40 in nearby Jensen, UT, runs daily trips through Split Mountain Gorge as well as multi-day trips in Col-

UTAH

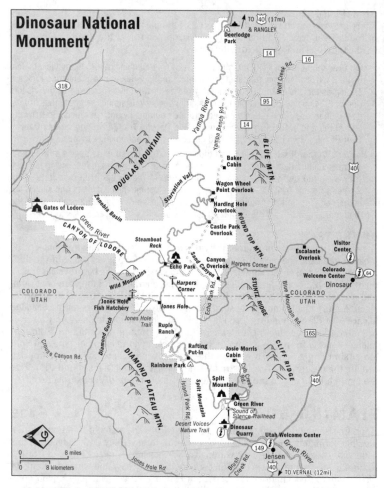

Dinosaur National Monument

orado and Utah. (☎800-824-0150. Open M-Sa 8am-6pm, Su 8am-5pm. Trips leave daily at 9am from outside the Adrift Adventures store. One-day trip $66, child $55. Advance reservations recommended.)

It is possible for experienced river runners with their own equipment to gain access to Dinosaur National Monument's rivers, but this requires a lot of fore-thought and planning, and quite a bit of luck. Applications for permits to the site ($15 non-refundable fee) must be filed by February 1 for summer trips, with permits granted by lottery. In 2003, only 300 seasonal public permits and two private permits per day were randomly awarded to a pool of some 4500 applicants. Applicants are notified of lottery selection by March 1 and must then submit a second-ary application. The winners must pay an extra fee for the permits (one-day $25, multi-day up to 5 days $125, each additional day $35) and follow a list of park reg-ulations for boating. Call 970-374-2468 for more info and application requests (office open M-F 8am-noon).

ON THE ROAD

There are two paved scenic driving tours of the park, as well as an extensive web of four-wheel-drive and high-clearance roads. Inquire at the Visitors Center for road conditions and specific driving advice.

Cub Creek Scenic Drive (22 mi. round-trip, 1-3hr.). Beginning at the Quarry Visitors Center, this drive winds past striking mountains, ambling rivers, and prehistoric rock art, ending at the Josie Morris Homestead. A guide to the drive (available at the Visitors Center; 50¢) points out notable features along the way. Examine the mysterious lizards, goats, princesses, and hunters carved into the boulders by ancient artists. Stretch your legs at the end of the drive, either on the **Hog Canyon Trail** (1 mi.) or the **Box Canyon Trail** (¼ mi.). Both hikes are easy and descend into breathtaking canyons.

Harper's Corner Road (62 mi. round-trip, 2-4hr.). This paved route begins at the Headquarters Visitors Center and climbs to a spectacular vantage point for viewing the canyons sculpted by the Green and Yampa rivers. At road's end, the moderate 2 mi. **Harper's Corner Trail** leads to one of the park's most magnificent views and should not be missed. The Park Service warns that open domestic cattle grazing occurs along the road, creating a serious driving hazard for cars traveling at high speeds.

ON THE TRAIL

Exploring the monument on foot provides a way to dodge summer sightseers, as most tourists see the park from their cars. It also gives a good sense of the difficulty of desert travel; pack plenty of water and sunscreen. The **Desert Voices Trail** (2 mi. round-trip) is a moderate hike that departs from the Split Mountain boat ramp and provokes reflection on the desert environment with a series of interpretive signs. A more challenging glimpse of desert environs faces hikers on the **Sound of Silence Hike** (2 mi. round-trip), along which you must navigate using only a series of landmarks; there is no trail, except the footprints of other hikers. Sound of Silence departs from Cub Creek Rd. halfway between the entrance gate and Split Mountain Campground. To witness the fertile riverside ecosystems that flourish despite the desert heat, try the stream-side **Jones Hole Trail** (8 mi. round-trip). This moderate hike begins at the Jones Hole Fish Hatchery, off of Jones Hole Rd.

FLAMING GORGE ☎ 435

Upon first seeing the fading light of the sunset turn the walls of Red Canyon to a dazzling vermilion, one-armed Civil War veteran John Wesley Powell declared this wide waterway flowing from Wyoming to Northeastern Utah a "Flaming Gorge." Natural beauty alone, however, didn't satisfy the electricity and water demands of the Bureau of Reclamation; a BOR dam in Flaming Gorge near Red Canyon completed in 1964 as part of the Colorado River Storage Project now generates power for 150,000 homes. Today, the reservoir and over 200,000 surrounding acres, ranging from alpine wilderness and dramatic canyons in the south to high desert in the north, are protected as the Forest Service's Flaming Gorge National Recreation Area. Outdoors enthusiasts, especially boaters and fishermen, descend into the gorge every summer and fall to fish for its world-class rainbow, brown, cutthroat, and cutbow trout.

■✻🚻 ORIENTATION & PRACTICAL INFORMATION

From Vernal, UT, follow scenic byway U.S. 191 north to the recreation area. Signs explain the geologic history of the area along the spectacular ascent through the foothills. The reservoir extends as far north as Green River, WY, and is also accessible from I-80. A recreation pass ($2 per day, $5 per 16 days) can be obtained at

"SCIENCE FIRST, MEN!" In early June, 1869, intrepid explorer and avid naturalist John Wesley Powell, missing an arm and tied to his boat, led a team of eight "mountain men" into the Gates of Lodore at the northern tip of today's Dinosaur National Monument. Powell, the self-reliant, decorated Civil War hero, professor of natural history, and later director of the US Geological Survey, lived the rugged, independent life that makes the modern outdoorsman feel envious and downright feeble. Yet, despite the heroics involved in leading a team down the treacherous waters that had ruined earlier expeditions, Powell downplayed the adventurousness of his mission, claiming it was all in the name of science. In the face of constant danger he insisted on taking scientific measurements, and at journey's end his main regret was not the hardship for himself and his men, but instead that they hadn't taken enough data. His crew probably thought him crazy, as demonstrated by the incident at Disaster Falls in Lodore. One of the ships capsized and broke apart on the rocks, but the cabin remained intact, wedged next to a large boulder downstream from the falls. Fearing the loss of all of his precious barometers (they'd all been foolishly stored in one boat), Powell sent several men out into the raging river on a recovery mission. When the men reached the boat, they began shouting ecstatically. As Powell recounts in his journal, he was surprised to see such exuberance over the recovery of the scientific instruments that his men considered utterly ridiculous. They were in fact celebrating the discovery of an intact whiskey barrel, which was dragged joyously back to shore. To Powell's relief, they also remembered to retrieve a few of the barometers. No hardship too great in the quest for knowledge. Or whiskey, as the case may be.

the **Flaming Gorge Visitors Center,** on U.S. 191 atop the Flaming Gorge Dam, or at most stores surrounding the Gorge, such as the Flaming Gorge Lodge. The Visitors Center also offers free tours of the dam and power plant. Since September 11, 2001, security has been much tighter, but the tour is still enjoyable. For $0.25 those taking the tour can buy fish food and feed trout at the bottom of the dam. (☎885-3135. Open daily 8am-6pm; off-season 10am-4pm. Tours start at 9am, last one leaves at 3:45pm.) A few miles off U.S. 191 and 3 mi. off Rte. 44 to Manila, the **Red Canyon Visitors Center** hangs 1360 ft. above the reservoir, offering breathtaking views into the canyon. (☎889-3713. Open late May to Aug. daily 10am-5pm.) Gas and other services cluster around the dam and the towns of Manila and Dutch John, UT. Medical care awaits in Vernal at **Ashley Valley Medical Center,** 151 W. 200 N. (☎789-3342). **Post Office:** 4 South Blvd., in Dutch John (☎885-3351. Open M-F 7:30am-3:30pm, Sa 8:30-11am and 1:45-3:15pm.) **Postal code:** 84023.

ACCOMMODATIONS & CAMPING

While camping is cheaper, indoor lodging exists at **Red Canyon Lodge ❸,** 2 mi. before the Visitors Center on Rte. 44. This lodge offers location, views, and year-round activities more in line with a luxury resort, touting itself as a civilized way to enjoy the great outdoors. Well-appointed cabins are available at moderate prices for groups. (☎889-3759; www.redcanyonlodge.com. Private lake stocked with trout; horseback riding in the summer; inviting, gourmet family-style restaurant. 2-person cabins with restrooms $95; 4-person $105; rollaway beds $6 per night.) Twenty-eight miles north on Rte. 44, the town of **Manila** boasts a collection of motels, though they are pricey. In town, the **Steinnaker Motel ❷,** at the intersection of Rte. 43 and 44, offers five rooms that are cramped but clean, one with a kitchenette. (☎784-3104. Check-in at the Chevron station. Reservations recommended but not required. Singles $36; doubles $44; tax included.)

UTAH

Camping in the area is scenic and accessible. The Visitors Centers offer sound advice on how to pick from the over 30 campgrounds spread around the lake. A number of sites can be reserved by calling ☎ 877-444-6777 at least five days in advance. The 19 secluded sites at **Dripping Springs ❶**, just past Dutch John northeast on Rte. 191, are some of the most coveted due to their prime fishing location. Though a forest fire consumed this area in 2003, it has been rebuilt. (Sites $14. Pit toilets, water available early May to mid-Oct.; open with no fee rest of year. Reservations accepted.) **Canyon Rim ❶**, on the road to the Red Canyon Visitors Center, offers a feeling of high-country camping with nearly vertigo-inducing views of the nearby red-walled gorge and convenient access to the Canyon Rim Trail. ($14. Pit toilets, water available mid-May to mid-Sept.; after that, open with no fee untill snow forces closure.) Several miles past Dutch John, the popular **Mustang Ridge Campground ❶** lies just above an excellent swimming hole and a boat ramp. ($16. Water, flush toilets. Open mid-May to mid-Sept.) The immense **Firefighter's Memorial Campground ❶**, on Rte. 191 south of the dam, has numerous large, shady sites, some with hillside views of the reservoir. ($14. Water, pit toilets. Open mid-May to mid-Sept.) Free showers are available at **Deer Run, Cedar Springs, Firehole,** and **Mustang Ridge** ($3 for non-campers).

🔫 OUTDOOR ACTIVITIES

FISHING & BOATING. The Flaming Gorge Reservoir and the Green River below the dam offer some of the best trout fishing in the US; it's not unusual to have a 20-fish day on the river's A section. *(Fishing permits $8 first day, $6 each additional day. Available at Flaming Gorge Lodge, Dutch John Recreation Services, and most Manila stores.)* **Cedar Springs Marina,** 2 mi. before the dam, rents pontoon, ski, and fishing boats and offers guided fishing trips. *(☎ 889-3795. Open daily 8am-6pm. 10-person pontoon boats from $120 for 3hr., $200 per day. 6-person ski boats $130/$220; skis $15 per day. 6-person fishing boats $50/90.)* Nearby, **Flaming Gorge Lodge** rents fishing rods and has summer employment opportunities. The Lodge offers housing for employees; more info is on the website. *(☎ 889-3773; www.fglodge.com. Open daily 6:30am-10pm. $10 per day for demos, fly fishing rods $5 per day, flies not included.)* **Lucerne Valley Marina,** 7 mi. east of Manila off Rte. 43, hosts fishing contests on some of the best-regarded stretches of the Green River. *(☎ 784-3483. Visitors can rent a 14 ft. fishing boat for $75 a day. Open daily 7am-9pm. $50 deposit required.)*

RIVER RUNNING. The stretch of the **Green River** from the base of the **dam** to the **Gates of Lodore** in Dinosaur National Monument (p. 263) does not require a permit and contains several named rapids of the Class II and III varieties. Below the dam, management of the river is divided into three sections: **Spillway to Little Hole, Little Hole to Indian Crossing,** and **Indian Crossing to the Gates of Lodore.** The first section, a popular, 7 mi. trip, can take 1-3hr., depending on outflow from the dam (daily outflow can range from 830 to 4500 cubic feet per second). There is no camping between the Spillway and Little Hole. The next section, 7.5 mi. from Little Hole to Indian Crossing, demands 3-4hr. of float time and is speckled with developed campsites available to rafters. **Cottonwood** is located about 1.5 mi. below the dam and is reservable. **Grasshopper 1 and 2** are non-reservable and rest about 2.5 mi. below the dam. Both sites accommodate groups of 10 but have no toilet facilities. Fewer rafters continue on for the remaining 30.8 mi. to the Gates of Lodore, although no permit is required until the boundary of the National Monument. For more info on floating the Green, contact the **Flaming Gorge Ranger District.** *(At the corner of Rtes. 43 and 44 in Manila. ☎ 784-3445. Open M-F 8am-4:30pm.)*

Several companies rent rafts to self-guided rafters and provide shuttle services up and down the waterway. **Green River Outfitters,** at the Rte. 66 gas station in

Dutch John, offers guided fishing trips, in addition to raft rental and shuttle services. (☎ 885-3338. *2-person kayak $30 per day; 6-, 7-, 8-, 10-, and 14-person rafts $45-80. Moving a vehicle from the dam to Little Hole costs $25.*) The **Flaming Gorge Recreation Service,** at the Conoco Station in Dutch John, rents the same sort of equipment. (☎ 885-3191. *2-person kayaks $39 per day; 7-person rafts $49 per day, 8-person rafts $59. Shuttling between the dam and Little Hole costs $47, to move a vehicle $32. Waverunners $150 per day.*)

HIKING AND BIKING. Although most reservoir recreationalists stick to boats, water skis, and fishing poles, the area offers an extensive network of hiking and biking trails clustered around Greendale. **Canyon Rim Trail,** a moderate 5 mi. one-way hike, has access points at the Red Canyon Visitors Center and the Red Canyon, Canyon Rim, Green Lake, and Greendale campgrounds. From the Canyon Rim Campground Visitors Center, the trail traces the edge of Red Canyon for about a mile before splitting in two. The left fork, which is more desirable for its vistas, follows the rim of the canyon, while the right cuts inland to Green Lake before the trails meet up again and continue to the Greendale Overlook. Starting at Canyon Rim Campground, the trail can also be done as a 2.7 mi. loop. Another popular hike begins at **Dowd Mountain** and descends 1500 ft. into Hideout Canyon over the course of 5 mi. To access the trail, turn at signs for the mountain off Rte. 44 south of Manila. The first mile is relatively flat and boasts spectacular views of the gorge. Beginning at the base of the dam, the **Little Hole Trail** follows the Green River savors the beauty of the river for 7 mi. to Little Hole. The trail is mostly flat and offers beautiful scenery and excellent wildlife viewing opportunities.

All hiking trails in the recreation area also allow mountain bikers. The strenuous **Elk Park Loop** (20 mi.) departs Rte. 44 at the signs for Deep Creek Campground, follows the Deep Creek Rd. to Forest Rd. 221 and Forest Rd. 105, skirts Browne Lake, and then runs single-track along the **Old Carter** and **South Elk Park Trails.** For more info on hiking and biking trails, grab the helpful pamphlets available at the Visitors Centers and the Flaming Gorge District Ranger Station.

For the traveler in search of yet more spectacular geology, the **Sheep Creek Geologic Loop,** an 11 mi. scenic backway off Rte. 44, 11 mi. south of Manila, winds through Sheep Creek canyon lined with towering, red Moenkopi rock formations, sculpted strata, and desert wildlife such as antelope and rabbit.

HIGH UINTA WILDERNESS ☎ 435

The High Uinta (you-IN-tah) Wilderness Area offers a welcome respite from the crowded trails of the Wasatch Range. Within its 460,000 acres, it contains 500 lakes and several 13,000 ft. peaks, including Kings Peak, Utah's highest. Parts of the Uintas suffer from the same popularity and overuse as the Wasatch Front, but for the backpacker willing to wander off the beaten path, the Uintas reward with some of Utah's most pristine alpine environments. The mountain range itself differs from all others in the region, and most ranges in the US, with its east-west rather than north-south orientation. Powerful, high-angle faulting lifted the 600-million-year-old Uinta parent rocks while glaciers sculpted the terrain, combining to create a striking and varied topography. The resulting mountain block shelters a rich variety of wildlife, including beaver, porcupine, moose, trout, elk, and black bears.

■■ ☷ ORIENTATION & PRACTICAL INFORMATION

The High Uinta Wilderness Area covers a substantial portion of northeastern Utah and is therefore accessible from several different highways and trailheads. The most heavily used sections of the wilderness are the **Mirror Lake Scenic Byway** in the western corner and the **Henry's Fork/Kings Peak** area in the northeast. The **Wasatch-Cache** and **Ashley National Forests** jointly administer the wilderness. Depending on your planned destination, the following ranger stations oversee the area and are of help to visitors: in the west, **Kamas Ranger District**, 50 E. Center St. (☎783-4338; open M-F 8am-4:30pm); in the east, **Vernal Ranger District**, 355 N. Vernal Ave. (☎789-1181); and in the south, **Roosevelt Ranger District**, 244 W. U.S. 40 (☎722-5018).

Small, rural **Kamas** serves as a gateway to the western portion of the wilderness. The town has gas stations, restaurants, and lodging spread out along Rte. 34, although camping is in the Uintas themselves. To stock up on groceries before heading into the woods, stop by **Kamas Food Town**, a large, full-service grocer at 145 W. 200 S (☎783-4369; open M-Sa 7am-9pm, Su 9am-7pm).

⚡ OUTDOOR ACTIVITIES

WESTERN UINTA WILDERNESS

By far the easiest access to the western portion of the wilderness area is the Mirror Lake Scenic Byway. The byway (also known as **Rte. 150**) leaves Kamas and meanders 46 mi. through high alpine-scapes and past mountain lakes to the northern edge of the Wasatch-Cache National Forest. In summer, there is often still snow on the road, at least at the higher elevations. The road skirts the wilderness, with several trailheads yielding access to truly remote lands. Two ranger stations serve the Lake Scenic Byway: one is the **Kamas Ranger District**, on Rte. 150 in Kamas, and the other is the **Bear River Ranger Station**, on Rte. 150 at the northern limit of the national forest. Both stations provide ample information on camping, and scenic opportunities in the area, including a very detailed mile-by-mile guide to the scenic byway ($8). Travel along the byway requires a pass ($3) available at both ranger stations.

Both developed and primitive campsites line the length of the scenic byway at regular intervals. All developed sites have pit toilets and potable water, but none have showers. By far the most popular campground, **Mirror Lake ❶**, at mile 31.5, lies on the banks of the byway's namesake. (79 sites. $12, $5 per extra vehicle.) For the crowd-averse, both **Washington Lake ❶** (36 sites; $12) and **Trail Lake ❶** (60 sites; $12) campgrounds, at mile 25, offer shady sites on the shores of tranquil lakes. Many primitive sites can easily be seen from the byway itself, and are the best free camping bet for those lacking the high clearance needed to explore the more remote Forest Service roads.

Several popular **day hikes** lie along the byway. The **Ruth Lake Trail** (2 mi. round-trip, easy to moderate, 1½hr., water on trail) begins at mile 35 of the drive and climbs gently only 200 ft. to the lake (10,300 ft.). The **Bald Mountain Trail** (4 mi. round-trip, strenuous, 2½hr., no water available on trail), begins at mile 29 and leads from the trailhead at Bald Mountain Pass (10,715 ft.) to Bald Mountain Peak (11,943 ft.). The summit provides dazzling views of the westernmost peaks of the High Uintas. For other hiking and backpacking trails, the well-marked **Mirror Lake, Highline, Wolverine, Christmas Meadows,** and **East Fork Bear River** trailheads all provide ready trail access.

EASTERN UINTA WILDERNESS

Reaching trailheads that access the eastern part of the wilderness is much harder than from the scenic byway in the west. Trailheads surround the wilderness area, but reaching many of them demands travel on washboard Forest Service roads. Access to the southern and eastern trailheads begins from Rte. 87 north from Duchesne or Rte. 121 north from Roosevelt. Two Wyoming towns, **Mountain View** and **Lonetree,** serve as gateways to trailheads in the northeast.

A ROYAL ROMP FIT FOR A KING Despite inconvenient access, the trailhead leading to Utah's highest summit, Kings Peak (13,528 ft.), is routinely packed during summer months. A shot at conquering Utah's highest begins in Lonetree, WY. First, stock up on provisions and fill up with gas. If approaching from I-80 in Wyoming, Mountain View provides the last services. From Flaming Gorge in Utah, Manila has the last gas stations and markets. The sign for Rte. 290 lies hidden off Rte. 414, the major thoroughfare. To find the turn, clock 22 mi. from Mountain View, WY and take the right onto gravel past the first cluster of buildings. On Rte. 290 S, the sign for Henry's Fork Trailhead appears immediately. Follow signs for Henry's Fork and Forest Service Rd. 077 to the trailhead, where there are four campsites and a pit toilet. The hike to the summit requires at least two days, stretching 32 mi. from trailhead (9400 ft.) to summit along the most traveled route. The 11 mi. from Henry's Fork to the basin below Gunsight Pass (11,800 ft.) is relatively easy and heavily traveled. Ford Henry's Fork via the footbridge at Elkhorn Crossing and continue toward Gunsight. At Gunsight, the main trail dips into Painter Basin before climbing back up to Anderson Pass (12,600 ft.). From here, the summit lies nearly 1 mi. to the south, along a ridge that requires trailless scrambling over boulders. The main route demands very fit lungs and legs, but no technical expertise. An alternate route diverges from the main trail at Gunsight Pass, skirting the shoulder of an unnamed peak to arrive at Anderson Pass more quickly and directly. This route requires extensive scrambling over talus and a difficult, non-technical climb over a small cliff. Many cairns make the first half of the route easy to follow, but once you're on the shoulder, a map is absolutely necessary. Inexperienced mountaineers should stick to the main trail, especially on the way down. Most Kings Peak hikers spend a night or two near Henry's Lake. Enough snow melts by July 1 to clear the summit route, and it remains open until the first autumn snowfall. Afternoon thunderstorms are a danger that make summiting in the morning an absolute necessity. Topo maps are available from local ranger stations.

Most people focus on Kings Peak when hiking in the eastern Uintas. For more ideas on places to hit, stop by the Forest Service offices in the towns of Roosevelt or Vernal (see p. 258). Hikers tackling the wilderness from the north should definitely stop by the Mountain View Ranger Station, 321 Rte. 414 in Mountain View, WY, for information on hikes in the area as well as updates on trail conditions. (☎ 307-782-6555. Open M-F 8am-4:30pm.) All camping within the eastern wilderness area of the Uinta Wilderness is primitive, but many trailheads have basic toilet facilities. For a unique way of "roughing it," consider spending a night at the primitive **Spirit Lake Lodge ❸**, nestled east of the wilderness area in a high basin surrounded by commanding peaks. The lodge, decorated with a blend of diner kitsch and hunting trophies, serves three full meals a day and offers guests a stable of horses for riding as well as a fish-filled alpine lake. (☎ 880-3089. No running water and 2hr. of electricity per day. Cabins start at $34. Horse rides $10 per hr.; boat rentals $30 per day.)

EAST CENTRAL UTAH

Extreme sports, ranching, and wilderness solitude mix in the area around Moab in eastern Utah to form a wacky Western concoction as enigmatic as the state of Utah itself. The area's various parks are by far its biggest draws. Remote Canyonlands National Park makes a counterpoint for easily accessible Arches, with the La Sal Mountains providing a scenic backdrop to both.

MOAB ☎ 435

A town with few historic buildings or cultural attractions in the traditional sense, Moab may at first seem an unlikely major tourist destination—until you look up to the towering sandstone of the Moab and Swiss Cheese Rims just beyond the city limits, that is. As has always been the case, the canyonlands that surround Moab are the real draw for residents and visitors alike.

Moab first flourished in the 1950s, when uranium miners rushed to the area and transformed the town from a quiet hamlet into a gritty desert outpost with a phosphorescent glow that hasn't left the town since. These days, the mountain bike has replaced the Geiger counter as the main tool of outdoor recreation, and heavily laden SUVs lurch into town filled to the brim with passengers eager to bike and climb the red slickrock, raft whitewater rapids, and explore surrounding Arches and Canyonlands National Parks. The town itself has changed to accommodate the new arrivals; countless cafes and t-shirt shops now fill the rooms of the old uranium building on Main St. The influx of the earthy outdoors crowd has also had the political effect of making the town of Moab one of the most liberal in all of Utah.

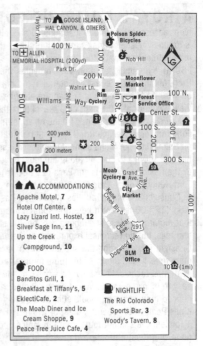

Moab

🏠🏕 ACCOMMODATIONS
Apache Motel, **7**
Hotel Off Center, **6**
Lazy Lizard Intl. Hostel, **12**
Silver Sage Inn, **11**
Up the Creek
   Campground, **10**

🍎 FOOD
Banditos Grill, **1**
Breakfast at Tiffany's, **5**
EklectiCafe, **2**
The Moab Diner and Ice
   Cream Shoppe, **9**
Peace Tree Juice Cafe, **4**

🍸 NIGHTLIFE
The Rio Colorado
   Sports Bar, **3**
Woody's Tavern, **8**

TRANSPORTATION

Canyonlands Field (☎259-7421), 18 mi. north of town on U.S. 191, offers charter plane service to Western hubs, through operators like **Redtail Aviation** and **Great Lakes Airlines.** Flights to Denver, Salt Lake City, and Phoenix can run as low as $100 with advance reservation. The closest **Amtrak** (☎800-872-7245) and **Greyhound** (☎564-3421, 800-454-2487) stations are in Green River, 52 mi. northwest. Some hotels and hostels pick up from the train or bus for a fee. **Bighorn Express** (☎888-655-7433) makes a daily trip to and from Salt Lake City airport, stopping in Green River and Price en route. Shuttles depart the Ramada Inn, 182 S. Main St. (Departs Salt Lake City airport at 2pm, departs Moab at 7:30am. 4½hr. trip. $56 each way.)

A car is a handy tool for exploring Moab and its environs but, unlike the case for the rest of southeastern Utah, is not necessity. **Roadrunner Shuttle** (☎259-9402) and **Coyote Shuttle** (☎259-8656) can take you where you want to go on or off-road in the Moab area; both specialize in bike ($10-12), river ($30-40), and airport ($23) shuttles but accommodate other needs as well. **Thrifty Car Rental,** 711 S. Main St. (☎259-7317), in the Moab Valley Inn, offers cars and 4x4s and one-way rentals to a number of Colorado and Utah destinations. If you're hankering for an off-road excursion, **Farabee 4x4 Rentals,** 397 N. Main St., Unit #4 (☎259-7494), and **Slickrock Jeep Rentals,** 284 N. Main St. (☎259-5678), are both good choices.

◢◪ ■ 🖈 ORIENTATION & PRACTICAL INFORMATION

Moab sits 30 mi. south of I-70 on U.S. 191, just south of the junction with Rte. 128. Grand Junction is 112 mi. northeast, and Monticello is 53 mi. south. The town center lies 5 mi. south of the entrance to Arches National Park and 38 mi. north of the turnoff to the Needles section of Canyonlands National Park. U.S. 191 becomes Main St. for about 5 mi. through downtown. Drivers eastbound into Moab on I-70 who don't mind a few extra miles should take exit 212, which leads past the shambles of Cisco to Rte. 128. This jewel among desert roads parallels the sparkling Colorado River, affording vistas of the La Sal Mountains and red rock towers for 45 mi. until it terminates at U.S. 191 just north of Moab. Sites along Rte. 128 have been featured in numerous westerns, including John Wayne's *Rio Grande* (1950) and *The Comancheros* (1961).

Visitor Info: Moab Information Center, 3 Center St., at the intersection of Center and Main St. (☎259-8825, 800-635-6622). This umbrella organization for the Chamber of Commerce, the **National Park Service,** the **US Forest Service,** and the **BLM,** doles out copious information on the city and the surrounding outdoors. (Open daily Jan.-Feb. 9am-5pm, Mar. 8am-7pm, Apr.-May and Oct.-Nov. 8am-8pm, June-Sept. 8am-9pm, Nov.-Dec. 9am-5pm.) While the Visitors Center has info to spare, specific information about Forest Service land can be found at the La Sals office of the **Forest Service,** 62 E. 100 N. (☎259-7155), and the **Moab BLM** office, 82 E. Dogwood Dr. (☎259-6111).

Laundry: Country Clean Laundromat, 588 S. Kane Creek Blvd. (☎259-3987). Open daily 7am-9pm.

Weather and Road Conditions: ☎801-524-5133, 800-492-2400.

Emergency: ☎911 or 259-8115. **Police:** 125 E. Center St. (☎259-8938).

Crisis Center: Seekhaven Family Crisis and Resource Center, ☎259-2229.

Medical Services: Allen Memorial Hospital, 719 W. 400 N (☎259-7191).

Internet Access: Free at **Grand County Library,** 25 S. 100 E (☎259-5421). Open M-W 9am-9pm, Th-F 9am-7pm, Sa 9am-5pm.

Pharmacy: 425 S. Main St. (☎259-8971). Open M-F 9am-7pm, Sa 9am-6pm.

Post Office: 50 E. 100 N (☎259-7427). Open M-F 8:30am-5:30pm, Sa 9am-1pm. **Postal code:** 84532.

🖈 ACCOMMODATIONS

Chain motels clutter Main St., but Moab is generally not cheap and fills up fast in spring and summer, especially on weekends. Off-season rates can fall by half.

Lazy Lizard International Hostel, 1213 S. U.S. 191 (☎259-6057; www.gj.net/ ~lazylzrd). Look for the "A1 Self Storage" sign 1 mi. south of Moab on U.S. 191. Well-maintained hostel whose owners go out of their way to be helpful. The kitchen, VCR, extensive video library, laundry, and hot tub are at guests' disposal and draw a mix of college students, international backpackers, and aging hippies. 24 dorm beds, 11 private rooms, 8 cabins, and tent camping area. Showers for non-guests $2. **Internet access** $1 per 10min. Reception 8am-11pm, late arrivals can be arranged. Check-out 11am. Reservations recommended for spring and fall weekends. Dorms $9; private rooms for 1 or 2 from $22; cabins sleeping up to 6 $27-47; tent sites $6. ❶

Hotel Off Center, 96 E. Center St. (☎259-4244), a block off Main St. This converted office building rents eclectically lavish rooms accented with antique items such as a miner's hat, fishing nets, and a Victrola. The gracious owners are continually renovating, to the delight of the many returning guests. Shared bath and kitchen. Open roughly Mar.-Nov. 4 bed dorm $12; singles $39; doubles $49, additional person $5. ❶

Silver Sage Inn, 840 S. Main St. (☎259-4420). The best rates in town for simple, clean rooms in a small, somewhat institutional building. Reception 7am-midnight. Check-out 11am. Apr.-Oct. singles $40; doubles $45. Nov.-Mar. $25/$30. ❷

Apache Motel, 166 S. 400 E (☎259-5727, 800-228-6882). Sleep where John Wayne slept. Follow the proud signs and hitch your horse outside a quiet, spotless room before heading into town to maintain law and order. When you're all done, wash off the red dust in the swimming pool. Reception 7am-11pm. Check-out 11am. Rooms $32-85, depending on business. AAA discount. ❷

📷 CAMPING

One thousand campsites blanket the Moab area, so finding a place to sleep out under the stars shouldn't be a problem, even in busy seasons. Most private campgrounds target RVs, but tenters can find dozens of sites along the river and some select private grounds. Pure water is available at Matrimony Spring, a literal watering hole treasured by locals, near the intersection of U.S. 191 and Rte. 128.

Goose Island, Hal Canyon, Oak Grove, and **Big Bend,** along Rte. 128 (☎259-2100). This series of developed campgrounds lines the south bank of the Colorado River 3-9 mi. northeast of town. Many sites are shaded, and the location couldn't be better. Picnic tables and fire pits, but no hookups or showers. Check-out noon. Sites $10. ❶

Negro Bill, Drinks Canyon, Upper Big Bend, Rte. 128 (☎259-2100). For those willing to rough it, these semi-developed camping areas are interspersed among the more developed sites on Rte. 128. The flat, shaded sites at Negro Bill are the best. Fire rings and pit toilets. Check-out noon. Sites $5. ❶

Up the Creek Campground, 210 E. 300 S (☎259-6995). This shady, secluded campground, just a walk away from downtown, caters solely to tent camping, unlike the RV-oriented sites that rule in town. 20 sites. Showers $5 for non-guests. Check-out 11am. Open Mar.-Oct. $10 per person. ❶

🍴 FOOD

Moab's eateries cover a more cosmopolitan range than most Utah towns of its size to accommodate discerning visitors and many budgets. **City Market,** 425 S. Main St., is a great choice for groceries and quick deli meals. (☎259-5181. Open daily 6am-midnight, deli 6am-7:30pm.) Another option is **Moonflower Market (Moab Community Coop),** 39 E. 100 N, an oasis of organic and health food. Check the bulletin board inside the market for apartment listings and rides all over the West. (☎259-5712. Open M-Sa 9am-8pm, Su 10am-3pm.) On summer Saturday mornings, check out the **Farmer's Market** at the Swanny City Park from 8-11am. Restaurants in Moab tend to close by 10pm.

The Moab Diner and Ice Cream Shoppe, 189 S. Main St. (☎259-4006). The retro booths might take you back to the 50s, but the food certainly won't. The menu features various veggie specials and tasty green chili ($4-10). Grab breakfast here and you'll be set until dinnertime. Open Su-Th 6am-10pm, F-Sa 6am-10:30pm. ❷

EklectiCafe, 352 N. Main St. (☎259-6896). Look for the coffee cup mosaic out front. All the weariness of the road dissipates here amidst the greenery and folk art of the shady front deck. A wide array of pastries, coffee drinks made with organic, fair trade beans, breakfasts ($3-7), and lunch options ($4-8) are available to go, but you'd be passing up on unbeatable atmosphere that includes live roots music Su morning and whenever the spirit moves a local musician. Open M-Sa 7am-2:30pm, Su 7am-1pm. ❶

Peace Tree Juice Cafe, 20 S. Main St. (☎259-8503). After a day in the desert, cool off here with a smoothie or fresh juice ($2.50-5). More substantial fare is also served, including a wide variety of vegetarian delights, wraps and salads ($4.50-6), and day-starters ($1.50-5.50). Open daily 8am-6:30pm. ❶

Breakfast at Tiffany's, 90 E. Center St. (☎259-2553). Audrey Hepburn would be proud of this hole-in-the-wall adding a little Fifth Ave. flare to an otherwise Western town. The creative fare ($4-7) defies the bacon-and-eggs standard; the almond french toast ($5.25) and catfish and eggs ($7) are favorites. Open M-F 7am-2pm, Sa-Su 7am-11:30am; open for appetizers F-M 7pm-closing. Cash only. ❶

ENTERTAINMENT & NIGHTLIFE

Every September starting on Labor Day weekend and continuing the next two weeks, the **Moab Music Festival** brings a variety of acts to several stunning venues against canyon country's scenic backdrop. For tickets and information, call ☎259-7003 or visit www.moabmusicfest.org. The **Moab Fat Tire Festival,** which takes place around Halloween, is one of the best times for mountain bikers to visit. Guided rides and celebrity guests add excitement to this benefit for the Moab Trails Alliance. (☎260-1182; www.moabfattirefestival.com.)

Moab's bars resound with rollicking fun on weekend nights starting at about 9pm. **The Río Colorado Sports Bar,** 100 W and Center St., is the place for live music on Friday and Saturday nights during spring and fall, and one of the few places in town serving hard drinks. (☎259-6666. Open daily 4-9pm, bar until 1am.) **Woody's Tavern** at Main St. and 200 S also serves the hard stuff, filling up with pool players and others looking for a rough-and-tumble rager to live music. (☎259-9323. Open M-Sa 2pm-1am, Su 11am-midnight. Live blues and rock F-Sa, with cover.)

OUTDOOR ACTIVITIES

Moab can serve as home base for almost any conceivable desert activity, and in many cases is the preeminent locale. For **mountain biking, rafting, hiking, rock climbing, canyoneering,** and **four-wheeling,** it doesn't get much better.

MOUNTAIN BIKING

More than any other destination in the West, Moab is synonymous with mountain biking. More people come to ride Moab's **Slickrock Trail** than any other route in the world, but it is only one of many fantastic rides in the area. Other routes provide equally challenging biking and views without the sometimes overwhelming crowds. For example, you can try the epic 143 mi. **Kokopelli Trail,** which also begins near Moab and passes through desert and canyon on its way to Grand Junction, CO. In all cases, be sure to ride only on open roads and trails, stay clear of crypto-biotic soil, and protect water sources. The desert environment may seem tough, but it recovers slowly from the impact of thousands of mountain bikers.

There is no shortage of bike shops in Moab, and all charge similar rates for rentals: $32-35 per day for front suspension, $38-40 for full suspension, $50 for top-end demos. **Rim Cyclery,** 94 W. 100 N, holds a strong reputation as the shop that started it all in Moab. (☎259-5333. Open Su-Th 9am-6pm; summer F-Sa 8am-6pm; winter 9am-6pm for ski/snowshow rentals. Ask about cross-country and backcountry skiing in the La Sals.) For those interested in renting a bike for multiple days, **Poison Spider Bicycles,** 497 N. Main St., has reduced rates. (☎259-7882, 800-635-1792; www.poisonspiderbicycles.com. Open daily 8am-6pm.) Other Main St. outfitters, including Moab Cyclery and Chile Pepper Bike Shop, offer mountain bike tours in the surrounding area as well as in Canyonlands National Park. Several Warner

Brothers' cartoon-inspired companies provide shuttle service to bikers: **Coyote** (☎259-8656), **Roadrunner** (☎259-9402), and **Acme** (☎260-2534). Popular destinations cost $10-12 per rider, and some companies charge a minimum rate per trip. Riders should carry plenty of **water** and consult the incredibly useful set of topo maps, **Moab East** and **Moab West** ($10 each), which describe numerous rides in reliable detail and show elevation profiles. An excellent local trail guide is *Rider Mel's Mountain Bike Guide to Moab.*

Slickrock Trail (9.6 mi. round-trip, with a 2.2 mi. practice loop). The trailhead is on Sand Flats Rd., 2.3 mi. from its intersection with Millcreek Dr., which begins on 400 E in town. The loop tackles the intense terrain of Moab's slickrock and shows off the spectacular scenery, constantly changing elevation as it traverses the red sandstone above Moab and the Colorado River. Rideable year-round, although the lack of shade increases the heat stroke potential. Sand Flats Recreation Area fee $3.

Porcupine Rim (21 mi. one-way). A favorite among locals, the Porcupine Rim ride is a challenging one that embarks from near two metal stock tanks on the north side of Sand Flats Rd., 11 mi. from Moab. After a 4 mi. climb to High Anxiety Viewpoint and outstanding views of Castle Valley, the trail descends on jeep roads and technical singletrack for 10 mi. until it reaches Rte. 128, 7 mi. from Moab. A shuttle is desirable, but the ride can be done as a 32 mi. loop.

Poison Spider Mesa (12 mi. round-trip). The trailhead for this moderate route is on Potash Rd. 279 (Rte. 279) at the "Dinosaur Tracks" sign. The climb up onto Poison Spider Mesa and Little Arch is tough but rewards riders with a thrilling descent. The confident can choose the challenge of the exposed and vertigo-inducing Portal Trail, which turns the ride into a loop and should not be attempted by any but the most skilled riders. 860 ft. elevation gain on the way in. Rideable year-round, though sandy in the summer.

Gemini Bridges (14 mi. one-way). This trail begins on Rte. 313, 12.6 mi. from its intersection with U.S. 191 north of Moab. Besides a brief ascent out of Little Canyon, riders enjoy long downhills on this pleasant entry-level route which passes the formations of Gemini Bridges and Gooney Bird Rock and provides spectacular views of Arches and Behind the Rocks. The trail emerges on U.S. 191 north of Moab. A shuttle is necessary, or the ride turns into a 50+ mi. loop.

Amasa Back Trail (21 mi. round-trip from town). A highly technical ride beginning with the "stairs," a steep series of descending rock stairs, and requiring several stream crossings and intense hillwork. The trail affords views into Canyonlands National Park and Dead Horse State Park, as well as a look at the mining operations along Potash Rd. The trail begins ¼ mi. beyond the end of the pavement on Kane Creek Rd.

RIVER RUNNING

Next to mountain biking, rafting on the Colorado River is Moab's biggest draw. Every day, busloads of visitors are whisked north along Rte. 128 to the **Fisher Towers** put-in. For those in search of bouncier thrills, May and June bring big water in the Colorado's **Westwater** and **Cataract Canyons.** Westwater trips range from one ($125) to three days ($435), while Cataract and other longer stretches of the Colorado can be explored on multi-day trips. Countless raft companies based in Moab offer trips catering to every imaginable type of rafter, from the four-year-old first-timer to the wily Class V+ veteran. For basic day-long trips, reservations are rarely necessary, and all the outfitters offer essentially the same trips. **Canyon Voyages Adventure Company,** 211 N. Main St. (☎259-6007 or 800-733-6007; www.canyonvoyages.com), **Tag A Long Expeditions,** 452 N. Main St. (☎259-8946 or 800-453-3292), and **Western River Expeditions,** 1371 N. U.S. 191 (☎259-7019 or 800-453-7450), all have good reputations and are well established. You can choose between a full-day voyage ($44-49 including lunch, children $33-37) and a half-day excursion ($33-36, children $26-29). The superb guides who work at **OARS/North American River Expedi-**

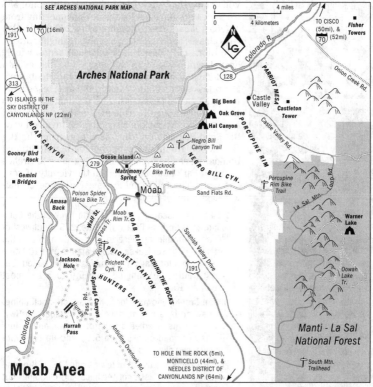

Moab Area

SEE ARCHES NATIONAL PARK MAP

TO (70) (16mi)

TO ISLANDS IN THE SKY DISTRICT OF CANYONLANDS NP (22mi)

Arches National Park

TO CISCO (50mi), & (70) (52mi)

Fisher Towers

Colorado R.

Onion Creek Rd.

PARRIOT MESA

Castle Valley

Castleton Tower

PORCUPINE RIM

Castle Valley Rd.

Big Bend

Oak Grove

Hal Canyon

Negro Bill Canyon Trail

NEGRO BILL CYN.

Gooney Bird Rock

Goose Island

Gemini Bridges

Matrimony Spring

Slickrock Bike Trail

Moab

Sand Flats Rd.

Porcupine Rim Bike Trail

Amasa Back

Poison Spider Mesa Bike Tr.

Wall St.

Kurrah Pass Rd.

Moab Rim Tr.

MOAB RIM

Spanish Valley Drive

La Sal Mtn.

Loop Rd.

Warner Lake

Jackson Hole

Kane Springs Canyon

Prichett Cyn. Tr.

PRICHETT CANYON

HUNTERS CANYON

BEHIND THE ROCKS

191

Oowah Lake Tr.

Hurrah Pass

Colorado R.

Anticline Overlook Rd.

TO HOLE IN THE ROCK (5mi), MONTICELLO (44mi), & NEEDLES DISTRICT OF CANYONLANDS NP (64mi)

South Mtn. Trailhead

Manti - La Sal National Forest

0   4 miles
0   4 kilometers

tions, 543 N. Main St. (☎259-5865, 800-342-5938), are specialists in extended expeditions in the area, ranging from overnights in Cataract Canyon to week-long journeys and beyond.

Those who prefer to tackle the turbid water in a more independent and hands-on fashion should consider cruising in an inflatable, touring, or whitewater kayak. All three rent for $35 per day at **Canyon Voyages,** but prior experience is required for the more technical boats. One-way river shuttles can be arranged with the rental, as well as one- to three-day courses in whitewater kayaking (from $210 including equipment rental). Most of the extended trips offered by Canyon Voyages and OARS allow the option of paddling a kayak through flatwater sections.

ROCK CLIMBING

Unsurprisingly, Moab and its environs are a climbing paradise that beckons climbers from all over the world. While many of the routes challenge expert climbers and require a great deal of technique, beginners with a little grit and determination can scale the red rock too. **Pagan Mountaineering,** located in McStiff's Plaza on S. Main St., has a good selection of gear for sale or rent and can provide info on area climbs. (☎259-1117. Open M-Sa 10am-7pm, Su 10am-5pm, shoe/harness/helmet rental $5 each.) The folks at **⊠Moab Cliffs and Canyons,** 63 E. Center St., initiate the inexperienced and hone the skills of the more practiced. From a vertical wall or atop an exhilarating 400 ft. tower, the price of hiring a guide's individualized instruction will feel well worth it. (☎259-3317 or 877-641-5271; www.cliffsandcan-

WHERE THE SUN DON'T SHINE

The up-and-coming sport of **canyoneering**, which combines hiking, swimming, wading, boulder hopping, rock climbing, and rappelling, is steadily gaining popularity among adventurers. Though the story of Aron Ralston (p. 364) highlights the sport's dangers, canyons are more safely tackled in small groups rather than solo. As the tourist hoards crowd hotspots like the Grand Canyon, canyoneering satisfies its enthusiasts' needs for solitude, escape, and a physical challenge, and Utah's thousands of exquisitely twisting canyons make an unparalleled natural playground. Most are wholly inaccessible to those without the proper equipment and technical skill, and paved roads will never reach them.

Some call canyoneering the next big thing in adventure sports. The best spots include Canyonlands, Zion, Escalante, San Rafael Swell, Arches, and Cedar Mesa. There are links to photographs and descriptions of these areas at www.canyoneeringusa.com. For a more detailed introduction to the sport, try the free "Intro to the Canyons Booklet" (www.canyoneering.net). In the Moab area, contact **Moab Cliffs and Canyons** about guided excursions. (Half-day trips $90 per person for two, $75 for 3 or more; full-day $150/$120. Ephedra's Grotto: 2.5 mi., 4-5 hr., year-round. Hypatia Canyon: 4 mi., 6-7 hr., Sept.-May.)

yons.com. Half day of climbing $100 for one, $85 each for two, $65 each for three. Canyoneering from $85/65.) **Moab Desert Adventures** (☎260-2404) also runs classes and guided trips at slightly higher prices. Eric Bjornstad's **Desert Rock guidebook series,** widely available in bookstores and gear shops, delves into the details of many of the routes in the Moab area. Countless sport climbs exist in the area, especially up in the **La Sal Mountains,** where summer climbers escape the stifling desert heat. For those interested in getting on the rock in a slightly less involved way, **Big Bend Boulders** on Rte. 128 across from the Big Bend Campground has great bouldering. Additional bouldering can be found near the entrance to Arches National Park and quite likely in the vicinity of your campsite. The following areas are considered hallowed ground by climbers:

Wall Street, located along the north bank of the Colorado, rises up from Potash Rd. (Rte. 279) northwest of Moab. Conveniently close to town and shaded in the afternoon, the vertical sandstone affords over 100 one-pitch routes for crag-style climbing (some bolted, but most traditional) ranging from 5.6 to 5.12, most around 5.10.

Indian Creek, renowned for world class **crack climbing,** is reached by a 50 mi. drive south of Moab on Hwy. 211 near the Needles district of Canyonlands. Hundreds of famed cracks from 5.10 and up captivate experienced climbers.

Fisher Towers, northeast of town along Rte. 128 on the Colorado, is a classic for technical aid climbing, but most routes require extensive gear and a great deal of faith in the crumbly-looking Cutler sandstone. Notable exceptions are **Ancient Art Tower,** a formation straight out of Dr. Seuss, whose more moderate corkscrew summit can be free-climbed, and the one-pitch route at the trailhead on **Lizard Rock.**

Castle Valley, also along Rte. 128, 5 mi. west of Fisher Towers, features towers of calcified Wingate Sandstone recognizable as the epitome of desert free climbing. The most classic, **Castleton Tower,** a symmetrical 400 ft. monolith, can be ascended along routes ranging from 5.9 to 5.12. A host of other superb formations include **the Rectory, the Priest, the Nuns, Sister Superior,** and **Parriott Mesa.**

Ice Cream Parlor, just west of town on Kane Creek Rd., offers routes from 5.6-5.11. The crag is visible on the left hand side of the street 3.6 mi. beyond the cattleguard (8.6 mi. from the beginning of Kane Creek Rd. at the McDonalds just south of the main section of town). If you come to where the canyon opens up, you've gone too far. Across the street from Ice Cream Parlor, **Space**

Tower is a long, single-pitch 5.9 route. Kane Creek Rd. is also home to more advanced climbing areas such as Abraxis Wall and the Cirque of the Climbables, home to the famous "tombstones."

HIKING

Amazing hiking abounds in the Moab area, and whether you're looking for a few peaceful hours or a full-day slog, the options are nearly endless. The **La Sal Mountains,** which lie east of Moab and rise to heights of over 12,000 ft., are often forsaken for the allure of the nearby slickrock, but offer incredible wilderness. More info on hikes around Moab and in the La Sals is available at the Moab Info Center.

IN THE LA SALS. The **South Mountain Trail** is on the La Sal Pass Rd. about ¼ mi. from the **Brumley Creek-La Sal Springs Trail.** This moderate hike, passable May through October, is one of the most scenic in the La Sals, circumscribing the 11,535 ft. South Mountain. The trail passes through varied terrain and crosses a number of basins. The route ends at La Sal Rd., about 4 mi. east of where it begins, so the hike can be made into an approximately 9 mi. loop. The **Oowah Lake-Clarks Lake Trail** begins on Geyser Pass Rd. south of Haystack Mountain. An easy hike passable May through October, it climbs down from 10,000 ft. along the **Geyser Pass Road** to 8800 ft. at **Oowah Lake,** passing through aspen, fir, and picturesque meadows. The 3 mi. one-way trail may be combined with the **Boren Mesa Trail** and a portion of the Geyser Pass Rd. to make an enjoyable 9 mi. loop. A short shuttle would allow for a bypass of the road section. Although not one of the highest cluster of peaks, **Manns Peak** is a highly accessible day-hike and offers amazing views all the way to the San Juan Mountains on a clear day, as well as a view of Moab and the surrounding canyons below. The trailhead is accessible from Geyser Pass Rd.

AROUND MOAB. The **Portal Overlook Trail** (980 ft. elevation gain) begins at JayCee Park Recreation site on Rte. 279, 4.2 mi. west of its junction with U.S. 191. This moderately easy 4 mi. round-trip trail, hikeable year-round, climbs above the Colorado to a panoramic view of the Moab Valley, the La Sal Mountains, and the Colorado River. Much of the trail follows cairned ramps of Kayenta sandstone to the breathtaking destination. The trailhead for the **Negro Bill Canyon Trail** (330 ft. elevation gain) is located on Rte. 128, 3 mi. east of its junction with U.S. 191. An easy 4 mi. round-trip jaunt hikeable year-round, it follows a perennial stream up Negro Bill Canyon. The 243 ft. Morning Glory Bridge, the sixth longest natural rock span in the US, spans a side canyon approximately 2 mi. up. For a bird's-eye view of the Behind the Rocks area sandstone fins, hike up the **Hidden Valley Trail,** accessible by driving 3 mi. south from town on U.S. 191, turning right onto Angel Rock Rd., and right again onto Rimrock Rd. This moderate trail climbs 680 ft. over 2 mi. up, the first 500 ft. rise coming in the first mile, to a broad shelf between the higher Moab rim and Spanish Valley below to the east. By continuing onto the Moab Rim jeep and mountain bike trail, the hike can be extended 3 mi. to the Colorado River. About 4.7 mi. down Castle Valley Rd. off Rte. 128 east of Moab, the **Castleton Tower Approach Trail** has panoramic views of Castle Valley, its numerous lovely sandstone formations, Porcupine Rim, and the La Sals to the south. Of course, the view from the summit of Castleton Tower 400 ft. above is even better, but you'll have to bring rock climbing gear to fully enjoy this 2.5 mi. round-trip. (1300 ft. elevation gain.)

FOUR-WHEELING

There are thousands of miles of jeep trails in Grand County. Unless you have previous experience off-roading, most of these routes are not the sort of thing that you'll want to dive (or drive) right into. The Visitors Center can provide info specific to your vehicle's and your own abilities. Popular easier routes include **Gemini**

Bridges, beginning on U.S. 191 just south of its intersection with Rte. 131, and some routes in the **Behind the Rocks** area. The second-best option is to let someone else do the driving for you. Numerous companies throughout town offer tours of the backcountry on a daily basis and are willing and able to take you on the area's most extreme paths. Of course, count on extreme prices. **Farabee Adventures, Incorporated,** 401 N. Main St. (☎259-7494, 888-806-5337), and **Dan Mick's Guided Tours,** 600 Millcreek Dr. (☎259-4567), specialize in four-wheel-drive excursions.

ARCHES NATIONAL PARK ☎435

"This is the most beautiful place on earth," novelist Edward Abbey wrote of Arches National Park. Although the number of visitors has increased from around 25,000 in Abbey's day to nearly 800,000 today, little else has changed since that time. Thousands of sandstone arches, spires, pinnacles, and fins tower high above the desert, creating a scene of overwhelming grandeur. Some arches are so perfect in form that they appear to have been constructed by some ancient civilization. The reality may be even more astounding: over the course of millions of years, bits and pieces of the porous sandstone that characterizes this area were broken off in cycles of freezing and thawing, and what remained was then sculpted by ice and water into its current flowing form. Deep red sandstone, green piñon, juniper trees, and the occasional ominous thundercloud set against a strikingly blue sky combine to form an unforgettable palette of color. However, the tableau shouldn't be fully appreciated with museum-like reserve from behind tinted automobile windows. Throw yourself into this natural painting and explore the magnificent landscape on foot for yourself.

AT A GLANCE: ARCHES NATIONAL PARK	
AREA: 76,519 acres.	**GATEWAY TOWNS: Moab** (p. 272).
FEATURES: Arches!	**CAMPING:** Devil's Garden $10.
HIGHLIGHTS: Driving to the Windows, Delicate Arch, and Devil's Garden; hiking to Delicate Arch.	**FEES:** Weekly entrance pass $10 per carload, $5 per pedestrian or cyclist.

ORIENTATION & PRACTICAL INFORMATION

Although no public transportation serves Arches, a number of shuttle bus companies, including **Roadrunner Shuttle of Moab** (☎259-9402), travel to the park. The park entrance is on U.S. 191, 5 mi. north of Moab and 25 mi. south of the junction of U.S. 191 and I-70. An 18 mi. paved road bisects the park and, along with two roads, offers access to the most popular formations, viewpoints, and hiking trails. The **Visitors Center,** just beyond the entrance station to the right, has interesting exhibits and rangers on duty. (☎719-2299. Open daily 8am-4:30pm; extended hours Mar.-Oct.) For **weather and road info,** call ☎800-492-2400 (Utah) or ☎877-315-7623 (Colorado). Write to the Superintendent, Arches National Park, P.O. Box 907, Moab, UT 84532 for more info or check the website (www.nps.gov/arch).

WHEN TO GO. While many visit in the summer, 100°F temperatures make hiking difficult. If you do plan to hike in the summer, be sure to bring plenty of water. The best time to visit the park is in the spring and fall, when temperate days and cool nights combine to make for a comfortable stay. In the winter, occasional white snow provides a brilliant contrast to the red-rock arches.

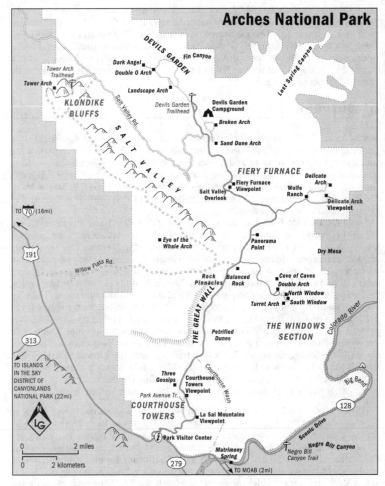

Arches National Park

CAMPING

The park's only campground, **Devil's Garden ❶,** has 52 excellent campsites nestled amid piñon pines and giant red sandstone formations. The campsite is within walking distance of the Devil's Garden and Broken Arch trailheads; however, it is a long 18 mi. from the Visitors Center. Sites are first-come, first-serve except for large groups, and the campground tends to fill every night. At the time of publication, Devil's Garden was considering a reservation system; check the park website for more information. (☎719-2299. Bathrooms, water, no wood gathering. Open year-round. 1-week max. stay. Sites $10.)

If the heat becomes unbearable at Arches, the aspen forests of the **Manti-La Sal National Forest** offer respite. Take Rte. 128 along the Colorado River and turn right at Castle Valley, or go south from Moab on U.S. 191 and turn left at the sign for the

Loop Rd. and Ken's Lake (Old Airport Rd.). There are a number of campgrounds here including **Warner Lake ❶**, where beautiful sites rise 4000 ft. above the national park and are invariably several degrees cooler (sites $10; Oowah Lake sites free). Oowah, a 3 mi. drive from the Geyser Pass Rd., is a rainbow trout haven. Fishing permits are available at stores in Moab and at the Forest Service Office, 62 E. 100 N, for $5 per day. Contact the Manti-La Sal National Forest Moab/Monticello Ranger District (☎259-7155).

▚ OUTDOORS

HIKING. While the red slickrock vistas from the road may seem unbeatable, the park's eponymous arches are best appreciated up close. To experience them more intimately, load up on water and sunscreen and seek out the formations on foot. For detailed maps and info on hiking, ask a ranger at the Visitors Center. Hiking in the park is hard to beat, especially in the cool days of spring and fall. **Stay on trails;** the land may look barren but the soil actually contains cryptobiotic soil crust that is easily destroyed by footsteps.

The 3 mi. **Delicate Arch** Trail leaves from the Wolfe Ranch parking area, 1.2 mi. off of the main road. Much of this strenuous hike follows cairns over exposed slickrock, offering excellent views of the surrounding terrain. The exquisitely eroded arch is best appreciated on foot from beneath. Hikeable year-round except when wet, the round-trip takes two to three hours. For a longer, more challenging alternative, the 7.2 mi. round-trip **Devil's Garden Trail** takes three to five hours, beginning at the Devil's Garden parking area at the end of the main road. The hike requires some scrambling over rocks, but eight arches visible from the main trail are a fitting reward. Start early in the morning or at the end of the day for fewer people, better lighting, and cooler temperatures, but don't attempt it in wet or snowy conditions. Exploring one of the more remote and less crowded areas of the park, the 3.4 mi. round-trip **Tower Arch Trail** begins at the Klondike parking area on Salt Valley Rd. This moderate, two to three hour hike ascends a steep but short rock wall before meandering through sandstone fins and sand dunes. Salt Valley Rd. is often washed out, so check with the Visitors Center before departing.

DRIVING. The 18 mi. main park road cruises past must-see attractions of Arches for those lacking the time or inclination to brave the desert heat. The park boasts the most accessible concentration of natural arches on the planet, and many are pinpointed on the free map and guide passed out at the entrance station. Leaving the Visitors Center, the drive comes first to **Courthouse Towers** and **Park Avenue,** whose sheer faces are strangely reminiscent of a mainstreet facade from a movie set. A 1 mi. trail promenades down this stretch before meeting up again with the park drive. The road then passes **Petrified Dunes, The Great Wall,** and **Rock Pinnacles** before arriving at the gravity-defying **Balanced Rock.** Immediately after the turn-out for Balanced Rock, a spur road heads out to the fantastic **Windows** section. Here it seems that everywhere you turn another arch comes out of the woodwork, and an easy 1 mi. trail allows visitors to get up close and personal with such goliaths as **North Window, South Window,** and **Turret Arch.** Visitors occasionally encounter petroglyphs left on the stone walls by the Ancestral Puebloans and Utes who wandered here centuries ago. Two and a half miles north of the turnoff to the Windows, another spur road sets out for the Delicate Arch. A trail climbs up to the arch, but to view the spectacular formation without the long hike, take the **Delicate Arch Viewpoint Trail** from its parking area. Beyond the Delicate Arch turnoff is the maze of **Fiery Furnace.** *(Access to this labyrinth of canyon bottoms beneath cliffs and monoliths requires an additional fee. Rangers lead small groups twice daily in season on moderately strenu-*

ous 2½-3hr. hikes. Reservations must be made at the Visitors Center in person, but no phone or mail requests and no more than seven days in advance. Tours often fill up 1-2 days early. $8, children $4.) At the road's end lies **Devil's Garden,** a wonderland of rock.

OTHER ACTIVITIES. Rock climbing is also popular in the park. A number of guide books provide specific info on routes. None of the features named by the United States Geological Services (USGS) may be climbed, but an abundance of ascents await the vertically-inclined, including **Owl Rock,** a 100 ft., 5.8 single pitch in the Garden of Eden climbing area, and **The Three Penguins,** a popular two-pitch, 120 ft. route (5.9) in the Central Chimney area. All park routes are detailed in the *Desert Rock Guidebook* series, which is sold at the Arches Visitors Center and bookstores in the region.

GREEN RIVER ☎ 435

The town of Green River (pop. 860) straddles the calm section of the waterway famous for its raging rapids to the north and south. An oasis in the vast desert traversed by the interstate, Green River once acted as a robber's roost, a remote desert hideout for the Wild Bunch and other outlaws. A historic crossroads from the early days of the Denver-Río Grande Railroad to the construction of Interstate 70, today Green River survives as a center for rafting the Green and Colorado and, believe it or not, melon farming. If you're in town for the August harvest or the September festival that follows, the watermelon and cantaloupe can't be missed.

■�◪ ORIENTATION & PRACTICAL INFORMATION. Green River lies along I-70 just east of its intersection with U.S. 191 N, 185 mi. southeast of Salt Lake City, 102 mi. west of Grand Junction, CO, and 160 mi. east of the junction of I-70 and I-15. Main St., the only thoroughfare in town, runs between two exits off I-70. The town is home to **Greyhound** (☎564-3421 or 800-231-2222) and **Amtrak** (☎800-872-7245). Buses stop at the **Rodeway Inn,** 525 E. Main St., on their way to Salt Lake (185 mi.), Las Vegas (400 mi.), or Denver (350 mi.). The train, which stops at the south end of Broadway, comes through once a day in each direction, bound for Salt Lake City or Denver. You may have to ask the conductor for it to stop in town.

The **Visitors Center,** located in the **John Wesley Powell Museum,** 885 E. Main St., is well stocked with brochures about town services and the surrounding outdoors. (☎564-3526. Open June-Aug. daily 8am-8pm; Sept.-May 8am-5pm.) The adjacent museum captivates history buffs and others with river lore and a slideshow with narrated excerpts from Powell's journals. In addition, artifacts from Powell's expedition line the museum, including a replica of his boat, the Emma Dean. (☎564-3427. $2, youths $1. Same hours as Visitors Center.) There's a **laundromat** at the Shady Acres RV Park and Campground, 350 E. Main St. (☎564-8290. Open daily 6am-11pm. Non-campers may ask to use the facilities.) Other services include: **weather and road conditions,** ☎800-492-2400; **Emery County Sheriff,** 48 Farrer St. (☎564-3431); **Green River Medical Center,** 305 W. Main (☎564-3434); free **Internet access** at the **Green River City Library,** 85 S. Long St. (☎562-3349; open M-F 10am-6pm); and the **post office,** 20 E. Main St. (☎564-3329; open M-F 8:30am-noon and 1-4:30pm, Sa 8:30-11:30am). **Postal code:** 84525.

▌◖ ACCOMMODATIONS & FOOD. Main St. is lined with budget motels. One of the cheapest is **Budget Inn ❷,** 60 E. Main St. Located across the street from the Green River community park, the inn offers access to the **Internet,** large rooms with queen size beds, cable TV, and new A/C units. (☎564-3441. Open 24 hrs. Singles $24-29; doubles $5 more.) **Robbers Roost Motel ❷,** 225 W. Main St., offers clean, basic rooms with shower/bathtub combinations and the added bonus of a pool. (☎564-3452. Reception 7am-2am. Check-out 10:30am. Singles $29; doubles $39.

Rates drop in winter.) **Green River State Park ❶**, 145 S. Green River Blvd., has 40 grassy sites and showers, making for a relaxing spot to recuperate from a day on the river. (☎ 564-3633. Check-in 3pm, check-out 2pm. Sites $14. No hookups.)

Ben's Cafe ❶, 115 W. Main, dishes out ample portions of Mexican and American food as jukebox tunes fill your ears. Bargain breakfasts range $3.75-7, while lunch runs $5-8. (☎ 564-3352. Open daily summer 7am-11pm; winter 7am-10pm.) For the second-best option in town, head to **Ray's Tavern ❷**, right next door at 26 S. Broadway. Rafting t-shirts adorn the walls above diners helping themselves to ½ lb. burgers ($5.70 with fries) and pizzas ($9-14) at tree-trunk tables. (☎ 564-3511. Open 11am-10pm.) During harvest season in August, look for melon stands along Main St., where fresh fruit costs 17¢ per pound.

🄺 OUTDOOR ACTIVITIES. As its name implies, the town of Green River's grandest offering is the Green River itself. Numerous rafting trips depart frequently from late spring through early fall. Two reputable local outfitters are **Moki Mac River Expeditions**, 100 S. Sillman Ln. (☎ 564-3361 or 800-284-7280), and **Holiday Expeditions**, 1055 E. Main St. (☎ 801-266-2087 or 800-624-6323). Both companies offer a day trip on the Green River (for about $55) as well as multi-daytrips on multiple rivers, including the Green, the Colorado, and other regional waterways. For the truly adventurous, Holiday Expeditions also features expeditions combining rafting with mountain biking.

To see the spectacular terrain of this country gripping your steering wheel in your hands rather than a canoe or kayak paddle, the **Green River Scenic Drive** is an appealing (and completely dry) option. This short drive follows the course of the Green River all the way through Gray Canyon for almost 20 mi., offering plenty of diversions for those interested in biking, hiking, swimming, and camping along the way. From the center of town, head east to Hastings Rd. and turn left. Eight miles down the road, at Swasey Beach, the pavement ends, but the road stays just above the river for the remainder of the drive, leading finally to a rock formation bearing a likeness to Queen Nefertiti.

Thanks to an uplift 40-60 million years ago and the subsequent forces of erosion, the spectacular topography of the **San Rafael Swell** is a wonderland for hikers, backpackers, and bikers. This kidney-shaped area located off I-70 19 mi. west of Green River has been designated a Wilderness Study Area (WSA) by the BLM and is up for inclusion in the National Park system as a National Monument, though the decision is still pending. The Visitors Center in Green River provides information on road conditions and a free guide to the **San Rafael Desert Loop Drive,** which begins just south of town and follows the river to **Horseshoe Canyon,** an extension of Canyonlands National Park. It then links up with Rte. 24 to skirt the edge of the sawtooth ridge that marks the eastern rim of the swell, called **San Rafael Reef,** before intersecting with I-70. This 100 mi. scenic drive can be combined with the Bicentennial Highway (Rte. 95) departing from Hanksville. **Backcountry camping** is usually allowed along the route (check with the BLM in advance), and developed sites are available for a fee at **Goblin Valley State Park** south of the swell near Temple Mountain and Crack Canyon just off Rte. 24. For more info on San Rafael, visit www.emerycounty.com.

Crystal Geyser, about 10 mi. south of town, erupts every 14-16hr. for about 30min. at a time, shooting a jet of water as high as 80 to 100 ft. into the air. Environmental purists may be surprised to learn that the seemingly natural scenic phenomenon owes its origin to the oil extraction industry; the geyser was formed in 1936 not from natural breaks in the earth but after a petroleum test well was drilled on the riverbank. To get to the geyser, head east on Main St. from town, continue over I-70, and turn left onto the first frontage road. After 2.7 mi., turn right and continue 4.4 mi. to the geyser.

CANYONLANDS NATIONAL PARK   ☎ 435

Those who make the trek to Canyonlands National Park are rewarded with a pleasant surprise: the near complete absence of people. The sandstone spires, roughly cut canyons, and vibrantly colored rock layers of this awe-inspiring landscape are often passed up by those on a strict time budget, which is fine with many visitors. Without the onslaught of RVs and tour buses typical of most popular parks, some of the wildest land in the lower 48 gets room to breathe. When the park was established in 1964, much of the territory had yet to be mapped or fully explored, and was traveled only by Native Americans, cowboys, outlaws, and miners. In some sections of the park, not much has changed. Due to the park's sheer size and awe-inspiring panoramas, those willing to get off the beaten path will experience a vast beauty unlike that of any other park. Like the Utes, mountain men, and fortune-hunters that came before them, visitors must come well prepared—there are few amenities in the park, and those who venture out commit themselves to a real outdoor experience.

UTAH

AT A GLANCE: CANYONLANDS NATIONAL PARK

AREA: 337,598 sq. acres.

FEATURES: Green and Colorado Rivers, The Needles, Island in the Sky, The Maze.

HIGHLIGHTS: Hiking in the Needles, off-roading on White Rim Road, touring Horseshoe Canyon.

GATEWAY TOWNS: Moab (p. 272), Monticello.

CAMPING: Squaw Flat Campground (The Needles) $10, Willow Flat Campground (Island in the Sky) $5; permits required for overnight backcountry travel.

ENTRANCE FEES: Weekly pass for vehicles $10, pedestrians and bikers $5.

✴ ORIENTATION

The Green and Colorado Rivers divide the park into three districts and together comprise the fourth. Because each region is essentially self-contained, once you've entered one district, getting to another requires retracing your steps and reentering the park, a trip that can last from several hours to a full day. To get to the **Needles,** take Hwy. 211 W from U.S. 191, about 40 mi. south of Moab or 14 mi. north of Monticello. Farther north, **Island in the Sky** is the most easily accessible district from Moab—the entrance station and Visitors Center sit about 22 mi. southwest of the Hwy. 313 W turnoff from U.S. 191, 10 mi. north of Moab. To reach the **Maze** district from I-70, take Rte. 24, 15 mi. west of Green River, 29 mi. to a turnoff just south of the entrance to Goblin Valley State Park. The **Rivers** district features great stretches of flat water and some world-class rapids. Above the confluence, both rivers remain calm as they wind their way through the layered sandstone, cutting two deep canyons. The power of their combined flow in the southern portion of the park makes for incredibly fast and powerful whitewater raging through Cataract Canyon. For more info on rafting in Canyonlands, visit the rafting companies based in Moab (p. 272).

WHEN TO GO Summer temperatures in Canyonlands often top 100°. Spring and fall are the best times of year for hiking and backpacking, with highs ranging 60-80°. Be aware, however, that temperatures fluctuate greatly over the course of a day, and it is not unusual for an 80° day to turn into a 40° night. Although there is not much snowfall in Canyonlands, winter highs range 30-50°, with lows of 0-20°, and even a little bit of snow can render much of the park impassable.

▓ PRACTICAL INFORMATION

Coyote Shuttle (☎259-8656) and **Roadrunner Shuttle of Moab** (☎259-9402) both provide taxi service to the Needles and Island in the Sky districts. Before plunging into the different districts, visit Monticello's **Multiagency Visitors Center,** 117 S. Main (☎587-3235, 800-574-4386; open M-F 8am-5pm, Sa-Su 10am-5pm), or the **Moab Information Center,** 3 Center St. (☎259-8825, 800-635-6622. Open July-Aug. daily 8am-9pm, Sept.-Oct. and Apr.-May 8am-7pm, Nov. 9am-7pm, Dec.-Mar. 9am-5pm, May-June 8am-8pm.) The **Bureau of Land Management** presides over the Green and Colorado upstream from the park. For more info, contact the **Grand County Travel Council** (☎800-635-6622) or the **Moab Area BLM Office** (☎259-6111). For recorded river flow info, call ☎801-539-1311, and ☎800-492-2400 or 964-6000 for **weather and road conditions.** Moab's **Rim Cyclery,** 94 W. 100 N (☎259-5333), and **Pagan Mountaineering,** 88 E. Center St. (☎259-1117), offer a full range of outdoor gear. There is no **gas** or food available in the park, and no **water** available in Island in the Sky or the Maze. Write to Canyonlands National Park, 2282 S.W. Resource Blvd., Moab, UT 84532, or call ☎259-7164 for more info.

NEEDLES REGION

The Needles region, named for its Cedar Mesa sandstone spires, offers unparalleled hiking amid arches, canyons, and Native American ruins. Hiking and four-wheel-drive trails offer excellent views of the rivers and make for some of the best day trips and overnight treks in the park.

▓ PRACTICAL INFORMATION.

The **Needles Visitors Center,** 35 mi. west of U.S. 191, is a good place to fill up on water and chat with rangers before setting out. (☎259-4711. Open Mar.-Oct. daily 8am-5pm; Nov.-Feb. 8am-4:30pm.) Services including an **ATM, grocery store, hospital,** and **post office** are available in **Monticello,** 50 mi. southeast of the park. **Water** is available at the Visitors Center and Squaw Flat Campground. Just outside the park boundary and 1 mi. from the Visitors Center, the solar-powered **Needles Outpost** has expensive groceries and gas, and a small **restaurant ❶** from March to December (menu items $5-8.50). **Camping ❶** ($15) and showers (non-guests $5, guests $3) are also available here. (☎979-4007. Open daily 8:30am-5pm, with extended spring and fall hours.)

▓ CAMPING.

Squaw Flat Campground ❶, 4 mi. west of the Visitors Center on a well-marked spur of the main park drive, offers 33 sites shaded by scattered piñon-juniper trees and surrounding sandstone pinnacles and alcoves. (☎259-4711. Flush toilets and running water. No wood gathering. 14-night max. stay. Check-out 11am. Sites $10.). For great overlooks at elevations above 8000 ft., camp in the **Monticello District** of the **Manti-La Sal National Forest,** south of Needles. The sites in the forest are almost always cooler than those in the park. Two campgrounds are easily accessible from Hwy. 211: **Buckboard ❶,** 11.5 mi. south of Hwy. 211 (16 sites, 10 with full hookup; $9), and **Dalton Springs ❶,** 13 mi. south of Hwy. 211 (18 sites, 16 with full hookup; $9). Both are open from late May to October.

▓ HIKING.

Hiking options from the Needles area are more developed than in any other district, and numerous itineraries are possible along the interconnecting trails. The majority of trails traverse a mixture of slickrock and sandy washes surrounded by the surreal landscapes of the Needles themselves. Almost any hike in this region is bound to be a good one, but a few favorites stand out.

One of the more popular routes is the moderate **Chessler Park Loop,** which travels through prime slickrock country en route to the spectacular Chessler Park, 960 acres of grassy meadows surrounded by magnificently rainbowed hoodoos. Start-

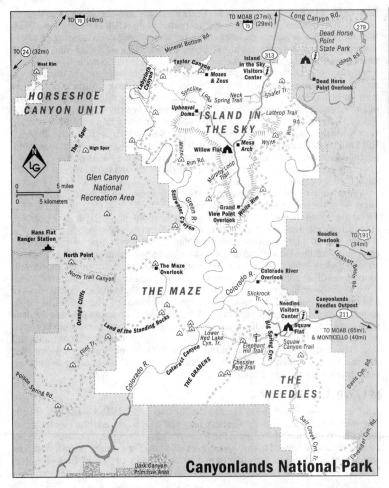

TO 70 (49mi)

TO 24 (32mi)

West Rim

Long Canyon Rd.

TO MOAB (27mi),
& 70 (29mi)

279

Dead Horse
Point
State Park

Potash Rd.

Mineral Bottom Rd.

Taylor Canyon

Labyrinth Canyon

Moses
& Zeus

Island
in the Sky
313 Visitors
Center

Dead Horse
Point Overlook

HORSESHOE
CANYON UNIT

Syncline Loop

Neck
Spring Trail

Shafer Tr.

Upheaval
Dome

ISLAND IN

THE SKY

Lathrop Trail

White Rim
Rd.

The Spur

High Spur

White Rim Rd.

Willow Flat

Mesa
Arch

White Rim

N
LG

0   5 miles

0   5 kilometers

Glen Canyon
National
Recreation Area

Green R.

Stillwater Canyon

Murphy Loop
Trail

Grand
View Point
Overlook

White Rim

Hans Flat
Ranger Station

North Point

North Trail Canyon

THE MAZE

The Maze
Overlook

Colorado R.

Colorado River
Overlook

Needles
Overlook

TO 191
(34mi)

Lockhart Basin Rd.

Orange Cliffs

Land of the Standing Rocks

Flint Tr.

Lower
Red Lake
Cyn. Tr.

Slickrock
Tr.

Needles
Visitors
Center

Canyonlands
Needles Outpost

211

Squaw
Flat

Big Spring Cyn.

Squaw
Canyon Trail

TO MOAB (65mi),
& MONTICELLO (40mi)

Poison Spring Rd.

Colorado R.

Cataract Canyon

THE GRABENS

Elephant
Hill Trail

Chessler
Park Trail

THE

NEEDLES

Davis Cyn. Rd.

Salt Creek Cyn. Tr.

Lavender Cyn. Rd.

Dark Canyon
Primitive Area

Canyonlands National Park

ing at the base of Elephant Hill, the 11 mi. round-trip hike encircles the meadow
and winds through a series of deep, narrow fractures along the way. The **Druid Arch**
hike follows the Chessler Park Loop for a few miles before branching off on its
own into Elephant Canyon and the arch itself. The moderately difficult 11 mi.
round-trip route provides some of the most spectacular views in the Needles
Region as it makes its way up a steep climb that requires both a ladder and some
scrambling to the arch.

A moderate 7.5 mi. trail connects **Big Spring** and **Squaw Canyon**. The trailhead is
located along Squaw Flat Loop "A." Rambling through varied terrain in two canyons, this trail serves as an excellent introduction to the Needles Region. The section between the two canyons climbs steep grades along exposed slickrock
benches and is very dangerous when wet. The shorter **Slickrock Trail** (2.4 mi. round-
trip) departs from a well-marked turn-out near the end of the park drive. The trail
itself offers several viewpoints of the river canyons and surrounding terrain.

OTHER OUTDOOR ACTIVITIES. There is no shortage of **backpacking** opportunities in the Needles. Make sure you get a permit at the Visitors Center before setting out ($15; reservations recommended for spring and fall), and bring plenty of water; reliable water sources are scarce. The challenging 22.5 mi. one-way **Salt Creek Canyon Trail** begins at Peekaboo Camp and plunges into some of the wildest terrain in the district. It follows the canyon's main drainage through dense brush and cottonwood groves before picking up an old four-wheel-drive trail. Those without high-clearance four-wheel-drive vehicles can begin the hike 3.5 mi. north of Cave Spring at Peekaboo or at the southern end of the canyon at Cathedral Butte. Allow two days to complete the one-way trip and camp at semi-developed sites along the way. The 18.9 mi. **Lower Red Lake Canyon** hike begins at the Elephant Hill Trailhead. This strenuous route climbs through the Grabens before descending the steep talus slope of Lower Red Lake Canyon to the banks of the Colorado, affording great views of the river and the Maze on the opposite bank. Allow two days; the only camping is dispersed.

A multitude of **rock climbing** routes are easily accessible throughout the park, but none of the routes are bolted and most are difficult to top rope, so they are not for beginning climbers. Talk to a park ranger for more info. Myriad rock outcroppings attract amateur and hard core boulderers from far and wide.

More than 50 mi. of backcountry roads blanket the Needles, providing access to campsites, trailheads, and natural wonders, and some great rides for high-clearance **four-wheel-drive** vehicles. The **Elephant Hill** route is one of the most difficult four-wheel-drive roads in Utah and should not be attempted by inexperienced drivers. Those willing to risk life and limb are rewarded with spectacular views and access to some of the more remote parts of the area. The road also offers some challenging riding for mountain bikers. The more moderate **Colorado Overlook** route presents a four-wheeling experience better suited for less seasoned drivers, as well as some excellent biking. The last 1.5 mi. of the road has large rocks and stair-step drops. Elephant Hill and the Colorado Overlook are both free for day-use, but routes through Horse Canyon and Salt Creek to Peekaboo require day-use permits, as does overnight use.

ISLAND IN THE SKY

A towering mesa within the "Y" formed by the two rivers, Island in the Sky affords fantastic views of the surrounding canyons and mountains and the easiest drive-through experience of the park for travelers short on time. For those staying longer, the abundance of hiking and jeep roads make for a more in-depth visit. The peninsular mesa connects to a plateau by an isthmus or "neck" that stretches between two canyons and is just wide enough to allow the road to pass over.

PRACTICAL INFORMATION. The **Island in the Sky Visitors Center**, 25 mi. southwest from the intersection of U.S. 191 and Rte. 313, provides info and sells the only **water** in this area of the park. (☎259-4712. Open Apr.-Oct. daily 8am-6pm, Nov.-Mar. 8am-4:30pm.) Moab (p. 272), 32 mi. from the park, provides many services, including **banks, grocery stores,** a **hospital,** and a **post office.**

CAMPING. Willow Flat Campground ❶ sits atop the mesa, approximately 8 mi. south of the Visitors Center on a well-marked 1 mi. turnoff from the park drive. At 6000 ft., the campground provides respite from the heat of the surrounding countryside. (12 sites. Pit toilets, no water. 14-night max. stay. Check-out 10am. Sites $5.) **Dead Horse Point State Park ❶** on Rte. 313, 22 mi. south of the junction with U.S. 191, pampers campers with its share of astounding sights, including a view of the Colorado that may surpass any in the Island of the Sky. (21 sites. Water, hookups, and covered picnic tables. Sites $14, including park admission. **Visitors Center** open daily 8am-5pm. Entrance fee $7.) For more info, write the Park Superintendent, Dead Horse Point State Park, Box 609, Moab, UT 84532. (☎259-2614, 800-322-3770. Open daily 6am-10pm.) Free camping is allowed in designated **primitive campsites** on BLM land along Rte. 313 east of the park. Know that the BLM's hospitality extends to mining companies, who make an occasional ruckus in the area.

■ **HIKING.** Trails on the Island in the Sky offer spectacular views, and a short hike makes a satisfying diversion. Routes that drop below the mesa top tend to be primitive and rough. Hikes are marked with cairns and signs at junctions and trailheads and may be tackled without a day-use permit. The **Neck Spring Trail** begins across from the overlook just south of the Neck. This moderate 5 mi. round-trip hike stays on the mesa top as it loops above the Taylor Canyon, which makes the northern "moat" of Island in the Sky. The trail passes a spring that was used by ranchers, as well as relics of these operations. (300 ft. elevation change. Hikeable year-round.) The moderate 8 mi. round-trip **Syncline Loop** begins at the end of the park road at the Upheaval Dome Trailhead and encircles the breathtakingly surreal **Upheaval Dome,** in addition to providing access to both the Green River and the crater. A 3.5 mi. spur leaves the trail about halfway through and heads west to the White Rim Rd. and the Green River. Near this point, a 1.5 mi. spur strikes out into the middle of the crater's moonscape. (1300 ft. elevation change.)

Starting at the well-marked trailhead along the Grand View Point Spur, the **Murphy Loop** crosses the mesa top before dropping down Island in the Sky and heading out onto Murphy Hogback, which features excellent views of the White Rim and surrounding canyons. The moderately strenuous 10.5 mi. route then follows White Rim Rd. for a little over 1 mi. before climbing back up to the mesa top. (1500 ft. elevation change. Hikeable year-round.) The strenuous **Lathrop Canyon** hike drops off Island in the Sky and descends to the banks of the Colorado River. The 17 mi. round-trip route passes through varied terrain from the grasslands of the mesa top across the slick sandstone of its red rock sides to the sandy washes and groves of cottonwoods leading to the mighty river. Find the well-marked trailhead on the main park road in the large meadow south of the Neck. Bring plenty of water for this long trip, which can be done in two days or one long day. (2000 ft. elevation change. Hikeable year-round.)

■ **OTHER OUTDOOR ACTIVITIES. Backpacking** routes in Island in the Sky aren't as developed or varied as the routes in the Needles, but some good treks still exist. **Taylor Canyon,** which drops from the Island in the Sky to the Green River, offers a good overnight hike, combining the Alcove Spring Trail and the four-wheel-drive road that heads from the White Rim up to Taylor Camp. A loop route including **Upheaval Canyon** is also a good option. Backpacking permits ($15) are required and can be obtained at the Visitors Center.

As is true with the other districts in Canyonlands, four-wheel-drive vehicles and mountain bikes share the same routes because mountain bikes are not allowed on hiking trails. The 100 mi. **White Rim Road** offers premier off-roading in Canyonlands for both drivers and bikers. Spectacular views of the Colorado and Green Rivers, the surrounding canyons and mountains, and Island in the Sky are omnipresent along the route. The full loop usually takes two to three days for vehicles and three to four days for mountain bikes. The trail is moderately difficult for both bikes and cars, and some sections, including the Lathrop Canyon Rd., Murphy's Hogback, Hardscrabble Hill, and the Mineral Bottom switchbacks, are challenging. Reservations are required for four-wheel-drive trips, and permits are required for over-night trips ($30). Drivers and cyclists must stay in designated campsites.

THE MAZE

The most remote district of Canyonlands National Park, the rugged Maze is, as its name implies, a veritable hurly-burly of twisted canyons made for *über*-pioneers with four-wheel-drive or a yen for rough backcountry walkabouts. The BLM roads that go east from Rte. 24 to the Maze provide nearest access to the outlying Horseshoe Canyon, which boasts some of the most significant rock art in North America, including life-size human depictions.

🛈 PRACTICAL INFORMATION. The **Hans Flat Ranger Station,** 75 mi. from I-70 and 60 mi. from the junction of Rte. 24 and 95 in Hanksville, is an invaluably informative resource for Maze exploration, though it has **no services** or **water.** (☎259-2652. Open daily 8am-4:30pm.) Green River, approximately 90 mi. north on I-70, offers most services, including an **ATM, grocery store,** and **post office.** Hanksville, 60 mi. south of Green River on Rte. 24, provides more limited services. No permanent water sources are available, and none of the hiking trails in the region are wheelchair accessible. There are no entrance fees in the Maze district.

⛺ CAMPING. There is no developed campground in the Maze area that is comparable to those in the Needles and Island in the Sky districts, but numerous **primitive campgrounds** dot the terrain. Some of the most popular campgrounds for all those visitors embarking on (relatively) brief excursions into the Maze include North Point, High Spur, and Maze Overlook. All campgrounds operate on a first come, first served basis.

◎ SIGHTS. Horseshoe Canyon, a detached unit of Canyonlands, boasts some of the very best rock art in all of North America. The **Great Gallery** includes well-preserved, life-sized figures adorned with countless detailed designs. Horshoe Canyon sits approximately 30 mi. east of Rte. 24 on a spur off the road heading to Hans Flat Ranger Station. Visitors may stay at the **campsite** on BLM land at the West Rim trailhead; it is a basic site with a pit toilet and no water capabilities. Those looking for a guided tour should take the 6hr., 6.5 mi. guided **hike** into Horseshoe Canyon that leaves the West Rim trailhead at 9am on Saturday and Sunday from April to October. This trail, dropping 750 ft. into the canyon, can also be hiked without a ranger escort. **Be sure to bring plenty of water.**

🏞 OUTDOOR ACTIVITIES. Like everything else in the Maze, **hiking** trails are primitive. Many lead to viewpoints and into canyons, but tend to be marked either with cairns or not at all, and are accessible only by four-wheel-drive roads. Many canyons look alike and require basic rock climbing skills in order to gain access. A topographic map is essential. One multi-day route readily accessible to standard vehicles is **North Trail Canyon.** The hike begins for those with two-wheel-drive at the **North Road Junction,** 2.5 mi. southeast of the Hans Flat Ranger Station. This moderately strenuous 30 mi. round-trip route drops through steep, rocky terrain from the Orange Cliffs mesatop into Elaterite Basin before heading out to the stupendous views of the Maze Overlook. (1000 ft. elevation change. Hikeable year-round.)

Four-wheel-drive roads in the Maze district are extremely difficult and should not be attempted by inexperienced drivers. Visitors should be aware that all routes present considerable risk of vehicle damage and come prepared to make basic repairs (see **The Desert and Your Car,** p. 67). In addition, drivers must provide their own toilet systems. For those seasoned veterans undeterred by all the obstacles the Maze throws at drivers, the region offers a considerable network of roads that lead to myriad canyons and vistas. The **Flint Trail** is the most popular trail in the district but is closed in winter due to its extremely slippery clay surface.

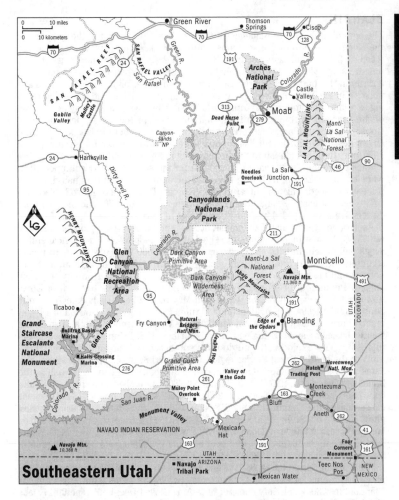

Southeastern Utah

SOUTHEASTERN UTAH

This less-traveled corner of the otherwise well-visited Utah shelters a few of the state's more unknown wonders, including Valley of the Gods and Natural Bridges parks as well as the downright spine-tingling Moki Dugway drive. All of this natural wonder is interspersed with several cookie-cutter small towns that are really little more than places to spend the night and/or gas up. With otherworldly landscapes, these truly off-the-beaten track destinations inspire a departure from the crowds at the Fab Five chain of Southern Utah national parks, the enormity of the Navajo Nation to the south, or the hell-bent recreational spirit of Southwest Colorado's San Juan Mountains.

BLANDING ☎435

The agricultural town of **Blanding** (pop. 3600) lies 44 mi. south of the entrance to the Needles section of Canyonlands National Park, 45 mi. northwest of Hovenweep (p. 359), 47 mi. east of Natural Bridges (p. 296), and 73 mi. northeast of Monument Valley (p. 136). Its broad, tree-lined streets and expanses of green lawns are a rarity in this part of the world. Blanding supplies the full gamut of services and makes a home base for the Four Corners, southeastern Utah, and Navajoland, acting as a larger neighbor to charming Bluff, UT. The town is a gateway to the Trail of the Ancients, a rough loop from Blanding west to Natural Bridges, south to Goosenecks State Park, east to Hovenweep, and back. **AAA (Arches, Anasazi, ATV) Adventures,** 429 S. 200 E., thrills adventure-seekers with outstanding scenic-guided ATV tours from Blanding into the surrounding mountains and deserts. Experience Arches National Monument or Anasazi from the seat of a fully equipped four-wheeler. (☎678-2838 or 678-3224; www.aaa-adventures.com. Full- or half-day trips, price varies according to number in party; contact Ben Black or Lloyd Nielson.)

The nearest **buses,** though, run through Green River on I-70. The recently built **Visitors Center** on U.S. 191 at the northern edge of town contains helpful info about the surrounding area, has free **Internet access,** and hosts a small pioneer museum. (☎678-3662; www.blandingutah.org. Open M-Sa 8am-8pm.) Archaeological enthusiasts will delight in **Edge of the Cedars State Park,** 660 W. 400 N, home to reconstructed Ancestral Puebloan ruins, an informative museum with an array of pottery and baskets, and a display of the history of San Juan County from the ancient Pueblo culture through the Navajo and Ute cultures to the first Euro-American settlers. (☎678-2238. Open mid-May to mid-Sept. daily 8am-7pm; mid-Sept. to mid-May 9am-5pm. Museum and ruins $2, vehicles $5.) Housed in a refurbished barn, the **San Juan County Multi-Agency Visitors Center** (also known as the **Frontier Museum**), at 232 S. Main St., 21 mi. north on U.S. 191 in Monticello, is a useful resource for exploring the outdoors of southeastern Utah and can direct questions to the nearby **Forest Service regional office.** (☎587-3235. Open Apr.-Sept. M-F 8am-5pm, Sa-Su 10am-5pm; Oct.-Mar. M-F 8am-5pm.) You can do a wash at the **Blanding Laundromat,** 225 E. 100 N. (☎678-2786. Open M-Sa 8am-10pm, Su 8am-8pm.) Services include: **police,** 62 E. 200 S (☎678-2334, after hours 678-2916); **medical services** at the Blanding Clinic, 818 N. and 400 W. (☎678-2254) or **San Juan Hospital,** 364 W. 1st St. in Monticello (☎587-2116), 21 mi. north on U.S. 191; free **Internet access** at **San Juan County Library,** 25 W. 300 S (☎678-2335; open M-Th noon-7pm, F 2-6pm, Sa 10am-2pm); and **post office,** 90 N. Main (☎678-2627. Open M-F 8am-4:30pm, Sa 8am-noon.) **Postal code:** 84511.

The **Blanding Sunset Inn** ❷, 88 W. Center St., has friendly management and basic, phoneless rooms for as cheap as they come. (☎678-3323. Check-out 11am. Singles $25; doubles $30-33. Slightly cheaper Mar.-Apr. Closed Dec.-Feb.) The **Cliff Palace Motel** ❷, 132 S. Main St., must have been posh when it was built in the 1955, but time has taken its toll. (☎678-2264 or 800-553-8093. Reception 4-11pm. Check-out 11am. Singles $29; doubles $38; lower in winter.) Nine miles north of town on U.S. 191, near the Manti-La Sal National Forest, is the **Devil's Canyon Campground** ❶ (33 sites; water, pit toilets, and picnic tables. $10). On U.S. 191 at 1888 S., **Blue Mountain RV Park** has 26 sites with hookups and 15 tent sites with picnic tables, water, flush toilets and showers. (☎678-2570. Fee based on availability, so call ahead.)

A better bet for meals is to head north 21 mi. to Monticello. The **MD Ranch Cookhouse** ❷, 380 S. Main St. in Monticello, serves up hearty breakfasts ($3-8), lunches ($5.25 specials), and dinners with all the fixings ($8-13), in an inviting atmosphere. (☎587-3299. Open daily 8am-2pm and 5-10pm.) Unfortunately, Blanding doesn't have as many dining options as it does motels. For sandwiches ($5-7), burgers and salads ($5.50-8), and hearty dinners ($9-16), try the **Homestead Steakhouse** ❸, 121 E. Center St. (☎678-3456. Open M-F 11am-9:30pm, Sa-Su 4:30-9:30pm.)

VALLEY OF THE GODS

To enter the Valley of the Gods is to envision a land where sandstone spires tilt like drip castles at the beach. Here the term outback finds its American definition in the rugged expanse of scenic desert, cut only by washes of flash floods, horse trails, and the tracks of other 4x4 adventurers. The valley's towers are not as tall as those of their more famous southern neighbor in Monument Valley, and the buttes, with their red crumbling sides, seem rougher, hewn with less precision. However, for all the quirks of these less photographed siblings, Valley of the Gods surpasses Monument Valley in terms of its liberating solitude, its miraculous sweeps of natural grandeur, and its impression of a kind of heaven on earth.

An incredible 17 mi. drive departs from U.S. 163, about two-thirds of the way between the towns of Bluff and Mexican Hat and runs through the valley, emerging on Rte. 261 at the base of the **Moki Dugway** (p. 293), about 6 mi. west of the intersection of 163 and 261. The dirt track is generally passable by all cars, but watch for loose rock and rough sections across washes, and don't attempt the drive if the route is wet. The drive only takes about 1hr., but be sure to allow time for jaunts away from the car. You'll feel like you're the only person for miles.

Although this remote route bears no services, travelers interested in spending a heavenly night or two in these divine stomping grounds might consider splurging on a stay at the **Valley of the Gods Bed and Breakfast ❺.** The friendly owners of this charming 1930s homestead treat guests to lavish lodging in four exquisitely decorated rooms with private bathrooms that feature stone-laid showers. Guests enjoy a full breakfast and an unbeatable location flanked on all sides by rock and sky. (☎970-749-1164; www.valleyofthegods.cjb.net. Singles $85; doubles $100-110. Located ½ mi. from Rte. 361 on Valley of the Gods Rd.)

On your way back to U.S. 163, be sure to check out the geology of **Gooseneck State Park.** About 1 mi. west of the intersection of Rte. 261 and 163, a road leads about 4 mi. south to this remarkable lookout over the San Juan River. In the deepest and most dramatic example of an entrenched meander in the US, the river winds its way over 6 mi. while only traveling a little over 1 mi. as the crow flies. The rock exposed by the river's relentless carving 1000 ft. below the lookout is some of the oldest in the country. Use caution as there are many loose rocks and high ledges. No barrier exists at the canyon's edge.

MOKI DUGWAY & MULEY POINT

The desolate Rte. 261 winds south from Rte. 95 and Natural Bridges National Monument, climbing into the San Juan River Valley and off of the Cedar Mesa, but this is no ordinary descent, even for the West. Most of the 34 mi. road is solid asphalt, but a 3 mi. stretch dropping a precipitous 1,200 ft. down the sandstone side of Cedar Mesa remains unpaved. This section teeters over spine-tingling drop-offs and negotiates five-mile-per-hour hairpin turns while providing glorious views of the San Juan River and Monument Valley. The mere thought of uranium trucks that made the same descent 50 years ago inspires awe but should not distract you from the task at hand: drivers must strike a balance between sights and safety.

Immediately at the top of the dugway on the left-hand side of the road is the unmarked, unpaved turnoff for Muley Point, which succeeds in the seemingly impossible mission of providing even more astounding vistas. This overlook hangs on the edge of Cedar Mesa at the end of a 5 mi. road, lying within **Glen Canyon National Recreation Area.** The panorama visible from the point encompasses the **Henry Mountains** and **Glen Canyon** to the west, the **San Juan River** and **Monument Valley** to the south, and **Sleeping Ute Mountain** and the western tip of the Rockies to the east. Except when wet, the graded, mostly level road is easily passable by any vehicle that already made it up onto the mesa.

TIME: 3hr. driving time

DISTANCE: 112 mi.

SEASON: year-round

The scenic 122 mi. stretch of Rte. 95 between Blanding and Hanksville, known as the **Bicentennial Highway** because it was built in 1976 (the US' 200th anniversary), is a pleasure to cruise, with little chance of tailgating traffic. From the cliff dwellings of the Ancestral Puebloans to the modern-day engineering feats of Lake Powell, the heights of the Henry Mountains to the canyon bottoms of Natural Bridges, Rte. 95 tours a cross-section of southern Utah. The highway mirrors part of the route taken by Mormon settlers as they pushed into this uncharted part of the state. Traveling past natural and cultural highlights, this scenic drive packs an interactive anthropology, geology, and history lesson into an afternoon.

Unlike many of the Southwest's other scenic routes, Rte. 95 is not a dusty, twisting desert road but instead a well-maintained, state-funded highway. Instead of potholes, a driver's biggest concern is fuel—the only town along the drive is tiny Fry Canyon, 40 mi. from Blanding. Outside Fry Canyon, gas is scarce, and stations in the hamlet are not open 24hr. Do yourself a favor by filling up in Blanding.

1 BEAR'S EAR PASS. Seven miles west of Blanding on Rte. 95, a sign for **South Cotton-wood National Forest Access** indicates a road that leaves the highway, climbing north up the southern slopes of the Abajo Mountains. The pavement ends after several miles, and the terrain changes dramatically as the road rises. Before long, the slopes are blanketed with lush grass shaded by massive birches. After miles of travel in the surrounding semi-arid terrain, this oasis is a welcome surprise. After 26 mi., the road passes between twin buttes dubbed the **Bear's Ears** before descending 6 mi. to Rte. 275, the access road to Natural Bridges. All told, the 32 mi. route should take about 1-2hr. and is easily passable in good conditions.

2 BUTLER WASH RUINS. The turnoff for these well-preserved **Ancestral Puebloan cliff dwellings** lies about 10 mi. west of Blanding on the right-hand side of the road. The once-rich soil of the canyon floor below provided the Ancestral Puebloans with arable

ROAD TRIP

land for farming crops. A 1½ mi. hike leads to an overlook of the ruins, which are tucked underneath an overhang at the head of **Butler Wash.** These ruins bear many similarities to the sites at Mesa Verde but also share similarities with Kayenta culture sites like those found at Navajo National Monument.

❸ COMB RIDGE. The slope beyond the Butler Wash site is part of this impressive ridge, which once ran unbroken on a north-south axis through much of southeastern Utah. A bit farther south, the highway blasts through this wall of sandstone, catering to modern travelers. The Hole-in-the-Rock pioneers were not so lucky and had to make their way down to Bluff, UT to find a way through. The ridge, like a tsunami of rock, is even more impressive when viewed from the west, so make sure to take a look behind you once you've passed through the road-cut.

❹ MULE CANYON INDIAN RUINS. These Ancestral Puebloan ruins, which flank the highway about 20 mi. west of Blanding, have been carefully reconstructed by the University of Utah and give a good sense of a small mesa-top village. An interesting exhibit explains many aspects of Basketmaker and Ancestral Puebloan culture. You can set up **camp** for free at this spot.

❺ NATURAL BRIDGES NATIONAL MONUMENT. 35 mi. west of Blanding, Rte. 275 diverges to the geological wonders of Natural Bridges (p. 296).

❻ DARK CANYON. Fifty miles west of Blanding is the **Fry Canyon Lodge,** which provides expensive gas to go along with expensive "backcountry" dining and accommodations. About 10 mi. farther, the highway crosses over a small wash, just before **San Juan County Road 2061,** which climbs into and out of White Canyon, heading north to Dark Canyon and some of the most remote canyoneering and hiking in the country. This road should not be attempted without a high-clearance vehicle. Contact the San Juan Resource Center in Monticello (☎ 587-1500) for more info.

❼ GLEN CANYON NATIONAL RECREATION AREA. Rte. 95 crosses into the recreation area where a well-marked access road to the lake and White Canyon immediately turns off to the left. The road then crosses White Canyon before coming to the Farley Canyon turnoff about 70 mi. from Blanding and then spanning the Dirty Devil River near the town of **Hite** (water, gas, groceries, marina, and campground). If Hite's crowds and noise don't suit you, seek solitude along the lake at the end of one of three unpaved roads which leave Rte. 95 in succession southeast of Hite. Just west of the turnoff for Dark Canyon, **Blue Notch Canyon Road** winds up numerous switchbacks to the incredibly blue mesa top. The road, marked C.R. 2061, can be tough on cars and may force a turnaround after 11 mi., but eventually peters out at the lakeshore. **White Canyon** and **Farley Canyon** provide easier, if somewhat less scenic, access to Lake Powell a few miles closer to Hite. The **campgrounds ❶** here, like the ones at Hite and the end of Blue Notch Canyon Rd., are primitive and charge a $6 fee.

❽ HENRY MOUNTAINS. After crossing the once-mighty Colorado where it pools behind the reservoir, Rte. 95 climbs out of canyon country and parallels the majestic Henry Mountains, the last mountain range in the contiguous US to be named and explored. About 100 mi. northwest of Blanding and 20 mi. south of Hanksville, the **Bull Creek Pass National Backcountry Byway** leaves Rte. 95 to the west and climbs into the mountains. There are a number of campsites on this drive and some spectacular scenery—you might even see a herd of wild bison! Parts of the road are okay for cars, but don't attempt the entire 56 mi. loop without a high-clearance, four-wheel-drive vehicle. Contact the BLM in Hanksville (☎ 542-3461) for more info.

ROAD TRIP

GRAND GULCH PRIMITIVE AREA

This 52 mi. stretch of wild land from the top of Cedar Mesa to the banks of the San Juan River features the largest concentration of **Ancestral Puebloan ruins** and artifacts in Utah. These archaeological attractions, as well as the scenery of Grand Gulch, make it a popular destination for backpackers. The **Kane Gulch Ranger Station,** on Rte. 261, 4 mi. south of the intersection with Rte. 95, provides permits and area info. (Open Mar. to mid-June and Sept.-Oct. irregular hours; best chance at catching them 8am-noon. Day-use permits $2; overnight $5; weekly $7.) The spring and fall are the best times to visit; during the summer, temperatures frequently exceed 100°F. **Grand Gulch,** home to some of the most well-preserved remains, is 4 mi. from the ranger station and makes for a good day hike. For more info, call the San Juan Resource Area BLM Office in Monticello (☎ 587-1532).

BLUFF   ☎ 435

Nestled among the sandstone canyons, the tiny town of **Bluff** (pop. 300), 35 mi. from Hovenweep (p. 359), 65 mi. from Natural Bridges (p. 296), and 51 mi. from Monument Valley (p. 136), welcomes the budget traveler with a few more services than underwhelming Mexican Hat to the south. In addition, tiny Bluff boasts a thriving artist community, a popular Bluff Hot Air Balloon Festival in the Valley of the Gods in January, a rodeo in June, and in September the Utah Navajo Fair which features an Indian dance competition. The **Cottonwood Wash...and Dry,** U.S. 191, is a good place to purge the painted desert from your clothes. (☎ 672-2281. Open daily 9am-9pm.) In case of **emergency,** call the **San Juan County Sheriff** (☎ 587-2237). There's also a **post office,** 55 N. 500 E, on U.S. 191. (☎ 672-2228. Open M-F 8:15am-noon and 1:30-4:30pm, Sa 10:30am-12:30pm.) **Postal code:** 84512.

The **Sand Island Campground ❶,** on a well-marked road off U.S. 191 south of Bluff, is a great spot on the banks of the San Juan River and a nearby wall of petroglyphs. Within the campground, camp A's sites have the better value. (☎ 587-1500. 24 sites. 14-day maximum. Check-out 2pm. $6.) Inexpensive, comfortable lodges and motels line U.S. 191, including the **Recapture Lodge ❸,** which has a pool and hot tub. (☎ 672-2281. Singles $40; doubles $50.) The lodge arranges, through Buckhorn Llama Co. Inc. (www.buckhorn@llamapack.org), llama pack trips overnight into the canyons and mesas. There are a number of spots to eat for such a small town, especially the **Twin Rocks Cafe ❷,** 913 E. Navajo Twins Dr., which has good veggie options ($5-9) and some great Navajo fry bread. (☎ 672-2341. Open daily 7am-10pm.) Bluff also serves as the put-in for many **rafting trips** on the San Juan River. The river is run less than many others in the area but features Class II and III rapids, as well as Ancestral Puebloan ruins. Contact **Wild Rivers Expeditions** (☎ 800-442-7654, 672-2200), the oldest and largest company in the area, for more info.

NATURAL BRIDGES
NATIONAL MONUMENT   ☎ 435

Forty miles from the nearest town and 25 mi. from luxuries such as gas, the remote Natural Bridges National Monument remains a relatively tourist-free destination, though much more crowded now than it was in the days when prospectors wandered this land in search of gold or when early inhabitants etched petroglyphs and handprints on canyon bottom's sandstone. The first federally protected land in Utah, the national monument boasts three of the world's largest natural bridges, each spanning between 180 and 268 ft., produced by geological uplift and the erosive action of the water below them. While most visitors confine themselves to the road on the canyon rim, the best way to really appreciate the size and shape of these natural wonders is to take the plunge and view them from underneath.

■ ☷ ORIENTATION & PRACTICAL INFORMATION. With the closest **Greyhound** and **Amtrak** stations several hours north in Green River, a **car** is essential to get to Natural Bridges. The entrance road to the monument, **Route 275**, departs from Rte. 95, 35 mi. northwest of Blanding and 45 mi. southeast of Hite on Lake Powell, and can be reached from almost every direction. The nearest gas is 25 mi. west at Fry Canyon and much more expensive than in surrounding towns. The park's paved, 9 mi. long one-way loop, the **Bridge View Drive**, passes the overlooks and trailheads to each of the three major bridges.

The **Visitors Center**, 4.5 mi. along Rte. 275, runs a slide show and hosts some interesting exhibits. More importantly, it represents the closest resource next to Blanding in an emergency and the only spot where you can fill up on **water**. (☎ 692-1234. Open Mar.-Oct. daily 8am-6pm; Nov.-Feb. 8am-5pm. Weekly park entrance $6 per vehicle, $3 per hiker or biker. National Parks Passes accepted.) For weather and road conditions, call ☎ 800-492-2400. For more info, write the Superintendent, Natural Bridges National Monument, Box 1, Lake Powell, UT 84533.

You can sleep under the stars at the **Natural Bridges Campground ❶**, less than 1 mi. west of the Visitors Center on the park road. Thirteen shaded primitive sites set amid piñon pines accommodate up to nine people each and include grills and picnic tables, but no water. (First-come, first-serve. $10.) **Free camping** is available on BLM land along a gravel road that begins at the intersection of Rte. 95 and Rte. 261, 6 mi. from the Visitors Center. The sites, though unmarked and without facilities, are flat and provide shade.

◖ ☷ SIGHTS & HIKES. All three bridges are spectacular and each displays unique and striking features. Through a remarkably educative natural coincidence, each structure represents a stage in a bridge's typical erosive progression. **Kachina**, still thick and bulky but eroding rapidly, is a youngster; **Sipapu**, with its long, curving span is middle-aged; and **Owachomo**, exhilaratingly thin, is an old-timer. Each is visible from overlooks along the park drive but can be more intimately explored via short trails that drop beneath the canyon rim.

Hearty hikers who want to escape the crowds while visiting each of the three bridges delight in the often overlooked **trail** that follows the floors of **White** and **Armstrong Canyons**. An 8.6 mi. loop completed by a trail network across the mesa top departs from any of the three major parking areas, but park officials recommend taking the Sipapu trail since the ascent from Owachomo Bridge is easier that the other two options. The trail itself, unmaintained but easy to track, follows the canyon floor for the 6 mi. separating Sipapu and Owachomo. About 1 mi. south of Sipapu Bridge, the Horsecollar Ruins sit tucked into the western canyon wall and are accessible by a short scramble. South of Kachina Bridge the trail rises out of the canyon, skirting an impassable dry waterfall. The loop can be shortened to 5.5 mi. to include only two bridges, but once you've dropped into the canyon you won't want to leave short of the third.

Visitors shorter on time or looking for the challenge of hiking down and out of the canyon multiple times can take advantage of the shorter trails leading from parking areas to each of the bridges. The 1.2 mi. round-trip **Sipapu Bridge Trail** drops 500 ft. to the floor of **White Canyon**. The trail is moderately strenuous and requires hikers to negotiate a number of ladders while making their way down the sandstone walls of the canyon. The next major stop on the drive is the **Horsecollar Ruin Overlook**, a .6 mi. trail with little elevation change which heads out to the canyon's edge above well-preserved Ancestral Puebloan dwellings. The **Kachina Bridge Trail** descends 400 ft. over ¾ mi. to the valley floor for impressive views of the massive Kachina as well as some petroglyphs. The trail includes some difficult sections with steel handrails. The **Owachomo Bridge Trail** is the easiest in the park, descending 180 ft. over .3 mi. to end beneath this svelte formation.

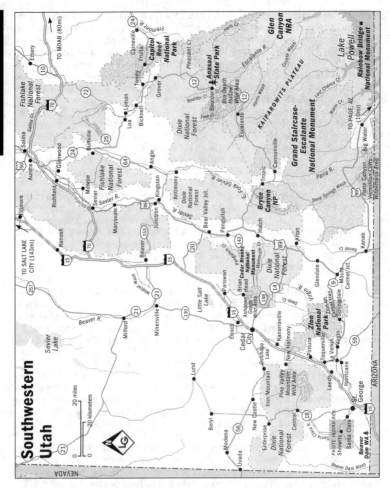

Natural Bridges was once home to the largest solar array in the world, a one-acre, 100-kilowatt photovoltaic (PV) system near the Visitors Center that used the monument's 300 annual days of sunlight to test the viability of solar power. The array can be toured with help from a ranger; no reservations are required.

PARKS OF SOUTH CENTRAL UTAH

Bryce Canyon, Zion, and Capitol Reef National Parks lie in a northeast-to-southwest-oriented line running through the southern portion of the state, connected by Rte. 9, U.S. 89, and Rte. 12. These popular parks are dwarfed by Grand Staircase-Escalante National Monument, the new kid on the block, sprawling south and east of Bryce Canyon and west of Capitol Reef. To the north of Rte. 12 between Bryce and Capitol Reef, the Dixie National Forest covers much of the Aquarius Plateau.

ZION NATIONAL PARK ☎435

Russet sandstone mountains loom over the millions of visitors who flock to Zion National Park each year in search of the promised land, and rarely does Zion disappoint. The narrow Virgin River, whose watery fingers continue to sculpt the smooth white and pink rock monuments, deserves credit for cutting through thousands of feet of sediment over the course of 13 million of years and thus creating the spectacular canyon we see today. In the northwest corner of the park, the walls of Kolob Terrace tower thousands of feet above the river. Elsewhere, branching canyons and rock formations showcase erosion's unique artistry. In the 1860s, Mormon settlers came to the area and enthusiastically proclaimed that they had found Zion, the promised land. Brigham Young disagreed, however, and declared that the place was awfully nice, but "not Zion." The name "not Zion" stuck for years until a new wave of entranced explorers dropped the "not," giving the park its present name. Zion might very well be the fulfillment of biblical prophecy for the throngs of outdoor recreationalists that visit each year. With hiking trails nonpareil and challenging and mysterious slot canyons set against a tableau of sublime rock faces, visiting Zion can be a downright spiritual event.

AT A GLANCE: ZION NATIONAL PARK

AREA: 147, 551 acres.

FEATURES: Zion Canyon, Virgin River, Great White Throne, Checkerboard Mesa, Kolob Canyons.

HIGHLIGHTS: Riverside Walk, Angel's Landing, Observation Point, canyoneering in the The Narrows.

GATEWAY TOWNS: Springdale (borders park), St. George.

CAMPING: South and Watchman Campgrounds $14-16, Lava Point free, $5 permit for overnight backcountry travel.

ENTRANCE FEES: Vehicles $20; individuals (pedestrian, bicycle, or motorcycle) $10. Kolob Canyons $10, individuals $5.

▣ TRANSPORTATION

Access to the park without your own vehicle is limited, as no bus line provides service to Springdale. **Greyhound** (☎800-231-2222) has added service as far as Hurricane, while **Zion Canyon Transportation** (☎877-635-5993) has 24hr. shuttle service from St. George to Zion (one-way $15, round-trip $27).

No unauthorized traffic is allowed to travel the Zion Canyon Scenic Drive from April to October. **Free shuttles** run between Springdale, the Visitors Center, and Temple of Sinawava (the northmost stop in the canyon). Shuttles leave from Majestic View at the western end of Springdale and make six stops along Hwy. 9 heading to the park entrance from mid-May through Labor Day daily 5:30am-11:15pm (buses every 20min. 6:40-7am; 10-15min 7am-10pm; and 30min. 10-11pm), and Apr. through mid-May and Labor Day through late Oct. daily 6:30am-10:15pm (buses every 10min. 7-11am and 4-9pm and every 15min. 11am-4pm and 9-10pm). Shuttles leave from the park Visitors Center bound for the Temple of Sinawava on Zion Canyon Scenic Drive, making nine stops, from mid-May through Labor Day daily 5:45am-10:30pm (buses every 30min. 6:30-7am; 10-15min. 7-9am; 6-10min. 9am-8pm; 15min. 8-9pm; and 30min. 9-10:30pm; last bus departs the Temple of Sinawava at 11pm). From Apr. through mid-May and Labor Day through late Oct., shuttles run daily 6:45am-9:30pm (every 15min. 6:45-8:30am; 7-10min. 8:30am-8pm; and 15min. 8am-9pm; last bus departs Temple of Sinawava at 10pm). There's **parking** at the Visitors Center, but the Park Service advises leaving cars in Springdale and taking the shuttle. Their lot generally fills entirely between 10am and 3pm in summer. **Gas** awaits just outside both the east and south park entrances.

WHEN TO GO. Crowds of hikers, backpackers, and camera-toting tourists flock to Zion between Memorial Day and Labor Day and show up in sizeable numbers until Columbus Day, overcrowding campgrounds and parking lots. For the visitor with a more flexible travel schedule, the cool, wet Zion spring and the clear, mild fall offer a less crowded park and a more comfortable climate. Between May and October, daily high temperatures range from 70-105°F with lows 45-75°F. Afternoon thunderstorms are common in July and August, the park's two hottest months. In the late fall and early spring, temperatures range from 45°F at night to 80°F during the day. Even in the midst of winter, highs are often above 40°F with temperatures dipping below freezing some nights.

ORIENTATION

The main entrance to Zion is in **Springdale,** on Hwy. 9, at the south end of the park along the **Virgin River,** about 45 mi. northeast of St. George and 160 mi. northeast of Las Vegas. Cedar City is about 60 mi. north on the way to Salt Lake City (325 mi.). Coming from the south take the **Hurricane** ("Hurakin") exit (#16, Hwy. 9), or from the north, the **La Verkin** exit (#27, Hwy. 17). From Springdale Hwy. 9 continues through the park and connects with Zion's eastern border via a mile-long tunnel. Approaching from the east, pick up Hwy. 9 from Hwy. 89 at Mt. Carmel Junction. In Zion Canyon itself, the **Scenic Drive** accesses many of the park's best trails, most spectacular views, and **Zion Lodge.** To reach the less-visited **Kolob Canyons** in the northwest corner of the park, take exit 40 off I-15. This entrance connects with Zion Canyon only via the rubber soles of your hiking boots.

Zion divides neatly into three distinct districts. In **Zion Canyon** proper, the heart of the park, visitors stand awestruck in the shadows of towering crags like **The Great White Throne, Angels Landing, The Temple of the Virgin,** and the **Temple of Sina-wava.** This is Zion at its postcard-picture best. To the north and west of Zion Canyon, separated by the Kolob Terrace, lie Kolob Canyons, home to the immense **Kolob Arch** and some of the parks most pristine wilderness. In the park's southeastern corner, the **Zion-Mt. Carmel Highway** winds past sculpted slickrock and colorful mesas. All three areas lend their own unique insights into the haphazardly creative power of plate tectonics, rain and ice, and raging rivers.

PRACTICAL INFORMATION

The new, ecologically harmonious **Zion Canyon Visitors Center,** just inside the south entrance, houses an information desk, bookstore, backcountry permit station, and a number of captivating exhibits on the park's surrounding grounds. (☎772-3256; www.nps.gov/zion. Open daily Memorial Day-Labor Day 8am-7pm; mid-Apr. through Memorial Day and Labor Day-Sept. 8am-6pm; and Oct. through mid-Apr. 8am-5pm.) At the northwest entrance to the park, the **Kolob Canyons Visitors Center** offers books, maps, and info on the Kolob Canyon Scenic Drive and the surrounding trail system. (☎586-9548; www.nps.gove/zion. Open daily Memorial Day-Labor Day 7am-7pm; mid-Apr. through Memorial Day 7am-6pm; Labor Day-Sept. 7am-6pm; and Oct. through mid-Apr. 8am-4:30pm.) Pick up a copy of the *Zion Map & Guide* for up-to-date information about exploring the park.

Outside the main entrance, in Springdale, is the **Happy Camper Market,** 95 Zion Park Blvd., which sells everything a visitor to the park could want, including camping supplies and produce and meat for making meals. (☎772-3402. Open Tu-F 7:30am-10pm, Sa-M 7am-10pm.) Grab adventure gear at **Zion Outdoors,** 868 Zion Park Blvd. (☎772-0630. Open daily mid-Mar. through Oct. 9am-9pm; mid-Feb.

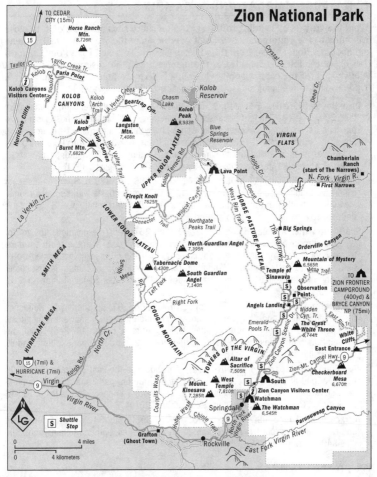

Zion National Park

through mid-Mar. and Nov. 10am-7pm; closed Dec. through mid-Feb.) In case of an **emergency,** call ☎911 or 772-3322. The nearest hospitals are in the towns of St. George, Cedar City, and Kanab, so for **medical service** you'll have to head to **Zion Canyon Medical Clinic,** on Lion Blvd. (☎772-3226, 772-3435. Open May-Sept. 9am-5pm, Oct.-Apr. Tu and Th 9am-5pm.) Other services include: **Zions Bank,** 921 Zion Park Blvd., with **24hr. ATM** (☎772-3274; open May-Oct. M-F 9am-4pm, Nov.-Apr. M-F 9am-2pm); **ATM** at **Zion Lodge** in the park; **Zion Park Laundry,** 855 Zion Park Blvd. (☎772-3251; open daily 7am-8pm); **pharmacy** at **Lin's Marketplace,** 1120 W. State, in Hurricane (☎635-3840; open M-F 9am-9pm, Sa 9am-7pm; store open daily 6am-midnight); **Internet access** at **Leon Lewis Public Library,** 898 Zion Park Blvd. (☎772-3676; open M, W, F 10am-6pm; Tu, Th 10am-9pm; Sa 10am-5pm); and **post offices** at Zion Park Lodge (☎772-3213; open M-F 8am-4:30pm, Sa 8am-noon) and 624 Zion Park Blvd. in Springdale. (☎772-3950. Open M-F 7:30am-11:30am and 12-4pm, Sa 9am-noon.) **Postal code:** 84767.

UTAH

 ACCOMMODATIONS & CAMPING

Avoid the crowds by heading to the six free **primitive sites** at Lava Point, in close proximity to the panoramic Lava Point overlook and the Western Rim Trailhead and about an hour's drive from the Visitors Center. To reach Lava Point, turn off Hwy. 9 onto Kolob (Terrace) Rd. at the sign for the Kolob Reservoir in Virgin and follow signs for the campground, which is a little more than 20 mi. from Hwy. 9. (Open roughly May-Oct. Vault toilets, fire grates, tables; no water.)

Dixie Hostel (HI-AYH), 73 S. Main St. (☎ 635-8202; www.dixiehostel.com), a little more than 20 mi. west of Zion in Hurricane. This bright, airy, and immaculate hostel is a back-packer's haven. Large common areas and a shady patio, and a short trip from Lake Powell, the North Rim of the Grand Canyon, and Bryce. Greyhound stops here on its way to Las Vegas and Salt Lake City. Linen, laundry, kitchen, and continental breakfast. **Internet access** $1 per hr. 3-day max. stay. Dorms $15; singles $35. ❶

El Río Lodge, 995 Zion Park Blvd. (☎ 772-3205, 888-772-3205). Springdale's least expensive indoor accommodations. The lodge welcomes guests with spotless rooms, incredible attention to detail, and dazzling views of the Watchman Face. Singles $47; doubles $52; winter rates dip to around $35. ❸

South and Watchman Campgrounds (☎ 800-365-2267; http://reservations.nps.gov for Watchman reservations Apr.-Oct. up to 5 months in advance.). Near the south entrance to the park. More than 300 sites, but campgrounds still fill quickly in summer; arrive before noon to ensure a spot. Watchman takes reservations, but South is first-come, first-serve. Water, toilets, and sanitary disposal station. Sites $14, full hook-up $16. Open year-round. ❶

Zion Canyon Campground, 479 Zion Park Blvd. (☎ 772-3237), in Springdale. Refreshes the weary, hungry, and filthy with a convenience store, pizzeria, showers (non-guests $3), pool, and coin-op laundry facilities. Office and store open daily 8am-10pm, off-season 8am-6pm. Sites for two $18; full hookups $22-25; $3.50 per additional adult, $2 per additional child under 15. ❶

Zion Frontier Campground (☎ 648-2154), ¼ mi. outside the east entrance. Sits 1000 ft. higher and about 10°F cooler than the sites inside the park, and offers a laundro-mat, showers, restaurant, and gas station. Office open 24hr. 60 tent sites, $12; 19 hookups, $20; tepees and a hogon, $20; cabins $25. ❶

Terrace Brook Lodge, 990 Zion Park Blvd. (☎ 772-3932, 800-342-6779). Offers clean and reasonably inexpensive rooms, some with kitchenettes, and a swimming pool. Sin-gles $49-55; twin beds $65-71. AAA discount. ❸

▶ FOOD

The **Zion Lodge,** located in Zion Canyon halfway to the Temple of Sinawava, houses the only in-park concessions. Inside, the cafeteria-style **Castle Dome Cafe** ❶ serves standard hamburgers, salads, and deli sandwiches. (Open daily Apr.-Oct. 10am-7pm. Burgers $3-5, salads $3-6, subs $5-7.) On the lodge's second floor, the **Red Rock Grill** ❷ cooks up a breakfast buffet ($8), reasonable salad, sandwich, and burger lunches ($5-8), and pricey dinners ($12-22), with entrees like Ruby Mountain Trout. (☎ 772-3213. Open daily 6-10am, 11:30am-2:30pm, and 4:30-10pm.) For tree-ripened organic peaches, apples, and apricots, head to the **Springdale Fruit Company Market,** 2491 Zion Park Blvd. (☎ 772-3222. Open in season daily 8am-8pm.)

Sol Foods, 95 Zion Park Blvd. (☎ 772-0277). Connected with the Visitors Center by foot-bridge. Locally owned with an exceptionally friendly staff. On top of big breakfasts ($4-6), well-crafted sandwiches, and juicy burgers ($5-6), Sol Foods boasts veggie options. Open daily mid-Feb. through Dec. 7am-9pm, Jan. through mid-Feb. 8am-8pm. ❶

CABLE GUYS Imagine how the sandstone monuments of Zion Canyon would look as you glance back over your shoulder while descending rapidly over 2000 ft. on a thin cable and at the mercy of whoever is controlling the brakes. Such were the rides on the **Cable Mountain Draw Works** during the 1910s and 20s. Spanning a 2000 ft. vertical drop from the summit of Cable Mountain to what is today the Weeping Rock shuttle stop, the cable first carried lumber from the high mesa of the east rim to the valley floor in 1901. From their arrival, settlers in Springdale, an area forested only by poor-quality cottonwoods, had been unable to access the forests on the canyon rim. They had been forced to haul lumber from as far away as Arizona's Kaibab Forest—a task that could take as long as two weeks per load. When Brigham Young visited the area in 1863, he prophesied that, one day, lumber would descend from the cliffs "like a hawk flies." Such colorful imagery inspired young David Flanigan to begin construction on the cable works around 1898. By 1901, lumber traveled from peak to valley in less than 3 min., allowing more efficient construction. According to Flanigan's diary, the cable work's first passenger, a family dog, was "real scairt" after its ride. Falling 2000 ft. in 2½min. was quite a thrill, and lumber workers regularly used the works to travel to and from the mesa. In 1930, the National Parks Service removed the cable, fearing injury to visitors. Now, watching the escarpments' heights receding rapidly into the blue sky above is an experience that promises to be a Zion visitor's last.

Oscar's Cafe, 948 Zion Park Blvd. (☎ 772-3232). A local favorite, Oscar's vends innovative Mexican entrees ($10-13), juicy garlic burgers ($8-11), and tasty breakfasts ($4-8) in a funky venue. Open daily Mar.-Oct. 6:30am-10:30pm, Nov.-Feb. 7:30am-10pm. ❷

Zion Pizza and Noodle Company, 868 Zion Park Blvd. (☎ 772-3815). Carbo-craving backpackers camp out here to devour pasta platters ($10) and unique pizzas ($9-14) such as The Virgin. Open daily for dinner at 4pm. ❷

■ HIKING & BACKPACKING

Zion offers a wide variety of trails suitable for a broad spectrum of ability levels. Within Zion Canyon, some trails meander peacefully near the banks of the Virgin River; others scale the canyon walls and will have you praying for a stray mule to show up. The park's famous slot canyons challenge the adventuresome, and a number of backcountry treks traverse spectacular and varied terrain. As always, prepare yourself thoroughly for the trails. Zion is situated in a desert; heat exhaustion and dehydration are constant threats. Drink copious amounts of water, apply sunscreen liberally, and avoid hiking at mid-day. Any hiking itineraries that include portions in slot canyons or other terrain prone to flash flooding should begin with a check of the day's forecast at a Visitors Center.

DAY HIKING

Riverside Walk (2 mi. round-trip, 1-2hr.). Zion's most traveled trail, on busy summer afternoons the Riverside walk can resemble a city sidewalk. This easy trail begins at the last shuttle stop, the Temple of Sinawava, and follows the Virgin River upstream between towering sandstone cliffs and gardens of hanging wildflowers in the spring and summer. A concrete surface makes the trail accessible to anyone. Many hikers walking through the mid-day heat cool off at trail's end with a quick dip in the Virgin. From the end of Riverside path, day-hikers can venture up into the **Narrows** (p. 306).

Watchman (2 mi. round-trip, 2-3hr.). Embarking from the Watchman Campground (0.75 mi. south of the Visitors Center) and less crowded than many other short Zion trails, this moderate hike climbs to a shelf adjacent to the mammoth Watchman (6545 ft.). From here, hikers have excellent views of West Temple and The Temple of the Virgin across the canyon, the Watchman above, and Springdale below. Hiking in the late afternoon or early evening avoids the searing mid-day heat and sun exposure. 350 ft. elevation gain.

Emerald Pools (round-trip distances vary 1.2-3.1 mi., 1-3hr.). Accessing several sparkling pools and waterfalls, this matrix of trails allows trips of various lengths and difficulties. Trails to the pools can be joined at both the Zion Lodge and Grotto shuttle stops. The easy 0.6 mi. one-way leg between Zion Lodge and Lower Emerald Pool is paved all the way. From here, trek up to the Middle Pools and loop back to the canyon floor without retracing your steps. A short (0.3 mi.) spur connects the Middle and Upper Pools. Though the trails are heavily used and easy to follow, the surrounding terrain is dangerously steep and slippery. Trail gains 70-350 ft. depending upon destination.

Hidden Canyon (2 mi. round-trip, 3-4hr.). Originating at the Weeping Rock shuttle stop, this moderately difficult trail, etched into the solid sandstone face, winds rapidly to the mouth of Hidden Canyon, providing excellent views of the Great White Throne. The canyon itself is a magnificent example of the artistic talent of erosive water. At trail's end, hikers can scramble another 1.8 mi. up between the narrow slot walls. 850 ft. elevation gain. Not recommended for acrophobes.

Angels Landing (5 mi. round-trip, 4-5hr.). This trail packs a lot of climbing into a short distance, making it one of the park's most strenuous day-hikes. But incomparable views at the end make achy legs and wheezy lungs seem inconsequential. The trail begins at the Grotto shuttle stop and picks its way up sandstone face, traveling through the famous "Walters Wiggles," a series of tight switchbacks carved out of the rock in the 1920s, before reaching Scout Lookout after 1.8 mi. From Scout Lookout, the route to the summit traverses a ridge that drops off to the valley floor on both sides. Chains and carved steps provide ample assistance in making it to the top, where magnificent views await. 1500 ft. elevation gain. Not recommended for acrophobes.

Observation Point (8 mi. round-trip, 5-6hr.). Ascending from the Weeping Rock shuttle stop, the highly strenuous yet well-maintained trail to Observation Point climbs through Echo Canyon before reaching steep sandstone slopes that look out over East Mesa. The trail winds its way to the canyon rim en route to a staggeringly beautiful vantage point. From a grove of ponderosa pine, Gambel Oak, and Manzanita, this towering overlook rewards determined climbers with sweeping views of Zion Canyon. This trail may be inadvisable for those afraid of heights. 2150 ft. elevation gain.

Kolob Arch (14.4 mi. round-trip, 8-9hr.). This strenuous hike departs the Kolob Canyons Scenic Drive at Lee Pass, 3.5 mi. from the Visitors Center, and follows the picturesque Timber and La Verkin Creeks to Kolob Arch, the world's largest free-standing arch (at 319 ft. in length). The trail runs through the heart of the Kolob Canyons district, passing between towering sandstone faces and past cascades, pools, and numerous springs, before climbing to the arch for a total elevation gain of 700 ft. Give yourself plenty of time and water on this long route, or get a backcountry permit (limited to 15 per day) to turn it into an overnight excursion (numerous campgrounds line the creek).

BACKCOUNTRY HIKING

The park requires permits ($5 in 2003, but fees may increase) obtainable at both Visitors Centers for day-travel on routes in technical canyons and for backcountry camping. Popular hikes like the West Rim have limits on the number of trail-users per day; permits are available up to three days in advance. Backcountry permits may soon be available on-line. For extensive info on backcountry routes and procedures, pick up a copy of the *Zion Backcountry Planner* at either Visitors Center and visit the **Backcountry Desk** (open daily Memorial Day-Labor Day 6:30am-7pm; mid-Apr. through Memorial Day and Labor Day-Sept. 6:30am-6pm; Oct. through mid-Apr. 8am-5pm) in the **Zion Canyon Visitors Center. Water** is not always available along the trails depending on the season. Check the water source board at the Backcountry Desk in Zion Canyon Visitors Center before departing. On the other hand, too much rain poses the problem of potential flash floods throughout the year. Make sure you know current conditions and weather forecasts.

Most backcountry hikes in Zion are one-way, requiring either a two-vehicle shuttle or a shuttle service. Several companies run shuttles to and from the Zion backcountry, including **Zion Canyon Transportation** (☎ 877-635-5993).

West Rim Trail (14 mi. one-way). Starting up on the Kolob Plateau in the park's north central area, this moderately strenuous 2-day trek follows the West Rim of Zion Canyon to the Grotto picnic area. The trail grants bird's-eye views of narrow slot canyons and Zion monoliths. Because of these vistas, the route hosts more hikers than any backcountry trail; the backcountry office issues only 9 overnight permits per day. Established backcountry sites lie along the trail. To begin, head north from Virgin along Kolob Rd. and turn right at the signs for Lava Point Campground. Bear left past the lookout and follow the steep dirt road to the trailhead. The hike opens by tracing the edge of the Horse Pasture Plateau. Going south, the first 8 mi. are relatively constant in elevation, but the last 5 mi. drop dramatically over 3500 ft. Three springs usually provide water along the way, but check the water source board at the Backcountry Desk to be sure.

East Rim Trail (10.5 mi. one-way). This strenuous through-hike connects the park's east entrance (5700 ft.) with the Weeping Rock shuttle stop (4360 ft.). From either end, the trail climbs to Stave Spring Junction and offers views of Angels Landing and The Great White Throne in Zion Canyon. In late spring and early summer, wildflowers blanket the Zion uplands. An energetic adventurer could climb up to Stave Spring and arrive 7hr. later in Zion Canyon.

Wildcat Canyon Trail (6 mi. one-way, 4hr. or more depending on the route). A moderate hike traveling from Kolob Rd. to Lava Point, this little-used 500 ft. climb traverses part of the Kolob Plateau. Views of dark, basaltic lava flows along the trail contrast Zion's red and white sandstone hue. The hike extends into an overnight with the addition of the 1.2 mi. Northgate Peaks Spur Trail. To find the trail, follow the Kolob Rd. north from Virgin past Maloney Hill to the well-marked trailhead. Combined with the Hop Valley, Connector, and Western Rim trails, Wildcat Canyon can serve as a leg on a multi-day backcountry trip through some of the park's most scenic terrain.

Hop Valley Trail (6.7 mi. one-way, 4-6hr.). Beginning from the Kolob Rd. just within the park's western boundary, this excursion accesses La Verkin Creek and the Kolob Arch from the southeast. Backcountry restrictions assure a relatively uncrowded hike, with only 3 groups allowed per day. The trail winds through alpine meadows before dropping steeply to La Verkin Creek. Cattle may wander into the park in the summer; their trails helpful with route-finding along the stream, which sometimes disappears into the sand. Water can be scarce. 3 established campsites sit on the hillside above La Verkin Creek.

CANYON HIKES & CANYONEERING

Descending thousands of feet between narrow sandstone walls provides an exhilarating glimpse of the forces that shape the Western landscape, and Zion's slot canyons are some of the world's most famous. The Park Service prohibits commercial guiding inside the park, so canyoneers must come equipped with their own ropes, hardware, and savoir-faire. For detailed info on canyoneering, consult the Zion Canyon Visitors Center's Backcountry Desk. A limited number of people are allowed to tackle the park's most popular canyon routes each day. Permits for hiking the Narrows from top to bottom (north to south) are available at the backcountry desk when it opens the day before the proposed trip. For the Subway, hikers must apply to a lottery three months in advance, though a limited number of walk-in permits are available a day in advance.

The Narrows (16 mi. one-way, 1-2 days) is a Zion classic that follows the Virgin River from the park's northern border to the Temple of Sinawava. More than 60% of the hike is actually in the river, ranging in depth from ankle-deep to mid-chest. During the colder winter months, the hike requires a wetsuit and other protective clothing. The corridors, despite their scenic beauty, present a potentially lethal flash-flood threat; all hikers attempting the Narrows should check on the antici-pated weather in advance. Even with a promising weather report, sudden summer thunderstorms anywhere in the Virgin River basin can cause sudden downriver flash flooding. Walking sticks and sturdy hiking shoes are highly recommended, as they will protect trekkers from ankle sprains on terrain described as "hiking on slippery bowling balls." **The Narrows Outfitting** at **Zion Adventure Company**, 36 Lion Blvd., rents hiking packages that include Neoprene socks, canyoneering shoes, and walking sticks ($16), with the addition of dry suits (package $35) for early or late season excursions. (☎772-1001; www.zionadventures.com. Open daily Mar.-Nov. 8am-8pm, Dec.-Feb. by appointment.)

The most popular, and easiest, way to hike the Narrows begins by hiking up the Virgin River past the end of the Riverside Walk. The canyon walls soon narrow for a thrilling effect. Several views of the Narrows at their most majestic are within a couple of hours' reach. Other hikers choose instead to shuttle to the northern end of the park, join the Virgin River at the Chamberlain Ranch, and complete the hike either in one gruelling 12hr. day or as an overnight trip. Twelve coveted campsites serve backpackers about halfway between the Chamberlain Ranch and the River-side Walk. As the hike is one-way, starting at Chamberlain Ranch requires either a two-car shuttle or some sort of commercial service. To reach the trailhead, turn north off Hwy. 9 two miles east of the park's east entrance at the sign for "Zion Ponderosa Resort and Ranch." Though the first half of the roughly 20 mi. road to Chamberlain Ranch is paved, the dirt portion is impassible by all vehicles when wet. Four-wheel-drive is recommended. A number of companies run daily shuttles to the trailhead for about $25 per hiker. **Zion Canyon Transport** (☎877-635-5993) departs from the Zion Canyon Visitors Center at 6am daily, and sometimes runs at 9am if enough people sign up ($30 per person). **Springdale Cycles**, 1458 Zion Park Blvd. (☎800-776-2099), offers shuttle service departing from their shop at 6:45am daily. **Zion Adventure Company,** 36 Lion Blvd. (☎772-1001), has 6 and 9am departures from their store. Only 80 hikers per day receive day-permits to hike south from Chamberlain Ranch, and only twelve permits per day are issued for overnight trips. No reservations accepted; hikers must obtain permits at the Backcountry Desk the day before departing.

Traveling the length of the Left Fork of North Creek, **The Subway** (4.5-9.5 mi. one-way) involves scrambling over boulders, rappelling down rock faces, and swim-ming in frigid pools in the narrow gaps between sandstone walls. There are two route options for this trek: down from the top or up from the bottom. The bottom route begins at the Left Fork Trailhead off Kolob (Terrace) Rd., travels 4.5 mi. up the canyons before returning the same way, and requires route-finding skills, stream crossings, and boulder scrambles. The alternate top-down route is much more intense; it starts at the Wildcat Canyon Trailhead (also off Kolob Canyon Rd.), travels 9.5 mi. to the Left Fork Trailhead, and requires at least 60 ft. of rope or webbing for rappelling. The thrill of traversing such wild terrain attracts droves of hikers, but the Park Service limits use of the trail to just 50 people per day. Thirty of these permits are available via a special reservation system. Reservations for The Subway must be made at least three months in advance; hikers are notified one month before their departure date if their reservation has been accepted. Visit www.nps.gov/zion or call ☎772-0170 for more info. Twenty permits go to walk-ins each day (non-refundable permit fee $5), but get in line bright and early, as one hiker can take them all.

▓ OTHER OUTDOOR ACTIVITIES

MOUNTAIN BIKING. Inside the national park, bicycles can travel only on park roads; no trail riding is permitted. The Zion Canyon Scenic Drive, closed to car traffic, makes for an excellent ride, allowing cyclists to avoid the pseudo-urban experience of crowds and obstructed views found on shuttle rides into the canyon. Trail riding is available just outside of the park along the extensive trail system on **Gooseberry Mesa.** The advanced terrain challenges more experienced enthusiasts, and the views of Zion make the rides all the more rewarding. Ask for trail directions and info at **Springdale Cycle,** 1458 Zion Park Blvd., which offers high-quality bike rentals, as well as single and multi-day tours. (☎ 772-0575, 800-776-2099; www.springdalecycles.com. Open M-Sa 9am-7pm. Front suspension full day $35, half day $25; full suspension $45/$35; kids $10/$7.)

DRIVING THE ZION-MT. CARMEL HIGHWAY. Although Zion cannot be fully experienced from any moving vehicle, this cross-section through the park provides an excellent overview of its varied terrain. Following the Virgin River into Zion Canyon in the shadow of towering sandstone faces, Hwy. 9 passes the **Zion Museum,** which shows an introductory film about the park every half hour and has some interesting exhibits on Zion's history. (Open Memorial Day-Labor Day 8am-7pm; mid-Apr. through Memorial Day and Labor Day-Sept. 8am-6pm, Oct. through mid-Apr. 8am-5pm.) The highway then begins to climb the eastern wall toward Zion Arch. After passing through the remarkable, mile-long Zion Canyon Tunnel, the road winds its way by dazzling slickrock domes and mesas. A panoply of soft reds and whites contrasting the brilliant hues of the canyon greets travelers around every bend. Scenic pull-outs at striking viewpoints, like Checkerboard Mesa, a formation adorned with symmetrical square panels of pink and white, allow for quick snap shots.

TUBING & ROCK CLIMBING. On scorching summer days, many Zion visitors enjoy the cooling waters of the lower Virgin River. **Zion Tubing,** 180 Zion Park Blvd., rents tubes for floating a 2.5 mi. segment of the lower Virgin and provides shuttle service. (☎ 772-8823. Open mid-May through mid-Sept. daily 10am-4:30pm; tube and shuttle $14, additional rides $3.) For a more intense afternoon, visit the Zion Adventure Company (p. 305), which offers introductory canyoneering course in narrow slot canyons just outside the park. (Half-day $99, full day $199, 3-day all-inclusive $495.) Rock climbers often scale the enormous sandstone faces of Zion Canyon, considered to be the best big wall climbing in the lower 48 outside Yosemite. Most faces are too hot for long routes in the summer, but the mild spring and fall are a different story. Less ambitious or experienced climbers can test their mettle at several areas throughout the canyon. Consult one of the climbing guide books available at the Visitors Center or the Backcountry Desk for more info. **Zion Rock and Mountain Guides,** 1416 Zion Park Blvd., is also a great resource. (☎ 772-3303.)

BRYCE CANYON NATIONAL PARK ☎ 435

One of the West's most vivid landscapes, Bryce Canyon brims with haunting, slender rock pinnacles known as hoodoos. What it lacks in Grand Canyon-esque magnitude, Bryce makes up for in intricate beauty. Early in the morning or late in the evening, the sun's rays bring the hoodoos to life (especially when witnessed from overlooks like Inspiration Point), transforming them into stone chameleons. The first sight of the canyon is breathtaking: as Ebenezer Bryce—a Mormon carpenter and early pioneer with a gift for understatement—put it, the canyon is "one hell of a place to lose a cow."

AT A GLANCE: BRYCE CANYON NATIONAL PARK

AREA: 35,835 acres.	**GATEWAY TOWNS:** Tropic, Panguitch.
FEATURES: The main amphitheater of Bryce Canyon, Paunsaugunt Plateau, Pink Cliffs, countless hoodoos.	**CAMPING:** Park campgrounds $10, backcountry camping permit $5.
HIGHLIGHTS: View the Bryce sunset from Inspiration Point, hike the Peeka-boo/Navajo Loop, cross-country ski the Under-the-Rim trail in complete solitude.	**FEES:** Weekly pass $20 per car, $15 if parking outside the park; $10 per bike or pedestrian.

ORIENTATION & PRACTICAL INFORMATION

Coming from the west, Bryce Canyon National Park lies an approximately 1½hr. drive east of **Cedar City** (see p. 328); you can take either Rte. 14 or Rte. 20 to U.S. 89. Driving from the east, take I-70 to U.S. 89 and turn east on Rte. 12 in Panguitch. Most visitors arrive at Bryce Canyon from the south, taking U.S. 89 to Rte. 12 after visiting Lake Powell, the Grand Canyon, or Flagstaff, AZ.

Public Transportation and Parking: During the summer, **parking** inside the park varies from crowded to non-existent. To assuage the traffic problem, the Park Service has implemented a shuttle system—though it only runs from 9am-6pm, so you'll miss the sunset—serving the viewpoints around Bryce Amphitheater, the Visitors Center, and Ruby's Inn. Private vehicles can travel park roads, but the Park Service offers a $5 admission discount to those who park at **Ruby's Inn** (a pricey lodging option just north of the park entrance) and ride the shuttle into the park. Buses run roughly every 10-15min. and are worth the small hassle so long as you return before 6pm.

Visitor Information: The **Visitors Center** (☎834-5322) lies just inside the park. A help-ful backcountry desk provides info on recreation opportunities in the area. Open June-Aug. daily 8am-8pm; Apr.-May and Sept.-Oct. 8am-6pm; Nov.-Mar. 8am-4:30pm.

Groceries: Doug's Place Grocery Store (☎679-8600), 141 N. Main St. in Tropic, UT, 7 mi. east of the Rte. 12 and 63 junction. Has the best selection of any area grocery store with affordable prices and favorites like Nutella. Open in summer daily 7am-9:30pm.

ATM and Currency Exchange: In the lobby of Ruby's Inn. Ruby's also has a gas station, large gift shop, and market for snacks (☎834-5341).

Showers and Laundry: The **Bryce Canyon General Store,** at Sunrise Point. Purchase shower tokens at the register. Open in summer daily 8am-8pm. Showers $2 per 10min.

Internet Access: Terminal located in the lobby of Ruby's Inn ($1 per 4min.). Free at the **Panguitch Public Library,** 25 S. 200 E, a 25 mi. jaunt from the entrance to the park. (☎676-2431. Open M-F 1-6pm.)

Post Office: In Ruby's Inn Store (☎834-8088). Window open M-F 8:30am-noon and 12:30-4:30pm. No credit cards accepted. A second post office is inside the Bryce Can-yon Lodge and only open in summer. **Postal code:** 84717.

 WHEN TO GO. Peak visitation occurs in the late spring, summer, and fall until snow descends in earnest on the park. Because much of the park is situ-ated in the high country, summer highs are only moderate (in the 80s), and an average of 95 in. of snow blankets the high country each winter.

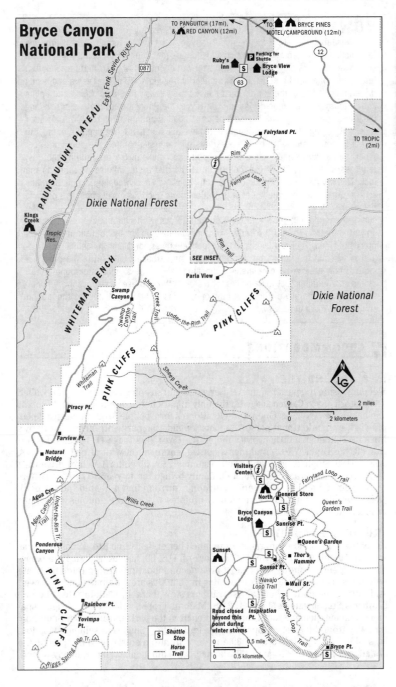

Bryce Canyon National Park

UTAH

TO PANGUITCH (17mi), & RED CANYON (12mi)

TO: BRYCE PINES MOTEL/CAMPGROUND (12mi)

12

Parking for Shuttle

Ruby's Inn

Bryce View Lodge

63

Fairyland Pt.

TO TROPIC (2mi)

Rim Trail

Fairyland Loop Tr.

PAUNSAUGUNT PLATEAU

East Fork Sevier River

087

Dixie National Forest

Kings Creek

Tropic Res.

Rim Trail

SEE INSET

Parla View

WHITEMAN BENCH

Swamp Canyon

Sheep Creek Trail

Swamp Canyon Trail

Under-the-Rim Trail

PINK CLIFFS

Dixie National Forest

Whiteman Trail

PINK CLIFFS

Sheep Creek

Piracy Pt.

N
LG

0   2 miles

0   2 kilometers

Farview Pt.

Natural Bridge

Agua Cyn.

Under-the-Rim Tr.

Willis Creek

Agua Canyon Trail

Ponderosa Canyon

PINK CLIFFS

Rainbow Pt.

Yovimpa Pt.

Riggs Spring Loop Tr.

S Shuttle Stop

--- Horse Trail

Inset

Visitors Center

North

General Store

Bryce Canyon Lodge

Sunrise Pt.

Fairyland Loop Trail

Queen's Garden Trail

Queen's Garden

Sunset

Thor's Hammer

Sunset Pt.

Navajo Loop Trail

Wall St.

Peekaboo Loop

Road closed beyond this point during winter storms

Inspiration Pt.

Rim Trail

Bryce Pt.

0   0.5 mile

0   0.5 kilometer

HOW DO YOU HOODOO? Sweating under the scorching summer sun during a walk through Bryce Canyon, it's hard to visualize the wintry ice responsible for the amphitheater's striking hoodoo formations. How could water create such a dramatic, almost cave-like topography in dry desert plateau that receives less than 18 in. of annual precipitation? The answer begins 10-15 million years ago, when powerful collisions of the earth's crust caused the extensive series of faults and uplifts known today as the Colorado Plateau. At Bryce, the Paunsaugunt Plateau rose along fault lines from the surrounding sediments to heights approaching 10,000 ft. At such an elevation, nighttime winter temperatures average well below freezing, but during the day, year-round sunlight lifts temperatures high enough to melt the snow and ice. When the snow, having melted and seeped into cracks in the rock during the day, refreezes at night to ice, it expands by up to 9% and exerts intense pressure on the rock. This process of melting and refreezing, known as frost wedging, occurs as many as 200 times per year. The linear organization of the hoodoos results from this process because most of the cracks in the rocks are straight fault-created lines. During the spring thaw, melting snow and ice also help to sculpt the hoodoos. Run-off travels down the plateau toward the Paria River, eroding the surface by both the mechanical process of lifting rock particles and the chemical process of dissolving calcium carbonate particles in the limestone. The more calcium carbonate present in the rock, the more rapidly it erodes. Some areas of limestone contain less calcium carbonate than others and remain intact while gullies form around them. These less-concentrated limestone rocks eventually become the tops of hoodoos, called capstones, as the ground surrounding them erodes away.

ACCOMMODATIONS

IN & AROUND THE PARK

Sleeping inside the park requires either a tent and sleeping bag or a very fat wallet. The historic **Bryce Canyon Lodge ❾,** the only in-park hotel, offers motel-style rooms and cabins. (☎834-5361. Open Apr.-Oct. Rooms for 2 people $100; cabins for 2 people $111; each additional person $5.) Just outside the park entrance is the Ruby's Inn's less expensive little-brother motel, the **Bryce View Lodge ❸.** Located just off Rte. 63, the Bryce View combines a convenient location with affordable prices. (☎834-5180. Singles and doubles $60 in summer, $44 in winter.) A short drive west on Rte. 12 is the **Bryce Pines Motel ❸,** family-owned for 45 years. The Pines offers quite spacious and newly renovated rooms surrounding a heated indoor pool. (☎800-892-7923. Singles $50; economy doubles $64; deluxe doubles $75. Rates drop as much as $20 in winter.)

TROPIC & PANGUITCH

Away from the park, room rates drop; much better deals line Rte. 12 in Tropic, as well as Panguitch, 23 mi. west of the park on U.S. 89, has more than 15 inexpensive, independent motels. For most area accommodations, room rates fluctuate with the season and tourist flow. Winter rates in this area are much, much lower, and during summers when tourist traffic is slow, bargain walk-in rates abound. ▧**Bybee's Steppingstone Motel ❷,** 21 S. Main in Tropic, offers clean, bright, spacious, and inexpensive rooms only minutes from the park entrance, but thankfully far away from the chaotic tourist bustle. (☎679-8998. Singles in summer $40; doubles $45.) In Panguitch, a mere 30min. drive from the entrance to the park is the ▧**Marianna Inn ❸,** 699 N. Main. Marianna boasts immaculate, large, newly remodeled rooms with amenities such as porch swings for relaxing on hot summer days and a hot tub for warming up on chilly fall afternoons. The Inn also has one fully equipped, handicapped-accessible room. (☎676-8844. Singles $45 in summer, $30 in winter; doubles $60.)

▓ CAMPING

North and **Sunset Campgrounds ❶,** both within 3 mi. of the Visitors Center, offer toilets, picnic tables, potable water, and 216 sites on a first-come, first-served basis (sites $10). Arrive early to claim a good site, as many spots are uncomfortably close to neighbors (of which you're sure to have many in Bryce Canyon) or situated inconveniently on sloping ground. The North Campground is located much closer to the rim, for those campers looking for convenience. No RV hookups are available inside the park, but the North Campground has a $2 dump station.

Two popular campgrounds lie just west of Bryce on Rte. 12 in the Dixie National Forest. The **Kings Creek Campground ❶** is 11 mi. from Bryce on Forest Service Rd. 087, just off Rte. 12 (look for signs pointing to the Tropic Reservoir). The grounds feature very spacious sites and allow visitors to refresh themselves on hot summer days with a quick dip in the Tropic Reservoir, just a stone's throw from the campground. Group sites are also available, but with reservations only. (☎800-280-2267. Sites $10. Drinking water, flush toilets. Open May 21 through Labor Day.) West of the park on Rte. 12, the **Red Canyon Campground ❶** has 36 well-developed sites doled out on a first-come, first-served basis, all amid the glory of the striking red rocks. The campground lies rather close to the road, but the shade and scenery make it a prime location. (Sites $11. Drinking water, flush toilets. Showers $2 per 8min.) For an affordable RV hookup near the park, try the **Bryce Canyon Pines Campground and RV Park ❶,** on Rte. 12 several miles west of the Rte. 63 junction and across the street from Pines Restaurant. (☎800-892-7923. Wooded and shady tent sites $17. Hookups $23.)

▐ FOOD

Inside and immediately surrounding the national park, feeding options are scarce. A hot dog ($2) or a packaged sandwich ($3) awaits famished tourists at the **Bryce Canyon General Store ❶** at the Sunset Point overlook (open daily 8am-8pm). To fill up in preparation for your next hike, feast on reasonably priced burgers ($5-6) and sandwiches ($5.50-6.50) at the **Bryce Canyon Lodge Dining Room ❶.** There are limited veggie options, besides the generic pizza slice. (☎834-5361. Open daily 6:30-10:30am, 11am-3:30pm, 5:30-9:30pm.)

With a little driving time, more affordable and varied food alternatives multiply. An unlimited supply of thick, golden-brown pancakes ($2) await starving passersby at the **Hungry Coyote ❶,** on N. Main in Tropic. Bring an enormous appetite if you hope to finish more than two or three of these monsters. The all-you-can-eat options continue with dinner, when customers can choose from an all-you-can-eat soup and salad bar for just $8. (☎679-8811. Open Apr.-Oct. daily 6:30-10:30am and 5-10pm.) Several miles west of the park on Rte. 12 is the **Bryce Pines Restaurant ❸,** which earns its distinction as a local favorite by serving delicious home-cooked meals complemented by fresh soups and an endless selection of always-fresh homemade pies. (☎834-5441. Open in summer daily 6:30am-9:30pm. Sandwiches $5-8; dinner entrees $13-19.) Twenty-three miles west of the park in Panguitch, **Grandma Tina's Spaghetti House ❷,** 525 N. Main, specializes in hearty Italian eating with a vegetarian emphasis. (☎676-2376. Open in summer daily 7am-11pm. Lunch pastas $5-6; dinners $10-12.)

SEEING STARS

At Bryce Canyon, the stars were frequently so bright at night that camping didn't even require a flashlight, making it a phenomenal spot for stargazing.

About two hours after sunset, before the stars appear, the casual observer can catch a rare glimpse of Earth's penumbra. As light from the setting sun fades from the highest clouds, a violet band will appear directly above the eastern horizon—this is the fleeting projection of the edge of the Earth's shadow onto the atmosphere. Momentarily it will give way to darkness.

The first twinkle to appear will be a planet, followed by Vega, Arcturus, and other bright stars. Soon a billion stars combine in the night sky, forming what looks like a long cloud of light—the Milky Way. Wait even longer and Bryce Canyon will be dark enough to see 527 quadrillion miles (2.2 million light years) to the Andromeda Galaxy. Rarely seen without a telescope, the Andromeda Galaxy is the largest (diameter: 110,000 light-years) and most distant object your naked eye will ever see. Trace your eye from the middle star of the Big Dipper's handle through the North Star, past the zigzag-shaped Cassiopeia until you come to a fuzzy bunch of stars forming a brilliant cloud of light.

–Brendan Reed

⚑ OUTDOOR ACTIVITIES

The 18 mi. park road travels south from the Visitors Center, offering a variety of vantage points from which to gaze out upon the land beyond the Paunsaugunt Plateau. Some viewpoints like **Sunset, Sunrise,** and **Natural Bridge** offer close-up views of notable formations like **Thor's Hammer** (a rock sitting atop a narrow shaft that resembles the weapon of the mythological figure). Other places like **Bryce** and **Inspiration Points** deliver panoramic views of the entire Bryce amphitheater. For some fabulous photographs of the amphitheater, catch the light of the rising or setting sun from Inspiration Point as it illuminates the hoodoos. The final two viewpoints along the drive, **Rainbow** and **Yovimpa Points,** impart views extending on a clear day over 100 mi., all the way out to the North Rim of the Grand Canyon. On wintry days, only the curvature of the earth limits the eye's reach into the Black Mesas of Northern Arizona over 200 mi. away.

As awe-inspiring as the vast forest of **hoodoos** may appear from the rim of the alcove, individual hoodoos seem to betray peculiar quirks and oddities when seen up close. The best way to appreciate these towering spires is by descending into the amphitheater, either by foot or on horseback. Several companies offer mule trail rides in and around Bryce Canyon, although only **Canyon Trail Rides,** inside the Bryce Canyon Lodge, offers trips that travel to the canyon floor. (☎679-8665. 2hr. rides $30, half-day $45.) For yet another perspective on the famous hoodoos, try a helicopter flight from **Helivision,** located at Ruby's Inn. (☎834-5341. 15-20min. fly-overs from $55 per person; 2-person min. Longer flights over all of Bryce Canyon and into Grand Staircase-Escalante also available.)

During winter months, a thick blanket of snow covers the Bryce landscape, painting the amphitheater's bizarre spires a resplendent white. Park visitation invariably shoots up in late October as travelers flock to see this marvelous display created by the season's first snow. **Cross-country skiers** enjoy these snowy views all winter long while traversing several established trails along the Canyon Rim. **Skiers should remember to beware of cornices, fragile cusps of snow forming along the canyon edge that can collapse without warning.** Although **biking** inside the park is limited to paved surfaces, the Red Canyon region of the Dixie National Forest that rings the park offers some respectable rides. The **Visitors Center,** on Rte. 12 west of Bryce, has more info. (☎676-2676. Open summer daily 8am-6pm.)

DAY HIKING

Hiking in Bryce is fantastic, but visitors traveling from sea level should remember that at park elevation (8000-9000 ft.), the air is thinner, and climbing several hundred feet back up to the rim is likely to be at least twice as hard as descending. The park's guide, called the *Hoodoo*, offers short descriptions of Bryce hikes. For more detailed info, ask a ranger in the Visitors Center or pick up a copy of *Bryce Canyon National Park: Day Hikes and Backpacking Trails* ($2), published by the Park Service and Bryce Canyon Natural History Association.

Rim Trail (5.2 mi. one way, 2-3hr.). Tracing the edge of the spectacular Bryce amphitheater, this moderately strenuous trail travels from Bryce Point (8280 ft.) to Fairyland Point (7804 ft.). Between Sunrise and Sunset Points (½ mi. one way), the flat and paved trail is wheelchair accessible. As no shuttle service is available at Fairyland Point, hikers in search of an easy stroll may wish to take the shuttle back to their cars from Sunrise Point (a 2.7 mi. one-way trip) rather than continue on. However, the segment between Sunrise and Fairyland Points (5 mi. round-trip) is less crowded. Along the entire route, looking east affords breathtaking views of the hoodoos and the distant Aquarius Plateau. Light shines most beautifully on the hoodoos and less severely on you early in the morning and late in the afternoon.

Navajo Loop (1.3 mi. round-trip, 1-2hr.). This steep, moderately strenuous hike is made famous by postcards depicting majestic Douglas Fir trees growing between the towering limestone walls of "Wall Street," a narrow slot canyon. The route begins at Sunset Point (8000 ft.) and descends 521 ft. over a series of tight switchbacks to a junction with Queen's Garden Trail before climbing back via a different trail. En route, hikers get close-up views of the precarious Thor's Hammer hoodoo and relief from the blistering heat inside Wall Street. An alternate route picks up the Queen's Garden Trail at the bottom, following it up to Sunrise Point and then following the Rim Trail (½ mi.) back to Sunset. Trail guide available in the Visitors Center.

Queen's Garden Trail (1.8 mi. round-trip, 1-2hr.). One of Bryce's easier trails, the hike begins at Sunrise Point (8017 ft.) and descends slowly 320 ft. to the Queen Victoria Pinnacle, a rocky spire resembling a queen on her throne. To hike back, follow the same path you descended or pick up the Navajo Loop Trail at the base for more variety.

Peekaboo Loop Trail (5½ mi. round-trip from Bryce Point, 3-4hr.). Descending roughly 1000 ft. from Bryce Point, this highly strenuous, breathtaking hike weaves through a forest of hoodoos and firs, providing some of the best views in the park. The 1.1 mi. trail from Bryce Point to the Peekaboo Loop winds down an exposed face and offers a remarkable panorama of the amphitheater and the town of Tropic below. Hikers can continue up the same path back to Bryce Point after completing the 3 mi. loop, but a better option is to connect the trail with the Navajo Loop and return via Sunset Point. For the most spectacular hoodoo-viewing, take a left on the Peekaboo Loop after descending from Bryce Point and observe the Wall of Windows and Three Wise Men. At the junction after 1.7 mi., follow the signs to the Navajo Loop and turn left at the intersection with that trail. This route ascends to Sunset Point and the canyon rim via the famous "Wall Street" slot canyon. From there, hikers can return to their cars at Bryce Point via the shuttle or the Rim Trail.

BACKPACKING

Nearly all visitors to Bryce Canyon remain high above the amphitheater, perhaps venturing on a few day hikes amongst the hoodoos but leaving the national park's backcountry largely untrodden. Backpacking offers much different scenery than dayhiking. Multi-day treks escape the amphitheater's hoodoos and sand hills for high alpine forests and meadows. The Park Service regulates backcountry use and camping with a permit system. **Backcountry permits** ($5) are available at the Visitors Center and are issued beginning at 8am the day before the proposed trip. Before making plans, stop by the Visitors Center to discuss your route with a ranger and pick up a copy of the free *Backcountry Hiking and Camping Guide*. Bryce has two main backcountry trails:

The **Riggs Spring Loop** (9 mi., 1-2 days) explores the remote southern portion of Bryce Canyon National Park, beginning at the Rainbow Point parking area and descending 1700 ft. to the Pink Cliffs heading toward Riggs Spring (7443 ft.). After 5.7 mi., the trail joins the Under-the-Rim Trail (see below) to return to Rainbow Point. Three designated campsites lie separated widely along the trail. The short distance involved makes the loop an excellent choice for the time-crunched backpacker—a cool, late afternoon hike provides access to remote campgrounds, and an early morning return allows for quick turn-around to the next destination. As a day hike, however, the trail proves much more strenuous, with a total of 3400 ft. of elevation change. As the summer heat often bakes all moisture out of the surrounding landscape, check with the Visitors Center before departing to find out if there is water at Riggs Spring.

The **Under-the-Rim Trail** (23 mi. one-way, 3-4 days), Bryce's backcountry thoroughfare, travels south-north, paralleling the park road. Because so few visitors travel the Bryce backcountry, the trail remains mostly uncrowded even in the busy summer, affording a real taste of solitude as it winds through forests and meadows. From Rainbow Point at the southernmost end of the park to Bryce Point, the trail descends a total of 2000 ft. over the course of some 19 mi., occasionally traveling up moderate inclines. Eventually it gains regaining roughly 1500 ft. in the last 4 mi. Several connector trails descending from the rim provide options for hikes of variable lengths in the area. Water sources are intermittent and unreliable here; check with the Visitors Center for water availability and to reserve a campsite before departing. Though shuttles no longer serve the southern portion of the park, hikers can often get rides back to their cars at Rainbow Point from other visitors. Hitch-hiking within the park is prohibited, but the rangers at the Visitors Center can arrange pick-up.

GRAND STAIRCASE-ESCALANTE ☎ 435

The last virgin corner of US backcountry to be captured by the cartographer's pen, Grand Staircase-Escalante National Monument remains remote, rugged, pristine, and enchanting. This 1.9 million-acre expanse of painted sandstone, high alpine plateaus, treacherous canyons, and raging rivers shelters diverse areas of geological, biological, and historical interest. The name "Grand Staircase" refers to the exposed layers of stratigraphy, layers of rock rising in a colorful and continuous series of cliffs from Lake Powell to Bryce Canyon. Unique biological communities flourish in isolation, ranging from fragile cryptobiotic crusts to hardy, 1400-year-old pines. Human occupation and use of the area likewise has a varied history, from the Ancestral Puebloan and Fremont cultures, who left petroglyphs, granaries, and pottery, to the Mormon pioneers, who fought the desert mile-by-mile in establishing Hole-in-the-Rock Trail. The western portion of the monument guards the impressive and inspiring Vermilion Cliffs, while the southern borders the labyrinthine Paria Canyon Wilderness and the geologically spectacular, rainbow-colored East Kaibab Monocline. On the high Kaiparowits Plateau in the central area of the monument, invaluable fossils provide scientists with their only current insights into certain Cretaceous mammals. In the east, the Escalante River provides terrain for countless challenging and scenic hiking opportunities through narrow slot canyons and fertile riparian areas. All of these outstanding features, hidden away in wild expanses of sandstone, make the monument one of the most intriguing and mysterious areas of the west.

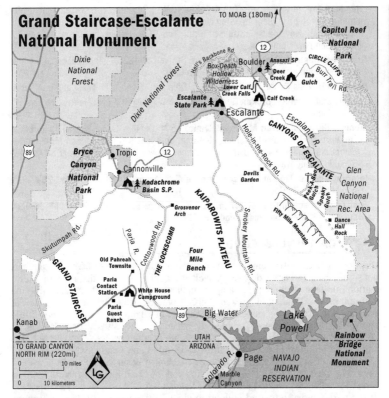

Grand Staircase-Escalante National Monument

TO MOAB (180mi)

Dixie National Forest

Capitol Reef National Park

CIRCLE CLIFFS

Hell's Backbone Rd.

Box-Death Hollow Wilderness

Boulder

Anasazi SP

Deer Creek

Burr Trail Rd.

The Gulch

Dixie National Forest

Lower Calf Creek Falls

Escalante State Park

Calf Creek

Escalante

CANYONS OF ESCALANTE

Escalante R.

89

Bryce Canyon National Park

Tropic

12

Cannonville

Hole-in-the-Rock Rd.

Devils Garden

Glen Canyon National Rec. Area

Kodachrome Basin S.P.

KAIPAROWITS PLATEAU

Peek-a-boo Gulch

Spooky Gulch

Grosvenor Arch

Smokey Mountain Rd.

Fifty Mile Mountain

Dance Hall Rock

THE COCKSCOMB

Paria R.

Cottonwood Rd.

Four Mile Bench

Skutumpah Rd.

GRAND STAIRCASE

Old Pahreah Townsite

Paria Contact Station

White House Campground

Paria Guest Ranch

Big Water

Lake Powell

Rainbow Bridge National Monument

Kanab

TO GRAND CANYON NORTH RIM (220mi)

UTAH
ARIZONA

Colorado R.

Page

NAVAJO INDIAN RESERVATION

Marble Canyon

0   10 miles
0   10 kilometers

LG

UTAH

ORIENTATION & PRACTICAL INFORMATION

An entire lifetime could be spent wandering the 1.9 million acres of the Grand Staircase. As such, several communities serve as gateways to different portions of the monument. In the north, scenic **Route 12** travels between **Bryce,** located approximately 50 mi. northwest (see p. 307), and **Capital Reef National Park** (p. 320), located approximately 75 mi. north. It passes through the towns of **Escalante** and **Boulder, UT** and offers prime access to the Escalante River and its canyons. In the south, well-paved **Route 89** cuts into the monument above **Lake Powell** (p. 87) and provides easy access to **Cottonwood Canyon Road,** the best road from which to experience the heart of the national monument.

Visitor Information: Escalante Interagency Visitors Center, 755 W. Main (☎826-5499), in Escalante. Within the hub for Grand Staircase-Escalante info, helpful and friendly staff steer eager hikers to appropriate routes and dissuade the over-ambitious from attempting Box-Death Hollow in the middle of monsoon season. Open mid-Mar. to Oct. daily 7:30am-5:30pm; Nov. to mid-Mar. M-F 8am-4:30pm. Two info centers are located strategically on either end of the Cottonwood Canyon Rd. In the South: **Paria Contact Station,** 30min. west of Lake Powell on U.S. 89. Open Mar.-Nov. daily 8:30am-4:15pm. In the north: **Cannonville Visitors Center,** 10 Center St. (☎679-8981), near Rte. 12 in Cannonville. Open Mar.-Nov. daily 8am-5pm. **Grand Staircase-Escalante**

Headquarters in Kanab, UT, 745 Rte. 89E (☎435-644-4680), is a clearinghouse of information for those planning extended day visits at the national monument. Open late March to mid-Nov. daily 7:30am-5:30pm. The **BLM** website is also quite helpful: www.ut.blm.gov/monument.

Groceries: Bestway Groceries, 9 W. Main St. (☎826-4226). Stocks Escalante's only selection of grocery items. Open M-Sa 8am-8pm.

Bank/ATM: Wells Fargo, on W. Main St. in Escalante. 24hr. ATM. Open M-F 9am-3pm.

Laundry and Showers: Broken Bow RV Park, on W. Main St. in Escalante. Showers $4; coin-op laundry.

Medical Services: Kazan Memorial Clinic, 65 N. Center St. (☎826-4374), in Escalante. Visiting physicians from Panguitch treat both locals and visitors on M, W, and F. Doctors are available Tu and Th at the **Bryce Valley Clinic,** 10 W. Center St. (☎679-8545), in Cannonville.

Internet Access: Free at the **Escalante Public Library,** 90 N. 100 W (☎826-4200). Open M-F 2:30-6:30pm.

Post Office: Escalante Post Office, 230 W. Main (☎826-4314). Open M-F 8:30am-4pm, Sa 8:30am-noon. **Postal code:** 84726.

■■ CAMPING & FOOD

Dispersed backcountry camping is permitted in most sections of Grand Staircase, but some restricted areas do exist. Check at the Interagency Office for more information on these. A number of campgrounds serve the Escalante area. Within the monument, the 13 shaded sites at the **Calf Creek Campground ❶,** 15 mi. east of Escalante on Rte. 12, accesses the Calf Creek Falls Trail. ($7. Flush toilets, drinking water.) Six miles east of Boulder, the seven primitive sites at **Deer Creek ❶** lie off the scenic Burr Trail Rd. ($4. Pit toilets, no drinking water). Two state parks adjoining the monument provide more developed and expensive sites. West of Escalante in Cannonville, the stunning **Kodachrome Basin State Park ❶** boasts 27 sites ($14. Showers, flush toilets, drinking water). Camping at **Escalante Petrified Forest State Park ❶,** located just west of Escalante off Rte. 12, allows exploration of the park's petrified wood collection via a 1 mi. nature trail. ($14. Showers, flush toilets, water.)

There are hardly any services within the borders of the national monument, so the town of Escalante serves as a remote outpost for those looking to recuperate from long days spent roaming virgin territory. On the terrace in front of the ▣**Trailhead Cafe ❶,** 100 E and Main St. in Escalante, relax to soothing reggae beats or classic rock anthems as you sip an herbal smoothie ($3). This local hangout serves espresso, masterfully grilled sandwiches ($5-7), and delicious baked goods. (☎826-4714. Open Apr.-Nov. daily 7:30am-10pm.) Also in town, **Escalante Outfitters ❷,** 310 W. Main St., caters to the backpacker/hiker crowd, welcoming the desert-dirtyback to civilization with seven simple yet elegant cabins. A small camping supply shop has film and a cafe with delicious pizza. (☎826-4266. Cabins $25, tents $10; subs $4-5, pizza from $10.)

◤ OUTDOOR ACTIVITIES

Any trek or drive into the monument, whether for an afternoon or a month, should begin at the Escalante Interagency Office. The extensive map collections and route knowledge offered by the staff help ensure both safety and fun. In addition, individual hiking without a guide is not advised without a firm grasp of the area's landscape and geographic organization.

UTAH

 GRAND STAIRCASE PRECAUTIONS. Venturing into Grand Staircase-Escalante National Monument intimidates even the most experienced hikers and backpackers. Before traveling inside the monument, check for road conditions and weather forecasts at any one of the Visitors Centers; many roads, including Cottonwood Canyon Rd., are extremely dangerous in mildly bad weather conditions and impassible during rainstorms. Finding water is always difficult, yet deadly flash floods can strike without warning during summer. Don't come to the monument expecting to find a network of developed trails; every hike requires detailed topo maps and route-finding, and most require scrambling across rugged, rattlesnake-infested terrain. Because summer temperatures climb dangerously high, most hikers visit in spring and fall. For the well-prepared and informed hiker, Grand Staircase-Escalante National Monument represents a remote swath of the wild American West, ripe for exploration; for the careless and unprepared, the monument can mean death or serious injury.

Owing to the rugged nature of the monument, a guided trip is perhaps the best way to make the most of a visit to Escalante. **Excursions of Escalante,** with offices in the Trailhead Cafe at 125 E. Main St. (☎800-839-7567; www.excursions-escalante.com), provides professional yet relaxed guide services that are tailored to meet the client's needs. Even a short, inexpensive half-day hiking trip ($45) offers an up-close, physically challenging look at some breathtaking slot and box canyons. Extreme slot canyon adventures and overnight treks are also available. Mention *Let's Go* for a 15% discount. A new guide service focused on exploring the slickrock wonderlands of Escalante is **Earth Tours** (☎691-1241; www.earth-tours.com). This specialized outfit, run from Boulder, UT, is led by a former university geology professor, Dr. Keith Watts, and prides itself on customizing 5-6 person private tours to meet clients' interests and abilities. Prices vary so inquire in advance. **Escalante Outback Adventures** (☎877-777-7988), in the Utah Canyons Shop at 325 W. Main, handles local hiker shuttle services ($1 per mi.). The service is pricey for individual hikers, but it's a good bargain for a group. This outfitter also conducts various guided tours: a sunset tour ($38), an archaeological tour ($32), and a slot canyon tour ($65).

HIKING & BACKPACKING

A **free backcountry permit** is required for all multi-day trips into the monument. The most popular destination for backpacking trips is the **Canyons of Escalante,** in the eastern portion of the monument. Cutting through the slickrock toward Lake Powell, the Escalante and its feeder drainages create a practically endless series of canyons ripe for exploration. Many routes require technical canyoneering skills. Primary access to the canyons of Escalante comes via the **Hole-in-the-Rock Road,** heading south from Rte. 12 east of Escalante. The southern stretches of the road require four-wheel-drive, but access to the popular **Peek-A-Boo** and **Spooky** slot canyons is available to two-wheel-drive vehicles. For one of the most challenging routes in the area, inquire about the **Box-Death Hollow** at the Interagency Office in Escalante. This 30 mi. trek through **Death Hollow Wilderness** travels through narrow slot canyons north of town and earns its name from frequently lethal flash floods. The hike should not be underestimated, as it involves technical climbing skills and long stretches of swimming with a heavy pack through stagnant pools.

Travelers with enough time for an afternoon's constitutional can hike the 3 mi. one-way trail to the cascading, 126 ft. **Lower Calf Creek Falls,** the only developed route in the monument. The trail originates at the Calf Creek Campground, on Rte. 12 halfway between Boulder and Escalante, and generally takes 3-4hr. round-trip.

ON THE EDGE

t was the one section I didn't bother to read. My mom gave me one of those survival books, and I had dutifully memorized key sections on stopping runaway camels and alien abduction. The chapter on what to do if your car is hanging off the edge of a cliff, though, struck me as contrived. If your car's hanging off a cliff, I thought, you're screwed. Next page.

At 8:30pm on June 18, 2002, my friend Matt was driving down the dirt road through Nine-Mile Canyon on the way from Vernal, to Price. A car appeared around a blind corner. We swerved right, into a ditch. The front right tire hit a small boulder and the rear of the car swung right, slamming into canyon wall as we skidded diagonally across the road. I closed my eyes before we bounced off the other vehicle and came to rest tilted backwards at a steep 45° angle, the right front tire two feet off the ground.

A second elapsed. I opened the door and got out, slowly, deliberately. Matt forced his door open and squeezed through. I looked down. One hundred feet.

At that moment a joyous feeling welled up in me and persisted long after the fact. Standing in the middle of the dirt road, Matt and I embraced each other. Later the car would be winched back onto the road, loaded onto a truck, and taken away. Life would go on, a little more real.

–Evan North

DRIVING & FOUR-WHEELING

Travelers passing through the Escalante area en route to national parks east and west have a variety of options for getting a brief glimpse of the monument's wild beauty. Tracing the quite picturesque slickrock hills between Boulder and Escalante, scenic ■**Route 12** is arguably one of the Southwest's most spectacular stretches of highway. The views are transcendent as the road crests and plunges among sculpted sandstone rises, skating atop a narrow ridge before descending into the tranquil farming community of Boulder. The 40min. needed to complete this 28 mi. drive are likely to inspire a summer's worth of enchantment.

Another route between Boulder and Escalante, the **Hell's Backbone Road** climbs high into the Dixie National Forest for spectacular views of the Death Hollow area and the colorful Escalante slickrock. The well-maintained and graded dirt road is friendly toward any vehicle. As magnificent as the views along the 45 mi. route may be, don't miss Rte. 12 between Boulder and Escalante to see them.

Starting from Boulder, the paved, one-way ■**Burr Trail Road** descends 31 mi. into a spectacular red-walled gulch before emerging onto the Circle Cliffs and a breathtaking series of red, white, purple, yellow, and orange dunes. From there it continues east toward the looming monuments of **Capitol Reef National Park** (p. 320). The paved surface ends at the park boundary, and though two-wheel-drive vehicles should not descend the switchbacks into Capitol Reef, a picnic table with a view awaits a few navigable miles down the gravel road. For those willing to make an early start, the morning light brings the red rocks and rainbow dunes to life. The route is manageable without a high-clearance vehicle, but as always rangers recommend inquiring about road conditions prior to your drive.

If passing through Escalante around lunchtime, feel free to picnic among the sculpted natural statues at **Devil's Garden.** Splendid slickrock formations and bizarre hoodoos await travelers here, 13 mi. down the **Hole-in-the-Rock Road.** While the road surface alternates between gravel washboard, sand, dried mud, and slickrock, the first half is generally passable to most cars.

Traveling the 50 mi. between Cannonville and Rte. 89, the popular **Cottonwood Canyon Road** cuts through the **Cockscomb,** a remarkable fissure in the earth's crust delineated by sawtooth edges. Though often passable to two-wheel-drive vehicles, the road surface is treacherous and marked by large sandy patches. Inquire at the Cannondale Visitors Center or the Paria Contact Station for road conditions.

Other more remote **four-wheel-drive roads** criss-cross the monument, providing a day's or several days' worth of pristine desert scenery. Check at the Interagency Office for info on traveling the Monument's backcountry roads.

The area just south of **Cannonville** contains several other easily accessible parks and outdoor experiences. At the northern tip of the Cottonwood Canyon Rd., 9 mi. south of Cannondale and Rte. 12, **Kodachrome Basin State Park** (☎ 800-322-3770) preserves the unique, solidified spires of ancient geysers. Seventeen miles south of Cannondale along a passable stretch of the Cottonwood Canyon Rd. stands **Grosvenor Arch,** an unusual and rugged double span.

PARIA CANYON WILDERNESS   ☎ 435

South of Grand Staircase-Escalante National Monument, the Paria River cuts through a wild region of petrified sand dunes to create a gallery of slickrock canyons and buttes. Eons of erosive wind and water in this region have sculpted sensuous and ethereal formations such as **The Wave,** which now dot the landscape all around the river's path.

ⁿ⚇ ACCOMMODATIONS & FOOD. Two miles past the contact station on a gravel road lies **White House Campground** and **Trailhead ❶.** Walk-in sites ($5) have pit toilets and fire pits. The trailhead is the northernmost access point for the Paria Canyon Wilderness Area. Down the dirt road at ▨**Paria Canyon Guest Ranch ❶,** a hip, remodeled farm welcomes a young and international crowd. The ranch entertains its guests with trail rides ($20 per hr.), a climbing wall/adventure course, and a clubhouse with two turntables and 1000 LPs. On summer nights, European teenagers traveling across the country throb to techno beats in this surreal wood-panelled lounge. (☎ 689-0398; www.pariacampground.com. Guest showers $1, nonguests $2. Dorms $12; campsites $15 per vehicle. Private room available.)

Just west of the contact station at mile marker 21, the friendly, hospitable proprietors of **Paria Outpost Restaurant and Outfitters** (☎ 928-691-1047; www.paria.com) help visitors feel right at home. The Outpost and Outfitters provide guide services to both Glen Canyon and Grand Staircase-Escalante National Monument, hiker shuttle service to trailheads and the town of Lee's Ferry, Utah, a charming **room for rent ❷** ($40), and a **restaurant ❶** with an endless Western-style buffet that draws locals from Page on Friday and Saturday (served 5-8pm; $12).

◨⚐ SIGHTS & OUTDOOR ACTIVITIES. For info on the wilderness, permits, camp fees, and weather forecasts or to fill up on drinking water, visit the **Paria Contact Station** at mile marker 21 on Rte. 89, within 3 mi. of the Cottonwood Canyon Rd. turnoff and 30min. west of Lake Powell on U.S. 89. (Open Mar.-Nov. daily 8:30am-4:30pm.) The swirling slickrock patterns in the **Coyote Buttes** area draw more eager visitors than resources can support, prompting the BLM to place strict limitations on daily use. Only 20 people are allowed to make the 3 mi. trek to **The Wave** each day. Ten **permits** ($5 per person per day) are made available at the Paria Contact Station at 9am the morning before the proposed hike during high season, April and May, and then again in October a waiting line forms by 8:30am; the other 10 may be reserved 6 months in advance on the Paria website (https://az.blm.gov/paria). Additional hikes include the 16 mi. journey through narrow **Buckskin Gulch,** said to be the longest slot canyon in the world, and the serene 38 mi. trek through the **Paria Canyon** itself. In some areas, the canyon narrows to as little as 10 ft. wide. Come prepared with plenty of water and sunscreen, and remember that flash floods can be the result of storms over 50 mi. away. Inquire with the Paria Contact Station regarding weather forecasts and do not chance a journey into the canyon if the forecast is for rain of any kind, especially in July and August.

CAPITOL REEF NATIONAL PARK ☎ 435

The chief virtue of Capitol Reef, named in part because one of its mountains resembles Washington, D.C.'s Capitol Dome, is that it grants visitors a sampling of all the impressive aspects of southern Utah. A microcosm of the Colorado plateau's parks, this is the one most visited by Utahns themselves, where the highlights of the Grand Circle shine: hoodoos, arches, natural bridges, and narrow slot canyons, all in one place. A geologist's fantasy and the Reef's feature attraction, the 100 mi. Waterpocket Fold, with rocky peaks and pinnacles, bisects the park's 378 sq. mi. and presents millions of years of stratified natural history. Many of the settlers who gave the Reef its name were former seamen who called anything difficult to cross a reef. After much effort and innovation, they navigated their way through the treacherous but magnificently colored cliffs of what the Navajo call the "Land of the Sleeping Rainbow." They sunk their roots into the fertile soil along Fremont River, planting a variety of fruit trees amid the geological wonders, and the town that sprang up was aptly named Fruita. Now the spot serves as a base for the park's services, and over 100 years later, visitors still enjoy the fruits of their predecessors' labors.

AT A GLANCE: CAPITOL REEF NATIONAL PARK

AREA: 241,904 acres.	**GATEWAY TOWNS:** Torrey, Caineville.
FEATURES: Waterpocket Fold, Fremont River.	**CAMPING:** Fruita Campground $10; free permit required for backcountry camping, and camping at Cedar Mesa and Cathedral Valley.
HIGHLIGHTS: The park's scenic drive, backcountry hiking, fruit picking at the Fruita orchard.	
	FEES: Entrance free; scenic drive $5.

✦ ORIENTATION

East of Zion and Bryce Canyon and west of Arches and Canyonlands, Capitol Reef, the middle link in the Fab Five chain of national parks, is unreachable by train or bus. The closest Amtrak and Greyhound stops are in **Green River.** For a fee, **Wild Hare Expeditions** (p. 324) will provide a shuttle between Richfield and the park. The park extends over 50 mi. north to south but on average is no more than 10 mi. wide. **Route 24,** the main route through the park, crosses at one of the wider portions, providing access to the Visitors Center, campground, and scenic drive in Fruita as well as a number of sights and trailheads. In addition, a number of secondary roads, including the **Notom-Bullfrog Road** and **Burr Trail Road,** offer more secluded experiences of this area.

WHEN TO GO. With low humidity all year, there is no bad time to visit Capitol Reef. Summers bring highs in the upper 90s, with significantly cooler evenings, while the spring and fall are temperate, their highs averaging in the 60s. Beware of thunderstorms, and their attendant flash floods, in July and August.

▤ PRACTICAL INFORMATION

The **Visitors Center,** on Rte. 24, 11 mi. east of Torrey and 19 mi. west of Caineville, is equipped with free trail brochures, info on daily activities, and plenty of maps for sale. (☎425-3791. Open June-Aug. daily 8am-6pm, Sept.-May 8am-4:30pm.) For more info, contact the Superintendent, Capitol Reef National Park, Torrey, UT 84775, or call ☎425-3791. Other services include: **weather and road conditions, ☎**425-

GARDEN OF EATIN' Intrepid Mormon settlers must have known that Brigham Young had found the Promised Land when they emerged out of the deserts of southern Utah and stumbled across the bountiful **orchards** of their brethren homesteaders in **Fruita,** on the Fremont River. Cherry, apricot, peach, and apple trees were first planted by pioneers in the 1880s and provided sustenance for this small town, which was rarely home to more than ten families. Today, a two-person orchard crew maintains the 2700 trees in Capitol Reef solely for the enjoyment of park visitors. The cherry harvest kicks off in early June, followed by apricots (late June to mid-July) and peaches and pears (Aug. and early Sept.), finishing off with apples (Sept. to mid-Oct.). While in the orchards, visitors are welcome to eat as much ripe fruit as they want, but cash is necessary to take some home. Either way, you're likely to enjoy solitude in the orchards, with the company of only a deer or two if you're lucky. Call the Capitol Reef Visitors Center (p. 320) and listen for prompts that will take you to the fruit harvest hotline for updated information on the ripe and juicy offerings.

3791; **Wayne County Medical Clinic,** 128 S. 300 W (☎425-3744), 19 mi. west of the Visitors Center in downtown Bicknell; and the **post office,** 222 E. Main. (☎425-3488. Open M-F 7:30am-1:30pm, Sa 7:30-11:30am.) **Postal code:** 84775.

ACCOMMODATIONS & FOOD

Torrey, a sleepy town 11 mi. west of the Visitors Center on Rte. 24, has the nearest lodging and restaurants to the park. The friendly **Sandcreek Hostel ①,** 540 Rte. 24, features an espresso and smoothie bar, organic produce and local crafts, and remarkably inexpensive rates. A single dorm room houses eight comfy beds, a minifridge, and a microwave. There are also 12 tent sites, 12 hookups, and two rustic cabins that sleep up to four people. (☎425-3577; www.sandcreekrv.com. Nonguest showers $4. Linens $2. Reception 7:30am-8pm. Check-out 11am. Open Apr. to mid-Oct. Dorms $10, tent sites $11, hookups $16-18, cabins $28-34.) Down the road, the **Capitol Reef Inn and Cafe ②,** 360 W. Main, puts guests up in Southwest-themed rooms with jacuzzis and handmade furniture, while featuring one of the best **restaurants** in town. Fresh local produce and lush salads ($8-11) dot the menu. Try the grilled trout sandwich on a bagel with cream cheese for $7.75. (☎425-3271. Reception 7am-10pm. Check-out 11am. Open Apr.-Oct. Rooms $40, each additional person $4.)

Across the road from a Best Western, **Rim Rock Restaurant ③,** 2523 E. Hwy. 24, rests on a cliff with stunning views of the expanses at the entrance to Capitol Reef. The kitchen turns out the best cuts of steak for miles around ($14), and the lodge has rooms ranging $49-$79. (☎425-3388; www.therimrock.com. Open for dinner Apr. to mid-Nov. daily 5-10pm.) A stone's throw from the hostel, **Cafe Diablo ③,** 599 W. Main, dishes out pricey but extraordinary gourmet Southwestern fare. Turn the tables on sidewinders by ordering the rare and unusual rattlesnake cake for $8. (☎425-5070; www.cafediablo.net. Open daily 5-11pm.) Greasier offerings await at **Brink's Burgers ①,** 163 E. Main. (☎425-3710. Open daily 11am-9pm. Take-out available. Entrees $2-5. Cash only.)

CAMPING

The park's campgrounds offer sites on a first-come, first-serve basis. The main campground, **Fruita ①,** 1.3 mi. south of the Visitors Center off Rte. 24, contains 71 sites with drinking water and toilets, but no showers. The campground is nestled between two orchards, and visitors can eat all the fruit, usually apricots and cherries, they want (sites $10). **Cedar Mesa Campground ❶**, on the Notom-Bullfrog Rd. (half paved, accessible by passenger car except when wet), and **Cathedral Valley ❶**, in the north, have five sites each. Both are free, but without water. Cathedral is accessible only by high-clearance four-wheel-drive vehicle or a long hike

❧ HIKING

The park greets hikers and backpackers with virtually limitless possibilities, sheltering trails for every level of outdoorsman. Bicycling is allowed only on established roads in the park, many of which are sandy, so sticking to foot is generally the best tactic for exploring Capitol Reef. On all hikes, be aware of the weather and consider the possibility of flash floods. **Water** is available in the park at the Visitors Center, picnic area, and Fruita Campground.

In the less frequented northern and southern sections of Capitol Reef, all hikes are considered backcountry travel. Before you set out for overnight trips, be sure to get a **free backcountry permit** at the Visitors Center. In the north, Cathedral Valley features an incredible moonscape of natural monoliths and pinnacles. A four-wheel-drive, high-clearance vehicle is recommended to drive on all of the roads here, but you can hike either on the roads or overland from Rte. 24 and enjoy the solitude of the most remote region of park. Along the Notom-Bullfrog Rd., a number of strenuous hikes head up the washes that descend from the Waterpocket Fold. **Burro Wash, Cottonwood Wash, Sheets Gulch**, and **Muley Twist Canyon** are all exciting possibilities for both day hikes and longer forays into the backcountry. Some of these washes may require wading or scrambling. Be sure to consult with a park ranger before setting off. Worthwhile hikes in close proximity to Rte. 24 and the Visitors Center include:

Capitol Gorge Trail (2 mi. round-trip, 2-3 hr.). This easy hike on mostly level, narrow wash bottom runs off the Scenic Drive. Trekking through sheer canyon walls brings you to the Pioneer Registrar, a list of names of Fruita settlers cast onto well preserved rock walls. The trail rises over the middle 0.2 mi. to a series of tanks—water pockets that collect rainfall.

Chimney Rock Trail (3.5 mi. loop, 3-4hr.). This moderate loop trail departs from a turnoff on the north side of Rte. 24 at the west entry of the park and climbs a set of switchbacks to an upper loop that traverses cross-sections of Capitol Reef's unique geology. Great views of Chimney Rock and panoramas of the Waterpocket Fold. 600 ft. elevation gain. Hikeable year-round, except when very wet.

Rim Overlook and Navajo Knobs Trail (4.5-9 mi. round-trip, entire route 4-8 hr.). This hike, one of the more challenging maintained routes in the park, departs from the Hickman Bridge parking area and climbs to the canyon rim above the Fremont River. Huge domes of the reef tower over the trail, while views of the valley below reward upward trekkers. The vista from the Rim Overlook at 2.3 mi. is fantastic, and from Navajo Knobs (4.5 mi. in) you'll have a sweeping 360-degree panorama. 1600 ft. elevation gain. Treacherous when wet.

Frying Pan Trail (5 mi. one-way, 4-5hr.). The trailhead, as well as that for the Cohab Canyon Trail, sits across from the Hickman Bridge parking lot, 2 mi. east of the Visitors Center. This moderately strenuous trail parallels a portion of the Waterpocket Fold atop Capitol Reef for a good one-way trip (requiring a two-car shuttle), although it can be combined with the Grand Wash Trail for a loop (including a portion of the highway). A short ½ mi. spur heads out to the inconspicuous but lovely Cassidy Arch. May also be hiked south to north from the Grand Wash parking area. 1000 ft. elevation gain. Exposed to wind and weather, especially in the winter.

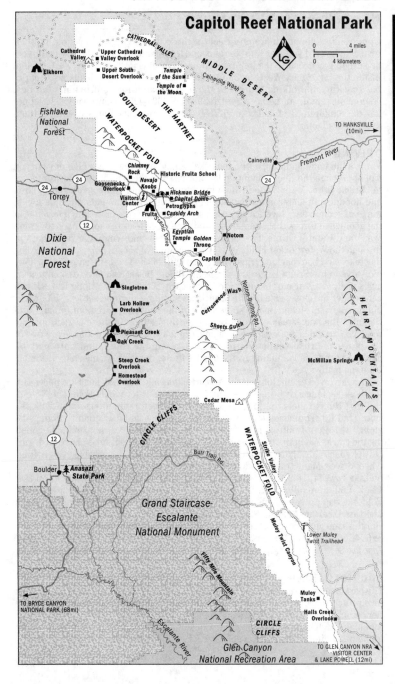

Capitol Reef National Park

UTAH

⚠ OTHER OUTDOORS ACTIVITIES

Opportunities abound in Capitol Reef for those who are eager to set out on their own. However, if you just want to relax and let someone else lead the way for you, be sure to pay a visit to the helpful **Wild Hare Expeditions**, 2600 E. Hwy. 24, located inside the large Best Western Capitol Reef Resort. Wild Hare leads a variety of backpacking and hiking tours into the park, in addition to providing the best equipment rentals in the area. (☎425-3999, 888-304-4273. Hours vary. $40-50 per half day, children $35; full day $60-75/$50. Scenic drives and four-wheel-drive tours are also available.)

DRIVING

While a full understanding of the remarkable land here requires a hike or two, you can appreciate the Reef's haunting landforms from the seat of your car on the 20 mi. **Scenic Drive.** A 1hr. round-trip jaunt through red and white sedimentary cliffs and hoodoos, the alternately paved and improved dirt route cuts through a wide range of sedimentary layers as it progresses south, giving a more tangible sense of the geological forces that shaped the land. The drive features spur roads to Grand Wash and Capitol Gorge, two of the more narrow and windy canyons that cut through the Waterpocket Fold, as well as a number of access points for rewarding day hikes and backpacking trips. One mile south of the Visitors Center on the Scenic Drive in the Fruita Historic district, the **Gifford Homestead** *(open daily in summer)* gives visitors a sense of pioneer life in the early 20th century. Along Rte. 24, you can ponder the closet-sized **Fruita Schoolhouse** built by Mormon settlers, 1000-year-old petroglyphs etched on the stone walls of the canyon by Fremont Indians, and Behunin, the homestead of an early pioneer. In addition to these attractions, the road also provides its fair share of sights. Chimney Rock and the Castle are two of the more abstruse sandstone formations along the route, and both may be explored up close via hiking trails. **Capitol Dome,** the park's namesake, is visible from the highway.

More involved excursions on the **Notom-Bullfrog** and **Burr Trail Road** are necessary for those seeking a truly in-depth experience of the Waterpocket Fold. The Notom-Bullfrog Rd. parallels the fold for almost 30 mi. before its intersection with the Burr Trail Rd. Trailheads for several good day hikes and backcountry outings lie along the Notom-Bullfrog. In good weather, cars should have no trouble negotiating the track. When the weather gets wet, however, the bentonite clay transforms Dr. Jekyll into Mr. Hyde, at times rendering the dirt roads impassable even in four-wheel-drives. Many travelers do not follow the road all the way to Bullfrog Marina on **Lake Powell** (p. 87), and instead take the Burr Trail Rd. west to Boulder on Rte. 12 (130 mi. loop; allow a full day). The only route that climbs the Waterpocket Fold, the trip passes through both Capitol Reef and the adjacent, desolate **Grand Staircase-Escalante National Monument** (p. 314). The **ferry service** at Bullfrog Marina shuttles cars and people 3.1 mi. across Lake Powell to Hall's Crossing on Rte. 276. (☎684-3000, call ahead to confirm that the ferry is running. Mid-May to mid-Sept. daily 8am-7pm; mid-Sept. to May 8am-3pm and 5-7pm. Cars $12, motorcycle $5, person/bike $3.)

ROCK CLIMBING

The park boasts a great deal of excellent rock climbing. Since you need to use your own protection and route-finding skills, the climbs aren't for beginners. For experienced climbers, Capitol Reef's soft sandstone provides a nice vertical stopover for single-pitch climbs rated 5.7-5.11. Consult a park ranger to match your ability to the right climbs, and study a guidebook before setting out.

INTERSTATE 15

One of Utah's most-traveled thoroughfares, Interstate 15 zips red-rock-hungry tourists straight from Salt Lake City to the Grand Circle of parks spread across southern Utah and northern Arizona. The towns along the interstate don't offer much at all, but Cedar Breaks's excellent amphitheater and the Bard's work performed live on stage in Cedar City merit a stop en route to the outdoors enthusiasts' promised land.

PROVO ☎801

Fishermen flock to the town of Provo for its world-class fly fishing—and indeed, the healthy rainbow, cutthroat, brown, and cutbow trout pulled from the Provo River never disappoint fishing enthusiasts. Sandwiched between the state's largest freshwater lake, Utah Lake, and the impressive and imposing wilderness around Mt. Timpanogos, strip-mall-laden Provo and her sister city, Orem, feel like suburban civilization at its most commercial. Less than an hour south of Salt Lake on I-15, Provo and Orem are excellent staging grounds for the wilder destinations to the south and east.

■ ⁊ **ORIENTATION & PRACTICAL INFORMATION.** Provo's downtown lies at the junction of **Center Street** and **University Avenue** and has several retail stores, banks, and high-end restaurants. To find anything else in Provo, be prepared to navigate a virtual maze of malls. Most retail and restaurant developments crowd along University Ave., State St. (500 W), and University Pkwy. To escape the concrete jungle, follow University Ave. (Rte. 189) through town to Bridal Veil Falls, Sundance Resort, and the Mt. Timpanogos area. **Greyhound,** 124 N. 300 W (☎373-4211) serves Provo. Bike-carrier-equipped **UTA buses** (☎287-4636) travel on major Provo thoroughfares. The **Utah County Visitors Center,** 51 S. University Ave., has area info. (☎370-8393. Open M-F 8am-5pm, Sa 9am-5pm.) **Internet access** awaits at the **Provo County Library,** 500 N. University Ave. (☎852-6650. Open M-Sa 9am-9pm.) Other services include: **police,** 352 W. Center St. (☎852-6210); **Seaside Laundromat,** 300 S. and Freedom Blvd. (☎375-0900; open M-Sa 7am-11pm, last load in by 9:30pm); **Utah Valley Regional Medical Center,** 1034 N. 500 W (☎333-7850); and the **post office,** 95 W. 100 S, downtown. **Postal code:** 84601.

⁊ **ACCOMMODATIONS.** Downtown Provo has its fair share of inexpensive lodging. The **Provo Traveler's Motel ❷,** 469 W. Center St. (☎373-8248), keeps small rooms ($29-89) on a retail- and restaurant-crowded street in the heart of town. The **Safari Motel ❷,** 250 S. University Ave., furnishes some of its large rooms with microwaves and refrigerators. (☎373-9672. Singles $37, doubles $45.) Tree-speckled plots welcome tent campers and RVs at the **Lakeside RV Campground ❶,** near Utah Lake State Park at 4000 W. Center St. (☎800-906-5267. Pool on premises. Tent sites $16, full hookups $23.)

⌂ **FOOD.** Provo has a wide variety of chain restaurants, in addition to a few diamonds in the rough. Downtown's **Lotus Garden ❷,** 56 W. Center St., (☎374-1626), serves a buffet lunch ($7) large enough to require navigational skills. It features a small sushi bar and a stir-fry station. Also downtown, Ghandi-inspired **Guru's ❶,** 45 E. Center St., vends Southwestern food, such as the twin-taco-and-one-enchilada meal ($6), while promoting youth leadership and life skills. Proceeds go to Guru's Foundation. (☎377-6980. Open M-Th 11am-9pm, F-Sa 11am-10pm.)

◙ ♫ **SIGHTS & OUTDOOR ACTIVITIES.** The quite impressive **North American Museum of Ancient Life** (☎768-2300), at Thanksgiving Point, north of Provo on I-15 off exit 287, displays the world's largest collection of dinosaur skeletons, including a 110 ft. Supersaurus. Outdoor activities in the area are focused around Mt. Timpanogos and the surrounding Uinta National Forest (see p. 269 for more on this wilderness). For swimming and boating on scorching summer days, follow the crowds of locals to the **Utah Lake State Park** at the western end of Center St.

TIMPANOGOS CAVE NATIONAL MONUMENT

Accessible solely via Rte. 92 20 mi. south of Salt Lake City off I-15, exit 287; Rte. 92 also connects with Rte. 189 northeast of Provo. ☎756-5238. Open mid-May to late Oct. daily 7am-5:30pm. 3hr. hikes depart daily 7am-4:30pm every 15min. $6, ages 6-15 $5. Golden Age Passport and ages 3-5 $3, ages 2 and under free.

Legend has it that a set of mountain lion tracks first led Martin Hansen to the mouth of the cave that today bears his name. **Hansen's Cave** forms but one third of the cave system of American Fork Canyon, collectively called Timpanogos Cave. Situated in a rich alpine environment, Timpanogos is a true gem for speleologists (cave nuts) and tourists alike due to the presence of 43 different types of formations, including one of the highest concentrations of helictites in the world. These gravity-defying formations look like weeds pulled from the ground but are made of exotic, light-catching stone.

Though early miners shipped boxcar loads of stalactites and other mineral wonders back east to sell to universities and museums, enough remain to bedazzle guests for the 1hr. walk through the caves. Today, the cave is open to visitors only via ranger-led tours. The **visitors center** dispenses tour tickets and info on the caves. Summer tours tend to sell out by early afternoon; reservations for busy summer weekends should be made as early as 30 days in advance. In less busy times, reservations are accepted up to the day before the tour. Bring water and warm layers: the rigorous hike to the cave climbs 1065 ft. over 1.5 mi., but the temperature remains a constant 45°F inside.

UINTA NATIONAL FOREST

Engulfing the National Monument, the forest provides terrain for outdoor exploration in the mountains of the Wasatch Range. The **Alpine Scenic Drive (Route 92)** leaves the Visitors Center and heads southwest through endless aspen groves, providing excellent views of Mt. Timpanogos and other snowcapped peaks. The 20 mi. drive traverses a slew of switchbacks, takes close to 1hr. in one direction, and passes many trailheads. The Forest Service charges $3 for recreation along the road on national forest land (pass good for three days). The climb to the summit of sheer Mt. Timpanogos (11,749 ft.) starts either from the Aspen Grove Trailhead (6860 ft.) or from the Timpooneke Trailhead (7260 ft.). The Timpooneke Trail (16.2 mi. round-trip to the summit) lies on the cave side of the scenic drive and meets the summit trail at Emerald Lake. The Aspen Grove Trail (19.8 mi. round-trip to the summit) ascends from the other side of the scenic drive, climbing 6.9 mi. to Emerald Lake and the summit trail. Both hikes are very strenuous and can be treacherous in spring or early summer when precipitous rock faces and slick snowfields make for a deadly combination. Expect the ascent to require at least a full day, and though the trails are reasonably well marked, rangers recommend bringing a map and compass and preparing for severe weather.

The Silver Lake Trail (3.6 mi. round-trip, 4hr.) offers a pleasant afternoon's hike, climbing from 7600 ft. to 9000 ft. Find the trailhead in the North Fork of American Fork Canyon, on Forest Rd. 9, just before the **Granite Flat Campground ❶.** Those camping in this area should store food out of the reach of bears (see **Bears**, p. 70). For more info, pick up a trail guide at the Pleasant Grove Ranger District (☎785-3568), 390 N. 100 E, Pleasant Grove.

The ranger district also has info on the campgrounds in the area (☎800-280-2267 for reservations; sites $11-13). **Backcountry camping** throughout the forest requires no permit or fee as long as you respect minimum-impact guidelines. While the National Park Service completely forbids camping within the national monument itself, **Little Mill Campground** ❶, on Rte. 92 past the monument, provides an excellent jumping-off point from which to beat the Timpanogos Cave crowds. ($11. Open early May-late Sept.) Once in the Wasatch, the most basic services are extremely limited. Rte. 89 has gas stations, supermarkets, and fast food in Pleasant Grove and Orem.

SUNDANCE RESORT

Located just a short drive up Rte. 189, actor Robert Redford's legendary **Sundance Resort,** named in the spirit of his role in the award-winning film *Butch Cassidy and the Sundance Kid* (1969), boasts 450 acres of pristine Utah powder and surprisingly reasonable lift ticket rates. Sundance is one of the best lesser-known ski resorts in the country, and while lodging rates are sky high, nearby Provo makes a good base for exploring the region. Three lifts provide access to a wide variety of terrain over a vertical drop of 2150 ft. UTA buses provide transportation between Provo's Mt. Timpanogos Transit Center and Sundance 8am-6pm daily; call for more information on routes and schedules, as these change seasonally. A year-round resort, summers in Sundance promise excellent hiking, biking, and horseback riding opportunities. (☎255-4107, 888-743-3882; www.sundanceresort.com. Full-day lift ticket M-F $28, Sa-Su $34, children $16, seniors $10. Ski and snowboard rentals available. Open late Nov. to early Apr. 9am-4:30pm. Sundance also offers 15 mi. of groomed nordic trails and 6 mi. of separate snowshoe trails. Nordic trail fee $11, nordic ski/boot rentals $18, snowshoe rentals $10.) Founded by former employees of the Sundance Resort, **■Rocky Mountain Outfitters** is a superb all-service year-round outfitter in the Provo area. They customize fly fishing trips, horseback riding, snowmobiling, and even stage coach dinners and sleigh rides in the gorgeous and magical valley of Soldiers Hollow in nearby Midway. Mention *Let's Go* for a 10% discount. (☎435-654-1655; www.rockmtnoutfitters.com. Half-day guided fishing $135 for two or more persons. Horseback riding from $38 per half day.)

BEHIND THE SCENES AT SUNDANCE

Every year, the prestigious **Sundance Film Festival** takes place over ten days in January, usually starting around the 15th of the month. Fledgling and big-name directors alike come from around the country and overseas to screen their cinematic brain-children before the discerning festival jury. Park City hosts most of the screenings, but a handful of films are shown in the 160-seat theater of the Sundance Institute at North Provo Canyon's Sundance Resort. The event is especially attractive to filmmakers because of its meeting houses in Park City, where filmmakers schmooze and network, demonstrate new technology, attend countless parties and receptions, and even do yoga.

If you're submission didn't make the cut this year, you can still get a behind-the-scenes view of the festival as one of the over 1000 **volunteers** who work the festival each January, doing everything from office work to driving airport shuttles to working on film crews (if experienced). The Sundance Institute reviews volunteer applications for the festival in October, although it needs volunteers at the institute year-round. Visit its website (**http://institute.sundance.org**) for more information on job and volunteer opportunities at the festival.

CEDAR CITY ☎435

Southern Utah's college town, Cedar City, with its vibrant, historic Main St. and youthful feel, is as close as you can get to a cultural center in this part of the state. With a well-manicured park and interesting shops and restaurants, downtown exudes energy, especially when summer crowds pour in for the annual Shakespeare Festival. To the east, Brian Head and the Dixie National Forest lure visitors with endless views and stellar hiking and biking, while the fantastic red sandstone sculpture garden of Cedar Breaks National Monument will inspire wonder at the creative powers of the environment.

▐ TRANSPORTATION. Skywest Airlines (☎586-3000, 800-453-9417) flies to **Salt Lake City** (3 times daily, $150 one-way) out of **Cedar City Regional Airport,** 2281 W. Kitty Hawk Dr. (☎867-9408), west of town along Airport Rd. off of 200 North St. **Greyhound,** 2569 N. Main St. (☎586-0627, 800-231-2222), stops in Cedar City at Steaks & Stuff north of town on its way up and down the I-15 corridor. To: **Salt Lake City** (4hr., 2 per day, $41); **Las Vegas** (3hr., 5 per day, $32); and **Denver** (8-10hr., 3 per day, $87). **Cedar Area Transportation Service** (CATS, ☎559-RIDE/7433), runs buses throughout town (M-F 7am-5:30pm, Sa 10am-5:30pm. $1.) **Cedar City Cabs & Shuttles** (☎888-658-CABS/2227) and **Iron County Shuttle & Taxi** (☎865-7076), provide service throughout southwest Utah. For car rentals, **Alamo** (☎888-426-3299, 586-4004), **Avis** (☎867-9898), and **National** (☎888-868-6204 or 586-4004), have all set up shop in the airport. In town, **Speedy Rentals,** 650 N. Main St. (☎586-7368), rents less pristine vehicles. (From $40 per day. 21 and over, with a major credit card. Open M-F 9am-5pm, Sa 9am-noon.)

▐ ORIENTATION. If you're driving south along Interstate 15, Cedar City will be southwestern Utah's first major jumping-off point for outdoor exploration. The town is over 260 mi. southwest of **Salt Lake City** and 175 mi. northwest of **Las Vegas** (when coming via St. George 50 mi. to the south). In town, **Main Street** is the main drag, and **Center Street** and **200 North Street** are the major cross streets. Run-down stripmalls are juxtaposed with classic old downtown buildings all along Main St., while new commercial development has sprung up at the Providence Center south of town along I-15.

▐ PRACTICAL INFORMATION. The **Iron County Visitors Center,** 581 N. Main St., has a friendly staff and a host of brochures and maps with information on various outdoor opportunities and other activities in the region. (☎586-5124, 800-354-4849. Open June-Aug. M-F 8am-7pm, Sa 9am-1pm; Sept.-May M-F 8am-5pm.) For **outdoor information,** pay a visit to the **Forest Service's Cedar City Ranger District** offices, 1789 N. Wedgewood Ln. (☎865-3200. Open M-F 8am-5pm.) Alternatively, you can try the equally helpful **Cedar City BLM,** 176 East D.L. Sargent Dr., off Commercial Canyon Ave. and located just north of town. (☎586-2401. Open M-F 7:45am-4:30pm.) For bike rental, check out **Cedar Cycle,** 38 E. 200 South St. (☎586-5210. Open M-F 9am-5pm, Sa 9am-2pm.) There is plenty of **outdoor gear** for sale or rent at the aptly-named **Mountain Shop,** 1067 S. Main St. (☎586-7177. Open M-F 10am-7pm, Sa 10am-6pm.) Cedar City's services include: **Zions Bank,** 3 S. Main St. (☎586-7614; open M-Th 9am-5pm, F 9am-6pm; drive-through window M-F 9am-6pm, Sa 9am-1pm.), with **24hr. ATM; emergency** (☎911); **Cedar City Police,** 2132 N. Main St. (☎586-2955); **Valley View Medical Center,** 1303 N. Main St. (☎868-5000); **pharmacy** at Wal-Mart, 1330 S. Providence Center Dr. (☎586-0155; open M-F 9am-9pm, Sa 9am-6pm, Su 11am-5pm. Store 24hr.); **Raindance Cleaners Laundromat,** 434 S. Main St. (☎586-6964; open M-Sa 8am-10pm, last load 9pm); free **Internet access** at the **Cedar City Memorial**

Library, 136 W. Center St. (☎586-6661; open M-Th 9am-9pm, F-Sa 9am-6pm); and the **post office,** 333 N. Main St. (☎586-6701. Open M-F 8:30am-5:30pm, Sa 8:30am-12:30pm.) **Postal code:** 84720.

⏚ ☐ ACCOMMODATIONS & FOOD. Economy motels flourish on Main St., sustained by the traffic up and down I-15. **Abbey Inn ❹,** 940 W. 200 North St. (☎586-9966, 800-325-5411), presents some of the town's most luxurious lodgings. With a complimentary deluxe breakfast bar, indoor pool and spa, guest laundry, refrigerators, microwaves, and coffee makers in renovated surroundings, you get more than your money's worth. (Rooms with king or double queens from $65. AAA, AARP, and senior discounts.) For spacious, spotless rooms and friendly service, try **Cedar Rest Motel ❷,** 479 S. Main St. (☎586-9471. Singles from $30; doubles from $36.) Escape the heat on Hwy. 14 at the convenient **Cedar Canyon Campground ❶** (8100 ft.), 13 mi. east of town, which has 19 shady sites with water and vault toilets ($8). Camping is also available in the **National Monument** (p. 330).

While fast-food joints populate the area near I-15 interchanges, downtown Cedar City shelters high-quality, budget-priced dining. For lunch, dinner, and late-night snacks, **The Pastry Pub ❶,** 86 W. Center St., is a Cedar City fixture. The medieval decor belies a very modern menu with creative sandwich ($3.50-5) and salad ($5) options, along with all sorts of liquid concoctions. Choose your poison carefully. (☎867-1400. Open M-Sa 7:30am-10pm, during the festival M-Sa 7:30am-midnight.). **Lupitas ❶,** 453 S. Main St., serves the most authentic Mexican food in town in a laid-back setting. Favorites like *carnitas* or *carne asada* with rice and beans make tasty dinners ($6.25-8.50), while the *taquitos* (3 for $4.50) are perfect to go. (☎867-0945. Open M-Th 10am-9pm, F-Sa 10am-10pm.) To go your own way, stop by **Smith's,** 633 S. Main St., for supplies. (☎586-1203. Open 24hr.)

⏛ ENTERTAINMENT. Every summer, thousands of travelers from around the country descend on Cedar City for a drama fix at the annual ▨**Utah Shakespearean Festival.** Held in a traditional Elizabethan theater and several other venues on the Southern Utah University campus between mid-June and mid-October, the Tony-Award-winning festival presents not only several Shakespearean selections but also a repertoire of modern works. Between two and five shows are performed daily during the festival. (☎800-752-9849; www.bard.org. Tickets $12-44, student rush tickets 30min. before show 50% off.)

⏛ HIKING. The 6750-acre **Ashdown Gorge Wilderness Area,** administered as part of the **Dixie National Forest,** abuts the western edge of **Cedar Breaks National Monument,** east of Cedar City. This entire area shelters an excellent arena for experienced backcountry hikers and backpackers who want a chance to explore dramatic canyons and approach the Cedar Breaks monument from the ground up. Trailheads leading into the wilderness depart from both Hwys. 14 and 143; trails are fairly clearly marked. Maps and extensive information on the wilderness area are available at the Forest Service's Ranger District offices back in Cedar City (see **Practical Information,** above).

A popular and challenging hike in the wilderness area is the **Rattlesnake Trail.** This trek departs from Hwy. 143 at 10,460 ft., just beyond the northern boundary of Cedar Breaks National Monument, and descends over 3600 ft. to the base of the monument's excellent natural rock amphitheater. Traveling 5 mi. one-way, it parallels the rim of the amphitheater early on, offering endless views of both the brilliant colors of Cedar Breaks and the equally spectacular **Ashdown Gorge.** The trail's end joins the 2.5 mi. **Potato Hollow Trail,** which connects with Forest Road 301. This latter trail is immediately accessible off Hwy. 148 and is meant for those interested in through-hiking and shuttling cars. The hike can be done in one very long day, but it's much more manageable as an easy two-day trip. Hikers should be aware that Ashdown Gorge is prone to flash flooding.

East of Cedar City, the **Virgin River Rim Trail** readies visitors for Zion National Park, sprinkling its striking views of the Virgin River headwaters with those of the distant Zion Canyon monuments. The entire trail lasts 32 mi., beginning at **Woods Ranch** just before the Cedar Canyon Campground on Hwy. 14 (12 mi. from Cedar City) and ending at **Strawberry Point** along Forest Service Road 058. There are several secluded campsites along the route, which makes a great 3-4 day trip. For hikers interested in shorter excursions, several trails around **Navajo Lake** represent more modest treks, including the **Cascade Falls Trail**, which climbs to the awesome **Cascade Falls.** To reach Navajo Lake, drive 25 mi. on Hwy. 14 east of Cedar City and turn right on the Navajo Lake Rd.

⛷ **SKIING.** North of Cedar Breaks National Monument on Hwy. 143, about 30 mi. from Cedar City, lies **Brian Head Resort**, a quiet ski hamlet and mountain biking resort. The slopes envelop two mountains towering above town, **Brian Head Peak** and **Navajo Peak,** sporting varied terrain for skiers and snowboarders of all abilities. Eight lifts serve 500 skiable acres and a 1707 ft. vertical drop. The base boasts Utah's highest resort elevation at 9600 ft., and 425 in. of snow fall annually on the mountain. Fifty runs (30% beginner; 40% intermediate; 30% advanced) adorn the mountain. (☎677-2035; www.brianhead.com. Ski season mid-Nov. to early Apr. Slopes open daily 9:30am-4:30pm; night skiing F-Sa 3:30-9pm, holidays until 10pm. Full-day pass $39, half-day $34; seniors and ages 6-12 $26/$23. Adult ski rental packages $25, child packages $16; adult snowboard rental packages $30, child packages $25.) During summer months, Brian Head gives **mountain bikers** over 200 mi. of sizzling singletrack. The resort runs a shuttle service ($13) to area trailheads, and Friday to Sunday a chairlift (all day $16, single ride $8) whisks bikers to higher elevations. (☎677-3101. Open late-May through mid-Oct. daily 8:30am-5pm. Bike rental $34 per day.). A free brochure entitled **Bike & Hike Brian Head,** available at the resort offices on Hwy. 143 and the Cedar City Visitors Center, has listings of area trails. **Georg's,** 612 S. Hwy. 143, has been a Brian Head fixture since 1965, renting skis in the winter ($25 per day) and full-suspension bikes ($32) in the summer, all the while supplying heaps of Austrian cheer. (☎677-2013. Open 8:30am-6pm.)

CEDAR BREAKS NATIONAL MONUMENT

Shaped like a gigantic amphitheater, the semicircle of canyons that makes up Cedar Breaks National Monument measures more than 3 mi. in diameter and 2000 ft. in depth. The red, yellow, and even purple layers of sediment are emphasized by a gallery of spires, columns, and arches, all cut by the erosive powers of water, ice, and wind as forces deep within the Earth slowly lifted the Markagunt Plateau upwards. To reach this geological spectacle, take Hwy. 14 east from Cedar City for 17 mi., then go north on Hwy. 148 4 mi. to the entrance station. ($3; under 17 free.)

Tourists travel to the Monument almost exclusively for the view, most easily reached by parking at the Visitors Center and walking to Point Supreme or by stopping at one of several vistas along the 5 mi. stretch of scenic Hwys. 148 and 143 within the monument. Cedar Breaks maintains two trails that provide for a more detailed experience. Originating at the **Chessman Ridge Overlook** (10,467 ft., 2 mi. north of the Visitors Center), the popular 2 mi. round-trip **Alpine Pond Trail** leads to a spring-fed alpine lake whose waters trickle through the breaks, incrementally eroding the landscape as they descend toward the Great Basin. The hike takes 1-2hr.; an instructive trail guide is available at the Visitors Center or trailhead ($1). The 4 mi. round-trip **Ramparts/Spectra Point Trail** departs from the Visitors Center at 10,350 ft. and traces the edge of the amphitheater through a bristlecone grove to two breathtaking viewpoints. Call ☎586-9451 or visit www.nps.gov/cebr for more info about the park.

The **Visitors Center** (☎586-0787; open May-Sept. daily 8am-6pm) is located just beyond the entrance station at 10,350 ft. on the amphitheater rim near the spectacular vantages of **Point Supreme.** The Park Service holds geology talks (daily 10am-5pm) and guided hikes from the Visitors Center (Sa-Su 10am) for a more in-depth look at the monument. Nestled about ½ mi. north of Point Supreme on Hwy. 148 is a 28-site **campground** ❶ that hosts ranger-led evening programs. (10,200 ft. Open June to mid-Sept. Water and flush toilets. Sites $12.) The nearest **gas, food,** and **lodging** are in Cedar City and Brian Head.

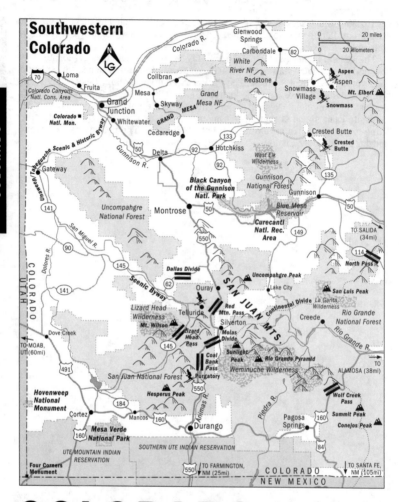

Southwestern Colorado

With the world's largest hot springs, Ancestral Puebloan ruins in barren desert, high-speed gondolas flying up forested mountains, extreme skiing, and raging rivers, southwestern Colorado offers a diverse travel experience unified by the truly wild country around every corner and behind every bend. Bounded by Pagosa Springs in the east and Grand Junction to the north, this rectangle of mountains, canyons, forests, and deserts is home to two national parks and the vast

COLORADO

Uncompahgre and San Juan National Forests. Whether bombing down uncrowded ski slopes at Purgatory and Telluride or tearing up whitewater on the Animas and Gunnison Rivers, travelers are sure to find challenges that push their skills and strength to the limit. The San Juan Mountains have several of Colorado's 14,000 ft. peaks; the San Juan Skyway, blazing a path straight through the mountains, offers access to myriad hiking and biking trails, like the 500-mile Colorado Trail between Durango and Denver. Welcome to an outdoorsman's dream come true.

Amid the untamed wilderness, signs of civilization are reminiscent of the cultures that have lived in southwestern Colorado for thousands of years. The Ancestral Puebloan cliff dwellings at Mesa Verde and the ruins at nearby Hovenweep attest to the state's ancient human presence. Vestiges of an era when the dream of striking it rich enticed optimistic souls, the steam railroad still runs between Durango and Silverton and mines dot the Unaweep/Tabeguache Scenic Byway.

The communities of southwestern Colorado stand as evidence of the population's relationship with the great outdoors. From fans at Telluride's myriad music festivals to ranchers herding cattle across vast alpine expanses, interaction with the natural world is vital to everyday life. For travelers yearning to discover themselves in the woods, the wilds of southwest Colorado beckon.

COLORADO

▧ HIGHLIGHTS OF SOUTHWESTERN COLORADO

MOUNTAIN BIKING. Durango, Crested Butte (p. 371), and others in the San Juans boast mind-blowing (and lung-bursting) terrain for mountain biking.

RUINS. Cliff dwellings at **Mesa Verde** (p. 356) delight the eye and boggle the mind.

OURAY. Hot springs and chilly ice climbing in the "Switzerland of America" (p. 350).

SAN JUAN RANGE

Ask Coloradans about their favorite mountain retreats, and they'll most likely name a peak, lake, stream, or town in the San Juan Range of southwestern Colorado. Durango is an ideal base camp for forays into these mountains, and northeast of town, the Weminuche Wilderness tempts the hardy backpacker with vast expanses of rugged terrain where sweeping vistas stretch for miles. Moreover, the San Juans are loaded with campgrounds and hostels, making them one of the more economical places to visit in the Southwest.

DURANGO   ☎970

In its heyday, Durango was one of the main railroad junctions in the Southwest. Walking down the thoroughfare today, it's easy to see that it remains a crossroads. Dread-locked, hemp-clad youths share the sidewalks with weathered ranchers in ten-gallon hats and stiff Wranglers, while toned pro mountain bikers rub shoulders with camera-toting tourists. What brings them together is a zeal for the wilderness that engulfs the town. Durango was for some time the home of more professional mountain bikers than anywhere else. Whether you choose to enjoy the flora, rope doggies at the rodeo, bike the San Juans, or ride the narrow gauge railroad, you're bound to spend a good chunk of your time in Durango's great outdoors.

▉ TRANSPORTATION

Flights: Durango/La Plata County Airport, 1000 Airport Rd. (☎247-8143), 14 mi. southeast of downtown along U.S. 160. Flights to Durango can be quite expensive, so flying into regional hubs such as Denver or Phoenix may make more sense.

COLORADO

Buses: Greyhound, 275 E. 8th Ave. (☎259-2755). Runs 1-2 times per day to: **Albuquerque** (5hr., $40-42); **Denver** (11½hr., $58-60); **Grand Junction** (5hr., $32-35). Station open M-F 7:30am-noon and 3:30-5pm, Sa 7:30am-noon, Su and holidays 7:30-10am.

Public Transportation: The Durango Lift (☎259-5438) runs trolleys along Main Ave. every 20min. Memorial Day-Labor Day daily 7am-10:40pm. Call for off-season service. Fare $0.50. Three transit loops connect Main Ave. to outlying areas like the fairgrounds on the South Durango/West loop and Fort Lewis College/Durango Mall on the FLC South loop. (☎259-LIFT, outlying routes run approx. M-Sa 6:30am-6:30pm. $1, seniors $0.50.)

Taxis: Durango Transportation (☎259-4818 or800-626-2066). Base rate $2 per mi. plus $2 per person.

Car Rental: Rent-A-Wreck, 21760 W. U.S. 160 (☎259-5858 or 800-682-5858). Starting at $30 per day.

▆✷ ☑ ORIENTATION & PRACTICAL INFORMATION

The largest town in southwestern Colorado, Durango lies alongside the Animas River at the intersection of **U.S. 160** and **U.S. 550.** In general, count on streets running perpendicular to avenues, but don't get thrown off by the fact that **Main Avenue** is always called "Main St." The other central drag, **Camino Del Río,** forks from Main Ave. at **14th Street** and runs diagonally for several blocks parallel to the river. Main Ave., with its trading posts in Victorian downtown (between 5th and 14th St.) and motels on its northern stretch, coddles busloads of tourists, while Camino Del Río, with supermarkets and hardware stores, caters to locals.

Visitor Info: Durango Area Tourism Office, 111 S. Camino del Río (☎247-3500, 800-525-8855; www.durango.org), on the southeast side of town at Santa Rita Park along Rte. 160. Offers info on accommodations, food, sights, and the outdoors, with the added bonus of a free phone for local calls. Open M-Sa 8am-5:30pm (M-F until 6pm in summer), Su 10am-4pm. For outdoors info, inquire at the staffed **Forest Service Desk** at the Visitors Center (☎385-1210) or visit the **San Juan Public Lands Center,** 15 Burnett Ct. (☎247-4874), in the Durango Tech Center on U.S. 160 W. Open Apr. to mid-Dec. daily 8am-5pm; mid-Dec. to Mar. 8am-4:30pm.

Equipment Rentals: Southwest Adventures, 1205 Camino Del Río (☎259-0370, 800-642-5389). Rents mountain bikes (hourly $8, daily $30-50) and climbing and backpacking gear. Guided hiking tours start at $55, mountaineering from $190, and mountain biking $50-90. Beginner/intermediate group climbing lessons available. (Half-day $65 per person, full-day $95. Advanced lessons $85/$150. Individuals can often join group classes). Open daily 8am-6pm.

Laundromat: King Center Laundry, 1127 Camino Del Río (☎259-2060), provides self-service facilities. Open daily 7am-9pm.

Weather Info: ☎264-6397. **Road Conditions:** ☎264-5555.

Emergency: ☎911. **Police:** 990 E. 2nd Ave. (☎385-2900).

Pharmacy: Wal-Mart, 1155 S. Camino Del Río (☎259-8788). Open M-F 8am-8pm, Sa 8am-6pm, Su 10am-4pm.

Medical Services: Mercy Medical Center, 375 E. Park Ave. (☎247-4311).

Internet Access: Free at the **Durango Public Library,** 1188 E. 2nd Ave. (☎385-2970). Wheel-chair accessible. Open M-W 9am-9pm, Th-Su 9am-5:30pm; June-Aug. closed Su.

Post Office: 222 W. 8th St. (☎247-3434). Open M-F 8am-5:30pm, Sa 9am-1pm. **Postal code:** 81301.

ACCOMMODATIONS

Alpine Inn, 3515 Main Ave. (☎247-4042 or 800-818-4042). One of the best budget digs in Durango with friendly managers. Spotless rooms, some with microfridges and microwaves. Reception 8am-10pm. Check-in and check-out flexible. Singles mid-May to mid-Sept. $42-74, mid Sept. to mid-May $28-32; doubles $58-84/$38-42. ❷

General Palmer Hotel, 567 Main Ave. (☎247-4747 or 800-523-3358; www.general-palmerhotel.com). Cheapest rates of the three Victorian hotels downtown. Located next to the Durango-Silverton train depot and within walking distance of most shops and restaurants. Continental breakfast included. Check-in 4pm, check-out 12pm. Rooms from $98 during the summer and $75 during the off-season; variety of suites available. ❹

Spanish Trails Inn & Suites, 3141 Main Ave. (☎247-4173; www.spanishtrails.com), across from City Market. Behind the adobe exterior by the noisy road, immaculate rooms with great bathrooms and kitchenettes await. Check-out 10:30am. Check-in around 2pm. Rooms range from $29-59, two-room suites $49-79. ❷

CAMPING

Junction Creek Campground, Forest Rd. 171 (☎247-4874). From Main Ave. turn west on 25th St. (Junction Creek Rd.), which becomes Forest Rd. 171 after 4 mi. Turn off left at signpost 1 mi. past the entrance. Basic sites and facilities in a breathtaking, forested mountainside setting above Junction Creek. For low-key hiking and biking, **Log Chutes Trails** run in near the campground. The **Colorado Trail** trailhead is nearby, on the left upon entering the National Forest. Drop down from campground into the creek to connect with the trail. 34 sites. 14-night max. stay. Open year-round, expect snow Dec.-Mar. $12 per vehicle, each additional person $6. 6 mi. farther up Forest Road 171 (¼ mi. past Animas Overlook), free dispersed camping allowed along the roadside. ❶

Hermosa Creek Campground, Country Rd. 201. Drive 10 mi. north of Durango on U.S. 550 to Hermosa Creek Rd. on left; immediate right on Country Rd. 201; after 3.9 mi., turn right. Primitive campground has only pit toilets and no defined sites. So deep in the woods above Hermosa Creek, you'll share it with only the cows. The **Hermosa Trail** provides access to vast tracks of roadless land and begins a few hundred feet up the road. For the more adventurous, numerous turnouts and spurs on the road up are good crash sites. 14-night max. stay. Open May-Oct., depending on snow. Free. ❶

Haviland Lake Campground, 18 mi. north of Durango on Hwy 550. Turn east from Hwy. 550 at the sign for Haviland Lake and follow the road less than a ½ mi. to the campground. Love-Hermosa Cliffs to the west serve as a backdrop to this beautiful lake campground, making for amazing sunrises. The lake teems with trout. 45 tent sites. $12, lakefront $14, with electrical hookup $15. Restrooms and water. ❶

FOOD

Some of Durango's eateries cater to the moneyed train crowd, but quality affordable eateries exist as well. Pick up groceries at **City Market's** two locations: Main Ave. (at 32nd St.) and Camino Del Río near 7th St. (both open daily 6am-midnight). **Nature's Oasis,** 1123 Camino Del Río, has organic goods (☎247-1988. Open M-Sa 8am-9pm, Su 8am-7pm; winter M-Sa 8am-8pm). There's fresh produce at the **Durango Farmers' Market** (Sa 8am-noon) in the First National Bank parking lot.

Johnny McGuire's Deli, 601 E. 2nd Ave. (☎259-8816). Choose among more than 25 sandwiches, all made with fresh-baked bread (regular $5.50, footlong $10), and you'll walk away satisfied. The Free Iron Willy and the 4:20 Vegan are local favorites. Take-out and delivery available. Open daily 7am-9pm. Cash only. ❷

Skinny's Grill, 1017 Main Ave. (☎382-2500). The best vegetarian eatery in town, Skinny's is a bargain, with nothing, including the meat and fish entrees, priced over $11. Enjoy large portions of such Southwestern treats as deep dish spinach enchiladas ($8) or fajitas ($10) in a bright, chilled-out setting. Don't pass up the award-winning desserts. Take-out is available, but you'd miss the lively waitstaff. Open Su-Th 11:30am-9pm, F-Sa 11:30am-10pm. ❷

Steaming Bean Coffee Co., 915 Main Ave., at 9th St. (☎385-7901). You'll find any coffee creation ($1-4) that your cosmopolitan palate could desire at this popular hangout, plus sandwiches ($5), tasty wraps ($3.50), and several light breakfast items (the croissants are excellent, $1-2). Open M-Th 6:30am-9pm, F-Sa 6:30am-9pm, Su 7am-8pm. ❶

Carver Brewing Co., 1022 Main Ave. (☎259-2545), between 10th and 11th St. A local favorite, Carver is famous for its pancakes and hospitality. They serves delicious fresh-baked bread and breakfast specials ($3-7) such as Southwest Benedict. Dinner is a pricier proposition, at $6-15 per entree. Open M-F 6:30am-10pm, Su 6:30am-1pm. ❸

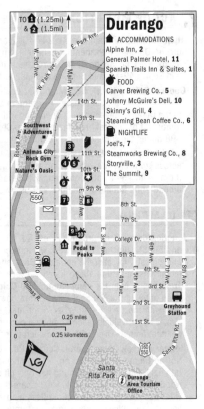

Durango

▲ ACCOMMODATIONS
Alpine Inn, **2**
General Palmer Hotel, **11**
Spanish Trails Inn & Suites, **1**

🍴 FOOD
Carver Brewing Co., **5**
Johnny McGuire's Deli, **10**
Skinny's Grill, **4**
Steaming Bean Coffee Co., **6**

🍸 NIGHTLIFE
Joel's, **7**
Steamworks Brewing Co., **8**
Storyville, **3**
The Summit, **9**

NIGHTLIFE & ENTERTAINMENT

The Summit, 600 Main Ave. (☎247-2324), near the train station. The ski-lodge atmosphere and frequent live music attracts the college crowd for some rowdy fun. Open daily 7pm-last customer.

Steamworks Brewing Company, 801 E. 2nd Ave. (☎259-9200). With live music and a DJ, the weekends at the Steamworks jump. On Saturday, be sure to check out ladies' night. All nights of the week, you can enjoy beer brewed on the premises. If you're hungry, the expensive but famous cajun boil ($17 for one person, $30 for two) is worth a try. Open Su-W 11-12am, Th-Sa 11-2am.

Storyville, 1150 B. Main Ave. (☎259-1475; www.storyvilledurango.com), For live music ranging from bluegrass to punk rock, check out Storyville on weekends. Before the kitchen closes at 10pm, try the excellent barbecue, which comes in portions from small to humongous. Happy Hour daily 3-6pm with $2.75 Fat Tire beer. Open M-Th 11am-10:30pm, F 11am-2am, Sa 5pm-2am.

Joel's, 119 W. 8th St. (☎385-0430). Filled with professionals by day, by night Joel's transforms into a chill hangout for local climbers and bikers. Martini bar $4-7, Tu and Sa $1 off martinis. Open M-Sa 4pm-2am, Su 6pm-2am.

SIGHTS

More a tourist attraction than a means of transportation, the **Durango and Silverton Narrow Gauge Train,** 479 Main St., runs up the Animas River Valley to the historic mining town of Silverton and has been in continuous operation since 1881. Old-fashioned, coal-fed locomotives wheeze through the San Juans, making a 2hr. stop in Silverton before returning to Durango. The train also offers excellent access to the Weminuche Wilderness, dropping off and picking up backpackers at various scenic points. (☎247-2733; www.durangotrain.com. Office open June to mid-Aug. daily 6am-8pm; mid-Aug. to Oct. 7am-7pm; Nov.-Apr. 8am-5pm; May 7am-7pm. Morning trains from Durango and afternoon trains from Silverton; 9hr. including stop, layover day optional; $60 mid-June to mid-Aug., $55 Sept. to early Oct.)

The **Durango Pro Rodeo Series** moseys into town every summer at the LaPlata County Fairgrounds, 25th St. and Main Ave. Rough riders saddle up on Tu, W, F, and Sa nights at 7:30pm following the 6pm barbecue. (☎247-2790. Mid-June to Aug. $12, under 12 $6. Barbecue $7.) Seven miles north on U.S. 550 at 6475 County Road 203, **Trimble Hot Springs** allows visitors to soak in pools with a great view of Missionary Ridge for $9. (☎247-0111; www.trimblehotsprings.com. Open summer daily 8am-11pm, winter Su-Th 9am-10pm, F-Sa 9am-9pm.)

OUTDOOR ACTIVITIES

Durango is surrounded by the **San Juan National Forest,** a famed locale for all kinds of outdoor pursuits. The **USFS headquarters** in Durango at 15 Burnett Ct., off U.S. 160 W, provides info on hiking, backpacking, biking, mountaineering, and skiing in the forest. (☎247-4874. Open Apr. to mid-Dec. daily 8am-5pm, mid-Dec. to Mar. 8am-4:30pm.) Pay them a visit, especially if you're planning a trip into the massive Weminuche Wilderness northeast of Durango. **Southwest Adventures,** 1205 Camino Del Río, provides guided hiking, backpacking, mountain biking, and rock climbing in the San Juans. (☎259-0370 or 800-642-5389; www.mtnguide.net.)

DAY HIKING
With the San Juan Mountains on all sides, trails around Durango abound, providing the opportunity for everything from a leisurely walk to an intense ascent. The **Colorado Trail,** which covers 468 mi. of the Rockies, starts in Durango on its way to Denver, and parts of this trek make for fun day hikes. Durango also offers access to some of the highest peaks in the lower 48 states. Although it is hard to go wrong hiking in this area, here are some of your best bets:

Animas City Mountain (6 mi. round-trip, 3-4hr. Peak 8175 ft.). From Main Ave., take 32nd St. west to W. 4th Ave. Turn right on W. 4th Ave. and follow it to the end to reach the trailhead. This easy and popular hike to the high points on Animas Mountain offers spectacular views of the Animas River Valley and Durango, as well as the chance to see elk and deer. Elevation gain 1800 ft. Hikeable year-round, snow-free Apr.-Nov., with some closures in winter depending on snow levels.

Haflin Creek Trail (7 mi. round-trip, 5-6hr.). Take 32nd St. east from Main Ave. and turn left on E. Animas Rd.; 5 mi. up on the right is a sign for the trailhead. Although forest fires have passed through the area in the past few years, this moderate hike is still well worth it. It ascends over 3000 ft. through several climatic zones, providing clear views of the valley and the La Platas to the west. Hikeable year-round, snow-free Apr.-Nov.

Perins Peak (5 mi. round-trip, 3½-4½hr.). From Main Ave., take 22nd St. west-bound, which becomes Montview Pkwy.; after 1 block, turn right on Leyden St. Follow it to the end and head west up the drainage past the last house. This difficult hike to the summit of Perins Peak requires a fair deal of bushwhacking and scrambling but rewards the with

THE LOCAL STORY

URANGO ROUGH RIDER

*Former world championship mountain biker **Ned Overend** lives in Durango, Colorado.*

Q: How did you end up here?
A: I was living in San Diego and took an ice climbing class in Ouray, CO (p. 350). So I drove from SD to Ouray. That's how I saw the San Juans and the Southwest.

Q: What's your favorite area ride?
A: If you ride one trail too much you get tired of it. I do most of my riding in the **Horse Gulch area**. It leads to several different areas. We have a trails group here, **Trails 2000**, which built a ton of trails, many in that area. I'll bet there's 10 mi. of singletrack out there and a ton of different loops. Not super-long climbs, but a lot of climbing.

Q: Your worst biking experience?
A: Tu races are called "Tuesday Night World Championships" here because people are so serious. There were 5 guys in front of me and guys attacking, and there was wood in the road I didn't see. I hit it with my front wheel, dropped my hands off the bars, landed head first on the pavement, flipped over, and slid down the road. My helmet was busted, but I was lucky...I had a stiff neck, a concussion, contusions on my face....

Q: Did it take you a long time to get back on the bike?
A: No, I got back fast...My eyes were swollen almost shut for a couple days but...you gotta get back on the bike.

(Continued on next page)

panoramic vistas above the tree line. There is a trail only for the lower half of the hike, which leaves the initial drainage and climbs the western valley wall after about ½ mi. Elevation gain 1700 ft. Advisable May-Sept.; the trail may be difficult to find at other times of the year. Closed seasonally to protect wildlife habitat.

Crater Lake Trail (a.k.a. #623, 5½ mi. one-way) is good for a long day hike or overnight. Beginning from the Andrews Lake day-use area 45 mi. north of Durango along Hwy. 550, the trail ascends 500 ft. up 31 switchbacks in the first mile, with great rewards. It continues through meadows and forestland, affording breathtaking views around every corner, including glimpses of Engineer Peak, Twilight Peak, and Snowdon Peak. Crater Lake is located at the base of Twilight Peak, and Snowdon Peak is also accessible from the Crater Lake Trail. Either of these peaks provides wide-ranging views of the Weminuche and beyond. Moderately difficult with an 800 ft. elevation gain.

BACKPACKING
The **Weminuche Wilderness** to the northeast of Durango lies in the heart of the San Juan Mountains, straddling 50 mi. of the Continental Divide. With an average elevation of 10,000 ft., the area offers some of the highest, most remote backcountry travel in the continental US. The closest road access is from trailheads near Lemon Reservoir and Vallecito Lake. One unique option available to backpackers out of Durango and Silverton is the Narrow Gauge Railroad (p. 337), which provides access to the Weminuche at its Elk Park and Needleton stops, as well as an open-ended pick-up. Much of the wilderness is above the treeline in sensitive alpine tundra. Numerous streams and creeks criss-cross it, and while some backcountry travelers swear by the water, without treating it you'll be tempting the Giardia gods. No permits required. An excellent guide to the Weminuche is *Walking in Wilderness: a guide to the Weminuche Wilderness*, by B.J. Boucher (1998). The **San Juan Mountains Association** (www.sjma.org) also publishes a free Weminuche guide. These and other guidebooks are available at the **San Juan Public Lands Center**. The Colorado Trail (p. 337), beginning west of Durango, provides an opportunity for fantastic extended trips in the Durango area.

MOUNTAIN BIKING
While mountain biking may have gotten its start in northern California, the sport came into its own in Durango. World-class riders swarm the streets in town, but the surrounding web of trails are geared toward a range of abilities. Bikes are available at **Hassle Free Sports**, 2615 Main Ave., but you must have a

driver's license and major credit card. (☎ 259-3874 or 800-835-3800. Open summer M-Sa 9:30am-6pm, Su 9am-5pm; winter daily 7:30am-7pm; spring and fall M-Sa 8:30am-6pm. Half-day $16, full-day $25. Full suspension $24/35. Ski rental packages $16-27 per day.) **Pedal to Peaks,** 598B Main Ave., specializes in downhill biking and rents bikes for $15 per half-day and $25 per full day. (☎ 259-6880. Open Mar.-Dec. M-Sa 9am-6pm, Su noon-5pm.) **Southwest Adventures** (p. 334) provides shuttles to popular mountain biking locations, rents bikes ($8 per hour, $30-50 daily), and operates bike tours ($50-90).

Hermosa Creek Trail (23½ mi. one-way, 3-5 hours). From Durango, travel north up Hwy. 550 to F.R. 578 (near Durango Mountain Resort). Park after 2 mi. near the junction to Forest Road 581. The ride begins by following Forest Road 581 for 5 mi. to the trailhead where the "epic singletrack" takes off to the south. The trail descends for 15 mi., with 1 mi. of steep uphill to keep you honest. It ends at the town of Hermosa, about 9 mi. north of Durango along Hwy. 550. Many moderately technical sections, one long, steep uphill, and two stream crossings (which can get to be waist-high in spring and early summer) make this a difficult ride. Elevation loss over 2,000 ft.

Dry Fork (9 mi. round-trip, 1-2hr.). Take U.S. 160 west 3.5 mi. to Lightner Creek Rd. (County Rd. 207); turn right and follow this paved road 1 mi. to County Rd. 208; follow the dirt road 2 mi. to a fork, bear right, and continue for 1 mi. to the Dry Creek trailhead to the left. This moderate ride along a loop of singletrack cuts uphill and downhill through the woods of Perins Peak Wildlife Area and includes a portion of the Colorado Trail. Elevation gain 1200 ft. Recommended May-Oct.

Around Perins Peak (18 mi. round-trip, 2-3hr.). This ride can begin right in Durango from anywhere on Main Ave. From Main Ave. head west on 25th St. for 3½ mi., over the San Juan National Forest boundary before turning left on the Colorado Trail. This advanced loop is a favorite of local riders and incorporates a portion of the Dry Creek ride listed above. The ride climbs a series of steep switchbacks, then rewards with scintillating downhill singletrack, and offers some awesome views. Route combines singletrack and road. Elevation gain 1500 ft. Recommended May-Oct.

Kennebec Pass (34 mi. one-way, 5-7hr.). This ride requires a drop-off or shuttle, or else it becomes a 50 mi. loop. Drive west of Durango on U.S. 160 and turn right after 10 mi. on Country Rd. 124; after 4 mi. the beginning of the ride coincides with the transition to dirt road. This expert ride cuts into the La Plata Mountains and includes 20 mi. of rugged Colorado Trail. A mountain biking classic and one hell of a trip. Elevation gain 4500 ft. Recommended July-Sept.

(Continued from previous page)

Q: Your best riding experience?
A: Probably winning the 1990 World Championships. I won some Nationals here also...but the Worlds—it's a pretty big deal.

Q: How is Durango different from other mountain biking hot spots?
A: The best thing about Durango is the variety. South of town it's high desert, rocky; north of town it's like alpine riding. To the west, trails are smooth shale. Northwest is the Colorado Trail, heading into trees and alpine stuff. From town you can get 3 different trail types.

Q: What are your favorite places to ride other than Durango?
A: **Crested Butte, CO** (p. 371) and **Moab, UT** (p. 272) are both great. Moab's views are incredible, and Butte's high alpine riding is some of the world's best. I like doing stuff that's different.

Q: How is competitive mountain biking different from road cycling?
A: The attitude of road cycling is affected by the draft. In biking there's not much advantage to drafting as speeds are slower and there's corners. You need to leave a little space. In mountain biking the strongest guy wins. In road biking it can be the guy with the strongest team or the best strategy. That can create a little animosity, especially between the teams. Mountain biking is pure fitness, which leads to more camaraderie among the riders. It's pure fitness and bike handling ability, not so much taking advantage of another guy by drafting his back wheel.

FLY FISHING

The many streams and rivers flowing from the San Juan Mountains draw anglers in search of the next record-breaking trout. The Animas, which runs through the city, is open to the public, as are the Piedra and San Juan Rivers a short drive away. There are also countless hike-in or drive-in alpine lakes in the area that nurture robust mountain trout. Try the San Juan Public Lands Office for suggestions or talk to the fishing experts at **Duranglers,** 923 Main Ave. This fly shop has the largest selection of equipment in the region and sets up wade or float trips. (☎385-4081 or 888-347-4346; www.duranglers.com. Half-day trips from $225, full-day from $265. Open mid-May to Aug. M-Sa 7am-8pm, Su 9am-5pm; Sept. to mid-May M-Sa 8am-6pm, Su 10am-4pm.)

ROCK CLIMBING

Though Durango is not known for its rock climbing, the town has access to many different levels and types of climbs in the immediate vicinity. In particular, there is an array of excellent bouldering for less experienced climbers, especially at the **Turtle Lake Boulders,** where both beginners and experts will find great problems (rated V0-V9). From Main Ave., take 25th St./Junction Creek Rd.; after approximately 5 mi., bear right on County Rd. 205; pass Chapman Lake to the right and you'll see the sandstone boulders on your left. North of Durango on Hwy. 550 there are several excellent climbing areas. **X-Rock** has routes rated from 5.5 to 5.12, with a well-marked access trail from the parking lot of Mercy Medical Center. Another easy access trail takes off from the dirt road to the left just beyond Mercy Medical. To get to the hospital, turn right on Park Ave. (where 17th St. should be on the grid). Equipment, guides, and advice on other climbing areas, stop by **Animas City Rock Gym,** 1111 Camino Del Río. (☎259-5700, 877-496-4227; www.animascity-rock.com. Workout pass for use of indoor facilities $6, shoe rental $8 per day, ropes and gear rental $12/with lesson $25; outdoor half-day $45, full day $75. Open M-F 6am-10pm, Sa-Su 10am-8pm; winter hours may vary.) Tim Kuss' *Durango Sandstone: A Guide to Area Freeclimbs* is an excellent book with more details about climbing around Durango.

RIVER RUNNING

The Animas River offers everything from family trips on placid Class II rapids to intense Class V battles, all within easy reach of the Durango area. If the prospect of rafting out in the untamed wilderness appeals to you, the rapids of the Piedra River are definitely worth exploring. **Flexible Flyers,** 2344 County Rd. 225, offers the cheapest trips in town on the Animas River. (☎247-4628 or 800-346-7741. 2hr. trips departing daily at 10am, noon, 2pm and 4pm. $20, under 15 $14. Full day trips departing at 10am. $60, under 15 $45. Reservations recommended.) The largest outfitter in the area, **Mild to Wild Rafting,** 701 Main Ave. (booth) or 1111 Camino Del Rio (office), runs trips on a wider array of rivers in the area, including the Upper Animas, allegedly the "toughest commercially rafted river," with Class III to V rapids depending on the season. (☎247-4789, 800-567-6745. Open daily 8am-8pm. Half-day mild trips $41, full day mild trips $65; children $32/55. Full day intense trips $105. Reservations recommended.) Both Flexible Flyers and Mild to Wild also offer daily rentals of inflatable kayaks from $30-90 depending on the length of rental. **Peregrine River Outfitters,** 64 Ptarmigan Ln., has been operating trips for almost 30 years in Durango and the surrounding areas, and currently offers Class I-V trips on the Animas, Dolores, San Miguel, San Juan and Piedra Rivers. Half-day ($35), full day ($75-200), and multi-day trips (call for prices and reservations) are all available. (☎385-7600 or 800-598-7600; www.peregrineriver.com.)

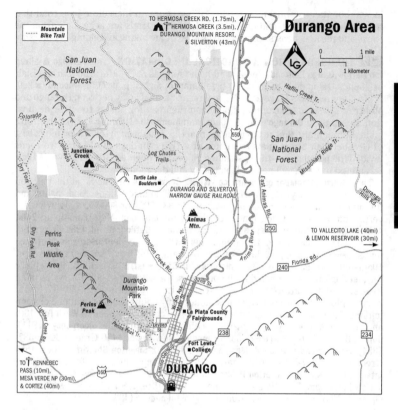

SKIING

Durango Mountain Resort, better known as **Purgatory,** sits 30min. north of town on U.S. 550 and hosts skiers of all levels (23% beginner trails, 51% intermediate and 26% expert). Lift tickets are $52 for full day and $40 for a half-day, with slight increases during holidays. (☎247-9000, 800-982-6103; www.durangomountainre-sort.com. Open late Nov. to early April depending on snow.) In addition to its 75 downhill trails (40 mi. groomed), Durango Mountain Resort boasts 10 mi. of cross-country ski trails at the **Purgatory Nordic Center,** 1 Skier Pl. (☎385-2114. Daily trail pass $8.50; combo lesson, rental, and trail pass $35.) Additional groomed cross-country trails are available at the **Pine River Valley Nordic Ski Club** at Vallecito Lake, 22 mi. from Durango. (☎884-9782; www.vallecitolakechamber.com. Free public use, donations appreciated.)

SILVERTON   ☎970

Silverton's old Town Hall and rickety county jail museum are telling reminders of the town's heyday as a mining center where silver was extracted by the ton. Now, instead of miners, Silverton's mountains draw thrill seekers of all types who cross paths with the rough-and-tumble locals along the town's ragged gravel roads and in wind-beaten establishments. The Alpine Loop, an incredible jeep road that traverses the Rockies, and other four-wheel-drive trails are accessible from the town, and the area boasts some of the most extreme hiking and skiing in Colorado.

▣▨ TRANSPORTATION & PRACTICAL INFORMATION. The **Durango & Silverton Narrow Gauge Railroad** (depot at 10th and Animas St., platform at 12th and Blair St.) sends trains daily to Durango (see **Durango: Sights,** p. 337). **Greyhound** (☎259-2755) stops at Teki's Place at 11th and Greene St. on its way between Durango and Montrose. Passengers can board here and then pay for tickets to either destination. Buses go to **Durango** (1hr., 7:30am) and **Montrose** (1½hr., 9:30am). Silverton's main thoroughfare, **Greene Street,** runs from U.S. 550 through town. One block east of Greene, **Blair Street** is also a center of activity. In days of old, the two roads divided the population—the upstanding citizens frequented Greene St. while Blair St. catered to those inclined to debauchery and decadence.

The **Silverton Chamber of Commerce Visitors Center,** 414 Greene St. at the junction of U.S. 550 and Hwy. 110, provides info about accommodations, food, sights, and the outdoors in Silverton and its environs. (☎387-5654 or 800-752-4494; www.silvertoncolorado.com. Open June-Sept. daily 9am-6pm, Oct.-May 10am-4pm.) **24hr. ATM** available at **Citizens State Bank,** 1218 Greene St. **Outdoor World,** 1234 Greene St., has a basic selection of outdoor equipment and an excellent assortment of area maps. (☎387-5628. Open daily June-Sept. 9am-6pm, Nov. 9am-5pm, Dec.-Apr. 10am-4pm, May 9am-5pm.) **The Explorer's Club Southwest,** 1332 Blair St., is the place for meeting others interested in the outdoors, for wilderness guide services of all kinds, and for advice and assistance in trip-planning. (☎387-5006; www.explorerclubsw.com. Open in summer daily noon-midnight, winter 3 or 4pm-midnight and may close later on busy nights) To do laundry head to **Wash Tub,** 10th and Greene St. (Open daily 8am-8pm.) Other services include: **emergency** (☎911); **police,** 306 S. Water St. (☎873-5326); **medical services** at 1450 Greene St. (☎387-5354); **weather and road conditions** (☎877-315-7623); **Silverton Sherriff's Office,** 1555 Greene St. (☎387-5531, office staffed M-F 9am-5pm, phone staffed 24hr.); free **Internet access** at the **Silverton Public Library,** 11th and Reese St. (☎387-5770. Open Tu-Th 11am-8pm, F-Sa 10am-5pm); and the **post office,** 138 W. 12th St. (☎387-5402. Open M-F 8:30am-4:30pm, Sa 11am-1pm.) **Postal code:** 81433.

▣▫ ACCOMMODATIONS & FOOD. The **Silverton Hostel ❶,** 1025 Blair St., offers cheap lodging year-round in clean and simple quarters with a colorful kitchen, all steps away from the owner's pottery studio. (☎387-0115 or 888-276-0088. Reception daily 8-11am and 4-10pm. Check-out noon. Dorms $14, in winter $10; private rooms $32-42/$25-30. Public showers $3.50. Reservations recommended late June-Aug. and holidays.) Guests at the 100-year-old **Teller House Hotel and B&B ❹** experience the more respectable side of Silverton's heyday in high-ceilinged Victorian rooms. The convenient location at 1250 Greene St. and full breakfast in the partner Green Table Cafe downstairs seal the deal. (☎387-5423 or 800-342-4338; mid-May to Sept. single with shared bath $64; double with shared bath $69; private bath $84/89; Oct. to mid-May $49 with breakfast.) The friendly manager of the **Prospector Motel ❸,** 1015 Greene St., provides cheap, clean rooms only a few blocks from most of the restaurants. (☎387-5466. Singles from $45 in summer, winter $25, doubles $30-70. Check out 10:30am.) The 26 sites at **South Mineral Campground ❶,** 4.5 mi. down County Rd. 7/Forest Rd. 585, off U.S. 550 2 mi. west of Silverton, is tucked away along Mineral Creek in the heart of the San Juans. Free dispersed camping is permitted in primitive sites along the road leading up to the campground, and these sites are a good staging ground for hikes in Ice Lakes Basin. (14-night max. stay. Open May-Sept. $12 per vehicle.)

Rocky Mountain Funnel Cakes ❶, 1249 Greene St., is the best spot in Silverton for tasty, inexpensive down-home cooking. Try the Mexican Funnel Cake, and don't forget to pinpoint your hometown on the wall map and peruse the vast selection of used books for sale. Those lucky enough to be in town on a Thursday morning will enjoy fresh donuts. (☎387-5450. Open Sept.-May daily 10am-7:30pm; June-Aug. 10am-9pm. Cash only.) For a slightly more upscale experience, head to **Handlebars Food & Saloon ❷**, 117 13th St. (just off Greene). Rare specimens of Jackalope and Furry Trout watch over as locals enjoy lunch specials ($8-12) by day and cold brews by night. Anyone sporting a handlebar moustache gets his Polaroid shot posted around the bar. (☎387-5395. Open May-Oct. daily 10:30am-10pm; saloon open daily 10:30-2am.) **The Explorer's Club Southwest ❸**, 1332 Blair St., serves as pub, grill, and meeting place for outdoor enthusiasts, offering diners a grill, menu of meats, seafood, tofu and veggies, and the liberty to concoct their own meals ($4-14 depending on ingredients). Enjoy the 62-in. TV—they claim it's the biggest in the county. (☎387-5006; www.explorersclubsw.com. Open in summer daily noon-midnight, winter 4pm-midnight. May stay open later on busy nights.)

◨ ▣ SIGHTS & ENTERTAINMENT. Next to the courthouse at the east end of Greene St., the **San Juan County Historical Society Museum** inhabits the 101-year-old county jail. Exhibits range from ancient outdoor equipment to a restored miners' boarding house accessed through a tunnel. (☎387-5838. Open late May to late Sept. daily 9am-5pm, Oct. 1 to mid-Oct. 10am-3pm. $3.50.) Just east of the museum, Rte. 110 forms the southern base of the scenic **Alpine Loop.** Four-wheel-drive vehicles are recommended for those wishing to tackle the entire loop, which crosses the high country between Silverton, Ouray, and Lake City. About 12 mi. northeast of Silverton on Rte. 110, the ghost town of **Animas Forks** can be reached easily by passenger car in the warm months. Go at dusk to avoid crowds and catch the site at its eeriest. Every year in June, the **Silverton Jubilee Folk Music Festival** hits the streets with rootsy flair. (www.silvertonfestivals.org. Tickets from $35.)

▨ OUTDOOR ACTIVITIES. The area surrounding Silverton presents excellent **hiking** options. For example, **Ice Lakes** is a moderate, 7 mi. round-trip climb beginning opposite the South Mineral Campground (see **Accommodations,** p. 342), 8 mi. west of Silverton. (2400 ft. elevation gain. Accessible June-Sept.) **Highland Mary Lakes** is a moderately difficult, 6 mi. round-trip hike above the treeline to a group of large alpine trout lakes. To get to the trailhead, follow Rte. 110 northeast of town for 4¼ mi.; turn right on Cunningham Gulch and continue 4 mi. to the head of the canyon. Be careful—the trail is easy to lose above treeline. (1650 ft. elevation gain. Accessible June-Sept.) A challenging hike or bike ride is the ascent of **Kendall Mountain** (13,066 ft.), which towers above the town. A four-wheel-drive jeep road begins near the Recreation Center in Silverton and climbs the mountain to within 250 ft. of the summit (13 mi. round-trip), after which a talus scramble is necessary for the ultimate views. For hikers, the **Deer Park Trail** breaks off from the jeep road at about 4 mi. Follow the trail around a ridge to Deer Park and continue straight to Kendall Gulch, which leads up to the peak. (12 mi. round-trip, 6-7 hours. Difficult; over 2500 ft. elevation gain. Recommended spring-fall.)

Kendall Mountain also provides one of the two main **skiing** opportunities in Silverton, and the town operates a single chairlift on winter weekends that is perfect for families. Contact **City Hall** for info. (☎387-5522. Lift tickets $6.) At the other end of the spectrum, the lift for **Silverton Mountain Ski Area** (☎387-5706; www.silvertonmountain.com) provides access to some of Colorado's most extreme **backcountry skiing** in winter and unparalleled views of the San Juans in summer. (Lift $15 in summer, guided skiing $99 per day, unguided permit $30.)

TELLURIDE ☎970

Site of the first bank Butch Cassidy ever robbed (the San Miguel), Telluride was very much a town of the Old West. Locals believe their city's name derives from a contraction of "to hell you ride," an at times prescient caveat issued to travelers to the once hell-bent city. Things have quieted down a bit—outlaw celebrities have been replaced with film celebrities, and six-shooter guns with cinnamon buns. Skiers, hikers, and vacationers come to Telluride to pump gold and silver into the mountains, and the town claims the most festivals per capita of any postal code in the US. During the summer and fall, Telluride is inundated by outsiders every few weeks, granting just enough time for the community to catch its breath before the next wave. Still, a small-town feeling prevails—rocking chairs sit outside brightly painted, wood-shingled houses, and dogs lounge on storefront porches.

▐ TRANSPORTATION

The town is most easily and economically accessible by car, via **Route 145** from the north or south. The **Telluride Airport,** 1500 Last Dollar Rd. (☎728-5313), charges a pretty penny for planes from Denver, Phoenix, Houston, Chicago, Dallas, and Newark ($250-500). The nearest bus station is **Greyhound** (☎249-6673) in Montrose, 65 mi. away. **Budget Rent-A-Car** deals from the airport (☎728-4642).

Getting around the town itself is fairly easy. The public bus line, called the **Galloping Goose,** runs the length of town on a regular basis, and out to the towns of Placerville and Norwood several times daily. (☎728-5700. May-Nov. every 20min. 7:30am-6pm, Dec.-Apr. every 10min. 7am-midnight. Town loop free, outlying towns $1-2.) A **gondola** runs from downtown to Mountain Village. (☎728-8888. Runs 7am-midnight. Free.) **Taxi** service from **Mountain Limo** serves the western slope. (☎728-9606 or 888-546-6894. Airport fare $8.)

◆ ❼ ORIENTATION & PRACTICAL INFORMATION

Telluride sits on a short spur of Rte. 145, about 127 mi. southeast of Grand Junction (p. 362) and 71 mi. northeast of Cortez (p. 354), in a box canyon nestled among high peaks. The main drag, **Colorado Avenue,** runs perpendicular to a series of streets bearing the names of trees. Fabulous **Mountain Village,** primarily a residential area, sits on the mountainside 2 mi. above town, accessible from Telluride by car via Rte. 145 south or the gondola which departs from **San Juan Street** on the south edge of town.

Visitor Information: Telluride Visitor Information Center, 630 W. Colorado Ave. (☎728-4431 or 888-288-7360). Office open M-Sa 9am-7pm, Su noon-5pm.

Equipment Rental: Downtown Telluride seems to have a gear store on every corner, and several of them rent mountain bikes. **Paragon Ski & Sports,** 213 W. Colorado Ave. (☎728-4525), has bikes, skis, and outdoor equipment all under one roof. Bikes from $18 per half-day, $35 per day; skis and boots $28 per day. Open summer daily 9am-7pm; ski season 8am-7pm; off-season 10am-4pm. **SlopeStyle,** 236 W. Colorado Ave. (☎728-9889, 888-RIDE-321, www.slopestyle.com), specializes in snowboards (rentals $35 per day, demo boards $45 per day, 20% off on 3-day rentals) and also rents full-suspension bikes from $26 per half-day and $39 per day, with multi-day and advanced reservation discounts. Open winter 8am-9pm and summer 9am-7pm.

Laundromat: Washateria, 107 W. Columbia Ave. (☎728-4360). Open daily 8am-9pm.

Weather Conditions: ☎240-4900, ext. 9901. **Road Conditions:** ☎249-9363. **Ski Conditions:** ☎728-7425.

Emergency: ☎911. **Police:** 160 S. Fir St. (☎728-3818).

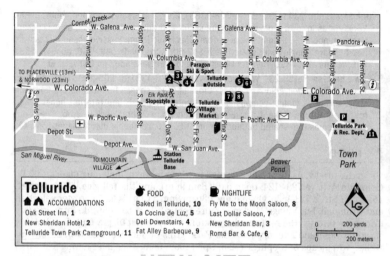

Telluride

▲■ **ACCOMMODATIONS**
Oak Street Inn, **1**
New Sheridan Hotel, **2**
Telluride Town Park Campground, **11**

🍴 FOOD
Baked in Telluride, **10**
La Cocina de Luz, **5**
Deli Downstairs, **4**
Fat Alley Barbeque, **9**

🍸 NIGHTLIFE
Fly Me to the Moon Saloon, **8**
Last Dollar Saloon, **7**
New Sheridan Bar, **3**
Roma Bar & Cafe, **6**

COLORADO

Rape Crisis Hotline: ☎ 728-5660.

Medical Services: Telluride Medical Center, 500 W. Pacific Ave. (☎ 728-3848).

Pharmacy: Sunshine Pharmacy, 236 W. Colorado Ave. (☎ 728-3601). Open daily 9am-9pm.

Internet: Wilkinson Public Library, 100 W. Pacific St. (☎ 728-4519). Offers 45 min. of free **Internet access,** a phone for free local calls, and a beautiful place to read and relax. Open M-Th 10am-8pm, F-Sa 10am-6pm, Su noon-5pm.

Post Office: 150 S. Willow St. (☎ 728-3900). Open M-F 9am-5pm, Sa 10am-noon.
Postal code: 81435. Those needing tickets or a camping pass on big festival weekends might get lucky asking around outside the post office, near the entrance to Town Park.

🏠🏕 ACCOMMODATIONS & CAMPING

If you're visiting Telluride during a festival, bring a sleeping bag; the cost of a bed is outrageous during any major holiday or celebration, and many public spaces morph temporarily into small tent cities.

▨ **Telluride Town Park Campground** (☎ 728-2173), east of downtown along Colorado Ave., offers affordable camping within walking distance of downtown. Particularly nice are the 5 primitive sites, which lie along Bear Creek removed from the road. Coin-op showers $1.50; water, bathrooms, and access to the full range of facilities in the park, including tennis and basketball courts, playing fields, pool ($3), and a kiddie fishing pond. 46 sites. 7-night max. stay. Open mid-May to mid-Oct., except the week of the Bluegrass Festival. Reception open M-Tu 8am-5pm, W-F 8am-8pm, Sa-Su 8am-4pm. $12 per vehicle; $10 primitive sites. ❶

Matterhorn (☎ 728-4211), 12 mi. south of town on Rte. 145. This campground provides a little distance from the hubbub of Telluride at the edge of the vast Uncompahgre National Forest. 28 sites with access to water, showers, and toilets. 7-night max. stay. Open late May-Sept. $12 per vehicle. Public showers $3. ❶

Priest Lake Campgrounds (☎ 728-4211), 14 mi. south of Telluride, and **Alta Lakes Campgrounds,** 18 mi. south of town, both offer free sites for camping with only primitive facilities. ❶

COLORADO

Oak Street Inn, 134 N. Oak St. (☎728-3383). Cozy, if sparsely appointed, rooms for the lowest rates in town. Convenient to the ski lift and downtown. Sports a sauna. Reception 9am-noon and 3-8pm. Check-in 4pm. Check-out 11am. Reserve ahead for festivals and holidays. Singles with shared bath $42-60, with private bath $66; doubles $58/$66; rooms about $20 more for Christmas and Bluegrass and film festivals. ❸

New Sheridan Hotel, 231 W. Colorado Ave. (☎728-4351 or 800-200-1891). William Jennings Bryan delivered his historic "Cross of Gold" speech from the hotel's front balcony. Luxurious rooms, complimentary gourmet breakfast, free **Internet access,** and roof-top hot tubs make it a sweet spot. Reception 24hr. Check-in 2pm. Check-out 11am. Rooms with shared bathroom from $90, approx. double during big festivals. ❺

◪ FOOD

Groceries are available at several small markets in town, including **Clark's,** 700 W. Colorado Ave. (☎728-3124; open daily 8am-9pm), and the **Telluride Village Market,** 157 S. Fir St. (☎728-4566. Open daily 7:30am-9pm.) Clark's has a greater selection and a full deli, but Village Market is more central. True to Telluride form, grocery prices are through the roof; stock up before arriving. **Hot Diggity Dogs** ❶, a hot dog stand on Colorado Ave. opposite Elk Park, grills up fat dogs that won't thin your wallet, with heaps of toppings. ($2-5. Open 10am-6pm; open later during festivals.)

La Cocina de Luz, 123 E. Colorado Ave. (☎728-9355 or 369-4555 for take-out/delivery). Behind Tequila Liquors. Tremendous portions of Mexican food ($5-10) and salads ($5-9) prepared with high-quality ingredients such as hand-made tortillas, free-range meat, and organic greens. Vegan friendly. Open M-Sa 9am-9pm. ❷

Deli Downstairs, 217 W. Colorado Ave. (☎728-4004). This subterranean nook feels like a food stand at a Grateful Dead show crossed with a New York City neighborhood deli. Energizing sandwiches ($6) and homemade veggie burgers ($5) keep young patrons boogying and biking for hours. Open daily 10am-midnight. Cash only. ❶

Baked in Telluride, 127 S. Fir St. (☎728-4775). Mellow bakery stocked with enough rich coffee, delicious pastries, pizza, sandwiches, and bagels to get you through an active weekend. The apple fritters ($2) are rightly famous and nightly dinner specials ($7-9) might be the best (and only) deal in town. Open daily 5:30am-10pm. ❶

Fat Alley Barbeque, 122 S. Oak St. (☎728-3985). The wooden benches and long tables are reminiscent of the sawdust saloons of yore, but Telluride's miners never ate BBQ ($5-17) like this. The town's large transplanted Southern population swears by the Carolina Pork sandwich ($7.50) and the sweet potato fries ($2 per ¼ lb.). Sides $2-5. Take-out available. Open daily 11am-10pm. ❸

◪ ♫ NIGHTLIFE & ENTERTAINMENT

Fly Me to the Moon Saloon, 132 E. Colorado Ave. (☎728-6666), shines with some of the area's freshest musical talent, and thrills groovers with its spring-loaded dance floor. Jam bands like Leftover Salmon and The String Cheese Incident have played many a free show here. Cover $1-5. Open daily 9pm-2:30am. Cash only.

Last Dollar Saloon, 100 E. Colorado (☎728-4800). Affectionately referred to as "the buck" by locals, this place is a town favorite. With the jukebox blaring and darts flying, it's not hard to see why. Beer $3-4. Open daily 11:30am-2am. Cash only.

Roma Bar & Cafe, 133 E. Colorado (☎728-3669). On busy weekends live music jams and the bar jumps. Open daily 11:30am-2:30pm and 5:30pm-2am. Dinner until 10pm.

The New Sheridan Bar, 231 W. Colorado Ave. (☎728-9100). Revelers drape along the velvet couches in the back room and shadow figures dance along the walls of the balcony. No smoking. Open daily 3pm-2am.

◘ FESTIVALS

Given that only 1900 people live in Telluride, the sheer number of festivals held in the town annually seems staggering. For general festival info, contact the **Telluride Visitors Center** (☎728-4431 or 888-288-7360). Gala events occur throughout the summer and fall, from the quirky **Mushroom Festival,** celebrated in late August, to the multi-sport challenge of the high-octane **360° Adventure** (mid-July), and, of course, the renowned **Bluegrass Festival.** (☎800-624-2422; www.planetbluegrass.com. 3rd weekend in June. Tickets $55 per day, 4-day pass $155.) One weekend in July is actually designated **Nothing Festival** to give locals a break from the onslaught of visitors and special events. The **Telluride International Film Festival** premiers some of the hippest independent flicks; *The Crying Game* (1992) and *The Piano* (1993) were both unveiled here. (☎728-4401. First weekend in Sept.) Telluride also hosts a **Jazz Celebration** during the first weekend of August (☎728-7009) and a **Blues & Brews Festival** (☎728-8037) during the third weekend in September. For some of these festivals, volunteering to usher or perform other minor tasks can result in **free admission** to events, concerts, screenings, and the like. Throughout the year a number of concerts and performances are staged at the **Sheridan Opera House,** 110 N. Oak St. (☎728-6363).

◪ OUTDOOR ACTIVITIES

Since the town lies sandwiched in the San Juans between Mount Sneffels Wilderness, the Lizard Head Wilderness, and the Uncompahgre National Forest, biking, hiking, and backpacking abound. Amazing vistas, ghost towns, and alpine lakes tucked away to the south also wow visitors. The mountain walls around town and through the valley offer various rock-climbing terrains, from bouldering to sport to traditional. These mountain passes also provide turf for some of the most extensive jeep adventures of any place in the US. For a relaxed Rocky Mountain high, take the **free gondola** to San Sophia station and hike, ski, or bike down.

HIKING

Telluride is built into the mountains, so it's not surprising that there are trails into the wilderness starting from the end of almost every street. Hikers share the trails with mountain bikers, so keep a wary eye and ear when approaching blind corners. As might be expected, most trails are very steep. For trail runners, an 8 mi. loop with significant flat sections starts up Jud Wiebe, veers left on Mill Creek, stretches flat for 2 mi., down the Mill Creek trail (exit by the Texaco west of town), and loops south to the River trail and back to town. Southwest of Telluride on Hwy. 145, the Lizard Head Wilderness beckons with excellent hiking opportunities easily accessible from the Matterhorn campground.

> **Bear Creek** (4-5 mi. round-trip, 2-3hr.). S. Pine St. ends at the trailhead. This easy hike up Bear Creek Canyon passes the remnants of old mining operations as well as some good bouldering spots before reaching Bear Creek Falls. 1050 ft. elevation gain. Recommended Apr.-Nov. Guide available at local bookstores.

> **Bridal Veil Falls** (3½ mi. round-trip, 2-3hr.). Trail begins at the eastern end of the Rte. 145 spur (Colorado Ave.). This moderate hike climbs 1200 ft. along a switchbacking jeep trail to the waterfall visible from almost anywhere in Telluride. At 365 ft., Bridal Veil is the highest waterfall in Colorado. Recommended May-Nov.

> **Wasatch Trail** (12 mi. loop, full-day). Hike or take a ride up the Bridal Veil falls jeep trail (four-wheel-drive essential) to the trailhead above the falls (next to the historic power plant). The trail follows the ridge south, crosses two alpine basins (covered in wildflowers during the summer) and makes a steep descent to join with the Bear Creek trail.

COLORADO

More a runway to the mountains and clouds than a terrestrial highway, the San Juan Skyway soars across the rooftop of the Rockies. Winding its way through San Juan and Uncompahgre National Forests, Old West mountain towns, and Native American ruins, the byway passes a remarkably wide range of southwestern Colorado's splendors. Reaching altitudes up to 11,000 ft., with breathtaking views of snowy peaks and verdant valleys, the San Juan Skyway is widely considered one of America's most beautiful drives. Travelers in this area inevitably drive at least parts of it as they head to destinations such as Telluride, Durango, and Mesa Verde. Several exhilarating unpaved mountain passes depart the main road and promise extreme off-road adventure for experienced four-wheel-drivers. A hard core cadre of cyclists embarks on the **"Death Ride"** every June near the full moon, attempting to complete the 236 mi. loop in a single day. Many sections of the skyway skirt steep drop-offs and involve driving curvy mountain roads. Call the San Juan (☎970-247-4874) or Uncompahgre (☎970-874-6600) National Forests to check road conditions or to inquire about driving the skyway.

A loop road, piggy-backing on Rte. 550, 62, 145, and 160, the skyway voyage can begin anywhere along the loop, at towns such as Durango, Ridgeway, or Cortez. Beginning in Durango, the skyway heads north along Rte. **550 N (Million Dollar Highway),** climbing into the San Juan Mountains and paralleling the Animas River.

1 DURANGO MOUNTAIN RESORT. 27 mi. north of Durango along the pastoral glacial valley of the Animas River, the **Durango Mountain Resort,** known popularly as **Purgatory,** offers outdoor adventures in any season. Skiers will enjoy 11 lifts, including a high-speed, six-person super chair serving 75 trails (23% beginner, 51% intermediate, 26% advanced) and 1200 skiable acres with a 2029 ft. vertical drop. (☎800-979-9742. Annual snowfall 260 in. Open late Nov. to early Apr. 9am-4pm. $55, under 12 $28.) When the heat is on, travelers can trade in their skis for a sled and test out the alpine slide or take a chairlift ride to access over 50 mi. of mountain bike trails. (Open mid-June to Aug. daily 9:30am-5pm. Slide ride $8; mountain bike lift $5, all day $15.)

2 MOLAS PASS & MOLAS LAKE. 15 mi. farther north on Rte. 550, the road peaks on the way to Silverton at Molas Pass (10,910 ft.). Breathe deep; researchers have allegedly documented the cleanest air in the US in Molas. On its way to Denver, the **Colorado Trail** crosses U.S. 550 here; pick up the trail at the pass or 1 mi. east at Little Molas Lake. **Molas Lake Campground ❶**, at the lake, 1.3 mi. north of the pass on U.S. 550, offers visitors 58 tent and RV sites ($14), cabins ($25), canoe rentals ($5 per hr.), horseback riding ($20 per hr.), showers, and picnic tables. (☎970-759-5557. Open mid-May to Oct. 8am-8pm.) The Molas Trail begins at the lake and after 4 mi. connects with the Elk Creek Trail, a popular access trail to the Weminuche Wilderness. On the other side of 550, a turn—off down a bumpy road treats visitors to the relative alpine solitude of **Little Molas Lake ❶**, where primitive campsites are free.

3 SILVERTON. Falling to 9310 ft., the road enters this easy-going town. Savvy drivers plan to avoid the 2hr. midday rush of tourists that pour off the narrow-gauge railroad to luncheon, shop, and gawk. (See p. 341)

4 RED MOUNTAIN PASS. Here the drive reaches its highest point at 11,018 ft. This stretch of road between Silverton and Ouray, called the "Million Dollar Highway" in reference both to its scenic splendor and mining yield, is one of the most avalanche-prone regions in Colorado. The snow shed a few miles outside of Ouray protects the road from the deadly **Riverside Chute,** one of 59 avalanche chutes along 550 between Ouray and Coal Bank Pass (south of Molas). This section of the drive also showcases stellar 14,000 ft. mountain peaks and defunct mines. The small and difficult to reach area around Red Mountain Pass once held over 200 inhabitants in six now-abandoned towns. In 1991, the Reclamation Act shut down most of the mines, but you can still see remnants in the most unlikely places.

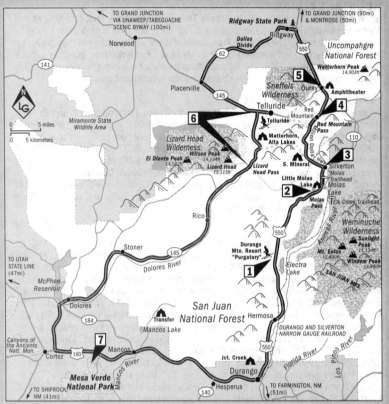

5 OURAY. The skyway's next stop is Ouray, also know as the "Switzerland of America." With fabulous views and hedonistic hot springs, this town is a relaxing stop for the weary. Indulge at one of the preponderant chocolate and ice cream shops, or soak at the public hot springs pool along the main road near the Visitors Center. (Open June-Aug. 10am-10pm, Sept.-May noon-9pm. $7.50, shower alone $2.) Ouray also features the world's only **Ice Park,** on Camp Bird Mine Rd. (☎970-325-4288; www.ourayicepark.com; free), with some of the best ice climbing anywhere. The season runs from mid-December to mid–March, with an ice festival in mid-January. Area guides include **Above Ouray Ice & Tower Rock Climbing School,** 450 Main St. (☎888-345-9061; www.towerguides.com), and **San Juan Mountain Guides,** (☎970-325-4925; www.ourayclimbing.com). In the summer, the ice walls turn into waterfalls at **Box Canyon Park.** (☎325-4464. Open daily 8am-dusk. $3, ages 5-12 $1.50.)

6 TELLURIDE. This spectacular, self-consciously chic community awaits travelers along Rte. 145. From the **Lizard Head Pass** and its access to the desolate **Lizard Head Wilderness,** the skyway runs along the Taylor Mesa through the quiet towns of Rico, Stoner, and Dolores. Rte. 145 connects with Rte. 160 between **Cortez** and **Mesa Verde National Park** (p. 356).

7 MESA VERDE NATIONAL PARK. Stunning **Ancestral Puebloan ruins** stand in this national park on top of a high plateau off Rte. 160. Moving east along Rte. 160, the skyway cuts through Mancos and finally returns to Durango (p. 333).

MOUNTAIN BIKING

Good biking trails include the **Mill Creek Trail** and **Deep Creek Trail** (starting at Jud Wiebe trailhead, 6½ mi. one way/18 mi. loop) west of town, which climb into the northern mountains. The **Telluride Trail** south of town ascends the ski mountain and bombs back down. Access the ride from its base or use the free gondola service (see **Transportation,** p. 344). The intense **Wasatch Trail,** beginning southeast of town at Bear Creek trailhead on S. Pine St., makes for a technical all-day outing.

FLY FISHING & RAFTING

Telluride's rivers and dirt roads are playgrounds for anglers, floaters, and drivers. Much of the San Miguel and Dolores Rivers permit public fishing. Stop by **Telluride Angler,** a full-service fly outfitter at 121 W. Colorado Ave., for advice or to schedule a trip. (☎728-3895 or 800-831-6230. Wade trips from $200 per half-day, $275 full day. Best deal with two people. Two-hour clinics available for $75 for 1-2 people. Rents rod, reel, and waders.) At the same location, **Telluride Outside** runs whitewater raft trips on the San Miguel River (Class II and III, half-day $65 per person, full day $115), jeep tours (half-day from $65, full day from $95), and mountain bike trips (half-day from $75, full day from $125).

SKIING

Telluride Mountain (☎888-605-2579; www.tellurideskiresort.com) is one of the premier American ski resorts. With 16 lifts, including 9 high speed, over 1700 skiable acres and 3500 ft. of vertical drop, the mountain challenges visitors with some of the most extreme skiing and snowboarding in Colorado without extreme crowding. The season generally runs from late Nov. to mid-Apr., with 309 in. of annual snowfall blanketing 66 trails (24% beginner, 38% intermediate, 38% advanced/expert). Even self-proclaimed atheists can be spied praying before hitting the Spiral Stairs and the Plunge, two of the Rockies' most gut-wrenching double black diamond runs. (☎866-287-5015. Nov. 26-Dec. 20 and Mar. 31-Apr. 6 fullday $51, half-day $40, children $29/$23; Jan. 6-Feb. 13 and Feb. 24-Mar. 30 $65/$51/ $36/$28; Dec. 21-Jan. 5 and Feb. 14-Feb. 23 $68/$54/$39/$31. Lifts open 8:45am-4pm.) For an even more intense experience, Telluride Helitrax (☎728-8377, 800-HELISKI; www.helitrax.com) offers Colorado's only heli-skiing. Paragon Ski and Sport, 217 W. Colorado Ave., rents bikes in summer and skis in winter. (☎728-4525. Open summers daily 9am-7pm; ski season daily 8am-7pm; off-season daily 10am-4pm. Bikes from $18 per half-day, $35 per day; skis and boots $28 per day.)

OURAY ☎970

For those fond of the vertical, Ouray is a wonderland. The intimacy of the snow-capped mountains and rocky cliffs prevents Ouray from growing more than a few blocks in either direction, preserving the old-time feel of this historic mining town. "The Switzerland of America," Ouray attracts outdoor enthusiasts to hike, mountain-bike, soak in natural hot springs, and explore some of the highest maneuverable mountain passes in the country by jeep. Recently, Ouray has become famous for its Ice Park, the oldest facility of its kind in the world. During winter, the Box Canyon cliffs, a narrow river gorge at the south end of town, are transformed into a continuous waterfall where expert ice-climbers come to compete in festivals that test their limits and awe onlookers.

◪◪ ORIENTATION & PRACTICAL INFORMATION. Ouray is oriented north/south along Hwy. 550, 9 mi. south of Ridgway and 23 mi. north of Silverton (p. 341) via the famous Red Mountain Pass through the San Juan Mountains. A car is essential to get into town. **Main Street** cradles most of the restaurants, hotels, and shops.

On the northern edge of town, the **Ouray Visitor's Center**, 1234 N. Main St., has excellent maps and information about the area. (☎325-4746 or 800-228-1876. Open M-F 9am-5pm, Sa 10-4pm, Su noon-4pm.) For more maps, trail advice, and gear, **Ouray Mountain Sports**, 722 Main St., is the right place to go. (☎325-4284. Open summer 9am-8pm, winter 9am-6pm, closed Tu and W in the off-season.) Medical facilities are limited. A **Nurse Clinic** is on 2nd St., but for more extensive medical care residents travel to **Mountain Medical Center**, 295 Hwy. 62, in Ridgway (☎626-5123. Office hours 9am-5pm, on-call 24hr.) or to hospitals in Montrose or Grand Junction. Other services include: free **Internet access** at the **public library**, 320 Sixth St. (☎325-4616. Open M-F 10am-5pm, Sa 10am-noon); **sheriff**, 541 4th Ave., behind the courthouse (☎325-7272); **24hr. ATM** outside Citizen State Bank of Ouray, 600 Main St. (☎325-4478, Lobby hours M-F 10am-4pm); coin-op **laundry** and public **showers** available at **Timber Ridge Campground**, just north of town on Hwy. 550; and **post office**, 620 Main St. (Open M-F 9am-4:30pm and Sa 9-11:30am. **Postal code:** 81427.)

⌐⌐ ACCOMMODATIONS & CAMPING. For such a small town, Ouray teams with luxury hotels. Least expensive is the **Historic Western Hotel ❸**, 210 7th Ave, the longest standing wooden hotel in Colorado (built 1891). Mark Twain is purported to have stayed here. (☎325-4645 or 888-624-8403. Singles $35; doubles $45. Both have shared bathrooms. Suites with private baths $75-85.) For a night of unabashed pampering and relaxation, reserve a room at the **Wiesbaden ❺**, at the corner of Sixth Ave. and First St. Guests enjoy access to in-house massages and Aveda spa treatments ($65-75 per hour for guests; non-guests $75-85), as well as the famous vapor caves below the hotel. (☎325-4347; www.wiesbaden-hotsprings.com. Check-in 2-9pm, check-out 10:30am with facility privileges for the rest of the day Rooms start at $120 per night.) **Ouray Hotel ❸**, 303 Sixth and Main St., provides clean, quiet, non-smoking rooms. (☎325-0500; www.montrose.net/ourayhotel. Singles $45; doubles $55-65; suites $80-100. Office open 10am-10pm.)

Perched high above Ouray to the south, **Amphitheatre Campground ❶** is a nearby option for camping in the National Forest, with 35 tent sites ($14). To get there drive 1 mi. south of town up a winding Hwy. 550. Turn right at the forest service sign for Amphitheatre Campground and weave 1 mi. up the paved road past several lookout points. (☎877-444-6777 for reservations. Pit toilets and water available.) North of town a ¼ mi. on Hwy. 550, **Timber Ridge Campground ❶** charges $10 for tent camping, with full hookups available for $23 and two-person cabins for $50. (☎325-4523. Free showers for guests. 6:30am-10pm. Late arrivals welcome.)

◘◙ FOOD & ENTERTAINMENT. Ouray has more restaurants than one would expect for a small town. The oldest establishment, 20-year-old **Pricco's ❶**, 736 Main St., offers a standard variety of soups ($3.50), salads ($4-9), sandwiches ($7-8), and burgers ($6-7). **Bombie's ❶**, 319 Sixth Ave., serves up "Ourayan cuisine" to go or to eat in his family-style dining area. The motto is "good food, fast." Ouray native Bombie spends all morning cooking tacos, burritos, and quesadillas ($2.50-7), and serves the food until it runs out, so get there early. (☎325-4101. Lunch 11am-3pm, dinner 5-7pm.) In the evening locals often hang out over a martini at the **Buen Tiempo ❷**, 515 Main St., which also has a vast array of Mexican food (entrees $10-16). (☎325-4544. Open M-Sa 11:30am-2pm for lunch, nightly 5-10pm for dinner. Closed for lunch in winter.)

Although Ouray was primarily a mining town in its early days, tourism existed from the beginning. In addition to the town's outdoors access, visitors come to enjoy the natural hot springs scattered in the mountains. Today the hot-springs have been developed into the **Ouray Hot Springs Pool**, 1220 Main St. This family-oriented facility includes lap-lanes, diving boards, a children's pool, and a hot tub section, all heated by natural springs. (☎325-7073. Summer 10am-10pm, Labor-

Memorial Day noon-9pm. $8, students and seniors $6, ages 3-6 $3, under 3 free). The **Weisbaden Hot Springs Spa and Lodgings** (p. 351) also provides public access to its vapor caves, soaking pool, and outdoor pool ($10 for 3 hrs.).

⚑ OUTDOORS. Ice climbing brings crowds to Ouray's doorstep, promising thrilling ascents up sheer ice cliffs. **Ouray Ice Park** (www.ourayicepark.com) sits directly south of town on Hwy. 550. Created in 1974, it was the first facility of its kind in the world. A couple locals looked at the skinny canyon carved by the Uncompahgre River and had the crazy idea to put water spouts along the canyon edges, producing artificial waterfalls that freeze and create an extreme-sports playland. With two spectator platforms, the area hosts high-level ice-climbing competitions. Today there are 150 ice-climbing routes at Ice Park, ranging from 80 to 140 ft. high. **Waterfall Ice** (WI2-WI6), along with mixed rock and ice climbs (M3-M9), is a diverse challenge. The area is free to use. Ouray grants access to natural waterfalls like the Ribbon, Gravity's Rainbow, and Horsetail Falls. Inquire at Ouray Mountain Sports for more info and an explanation of the ice climbing rating system.

Yankee Boy Basin is one of many alpine roads near Ouray whose stunning scenery promises thrills for **four-wheel** enthusiasts. A vast, winding network of jeep roads connects Hwy. 550 to towns across the mountains, such as Telluride to the west and Lake City to the East. An intermediate 4x4 challenge awaits along **Animas Forks Loop** (23 mi. south of Ouray on Hwy. 550). From Silverton, follow Hwy. 110 northeast. The road turns to dirt as it parallels the Animas Forks River. Proceed north 10 mi. after the pavement ends, bearing left to Animas Forks (passing the townsite of Eureka, beyond which the road deteriorates). Past Animas Forks, continue west and south for 15 mi. over Hurricane Pass, exiting back onto Hwy. 110, 7 mi. north of Silverton. Jeep rentals and tours are available from **Jeep Tours Ouray,** 701 Main. St. (☎325-4014 or 800-648-JEEP. Tours $45 half-day, $90 full day; rentals $120 per day.) Detailed jeep trail maps available at Ouray Mountain Sports or Jeep Tours Ouray.

CREEDE ☎719

The sole town in isolated, sparsely populated Mineral County, proud little Creede (pop. 300) brandishes its rich history and scenic splendor as tourism trump cards. Meanwhile, the friendly folks and thriving artistic community attest to the character and vitality held over from Creede's early days as a silver boomtown at the end of the 19th century. Today's visitors mine the mountains for a wealth of outdoor adventures and roam the narrow main street of town in the shadow of a canyon searching for a way to bring a piece of Creede home with them.

◰ ⊉ ORIENTATION & PRACTICAL INFORMATION. Creede lies smack dab in the center of the **Silver Thread Scenic Byway** that runs between Lake City and South Fork along Hwy. 149, accessible only by car. The town's main thoroughfare, **Main Street,** spurs off 149 and stretches for eight blocks.

The **Creede Chamber of Commerce,** 1207 N. Main, located next door to the courthouse, clues in visitors with helpful advice and maps. (☎658-2374; www.creede.com. Open summer M-F 9am-5pm; winter M-F 10am-4pm. Kiosk: 201 S. Main, mid-May to Sept. M-Sa 9am-5pm, Su 12-4pm.) The **USFS Ranger Station,** 304 Main St., sells detailed maps and books and dispenses permits. (☎658-2556. Open June-Aug. daily 8:30am-5pm; M-F only Sept. to mid-Oct. and mid-Apr. to May; W only mid-Oct. to mid-Apr.) **First National Bank (24hr. ATM),** lies further up Main St. Across from the Camber of Commerce is the **Cyber Stop,** the only **Internet** connection in town. (☎658-0235. $3.50 per 15 min. Open Memorial-Labor Day M-Sa 10am-7pm, Su noon-5pm.) **San Juan Sports,** 102 Main St., sells a large selection of outdoor gear, rents bikes and hiking equipment in the summer, and cross-country skis and snowshoes in the winter. (☎658-2359, 888-658-0851. Bike rental $13 per half-day, $19 per day. Open daily 9am-5:30pm, until 8pm on theatre nights in summer.) Services include: **sheriff,** 1201 N. Main St. (658-2600); **police/emergency** (☎911); the **Mineral County Health Clinic,** 802 Rio Grande Ave., west of Main St. (☎658-0929; doctor available M, Tu, and F 8am-5pm, W 8am-12pm. Nurse available Th 8am-5pm. 24hr. phone); **laundromat,** on 5th St. just off Main St.; **post office,** on Main St. near the bank. (Open M-F 8am-4:30pm, Sa 10am-12pm. **Postal code:** 81130.)

🎟🏠 ACCOMMODATIONS & FOOD. On Hwy. 149 southeast of town, the **Snowshoe Lodge and B&B ❸** sleeps guests comfortably in themed rooms, some with kitchenettes. John Wayne frequented Room 102. (☎658-2315. Continental breakfast included during the summer. Singles $36-59, doubles $44-70; 2-bedroom B&B suite $65-115. Public showers available for $5.) Downtown next to the theatre, the **Creede Hotel and B&B ❹** rents four rooms, two with balconies overlooking the town. (☎658-2608. Open early May to late Sept. Full breakfast included, $80-95.)

Campers will delight in the prospects around Mineral County, 96% of which is National Forest land. **USFS campgrounds ❶** (☎888-444-6777) dot the area, most $11-12. **Thirty-mile Campground ❶,** 20.1 mi. west on Hwy. 149, then left 11 mi. on Rio Grande Reservoir Rd., is a base for hikes up Weminuche and Squaw Creeks to the Continental Divide Trail. (35 sites with water, toilets, and trash collection. Reservations accepted. $12.) Closer to town, the **Rio Grande Campground and Fisherman Area ❶,** 8.4 mi. west on Hwy. 149 and then left on a dirt road for 1 mi., has four primitive sites and excellent fishing. (Toilets and water available. No reservations. Free.) Anyplace on Forest Service land is fair game for tenters, though, as long as they are sure to avoid open-range cattle.

Whether you plan on gazing in galleries or wading into the Rio Grande for trout, **Journeys ❶** will fix you a fantastic meal for about $5. Lounge there or order a box lunch to go. (☎658-2290. Open 7am-4pm, theatre nights until 8pm.) Because of the winter lull, many restaurants are open only in summer. The **Bear's Den ❶,** 704 La Garita Ave., one block east of Main. St., stays open year-round, serving hearty all-American breakfast, lunch, and dinner ($3-11). (Open M-Sa 7am-8:30pm, Su 8am-8:30pm; shorter winter hours.) For a more rambunctious setting, try the tacos and burritos at **Kip's Grille ❶,** on the patio of Tommyknocker Tavern off Main St. (☎658-0138. Open daily 11am-8pm, closed during winter.)

THE LOCAL LEGEND

VIGILANTE VENGEANCE

The breeze in many of Southwestern Colorado's old mining towns still carries a hint of the area's lawless history, from gun fights and poker games to the swindles of traveling con-artists. In tiny Creede, one of the favorite legends is that of Bob Ford, a western "businessman" who made a name for himself as the man who killed Jesse James in 1883. At the time, James was living under an alias in St. Joseph, Missouri. Instead of collecting the $10,000 reward, Ford was accused of murder, but later acquitted. He moved to Creede shortly thereafter and bought the town saloon.

For 10 years Ford lived in constant fear of retribution. It's said that "(he) always sat facing the door of his saloon with drawn revolver on the table," anticipating the day when a man might wander in and take his life. In 1892, a lone stranger on horseback named Ed O'Kelley ambled into town looking for Ford. An ominous melody wafted through Ford's bedroom window that night—"Jesse had a wife, she's a mourner all her life, Oh, the dirty little coward who shot Mr. Howard..."—and Ford knew the stranger was up to no good. The next morning O'Kelley burst into the saloon, guns blazing. Ford was dead before he could even defend himself. No one knows why O'Kelley wanted to avenge the death of James, but many Missourians considered him a hero.

♫ ☉ ENTERTAINMENT & SIGHTS. The well-known **Creede Repertory Theatre,** a troupe drawing acting talent from all over the world, puts up a new show almost weekly in the summertime. (☎ 658-2540; www.creederep.com. Mid-June to late Sept. shows nightly Tu-Su. $16-19.) To get an idea of what life was like in the old mines, step into one at the **Underground Mining Museum,** located past Main St. at the base of the Bachelor Loop. Guided tours of an old mine start at 10am and 2:30pm daily for $10. Throughout the day, a CD-guided tour is available. Bring a jacket; it's chilly in there. (☎ 658-0811. Open late May to early Sept. daily 10am-4pm, other months 10am-3pm. $6, children $4.) Check out the firehouse next door, the only one in the world that has an underground mine. From the Underground Museum, begin the 17 mi. **Bachelor Historic Loop,** a driving tour that encompasses mining sites, ghost towns, and glorious views of 14,000 ft. peaks. Follow the signs or purchase a guide for $1 at the Chamber of Commerce or the museum.

♦ OUTDOOR ACTIVITIES. Blessed by the waters of the Upper Rio Grande and vast tracks of La Garita and Weminuche Wilderness Areas, Creede brims with outdoor activities. Twenty-five miles west of town off Hwy. 149 on South Clear Creek Rd., the **Brown Lakes Wildlife Area** yields massive trout to patient anglers, though is often windy. The Coller section of the Rio Grande (between South Fork and Creede) has excellent fishing and is largely clear of private property. For an immediate thrill, try rafting the Rio Grande with **Mountain Man Tours,** on Hwy. 149 at the turnoff to downtown. (☎ 658-2663 or 658-2843; www.mountainmantours.com. Half-day trips departing at 9:30am and 2pm, $34.) Creede is strategically positioned to provide incredible access to famous hiking trails. The **Colorado Trail** to the south and the **Continental Divide Trail**—which forms an 80-mile semi-circle around the town—both begin nearby. Consequently almost every trail to the south, west, and east connect to the Continental Divide. Trails string through the wilderness and national forest and await intrepid hikers; ask at San Juan Sports for personal favorites. A difficult 14 mi. trek from Hanson's Mill Campground on USFS Rd. 650 west of town brings hikers or four-wheel-drivers to the bizarre **Wheeler Geologic Area,** which has volcanic rock eroded into unearthly forms.

CORTEZ   ☎ 970

Recently named one of the top ten pit stops in America, Cortez lives up to its title, for better or worse, with the gusto of a Southwestern ranching community. The motels and service stations lining U.S. 160 abut the great pasture lands of Montezuma Valley, suggesting that most of today's Cortez cowboys are less likely to be coiling a braided lasso than the hose of a gas pump.

▣ ♂ ORIENTATION & PRACTICAL INFORMATION. Cortez is 40 mi. north of Shiprock, NM and 46 mi. west of Durango (p. 333) at the junction of U.S. 160 and U.S. 491. These two highways represent the town's main thoroughfare, called **Main Street** downtown and **Broadway** on the stretch headed south. The **Cortez Municipal Airport** (☎ 800-872-7245), 2 mi. south on U.S. 160/491, offers prohibitively expensive flights from Denver and Farmington, NM. Getting to Cortez requires the use of a car; the nearest train (Gallup, NM) and bus (Durango) stops are many miles away. **Save-A-Buck Taxi** runs throughout town (☎ 749-5009. Open 9:30-2am).

Visitor information is available at the **Colorado Welcome Center and Cortez Chamber of Commerce,** 928 E. Main St. (☎ 565-3414. Open daily 8am-6pm late May to early Sept., 8am-5pm the rest of the year.) Ten miles north in Dolores, the **Mancos-Dolores District Forest Service Ranger Station and BLM,** 100 N. 6th St., provides lots of info on the outdoors. (☎ 882-7296. Open Apr.-Oct. daily 8am-4:30pm, Nov.-Mar. 8am-4pm.) Services include: **emergency** (☎ 911); **police,** 608 N. Park St. (☎ 565-8441);

Citizen State Bank, 77 W. Main St., with **24hr. ATM; Plaza Laundry,** 1419 E. Main (☎565-8467; open daily 8am-9pm, last wash 8pm); **Weather and Road Conditions,** ☎565-4511; **Southwest Memorial Hospital,** 1311 N. Mildred Rd. (☎565-6666); free **Internet access** at the **Cortez Public Library,** two blocks north of U.S. 160 at 202 N. Park on the corner of E. Montezuma Ave. (☎565-8117; open June-Aug. M-Th 10am-7pm, F 10am-4pm, Sa 10am-4pm); and the **post office,** 35 S. Beech St. (☎565-3181. Open M-F 9am-5pm, Sa 11am-1pm.) **Postal code:** 81321.

ACCOMMODATIONS & FOOD. Cortez has no lack of motel and fast-food options. Shag carpeting and veneer furniture make the budget rooms at **Ute Mountain Motel ❷,** 531 S. Broadway, a blast from the 70s. (☎565-8507. Reception 8am-11pm. Check-out 11am. Singles $26-32; doubles $30-42.) The **Sand Canyon Inn ❸,** 301 W. Main St., boasts a central location, immaculate rooms, and a pool to relieve the heat. (☎565-8562. Reception 24hr. Check-out 11am. Singles $36-51, doubles $44-65.) **McPhee Campground ❶,** 13 mi. north of Cortez on Rte. 184, has 64 sites above McPhee Reservoir and Montezuma Valley. The sites are part of a well-marked recreation area west of the Rte. 145/184 junction. (☎877-444-6777. Open May-Oct. Check-out noon. 30-night max. stay. Showers $2. Open tent sites $10-12.)

Francisca's ❷, 125 E. Main St., is a popular spot for Mexican food, and rightfully so. The white wicker gazebos are perfect for savoring large portions of fresh, original dishes. (☎565-4093. Take-out available. Entrees $5-9. Open Tu, W, Sa 4-10pm; Th-F 11am-10pm.) The adjoining **cantina** (☎564-1880) features unique nightly drink specials ($3.50-7.50) and a $3 appetizer menu. Just down the street, the **Main Street Brewery and Restaurant ❷,** 21 E. Main St., boasts its own Bavarian brewmaster, some great beers ($2-4), and innovative pub creations ($6-12) like the $9 Bratwurst Burrito. (☎564-9112. Take-out available. Open daily 4pm-midnight.) **Once Upon a Sandwich ❷,** 1 W. Main St., is a popular lunch spot offering generous meals, a friendly atmosphere, and good veggie options. Burgers and sandwiches are $5-7 and salads $6-7. (☎565-8292. Open M-F 11am-2:30pm, Sa 11am-2pm.)

OUTDOOR ACTIVITIES. Though not as exciting as Durango, Cortez offers quite a lot to do in the outdoors. The region combines Moab's slickrock with Durango's mountains, making for great **mountain biking.** To the north and east of town, a number of rides climb logging roads and singletrack into the foothills of the La Platas near Stoner and Mancos. West of Cortez, several rides traverse the desert mesa tops or follow the course of the Dolores River. Access roads to a number of the sites at **Hovenweep National Monument** (p. 281) also make for some excellent rides. The **San Juan National Forest Ranger Station** in Dolores, 100 N. 6th St. (☎882-7296), and **Kokopelli Bike and Board,** 30 W. Main St., are good resources. (☎565-4408 or 800-565-6736. Open May-Sept. M-Sa 9am-6pm, winter 10am-6pm. Bikes $20 per day, multi-day discounts available.)

A good beginner ride is **Boggy Draw Loop,** an 8.4 mi. loop of rolling singletrack with moderate climbs and steep descents in the middle section of the trail (357 ft. elevation gain). The ride starts 13 mi. from Cortez. Take Hwy. 145 north to Dolores and turn left on 11th St. Beyond the top of the canyon rim, switchbacks run for 3 mi. Go right on Road W and head east for 1 mi. Pass the cattle guard and park on the left. The trail takes off to the north. The trail is easy to follow, but keep in mind that logging roads cross the path about 6 mi. in. Allow 1-2½hr. for the ride.

The most famous ride in the area is the intermediate **Sand Canyon Trail,** which winds through the Canyons of the Ancients, providing close-up views of several well-preserved Puebloan ruins and expansive views. The trail is 11.1 mi. and can be ridden year-round, although the lack of shade makes it uncomfortable during the heat of summer. Get good directions from the Anasazi Heritage Center or Kokopelli Bike and Board because the trail is not always easy to find. It's espe-

COLORADO

cially important to stick to the trail to avoid crushing cryptobiotic soil that takes decades to grow back. From Cortez take Hwy. 160 west to Hwy. 491 and head south toward Four Corners. Take a right at the stoplight intersection with County Rd. G (at the M&M Truck Stop 3.1 mi. south of town). Go west 12.4 mi. into McElmo Canyon and the trailhead will be well marked on the right. Allow 1-3hr. for this ride, which sees a total 883 ft. elevation gain.

Advanced bikers will enjoy the **Phil's World Loop,** 8.1 mi. singletrack of short climbs, fast descents, technical riding, and jumps. The area is a jumble of smaller loops without good signage, so a trail map is essential. From Cortez take Hwy. 60 east about 4 mi. toward Mancos and watch for a shooting range on the left. Turn left beyond the shooting range onto a dirt road across from the "Montezuma Creek" sign. Park next to the fence on the left. The trail crosses BLM, state trust land, and private property. Allow 1-2hr. for the ride.

MESA VERDE NATIONAL PARK ☎970

Some of the most elaborate Pueblo dwellings found today, millennium-old sky-scrapers—or, more appropriately, rockscrapers—draw the largest crowds at this park of archaeological wonders. Fourteen hundred years ago, Native American tribes began to cultivate the relatively wet mesa tops of the area now known as Mesa Verde National Park. In the centuries that followed, these people (today called the Ancestral Puebloan, and formerly the Navajo term, Anasazi, or "ancient enemies") constructed a series of expansive cliff dwellings beneath the overhanging sandstone shelves surrounding the mesa. Then, around 1275, 700 years after their ancestors arrived, the Pueblo people abruptly left behind the dwellings whose eerie and stark beauty now captures the imagination of thousands of mar-velling visitors. Over 600 more years elapsed before local ranchers chasing stray cattle stumbled upon the magnificent ruins of Cliff Palace in 1888. Established in 1906, Mesa Verde National Park was the first, and remains the only, national park set aside exclusively for archaeological remains. Ravaged by wildfires in the sum-mer of 2000, parts of the park are marked by charred trees whose black silhouettes lend the now-recovering mesa a sense of the mysterious. Mesa Verde is not for the snap-a-shot-and-go tourist; the best sites require a bit of physical effort to reach.

AT A GLANCE: MESA VERDE NATIONAL PARK

AREA: 52,000 acres.	**GATEWAY TOWNS:** Cortez (p. 354), Mancos, Durango (p. 333).
FEATURES: Chapin and Wetherill Mesas.	
HIGHLIGHTS: Camping at Morefield Campground, wandering around the cliff dwellings at Chapin and Wetherill Mesas.	**CAMPING:** Morefield Campground $20.
	FEES: Weekly pass for vehicles $10, pedestrian or bike $5.

✴ ⁊ ORIENTATION & PRACTICAL INFORMATION

The park's sole entrance lies at its north end, ½ mi. from a well-marked exit for the park off U.S. 160, 10 mi. east of **Cortez** (see p. 354) and 8 mi. west of Mancos. The park's main road runs 21 mi. from the entrance station to Chapin Mesa and the park headquarters. Fifteen miles in on the main road, a branch road heads out 12 mi. to Wetherill Mesa.

An automobile is the best way to travel through the park, but no vehicles over 25 ft. in length are allowed on the road to Wetherill Mesa. There are two other options for intra-park transport. **Aramark Mesa Verde** runs daily bus tours. (☎529-4421 or 800-449-2288; www.visitmesaverde.com. Open mid-Apr. to mid-Oct. Half-day tours

Mesa Verde National Park

$32-34, under 12 $21-23; full day $53/$41.) A **tram** runs to Wetherill Mesa from the ranger kiosk in the parking lot. (May-Sept., 30min. ride every 30min., 9:30am-4pm. Free.) **Gas** is available only at Morefield Village, 4 mi. from the park entrance. Trailers and towed vehicles are prohibited past Morefield Campground; you'll have to park in the lot before the entrance station if you have either type of vehicle. Much of the park is **wheelchair-accessible.**

Several facilities within the park are equipped to aid visitors at various hours and times of the year. The **Far View Visitors Center,** 15 mi. in on the main road, offers plenty of helpful info on the park and is also the only place to buy tickets ($2.50) for guided tours. (☎529-5036. Open mid-Apr. to mid-Oct. daily 8am-5pm.) When the Visitors Center is closed during the winter, head to the **Chapin Mesa Archaeological Museum.** (☎529-4631. Open June-Sept. daily 8am-6:30pm; Oct.-May 8am-5pm.) In the summer if you arrive in the evening, the **Morefield Ranger Station** (☎564-6005) at Morefield Village is open daily from 5-8:30pm. Basic camping supplies and groceries are available at the **Morefield Village General Store.** (☎565-2133. Open mid-Apr. to mid-Oct. daily Memorial to Labor Day 7am-9pm, early and late season 8am-8pm.) Other services include: public **showers, laundry,** and **gas,** at Morefield Village (☎565-2407; open mid-Apr. to mid-Oct. 7am-9pm); **road and weather conditions** (☎529-4461); **general park information,** contact park headquarters (☎529-4465); and **post office,** Chapin Mesa by the park headquarters and museum. (☎529-4554. Open M-F 9am-4:30pm, Sa 10am-1:45pm.) **Postal code:** 81330.

WHEN TO GO. Snowy and icy conditions often make Mesa Verde an undesirable winter destination. Summer highs can hit the 90s, and afternoon thunderstorms are likely in July and August. The best times to visit are the late spring and early fall, when the weather tends to be fairly reliable and not too hot.

COLORADO

ACCOMMODATIONS & FOOD

Lodging in the park is pricey. Rooms at Mesa Verde's only motel-style accommodation, the **Far View Lodge ❺**, are costly and not particularly interesting. (☎ 592-4422 or 800-449-2288. June-Aug. $100+, Apr.-May and Sept.-Oct. from $93. Closed Oct. 31-Apr. 1.) Even the park's **Morefield Campground ❷**, 4 mi. from the entrance station, raises the cost of living, but with 452 beautiful, secluded sites equipped with running water and toilets, it might be worth it. Public showers and laundry are available at Morefield Village. (☎ 565-2407 or 800-449-2288. Reception Memorial-Labor Day 7am-9pm, early and late season 8am-8pm. Check-out 11am. Open Apr. to mid-Oct. Tent sites $20, RVs $26.) Outside the park, affordable overnight options—and food—abound in the nearby towns of **Cortez** (p. 354) and Mancos.

Two cafeterias are located within the Park boundaries. The **Spruce Tree Terrace Restaurant,** near the museum (open in summer daily 9am-6pm), and **Far View Terrace,** near the main Visitors Center, is open 6:30am-8pm in summer, with shorter winter hours. The **Knife Edge Restaurant ❶**, at Morefield Campground, has a $5.40 all-you-can-eat pancake breakfast (open Memorial-Labor Day daily 7:30-10am).

SIGHTS

A good starting point, the Far View Visitors Center is a 15 mi. drive from the entrance gate off Rte. 160. A comprehensive visitor's guide and tour tickets are available here, as well as the expertise of friendly park rangers. (☎ 529-5036. Open in summer daily 8am-5:30pm.) At the Visitors Center, two roads diverge and cut into the park: one heads to **Chapin Mesa,** which features the largest number of cliff dwellings, and the other runs to **Wetherill Mesa.**

The **Chapin Mesa Archaeological Museum,** along the first loop of the Chapin branch (before the dwellings), provides an overview of the Ancestral Puebloan lifestyle and is a good place to start before exploring the mesa. (☎ 529-4631. Open daily 8am-6:30pm; Oct.-May 8am-5pm.) Rangers lead **tours** of the cliff dwellings at Cliff Palace and Balcony House, each lasting about 1hr., departing every 30min. $2.50 tickets must be purchased at Visitors Center.) Tours of the spectacular **Cliff Palace** (Apr.-Oct. daily 9am-6pm) explore the largest cliff dwelling in North America, with over 150 preserved rooms, some of which are a few stories up and preserve plaster decorations in their interiors. The ticket-less can view the ruins only from an overlook along the road.

The impressive **Balcony House** is a 40-room dwelling 600 ft. above the floor of Soda Canyon; entrance requires climbing several ladders and squeezing through a tunnel. (Open mid-May to mid-Oct. daily 9am-5:30pm. Tickets required.) In addition, a few self-guided tours of sites are accessible from Chapin Mesa. **Spruce Tree House** is Mesa Verde's third-largest and most well-preserved cliff dwelling, and features a reconstructed *kiva*. This is the only dwelling open from November to March, when it is part of a free guided tour leaving from the museum. (Trail ½ mi. Open late May to early Sept. daily 8:30am-6:30pm, Apr.-May and Sept. to mid-Oct. 9am-6:30pm, mid-Oct. to early Nov. and Mar. 9am-5pm. Tours Nov.-Feb. daily 10am, 1, and 3:30pm.) About ½ mi. north of the museum on the road to Far View, the **Cedar Tree Tower** and **Farming Terraces Trail** (½ mi.) give a sense of what work was like on the mesa top. (Open daily 8am-sunset.) Three miles farther down the road and 2 mi. from the Visitors Center, the **Far View Sites** are comprised of five mesa-top villages. (Trail 0.8 mi. Open daily 8am-sunset.) A more low-key approach to Chapin Mesa is the self-guided **Mesa Top Loop Road,** passing a chronological progression of ruins from the 6th to the 13th century. (6 mi. Open daily 8am-sunset.)

The long drive out to Wetherill Mesa illustrates the various stages of regeneration occurring in the forest, which has suffered not only from the wild Pony Fire of 2000, but multiple other significant wildfires that have hit the area over the past century. From the ranger kiosk, 1½hr. tours of sprawling **Long House,** composed of 150 rooms and 21 *kivas*, include a tram ride that passes many sites. (Open late May to early Sept. daily 10am-5pm. Tickets required for tour but not for tram; ticket holders seated first when space is tight.) **Step House,** also located on Wetherill Mesa, features a well-preserved set of prehistoric stairs as well as pictographs. (Open late May to early Sept. daily 10am-5pm.) On both mesas, early morning visits tend to be less crowded and cooler.

▓ HIKING

In addition to the guided and self-guided tours, there are pleasant day hikes around the park, although none would challenge an experienced hiker. Most of these trails are much less frequented than the rest of the park and make for a nice respite from the crowds. Staying on established trails is critical to the preservation of Mesa Verde's archaeological remains.

The trails on Chapin Mesa require hikers to register at the Museum before setting out. **Petroglyph Point Trail** begins from the Spruce Tree House Trail and ends near the museum. This 2.8 mi. round-trip hike affords good views of the Spruce and Navajo canyons as well as a few petroglyphs. **Spruce Canyon Trail** begins from the Spruce Tree House Trail and ends at the Chapin Mesa picnic area. This 2.1 mi. hike follows the bottom of Spruce Canyon before climbing to the mesa top, giving hikers the chance to experience the range of Mesa Verde environments.

None of the three trails leading from Morefield Campground requires registering. **Prater Ridge Trail,** by far the most challenging in the park, begins and ends at the western side of the Morefield Campground. The 7.8 mile trail, composed of two loops (2.5 and 4 mi.) which can be done independently of each other for a shorter hike, climbs the east side of Prater Ridge through a few different types of vegetation and on a clear day provides incredible views of Montezuma Valley to the west and the La Platas to the east. Mule deer and birds flourish on Prater Ridge despite the scorched appearance of the trees charred in the Bircher Fire of 2000. **Knife Edge Trail** begins in the northwest corner of Morefield Campground and ends back at its start. A 3 mi. round-trip, this hike follows an old road along the front of the mesa and affords striking views of Montezuma Valley, particularly around sunset. **Point Lookout Trail** begins and ends at the parking lot in the northern tip of Morefield Campground. This 2.3 mi. hike, which switchbacks up the side of Point Lookout and offers good views of the Montezuma and Mancos Valleys, is a great spot to watch the sunrise or sunset.

HOVENWEEP NATIONAL MONUMENT ☎ 970

Hovenweep, from the Ute meaning "deserted valley," was aptly named by pioneer photographer William Jackson in 1874, and today it remains one of the emptiest regions in the US. Those who have made the trip to this strip of land spanning the border between Utah and Colorado since its founding in 1923 have relished the chance to explore the six groups of Pueblo ruins, dating back more than 1000 years, that still lean from canyon tops around the monument.

COLORADO

■ ▪ **ORIENTATION & PRACTICAL INFORMATION.** Desolate roads usher visitors to Hovenweep. From Utah or Arizona, follow U.S. 191 to its junction with Rte. 262 E (14 mi. south of Blanding, 11 mi. north of Bluff). After about 30 mi., watch for signs to the monument. From Cortez, CO (p. 354), go south on U.S. 160/491 to G Rd.; follow the signs to Hovenweep. The **Visitors Center** is accessible from both the Utah and Colorado sides. (☎562-4282. Open daily 8am-6pm, off-season 8am-5pm. $3 per person, $6 per car; National Parks Passes accepted.) There is no gasoline or food at the monument. Aneth, 20 mi. south, is the closest spot for these amenities. The **Hovenweep Campground ❶,** a few hundred yards after the Visitors Center, offers 30 scenic sites ($10) with shaded picnic tables. Water and toilets are available, but not hookups or showers. Campers must carry out trash.

▪ **OUTDOOR ACTIVITIES.** The most well-preserved and expansive remains, Square Tower Ruins, lie footsteps away from the Visitors Center. The 2 mi. round-trip Square Tower Loop Trail winds around Little Ruin Canyon, accessing Hovenweep Castle and the Twin Towers. A short spur trail, the ½ mile Tower Point Loop, accesses the ruins of a tower perched over the canyon. Both of these walks are relatively easy and give a good sense of the Pueblo ruins in a short amount of time. The canyon overlook is wheelchair friendly. For the more archaeologically inclined or those looking for a more serious hike, the outlying sites—Holly (8 mi. round-trip), Horseshoe & Hackberry, (10.6 mi. round-trip), and Cutthroat Castle (1.6 mi., in Colorado)—are isolated and provide more of a challenge to reach. A 4 mi. canyon-bottom trail runs one-way between the campground and the Holly ruins. All sites are accessible via dirt roads; a high-clearance four-wheel-drive vehicle is highly recommended. Directions to the outlying sites are provided at the Visitors Center. No biking is allowed anywhere on trails, but the monument's flat desert location makes hiking the premiere way to view the ruins.

PAGOSA SPRINGS ☎970

The Ute people called this spot *pah-gosa* (meaning "water" and "boiling"), believing that the springs were a gift from a divine source sent to heal them. Now the healing qualities of the mineral waters attract thousands of visitors from around the world each year. Pagosa Springs (pop. 1900), some of the world's hottest and largest, bubble from the San Juan Mountains 60 mi. east of Durango on Rte. 160. At the same time, the mountains, rivers, and forests near town hold their own appeal, and Pagosa Springs makes a fine base for excursions into the Rockies.

■ ▪ **ORIENTATION & PRACTICAL INFORMATION.** Pagosa Springs lies just west of the junction of Hwy. 160 and Hwy. 84 on the banks of the San Juan River. **Hwy. 160** is the main thoroughfare through town. West of downtown, a series of strip malls line the highway for several miles. In the heart of town, **Hot Springs Boulevard** runs perpendicular to Hwy. 160. The nearest airport and bus station are in Durango. The **Mountain Express** bus line, used mostly by locals, provides transportation along the highway and throughout downtown. (☎264-2250. M-F about every 1½hr. 6:30am-7:50pm. $0.50.)

The **Pagosa Springs Area Chamber of Commerce,** 402 San Juan St., just off Hot Springs Blvd., provides info on accommodations, food, and sights. (☎264-2363 or 800-252-2204; www.pagosaspringschamber.com. Open M-F 8am-6pm, Sa-Su 9am-5pm May-Oct., Nov.-Apr. Sa-Su 10am-2pm.) The **San Juan Ranger Station,** 180 Pagosa St., informs outdoor adventurers of the area's options. (☎264-2268. Open M-F 7:30am-5:30pm, Sa 9am-12:30pm and 1-3pm.) **Juan's Mountain Sports,** 155 Hot Springs Blvd., has a selection of outdoor equipment and **rents bikes** at $15 for 4 hrs.

or $25 for a full day. (☎264-4730 or 800-955-0273. Open June-Sept. M-F 9am-6pm, Sa-Su 10am-4pm; Oct.-May daily 7:30am-6pm.) Services include: **emergency** (☎911); **Piedra Laundromat,** 120 Piedra Rd. (☎731-4000); **road conditions,** ☎264-5555; **weather,** ☎264-6397/0930; **City Market Pharmacy,** several miles west of downtown at 63 N. Pagosa Blvd. (☎731-6000; market open daily 6am-10pm; pharmacist M-F 9am-7pm, Sa 9am-6pm); **Mercy Home Health and Hospice,** 35 Mary Fisher Clinic (☎731-9190), near the City Market; free **Internet access** at the **Sisson Library,** 811 San Juan St. at the corner of 8th St. (☎264-2208; open M-W 8:30am-6pm, Th 8:30am-7:30pm, F 8:30am-5pm, Sa 9am-3pm); and the **post office:** 250 Hot Springs Blvd. (☎264-5440. Open M-F 7:30am-5:30pm, Sa 9am-2pm). **Postal code:** 81147.

▉▢ ACCOMMODATIONS & FOOD. Pinewood Inn ❸, 157 Pagosa St., four

blocks from downtown, rents 25 wood-paneled rooms with cable TVs and phones, several with kitchens. (☎264-5715 or 888-655-7463. Reception 7:30am-11pm. Check-in 2pm. Check-out 11am. Singles $38-58; doubles $48-80.) **East Fork Campground ❶,** East Fork Rd., is a quiet spot 11 mi. east of town offering many shaded, rarely crowded sites with toilets and water faucets. (☎264-2268. 14-night max. stay. Open May-Sept. $8 per vehicle.) For a stay nearer the hot springs, splurge at the **Springs Resort ❹,** 165 Hot Springs Blvd., centrally located and granting 24hr. access to the springs and a private area of the San Juan River. (☎264-4168 or 800-225-0934; www.pagosahotsprings.com. Basic rooms $77-119. Non-guests $12.)

Daylight Donuts & Cafe ❶, 2151 W. Hwy. 160, dishes out big portions of classic breakfast and lunch fare for just $3-5.50. (☎731-4050. Open daily 6am-2pm.) **Pagosa Baking Company ❶,** 238 Hwy. 160, carries regionally produced foods and European cheeses. Organic produce from nearby Chimney Rock and Enchanted Valley Organic Farms doesn't disappoint. Daily breakfast and lunch specials ($1-6) include quiche, salads, and sandwiches made with fresh European-style artesian breads. (☎264-9348. Open M and W-Sa 7:30am-5pm, Su 8:30am-5pm.) For fine dining along the banks of the San Juan River, **JJ's Upstream Restaurant ❹,** 356 E. Hwy. 160, sits five blocks east of downtown, proffering a selection of steaks, seafood, wild game, and vegetarian entrees for $15 and up. (☎264-9100. Open for dinner year-round Su-Th 4-9pm, F-Sa 4-9:30pm; lunch June-Sept. M-Sa 11am-2pm; year-round Su brunch 9am-2:30pm.) The **Bear Creek Saloon and Grille ❶,** just off of Hwy. 160 at 475 Lewis St., is open daily for lunch and dinner serving burgers ($5-6), sandwiches ($5-7), nachos ($7), and more. The bar stays open late, providing pool, ping-pong, arcade games, karaoke on Wednesday, and live music Friday and Saturday nights. (☎264-5611. Open daily 11am-2am. Happy hour M-F 5-7pm.)

▨▨ SIGHTS & OUTDOORS. Follow the sulfur smell to The Springs, 157 Hot

Springs Blvd., beside the Chamber of Commerce, where 15 outdoor pools ranging from 89° to 114°F "relax the body and refresh the spirit." (☎264-2284 or 800-225-0934. Open daily 7am-1am. $12 per person.) Across the street at **The Spa,** hot spring water is pumped into indoor mineral baths. Access to an outdoor pool and hot tub are included in admission. (☎264-5910 or 800-832-5523. Open M-F 1-10pm, Sa-Su 8am-10pm. Pool closed every other W for cleaning. $8.) **Chimney Rock Archaeological Area,** 17 mi. west of Pagosa Springs on Hwy. 160 and Rte. 151 S., is a National Historical Site containing the ruins of a high-mesa Ancestral Puebloan village, where over 200 undisturbed structures have been found in a 6 sq. mi. area. (☎883-5359; www.chimneyrockco.org. Open daily mid-May to late Sept. 9am-4pm. 2½hr. tours leave at 9:30am, 10:30am, 1pm, and 2pm. $5, ages 5-11 $2.)

There is plenty of **hiking** around Pagosa Springs as well as easy access to the **Continental Divide Trail** from Wolf Creek Pass and the Weminuche Wilderness for longer **backpacking** trips. Some good treks near town include the **Cimarrona Creek Trail,** northwest of Pagosa Springs near the Cimarrona Campground, the **Quartz**

Lake Trail, east of town off Hwy. 84, and the **Anderson Trail,** which skirts Pagosa Peak north of town and includes the shorter trek to **Fourmile Falls.** Visit the **ranger station,** 180 Pagosa St. (☎264-2268), for more info, or pick up a guide to area hikes at the Chamber of Commerce office.

Excellent **mountain bike** trails criss-cross the area. You can begin **Willow Draw** (18 mi. loop) anywhere in downtown Pagosa Springs. From Hwy. 160, head south on Hwy. 84 to Mill Creek Rd. and follow the doubletrack dirt road across Mill Creek after the third cattleguard. This intermediate ride offers a sense of seclusion close to town. (700 ft. elevation gain. Recommended June-Oct.) To get to **Chris Mountain Trail** (8 mi. round-trip), turn north on Piedra Rd. from Hwy. 160, follow it for about 6 mi., turn left on FS 629 and follow it 4.5 mi. north through the woods to the "Steep and Narrow Road" sign. This doubletrack ascent's variety of challenging terrains tests technical skills. (800 ft. elevation gain. Recommended June-Sept.)

Wolf Creek Ski Area, 20 mi. east of Pagosa, claims to have the most snow in Colorado, and offers ample access to glades and bowls. Six lifts service over 1500 acres and 1600 ft. of vertical drop. (☎264-5639 or 800-754-9653; www.wolfcreekski.com. Adult full-day lift ticket $42, rental $13.)

WEST CENTRAL PLATEAU

After spending days marveling at the Front Range of the Rockies, many tourists access I-70 and propel themselves west at dizzying speeds, bypassing all of western Colorado and taking in only fleeting, auto-glass-distorted vistas. Paying homage to Grand Junction's self-proclaimed centrality, these road warriors might purchase a night's lodging before continuing west to Moab, Salt Lake City, southern Utah, or the Grand Canyon, but they don't know what they're missing. Featuring two spectacular canyons, a heavily forested mesa with beautiful lakes and campgrounds, and a city with budget lodgings and diverse food options, West Central Plateau merits a couple of days for exploring its little-known attractions.

GRAND JUNCTION   ☎970

Grand Junction gets its name from its seat at the junction of the Colorado and Gunnison Rivers and the nexus of the Río Grande and Denver Railroads. Today, the name aptly describes Grand Junction's role as a transportation hub for the masses heading to southern Utah and the Colorado Rockies. While the city doesn't have the reputation of some Colorado hot spots, its unique mix of cowboys and computers makes it worth a closer look if you've got the time to spare.

⬛ TRANSPORTATION

Flights: Walker Field Airport, 2828 Walker Field Dr. (☎244-9100), is the biggest airport in Western Colorado. Major airlines all fly to nearby hubs including **Salt Lake City, Phoenix,** and **Denver.**

Trains: Amtrak, 339 S. 1st St. (☎241-2733), heads daily to **Denver** (8hr., $49-85) and **Salt Lake City** (7hr., $45-77).

Buses: Greyhound, 230 S. 5th St. (☎242-6012), runs to: **Denver** (5½hr., 5 per day, $35-37); **Durango** (5hr., 1 per day, $35-37); **Las Vegas** (11hr., 3 per day, $65-69); and **Salt Lake City** (6hr., 1 per day, $46-49). **Grand Valley Transit** offers buses throughout the area. (☎256-7433. M-F 5:45am-7:15pm, Su 8:45am-6:15pm. $0.50.)

Taxis: Sunshine Taxi (☎245-8294).

Car Rental: All the usual car rental suspects are at the airport, including **Thrifty** (☎243-6626) and **Budget** (☎244-9155).

✈ ⚡ ORIENTATION & PRACTICAL INFORMATION

Grand Junction lies on the Colorado River near I-70, which runs northwest to Fruita (13 mi.) before crossing the Utah border and cutting southwest towards Moab (114 mi., 2hr. driving). Montrose lies 62 mi. to the southwest on Hwy 50. In town, streets run north-south, increasing in number from east to west, and avenues run east-west.

Visitor Info: The **Grand Junction Visitors Bureau**, 740 Horizon Dr. (☎244-1480, 800-962-2547), exit 31 off I-70, behind the Taco Bell, supplies high-quality city maps and allows visitors to check email briefly free of charge. Open May-Sept. daily 8:30am-8pm; Oct.-Apr. 8:30am-5pm. For **outdoor info** head to the **Bureau of Land Management**, 2815 H. Rd. (☎244-3000. Open M-F 7:30am-4:30pm.)

Outdoor Equipment: REI, 644 North Ave. (☎254-8970). Open M-F 10am-8pm, Sa 10am-6pm, Su 11am-5pm.

Laundromat: Holiday Cleaners Laundromat, 1251 N. 3rd St. (☎241-2594). Open daily 7:30am-11pm, last load 10pm.

Emergency: ☎911. **Police:** 625 Ute Ave. (☎242-6707).

Weather conditions: ☎243-0914. **Road conditions:** ☎245-8800.

Hospital: Community Hospital: 2021 N. 12th St. (☎242-0920).

Library and Internet Access: Mesa County Library, 530 Grand Ave. (☎243-4442). Open M-Th 9am-9pm, F-Sa 9am-5pm; Sept.-May also open Su 1-5pm.

Post office: 241 N. 4th St. (☎244-3400). Open M-F 7:45am-5:15pm, Sa 10am-1:30pm. **Postal code:** 81501.

⚑ ACCOMMODATIONS

If the relatively inexpensive options below are still too steep, camping is available at **Fruita State Park ❶,** 10 mi. west of downtown, off exit 19 from I-70, has 80 sites with showers and hookups (☎800-678-2267; $10-16; entrance fee $4 per day), at **Colorado National Monument** (p. 366), and also at the BLM's free **Rabbit Valley Campground ❶,** west of Fruita near I-70 (no water or facilities).

Hotel Melrose, 337 Colorado Ave. (☎242-9636, 800-430-4555; www.hotelmelrose.com), between 3rd and 4th St. Historic hotel beds travelers in the heart of the city. In addition to dorms, there are meticulously decorated private rooms. Reception 9am-1pm and 4-10pm; call if your arrival time is different. Check-out 11am. Dorms $20; singles $35, with private bath $50; doubles from $65. Reduced rates off-season. ❶

Daniel's Motel, 333 North Ave. (☎243-1084). Rents clean rooms, some including kitchenettes, within close driving distance of the downtown area. Check-out 10am. Singles $30-45, doubles $45-55. ❷

Two Rivers Inn, 141 N. 1st St. (☎245-8585), three blocks from downtown. 42 double-queen rooms, an outdoor pool, and a jacuzzi. Check-out 11am. $45-75 depending number of guests. ❸

◖ FOOD

For natural foods and a deli of organic, vegetarian, and vegan foods, **Sundrop Grocery and Garden Deli,** 321 Rood Ave., meets your needs. (☎243-1175. Open 9am-7pm M-Sa.) Thursday nights (4:30-8pm) in the summer see several blocks of downtown transformed into the **Farmer's Market Festival** (☎245-9697), complete with local produce, live music, and extended Main St. restaurant hours.

BETWEEN A ROCK
& A HARD PLACE

One day in late April of 2003, Colorado outdoorsman Aron Ralston, 27, biked and hiked his way to Canyonlands' Blue John Canyon for a little solo canyoneering. As he was descending into the 3 ft. wide, 100 ft. tall slot canyon, an 800 lb. boulder unexpectedly shifted. Ralston tried to get out of the way, but to no avail: his right arm was pinned.

He rationed the water and burritos he'd brought and hoped someone would happen by. After three days he ran out of water. By the fifth day, he'd run out options. His attempt to rig a pulley system to budge the rock had failed. His location inside the narrow, twisty canyon was so obscure that he didn't think searchers would ever find his body after he'd expired.

Desperate times called for desperate measures: Ralston then took out his pocket knife, broke two bones in his wrist, and cut off his arm beneath the elbow. He applied a pre-prepared tourniquet to stanch the bleeding, dropped down to the canyon floor, and stumbled out for safety. On his way out, he met three hikers who gave him food and helped him carry his pack. A little later a Utah Public Safety helicopter spotted the group, and the amazingly composed Ralston was flown to safety. His survival flabbergasted the world. He later would tell CNN, "I thought a lot about margaritas while I was out there."

Ying Thai, 757 U.S. 50 (☎245-4866), south of downtown. The best Thai for hundreds of miles in a homey setting. Lunch runs $6, while dinner goes for $9-15. Open Tu-F 11am-2pm and 5-9pm, Sa 5-9pm. ❷

Crystal Cafe, 314 Main St. (☎242-8843). Massive, mouth-watering breakfasts ($4-8) are the specialty here, but the hot lunches ($5.50-7) and decadent baked goods don't fall short either. Open M-F 7am-1:45pm (bakery until 3pm), Sa 8am-noon. ❶

Il Bistro Italiano, 400 Main St. (☎243-8622). This bistro tempts the palate with fresh, homemade pastas and breads. An attentive waitstaff, Italian music, and a candlelit dining room add up to a luxurious feel. Entrees $12-20. Open T-Su 11am-10pm. ❸

📻 NIGHTLIFE

A few cold brews and some gregarious social interaction are just what the doctor ordered after the jars and jolts of a day spent on the mountain bike trails. The presence of Mesa State College lends Grand Junction's nightlife scene a youthful enthusiasm, and weekend nights see local bars packed.

Rockslide Restaurant and Brew Pub, 401 S. Main St. (☎245-2111). Rockslide joins the avalanche of microbreweries blanketing the nation and serves as a town nightlife fixture. The Big Bear Stout comes in a half-gallon growler for $8.50. Half-price appetizers M-F 4-6pm. Open daily 10am-midnight.

The Sports Page, 103 N. 1st St. (☎241-4010). A typical sports bar with TVs and jerseys on the walls. F Afternoon Club (5-8pm) offers $1 pints and half-price appetizers. Happy Hour M-F 4-6pm and 10pm-midnight. W night local bands. F-Sa nights live band or DJ. Open M-Th 4pm-midnight, F-Sa 4pm-2am, Su 4-11pm.

The Mesa Theater, 538 Main St. (☎241-1717; www.mesatheater.com). Set in a converted theater, this dance club and concert venue features live music during summer weekends. W is under-21, Th college night with a DJ spinning R&B. Cover Th $6, concert tickets $12-50. Open W 8-11:30pm, Th 9pm-2am, F-Sa 8pm-1am, Su times vary.

Boomers, 436 Main St. (☎248-9022). Live blues and jazz on weekends, and dance-crazed Th nights alternate between salsa and swing lessons. Cover $3-10. Open F-Sa 11-2am, Tu-Th and Su 11am-midnight.

🏔 OUTDOOR ACTIVITIES

The Grand Junction area has a smorgasbord of outdoor activities close to town and even more within an hour's drive. Biking, hiking, river running, hunting, and fishing guides can be hired through **Fruita Outdoor Adventures** (☎260-5848). Expert climbing instructors and guides and rescue training courses are available at **Natural Progression Rock Guides** (☎434-8213, 877-434-8213; www.naturalprogression.com) or **Desert Crags and Cracks** (☎245-8513; www.desertcrags.com).

HIKING

The best **hiking** around Grand Junction awaits in the **Colorado Canyons National Conservation Area** just west of the Colorado National Monument. Pollock, Rattlesnake and Knowles Canyons all feature beautiful hikes. *(To find the Pollock Bench trailhead, take I-70 to exit 19 and head south 1.3 miles to Kings View Estates subdivision.)* Follow the Kings View Rd. west and look for signs to the trailhead. The trailhead for **Rattlesnake Arches Trail,** which provides views of many spectacular arches, is accessible from within Colorado National Monument. *(From the western entrance, drive 11 mi. along Rim Rock Drive to the sign for Glade Park. Just beyond this sign, turn right at Black Ridge Hunter Access Rd. Follow this road 14 mi. to the trailhead. High-clearance vehicles are recommended, and closures occur during winter.)*

East of Grand Junction, the Bookcliffs overlook the town. The **Mt. Garfield Trail** is a great option for a short hike to amazing views of this other-worldly rockscape. The hike gains 2000 ft. over 1.5 mi., taking about 1¼hr. up and 45min. down, and sometimes wild horse are visible from the top during winter and early spring. *(To reach the trailhead, take exit 42 from I-70 and travel south on 37 Three-tenths Rd. to G Seventenths Rd. Take a right and go west just under 2 mi. to 35 Five-tenths Rd. Turn right and cross I-70 to the trailhead.)* Maps of both Mt. Garfield and the Colorado Canyons National Conservation Area await at the BLM office (p. 363).

MOUNTAIN BIKING

A bevy of **mountain bike** shops offer advice and rent bikes. Downtown, **Ruby Canyon Cycles,** 301 Main St., is a full-service bike shop with full-day rentals of hard-tail bikes *($25 per day, $7 per hr.; $15 minimum)* and full-suspension *($35 per day, $8 per hr.; $15 minimum)*. Discounts apply for multi-day rentals. *(☎241-0141. Open M-F 9am-6pm, Sa 9am-5pm).* Out toward the Visitors Center on North Ave., **Board and Buckle Ski and Cyclery,** 2822 North Ave., rents mountain and road bikes at $25 per day. *(☎242-9285. Open summer M-F 9am-6pm, Sa 9am-5pm. Winter ski rentals 7am-7pm behind the back door if main store isn't open).*

There are three main trail areas that draw mountain bikers around Grand Junction: the Kokopelli area, the 18-Mile Rd. area, and the Tabeguache area. The Kokopelli area is a series of loops that tie into the first 5 mi. of the famous **Kokopelli Trail,** which stretches 143 mi. west to Moab, UT. *(To access Kokopelli, take exit 15 (Loma) west of Fruita 4 mi. Cross the highway to the south and proceed 1.5 mi. to Frontage Rd.; the trailhead sits ½ mile down the road.)* The excellent *Loops Map,* put out by the **Colorado Plateau Mountain Bike Trails Association (COPMOBA),** is available at the BLM office on Horizon Rd. near the airport.

In the **18-mile Road** area north of Fruita, popular trails include **Zippity, Primecut,** and **Joe's Ridge;** bike shops carry the excellent *Fruita Fat Tire Guide.* *(To get to this trail system, take exit 19 for Fruita off westbound I-70. Drive north into town and take a right on Aspen St. to N. Maple. Take a left and head north, following the same road as it turns into 17½ Rd. Turn right on N. Three-tenths Rd. and travel east .5 mi. to 18-mile Rd. Take a left and head north just over 2 mi. to the end of the pavement. Bathrooms and a kiosk are at the parking lot.)*

The **Tabeguache** area's trails connect to the first miles of the **Tabeguache Trail,** which runs 142 mi. from Grand Junction to Montrose and overlooks Unaweep Canyon in the early miles of the journey. **Andy's Loop** (6.6 mi.), the **Gunny Loop** (10.3 mi.), and **The Ribbon** (12.8 mi.) all leave from the parking lot on Monument Rd. *(To reach these strenuous rides, take exit 26 off I-70 and follow U.S. 6/50 to Broadway/Rte. 340 over the river to Monument Road. Turn left and continue 2.2 mi. to the parking area on the left.)*

COLORADO

COLORADO NATIONAL MONUMENT ☎970

Sitting on the outskirts of Grand Junction, Colorado National Monument is a 32 sq. mi. sculpture of steep cliff faces, canyon walls, and obelisk-like spires wrought by the forces of gravity, wind, and water. The monument serves as a playground for climbers, bikers, and hikers from the local area, and an appetite-whetting experience for travelers en route to the more thrilling destinations of Arches, Canyonlands, or the Rockies. The monument was established in 1911, largely due to the efforts and antics of one man, John Otto, who blazed most of the trails used today and badgered the government to protect this dreamworld of rock.

■ ▮ ORIENTATION & PRACTICAL INFORMATION. A car or bike is essential for exploring Colorado National Monument. Entrances lie at the east end, 5 mi. from Grand Junction on Monument Rd., and along Rte. 340 on the west end near Fruita (exit 19 off I-70). The 23 mi. **Rim Rock Drive** runs along the edge of red canyons across the mesa top between the two entrances, providing views of awe-inspiring rock monoliths, the Book Cliffs, Grand Mesa, and the city of Grand Junction. Check in at the monument's headquarters and **Visitors Center**, 4 mi. east of the western entrance, for info about ranger-led programs and a general orientation. (☎858-3617. Open June-early Sept. daily 8am-6pm; early Sept.-May 9am-5pm. Entrance fee $5 per vehicle, $3 per cyclist or hiker.) Both **Fruita** and **Grand Junction** (p. 362) provide a full range of services including equipment outfitters, ATMs, grocery stores, medical services, and post offices. For **weather and road conditions**, call ☎245-8800. **Water** is available at the Visitors Center, Saddlehorn Campground, and Devils Kitchen Picnic Area, near the eastern entrance.

▮ CAMPING. Saddlehorn Campground ❶, 0.5 mi. north of the Visitors Center, offers 50 beautiful sites on the mesa's edge and almost never fills up. Sites include tables and grills, and the nearby amphitheater hosts summertime ranger programs nightly. (☎858-3617. Water and bathrooms, but no showers. Open year-round. $10.) **Backcountry camping** is free and allowed anywhere over 0.25 mi. from roads and 100 yds. from trails. A **required permit** is available at the Visitors Center.

▨ HIKING. Although Rim Rock Dr. provides breathtaking views, the trails that criss-cross the monument are the only way to fully appreciate the scope and scale of this canyon country. Unlike some of the parks in the Southwest, the monument allows off-trail backcountry hiking for those travelers tired of roads and crowds.

For those with limited time in the park, there are a number of short walks that whisk hikers away from the road and immerse them in the terrain. The ½ mile round-trip **Window Rock Trail** leaves from a trailhead on the campground road and offers expansive vistas through piñon-juniper woodland over the Grand Valley, and views of Monument Canyon, Wedding Canyon, and many of the monument's major rock formations. The 1.5 mi. **Devil's Kitchen Trail** begins off the park drive just past the east entrance, and drops into No Thoroughfare Canyon and Devils Kitchen, a natural grotto surrounded by enormous upright boulders.

There are a number of options for longer hikes in the monument. Most of these trails are fairly primitive and marked with cairns. The **Serpents' Trail** follows "the Crookedest Road in the World," so named when it served as part of the main road to the high country during the first half of the 20th century. The moderately difficult 1.3 mi. route climbs more than 50 switchbacks from the trailhead, just beyond the Devil's Kitchen Picnic Area, before rejoining Rim Rock Dr. just north of the tunnel. (1000 ft. elevation change. 1.3 mi. with shuttle, 2.5 mi. round-trip.) The moderately strenuous 6 mi. **Monument Canyon Trail** is one of the park's most popular because it allows hikers to view many of the eerie, skeletal rock formations up close. The trail descends 600 ft. from the mesa top to the canyon floor and then wanders amid the giant rocks, including Independence Monument, Kissing Couple, and the Coke Ovens, until it emerges on Rte. 340 (Broadway/Redlands Rd.). A two-car shuttle conveniently allows for the trail to be done in one direction (downhill), but round-trip hikers enjoy the formations from multiple angles and can turn around whenever they fancy (ranging between 6 and 12 mi.) Find the trailhead along Rim Rock Drive, southwest of the Monument Canyon View. The **No Thoroughfare Trail** begins near Devil's Kitchen and follows the Devil's Kitchen Trail at its start. This strenuous 17 mi. out-and-back route accesses the most remote portion of the monument as it follows the streambed that cut No Thoroughfare Canyon and features several waterfalls during spring run-off. No Thoroughfare provides some of the monument's best shaded hiking and makes for a good overnight trip.

⚑ OUTDOOR ACTIVITIES. Amazing vistas await rock climbers visiting Colorado National Monument. The greatest attraction in the area is the 500 ft. **Independence Monument.** Routes on this massive tower accommodate all ability levels, including beginners. **Otto's Route** (5.9) is a popular beginner route, involving five pitches and a scramble.

UNAWEEP CANYON

The spectacular **Unaweep/Tabeguache Scenic and Historic Byway** winds its way 133 mi. through the heart of the Uncompahgre Plateau and some of the most varied terrain in Colorado. This drive follows Rte. 141 and 145 in the extreme western part of the state from **Whitewater** in the north (near Grand Junction) to **Placerville** on the San Juan Skyway in the south. Following the red rock canyons of the Dolores and San Miguel Rivers, the road passes the remains of prehistoric Native American cultures and long abandoned mining operations.

One of the most striking sections of this drive is its northern end, as the highway passes beneath the towering gray cliffs of the canyon. The streams that eroded the canyon cut through typical Colorado Plateau sedimentary layers to expose underlying igneous and metamorphic rocks. Additionally, Unaweep is the only canyon in the world with a divide in the middle and streams running out of both ends.

The canyon is as much a dream for **rock climbers** as it is for geologists, but unlike many choice climbing locales across the nation, Unaweep is virtually unknown among all but local climbers. Twenty-five miles of beautiful granite make up the walls of the canyon, whose crags, boulders, and cracks tempt novices and pros alike. There are routes of every level of difficulty, rating from 5.5 to 5.13, and of every length, from one-move bouldering problems to multi-pitch spine-tinglers. About 37 mi. of the northwestern wall of the canyon is climbable. Unfortunately, much of the area is private property, making access complicated or impossible. One sure bet is **Sunday Wall,** a popular section that rises 500 ft. in places. There is a pull-out on the right-hand side of the road 2.2 mi. from Divide Rd.; approximately 11 mi. from Whitewater, begin looking carefully for a sign on the right side and a small staircase that crosses a barbed-wire fence. Sunday Wall offers some quality crack climbing and a range of sport routes from 5.6-5.11. Local shops carry K.C. Baum's *Grand Junction Rock* and can be used to find more out-of-the-way areas.

The opportunities for outdoor recreation don't end with climbing, however; possibilities for **hiking, backpacking, and mountain biking** on BLM land and in the **Uncompahgre National Forest** abound. **Divide Road** (USFS), which leaves the northern section of the byway and traverses the Uncompahgre Plateau, accesses hiking and biking trails, and some choice sites for free **primitive camping,** such as **Dominguez ❶** (5 sites, vault toilets) and **Divide Fork ❶** (8 sites, potable water and vault toilets). There are no marked trails, and the BLM urges users to stay on pre-

COLORADO

existing trails, mostly created by ATV and motorcycle use. Passenger cars can navigate the early miles, but high-clearance, four-wheel-drive vehicles are recommended for most of this alternative route across the plateau.

The byway may be driven in 3-5hr., depending on stops made along the way, and is a good alternate route between Grand Junction and points south, particularly for travelers headed to **Telluride** (p. 344), **Cortez** (p. 354), and **Durango** (p. 333). The northern end of the byway is about 15 mi. south of Grand Junction off U.S. 50. The southern end of the byway leaves Rte. 62 in Placerville. For more info, contact the Bureau of Land Management, 2815 H Rd., Grand Junction, CO 81506 (☎ 244-3000) or the U.S. Forest Service, Main St., Norwood, CO 81423 (☎ 327-4261).

GRAND MESA

Covered in a coat of aspen and spruce, the largest flattop mountain in the world rises over 6000 ft. from the floor of Grand Valley with such grandeur and might that it seems like the Rockies' final proclamation against the flat, barren deserts to the west. Formed over millions of years by lava flows, glaciers, and the erosional forces of the Gunnison and Colorado Rivers, Grand Mesa today is sanctuary to a variety of plants and animals that thrive in a remote landscape of alpine forests, lakes, and lively streams. Outdoor nuts also find the area hospitable to hiking, biking, skiing, and fishing in the over 200 lakes that sparkle across the mesa.

The most popular hiking trail up on mesa is the **Crag Crest Trail** (10 mi.). The trail traverses Craig Crest for 6.5 mi. and provides stunning views of the surrounding area, including the Bookcliffs to the north, the Uncompahgre Plateau and the La Sal mountains to the west, and the San Juan and Elk Mountains to the east and south. The trail is accessible from two different trailheads: the east trailhead, approximately 4 mi. up Hwy. 121 from its junction with Hwy. 65; and the west trailhead, 1 mi. northwest of the **Grand Mesa Visitors Center.** The loop portion (an additional 3.4 mi.) allows for hikers to return to their starting point at a lower elevation. A car shuttle along Hwys. 65 and 121 is also an option. Good **trout fishing** can be found in most of the lakes atop the Mesa—consult *Fishing the Grand Mesa*, available at the Visitors Center and various lodges on the Mesa.

Powderhorn Ski Resort, 35 mi. east of Grand Junction on Grand Mesa, is small by Colorado standards but offers good deals and a less crowded alternative to some of its glitzier neighbors. The mountain has four lifts accessing 510 acres of terrain, 80% intermediate or higher, with a base elevation of 8200 ft. and a summit of 9850 ft., yielding 1650 ft. of vertical drop. Although the season only runs from December to March, Powderhorn receives over 250 in. of powder annually. (☎ 268-5700. Open Dec.-Mar. daily 9am-4pm. Ski rentals $15, snowboards $25. Full-day lift tickets $38, college students $31, ages 55-69 and 7-18 $28, over 70 $5, and under 6 free.)

The **Grand Mesa Scenic Byway (Route 65)** traverses 63 mi. between I-70 in the north and Cedaredge in the south, climbing to over 10,000 ft. before winding across the mesa top. Overlooking Ward Lake on Hwy. 65, the **Grand Mesa Visitors Center,** 40 mi. from I-70, supplies a wealth of information on outdoor activities. (☎ 856-4153. Open late May to mid-Oct. 9am-5pm.) A number of forest service campgrounds dot the landscape at heights between 8500 and 10,300 ft., providing a cool, shady escape from the heat down below. **Ward Lake ❶, Little Bear ❶,** and **Cobbett Lake ❶** sit beside the highway in shady groves and provide quiet sites amenable to tent campers looking for a base of exploration or a relaxing night's rest. (☎ 877-444-6777. 14-night max. stay. $12 per night. 60% reservations at Cobbett.) Bring groceries, or sit down to home-cooked meals at **Spruce Lodge Resort and Restaurant ❸** on Forest Service Road 121 near the Visitors Center, where cabins that sleep up to 6 are available for $100-170 per night, winter $85-159. (☎ 856-6240. Open 9am-9pm. Breakfast and lunch $5-8, dinner $9-17.) On a clear day, astounding views surround **Land's End Overlook** at the end of a 12 mi. spur road off the byway. Panoramas of hundreds of miles of terrain, including the San Juan Mountains to the south and Utah's canyon country to the west, turn jaws slack.

BLACK CANYON ☎970

Native American parents used to tell their children that the light-colored strands of rock streaking through the walls of the Black Canyon were hairs of a blond woman—if they got too close to the edge they would get tangled in it and fall. The edge of Black Canyon of the Gunnison National Park is indeed a staggering place, literally: watch for trembling knees. Over time, the Gunnison River slowly carved the 53-mile canyon, crafting a steep 2500-ft. gorge that can claim the greatest combination of depth, steepness, and narrowness of any canyon in North America. It wasn't until 1901 that a pair of brave souls on an air mattress explored Black Canyon. The Empire State Building, if placed at the bottom of the river, would barely reach halfway up the canyon walls. Christened by President Clinton in the fall of 1999, Black Canyon, the nation's youngest national park, has seen more tourists over the last few years, but it is still possible to enjoy the terrain in solitude, especially for those willing to get on hands and knees and explore the inner canyon.

◪ **PRACTICAL INFORMATION.** The Black Canyon lies 15 mi. east of the town of **Montrose.** The **South Rim** is easily accessible by a 6 mi. drive off U.S. 50 at the end of Hwy. 347 ($7 per car, $4 walk-in or motorcycle; National Parks Passes accepted); the wilder **North Rim** can only be reached by an 80 mi. detour around the canyon followed by a gravel road from Crawford off Rte. 92. This road is closed in winter. **Greyhound** (☎249-6673) shuttles once a day between Montrose and the **Gunnison County Airport,** 711 Río Grande (☎641-0060), and will drop you off on U.S. 50, 6 mi. from the canyon ($12). **Gisdho Shuttles** conducts tours of the Black Canyon and Grand Mesa from Grand Junction. (☎800-430-4555. 10-11hr. May-Oct. W and Sa. $39 including entrance fees.) A **Visitors Center** sits on the South Rim full of information on history, geology, and hiking. Free **permits** for inner-canyon treks can be filled out here. (☎249-1914, ext. 23. Open May-Oct. daily 8am-6pm, Nov.-Apr. 8:30am-4pm.) **Water** is available here and at the campgrounds. The **North Rim Ranger Station** also provides **permits** and advice. (Open sporadically.) Most services are in Montrose. Montrose **Visitors Center** (☎249-1726. Located at the Ute Indian Museum, at the corner of Chipeta Rd. and Hwy. 550. Open M-Sa 9am-4:30pm and Su 11am-4:30 between May 15 and Oct. 31st.) **Cimarron Creek,** 317 E. Main St., caters to your backcountry equipment and guiding needs. (☎249-0408. Open M-F 9am-6:00pm, Sa 9am-5pm.) Other services include: **weather and road conditions,** (☎249-9363); **police,** 435 S. 1st St. (☎252-5200); **crisis line** (☎626-3777); **Montrose Memorial Hospital,** 800 S. 3rd St. (☎249-2211); **laundry** at Highlander Laundry, 1347 E. Main St. (☎249-1741); public **showers** and laundry can be found at the Hanging Tree RV Park, 17250 Hwy. 550, across from the Ute Indian Museum/Visitor's Center (☎249-9966, showers $5); free **Internet access** at Montrose Public Library, 320 S. 2nd St. (☎249-9656. Open M-Th 10am-8pm, F 10am-6pm, Sa 10am-5pm.); Community First National Bank, 401 Main St., has the most central **24hr. ATM; Post office:** 321 S. 1st St. (☎249-6654. Open M-F 8am-5pm, Sa 10am-noon.) **Postal code:** 81401.

◪◪ **ACCOMMODATIONS & FOOD.** At the canyon, the **South Rim Campground** has 102 well-designed sites with pit toilets, charcoal grills, water, and some with paved wheelchair access. (Tent sites $10, full hookup $15.) The **North Rim Campground,** ¼ mi. past the ranger station, rarely fills and is popular with climbers. (13 sites. Water and toilets. $10.) If you're feeling adventuresome, turn right from the

COLORADO

LIKE A CHICKEN WITH ITS HEAD CUT OFF

Clutching the bird in one hand, the farmer in faded dungarees picks up the wood handle of the gleaming axe. He holds the chicken firmly against the worn chopping block and with one clean, smooth motion, brings the blade slicing down across the rough, golden skin of its scrawny neck. Blood spurts across his bare forearm as he releases the mass of twitching feathers and flailing feet. In a second, the beast is on its feet and races around the farmyard—for two years! When Mike, **The Headless Chicken,** was beheaded in Fruita, Colorado, sometime in the middle of the last century, things didn't go exactly as planned. Rather than falling to the ground, dead as a doornail after a run-in with a farmer's axe, Mike managed to survive for more than two years. His amazed owners fed him with a medicine dropper and Mike toured the country to rave reviews. Today all that remains of Mike's legend are the tales told by Fruita old-timers and a piece of sculpture in downtown Fruita, depicting the illustrious Mike in full stride.

entrance to the South Rim park and head down the 16% grade of E. Portal Rd. to find approximately 16 tent sites at the base of the canyon. (Water, toilets, grills; full hookup not available. $10.) Half-way down there are pull-offs to rest weary brakes. In the canyon, unimproved campsites are dispersed along a beach beside the river. Eleven additional hike-in only campsites are available in the **Gunnison Gorge National Conservation Area** northwest of Montrose. (☎240-5300, Bureau of Land Management. $5 for day-use of the gorge and $10 to camp, maximum 2 night stay.) Visitors register and pay at the trailheads. (See **Fly fishing**, p. 371, for driving directions and trail details.)

In town, many inexpensive motels line E. Main St./U.S. 50 east of downtown Montrose. At **Western Motel ❸,** 1200 E. Main St., a pool, hot tub, and continental breakfast make the clean, basic rooms a deal. (☎249-3481 or 800-445-7301. Reception 24hr. Check-out 10am. Singles from $50 in summer, $35 in winter; doubles and family units available.) The prices at **Traveler's B&B Inn ❷,** 502 S. 1st St., can't be topped in Montrose, although despite the name, no breakfast is served. (☎249-3472. Singles $34, with private bath $34-36; doubles $42.) The historic **Lathrop House Bed and Breakfast ❺,** 718 E. Main Street, offers comfortable, elegant rooms themed after the family that originally owned the house. Full breakfast served, along with wine and cheese in the evenings. (☎240-6075. Singles $89, doubles $99, private suite with kitchen available).

For tasty sandwiches ($5) and delightful omelettes ($6), head to the **Daily Bread Bakery and Cafe ❶,** 346 Main St. (☎249-8444. Open M-Sa 6am-3pm.) **Camp Robber Cafe ❸,** 228 Main St., caters to locals with its southwestern flare. Try the specialty Green Chile Pistachio Crusted Pork Medallions at $16.50 or the Grilled Chicken Cilantro Quesadilla for about $9. (☎240-1590. Open T-Sa 11am-3pm and 5-9pm, Sun 9am-2pm.) **Nay-Mex Tacos ❶,** 489 W. Main St., serves up tasty Mexican cuisine that's easy on the wallet. (Open M-F 11am-9pm, Sa-Su 9am-9pm. Tacos $1.25; tostadas $3, Mexican sweet bread 60¢.)

🧗 OUTDOOR ACTIVITIES. The spectacular 8 mi. **South Rim Drive** traces the edge of the canyon and boasts jaw-dropping vistas, including **Chasm View,** where you can peer 2300 ft. down the highest cliff in Colorado and across to the streaked **Painted Wall.** A little farther along, between the **Painted Wall** and **Cedar Point Overlooks,** a well-worn path leads to **Marmot Rocks,** which offer excellent **bouldering.** A detailed guide is available at the Visitors Center. Not surprisingly, the sheer walls of the Black Canyon make for a **rock climbing** paradise. This rock is not for beginners or the faint at heart, and all climbers must register at the Visitors Center. A couple of hiking routes skirt the edge of canyon and provide a more in-depth experience than the straight-forward overlooks can offer. On the South Rim, the moderate, 2 mi. round-trip **Oak Flat Loop Trail** begins near the Visitors Center and gives a good sense of the terrain below the rim. On the North Rim, the moderate, 7 mi. round-trip **North Vista Trail**, which begins at the North Rim Ranger Station, provides terrific scenic panoramas, such as the one at **Exclamation Point** (3 mi. round-trip), as well as some of the best inner-canyon views. At the end of the day, dropping over the edge of the canyon to reach the roaring **river** is the most rewarding of all. From the South Rim, you can scramble down the popular **Gunnison Route,** which drops 1800 ft. over 1 mi. Allow about an hour for the strenuous descent, and even longer for the climb out. Or, if you're feeling courageous, tackle the much more difficult **Tomichi** or **Warner Routes,** which make good overnight hikes. From the North Rim, **S.O.B., Long,** and **Slide Draws** cascade over the edge and serve as day hikes to the canyon floor. A free **wilderness permit** (from the South Rim Visitors Center or North Rim Ranger Station) is required for inner-canyon routes. Bring at least one gallon of **water** per person per day. For a relaxed, insider's view of the canyon, call ahead to reserve a **rafting** trip with **Gunnison River Expeditions** (☎ 249-4441, 800-297-4441, one-day float $200 per person). Reservations must be made at least 3-4 days in advance (some dates are reserved as early as a year ahead).

Anglers from all over Colorado trek to the Black Canyon to practice the art of **fly fishing** in a secluded, breathtakingly beautiful setting. Try a float trip, available through Gunnison River Expeditions, or hike in and camp along the riverbanks. **Gunnison Gorge National Conservation Area** is a particularly popular stretch of the river. Non-motorized boaters (namely canoers and kayakers) have access to the area via the Chukar Boater Put-In and the Gunnison Forks Boater Take-Out. The only land access is by hiking one of four trails from the rim of the gorge. The access roads are rough, to say the least. Some, especially Bobcat Rd., require four-wheel-drive; others are impassable when wet. Gunnison River Expeditions runs float fly fishing float trips in the Black Canyon (1-day $650 for two people, 2-day $1500, 3-day $2100) and 1-day walk-wade trips on the Gunnison ($275 per person).

CRESTED BUTTE   ☎970

In the heart of the Rockies and far from any interstate, the historic coal mining town of Crested Butte has been left alone by commercial developers to evolve at its own pace. The result is a place where laid-back residents pay more attention to trail and snow conditions than fattening up on the cash flow of tourists. A mecca for mountain bikers and the site of the Extreme Ski Championships, Crested Butte is perfectly situated for forays into the pristine wilderness spreading out in three directions from town. This self-proclaimed "Wildflower Capital of Colorado" delightfully defies the mold of commercial ski towns like Aspen and Vail.

▣ TRANSPORTATION

Getting to Crested Butte is easiest with a car, though the **Alpine Express Shuttle** runs from Gunnison Airport for $44 per person round-trip (☎ 800-822-4844; $50 minimum fare). Gunnison is accessible by Greyhound from all major cities and through **Gunnison County Airport** (☎ 641-2304). The local radio station in Crested Butte, **KBUT 90.3 FM** (89.9 FM in Gunnison), offers a ride-sharing service. Call ☎ 349-7444 to advertise space in your car or to ask for a ride. Once in town, **Mountain Express Buses** circulate regularly, offering free rides across town and up to the ski village at Mt. Crested Butte (every 10-40min. depending on season). Look for the schedule at any bus stop along the route or call ☎ 349-7318. After the bus shuts down in the evening, local taxis run the same route (☎ 349-0321. 10pm-2am. Fare $1.).

⬛ ⓘ ORIENTATION & PRACTICAL INFORMATION

Crested Butte lies at the end of Rte. 135, 28 mi. north of Gunnison. Its streets form a grid bisected by a creek which sometimes interrupts car access. **Highway 135** becomes Sixth St. when you enter town and carries visitors directly to the main intersection, referred to locals as "the four-way stop" (although it's not the only one). A left turn leads to the town's historic business district on **Elk Avenue**. Sixth St. becomes Gothic Rd. as the town gives way to mountains.

Tourist Office: Chamber of Commerce (☎800-545-4505; www.cbchamber.com). In the large building on the right at the main intersection of Elk Ave. and Rte. 135. Provides useful information and maps, including free hiking and biking trail maps. Open year-round daily 9am-5pm.

Bank: Also at the main four-way stop sits the **Community First Bank** (☎349-6606), with a **24hr. ATM.** Another branch is located in Mt. Crested Butte, 2 mi. north on Gothic Rd. Open M-Th 9am-5pm, F 9am-6pm.

Laundry: Coin-operated machines are available to the public at the Crested Butte International Hostel and Lodge (See **Accommodations**) from 8am-8pm.

Outdoor Equipment: 🔲**The Alpineer** (☎349-5210), located on the left just before the four-way stop coming into town, is stocked with a formidable selection of outdoor gear. In the summer they run a full bike shop, while in the winter they specialize in telemark and cross-country ski rentals. The knowledgeable staff can clue you into the best hikes and rides in the area. Father's Day Sale in mid-June. Open June to mid-Sept. and Dec. to mid-Apr. daily 9am-6pm, 10am-5pm otherwise.

Road Conditions: ☎245-8800.

Emergency: ☎911.

Police: The Crested Butte Town Marshal's office, 508 Maroon Ave. (☎349-5231), patrols within the city limits of Crested Butte. The Mt. Crested Butte Marshal's Office handles calls outside of town (☎349-6516). If no one answers, call the regional dispatch in Gunnison (☎641-8000).

Medical Services: The **Crested Butte Medical Center** is in the **Ore Bucket Building** at the corner of Maroon Ave. and Gothic Rd. (☎349-0321). Open daily 9am-5pm in the low season, 8am-8pm in the high season. **Elk Avenue Medical Center** is at 405 Elk Ave., near Fourth Ave. (☎349-1046). Open M-F 8:15am-8pm, Sa 8:15am-5pm.

Internet Access: Free at **Old Rock Community Library,** 507 Maroon Ave. (☎349-6535), next to the Marshall's office. From the four-way stop turn west onto Elk Ave., take the first right onto Fifth St., and look for the old schoolhouse with the bell tower. Open M, W, F 10am-6pm; Tu and Th 10am-7pm; Sa 10am-2pm.

Post office: 221 Elk Ave., (☎349-5568). Open M-F 7:30am-4:30pm. **Postal code:** 81224.

⬛ ACCOMMODATIONS

Devoid of chain motels, CB sleeps visitors in quirky B&Bs and a fantastic hostel. Campers will delight in the glut of free, spacious tent sites within 10 mi. of town.

🔲 **Crested Butte International Hostel and Lodge,** 615 Teocalli Ave. (☎349-0588 or 888-389-0588; crestedbuttehostel.com), 2 blocks north of the 4-way stop, a tidy stay in gorgeous, modern facilities. Its huge kitchen and bright common area make it an ideal base for exploring. No curfew or lockout. Breakfast ($1-5) and lock rental ($2). Showers for non-guests $5. Coin-op laundry. **Internet access** $2 per 15min. Room rates vary by season. Group discounts. Spacious 4-6 bed dorms $22 ($20 for multiple-night guests and HI members), doubles $55-89. Rooms for 3 or more $70-99. Roomy 3rd fl. apartment (sleeps up to 6) $125-210. Call ahead for specific prices and reservations. ❶

Purple Mountain Lodge, 714 Gothic Ave. (☎349-5888 or 800-759-9066; www.purple-mountain.com) puts up guests in high style on the east side of town. Decor of Martha Stewart and comfort of your favorite sweatshirt. Doubles with private baths $75-120. A family suite for 4-6 ($150) and duplex that sleeps up to 8, includes kitchen and laundry ($250-$375). Call for current rates. Full breakfast included, kitchen available. ❺

The Claim Jumper, 704 Whiterock Rd. (☎349-6471; www.visitcrestedbutte.com/claim-jumper). The proprietor, Jerry, has comprehensively outfitted all 7 themed rooms to a remarkable level of detail. For a real treat, try Jack's Cabin, with its sunroom and outdoor patio—just remember how to open the secret doors to get into the room with TV/VCR! All guests enjoy private bathrooms and an indoor hot tub, as well as a hearty breakfast. Rooms $99-139, with discounts in the off-season. ❺

CAMPING

The relaxed atmosphere of Crested Butte spells plenty of free camping for those willing to venture down dirt roads and up mountain passes. In addition to the sites listed below, traditional campgrounds with full facilities line **Cement Creek Road** and **Taylor Canyon Road,** south of town off Rte. 135.

Oh-Be-Joyful, located 5-6 mi. from the town center, doesn't disappoint with its brookside location and pit toilets. Take the first left as you drive north out of town onto Slate River Rd. and continue until you see the sign for Oh-Be-Joyful. Take the hairpin turn left to the water, or continue to higher sites if the road looks too rough. Free. ❶

Lake Irwin Campground (☎877-444-6777), a rough 9 mi. drive west of town, rewards guests with heavenly views from the alpine lake at over 10,000 ft. From the west end of Whiterock Ave., follow Kebler Pass Rd. until it forks. Take the left side and follow the signs to the campsite. $12 per vehicle with tent/camper, $6 per extra tent/camper. ❶

Gothic Campground (☎877-444-6777) is an excellent starting point for exploring hiking and biking trails north of town. Follow Gothic Rd. north 7 mi. from town, passing through the old townsite of Gothic and continuing until you cross the East River. Look for the campground ½ mile up the road to your left. 4 unimproved sites, suitable for tents or short RVs ($8). Additional camping at Washington Gulch trailhead up the road. ❶

FOOD

Crested Butte is home to more eateries than its size would suggest, so travelers have no trouble fueling up before or after a day on the trail. **Clark's Market,** located in the plaza on Rte. 135 at the south end of town, sells groceries. (☎349-6492. Open daily 8am-9pm.) Natural, organic and bulk foods are available at **Mountain Earth Whole Foods** just south of Elk Ave. on Fourth St. (☎349-5132. Open daily 8am-8pm.)

Paradise Cafe (☎349-6233), a long-time local favorite, bustles with business, contrary to its easy-going island theme. Enjoy a hearty breakfast ($3-6) or lunch ($5-7) inside or outdoors at the Paradise, located at Elk Ave. at 3rd in The Company Store building. Open daily 7am-3pm. ❶

The Secret Stash, 21 Elk Ave. (☎349-6245), at the west end of town. This joint aims to please, and succeeds. Try the eclectic pizzas ($8-17), salads and wraps ($3.50-8) and grilled wings (10 for $7). Sip a soy latte in the side garden or in the hippie's living room-like 2nd fl., with its cushy couches, mood lighting, and acoustic. Open daily 5-10pm, with additional lunch hours during the summer and winter seasons. ❸

Pitas in Paradise, 214 Elk Ave. (☎349-0897), a self-proclaimed "Mediterranean Cafe with Soul," wows diners with its delicious $5 gyros, $3-4 smoothies, and more. Watch your meal being made at the counter or wait for it in the backyard. Open daily 11am-9pm and until 10pm in the summer. ❶

NIGHTLIFE

True to its frontier roots, Crested Butte's saloons are where the extreme sports types come to trade tales of their exploits. Happy hour sees a bigger crowd than late-night because locals are tired from working or playing all day outside. Bars line Elk Ave., each with its own loyal clientele. **Kochevar's Bar and Saloon,** 127 Elk Ave. is still in the family after more than a century, and though gambling here is no longer legal, it still sports several pool tables and the relics of its gaming hall days, including ghosts that allegedly haunt the place. (☎349-6745. Happy Hour 3-7pm, Tu open mic night, live music during the summer. Open daily 11:30am-2am.) Those with late-evening munchies head to **The Last Steep Bar and Grill** for $4-7 appetizers and $6-8 specials. (☎349-7007. Open and Su-Th 11am-11pm, F-Sa 11am-midnight.) Hop between bars like **Eldo,** 215 Elk Ave. (☎ 349-6125; Happy Hour 4-8pm; open M-Sa 3pm-2am), **Talk of the Town,** 230 Elk Ave. (☎349-6809;

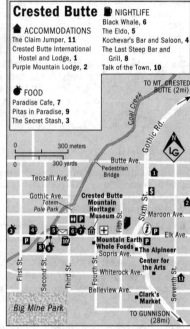

Crested Butte ■ NIGHTLIFE
Black Whale, **6**
🏠 ACCOMMODATIONS   The Eldo, **5**
The Claim Jumper, **11**   Kochevar's Bar and Saloon, **4**
Crested Butte International   The Last Steep Bar and
  Hostel and Lodge, **1**   Grill, **8**
Purple Mountain Lodge, **2**   Talk of the Town, **10**

🍎 FOOD
Paradise Cafe, **7**
Pitas in Paradise, **9**
The Secret Stash, **3**

Happy Hour 3-8pm; open 3pm-2am), and **Black Whale,** 330 Elk Ave. (☎349-0480. Open 6pm-2am.). The latter two are the best bets for late-night dancing.

It's not uncommon to land in Crested Butte during a festival, especially in the summer. Most notable are **Fat Tire Bike Week** in late June, the **Crested Butte Music Festival** in all of July, and the renowned **Wildflower Festival** in mid-July. The **4th of July** festivities and the early-August **Festival for the Arts** are local favorites. Throughout the summer and winter, local talent and touring companies grace the stage at the **Center for the Arts** (☎349-7487), located just south of the town park on Rte. 135.

OUTDOOR ACTIVITIES

Despite heavy tourist traffic, the landscape around Crested Butte remains pristine. And fortunately, land use regulations require that private property owners allow for public trails to cross their property at key junctures, providing expansive and unrestricted access to the valley for mountain-bikers, hikers, kayakers, fishermen, horse-back riders, and climbers. For guided trips of all kinds, consult **Alpine Outside** (☎349-5011) at 6th St. and Elk Ave. across from the Chamber of Commerce.

MOUNTAIN BIKING

Crested Butte claims to be one of the places this sport originated, and with the networks of rugged trails that lace the area, it's no surprise. The **Mountain Bike Hall of Fame,** located in the **Crested Butte Mountain Heritage Museum** (331 Elk Ave. ☎349-1880), features many locals, including the beloved restaurateur at Donita's across the street. **The Alpineer** (p. 372) and various other establishments around town rent bikes for reasonable prices, and **Crested Butte Mountain Guides** has guides for hire

(☎349-5430. Half-day $75 for 1-2 people, $25 each additional. Full day $130 for 1-2 people, $50 each additional). For more detailed trail descriptions, maps, and information about conditions, check **www.alpineer.com** or ask one of the local outfitters. A detailed trail map is available from the Chamber of Commerce.

Peanut Lake (3 mi. round-trip, ½hr.). From Crested Butte, follow Gothic Rd. north for ¼ mi. to Butte Ave. Turn left and continue to Peanut Lake and Mine. Return in reverse.

Lower Loop (9 mi. round-trip, 1½hr., continuing from the end of the Peanut Lake ride). Lower Loop extends north along the western side of the Slate River, providing some incredible views of the valley. Upper Lower Loop leads up the hillside, and Lower Lower Loop hugs the riverbank on the return.

Poverty Gulch (20 mi. round-trip, 3-4hr.). From Crested Butte, follow Gothic Rd. north for ½ mi. to Slate River Rd. (FS 734). After 7 mi., turn left onto FS 734.2A and climb towards Cascade Mt. for 2 mi. until hitting trail #404. Take a right and ride or hike to the stunning view at the top. Return in reverse.

Strand (7-10 mi. round-trip, 2hr.). Two miles south of Crested Butte on Hwy. 135, turn left on Brush Creek Rd. Follow Brush Creek for 2.5 mi. to a parking lot. The trailhead is 1 mi. further east from the parking lot. After a ¾ mi. climb up Farris Creek Rd., the Strand Hill ride veers off to the left at a fork in the road. Climb the dirt road to the beginning of a well-marked singletrack trail to the left.

Teocalli Ridge (15 mi. round-trip, 2.5hr.). The singletrack begins 5 mi. out on Brush Creek Rd. on the right (see directions to Strand). Expect a steep ascent and descent with incredible views before the trail empties onto West Brush Creek Rd., which can be followed south to Brush Creek Rd.

Trail #401 (24 mi. round-trip, 4hr.). Ride north from Crested Butte on Gothic Rd. through Mt. Crested Butte to Schofield Pass. Turn right onto trail #401 and climb along Mt. Belleview to the boundary of the Maroon Bells-Snowmass Wilderness Area. After descending to Schofield Pass Rd., continue on trail #401 to a four-wheel-drive road. Turn right, then left onto Hwy. 135. Head south back to Crested Butte.

SKIING

Three miles north of town, **Crested Butte Mountain Resort,** 12 Snowmass Rd., takes skiers to "the extreme limits," offering over 800 acres of bowl skiing. Many of the other 85 runs are less spine-tingling, but the panoramic views are inspiring. (☎800-544-8448; www.skicb.com. Open mid-Dec. to mid-Apr. Day passes around $50; ages 65-74 half-price; over 75 free; children 5-12 pay their age in dollars.)

HIKING

Just about any Crested Butte resident will gladly clue visitors into gorgeous hikes of all levels, many starting at the edge of town. The Chamber of Commerce has an excellent trail map detailing hikes in the area. Starting from town (next to the Nordic Center), **Green Lake** is a favorite picnic destination (6 mi. round-trip). The **Upper Loop** and **Peanut Lake** bike trails are friendly to hikers. North of town, the Judd Falls Trailhead serves as a starting point for the Copper Creek Trail, leading to Judd Falls (½ mi. one-way) and Copper Lake (4 mi.). The **Trailriders Trail** also begins from the same parking lot, leading to Rustler's Gulch (4 mi.) and Schofield Pass (8 mi.), which connect to a larger network. To get to the trailhead, either park along Gothic Rd. at the parking lot ¼ mi. beyond the townsite of Gothic or drive up the rough road ½ mi. to the actual trailhead.

An additional 4 mi. beyond Copper Lake on the Copper Creek Trail, Conundrum Hotsprings is a popular overnight trip for **backpackers** (it's above tree line, so watch the weather). Another favorite overnight is the trek through the Maroon Bells Peaks between Crested Butte and Aspen and back. Beginning at Schofield

Pass, the trip is approximately 13 mi. one-way, depending on the choice of West Maroon or East Maroon Pass, and takes hikers through some of the most photographed mountains in Colorado. The Alpine Express offers trailhead drop-off or pick up ($70) and charters from Aspen back to Crested Butte ($300). The KBUT ride-line facilitates car swaps between groups hiking in opposite directions.

FISHING

The wild trout of the Gunnison River Basin delight area fly fishermen. Much of the **East River** and its tributary **Taylor River** are public; access them from Rte. 135 and Taylor Canyon Rd. **Dragonfly Anglers,** a shop based at 307 Elk Ave. in Crested Butte, sells and rents gear and runs expert-led trips. (☎349-1228 or 800-491-3079; www.dragonflyanglers.com. Walk/wade trips: half-day $160 for 1, $210 for 2; full day $200/265. Float trips: half-day $230/265, full-day $255/295.) The **Three Rivers Resort** of Almont offers free 1hr. fly fishing clinics in Almont and Crested Butte (☎641-1303; www.3riversresort.com). Sign up in Crested Butte at **Alpine Outside,** a branch of Three Rivers Resort (☎349-5011).

WHITEWATER KAYAKING

The snow-covered peaks around Crested Butte produce torrents of spring run-off, meaning prime-time paddling for avid kayakers and rafters. During a short window of time in early June, perfect streamflow conditions transform **Oh-Be-Joyful** and **Daisy Creeks** (feeding into the Slate River)—as well as parts of the East River—into a whitewater challenge worthy of professional competition (Class V). Hike 4 mi. up the old mining road from Oh-Be-Joyful campground to watch experts taking on the waterfalls. More tame river running is along the Taylor and Gunnison Rivers, where Class I-IV stretches are perfect for learning or strengthening whitewater skills. Check www.mountainbuzz.com for flow levels. Three Rivers Resort offers kayak lessons for all levels. (2hr. $40 per person up to 5 people, half-day up to 3 people $135/$175/$215, full-day $225/$275/$325. See above.)

New Mexico

NEW MEXICO

In New Mexico, nature's eccentricities provide outdoor enthusiasts with the landscape they need to explore the limits of their abilities and interests. Skiers seek the fluffy powder and steep terrain around Taos, while hikers can choose anything from a one mile jaunt around the rim of Capulin Volcano to a week-long trek in the magnificent Gila Wilderness. Mountain bikers traverse the trails of Lincoln National Forest, Carson National Forest, the Sandía Mountains, and the Enchanted Circle, and river rats enjoy endless kayaking and rafting on the Río Grande Wild and Scenic River.

The New Mexico's myriad outdoor adventures find their foil in the art museums and galleries of Santa Fe, the nightclubs of Albuquerque, and the pueblos of northern New Mexico. With a rich cultural mosaic of Mexican, Native American, and European influence, historical and archaeological discovery is a never-ending process in New Mexico, and travelers would be remiss not to tap into this rich past. After all is said and done, save some time to wander across white sand dunes or relax in the bubbly warmth of natural hot springs. They don't call it "Land of Enchantment" for nothing.

⚜HIGHLIGHTS OF NEW MEXICO

ARCHAEOLOGY. Climb up 140 ft. of stairs and ladders to the Ceremonial Cave *kiva*, tucked into a cliff at **Bandelier National Monument** (p. 398). Hike between Ancestral Puebloan houses at **Chaco Culture National Historical Park** (p. 415).

OUTBACK. Spend a week or two backpacking in the **Gila Wilderness** (p. 428), one of the most remote wilderness areas in the country.

HIGH ROAD. Explore the churches, pueblos, and Spanish farming villages along this popular drive from Santa Fe to Taos (p. 404).

ALBUQUERQUE. Hit the town for the best nightlife in New Mexico (p. 383).

ALBUQUERQUE   ☎505

Albuquerque sits at the crossroads of the Southwest; anyone traveling north to Denver, south to Mexico, east to Texas, or west to California passes through this commercial hub. But as a destination in its own right, Albuquerque buzzes with history and culture, nurturing many ethnic restaurants, offbeat galleries, quirky cafes, and raging nightclubs. Route 66 may no longer appear on maps, but it's still alive and kicking here. Most residents still refer to Central Avenue as Rte. 66, and palpable energy radiates from this mythic highway—shops, restaurants, and bars on the thoroughfare conjure a distinctive spirit found nowhere else in the state. The University of New Mexico gives the town its young demographic, while the Hispanic, Native American, and gay and lesbian communities contribute to the cultural vibrance. Downtown Albuquerque may lack East Coast sophistication, but it has a cosmopolitan feel of its own, deriving from its unique juxtaposition of students, cowboys, bankers, and government employees. From historic Old Town to modern museums, ancient petroglyphs to towering mountains, travelers will be delighted at how much there is to see and do in New Mexico's largest city.

▐ TRANSPORTATION

Flights: Albuquerque International, 2200 Sunport Blvd. SE (☎244-7700), south of downtown. Take bus #50 from 5th St. and Central Ave., or pick it up along Yale Blvd. **Airport Shuttle** (☎765-1234) shuttles to the city ($12, 2nd person $5). Open 24hr.

Trains: Amtrak, 214 1st St. SW (☎842-9650). 1 train per day to: **Flagstaff** (5hr., $71-106); **Kansas City** (17hr., $98-207); **Los Angeles** (16hr., $58-120); **Santa Fe** (1hr. to Lamy; 20min. shuttle to Santa Fe, $34). Reservations required. Open daily 10am-6pm.

Buses: Greyhound (☎243-4435) and **TNM&O Coaches,** 300 2nd St. Both run buses from 3 blocks south of Central Ave. to: **Denver** (10hr., 4 per day, $64); **Flagstaff** (7hr., 4 per day, M-Th $41, F-Su $44); **Los Angeles** (18hr., 4 per day, $75); **Phoenix** (11hr., 4 per day, M-Th $43, F-Su $46); **Santa Fe** (1½hr., 4 per day, $10). Station open 24hr.

Public Transit: Sun-Tran Transit, 601 Yale Blvd. SE (☎843-9200; open M-F 8am-6pm, Sa 8am-noon). Pick up maps at Visitors Centers, the transit office, or the main library. Most buses run M-Sa 6:30am-8:30pm and leave from Central Ave. and 5th St. Bus #66 runs down Central Ave. $1, seniors and ages 5-18 $0.25. Request free transfers from driver.

Taxis: Albuquerque Cab, ☎883-4888.

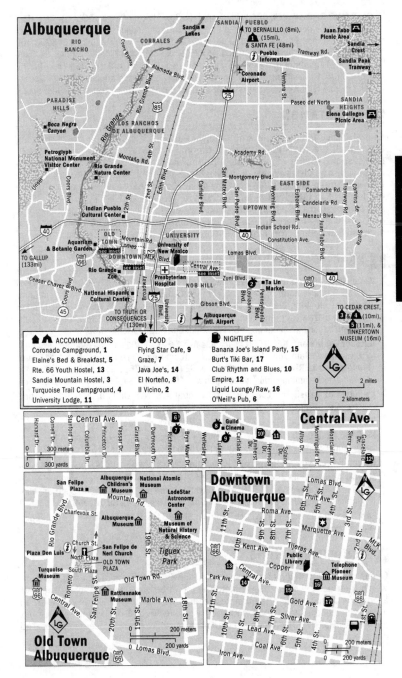

Car Rental: Rent-a-Wreck, 504 Yale Blvd. SE (☎232-7552 or 800-247-9556). Cars start-ing from $23 per day with 150 free mi.; $0.20 per additional mi.; starting at $120 per week. Insurance $11 per day, $70 per week. Must be 21+ with credit card or $250-500 cash deposit; under age 25 surcharge $3 per day. Open M-F 8am-5:30pm, Sa 8am-4pm, Su 11am-2pm. Reservations recommended. **Enterprise Rent-a-Car** (☎800-736-8222) has 10 locations in Albuquerque, including one at the airport. 21+ with license and major credit card. Rentals start at $31 per day. Most offices open M-F 9am-5pm.

▟ ORIENTATION

Central Avenue (Route 66), is still the main thoroughfare of Albuquerque, running through all the city's major neighborhoods. Central Ave. (east-west) and **I-25** (north-south) divide Albuquerque into four quadrants. All downtown addresses come with a quadrant designation: NE, NW, SE, or SW. The adobe campus of the **University of New Mexico (UNM)** spreads along Central Ave. from University Ave. to Carlisle St. **Nob Hill,** the area of Central Ave. around Carlisle St., features coffee shops, bookstores, used-CD stores, and art galleries. The revitalized **downtown** lies on Central Ave. between 10th St. and Broadway. Historic **Old Town Plaza** sits between San Felipe, North Plaza, South Plaza, and Romero, off Central Ave.

🛈 PRACTICAL INFORMATION

Visitor Info: Albuquerque Visitors Center, 401 2nd St. NW (☎842-9918 or 800-284-2282), 3 blocks north of Central Ave. in the Convention Center. Open M-F 9am-5pm. Recorded info 24hr. **Old Town Visitors Center,** 303 Romano St. NW (☎243-3215), in the shopping plaza west of the church. Open Apr.-Oct. daily 9am-5pm; Nov.-Mar. 9:30am-4:30pm. Airport **info booth** open Su-F 9:30am-8pm, Sa 9:30am-4:30pm.

Outdoor Equipment: REI, 1550 Mercantile Ave. (☎247-1191), at the Montano exit off I-25. Open M-F 9am-9pm, Sa 9am-7pm, Su 10am-6pm. Offers gear for sale and rent. **Mountains and Rivers,** 2320 Central Ave. SE (☎268-4876) sells kayaks, canoes, and camping/rock-climbing equipment. Open M-F 10am-6pm, Sa 9am-5pm, Su noon-5pm.

Laundromat: Wash Tub Laundry, 1105 Central Ave. NW. Open daily 6:30am-11pm. Last wash 9:30pm.

Police: 5408 2nd St. NW (☎761-8800), at Montano. **Emergency:** ☎911

Hotlines: Rape Crisis Center, 1025 Hermosa SE (☎266-7711). Center open M-F 8am-noon and 1-5pm, hotline 24hr. **Gay and Lesbian Information Line,** ☎891-3647. 24hr.

Hospital: Presbyterian Hospital, 1100 Central Ave. SE (☎841-1234), just east of I-25.

Internet Access: UNM Zimmerman Library (☎277-5761), at the heart of campus. Open fall and spring semesters M-Th 8am-midnight, F 8am-9pm, Sa 9am-6pm, Su 10am-mid-night; in summer M-Th 8am-9pm, F 8am-5pm, Sa 10am-5pm, Su 10am-9pm.

Post Office: 1135 Broadway NE, at Mountain St. (☎346-8044). Open M-F 7:30am-6pm. **Postal code:** 87101.

🏠 ACCOMMODATIONS

Cheap motels line **Central Avenue,** even near downtown. Though many of them are worth their price, be sure to evaluate the motel before paying. Many of the best accommodations in the Albuquerque area are found 20 min. outside of the urban insanity in sleepy Cedar Crest, 4 mi. north of exit 175 on I-40. During the October **Balloon Festival** (see **Nightlife and Entertainment,** p. 383) rooms become scarce, so call ahead to reserve.

▩ **Route 66 Youth Hostel,** 1012 Central Ave. SW (☎247-1813), at 10th St. Get your kicks at this friendly hostel located between downtown and Old Town. Dorm and private rooms are simple but clean. Key deposit $5. Reception daily 7:30-10:30am and 4-11pm. Check-out 10:30am. Ten easy chores required. Dorms $14; singles with shared bath $20; doubles $25; twin bed doubles with private bath $30. ❶

▩ **Sandía Mountain Hostel,** 12234 Rte. 14 N (☎281-4117). In nearby Cedar Crest. Take I-40 E to exit 175 and go 4 mi. north on Rte. 14. Call ahead and the owners will pick you up in Albuquerque. Only 10 mi. from the Sandía Ski Area, this large wooden building makes a great ski chateau, with a more mature feel than Rte. 66. Comfortable living room with fireplace and kitchen, plus a family of resident donkeys out back. Sandía hiking and mountain biking trails are just across the street. Linen $1. Coin-op laundry. Wheelchair accessible. Dorms $14; private cabins $32; camping $8. ❶

Elaine's Bed and Breakfast, (☎281-2467 or 800-821-3092; www.elainesbnb.com). Turn off Rte. 14 at the Turquoise Trail Campground's sign and follow the signs up the dirt road. A beautiful, cozy B&B nestled in the foothills of the Sandías. Owner Elaine dishes out amazing breakfasts and warm hospitality amidst wonderful views of the mountains. Rooms $85-139. ❹

Turquoise Trail Campground and RV Park (☎281-2005). Take I-40 E from downtown to exit 175 and go 4 mi. north on Rte. 14. A large campground in the Sandía Mountains with trails leading up into the Cibola National Forest. Tent sites are shaded by trees. Showers and laundry available. Office open daily noon-8pm. Tent sites $11, each additional person $2; 4-person cabins $26. ❶

University Lodge, 3711 Central Ave. NE (☎266-7663). About a 15min. walk from campus in the historic and cool Nob Hill district. Unusually cozy rooms with cable TV, A/C, free local calls, and access to a pool. Reception 24hr. Check-out 11am. Singles summer $33, winter $28; doubles $37/$33. AAA and AARP discounts. ❸

Coronado Campground (☎980-8256). About 15 mi. north of Albuquerque. Take I-25 to exit 242 and follow the signs. A pleasant campground on the banks of the Río Grande. Adobe shelters offer a respite from the heat. Toilets, showers, and water available. Office open daily 8am-5pm; see host to check in after hours. Tent sites $8, with shelters and picnic tables $18, full hookup $18-$20. Open W-M 8:30am-5pm, self-service pay station after hours. ❶

◨ FOOD

A diverse ethnic community, lots of hungry interstate travelers, and tons of chiles render Albuquerque surprisingly tasty. The area around **UNM** is the best bet for budget eateries. A bit farther east, the hip neighborhood of **Nob Hill** is a haven for yuppie fare, so head here if you're in the mood for avocado sandwiches and iced cappuccino. Grocery stores abound in Albuquerque, but for a more exotic selection stop by the **Ta Lin Market,** 230 Louisiana Blvd. SE, a grocery store-sized market carrying anything you can imagine (and plenty of things you couldn't if you tried) from Asia and South America. (☎268-0206. Open M-Sa 9am-6pm, Su 9am-5pm.)

▩ **Java Joe's,** 906 Park Ave. SW (☎765-1514). 1 block south of Central Ave., and 2 blocks from the Rte. 66 Hostel. This lively restaurant with a casual atmosphere has hearty wraps ($5), sandwiches ($5.50), salads ($4-5), and great breakfast burritos ($3). Lots of vegetarian dishes and occasional live music. Open daily 6:30am-3:30pm. ❶

El Norteño, 6416 Zuni (☎256-1431), at California. A family-run joint renowned as the most authentic and varied Mexican in town. The shrimp roasted with garlic is a treat, and their vast repertoire runs from chicken *mole* ($8) to *caldo de res* (a beef stew) to beef tongue ($7-9). Lunch buffet M-F 11am-2pm, $6. Open daily 8:30am-9pm. ❷

Graze, 3128 Central Ave. SE (☎268-4729). Patrons of Graze are encouraged to do just that: graze over the eclectic menu and eat what they like without the limits of conventional courses. The menu is highly seasonal but has featured udon noodles with a three mushroom sauce ($6), and a stuffed poblano pepper with a goat cheese and truffle sauce ($9). Chic but friendly; smallish servings. Open Tu-Sa 11am-11pm. ❷

Flying Star Cafe, 3416 Central Ave. SE (☎255-6633). This cafe soars beyond Starbucks to offer lattes, fancy pastries, and hearty lunches and dinners. An artsy crowd reads magazines and eats portobello mushroom sandwiches and Saigon wraps (both $7). Open Su-Th 6am-11:30pm, F-Sa 6am-midnight. ❷

Il Vicino, 3403 Central Ave. NE (☎266-7855). Some of the best budget Italian to be found anywhere. Combination pizzas ($6-8), calzones ($7-8), and lasagna ($7.25). Open Su-Th 11am-11pm, F-Sa 11am-midnight. ❷

 SIGHTS

OLD TOWN. When the railroad cut through Albuquerque in the 19th century, it missed Old Town by almost 2 mi. As downtown grew around the railroad, Old Town remained untouched until the 1950s, when the city realized that it had a tourist magnet right under its nose. Just north of Central Ave. and east of Río Grande Blvd., the adobe plaza today looks much like it did over 100 years ago, save for ubiquitous restaurants, gift shops, and jewelry vendors. Although a tourist trap, Old Town is an architectural marvel, and a stroll through it is worthwhile. **Walking tours** of Old Town meet at the Albuquerque Museum. *(1hr. Tu-Su 11am. Free with admission.)* On the north side of the plaza, the quaint **San Felipe de Neri Church,** dating back to 1706, has stood the test of time. *(Open daily 9am-5pm, accompanying museum open M-Sa 10am-4pm; Su mass in English 7 and 10:15am, in Spanish 8:30am.)* A posse of museums and attractions surrounds the plaza. To the northeast, the **Albuquerque Museum** showcases New Mexican art and history. The comprehensive exhibit on the Conquistadors and Spanish colonial rule is a must-see for anyone interested in history. Tours of the Sculpture Garden are available Tu-F at 10am and free with admission. *(2000 Mountain Rd. NW. ☎243-7255. Open Tu-Su 9am-5pm. $3, seniors and children $1. Wheelchair accessible.)* The museum also offers tours of the historic Casa San Ysidro in Corrales, NM. *(☎898-3915 for reservations.)* No visit to Old Town would be complete without seeing the **Rattlesnake Museum,** which lies just south of the plaza. With over 30 species ranging from the deadly Mojave to the tiny Pygmy, this is the largest collection of live rattlesnakes in the world. *(202 San Felipe NW. ☎242-6569. Open M-Sa 10am-6pm, Su 1-5pm. $2.50, seniors $2, Under 18 $1.50.)*

NEAR OLD TOWN. Two more museums lie just outside the main Old Town area but remain within easy walking distance. Spike and Alberta, two statuesque dinosaurs, greet tourists outside the kid-friendly **New Mexico Museum of Natural History and Science.** Inside, interactive exhibits take visitors through the history of life on earth. The museum features a five-story dynatheater, planetarium, and simulated ride through the world of the dinosaurs. *(1801 Mountain Rd. NW. ☎841-2802. Open daily 9am-5pm, closed M in Sept. $5, seniors $4, children $2; admission and Dynamax theater ticket $10/$8/$4.)* The **National Atomic Museum,** 1905 Mountain Rd. across from the **Albuquerque Museum,** tells the story of US nuclear weapons from Little Boy and Fat Man, the atomic bombs dropped on Hiroshima and Nagasaki, to the more sophisticated weapons of the Cold War. *Ten Seconds that Shook the World,* a documentary on the making of the atomic bomb, shows on the hour. *(☎284-3243. Museum open daily 9am-5pm. $4, seniors and children $3.)*

UNIVERSITY MUSEUMS. The University of New Mexico has a couple of museums on campus that are worth a quick visit. The **University Art Museum** features changing exhibits that focus on 20th-century New Mexican paintings and photography. (☎ 277-4001. *Near the corner of Central Ave. and Cornel St. Open Tu-F 9am-4pm. Free.)* **The Maxwell Museum of Anthropology** has excellent exhibits on the culture and ancient history of Native American settlement in the Southwest. (☎ 277-5963. *On University Blvd., just north of MLK Blvd. Open Tu-F 9am-4pm, Sa 10am-4pm. Free.)*

CULTURAL ATTRACTIONS. The **Indian Pueblo Cultural Center** has a bit of a commercial edge but still provides a good introduction to the history and culture of the 19 Indian Pueblos of New Mexico. The center includes a museum, store, and restaurant. *(2401 12th St. NW. ☎ 843-7270. Take bus #36 from downtown. Museum open daily 9am-4:30pm. Art demonstrations Sa-Su 11am-2pm, Native American dances Sa-Su 11am and 2pm. $4, students $1, seniors $3.)* The **National Hispanic Cultural Center** has an excellent art museum with exhibits that explore folk-art and surreal representations of Hispanic social and cultural life in America. *(1701 4th St. SW, on the corner of Bridge St. Open Tu-Su 10am-5pm. $3, seniors $2, under 16 free.)*

🎭 🎵 NIGHTLIFE & ENTERTAINMENT

If touring the Southwest has left you tired of small-town watering holes, Albuquerque will be a refreshing change. With intriguing bars, throbbing nightclubs, art houses, and a large university, Albuquerque has quicker blood coursing through its veins. Check flyers posted around the university area for live music shows or pick up a copy of *Alibi*, the free local weekly. During the first week of October, hundreds of aeronauts take flight in colorful hot-air balloons during the **balloon festival.** Even fervent landlubbers will enjoy the week's barbecues and musical events.

Most nightlife huddles on and near Central Ave., downtown and near the university; Nob Hill establishments tend to be the most gay-friendly. The offbeat **Guild Cinema,** 3405 Central Ave. NE, runs independent and foreign films. (☎ 255-1848. Open M-Th at 4:30 and 7pm, F-Su at 2, 4:30, and 9:15pm. $7. Students, seniors, and all shows before 5pm $5.)

Burt's Tiki Bar, 313 Gold St. SW (☎ 247-2878). Situated a block south of the Central Ave. strip of clubs, the difference shows in its friendlier, more laid-back atmosphere that doesn't try to be all things to all people. Surf and tiki paraphernalia line the walls and ceiling, while anything from funk to punk to live hip-hop takes the stage. Live music Tu-Sa and occasionally Su-M. No cover. Normally open Tu-Sa 9pm-2am.

Banana Joe's Island Party, 610 Central Ave. SW (☎ 244-0024), is the largest club in Albuquerque. With 6 bars, a tropical outdoor patio, a concert hall, and 1 big dance floor, Banana Joe's delivers nightlife to the masses. Nightly live music ranges from reggae to flamenco. DJ downstairs Th-Sa. Happy hour daily 5-8pm. 21+. Cover Th-Sa $5. Open Tu-Su 5pm-2am.

Club Rhythm and Blues, 3523 Central Ave. NE (☎ 256-0849). Great live music M-Sa with a crowd that's not afraid to get up and dance. World beat, latin, and, of course, blues dominate the music schedule; call ahead or check www.clubrb.com. 21+. Cover W-Th $5, F-Sa $7, Su $3. Open Tu-Su 8pm-2am.

O'Neill's Pub, 3211 Central Ave. NE (☎ 256-0564), in Nob Hill. Friendly neighborhood pub with 16 beers on tap, Guinness included, plus an great selection of bottled brews. The pub serves great hamburgers and sandwiches to a loyal crowd. Live music Tu and Sa 10pm-1am, Celtic tunes Su 5-8pm. Happy hour daily 4-7pm and 10pm-1am. 21+, unless accompanied by adult. No cover. Open M-Sa 11am-2am, Su 11am-midnight.

Liquid Lounge/Raw, 405 Central Ave. NW (☎843-7299), is one of Albuquerque's trendy, up-and-coming bars. This swanky joint has live DJs and a more upscale ambiance than the other downtown offerings. No cover. Open M-F 11am-2am, Sa 4pm-2am.

Empire, 4310 Central Ave. NE (☎255-1668; www.nmempire.com.), is relatively new on the gay scene, but already one of the new hotspots. With a decadent Greco-Roman theme and a solid mix of dance tunes, Empire is consistently good fun. No cover. Open W-Sa 4pm-2am, Su 2pm-midnight.

◪ HIKING

The **Sandía Mountains** offer hikes for all ages and abilities, but don't always provide solitude. Because of easy access from neighboring Albuquerque, the peaks are overrun by locals and tourists alike from spring through fall. Nevertheless, the 37,232-acre Sandía Mountain Wilderness does offer a brief respite from Albuquerque's auto-clogged insanity. To avoid trampling this heavily-used mountain range, stick to the trails. The **Forest Service Station** (☎281-3304) on Rte. 337 just south of I-40 at exit 175 has an excellent free guide to hiking in the Sandías.

Sandía Man Cave Trail (½ mi., 15min.). To reach the trail, drive halfway up Rte. 536 towards the Sandía Crest and turn right onto unpaved Rte. 165 at the Balsam Glade Picnic Area. The parking lot is on the right after 5 mi. Evidence of prehistoric humans has been discovered in the cave at the end. Bring a flashlight if you intend to explore.

La Luz Trail (7.7 mi. one-way, 5-6 hr.). This trail, which climbs the Sandía Crest, begins at the Juan Tabo Picnic Area. From exit 167 on I-40, drive north on Tramway Blvd. 9.8 mi. to Forest Rd. 333. From the trailhead, stay on Trail 137 for 6.8 mi. and turn left onto Trail 84, which leads to the crest. Despite the length and difficulty of this trail, it is one of the most heavily used in New Mexico, so it pays to avoid summer weekends. It can also be very hot in the late afternoon. Rather than hiking the full 15 mi. round-trip, hikers can drive or take the tram (p. 386) to eliminate one leg of the journey.

10-K Trail North (4.8 mi. one way, 3-5 hr.). The trail begins along Rte. 536, 11.6 mi. from the junction with Rte. 14, at a well-marked parking lot. Take the trail 2 mi. north; make a left and go 0.6 mi. on the Osha Loop, and then make another left onto 130N (the North Crest Trail), which you can follow 2.1 mi. to the crest.

North Crest Trail (12 mi. one way, 1-2 days). This route makes for a pleasant backpacking trip through the Sandía Wilderness. From Albuquerque take I-25 N to exit 242. Turn right after the ramp, drive east 4.9 mi. and turn right onto Tunnel Spring Rd. The road ends after 1.5 mi. From Tunnel Spring, the Sandía Crest Trail (#130) follows the ridge of the Sandía Mountains, offering great views all along the way. After about 12 mi. the trail reaches the Sandía Crest Recreation Area. Day hikers can arrange for a car pickup here; backpackers set up camp in the wilderness and return the way they came.

◪ OUTDOOR ACTIVITIES

Rising a mile above Albuquerque to the northeast, the crest of the **Sandía Mountains** is visible from just about anywhere in the city. The Spanish gave these mountains the name *sandía* (watermelon) due to their pinkish hue at sunset. The mountains' accessibility draws hikers, bikers, and rock climbers from spring through fall, while skiers and snowboarders schuss down the peaks in winter.

MOUNTAIN BIKING. The Sandía Mountains have excellent mountain biking trails. Warm up on the moderately easy **Foothills Trail** (7 mi.), which skirts along the bottom of the mountains, just east of the city. The trail starts at the Elena Gallegos Picnic Area, off Tramway Blvd. There are many other good trails in this area; check with REI (see **Practical Information,** p. 380) or any area bike shop for a map. The best biking, however, is south of I-40 in the Manzano Mountains; contact **Two**

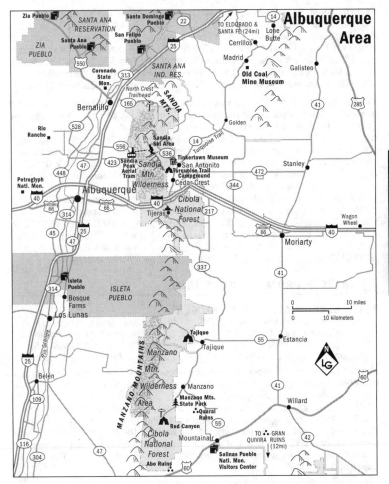

Wheel Drive, a bike shop at 1706 Central SE (☎243-8443) for a map of the trails. At the **Sandía Peak Ski Area,** bikers can take their bikes up the chairlift and then ride down on 35 mi. of mountain trails and rollers, covering all skill levels. *6 mi. up Rte. 536 on the way to Sandía Crest. ☎242-9133. Chairlifts run June-Aug. Sa-Su 10am-4pm. Full-day lift ticket $14, single ride $8. Bike rentals at the summit $38 per day. Helmets required.*

ROCK CLIMBING. The Sandía Mountains are blessed with thousands of feet of hard, granite cliffs, perfect for rock climbing. Many routes are accessible from the recreation area at the end of Rte. 536. There are also some good climbs along the foothills of the Sandías, near the Juan Tabo Picnic Area. The best spot for sport bolt climbing is along **Palomas Peak.** *The parking area is at the concrete blocks along Rte. 165 between Mile 15 and 14, 3 mi. north of the Capulin Spring Picnic Area on Rte. 536.* Albuquerque also boasts the **Stone Age Climbing Gym.** *4201 Yale Ave. NE. ☎341-2016. Open M-F noon-10pm, Sa 1-9pm, Su 1-6pm. M-F $7 before 3pm, $11 after; Sa-Su $13.*

SKIING. Sandía Peak Ski Area, only 30min. from downtown, is an option for those who can't head north to Taos or south to Ruidoso. Six lifts access 25 short trails (35% beginner; 55% intermediate; 10% advanced) on 200 skiable acres. The summit (10,378 ft.) tops a vertical drop of 1700 ft. ☎242-9133. *Snowboards allowed. Annual snowfall 125 in. Open mid-Dec. to mid-Mar. daily 9am-4pm. Full day $38, half day $29; ages 13-20 $32, under 13 and seniors $29.* There are also excellent cross-country skiing trails in the **Cibola National Forest,** where the North Crest and 10-K trails are popular.

SCENIC VIEWS. There are two ways to ascend Sandía Crest without breaking a sweat: the **Sandía Peak Aerial Tramway,** up Tramway Rd. from I-25 (exit 234), or Tramway Blvd. from I-40 (exit 167). Sandía Peak's is the world's longest aerial tramway and travels 2.7 mi. up the west face of the Peak to a height of 10,378 ft. The view overlooks Albuquerque and the Río Grande Valley—a panorama stretching 11,000 sq. mi. The ascent is especially striking at sunset. ☎856-6419. *Open June-Aug. and during the Balloon Festival daily 9am-10pm; Sept.-May Th-Tu 9am-8pm, W 5-8pm. During ski season Th-Tu 9am-8pm, W noon-8pm. $145, seniors $12, children $10.*

One can also drive an unforgettable 12 mi. to the top of **Sandía Crest** (10,678 ft.), amidst lovely forests of piñon and ponderosa pines, oaks, and spruce. A ranger station greets visitors at the top, as do views of Albuquerque and Cibola National Forest. A dazzling 1.8 mi. **ridge hike** connects the crest to the top of the tram. *To reach the road, take I-40 E to exit 175, turn north onto Rte. 14, and turn west after 6 mi. onto Rte. 536. ☎248-0190. Open June to mid-Oct. Th-Su 10am-4pm. $3 per vehicle parking fee.*

▣ DAYTRIP FROM ALBUQUERQUE

PETROGLYPH NATIONAL MONUMENT

To see the nearby volcanoes, take exit 149 off I-40 and follow Paseo del Volcán to a dirt road. The volcanoes are 4.8 mi. north of the exit. To reach the park itself, take I-40 to exit 154/Unser Blvd. and follow signs for the park. ☎899-0205. Park open daily 8am-5pm. Admission to Boca Negra Canyon M-F $1, Sa-Su $2; National Parks passes accepted.

Located at the edge of suburbia on Albuquerque's west side, this national monument features more than 20,000 images etched into lava rocks between 1300 and 1680 by Pueblo Indians and Spanish settlers. The park encompasses much of the 17 mi. West Mesa, a ridge of black basalt boulders that formed as a result of volcanic activity 130,000 years ago. The most easily accessible petroglyphs can be found via three short trails at **Boca Negra Canyon,** 2 mi. north of the Visitors Center. The **Rinconada Canyon Trail,** 1 mi. south of the Visitors Center, has more intricate rock art and is an easy 2.5 mi. desert hike along the base of the West Mesa. The best art awaits at the back of the canyon.

MANZANO MOUNTAINS

The Manzano Mountains southeast of Albuquerque were formed in the same geologic upheavals as the Sandías to the north. The range reaches heights of 10,000 ft. and contains lush forests of ponderosa pine, birch, oak, maple, and aspen. Manzano is Spanish for "apple"—when Spanish explorers came in the 1700s, they found apple trees, a plant not native to North America. In all likelihood, the apples had been obtained by Native Americans trading with other Spaniards. Despite their proximity to Albuquerque, the Manzanos receive little use, so campers and hikers can expect to find themselves alone with nature.

The 37,000-acre **Manzano Wilderness** is known for some wonderful hiking trails. To access the **Red Canyon Loop** (7.5 mi. round-trip, 4-6hr.), take Rte. 55 north to Manzano and go 6 mi. on Forest Rd. 253 to Red Canyon Campground. Trail 189 climbs through the forest for 3 mi. and reaches a junction with Trail 170. Take

Trail 170 for 1 mi. Here you can go west off the trail for a few hundred yards to the 10,003 ft. summit of Gallo Peak. From this vantage point, you can see nearly 100 mi. of the Río Grande Valley and the Jemez, Sandía, and San Mateo Mountains. Back on the trail for ½ mile, Trail 170 meets Trail 89 in a large meadow. Trail 89 returns to the trailhead through Red Canyon, passing two seasonal waterfalls. The **Albuquerque Trail** (3.2 mi. loop) is an easier hike through a grove of maple trees that turn brilliant colors in late October. The trail begins at a marked sign, 6.9 mi. east of the tiny town of Tajique along Forest Rd. 55.

The quiet town of **Mountainair** sits at the center of the Manzano Mountains region's attractions. To reach the town, take I-40 E to exit 175, drive 30 mi. south on Rte. 337, turn east onto Rte. 55 and continue 24 mi. into town. The **Forest Ranger District Office** in Mountainair sells topo maps and is a helpful resource for hiking and camping info. (☎847-2990. Open M-F 8am-4:30pm.) Those coming from Albuquerque and other points north should obtain this information at the ranger station on Rte. 337 just south of exit 175 on I-40. Located in Mountainair, the main **Visitors Center** for the **Salinas Pueblo Missions National Monument** orients visitors to the site and has info. At the time of the Spanish colonization in the 17th century, the Salinas Valley had a thriving Native American population. Catholic priests forced the natives to convert to Christianity and build massive stone churches. Harsh treatment by the Spanish, disease, and Apache raids led to the abandonment of these villages by the 1670s. The pueblo ruins are a fairly long, but worthwhile, drive from Albuquerque. Begin by watching the free 15min. video at the **Visitors Center,** 201 W. Broadway, in Mountainair. (☎847-2585. Open Jan.-Aug. daily 8am-6pm; Sept.-May 8am-5pm.) There are three ruins: **Gran Quivira** (☎847-2290), the largest site, is 25 mi. south of Mountainair on Rte. 55; **Abo** (☎847-2400) is 9 mi. west of Mountainair on U.S. 60; and **Quarai** (☎847-2290) is 8 mi. north of Mountainair on Rte. 55. (All 3 sites open June-Aug. daily 9am-7pm; Sept.-May 9am-5pm. Free.)

There are six developed campgrounds in the Manzano Mountain region of the **Cibola National Forest** as well as another campground operated by **Manzano Mountains State Park.** Thirty miles south of Tijeras off Rte. 55 and about 4 mi. up Forest Rd. 55 in Tajique, the free Tajique Campground has vault toilets but no drinking water. **Red Canyon Campground ❶,** 6 mi. west of Rte. 55 at the town of Manzano on Rte. 131/Forest Rd. 253, has vault toilets and drinking water (sites $7). The **Manzano Mountains State Park ❶,** 3 mi. up Rte. 131/Forest Rd. 253, has the most facilities, with flush toilets, running water, and RV sites. (☎847-2820. Tent sites $8, full hookups $14. Gates close at sunset.)

ROUTE 14: TURQUOISE TRAIL TO SANTA FE ☎505

The scenic and historic **Turquoise Trail** extends along Rte. 14 between Albuquerque and Sante Fe. Miners once harvested copious amounts of turquoise, gold, silver, and coal from the surrounding area, but the town suffered greatly during the Great Depression. Six miles north of I-40 and exit 175 on Rte. 14 is the turnoff for Sandía Crest and the unique **Tinkertown Museum.**

Following the highway another 26 mi. north on Rte. 14 brings you into the former coal-mining town of **Madrid** (*MA-drid*). In 1898, the town had one of the state's first electric power plants, and during the 1940s, the town's coal mines supplied operations in Los Alamos. Today, hippie refugees populate the town, cranking out offbeat art instead of minerals. **The Old Coal Mine Museum,** 2846 Rte. 14, has an interesting collection of relics from the days when Madrid was a booming coal town. (☎438-3780. Open daily 9:30am-5:30pm. $3, children $1.) The locally-revered **Mine Shaft Tavern ❷**, next to the museum, busts out the self-proclaimed "best burgers west of the Mississippi." (☎473-0743. Food served M, Tu, Th 11am-4pm; F-Su 11am-8pm. W special dinners 5-7pm. Bar open M-Th 11am-11pm, F-Sa 11am-2am,

Su 11am-midnight. Live music W 6-9pm, F 9pm-1am, Sa 2-6pm and 9pm-1am, Su 2-6pm.) If you need a pick-me-up on the road, **Java Junction,** 2855 Rte. 14, in the middle of town, offers lattes ($2.60), mochas ($3.10), as well as a selection of coffee-themed T-shirts and a one-room B&B upstairs. (☎438-2772. Open 7:30am-6pm.)

Three miles past Madrid is the ghost town of **Cerrillos.** In the 1880s this town, with 21 saloons and four hotels, was nearly chosen to be the state capital. The 83-year-old **Cerrillos Bar,** at Main St. and 1st St., hasn't changed a bit since then. (Open daily 10am-9pm.) Farther north on Rte. 14 is the **Garden of the Gods** rock formation. The trail ends 19 mi. north of Cerrillos at I-40, just south of Santa Fe.

SANTA FE ☎505

In today's Santa Fe, you're much more likely to encounter khaki-clad tourists than conquistadors, but it's still possible to find places with great character and authenticity. Traditional adobe buildings adorn narrow streets that wind and curve, and, unlike in any other Southwestern city, walking is still an adequate means of transportation. Founded by the Spanish in 1608, Santa Fe is the second-oldest city in the US and the only state capital to serve under the administrations of three countries. Lying at the convergence of the Santa Fe Trail, an old trading route running from Missouri, and the Camino Real ("Royal Road"), which originates in Mexico City, Santa Fe has always been a place of commerce and bustle. These days, art is the trade of choice, with Native Americans, native New Mexicans, and transplanted New Yorkers all hawking their wares on the streets and in the galleries surrounding the Central Plaza. In recent years, Santa Fe's popularity has skyrocketed, leading to an influx of gated communities, ritzy restaurants, and Californian millionaires. As a result, the city can be expensive, but the fabulous art museums, traditional churches, and mountain trails make it a worthwhile stop.

▐ TRANSPORTATION

Buses: Greyhound, 858 St. Michael's Dr. (☎471-0008). To: **Albuquerque** (1½hr., 4 per day, $10.50); **Denver** (8-10hr., 4 per day, $59); **Taos** (1½hr., 2 per day, $14). Open M-F 7am–9:45pm, Sa-Su 7-9am, 12:30-1:30pm, 3:30-5pm, and 7:30-9:30pm.

Trains: Amtrak's nearest station is in Lamy (☎466-4511, 800-USARAIL), 18 mi. south on U.S. 285. 1 train daily to: **Albuquerque** (1hr., $18-27); **Flagstaff** (7hr., $64-118); **Kansas City** (17hr., $83-198); **Los Angeles** (18½hr., $56-132). Call ☎982-8829 in advance for a shuttle to Santa Fe ($16). Open daily 8am-5pm.

Public Transit: Santa Fe Trails, 2931 Rufina St. (☎955-2001). Runs 9 downtown bus routes M-F 6am-11pm, Sa 8am-8pm, Su (routes 1, 2, 4, and M only) 10am-7pm. Most bus routes start at the downtown Sheridan Transit Center, 1 block from the plaza between Marcy St. and Palace Ave. Buses #21 and 24 go down Cerrillos Rd., the M goes to the museums on Camino Lejo, and #5 passes the Greyhound station on its route between St. Vincents Hospital and the W. Alameda Commons. $0.75, ages 6-12 $0.50; day pass $1. **Sandía Shuttle Express** (☎474-5696, 888-775-5696) runs from downtown hotels to the Albuquerque airport every hour on the hour 5am-5pm, and from Albuquerque to Santa Fe hourly 8:45am-10:45pm (one-way $23, round-trip $40). Reserve at least 4 days in advance. Open M-F 6am-6pm, Sa-Su 6am-5pm.

Car Rental: Enterprise Rent-a-Car, 2641 Cerrillos Rd. (☎473-3600). $45 per day, $240 per week. Must be 21+ with driver's license and major credit card. Open M-F 8am-6pm, Sa 9am-noon. **Advantage Rent-a-Car,** 1907 St. Michael's Dr. $35 per day, $175 per week. $15 per day surcharge for ages 21-24. Open M-F 7:30am-6pm, Sa 8am-4pm.

Taxis: Capital City Taxi, ☎438-0000.

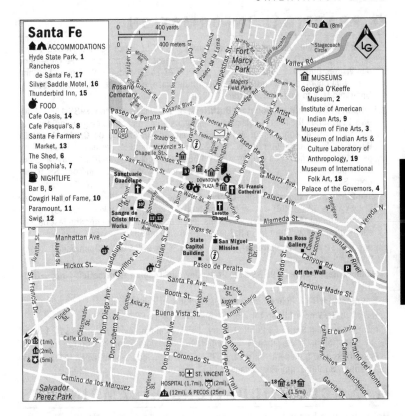

Santa Fe

🏠🏕 ACCOMMODATIONS
Hyde State Park, **1**
Rancheros
de Santa Fe, **17**
Silver Saddle Motel, **16**
Thunderbird Inn, **15**

🍴 FOOD
Cafe Oasis, **14**
Cafe Pasqual's, **8**
Santa Fe Farmers'
Market, **13**
The Shed, **6**
Tia Sophia's, **7**

🍸 NIGHTLIFE
Bar B, **5**
Cowgirl Hall of Fame, **10**
Paramount, **11**
Swig, **12**

🏛 MUSEUMS
Georgia O'Keeffe
Museum, **2**
Institute of American
Indian Arts, **9**
Museum of Fine Arts, **3**
Museum of Indian Arts &
Culture Laboratory of
Anthropology, **19**
Museum of International
Folk Art, **18**
Palace of the Governors, **4**

NEW MEXICO

✦ ORIENTATION

Santa Fe, abutting the jagged peaks of the **Sangre de Cristo Mountains,** stands at an elevation of 7000 ft., some 58 mi. northeast of the state capital at Albuquerque along Interstate 25. The streets of downtown Santa Fe seem to wind through the town without rhyme or reason; to navigate, it's helpful to think of the city as a wagon wheel, with the Plaza in the center of the wheel and major roads pointing outwards from the center like the spokes. **Paseo de Peralta** runs a full a loop all the way around the downtown area, and the main roads leading out towards I-25 are **Cerrillos Road, Saint Francis Drive,** and **Old Santa Fe Trail.** Except for the museums located southeast of the city center, most upscale restaurants and sights in Santa Fe are located within a cluster of a few blocks in the **downtown plaza** and just inside the loop formed by the **Paseo de Peralta.** The city's array of narrow streets make driving quite troublesome in Santa Fe; park your car in one of the lots and pound the pavement on foot. You'll find several public **parking lots** within walking distance of the plaza. Most convenient to the city's attractions is the municipal parking lot, just one block south of the plaza on Water St. between Don Gaspar Ave. and Shelby St. Metered parking spaces line both sides of the streets near the plaza (2hr. maximum). Parking is also available along the streets near the many art galleries on Canyon Rd.

🗹 PRACTICAL INFORMATION

Visitor Information: Visitors Information Center, 491 Old Santa Fe Trail (☎875-7400, 800-545-2040). Open daily 8am-6:30pm; off-season 8am-5pm. **Santa Fe Convention and Visitors Bureau,** 201 W. Marcy St. (☎800-777-2489, 955-6200). Open M-F 8am-5pm. **Info booth,** at the northwest corner of the plaza, next to the First National Bank. Open mid-May to Aug. daily 9:30am-4:30pm.

Equipment Rental: Wild Mountain Outfitters, 851 St. Michael's Dr. (☎986-1152, 800-988-1152), has the largest selection of hiking, camping and climbing gear in Santa Fe. Open M-Sa 9am-7pm, winter 9:30am-6pm, closed Su. **Sangre de Cristo Mountain Works,** 328 S. Guadalupe St. (☎984-8221), rents tents ($12 per day, $50 per 5-day period; $200 deposit) as well as sleeping bags and backpacks ($10 per day, $45 per 5-day period; $100 deposit) to prospective campers. Open M-F 10am-7pm, Sa 10am-6pm, Su noon-5pm.

Bike Rental: Sun Mountain Bike Company, located at 102 E. Water St. in the back of El Centro (☎982-8986; www.sunmountainbikeco.com), rents bikes for 1 day ($28), extended rental ($15 per day), and offers "night before" pick-up during the last hour of each business day. Open M-Sa 8:30am-6pm, Su 10am-5pm.

Laundromat: Adobe Laundromat, 411 W. Water St. (☎982-9063). Open daily 6:30am-9pm. Last wash 8pm.

Hotlines: Rape Abuse, ☎986-9111, 24hr. **Gay and Lesbian Information Line,** ☎891-3647.

Emergency: ☎911. **Police:** 2515 Camino Entrada (☎955-5033).

Hospital: St. Vincent Hospital, 455 St. Michael's Dr. (☎983-3361).

Internet Access: Santa Fe Public Library, 145 Washington Ave. (☎955-6781), 1 block northeast of the Plaza. Open M-Th 10am-9pm, F-Sa 10am-6pm, Su 1-5pm.

Post Office: 120 S. Federal Pl. (☎988-6351), next to the courthouse. Open M-F 7:30am-5:45pm, Sa 9am-1pm. **Postal code:** 87501.

🛏 🛏 ACCOMMODATIONS & CAMPING

Hotels in Santa Fe tend toward the expensive side. As early as May they become swamped with requests for rooms during **Indian Market** and **Fiesta de Santa Fe** (see **Festivals,** p. 393). Make reservations early or risk ending up homeless. In general, the motels along **Cerrillos Road** have the best prices, but even these places run $40-60 per night. For budget travelers, nearby camping is pleasant even during the summer and is much easier on the wallet. Two popular sites for free primitive camping are **Big Tesuque ❶** and **Ski Basin Campgrounds ❶** on national forest land. These campgrounds are both off Rte. 475 toward the Ski Basin and have pit toilets.

Thunderbird Inn, 1821 Cerrillos Rd. (☎983-4397). Slightly closer to town than the motel, and an excellent value (for Santa Fe, anyway). Large rooms, some with fridges and microwaves, all with A/C and cable TV. Reception 24hr. Summer singles $50-55, doubles $55-60; winter $39-44/$44-49. ❸

Silver Saddle Motel, 2810 Cerrillos Rd. (☎471-7663). Beautiful adobe rooms decorated with cowboy paraphernalia have A/C and cable TV. Reception 7am-11:30pm. Summer singles $67, doubles $72; winter $45/50. ❹

Rancheros de Santa Fe, 736 Old Las Vegas Hwy. (☎466-3482). Take I-25 N to exit 290 (Klein's Corner), turn left and make an immediate right onto Old Las Vegas Hwy. Proceed just over a mile to a big, friendly campground with 23 acres of land, swimming pool, laundry, groceries, and nightly movies. Tent sites in a secluded wooded area with fire pits and showers. Sites $19, full hookups $30; 2-bed rustic cabins $40. ❷

Hyde State Park Campground (☎983-7175), 8 mi. from Santa Fe on Rte. 475, has over 50 sites in the forest with water, pit toilets, fire rings, and shelters. Sites $10, hookups $14. No reservations for tent sites. ❶

🔾 FOOD

Spicy Mexican served on blue corn tortillas is the Santa Fe style. Wandering down sidestreets reveals the smaller Mexican restaurants where locals eat; grill carts in the plaza peddle fragrant fajitas ($3) and fresh lemonade ($1). **Albertson's,** 199 Paseo de Paralta, ½ mile northwest of the plaza in the De Vargas Mall, is the closest supermarket to downtown. (☎988-2804. Open daily 6am-midnight.) If you can't get enough of New Mexican cuisine, consider a 2½hr. cooking class at the **Santa Fe School of Cooking,** 116 W. San Francisco St. (☎983-7540. Courses $40-60.)

▩ **Santa Fe Farmers' Market** (☎983-4098; www.farmersmarketsnm.org/santafe), at the railyard near the intersection of Guadalupe St. and Paseo de Peralta, is a community focal point. Resident growers, bakers, and musicians gather on Saturdays to sell their wares. Fresh and organic produce, breakfast burritos ($3.50), and pastries ($3) are available. Open late Apr.-early Nov. Tu, Sa 7am-noon, Th at rodeo grounds 3-7pm. With less variety, mid-May to late Oct. Tu 7am-noon. Call to inquire about winter market. ❶

▩ **Tia Sophia's,** 210 W. San Francisco St. (☎983-9880). It looks and feels like a diner, but the food is exceptional. The most popular item is the Atrisco plate ($6)—chile stew, cheese enchilada, beans, *posole*, and a *sopapilla*. Open Tu-Sa 7am-2pm. ❶

▩ **Cafe Oasis,** 526 Galisteo St. (☎983-9599), at Paseo de Peralta. Take a break from the bustle of the city at this laid-back restaurant where all the food is organic and artistic expression is a way of being. Choose from several dining areas, including the Mushroom Room and outdoor patio garden. Creative dishes range from veggie enchiladas ($10.75) to *Samari* stir-fry ($13.50). Breakfast served all the time. Live music nightly. Open M-W 10am-midnight, Th-F 10am-2am, Sa 9am-2am, Su 9am-midnight. ❸

The Shed, 113½ E. Palace Ave. (☎982-9030), up the street from the plaza. Feels like a garden, even in the enclosed section. Lots of vegetarian dishes, like quesadillas ($6) and excellent blue corn burritos ($8.75). Meat-eaters will enjoy the amazing chicken enchilada verde ($10.75). Lunch M-Sa 11am-2:30pm, dinner M-Sa 5:30-9pm. ❷

Cafe Pasqual's, 121 Don Gaspar (☎983-9340). An intimate nook for healthy cuisine. Decorations evoke Oaxaca and complement the Free Range Organic Chicken Mole Enchiladas ($19). Open year-round 7am-3pm, 6-10pm. Reservations recommended. ❹

🅁🄻 NIGHTLIFE & ENTERTAINMENT

More mellow than those in Albuquerque, the bars in Santa Fe attract a mix of tourists, artists, bums, and millionaires. Here you might walk into a bar and booze with an investment banker and the sculptor who crafted the Pope's metal cross.

Cowgirl Hall of Fame, 319 S. Guadalupe St. (☎982-2565). Live music hoe-downs range from bluegrass to country. BBQ, Mexican food, and burgers served all evening, with midnight food specials. Ranch breakfast served weekend mornings. 12 microbrews on tap. Happy Hour 3-6pm and midnight-1am; Cowgirl Margaritas $3.50. 21+ after midnight. Cover up to $3. Open M-F 11am-2am, Sa 8:30am-2am, Su 8:30am-midnight.

Paramount, 331 Sandoval St. (☎982-8999). The only dance club around. Trash disco W is packed. Dance Sa, live music Tu, Th, Su. 21+. Cover $5-7, Sa $5-20. Open M-Sa 9pm-2am, Su 9pm-midnight.

Bar B, 331 Sandoval St. (☎982-8999), in back of Paramount. A futuristic setting with live music most nights. Cover $2-7. Open M-Sa 5pm-2am, Su 5pm-midnight.

MATTERS OF LIFE & DEATH

November 1's **Día de los Muertos Day of the Dead)** is a Southwestern holiday of colorful traditions. Visitors in Mexico are likely to see a raucous festival of mariachis and drunken revelry, and in urban areas the influence of the US's Halloween is visible in the witch and vampire costumes that children wear. North of the border, however, Mexican-Americans observe *Día de los Muertos* as a way of celebrating and preserving their heritage. Families construct altars in their homes and decorate them with candles, *papel picado* colorful tissue paper cut into intricate designs influenced by Aztec traditions), pictures of deceased relatives, flowers, and offerings of food. *Calaveras,* humorous skeleton figurines made of sugar or chick peas, are placed on the altar or given to children.

The goal of *Día de los Muertos* is primarily to honor and remember the dead, but the *Calaveras* and sometimes festive atmosphere serve another purpose: they help people accept death as a part of life and remind them that to fear death is to deny a natural and inevitable aspect of living.

If you're in southern New Mexico on November 1, the celebration at historic Mesilla near Las Cruces is a good one to attend. In the north there are usually several *Día de los Muertos* gallery events in artsy Santa Fe.

Swig (☎ 955-0400; www.i-swig.net), at the corner of Palace St. and Grant Ave. Climb up to the 3rd floor for an upscale, elevated club experience. Sip a martini ($5) on the intimate balcony of the bamboo room, chill in the blue room or the smoking room, or dance to techno in the red room. DJs W-Sa. Cover $5 for shows. Tu-Sa 5pm-1:30am.

◎ SIGHTS

The grassy **Plaza de Santa Fe** is a good starting point for exploring the museums, sanctuaries, and galleries of the city. Since 1609, this large plaza has been the site of religious ceremonies, military gatherings, markets, cockfights, and public punishments—now it shelters ritzy shops and packs of loitering tourists. Historic **walking tours** leave from the blue doors of the Palace of the Governors on Lincoln St. (May-Oct., M-Sa 10:15am. $10.)

MNM MUSEUMS. Sante Fe is home to six imaginative, world-class museums. Four are run by **The Museum of New Mexico** umbrella group. They all keep the same hours and charge the same admission. A worthwhile four-day pass ($15) includes admission to all four museums and can be purchased at any of them. (☎ 827-6463; www.museumofnewmexico.org. Open Tu-Su 10am-5pm. $7, under 16 free. The 2 downtown museums—Fine Arts and Palace of the Governors—are both free F 5-8pm.) Inhabiting a large adobe building on the northwest corner of the plaza the **Museum of Fine Arts** dazzles visitors with the works of major Southwestern artists, as well as contemporary exhibits of often controversial American art. (107 W. Palace Ave. ☎ 476-5072. Open daily 10am-5pm.) The **Palace of the Governors,** on the north side of the plaza, is the oldest public building in the US and was the seat of seven successive governments after its construction in 1610. The *haciendas* palace is now a museum with exhibits on Native American, Southwestern, and New Mexican history, with an interesting exhibit on Jewish Pioneers. (107 W. Palace Ave. ☎ 476-5100.) The most distinctive museums in town are 2½ mi. south of the Plaza on Old Santa Fe Trail. The fascinating **Museum of International Folk Art** houses the Girard Collection, which includes over 10,000 handmade dolls, doll houses, and other toys from around the world. The miniature village scenes are straight out of a fairy tale. Other galleries display changing ethnographic exhibits. (706 Camino Lejo. ☎ 476-1200.) Next door, the **Museum of Indian Arts and Culture Laboratory of Anthropology** displays Native American photos and artifacts. (710 Camino Lejo. ☎ 476-1250.)

OTHER PLAZA MUSEUMS. While Sante Fe's other museums have no affiliation with the MNM, they are just as worthwhile. The popular **Georgia O'Keeffe Museum** attracts the masses with O'Keeffe's famous flower paintings and some of her more abstract works. The collection spans her life and demonstrates her versatility. *(217 Johnson St. ☎946-1017. Open daily 10am-5pm. $8, under 17 and students with ID free; F 5-8pm free. Audio tour $5.)* Downtown's **Institute of American Indian Arts Museum** houses a collection of contemporary Indian art with a political edge. *(108 Cathedral Place. ☎983-8900. Open M-Sa 9am-5pm, Su noon-5pm. $4, students and seniors $2, under 16 free.)* The round **New Mexico State Capitol** was built in 1966 in the form of the Zia sun symbol. The House and Senate galleries are open to the public; the building also has an impressive art collection. *(☎986-4589. 5 blocks south of the Plaza on Old Santa Fe Rd. Open M-F 7am-7pm; June-Aug. Sa 8am-5pm. Free tours M-F 10am and 2pm.)*

CHURCHES. Santa Fe's Catholic roots are evident in the Romanesque **St. Francis Cathedral**, built from 1869 to 1886 under the direction of Archbishop Lamy (the central figure of Willa Cather's *Death Comes to the Archbishop*) to convert westerners to Catholicism. The architecture is especially striking against the desert. *(213 Cathedral Pl. ☎982-5619. One block east of the Plaza on San Francisco St. Open daily 7:30am-5:30pm.)* The **Loretto Chapel** was the first Gothic building west of the Mississippi, famous for its "miraculous" spiral staircase; see **Stairway to Heaven**, p. 394. *(207 Old Santa Fe Trail. ☎982-0092. 2 blocks south of the Cathedral. Open M-Sa 9am-5pm, Su 10:30am-5pm. $2.50, seniors and children $2.)* Southeast of the plaza lies the **San Miguel Mission**, at DeVargas St. and the Old Santa Fe Trail. Built in 1610 by the Tlaxcalan Indians, the mission is the oldest functioning church in the US. Also in the church is the San Jose Bell, made in Spain in 1356 and the oldest bell in the US. *(☎988-9504. Open M-Sa 9am-5pm, Su 10am-4pm; may close earlier in winter, 5pm mass Su only. $1.)*

GALLERIES. Santa Fe's most successful artists live and sell their work along Canyon Rd. To reach their galleries, depart the Plaza on San Francisco Dr., take a left on Alameda St., a right on Paseo de Peralta, and a left on Canyon Rd. Extending for about 1 mi., the road supports both galleries displaying all types of art and a number of indoor/outdoor cafes. Most galleries are open from 10am until 5pm. At the **Hahn Ross Gallery,** the work is hip, enjoyable, and way out of your price range. *(409 Canyon Rd. ☎984-8434. Open daily 10am-5pm.)*

A BIT OF CLASS. Old verse and distinguished acting invade the city each summer when **Shakespeare in Sante Fe** raises its curtain. The festival shows plays in an open-air theater on the St. John's College campus from late June to late August. *(Shows run F-Su 7:30pm. Number of shows per week varies; call to check the schedule. Reserved seating tickets $15-32; lawn seating is free, but a $5 donation is requested. Tickets available at show or call ☎982-2910.)* The **Santa Fe Opera**, on Opera Dr., performs outdoors against a mountain backdrop. Nights are cool; bring a blanket. *(7 mi. north of Santa Fe on Rte. 84/285. ☎800-280-4654, 877-999-7499; www.santafeopera.org. July W, F, Sa; Aug. M-Sa. Performances begin 8-9pm. Tickets $20-130, rush standing-room tickets $8-15; 50% student discount on same-day reserved seats. The box office is at the opera house; call or drop by the day of the show for prices and availability.)* The **Santa Fe Chamber Music Festival** celebrates the works of Baroque, Classical, Romantic, and 20th-century composers in the **St. Francis Auditorium of the Museum of Fine Arts** and the **Lensic Theater**. *(☎983-2075, tickets 982-1890; www.sfcmf.org. Mid-July to mid-Aug. Tickets $16-40, students $10.)*

▣ FESTIVALS

Santa Fe is home to two of the US's largest festivals. In the third week of August, the nation's largest and most impressive **Indian Market** floods the plaza. The **Southwestern Association for Indian Arts** (☎983-5220) has more info. **Don Diego de Vargas's**

NEW MEXICO

> ## STAIRWAY TO HEAVEN
> In 1873, under the guidance of Bishop Lamy and the Loretto Sisters, French and Italian masons began construction of a beautiful Gothic church in the heart of Santa Fe. After the building was finished, the sisters realized they had a problem: there wasn't room to build a staircase to the choir loft. Many carpenters tried, but each declared the task impossible. Rather than give up, the Loretto Sisters did what nuns do best—they prayed. According to legend, a gray-haired man appeared at the convent with a donkey and a tool chest. Using only a hammer, a saw, and a T-square, the carpenter built a wooden spiral staircase that made two 360° turns with no supporting pole in the center. When the sisters went to pay the man, he had vanished. Over the past 125 years, architects and structural engineers have been unable to explain how the staircase supports itself, and many agree that the wood is not from New Mexico. Some say the mysterious carpenter was St. Joseph himself.

peaceful reconquest of New Mexico in 1692 marked the end of the 12-year Pueblo Rebellion, now celebrated in the three-day **Fiesta de Santa Fe** (☎988-7575). Held in mid-September, festivities begin with the burning of the *Zozobra* (a 50 ft. marionette) and include street dancing, processions, and political satires. The *New Mexican* publishes a guide and a schedule of the fiesta's events.

🏔 OUTDOOR ACTIVITIES

There's a reason *Outside Magazine* bases itself in Santa Fe. The nearby **Sangre de Cristo Mountains** reach heights of over 12,000 ft. and offer countless opportunities for hikers, bikers, skiers, and snowboarders. The **Pecos** and **Río Grande** rivers make great playgrounds for kayakers, rafters, and canoers. Before heading into the wilderness, stop by the **Public Lands Information Center**, 1474 Rodeo Rd., near the intersection of St. Francis Rd. and I-25, to pick up maps, guides, and friendly advice. (☎438-7542, 877-276-9404; www.publiclands.org. Open M-F 8am-5pm, winter 8am-4:30pm.) The Sierra Club Guide to *Day Hikes in the Santa Fe Area* and the Falcon Guide to *Best Easy Day Hikes in Santa Fe* are good purchases for those planning to spend a few days hiking in the area.

HIKING. The closest trailheads to downtown Santa Fe are along Rte. 475 (Artist Rd.) on the way to the Santa Fe Ski Area. The **Chamisa Trail**, 4.5 mi. round-trip, leaves from a parking area 5.7 mi. north from Washington Ave. on Hyde Park Rd. (U.S. 475). The trail passes through open meadows and conifer forests, dropping down to end at the junction with Winsor Trail (#254) in an open meadow next to Tesuque Creek. Return to the parking area along the same trail, or for a change of scenery take Trail #183 for an easy second half of the return trip. For a longer loop, continue northeast on the **Winsor Trail** (which eventually leads up to the Santa Fe Ski Area) along Tesuque Creek for 1 mi. to the junction with **Bear Willow Trail** (#182). Follow Bear Willow east for 1 mi. and turn south on **Borrego Trail** (#150) to loop 4 mi. back to the parking area (7 mi. loop). For amazing views of the city, **Atalaya Mountain** (Trail #174) is an excellent choice. Beginning from the St. John's College parking lot off of Camino de Cruz Blanca Rd., the trail follows an arroyo for the first mile, then intersects with the **Atalya Mountain Trail** and climbs steeply. Increased residential development along the arroyo has decreased the wilderness appeal of the first mile. To bypass the area, start at the Atalaya Mountain Trailhead, approximately 0.75 mi. farther up Camino de Cruz Blanca.

During the past few years a new network of trails has been opened to the public. The **Dale Ball Trails**, 20 mi., provide many running, hiking, and biking loops only minutes from the town center. Parking lots are located on Upper Canyon Rd.

(accessible going south from the plaza on Old Santa Fe Trail) and Hyde Park Rd., left on Cerros Colorado Rd. The 4 mi. round-trip **Picacho Peak Trail** begins across Upper Canyon Rd. from the parking lot and involves many steep switchbacks during the last mile. Trails continue to be built, including a path from the top of Picacho Peak to the top of Atalaya. *(For more information about the Dale Ball Trails, contact the Foothills Forest Trust ☎983-9208.)*

Near the end of Rte. 475 and the Santa Fe Ski Area are trailheads that lead up into the 223,000 acre **Pecos Wilderness** (p. 399). For those in search of a day hike near Santa Fe, several trips lead into the adjacent **Santa Fe National Forest** from Artist Rd. A strenuous full-day climb to the top of 12,622 ft. **Santa Fe Baldy** (14 mi. round-trip) affords an amazing vista of the Pecos Wilderness Area to the north and east. The trailhead is marked on the left side of the road, 15 mi. northeast of Santa Fe on Rte. 475. Follow Trail 254 for 4.5 mi., then turn left on Trail #251, which leads up to the summit. Another good, strenuous hike is 12,000 ft. **Tesuque Peak** (12 mi. round-trip). The trail begins at the Aspen Vista Picnic Area, 13 mi. from Santa Fe on Rte. 475, and peaks at over 12,000 ft. From the parking area, the trail follows Forest Rd. 150 to the summit.

Sheltering one of New Mexico's most beautiful hikes, **Kasha-Katuwe Tent Rocks National Monument** has two short trails that wind through spectacular slot canyons towering over a hundred feet high. The slot canyon trail continues up the mesa: the view at top is worth triple the exertion. *(To reach the trailhead from Santa Fe, take I-25 S to exit 264. Turn right onto Rte. 16, go 8 mi., and turn right onto Rte. 22. To stay on Rte. 22, make a left into Cochiti Pueblo and then turn right onto Forest Rd. 266. The parking area is 5 mi. from the turnoff. ☎761-8700. Vehicles $5.)*

BIKING. Sun Mountain Bike Company rents bikes (p. 390) and offers guided tours. *($60 per day.)* Craig Martin's *Santa Fe Area Mountain Bike Trails* ($12) has detailed listings of 34 mountain bike trails in the area. The **Santa Fe Rail Trail** (12.6 mi. one-way) is the most popular local ride, following the tracks between Santa Fe and Lamy. To reach the trailhead from downtown Santa Fe, drive south on St. Francis Dr. and turn right onto Rabbit Rd. The dirt parking area is on the left just before the railroad tracks. Many bikers choose to ride the steep, 17 mi. **Route 475** between Santa Fe and the ski area. A loop connects Rte. 475 with the Winsor Trail/Chamisa Trail (see **Hiking**) for a moderately tough ride. A more challenging backcountry trip, climbing Forest Road 150 to the top of **Tesuque Peak** requires hard work on the uphill portion of the trail, but the downhill return trip is a just reward. On a bike, the **Atalaya Mountain** (**see Hiking**) is an advanced peak ride, climbing 1600 ft. over 3 mi. A good beginner trail is **Arroyo Chamiso** (6 mi. one-way, junctions with the **Winsor Trail**). The trailhead is the first large trailhead in the Santa Fe National Forest going north on Hyde Park Rd., lying 2 mi. beyond 10,000 Waves.

CLIMBING. Amazing climbing areas dot the Santa Fe region. **Vertical Ventures** offers guided climbing trips in various areas including the Jemez Mountains, El Rito, White Rock, the Y, the Sandía Mountains, and the Taos area. *(☎820-0919; www.verticleventuresinc.com. Full day 1 person $205, 2 people $150 per person, 3/$120, 4/ $105. Multi-day courses available. Call for reservations.)*

SKIING. Only 16 mi. northeast of downtown, **Ski Sante Fe** heats up the winters. Located in the towering Sangre De Cristo Mountains on Rte. 475, the ski area operates six lifts, including four chairs and two surface lifts, servicing 43 trails (20% beginner, 40% intermediate, 40% advanced) on 600 acres of terrain with a 1650 ft. vertical drop. *(☎982-4429. Snowboards welcome. Annual snowfall 225 in. Open late Nov. to early Apr. 9am-4pm. Lift tickets: full day $45, teens $37, children and seniors $33, half day $33. Rental packages start at $18.)*

TIME: 2-3hr. driving time

DISTANCE: 70 mi.

SEASON: year-round

Although most travelers zip between Santa Fe and Taos using the U.S. 285/Rte. 68 path through the Río Grande Valley (a.k.a. "The Low Road"), a far more scenic journey awaits along the High Road. This series of roads passes through the foothills of the Sangre de Cristo Mountains, past Indian pueblos, old Spanish villages, green pastures, and thick forests of Ponderosa pine, making it well worth the extra time. The entirely paved road begins at the intersection of U.S. 285 and Rte. 503, 15 mi. north of Santa Fe, and ends at the Rte. 518/68 intersection, 3 mi. south of Taos. Be sure to allow extra time for jaunts off the main road.

1 GETTING STARTED. From Santa Fe, head north on U.S. 285. The **Pojoaque Pueblo Visitors Information Center and Gift Shop,** 14 mi. from Santa Fe, has free maps of the High Road and brochures on all the pueblos of northern New Mexico. (☎455-3460. Open M-Sa 9am-5:30pm.) The actual pueblo of Pojoaque is preoccupied with running the lucrative **Cities of Gold Casino,** so there isn't much to see in the pueblo itself. Located on the road to Los Alamos 5.5 mi. west of Pojoaque, **San Ildefonso Pueblo** is famous for its distinctive black-on-black pottery. Visitors can browse the many pottery shops and take a self-guided tour around the central plaza. (☎455-3549. Visiting hours daily 8am-5pm. Vehicles $3.) To begin the High Road, turn right on Rte. 503, 1 mi. north of the Pojoaque Visitors Center.

2 NAMBE PUEBLO & WATERFALLS. Three miles past the start of Rte. 503, two signs point the way to Nambe Falls and Nambe Pueblo. Drive 1.8 mi. down the paved road and turn right to see the center of the pueblo, with its church and kiva, set off against the stunning backdrop of the **Sangre de Cristo Mountains.** The main attractions of this side-trip are the **waterfalls** and **campground ❶,** 6 mi. past the center of the pueblo at the end of the paved road. A 15min. hike leads to views of waterfalls.

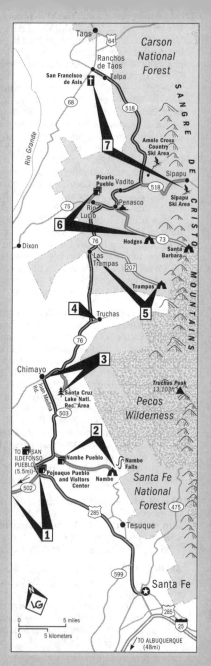

ROAD TRIP

396

(☎455-2304. Open Mar. to mid-Nov. 7am-8pm. Day use $5 per car, camping $20 per car, fishing $10 per person, photo permit $10.) Continuing on Rte. 503 past the Nambe Pueblo turn-off, the road climbs swiftly out of the thick lowland vegetation and curves through sandy-colored hills dotted intermittently with green shrubs. The Jemez Mountains rise to the left and the Sangre de Cristos to the right.

8 CHIMAYO. Five miles past Nambe Pueblo, turn left on **Juan Medina Road** (County Road 98) to get to Chimayo. At the end of Juan Medina Rd. turn right onto Rte. 76. For a side-trip to **Santa Cruz Lake Recreation Area ❶,** turn right after 2 mi. and follow the signs up the winding road to the lake. The BLM-run recreation area has fishing, boating, hiking trails, and camping, but no swimming. (☎758-8851. Day use $5 per vehicle, camping $9.)

4 TRUCHAS. The farming village of Truchas is 8 mi. up Rte. 76 from Chimayo. Though the highway bears left, it's worth a side-trip through the town to see the picturesque farms, meadows, and old houses, as well as Truchas Peak (13,103 ft.) and other high peaks of the Pecos Wilderness. Robert Redford filmed *The Milagro Beanfield War* (1987) in this village.

5 LAS TRAMPAS. Eight miles past Truchas in the tiny hamlet of Las Trampas stands the **San José de Gracia Church,** one of the finest Spanish Colonial churches in New Mexico. One mile past it, the 8 mi. Forest Rd. 207 leads to the free **Trampas Campground ❶.** From here, two 12 mi. round-trip trails lead into the Pecos Wilderness, Trail 30 leading to the San Leonard Lakes and Trail 31 heading for Trampas Lakes. Five miles farther along Rte. 76, turn left on Rte. 75 and then right after a half a mile for a short detour to the **Picuris Pueblo.**

6 PICURIS PUEBLO. Hidden in a valley of the Sangre de Cristo Mountains, Picuris Pueblo is the most highly elevated and geographically isolated of New Mexico's pueblos, and the people of Picuris will tell you that they were the last tribe to be "discovered" by the Spaniards. Pueblo residents celebrate the annual **San Lorenzo Feast Day** (Aug. 9-10) with dances, foot races, and church services. (☎587-2519 or 587-2957. Open daily 8am-5pm. Self-guided tour $3 per person, $5 with photo permit.)

Turn east onto Rte. 75 continue toward Taos. The turnoff for Rte. 73 leads to free **Hodges Campground ❶** and **Santa Barbara Campground ❷** ($12) in the **Carson National Forest.** Santa Barbara Campground serves as a trailhead for hikes into the northern Pecos Wilderness. **Carson Forest Camino Real Ranger District,** 15160 Rte. 75, just north of the turn in Penasco, sells maps and provides info on hiking and camping in the Carson National Forest. (Open M-F 8am-4:30pm.)

7 FINISHING UP. Past Penasco, Rte. 75 runs through the village of **Vadito.** Just after Vadito, Rte. 518 intersects with 75; turn left to continue to Taos, or continue on Rte. 75 for 6 mi. and a quick side-trip leading to the rustic **Sipapu Ski Area** (☎587-2240). The **Amole Cross Country Ski Area** (☎758-6200) sits 1.5 mi. north of the junction of Rte. 518. 18 mi. farther, Rte. 518 meets Rte. 68 in **Ranchos de Taos.** Turn left and drive a quarter of a mile to get to the San Francisco de Asis Church. This striking structure is one of the US's most photographed churches and has been immortalized by Georgia O'Keeffe and Ansel Adams. (☎758-2754. Church open M-Sa 9am-4pm.)

RIVER RUNNING. While the Río Grande doesn't actually flow through Santa Fe, there are a few outfitters in town that run rafting trips on it. **Santa Fe Rafting,** 1000 Cerrillos Rd. (☎988-4914 or 800-467-7238) and **New Wave Rafting Company,** 1101 Cerrillos Rd. (☎800-984-1444 or 984-1444) both offer guided half-day to three-day trips on rapids Class I-IV rapids. (Both companies half-day $40-50; full day $75-85.)

⚑ DAYTRIPS FROM SANTA FE

BANDELIER NATIONAL MONUMENT

Go 40 mi. northwest of Santa Fe off Rte. 502 on Rte. 4. Visitors Center: ☎672-3861, ext. 517. Open June-Aug. daily 8am-6pm; Sept. to late Oct. daily 9am-5:30pm; late Oct. to late Mar. 8am-4:30pm; late Mar.-May 9am-5:30pm.

Bandelier features the remains of spectacular cliff dwellings, stone houses, and ceremonial underground rooms called *kivas,* amid some of the most awe-inspiring scenery in New Mexico. The Ancestral Puebloan forefathers of today's Pueblo Indians inhabited this area between the 12th and 16th centuries, living in small villages of stone and mud houses and farming the fertile soil along the canyon floors. The **Visitors Center,** 3 mi. into the park at the bottom of **Frijoles Canyon,** has an archaeological museum and shows a short video. Just past the main entrance, **Juniper Campground ❶** offers the only developed camping in the park, with water and toilets (sites $10). Get a free permit at the Visitors Center for **backcountry camping.** Water is available year-round in Capulin Canyon, Upper Alamo Canyon, and Frijoles Canyon, making these popular spots to camp. Bandelier encompasses 33,000 acres of wilderness with over 70 mi. of backcountry trails. All visitors should start by hiking the 1.2 mi. **Main Loop Trail** to see the **cliff dwellings** and the ruins of the Tyuonyi Pueblo. Part of the trail is wheelchair accessible, but reaching the dwellings requires climbing narrow stairs. You can continue ½ mi. past the Main Loop Trail to the **Ceremonial Cave,** a *kiva* carved into a natural alcove.

More aggressive hikers will delight in Bandelier's offerings. **Frijoles Falls** (5 mi. round-trip) begins at the Visitors Center and follows the Frijoles Creek downstream 2½ mi. to the Río Grande. Upper Frijoles Falls, dropping 80 ft., is 1.5 mi. from the trailhead. The **Tsankawi Trail** (1.5 mi. round-trip) is in a different area of Bandelier from the Visitors Center. To reach the trail, turn right when leaving the park and follow Rte. 4 for 11 mi. Just past the third stoplight there will be a parking area on the right. The trail meanders along the top of a mesa and passes unexcavated cliff dwellings, pueblo ruins, and petroglyphs. Be wary of nasty weather on the exposed mesa. A multi-day backpacking trip, **Yapashi Ruin and Painted Cave** (22 mi. round-trip), leads into the Bandelier wilderness, climbing mesas and passing the unexcavated Yapashi Pueblo and the beautiful Painted Cave.

PECOS NATIONAL HISTORICAL PARK

The park is 30 mi. southeast of Santa Fe. From the city, take I-25 N to exit 299; drive east on Rte. 50, go right at the only intersection in Pecos, and drive 2 mi. south on Rte. 63. ☎757-6414, ext. 1. Open June-Aug. daily 8am-6pm; Sept.-May 8am-5pm. Entrance $3, under 16 free. National Parks passes accepted.

Before the time of the Spanish conquest, over 2000 natives lived here in high-rise adobe complexes. They grew corn, beans, and squash, traded extensively with nomadic Plains Indians, and partook in ritual religious ceremonies in *kivas.* Franciscan priests who arrived at the beginning of the 17th century forced the natives to abandon the *kivas* and embrace Catholicism. Today, visitors can take an easy 1 mi. walk through the ruins of the pueblo and its Spanish mission church. Two reconstructed *kivas* are open to the public and provide a first-hand look at ceremonial life in the pueblo. The **Visitors Center** has a tiny museum and a 10min. video.

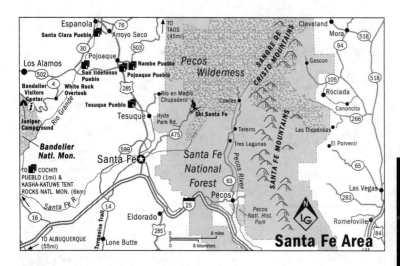

Santa Fe Area

NEAR SANTA FE

Offering countless galleries, restaurants, and old churches, Santa Fe is a must-see destination for travelers in New Mexico, but don't be surprised to find yourself anxious for a getaway from the pricey glamour of this artsy city. When the feeling strikes, you're in luck. Not far from Santa Fe, you can find hiking and solitude in the Pecos Wilderness, nuclear secrets in Los Alamos, archaeological sites and outdoor excitement in the Jemez Mountains, elk herds and volcanic valleys in Valles Caldera, and a quick taste of pueblos and old villages along the High Road to Taos.

PECOS WILDERNESS AREA ☎505

The Pecos Wilderness protects 233,667 acres of high country in the heart of the Sangre de Cristo Mountains, punctuated by the second highest peak in New Mexico, 13,103 ft. Truchas Peak. Winters are long and snowy, but from late spring to early autumn this is an ideal spot for backcountry hiking. The upper Pecos River is the premier trout-fishing area in the Southwest, so don't be surprised to find campgrounds crowded with Texan anglers. Once you get a few miles into the backcountry, you'll find yourself alone amid gorgeous mountains, forests, and rivers.

🚩 **PRACTICAL INFORMATION.** There are two main access roads into the Pecos Wilderness: **Route 475** from **Santa Fe** and **Route 63** from **Pecos,** 28 mi. southeast of Santa Fe. The trails along Rte. 475 tend to be more crowded because of their proximity to a major city. Prime fishing spots are located along Rte. 63 north of Pecos. Before heading into the wilderness, stop by the **Pecos Ranger District Office,** on Rte. 63 just south of Rte. 50, to pick up large topo maps ($7) and free descriptive trail handouts. (☎757-6121. Open June-Aug. M-Sa 8am-5pm, Sept.-May M-F 8am-4:30pm.) More info on the Pecos Wilderness is available at the **Public Lands Information Center** in Santa Fe (p. 394). **Santa Fe Fly fishers** hosts guided fly fishing from late spring to early fall along their private stretch of river above Tererro. (☎757-3294; www.santaflyfishers.com. Half-day trips: 1 person $200; 2 people, $250 per person. ¾ day: $250/$300. Full day: $300/$350. Additional fees for use of private water

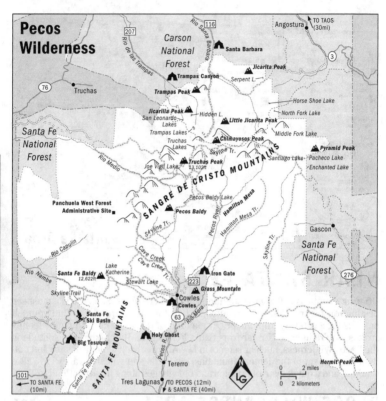

Pecos Wilderness

Carson National Forest

TO TAOS (30mi)

Angostura

Santa Barbara

Jicarita Peak

Serpent L.

Trampas Canyon

Trampas Peak

Truchas

Jicarilla Peak

San Leonardo Lakes

Hidden L.

Little Jicarita Peak

Horse Shoe Lake

North Fork Lake

Santa Fe National Forest

Trampas Lakes

Truchas Lakes

Chimayosos Peak

Middle Fork Lake

Skyline Tr.

Pyramid Peak

Rio Medio

Joe Vigil Lake

Truchas Peak 13,102ft

Santiago Lake

Pacheco Lake

Enchanted Lake

SANGRE DE CRISTO MOUNTAINS

Pecos Baldy Lake

Hamilton Mesa

Panchuela West Forest Administrative Site

Pecos Baldy

Pecos River

Hamilton Mesa Tr.

Gascon

Rio Capulin

Skyline Tr.

Cave Creek

Cave Creek Tr.

Santa Fe National Forest

Rio Nambe

Santa Fe Baldy 12,622ft

Lake Katherine

Stewart Lake

Iron Gate

Grass Mountain

Skyline Trail

Skyline Tr.

Cowles

Cowles

SANTA FE MOUNTAINS

Santa Fe Ski Basin

Holy Ghost

Rio Mora

Big Tesuque

Pecos R.

Hermit Peak

Santa Fe River

Tererro

N

Tres Lagunas

TO SANTA FE (10mi)

TO PECOS (12mi) & SANTA FE (40mi)

0   2 miles

0   2 kilometers

and for equipment rental.) Excellent fishing spots dot the Pecos River, and there are many designated river access pull-offs between Pecos and Tererro. Pools abound north of Tererro (a small community 14 mi. north of Pecos on U.S. 63), but be wary of private property. For required **fishing licenses** and **groceries,** stop by **Adelo's Town and Country,** at Rte. 63 and Rte. 50. (☎757-8565. Open M-Sa 9am-7pm, Su 9am-2pm. 1-day license $14, 5-day license $22.)

CAMPING. There are **National Forest Campgrounds ❶** along both Rte. 475 and Rte. 63. Campsites are available only on a first-come, first-serve basis. **Field Tract ❶,** 10 mi. north of Pecos, is the only campground with flush toilets ($8). **Holy Ghost ❶, Cowles ❶,** and **Iron Gate ❶** have several trailheads that lead into the wilderness area. Free **backcountry camping** in the park does not require a permit. The Pecos is a fee area, so pay stations sit at every trailhead ($2-8 for day use, $6-20 overnight).

HIKING & BACKPACKING. Though the Pecos remains a pocket of designated wilderness, the crowds that tread the area's trails every summer are not insignificant. Good stewardship and **Leave No Trace** hiking and camping techniques are required to keep the wilderness from showing the ill effects of recreational traffic (see **Leave No Trace,** p. 65). The main way to travel the wilderness is by foot (no bicycles), though horses are allowed on most trails. The remote wilderness lends itself more to overnight camping than day hiking, but there are a few options for ambitious day hikers. The **Cave Creek Trail** (6-10 mi. round-trip) follows a tributary of the Pecos River through thick conifer forest. To reach the trailhead, drive north 20 mi. from Pecos, turn left at Cowles, and cross the water. Go right at Panchuela Rd. and follow it to the Panchuela Trailhead. Trail 288 follows the Panchuela Creek 1.5 mi. to an intersection with Cave Creek. Turn left and follow Cave Creek to a series of caves where the creek flows underground. For a shorter hike, turn around after the caves; otherwise, the trail continues 2 mi. up a steep incline. The grassy **Hamilton Mesa** (10,000 ft., 3-10 mi. one-way) is accessible from a trailhead at Iron Gate Campground by Trail 249. The road to Iron Gate, about 30 mi. from Pecos on Rte. 63, requires a high-clearance vehicle. Drive 18 mi. north on U.S. 63 and turn right on Forest Rd. 233 toward Iron Gate campground. Those with cars can park at Jack's Creek Campground and hike 3 mi. up to Iron Gate, though this makes for a long day hike. Trail 249 leads 1.5 mi. to the mesa and another 8.5 mi. to Pecos Falls. Expect great views of the Sangre de Cristos from atop Hamilton Mesa.

Backpacking trails criss-cross large wilderness area. One of the most popular is the **Skyline Trail** (#257, 50 mi.), which makes a large loop around the highest terrain in the wilderness. The Skyline Trail passes some of the most scenic spots in northern New Mexico, including the **Truchas Peaks** and the **Trail Rider's Wall.** Many trails intersect this large loop, including the **Santa Fe Baldy Trail** (#254) from Rte. 475 near Ski Santa Fe and the **Cave Creek Trail** (#288).

LOS ALAMOS ☎ 505

Known only as the mysterious P.O. Box 1663 during the heyday of the Manhattan Project, Los Alamos is no longer the nation's biggest secret. With the infamous distinction of being the birthplace of the atomic bomb, Los Alamos used to house nuclear scientists and their families in a top-secret research camp. Now, it attracts visitors with its proximity to Valle Caldera Preserve, Bandalier National Monument, and the breathtaking Jemez Mountains.

◼️🔢 ORIENTATION & PRACTICAL INFORMATION. Overlooking the wide Río Grande Valley, Los Alamos hovers above the Pueblo and Bayo Canyons on fingerlike mesas, 35 mi. northwest of Sante Fe. **Los Alamos Visitors Center** dispenses info on Central Ave. just west of 15th St. (☎ 662-8105. Open M-F 9am-5pm, Sa 9am-4pm, Su 10am-3pm.) Services include: **police**, 2500 Trinity Ave. (☎ 662-8222); **Los Alamos Medical Center**, 3917 W. Rd. (☎ 662-4201. 24hr.); free **Internet access** at the **Mesa Public Library**, 2400 Central Ave. (☎ 662-8253. Open M-Th 10-9pm, F 10am-6pm, Sa 9am-5pm, Su 11am-5pm.); and the **post office,** 199 Central Park Sq. (☎ 622-2153. Open M-F 7:30am-5pm, Sat 8am-12:30pm.) **Postal Code:** 87544.

🔢🔃 ACCOMMODATIONS & FOOD. There are three hotels along Trinity Ave., catering more to the spending power of nuclear scientists than that of the budget traveler. All three charge $70-90 for a room. Fortunately, Forest Service campgrounds line U.S. 4 between Los Alamos and Jemez Springs. **Jemez Springs Campground ❶**, just over 22 mi. west of Los Alamos, charges $10 for one of its 52 sites. (Pit toilets, water, picnic area, and access to hiking trailheads.) For food, try the **Hill Diner ❷**, 1315 Trinity Ave., which serves delicious, low-priced American fare. (☎ 927-0373. Burgers and sandwiches $7-8.)

◼️ SIGHTS. Not to be missed in Los Alamos is the ▨**Black Hole**, 4015 Arkansas St., a store that sells all the junk the laboratory doesn't want anymore, including 50-year-old calculators, fiber-optic cables, flow gauges, time-mark generators, optical comparators, and other technological flotsam. Leave with your very own $2 atomic bomb detonator cable. (☎ 662-5053. Open M-Sa 10am-5pm.) In town, the

Bradbury Science Museum, at 15th St. and Central, explains the history of the Los Alamos National Laboratory and its endeavors with videos and hands-on exhibits. (☎667-4444. Open Tu-F 9am-5pm, Sa-M 1-5pm. Free.) The **Los Alamos Historical Museum,** at 20th St. and Central, has exhibits on what life was like for residents in this "secret city" during WWII. (☎662-4493. Open June-Aug. M-Sa 9:30am-4:30pm, Su 11am-5pm; Sept.-May M-Sa 10am-4:30pm, Su 1-4pm. Free.)

◪ **OUTDOOR ACTIVITIES.** In May 2000, the devastating **Cerro Grande Fire** burned 48,000 acres of forest and left 431 families homeless. Because of forest damage, many trails have been closed; visit or call the **Los Alamos US Forest Service Office,** 475 20th St., Suite B (☎667-5120; open M, W, F 9am-4:30pm), the **Jemez Springs Ranger Station** (☎829-3535; open M-Sa 8am-5pm), or the **Walatowa Visitors Center** (☎834-7235; open daily 8am-5pm) before setting off on a hike through the charred mountains behind Los Alamos. For a short hike with awesome views, try the **Blue Dot Trail,** which descends 1 mi. from White Rock Overlook to the Río Grande.

The mesas around Los Alamos offer **biking** and **climbing** opportunities. To rent a bike or purchase a map of local trails ($5), head to **D.O.M.E.,** 3801 Arkansas St., a biking and climbing outfitter. (☎661-3663. Open Tu-F 9am-6pm, Sa 10am-3pm. Mountain bikes $25 per day, $40 per 4-day weekend.) The 30 mi. road loop from Los Alamos to White Rock and Bandelier is a popular paved ride. **Pajarito Ski Area** has some excellent technical mountain biking. For area rock climbing info, contact the **Mountaineer Group** (☎665-0604). The cliffs below the White Rock Overlook have bolt routes that range from 5.8 to 5.12+. Another good spot for climbing lies along Rte. 502 just east of the intersection with Rte. 4.

NEAR LOS ALAMOS

The region surrounding the town of Los Alamos is one of extremes: the area around Jemez Springs sports verdant mountain springs, while fiery volcanic explosions hissed and sputtered eons ago to form the Valles Calderas. These relatively untrodden outdoors are easily accessed by travelers coming from either New Mexico's nuclear nook (Los Alamos) or from historic Santa Fe.

JEMEZ MOUNTAINS

Considering their location just north of the scrubby piñon pine forest around Santa Fe, mistaking the Jemez Mountains for a mirage in the desert is a pardonable offense. Affording outdoor opportunities and stunning scenery, the mountains are a hidden gem. The drive between Los Alamos and Jemez Springs on U.S. 4 winds up several paved switchbacks through some of the most beautiful forest in the area, providing a welcome rest from the raging sun. Easily accessible rock climbing areas flank the road, granting a reprieve from your spot behind the wheel. Hikes sprinkle the region, offering views and rewarding hikers with hot springs in several locations. Southwest near Jemez Springs the valley opens up into red rock mesas that will take your breath away. For a cheap, easy thrill, the view from the **White Rock Overlook** will knock your socks off. To reach the spot, take Rte. 4 to White Rock, NM; turn at the Conoco and immediately turn left onto Meadow Ln. Overlook Rd. is on the left after 1 mi.

Twenty-five miles west of Los Alamos and 13 mi. northeast of Jemez Springs on Rte. 4, a popular short hike carries you to the **Jemez Falls,** an idyllic pool and small cataract in the middle of the forest. The trailhead is located at the Jemez Falls Campground. The same trailhead provides access to the **McCauly Warm Springs,** 1.5 mi. one-way, mostly downhill. The warm springs are also accessible from a trailhead at Battleship Rock Picnic Area 4 mi. north of Jemez Springs Ranger Station. This 1.5 mi., one-way trail runs uphill for a moderate to difficult trek. Continuing from Jemez Falls campground, the trail extends onto **E. Fork Trail** (#137). From the campground, the E. Fork Trail heads east for 1 mi. where it encounters U.S 4 and the E. Fork Trailhead. The trail then continues farther east beyond the trailhead for 4.4 mi. to another junction with U.S. 4, passing a waterfall and a popular swimming hole en route. If you're up for taking a dip, try the **San Antonio Hot Springs.** From La Cueva, at the junction of U.S. 4 and U.S. 126, drive 4 mi. north to Forest Road 376, and continue north on 376 for 6 mi. Four-wheel-drive may be required to reach the parking area.

Excellent climbing spots lie further west in the Jemez Mountains as well. A good top-roping and instructional area is **Las Conchas,** visible from U.S. 4, 15-16 mi. northwest of Jemez Springs Ranger Station. Here, 8-10 anchor routes await, ranging in difficulty from 5.6-5.12. **Las Conchas Trail** leads to more traditional and sport climbing routes from 5.9 and up.

VALLES CALDERA

Between Los Alamos and Jemez Springs the forest breaks to provide a spectacular look at a vast volcanic valley. Home to the second-largest elk herd in the world (over 4000 head), the Valles Caldera was formed as a result of the eruption of an enormous mountain that collapsed upon itself, hurtling debris as far abreast as Kansas. The 89,000-acre preserve is made up of nine major valleys, a 15 mi. diameter rim, and central peaks formed by the continued upwelling of magma from the earth's core. After hundreds of years as a privately owned ranch, the land is seeing increasing, though closely monitored, opportunities for public access, its use highly controlled in an effort to preserve the untouched quality of the land. The available activities are constantly evolving (check www.vallescaldera.org for updates) and feature a handful of fee hikes. The most popular is the Cerro de Abrigo, a 7 mi. hike in the heart of the preserve that circles Abrigo Peak on old logging roads and provides views of the crater on all sides. Hikers are transported in vans twice a day (8:30am and noon) to the start of the trail and back (pick up at noon and 5pm). Two other paid hikes include the Rabbit Ridge, which climbs the ridge along the southern border (6-8 mi. round-trip, full day) and El Cajete, which leaves from mile marker 32. Valle Grande Hike is the only hike open for free use without reservations. The hike is a short 2 mi. round-trip descent through the forest to the edge of Valle Grande. Parking and trailhead rest between mile markers 42 and 43 on the right coming from Los Alamos before reaching the view of the valley. Fishing is available on the preserve. For $20—$10 use of the land and $10 fishing fee—a 1.5 mi. section of the San Antonio River can be reserved for a full day of private use (up to two people per section of river). Other summer activities include van and horse-drawn-wagon tours. Winter activities will include cross-country skiing and snowmobiling, among others. All use of the land requires payment and reservations, and many fill up weeks or months in advance; make reservations as soon as possible. To reserve an activity, visit www.vallescaldera.org or call the office at ☎ 866-382-5537.

NORTHEASTERN NEW MEXICO

Whether you're looking for an artist colony, a piece of living history, extreme skiing and hiking, or just a taste of the Wild West, northeastern New Mexico has got it all. The galleries and pueblos of Taos are by far the most touristed destinations of the region, but travelers would be remiss not to explore the hidden towns along the Enchanted Circle, hike the state's tallest mountain, relive wild shoot-outs in Cimarron, or wander the rim of the Capulin Volcano.

NEW MEXICO

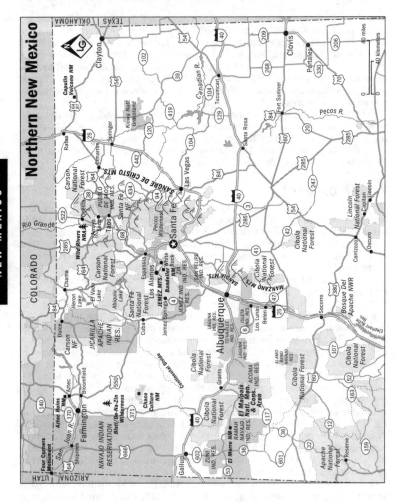

TAOS

☎505

Before 1955, Taos was a remote artist colony in the Sangre de Cristo Mountains. When the ski valley opened and the thrill-seekers trickled in, they soon realized that the area also boasted the best white water rafting in New Mexico, as well as some excellent hiking, mountain biking, and rock climbing. By the 1970s, Taos had become a paradise for New-Age hippies, struggling artists, and extreme athletes, and the deluge of tourists wasn't far behind. Today, Taos maintains an unlikely but enjoyable balance of ski resort culture, Bohemian spirit, and sunflower charm. To make the most of your time in Taos, spend a few days hiking in the Wheeler Peak Wilderness, biking through Carson National Forest, or taking a dip in the Hondo hot springs. For a more new age Western experience, travelers can head north to the village of Arroyo Seco, where locals practice yoga in the morning, hike in the afternoon, and discuss their favorite movies over coffee at the Gypsy 360 Cafe.

TRANSPORTATION

Only **Greyhound,** 1213A Gusdorf St. (☎758-1144), provides intercity transport, sending two buses daily to **Albuquerque** (3hr.; M-Th $25, F-Su $27), **Denver** (7½hr.; M-Th $62, F-Su $67), and **Santa Fe** (1½hr.; M-Th $13, F-Su $16). The local bus service, the **Chile Line,** runs every 15-30min. along Paseo del Pueblo from Ranchos de Taos, south of town, to and from the pueblo. In ski season, a bus runs from the center of Taos to the Ski Valley every 2½hr. (☎751-4459. Daily 7am-7pm. $0.50, ski shuttle $5.) **Taxi** service is offered by **Faust's Transportation** (☎758-3410) daily until 8:30pm. Rentals cars await at **Enterprise,** 1137 Paseo del Pueblo Sur. (☎737-0514. Open M-F 8am-6pm. $43 per day, $200 per week. Must be 21+, surcharge for drivers 21-24.)

ORIENTATION & PRACTICAL INFORMATION

Taos is located 79 mi. north of Santa Fe (p. 388), between the dramatic Río Grande Gorge and the mighty Wheeler Peak. **Paseo del Pueblo** (Rte. 68) is the main north-south thoroughfare in town, dubbed **"Paseo del Pueblo Norte"** north of Kit Carson Rd. and **"Paseo del Pueblo Sur"** to the south. Be aware that traffic on Paseo del Pueblo tends to move in inches during the summer and the ski season—use Rte. 240 and Upper Ranchitos Rd. as a bypass if possible. Drivers should park on **Camino de la Placita,** a block west of the plaza, or at meters on side streets. Several miles north on Paseo del Pueblo Norte, there is an important intersection: a right turn onto Rte. 150 leads to Arroyo Seco and Arroyo Hondo; straight onto Rte. 522 is the beginning of the Enchanted Circle (p. 413); and a left turn onto Rte. 64 West leads to the Río Grande Gorge Bridge and the earthships beyond it.

Visitor info is available at the **Chamber of Commerce,** 1139 Paseo del Pueblo Sur, 2 mi. south of town at the junction of Rte. 68 and Paseo del Cañon. (☎758-3873 or 800-732-8267. Open daily 9am-5pm.) The **Carson National Forest Office,** 208 Cruz Alta Rd., has free info on camping and hiking. (☎758-6200. Open M-F 8am-4:30pm.) Services include: **Pinch Penny Wash-O-Mat,** 823 Paseo del Pueblo Norte (☎758-1265; open M-Sa 7am-8pm, Su 7am-5pm); **police,** 107 Civic Plaza Dr. (☎758-2216); **emergency** (☎911); **Holy Cross Hospital,** 1397 Weimer Rd. (☎758-8883); **Internet access** ($1 per 30min.) at the **public library,** 402 Camino de la Placita (☎758-3063; open M noon-6pm, Tu-Th 10am-7pm, F 10am-6pm, Sa 10am-5pm); **post office,** 318 Paseo Del Pueblo Norte. (☎758-2081. Open M-F 8:30am-5pm.) **Postal code:** 87571.

ACCOMMODATIONS

Tourism is big business in Taos, which means that a room costs big bucks. Expect to pay upwards of $60 for a basic motel room. Camping and hostelling are much more economical options for those willing to stay a few miles outside of town. Taos also presents dozens of interesting B&B options starting around $70 per night. Visit www.taos-lodging.com for more information.

▨ **The Abominable Snowmansion Hostel (HI-AYH;** ☎776-8298). 8 mi. north of Taos in Arroyo Seco. Located on the road to Taos Ski Valley 9 mi. from the mountain, this hostel is packed with skiers all winter and accessible by public transportation only during the ski season. Tepees and tent camping in the backyard during summer. 2 kitchens, a pool table, and a fireplace in the common room. Reception 8am-noon and 4-10pm. Reservations recommended. Mid-Apr. to mid-Nov. dorms $15, non-members $17, weekly $95; dorm tepees $15/$17; private doubles $38-42; tent sites $12. Mid-Nov. to mid-Apr. dorms (breakfast included) $22, weekly $120; private rooms $40-52. ●

NEW MEXICO

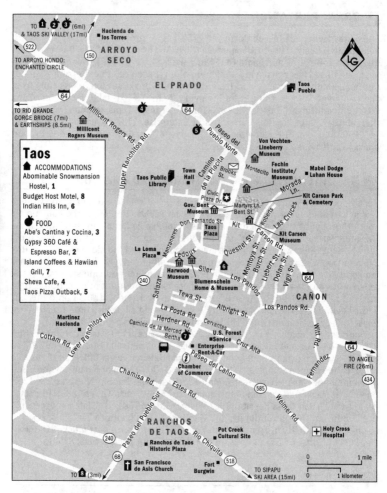

Taos

⬆ ACCOMMODATIONS
Abominable Snowmansion
  Hostel, **1**
Budget Host Motel, **8**
Indian Hills Inn, **6**

🌶 FOOD
Abe's Cantina y Cocina, **3**
Gypsy 360 Café &
  Espresso Bar, **2**
Island Coffees & Hawiian
  Grill, **7**
Sheva Cafe, **4**
Taos Pizza Outback, **5**

Budget Host Motel, 1798 Paseo del Pueblo Sur (☎ 758-2524 or 800-323-6009), 3¼ mi. south of the Plaza. The least expensive motel in Taos, with large, clean rooms in a beautiful building. Free continental breakfast. A/C, TV, free local calls. Singles $39-54, doubles $49-61. 10% discount for AAA, seniors, and veterans. ❸

Indian Hills Inn, 233 Paseo del Pueblo Sur (☎ 758-4293), 2 blocks south of the Plaza. The most affordable motel within walking distance of downtown. Cozy rooms behind an adobe facade have A/C and cable TV. Rooms range from $42 in low season to $59-99 during the summer and ski months. ❹

📷 CAMPING

Considering the price of lodging in Taos, sleeping under the stars is a particularly appealing option. The **Orilla Verde Recreation Area ❶**, 15 mi. south of Taos on Rte. 68, has five campgrounds in the scenic **Río Grande Gorge ❶**. (☎ 751-4899 or 758-

8851. Water and toilets available. Sites $7.) The **Carson National Forest ❶** has four campgrounds to the east of Taos on Rte. 64. Tent sites sit adjacent to a stream and are surrounded by tall pines on one side and piñon forest on the other. The closest two, **El Nogal** and **Las Petacas**, are 2 and 4 mi. east of Taos and have vault toilets but no drinking water. **Capulin Campground ❶**, 7 mi. east of Taos, and **La Sombra ❶**, 1 mi. farther, both have water and vault toilets. For more info, contact the Carson National Forest Office in Taos. (☎758-6200. Sites $12.50.) Campgrounds on the road to Taos Ski Valley have no facilities but rest by a stream in the high alpine forest. The Orilla Verde sites are near the put-in point for rafting, while the Carson National Forest and Ski Valley campsites are virtually roadside. While all sites can be a bit noisy by day, the river and roads go virtually unused at night.

Backcountry camping ❶ in the national forest is free and no permits are required. Dispersed camping is popular along Rte. 518 south of Taos and Forest Rd. 437, which branches east from Rte. 518. Park along the side of the road and set up camp a few hundred feet inside the forest. Make sure you aren't camping on private land. People planning on backcountry hiking should consider camping near **Lost Lake** in Latir Peak Wilderness or **Williams Lake** in Wheeler Peak Wilderness.

✍ FOOD

While many restaurants cluster around Taos Plaza and Bent St., cheaper fare dots the landscape north and south of town on Paseo Del Pueblo. Stock up at **Raley's Supermarket,** 710 Paseo del Pueblo Sur. (☎758-1250. Open daily 6am-midnight.)

- 🍴 **Island Coffees and Hawaiian Grill,** 1032 Paseo del Pueblo Sur (☎758-7777). Get leied in a grass hut at this tropical restaurant, where popular dishes include mango coconut chicken ($6), miso noodle soup ($6), and *lomi lomi* vegetables ($8). Many of the Polynesian and Southeast Asian dishes are vegetarian. Open M-Sa 10am-9pm. ❷

- 🍴 **Abe's Cantina y Cocina,** (☎776-8516), 6 mi. north of Taos on the road to Taos Ski Valley in the village of Arroyo Seco, a block up from the Abominable Snowmansion Hostel. Abe's is the place to go for cheap, delicious, homestyle New Mexican food. The breakfast burrito ($3.25) will keep you going all day, or try the tamales ($3.50) to cast off your hunger later on. Abe's doubles as Arroyo Seco's convenience store and watering hole. Open M-F 7am-6:30pm, Sa 7am-2pm, bar open untill around 10pm. ❶

- **Sheva Cafe,** 812B Paseo del Pueblo Norte (☎737-9290), prepares a wonderful selection of vegetarian Middle Eastern dishes including *falafel* ($4.50) and *borekas* ($3), with a focus on organic ingredients. Occasionally your hummus will be accompanied by trippy, live experimental music. Open M-F 7am-9pm, Su 10am-9pm. ❶

- **Gypsy 360 Café & Espresso Bar** (☎776-3166), 6 mi. north of Taos on the road to Taos Ski Valley in the village of Arroyo Seco. Right next to the Abominable Snowmansion Hostel, this pleasant little cafe dishes out tasty Asian-inspired fare in addition to keeping Arroyo Seco caffeinated. Shanghai chicken-noodle salad goes for $8.50, while Indonesian Pork costs $8.75. Open breakfast, lunch, and dinner; call for hours. ❷

- **Taos Pizza Outback,** 712 Paseo del Pueblo Norte (☎758-3112), 1 mi. north of the plaza. This pizza joint has an old gas pump and outdoor seating. Listen to good ol' rock 'n' roll music while scarfing down a giant slice of pizza ($4.50-6) or calzone ($8). Open June-Sept. daily 11am-10pm; Oct.-May M-Th and Su 11am-9pm, F-Sa 11am-10pm. ❷

🎵 NIGHTLIFE

The **Alley Cantina,** one block north of the Plaza at 121 Teresina Ln., inside the oldest building in Taos, is the most lively nightspot in town. This friendly bar has a pool table, couches, and an outdoor patio. Watch out for the ghost of Governor Bent's

Daughter. (☎758-2121. Live music W-Sa nights. 21+. Cover $3-5. Open M-Sa 11:30am-1am, Su 11:30am-11pm.) The 20-something crowd tends to skip the bars in favor of Taos's many coffee shops, especially **Caffe Tazza,** 122 Kit Carson Rd. (Live music three nights a week, open mic W 7-9pm, and poetry and prose readings most F nights 7-9pm. ☎758-8706. Open daily 6:30am-6pm, later if there's music.)

🔘 SIGHTS

ART MUSEUMS. Given its reputation as a haven for artists and art-lovers, Taos has a fitting number of reputable museums. The **Harwood Museum** houses works by early and mid-20th-century local artists, including a gallery of works by minimalist painter Agnes Martin, and a vast collection of art in the Hispanic tradition, including a striking Día de los Muertos (Day of the Dead) wood sculpture. *(238 Ledoux St.* ☎ *758-9826. Open Tu-Sa 10am-5pm, Su noon-5pm. $5.)* The **Millicent Rogers Museum** has an extravagant collection of Indian jewelry, textiles, pottery, and Apache baskets once belonging to Millicent Rogers, a glamour queen and socialite. *(1504 Millicent Rogers Rd. 4 mi. north of the Plaza on Rte. 64, turn left at the sign.* ☎ *758-2462. Open Apr.-Oct. daily 10am-6pm; Nov.-Mar. Tu-Su 10am-6pm. $6, students and seniors $5, under 16 $2.)*

HISTORIC SITES. Celebrated mountain man **Kit Carson** used Taos as a base for his many expeditions out on the frontier. The house where Carson and his wife lived between 1843 and 1868 has been preserved as a museum full of guns, saddles, and depictions of the life of rocky mountain fur trappers. *(113 Kit Carson Rd. One block east of the plaza.* ☎ *758-4741. Open daily 9am-5pm. $5, children $3.)* The **Governor Bent Museum,** in the house where Charles Bent was murdered during a Native American and Mexican uprising in 1847, displays many of Bent's personal belongings, Americana from the period, and an eight-legged lamb that could keep Stephen King awake at night. *(117 Bent St.* ☎ *758-2376. Open daily 10am-5pm. $2, children $1.)* The 🔲**Martinez Hacienda,** 2 mi. southwest of the plaza on Ranchitos Rd., is one of the few surviving Spanish Colonial mansions in the US. Built in 1804, this fortress-like adobe structure was home to the prosperous Martinez family and served as the headquarters of a large farming and ranching operation. The restored 21-room hacienda features excellent exhibits on life in the northernmost reaches of the Spanish Empire. *(2 mi. south of downtown on Ranchos Rd.* ☎ *758-1000. Open Apr.-Oct. daily 9am-5pm; Nov.-Mar. 10am-4pm. $5, children $3.)*

ARTS AND CRAFTS. Taos ranks second only to Santa Fe as a center of Southwestern art. Galleries located around the Plaza and Kit Carson Rd. include the **Lumina Gallery and Sculpture Garden,** which is more captivating than any art museum in town. Set in a stunning adobe home with five acres of rolling grassy lawn, gardens, and fountains, the cutting-edge contemporary paintings and sculptures here are superb. (The Lumina will soon be relocating to an equally picturesque location in Arroyo Seco, call ☎877-558-6462 for details.) Of the many arts-and-crafts shops in town, **Taos Drums** is unique. Here local craftsmen make wooden drums in the traditional Native American style. Performers Fleetwood Mac and Pearl Jam have made use of their creations. Take a free tour of the workshop and bang the largest drum in New Mexico, or attend one of the drum classes offered several times a week for $10. *(On Rte. 68, 5 mi. south of the Taos Plaza, look for the giant tepees.* ☎ *800-424-3786. Open M-Sa 9am-5pm, Su 11am-6pm.)*

TAOS PUEBLO. The five-story adobe homes of this pueblo are between 700 and 1000 years old, making it the oldest continuously inhabited settlement in the US. Taos Pueblo was named a UNESCO world heritage site in 1992, and remains the only pueblo in Northern New Mexico where the inhabitants still live traditionally, without electricity or running water. Guided tours depart daily May through September, and visitors can take self-guided tours all day. Highlights of the Pueblo include the **San Geronimo Church,** the ruins of the old church and cemetery, the adobe houses, and the kivas (ceremonial rooms). The **San Geronimo Feast Days** (Sept. 29-30) and the annual **powwow** (2nd weekend in July) are the most popular events of the year. (*¾ mi. north of the Plaza, bear right at the intersection and continue another 2 mi. to the Pueblo. Chileworks Buses stop at the Pueblo every 30min.-1hr. ☎758-1028. Open May-Sept. M-Sa 8am-4:30pm, Su 8:30am-4:30pm; Oct.-Apr. M-Sa 8am-4pm, Su 8:30am-4pm. $10, seniors $8, students $3, 12 and under free. Camera permit $10, video cameras $20.*)

OTHER SIGHTS. A number of natural hot springs bubble up along the Río Grande near Taos. One of the most popular is the **Stagecoach Hot Springs,** at the bottom of the Río Grande Gorge. From Taos, drive north 3 mi. and take Rte. 64 W towards the Gorge Bridge. After passing the airport turn right onto Tune Rd. Five miles down the road, go left at the fork and follow this road to the gorge's edge where you can park. The springs are a steep ¾ mile hike down into the gorge. The **Hondo Hot Springs** are located in Arroyo Hondo's portion of the gorge. The trail down to the springs is shorter and less strenuous than the one to Stagecoach. Clothing is optional in both of these hot springs.

⚡ OUTDOOR ACTIVITIES

Between skiing, rafting, hiking, biking, and rock climbing, Taos offers outdoor activities year-round. Due to the popularity of the **Taos Ski Valley,** Taos is the only town in New Mexico that is more crowded in the winter than in the summer.

HIKING

Wheeler Peak/#90 (15 mi. round-trip, 1-2 days). At 13,161 ft., Wheeler Peak is the highest point in New Mexico. The well-marked trailhead to this very strenuous hike awaits at the main Taos Ski Valley parking lot; the trail goes northeast for the first 2 mi. and then turns south towards Wheeler Peak at Bull-of-the-Woods Pasture. Thunderstorms are common near the summit and can be very dangerous—to avoid getting caught, start hiking as early in the day as possible. Since the trek is easiest as an overnight, consider camping in the forested valley 5 mi. from the trailhead.

Williams Lake/#62 (4 mi. round-trip, 3-5hr.). This short, moderate hike to an 11,000 ft. glacial cirque is an excellent half-day jaunt into the Wheeler Peak Wilderness. To reach the trailhead, drive to the Taos Ski Valley and turn south on Twining Rd. (it's off to the left in the parking lot). Follow the signs to the Bavarian Lodge and park at the marked trailhead. Williams Lake affords great views of Wheeler Peak and the surrounding mountains. The air on this trail is extremely thin: bring plenty of water and ascend gradually.

Devisadero/#108 (5 mi. round-trip, 2-3 hr.). The ideal hike for someone who wants to get out into the woods without driving far from Taos, the trail begins 3 mi. east of town on Rte. 64, across the highway from the El Nogal Picnic Area. The strenuous 5 mi. loop leads to the top of Devisadero Peak, revealing excellent views of Taos, the Río Grande Gorge, and the surrounding area.

Italianos Canyon/#59 (7.4 mi. round-trip, 4-6 hr.). This strenuous trail leads to the summit of 12,115 ft. Lobo Peak, offering sweeping views of the Wheeler Peak Wilderness and the Río Grande Valley. The trailhead is located along the road to the Taos Ski Valley (Rte. 150), 3 mi. east of Upper Cuchilla Campground.

Columbine Canyon/#71 (11.4 mi. round-trip, 6-8 hr.). This hike follows Columbine Creek through a picturesque canyon, with excellent views of Wheeler Peak further along. As a long trail that begins easy and gradually increases in difficulty, a shorter portion of the trail makes for an pleasant afternoon hike. The trailhead is at the back of the Columbine campground, west of Red River on Rte. 38.

STEEP THOUGHTS

Being from the coast of Florida, where the highest point in any given area is the local landfill, I find myself fascinated with mountains. I can't drive near a big peak without getting the urge to climb it, so when I reached Taos and saw Wheeler Peak towering above the village at a lofty 13,161 ft., it was obvious what I would be doing the next day.

Rather than pursue the conventional 15 mi. route, I got a tip that instead I could hike 4 mi. in to Williams Lake and simply head up the smooth slope to the peak. It would be a steep but non-technical climb. I started early, long before the sun came up over the mountains, and easily made the lake in under two hours. Standing on the shore of the lake, I looked up at the mountain reaching 2000 ft. above me and plotted my route in my mind.

The last 500 ft. looked craggy and treacherous, but an ascent up a smooth rock field followed by an up-ridge jaunt to the summit still seemed a reasonable proposition. As I climbed the steep pitch I was interrupted by fat marmots and chattering squirrels bounding over the rocks in defiance of my huffing and puffing, but it wasn't long before I reached the ridge. It was tougher than it had appeared from below, but I slogged on, believing it would get easier farther up.

(Continued on next page)

SKIING

Taos Ski Valley (☎776-2291), located 18 mi. north of town on Rte. 150, is the premier downhill ski destination in New Mexico and the brainchild of Swiss-born Ernie Blake. Blake chose this site in 1955 after an extensive aerial search to find the "perfect" mountain. His friends argued that the terrain was too difficult for American skiers, but Blake was confident that people could learn to ski with the right instruction. He was right, and Taos's **Ernie Blake Ski School** consistently ranks as one of the top ski schools in the land (call the Ski Valley or visit www.skitaos.org).

Taos is an extreme skier's delight—51% of the trails are most difficult, compared with 24% beginner and 25% intermediate. Receiving 312 in. of snow annually, the mountain boasts 898 skiable acres, 72 trails, a vertical drop of 2612 ft. serviced by lifts, and a 3274 ft. vertical drop for those willing to hike to the top of Kachina Peak. In the summer, sightseers can ride the ski lift for a view of the Wheeler Peak Wilderness. (24hr. snow report ☎776-2916. Nov. 22 to Apr. 7 9am-4pm; $51, ages 13-17 $40, 12 and under $31. Summer Th-Su 10am-4:30pm; $6, children $4.) Nearby ski areas Red River and Angel Fire promise less extreme terrain than Taos Ski Valley (p. 410). Cross-country skiing near Taos includes the Amole Cross-Country Ski Area, 17 mi. south of Taos on Rte. 518, and the Enchanted Forest Cross-Country Ski Area (☎754-2374 or 800-966-9381), 3 mi. east of Red River, the only full-service cross-country facility nearby, with 26km of groomed trails.

MOUNTAIN BIKING

The Taos area boasts some of the finest mountain biking in New Mexico. For bike rentals, visit **Gearing Up,** 129 Paseo del Pueblo Sur (☎751-0365; open daily 9:30am-6pm; bikes $35 per day, $90 per 5 days), or **Native Sons Adventures,** 1033A Paseo del Pueblo Sur (☎758-9342 or 800-753-7559; open daily 7am-7pm; bikes $20-35 per day, half price for longer rentals).

The best biking around Taos is in the Camino Real Ranger District, to the southeast of town. Many popular trails flank Rte. 518 including **La Cueva** and **Policarpio Canyon.** The strenuous 27 mi. **South Boundary Trail** (#164) is known as one of the top ten rides in the Southwest. To reach the start of the trail, take Rte. 64 east toward Angel Fire and turn south on Rte. 434, then turn right onto County Rd. B-1. The **West Rim Trail** is an easy one-way 9 mi. ride along the rim of the Río Grande Gorge, with great views of the river below and the Sangre de Cristos to the east. The trail begins at the west side of the Río Grande Gorge Bridge on Rte. 64. Gearing Up runs a shuttle that will take up to seven riders and their bikes to and from any site in the area for a total of $75 per ride. The Forest Service office has more information about area trails open to biking.

ROCK CLIMBING

Both **Mudd-n-Flood,** 134 Bent St. (☎ 751-9100), and **Taos Mountain Outfitters,** 114 South Plaza (☎ 758-9292), offer climbing gear and friendly advice. **Mountain Skills** (☎ 776-2222) has guided climbing trips. The best spot for top-rope climbing is **Dead Cholla,** on the west rim of the Río Grande Gorge. Sport and traditional climbs of 5.7 to 5.12 also abound at the site. **John's Wall,** in Arroyo Hondo, features sport and traditional climbs in the 5.8 to 5.11 range. Farther from Taos, the granite rocks in back of the water tower in **Tres Piedras** provides great bouldering and sport climbing. Another popular spot a little farther from Taos is the **Questa Dome,** north of Arroyo Hondo in Questa, which has top-quality granite bouldering.

RIVER RUNNING

The **Río Grande Gorge** extends 78 mi. through northern New Mexico and into Colorado. This section of river is administered by the BLM as a **Wild and Scenic River,** and it delights with the state's best whitewater rafting and kayaking. Many rafting outfitters operate out of Taos. **Los Ríos River Runners** (☎ 776-8854 or 800-544-1181), **Far Flung Adventures** (☎ 758-2628 or 800-359-2627), and **Native Sons Adventures** (☎ 758-9342 or 800-753-7559) all offer a range of guided half-day ($40-50) and full-day ($80-110) rafting trips, including the popular 15 mi. Class IV **Taos Box** and the 11 mi. **Lower Gorge,** which offers Class II-IV rapids. Kayakers may want to visit the **Río Grande Gorge Visitors Center,** 15 mi. south of Taos on Rte. 68, to get info on river conditions, as well as a helpful mile-by-mile guide ($15) to the Río Grande Gorge. (☎ 751-4889. Open Apr.-Oct. daily 8:30am-5pm.) The **Orilla Verde Recreation Area,** inside the Río Grande Gorge 15 mi. south of Taos on Rte. 68, has river access for boaters, a hiking trail, and five campgrounds along the Río Grande. (☎ 751-4899. Sites $7.) A popular two-day river trip incorporates Taos Box and the Lower Gorge, with a night of camping at Orilla Verde.

RED RIVER   ☎ 505

Red River attempts to re-create an Old West ambience, but the buildings merely generate a phony atmosphere that panders to the Disney-fied visions of vacationers. What redeems Red River, however, is its dramatic setting in a high mountain valley and the many available outdoor activities. Shops, restaurants, and accommodations line Rte. 38 and High St., one block to the north.

(Continued from previous page)

It didn't. After 350 ft. of vertical gain, the route became impassable without a belay, and I was without any equipment whatsoever. I scratched my head, knowing this could not be the path that had been described to me. I traversed a bit looking for an easier way up but found nothing. Vexed at having come within 200 ft. of the summit, I pulled out my GPS to at least mark the coordinates and altitude—and did a double-take when the altimeter read only 12,600 ft. Figuring the fancy gadget for miscalibrated, I reached for my camera to get some pictures of the spectacular view, only then realizing I was aiming my lens at a smooth peak rising at least 500 ft. higher than where I stood. Looking up from the lake, I had thought I was choosing the highest mountain, but in actuality I had somehow missed the highest one by a couple of peaks.

I retreated halfway down Not-Wheeler Peak to a huge snowfield I'd passed on the way up, and, leaving my concerns over my error in the thin mountain air, I launched myself down through the snow for some impromptu body-sledding. As the hard-won feet of elevation whizzed by, I found the humility to laugh at my mistake, and as I crashed gently into a snow bank at the bottom, I resolved never to do another peak without a map, no matter how obvious the route to the top might seem.

—Taylor Terry

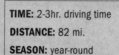

TIME: 2-3hr. driving time

DISTANCE: 82 mi.

SEASON: year-round

Rte. 522, Rte. 38, and U.S. 64 form a loop that circles Wheeler Peak and other summits of the Sangre De Cristos, offering endless opportunities for hiking and camping amid beautiful views and hidden towns. Seeing the snow-capped Sangre de Cristos in winter is particularly breathtaking. The circle itself takes about 2.5hr., but allow a full day or more to explore the many sites and activities along the route. Three miles north of town, a right turn leads to the Taos Ski Valley and a left turn leads to the **Río Grande Gorge Bridge.** Five miles farther, Rte. 522 passes through the small village of **Arroyo Hondo.** A left turn just after the bridge in town leads to the John Dunn Bridge, where rafters and kayakers put in their boats to run the Class IV **Taos Box** (see **Outdoor Activities,** p. 411).

1 QUESTA. Three miles north of the **Red River State Trout Hatchery,** where the state of New Mexico raises over 500,000 trout each year for stocking lakes and rivers, sits Questa. This unassuming town near the confluence of the Red River and the Río Grande grew up around a large molybdenum mine. The **El Seville Restaurant ❶,** at the intersection of Rte. 522 and Rte. 38, is a family-run restaurant with the finest Mexican food along the Enchanted Circle, famous for its delicious sopaillas. (☎586-0300. Open daily 7am-8pm. Dishes $4-7.) The **Carson National Forest Questa Ranger Station,** on Rte. 38, 1.5 mi. east of the Rte. 522 intersection, has info on hiking and camping in the northern section of the Carson National Forest. (☎586-0520. Open M-F 8am-4:30pm). Questa serves as an entryway to the remote **Latir Peak Wilderness** of the Carson National Forest. To reach the wilderness, take Forest Road 134 NE from Questa to the Cabresto Lake Campground. From here, trails lead to Baldy Mountain, Heart Lake, and Latir Peak. Heart Lake is an excellent spot for overnight backcountry camping. For more info, contact the Questa Ranger District.

2 WILD RIVERS NATIONAL RECREATION AREA. This rarely utilized park, 15 mi. northwest of Questa on Rte. 378, dazzles visitors with some of the most dramatic scenery in northern New Mexico. The **Chawalauna Overlook** provides views of the 800 ft. Río Grande Gorge, and **Junta Point** looks out over the confluence of the Red River and the Río Grande. The park has five campgrounds ❶ with sites along the rim of the Gorge, all with drinking water and vault toilets (sites $7). Backcountry camping ($5) is also permitted at designated shelters inside the gorge. Several excellent short hikes lead down into the Gorge. **La Junta** is the toughest but most rewarding, dropping almost 800 ft. in under 1 mi. of rocky trail before making a short jaunt to where the rivers meet. **Chiflo** presents a much smaller challenge, covering less than a mile round-trip and taking hikers part-way down to the Rio Grande for great views of the gorge. (For info, call the Taos BLM ☎ 758-8851. Day use 6am-10pm. $3 per vehicle.)

3 RED RIVER. Continuing east of Questa on Rte. 38, one begins to understand why this drive has been named the "Enchanted Circle." The highway weaves between pine-covered mountains, granting views of multi-colored cliffs and the Red River. Seven miles east of Questa, an enormous molybdenum mine is visible on the left side of the highway. The tourist-dominated village of Red River is just a few miles past the mine (see p. 411).

4 ELIZABETHTOWN. Leaving Red River, Rte. 38 climbs to Bobcat Pass (9820 ft.), the highest point on the Enchanted Circle. Eight miles out of Red River, the forest gives way to green meadows, and one can see the rocky top of Baldy Mountain (12,400 ft.) on the left side of the road and the snow-covered Wheeler Peak (13,161 ft.) to the right. The ghost town of Elizabethtown is 12 mi. southeast of Red River. Follow the signs to the **Elizabethtown Museum** to learn about the history of the town through photographs, mining tools, and a documentary video. (☎377-3420. Open daily 10am-5pm. Free.)

5 EAGLE'S NEST. A few miles past Elizabethtown rests the quiet town of Eagle's Nest. The main attraction is the large Eagle's Nest Lake, popular with fishermen year-round. Turn west on Rte. 64 to go to Cimarron Canyon State Park for hiking and camping (p. 414). Otherwise, turn east on Rte. 64 toward Taos.

ROAD TRIP

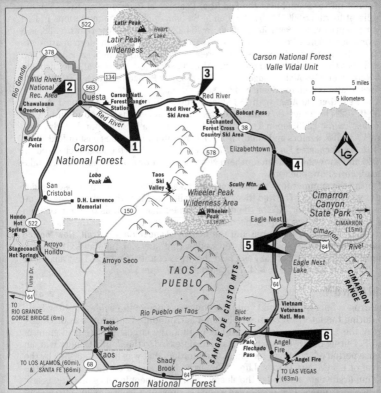

6 ANGEL FIRE. Eight and a half miles south of Eagle's Nest is the **Vietnam Veterans National Monument.** (☎377-6900. Visitors Center open daily 9am-7pm, chapel always open. Free.) South of the monument, Rte. 434 leads to the **Angel Fire Ski Resort,** with 68 trails on 445 acres of terrain and a vertical drop of 2077 ft., as well as over 11 mi. of cross-country ski trails. The **New Mexico Championship Mountain Bike Race** is held here every June; in the summer, bikers can take their bikes up the chairlift ($12) or run a dual slalom course. Bike rentals are available for $40 per day or $32 per half-day at the base of the lift. (☎377-6401. Open Dec. 14 to Mar. 24 daily 9am-4pm. Full-day lift tickets $43, teens $35, children and seniors $27; cross-country skiing $7 per day.)

West of Angel Fire, Rte. 64 climbs into the mountains again and enters the Carson National Forest. There are four campgrounds and numerous trailheads along the road. Beginning 1.5 mi. west of the Angel Fire turnoff, **Eliot Barker Trail,** a moderately strenuous 10 mi. round-trip hike, offers views of Angel Fire and the Wheeler Peak Wilderness. Just past the Eliot Barker Trail, Rte. 64 ascends to the 9100 ft. **Palo Flechado Pass.**

ROAD TRIP

Tourist info is available at the **Red River Chamber of Commerce** on Rte. 38 in the middle of town. (☎800-348-6444. Open M-Sa 8am-5pm.) Accommodations in Red River are pricey, but **River Ranch ❶/❸** (☎754-2293), west of town on Rte. 38, is a reasonable option, offering tent sites ($16), cabins ($42), and modern apartments ($62) in the summer. There are five Forest Service campgrounds (☎586-0520) on Rte. 38 between Red River and Questa. More upscale lodging is available throughout Red River. Call **Alpine Lodge** (☎800-252-2333) or **Pioneer Lodge** (☎800-542-0154) for reservations well in advance of ski season.

The **Red River Ski Area**, with 183 skiable acres, 58 trails, and a vertical drop of 1600 ft. (32% beginner; 38% intermediate; 30% advanced), is a good mountain for families. (☎754-2223. Open Thanksgiving to Easter daily 9am-4pm. Full day $43, ages 13-19 $38, seniors and children $29.) Three and a half miles east of Red River on Rte. 38, **Enchanted Forest** (☎754-2374 or 800-966-9381) is the largest cross-country ski and snowshoe area in northern New Mexico. For a unique experience, take a headlamp snowshoe tour.

During the summer low season, **mountain biking** takes over as the most popular activity in Red River. The Red River Ski area will take bikes to the top of the mountain for $9 per ride or $15 for the day. Be warned that the trails on the mountain are very difficult. Less experienced bikers should try the trails at the Enchanted Forest cross-country ski area and the nearby **Pioneer Canyon Trail. New Mexico Adventure Company,** 217 W. Rte. 38, rents bikes (half-day $25, full-day $35) and provides a free shuttle to Bobcat Pass, near the cross-country ski area. They also offer 3hr. **jeep tours** for $25. (☎754-2437. Open daily 8am-7pm.)

CIMARRON   ☎505

Cimarron is Spanish for "wild," and this town was one of the wildest in New Mexico during the late 19th century. The area surrounding Cimarron was originally part of the 1.7-million-acre Maxwell Land Grant, the largest private land grant in the US. During the 1870s, a series of land disputes led to the Colfax County War, an intense period of shootings, hangings, and murders that was finally quashed by the arrival of US Cavalry troops. Life in Cimarron has calmed considerably over the past hundred years, and today the sleepy town of 900 people relies on tourists and Boy Scouts from the Philmont Scout Ranch to prevent it from slipping into obscurity. As a result, this slice of the Old West, 54 mi. east of Taos and 41 mi. southwest of Raton, trumpets its cowboy origins at every opportunity. For more information, consult the **Cimarron Chamber of Commerce,** 104 N. Lincoln Ave., at Rte. 64. (☎376-2417. Open May-Oct. daily 9am-6pm; Nov.-Apr. M-Tu and Th-Sa 8:30am-5:30pm.)

The **St. James Hotel ❸,** on the corner of Rte. 21 and 17th St., is the most fascinating tourist attraction in Cimarron. The hotel was run by Henry Lambert, a Frenchman who both served as personal chef to General Grant and President Lincoln during the Civil War, and hosted a motley assortment of traders, ranchers, gamblers, and thieves. Jesse James, Wyatt Earp, and Doc Holiday all slept here, and Buffalo Bill and Annie Oakley planned their Wild West show here as well. Twenty-six men were shot dead in the hotel and, according to the staff, their ghosts still haunt the rooms. Guests are not allowed in Room 18 for fear of an angry ghost named TJ, who won the place in a poker game but was shot before he could claim the pot. The old Victorian rooms at the St. James are pricey at $90-120 per night, but annex rooms run $60-100. Even if you can't afford a stay, be sure to take a free self-guided tour. (☎376-2664. Complimentary continental breakfast 7-11am.)

The headquarters of the 130,000 acre **Philmont Boy Scout Ranch** is 4 mi. south of Cimarron on Rte. 21. The land was given to the Boy Scouts in 1941 by Oklahoma oilman Waite Phillips. The Scouts conduct daily tours of Phillips' mansion, **Villa Philmonte,** during the summer. (☎376-2281. Tours June-Aug. daily 8am-5pm every half hour. $4 donation requested.) The Boy Scouts also operate the **Kit Carson Museum** (7 mi. south of Philmont Headquarters on Rte. 21), a hacienda on the Santa Fe Trail dating to the 1850s where Kit Carson lived for four years. (Open daily June 1-Aug. 22 8am-5pm. Free.) **Cimarron Canyon State Park** (☎377-6271), 15 mi. west of Cimarron on U.S. 64, contains a scenic 8 mi. stretch of the Cimarron River. The park offers four campgrounds ($10) along the river with running water and flush toilets. The 7 mi. round-trip **Clear Creek Canyon Trail** follows a tributary up the side of the canyon, passing four waterfalls and offering views of the Sangre de Cristo Mountains to the north and south.

Johnson's Cabins ❸, 161 W. 13th St., rents two-person cabins on the Cimarron River with full kitchens and baths. There are only three cabins, so reserve in advance. (☎376-2210. $49.) **Camping** is available at **Cimarron Canyon State Park ❶**, 12 mi. west of Cimarron on U.S. 64. (☎377-6271. Sites with flush toilets and sink $10.) Food options are scarce in Cimarron, but the **Coffee Shop ❶** in the St. James Hotel has decent sandwiches ($4-7) and $6-7 Mexican fare (open daily 7am-9pm, dining room closed M in winter). Summer visitors can enjoy the **Burrito Banquet ❶**, a roadside stand across from the Chamber of Commerce that peddles homemade burritos ($2.50-4) and awesome green chile. (Open Memorial to Labor Day 10am-2pm.)

CAPULIN VOLCANO NATIONAL MONUMENT

The grassy plains of northeastern New Mexico are interrupted by the mountains and mesas of the 8000 sq. mi. Raton-Clayton Volcanic Field, which has been sporadically active over the past nine million years. Capulin Volcano, which erupted around 60,000 years ago, is one of the most recent eruptions in the field. Although the eruption lasted only a few years, in that time volcanic rock fragments accumulated to form a symmetrical cinder cone rising 1400 ft. above the surrounding plains. After the eruption ended, soil accumulated on the surface of the mountain, so that today the volcano is covered by piñon, juniper, cactus, and many shrubs. Deer, rodents, hummingbirds, and snakes all inhabit this ecosystem, and summer days occasionally bring swarms of ladybugs to the summit.

At the base of the mountain, the **Visitors Center** shows a 10min. introductory video. From here, a 2 mi. drive leads to the top of the cinder cone. A 1 mi. hike circles the rim of the crater, and a 0.2 mi hike leads down to the center of the crater. From the highest point on the rim trail, there are great views of four states. To get to the volcano, drive 30 mi. east of Raton on U.S. 64 and 3 mi. north of the village of Capulin on Rte. 325. (☎278-2201. Open summer daily 7:30am-6:30pm, winter 8am-4:30pm daily. $5 per vehicle.)

NORTHWESTERN NEW MEXICO

Offering a chunk of the Navajo Nation, the Bisti Badlands, ancient indigenous dwellings at Chaco Canyon, and unique lava formations at El Malpais, northwestern New Mexico has much more to it than the stretch of Rte. 66 that too-often simply shuttles travelers between the Petrified Forest and Santa Fe. Stray from the highway to explore the area's diverse landscape and cultural offerings.

CHACO CULTURE NATIONAL HISTORICAL PARK ☎505

Sun-scorched Chaco Canyon served as the first great settlement of the Ancestral Plebeians. The ruins here, which date from the ninth century, are among the most well preserved in the Southwest. The skill and craftsmanship with which Chacoans built the monumental masonry buildings that lie at the floor of the canyon have played a critical role in their preservation. They planned the multiple stories of these enormous structures before the first brick was laid, and positioned their "great houses" in accordance with solar and lunar patterns. The most celebrated of these ancient works of "public architecture" is Pueblo Bonito, a massive D-shaped structure with many interior *kivas* and two plazas.

The Chacoans did not limit the scope of their expertise to a single valley, but spread their ideas and culture through trade and communication across a vast region of the present-day Southwest and Mexico. The historical and cultural sacredness of Chaco Canyon was recognized in 1987, when it was designated a World Heritage Site. Today Chaco is revered by visitors from around the world who venture out into the desert, as well as by the Hopi, Navajo, and Puebloan peoples who consider the canyon part of their sacred homeland.

▣ ☷ ORIENTATION & PRACTICAL INFORMATION. Chaco Canyon lies 92 mi. northeast of **Gallup** (p. 418). From the north, take Rte. 44/550 to the road marked Chaco Culture National Historical Park (Old NM 44). The road intersects with U.S. 550 (3 mi. east of **Nageezi** and 50 mi. west of **Cuba**), right next to a Red Mesa Express gas station and convenience store. After 5 mi. turn right onto an unpaved road and follow signs to Chaco for 16 mi. From the south, take Rte. 9 from **Crownpoint** (home of an **ATM** and the nearest **grocery store**) 36 mi. east to the marked park turn-off in Pueblo Pintado; turn north onto unpaved Rte. 46 for 10 mi.; turn left on County Rd. 7900 for 7 mi.; turn left onto unpaved County Rd. 7950 and follow it 16 mi. to the park entrance. You can also take Rte. 57 straight north from Rte. 9 into the park.

Though a car is the only practical means by which to reach Chaco Canyon, many roads remain unpaved. While bumpy and sprinkled with washes, the roads are usually passable by all cars. After heavy rains a wash may be running, especially during late summer, rendering the muddy roads impassable. Call the park (☎786-7014) in advance to inquire about the conditions or call ☎888-386-7637 for more general **weather and road info**. There is **no gas or food** in the park. The nearest gas is at the Red Mesa Express on U.S. 550. There is also an ATM inside the store.

The **Visitors Center,** at the east end of the park, has an excellent museum that exhibits Ancestral Puebloan art and architecture. Pay the entrance fee and stock up on water here. All the ruins have interpretive brochures at their sites that can be purchased for $0.50-0.75. (☎786-7014. Open June-Aug. daily 8am-5pm; Sept.-May 8am-5pm. $8 per vehicle.) In case of an **emergency,** call ☎786-7060. The nearest **post office** is in Nageezi, 25 mi. northeast of the park.

☷ ☷ ACCOMMODATIONS & CAMPING. Circle A Hostel ❶, just northwest of Cuba, promises friendly, cheap lodging relatively close to Chaco. A worthwhile retreat in itself, Circle A is a converted ranch house and a common stop-over for hikers seeking a rest from trails that pass right next to the property. The ranch sits 5.1 mi. east of U.S. 550 on Los Piños road; follow the signs along Los Piños. (Dorm $18, private rooms $38-48, tent $15, includes use of facilities. Group use available. Reservations recommended.) In Farmington, 75 mi. north, the **Sage Motel ❷,** 301 Airport Dr., keeps clean rooms with microwaves and fridges for rock-bottom prices. (☎325-7501. Reception 24hr. Check-out 11am. Singles $25, doubles $32, triples $40, quads with 2 bathrooms and a kitchenette $50.) Next door, the **Journey Inn ❷,** 317 Airport Dr., also promises a good and cheap night's sleep. (☎325-3548. Singles $30, doubles $35.) The **Gallo Campground ❶,** a little more than 1 mi. from the Visitors Center in Chaco, offers serene desert camping for $10 per site; register at the campground. The 48 sites have access to tables, fireplaces, and central toilets. For those bedding down at the park, the observatory has stargazing for visitors three nights a week. Call ahead for available nights. Gallo campground fills up quickly, so visitors without reservations should make other plans for the night.

The Case for Ancient Astronomy at Chaco

On July 4, 1054, a seemingly new object appeared in the constellation Taurus, an object so bright that it could be seen during the day for almost a month. A star in Taurus had gone supernova; the explosion created the famous Crab nebula and pulsar. The only known written record of this event comes from the Sung-Shih, the dynastic records of the Sung Dynasty of China; why no European or Middle Eastern chronicle mentions the 1054 supernova remains a mystery. Nearly as mysterious is whether the supernova was also observed and recorded by the Ancestral Pueblo peoples (also referred to as Anasazi Indians), who inhabited Chaco Canyon in the middle of the 11th century.

From the mid-9th to the mid-12th century, Chaco Canyon was the political, economic, and ceremonial center of a "Chacoan world" that encompassed the Chaco Plateau and the San Juan Basin, and is now referred to as the Four Corners area. An irrigation system helped support an estimated population of between 2000 and 5000 people in the arid desert in and around Chaco, and more than 400 miles of roads linked the Canyon to 75 smaller settlements. Copious archaeological evidence, including macaw skeletons and seashells, suggests that trade contacts came from as far as Mexico. However, the great civilization centered on Chaco Canyon did not have a written language, and this is one major reason the question of whether the supernova was recorded at Chaco has remained unresolved.

The proposed records of the supernova in the American Southwest are rock art, making them often difficult to date and interpret. At Chaco, the ceiling of a cave near Penasco Blanco, one of the Canyon's "great houses," contains a pictograph, or pigment painted onto the rock face, of a moonlike crescent and a star; pictographs of a human hand and the sun are also nearby. Just before dawn on July 5, 1054, the new supernova and a crescent moon would have appeared, very near each other, in the sky over Chaco Canyon. This fact, combined with the overall rarity of crescents in Southwestern rock art, has led some scholars to consider the pictograph a record of the 1054 supernova. Yet the identification is almost impossible to confirm. Any given rock-art site contains pictographs that span centuries, and it is often difficult to establish which pictographs were created at the same time. Also, even if the pictograph is accepted as a depiction of the supernova-moon conjunction, that conclusion would yield little insight into the Chacoans' motivation for recording such a phenomenon.

Chaco Canyon has a number of sites with less ambiguous connections to specific astronomical phenomena, particularly solar solstices and equinoxes. Some of the niches in the Great *Kiva* at Casa Rinconada may be aligned to be illuminated at the summer solstice, and at least three different spots on the mesa top—near Wijiji, Pueblo Bonito, and Casa Rinconada—have been identified as possible solstice markers or solstice-observing stations. *Kivas* are circular ceremonial structures, built into the ground and accessed via a roof ladder. At unexcavated sites, *kivas* are identifiable as circular depressions, often located near room blocks or in plazas. One mesa-top location is identified with a pictograph usually interpreted as a sun or morning star; the petroglyphs marking the other two locations are less obviously associated with the sun.

Near the top of Fajada Butte, a 135m rock tower near the southern entrance to the Canyon, is Chaco's "sun dagger," an arrangement of three enormous sloping stone slabs and two petroglyphs that marked both solstices and equinoxes. Near noon on the summer solstice, a moving "dagger" of sunlight bisects the larger, spiral petroglyph, while on the winter solstice, two daggers of light frame the same spiral; on the equinoxes, a smaller dagger of light bisects the snake petroglyph. The light show was discovered in 1977, and now the site is visited only once a year to monitor its condition. Recently, the National Park Service established a small observatory at the Chaco Canyon Visitors Center to take advantage of the same dark skies observed by the Ancestral Pueblo peoples who built the great houses of Chaco.

Claudia Cyganowski graduated from Harvard University with a degree in Astronomy. She has participated in archeological field research in Southwestern Colorado and Copán, Honduras, and has researched the significance of astronomy and the calendar in classic Maya society, the Zapotec hieroglyphic writing system, and other archaeological topics.

🄖 **SIGHTS.** The largest pueblos are accessible from the main loop road. Although there are only five primary pull-offs on this 9 mi. road, several hours or an entire day should be dedicated to seeing the sites. The first of the six major Chacoan cultural sites, **Una Vida,** is accessed via a trail beginning at the Visitors Center. Most of the site is unexcavated, providing a good glimpse at what the other ruins must have been like before the archaeologists got their hands on them. There are also some excellent petroglyphs on the canyon wall above the site. The first site on the loop road is **Hungo Pavi,** where relatively small-scale ruins serve as an introduction for the monumental "great houses" to come. The second set of ruins is **Chetro Ketl,** which ups the ante with its raised plaza and vast *kiva*, a circular prayer room used in religious rituals. Nearby **Pueblo Bonito** is the canyon's largest pueblo; it was once four stories high and contained more than 600 rooms. **Pueblo del Arroyo,** built relatively quickly toward the end of the Chacoan ascendancy, is the next site. Finally, on the south side of the canyon, **Casa Rinconada** features a "Great *Kiva*," one of the largest in the Southwest.

🄟 **HIKING.** Opportunities for backcountry hiking in the park are plentiful, and several excellent trails lead to more remote ruins. All the treks are hikeable year-round. Stay on designated trails, and be sure to snag a **required backcountry permit** from the Visitors Center before heading out (free). The **Wijiji Trail** explores a great house built around 1100. Starting at the Wijiji parking area 1 mi. east of the Visitors Center, this easy hike makes for a 3 mi. round-trip. The moderately difficult 5.4 mi. round-trip **Pueblo Alto Trail** offers stunning overlook views of Pueblo Bonito and the other great houses, as well as exploring feats of Chacoan engineering on the mesa top (elevation gain 250 ft., 2-3 hr). The **Peñasco Blanco Trail** is the longest trail in the park, heading deep into Chaco Canyon and providing a perspective on the many cultures who have lived and traveled here. The trail ends at the unexcavated great house, Peñasco Blanco. A short side trail near the end leads to a small yet spectacular pictograph of a supernova. The trailhead is located at the Pueblo del Arroyo parking area. (6.4 mi. round-trip. 3-4 hrs.) Finally, the **South Mesa Trail** climbs high above the canyon onto South Mesa from the trailhead at the Casa Rinconada parking area and explores another great house, Tsin Kletzin. The entire trail affords spectacular panoramas of the canyon and San Juan Basin. (4.1 mi. round-trip. 2-3 hr.)

GALLUP ☎505

Gallup, located at the intersection of I-40 and Rte. 491, falls into the unfortunate class of Western cities that seem to have been built too quickly, filling their cultural void with an empty supermarket-and-styrofoam-cup modernity. However, Gallup's idyllic location amidst colorful granite and sandstone cliffs and its proximity to the Petrified Forest National Park (p. 127), the Navajo Reservation (p. 129), Chaco Culture National Historic Park (p. 415), and the El Morro and El Malpais National Monuments (p. 420) partly redeem it for the traveler. Gallup is also a good base for exploring the Four Corners region.

🄵🄿 **TRANSPORTATION & PRACTICAL INFORMATION. Gallup Municipal Airport** offers flights daily to Denver and other New Mexico cities on **Mesa Airlines** (☎722-5404 or 800-235-9292). **Amtrak,** 201 E. Rte. 66 (☎800-872-7245), chugs two trains through Gallup daily. (Eastbound train departs 9:03am; westbound train departs 7:36pm.) **Greyhound,** 201 E. Rte. 66 (☎863-3761), runs to **Albuquerque** (2½hr., 4 per day, $21) and **Flagstaff** (4hr., 4 per day, $37). Another good option is the **Navajo Transit System,** 201 E. Rte. 66., which sends buses a few times daily to various points around the Navajo Nation. (☎928-729-4115. Call for more info.)

Luna's Taxi (☎722-9777) services the Gallup area. **Price King Rent-a-Car,** 2000 S. 2nd St. (☎772-7701), offers vehicles from $30 per day.

Gallup Visitors Center, 701 Montoya Blvd., off Rte. 66, has info on all of New Mexico. (☎863-4909 or 800-242-4282; www.gallupnm.org. Open daily 8am-5pm, June-Aug. 8am-6pm) Other services include: **Pronto Laundry,** 2422 E. Rte. 66 (☎863-2207); **weather and road conditions** (☎863-3811); **police,** 451 State Rd. 564 (☎722-2231); **crisis line** (☎800-721-7273); and **Rehoboth McKinley Christian Hospital,** 1901 Red Rock Dr. (☎863-7000). Free **Internet access** is available at the **Octavia Fellin Library,** 115 W. Hill St. (☎863-1291. Open M-Th 9am-8pm, F 10am-6pm, Sa 9am-6pm.) The **post office** is at 950 W. Aztec. (☎722-5265. Open M-F 8:30am-5pm, Sa 10am-1:30pm.) **Postal code:** 87301.

◪◨ ACCOMMODATIONS & FOOD. Old Route 66, which runs parallel to I-40 through downtown, is lined with dirt-cheap motels (often with emphasis on the dirt), while the chains cluster on the western edge of town. The best place to stay in town, hands down, is **El Rancho Hotel and Motel ❸,** 1000 E. Rte. 66. You'll find a step up in price from most other options, but a leap up in quality. The who's-who of the silver screen all stayed here (John Wayne, Jack Benny, Kirk Douglas) and had rooms named after them. (☎863-9311. Singles $47; doubles $55.) One of the best spots for those watching their bottom line is the **Blue Spruce Lodge ❷,** 119 E. Rte. 66, with clean, well-maintained rooms. (☎863-5211. Singles $24; doubles $26.) You can pitch a tent in the shadow of red sandstone cliffs at **Red Rock State Park Campground ❶,** Rte. 566, which offers access to hiking 5 mi. east of town off Rte. 66. During the warmer months Red Rock is often the site of concerts, rodeos, and motorcycle races—call ahead to make sure the park is open for regular camping. (☎863-1329. 142 sites with showers and hookups. Tent sites $10, hookups $14.)

A number of diners and cafes line both sides of I-40. **Oasis Mediterranean Restaurant ❷,** 100 E Rte. 66, has Mediterranean fare with a slight Southwestern kick. (Open M-Sa 10am-9pm.) **The Ranch Kitchen ❷,** 3001 W. Rte. 66, has filling breakfasts, sandwiches and burgers ($5-7), and steaks. (Open summer 7am-10pm, winter 7am-9pm). **Panz Alegra ❷,** 1201 E. Rte. 66, is a notch above the rest of the Mexican food in town, with good deals on traditional dishes ($7-10), as well as steaks. (☎722-7229. Open M-Th 11am-10pm, F-Sa 11am-11pm.) **Wild Sage People's Market,** 610 E. Pershing, is a respite from the rest of gastronomic Gallup, offering a good selection of organic foods and pasta, and grains in bulk quantities. (☎863-5383. Open Tu-F 1pm-7pm, Sa 10am-6pm.)

HIGHWAY TO HELL

My first try at locating Hwy. 49 left me scratching my head, wondering what each gas station attendant knew that my map did not. But the mystery of Hwy. 49 is easily, if oddly, explained. For 77 years Hwy. 491 was actually Hwy. **666,** the sixth tributary of famous Rte. 66. The two-lane Devil's Highway, as it was called until May 31, 2003, linked **Gallup, NM,** to the arid outskirts of the **Navajo Reservation.**

The name was changed after a coalition of politicians led by New Mexico Governor Bill Richardson argued to federal authorities that the dangerous highway needed a new name and physical improvements. Some linked the high accident rate on 666 to a verse from the Bible's Book of Revelations that associates the number with Satan, though it likely stemmed more from poor road quality and sharp turns than the influence of the damned. Many area maps have yet to reflect the switch, which will cost $10,000 in new signs alone.

Locals hope renaming Devil's Highway will sweep in prosperity like a G.O.D. 18-wheeler. Others fear it will sap the region of some of its uniqueness and tourist appeal. Only time will tell if the swap is a blessing or a curse, but if you're driving on Hwy. 491 and see a red-horned, spiky-tailed stranger, you'll know that your map isn't the only one outdated.

—Brendan J. Reed

EL MORRO NATIONAL MONUMENT ☎505

Drawn by a nearby spring while traveling through what is now New Mexico, Native Americans, Spanish explorers, and Anglo pioneers left their inscriptions on a giant sandstone bluff. Its signatures dating back to 1605, **Inscription Rock** has been the center piece of El Morro National Monument since its founding in 1906. The monument offers two hiking options. The ½ mi. wheelchair-accessible **Inscription Trail** winds past the rock and large pool of rainwater that attracted visitors in centuries past, providing excellent views of the signatures and neighboring petroglyphs. The 2 mi. **Mesa Top Trail** climbs 200 ft. to the top of the rock before skirting the edge of an ancient pueblo. The trail is well-marked and affords impressive panoramas of the entire region. Trails close 1hr. before the Visitors Center. The monument is located just west of the Continental Divide on Rte. 53, 42 mi. west of Grants and 56 mi. southeast of Gallup. The **Visitors Center** includes a small museum and warnings against emulating the graffiti of old. (☎783-4226. Open daily 9am-5pm, occasionally later June-Aug. $3, under 17 free.) The small, tranquil **El Morro Campground ❶** has running water, primitive toilets, and is rarely full. (9 sites, 1 wheelchair accessible. Open year-round. $5 per site.)

EL MALPAIS NATIONAL MONUMENT ☎505

Home to a spectacle of converging lava flows and sandstone mesas, this 15-year-old national monument and its associated BLM land feature some of the Southwest's most unique and varied terrain, from miles of lava tubes to one of New Mexico's largest natural arches. Despite its spectacular landscape, the monument does not receive the traffic of some of its neighbors, making it a perfect spot to escape the crowds and head into some true wilderness.

◼🄌 **ORIENTATION & PRACTICAL INFORMATION.** Rte. 53 runs along the northwestern side of the monument, while Rte. 117 borders the eastern side. Both roads access the trailheads and are themselves excellent ways to see the diverse landscape. In addition, County Road 42, designated the **Chain of Craters Backcountry Byway,** runs into the monument's belly, but a high-clearance vehicle is recommended as the road is quite rough. A number of Visitors Centers are located throughout El Malpais and serve as invaluable resources for would-be explorers. Off I-40 at exit 85, the **Northwest New Mexico Visitors Center** sits at the northern part of the monument and is the best place to begin the venture. (☎876-2783. Open May-Sept. daily 9am-6pm; Oct.-Apr. 8am-5pm.) The park service's **El Malpais Information Center** (☎783-4774) is 23 mi. south of I-40 on Rte. 53, while the **Bureau of Land Management's Ranger Station** (☎280-2918) sits along Rte. 117 9 mi. south of I-40, off exit 89. (Both open daily 8:30am-4:30pm.) There is now one established campground at **The Narrows ❶**, which has five free sites with vault toilets. It is located off Rte. 117, and there is no water or electricity. **Backcountry camping ❶** is free in certain designated spots; check with rangers for specifics. Obtaining a permit at one of the Visitors Centers is required. For more info, contact any Visitors Center or write the National Park Service, 123 E. Roosevelt, Grants, NM 87020.

◪ **SIGHTS.** Rte. 117 runs by the most accessible wonders of the monument. The wheelchair-accessible **Sandstone Bluffs Overlook,** 10 mi. south of I-40 and 1 mi. south of the BLM station, offers panoramic vistas of the El Malpais lava flows and the surrounding landscape. Seven miles farther south, **La Ventana Natural Arch** is the largest of New Mexico's readily accessible natural arches. Less than 1 mi. farther along, Rte. 117 enters **The Narrows,** where lava flowed to the base of 500 ft. tall sandstone cliffs thousands of years ago.

■ **HIKING.** The **Narrows Rim Trail** provides excellent access to the landscape around the Narrows. The 6 mi. round-trip trail begins at the southern end of The Narrows, 21 mi. from I-40, and scrambles to the top of the rim, where spectacular views of the lava flows and La Ventana Natural Arch greet you. Rte. 53 accesses the heart of the monument's lava flows via a few good hiking trails. The **Zuni-Acoma Trail,** 16 mi. south of I-40, traces an ancient Anasazi trade route across four of the major lava flows and is part of the Continental Divide Trail. The strenuous hike is 15 mi. round-trip or 7.5 mi. one-way to Rte. 117. Four miles farther down Rte. 53, the **El Calderon Area** provides access to a relatively old lava flow and volcanic cinder cone. An easy 3 mi. loop passes by **Junction Cave,** sink holes, and trenches amid vegetation resilient enough to make a lava flow its home.

■ **OTHER OUTDOOR ACTIVITIES.** The **Big Tubes Area** on the Big Tubes Rd., off County Road 42 4.5 mi. south of Rte. 53, encompasses 17 mi. of lava tubes as well as a marked trail to two caves open to the general public, **Big Skylight** and **Four Windows.** Be sure to speak with a ranger about the necessary precautions of caving before setting out, and do not enter the caves alone. Farther south, Rte. 42 passes along a rift lined with 30 cinder cones, but the scenic 36 mi. drive necessitates a high-clearance vehicle. The **West Malpais Wilderness** and **Hole-In-The-Wall** offer opportunities for the most isolated backcountry experiences in the area. Hole-in-the-Wall is an island of ponderosa pines surrounded by a sea of lava, where many plant and animal species have adapted to the unique conditions. East of Rte. 117, backcountry hiking and camping abound in the Cebolla Wilderness.

SOUTHWESTERN NEW MEXICO

With some of the most remote wilderness in the region, southwestern New Mexico's large tracts of untraveled land make for a backcountry hiker's wonderland. While many towns in the region are comprised mostly of quiet residential areas, travelers can look to the outdoor opportunities and history of the area for flavor and appeal. Pull over to hike in the Gilas, rejuvenate yourself at the mineral baths of Truth or Consequences, to rejoin civilization in the historic town of Mesilla.

TRUTH OR CONSEQUENCES ☎ 505

In 1950, Ralph Edwards's popular radio game show, "Truth or Consequences," celebrated its tenth anniversary by renaming this small town, formerly Hot Springs, NM, in its honor. Every year on the first weekend of May, residents celebrate the name change with a fiesta that includes parades, rodeos, art displays, country music, high-energy drum circles, and canoe races. Today, T or C (pronounced "teeer-see") is a slow-paced, one-traffic-light town of 7500 folks. As its maiden name suggests, the town was a tourist attraction prior to the publicity stunt. Mineral baths play the role of the mythic fountains of youth, drawing visitors to a town filled with an ex-drifter, down-home spirit.

■ **TRANSPORTATION & PRACTICAL INFORMATION.** T or C sits approximately 150 mi. south of Albuquerque (p. 378) on I-25. Five miles north of town sits Elephant Butte Lake, a haven for outdoor enthusiasts in search of cooler waters. **Buses** depart and arrive from C.W.'s Premium Water and Ice, 8 Date St. **Greyhound,** in cooperation with **TNM&O Coaches** (☎ 894-3649), runs one coach daily from **Albuquerque** (3hr.; M-Th $27, F-Su $29) and two from **El Paso** (2hr.; M-Th $26, F-Su $28). The **Chamber of Commerce,** 400 W 4th St., has free maps and brochures about area accommodations and attractions. (☎ 894-3536. Open M-F 9am-5:30pm, Sa 9am-

1pm.) Services include: **24hr. ATM,** 509 Broadway, at the Bank of the Southwest; **police,** 401 McAdoo (☎894-1185, after hours 894-7111); **emergency** (☎911); **Davis Fleck Pharmacy,** 500 Broadway (☎894-3055; open M-F 9am-6pm, Sa 9am-3pm); **hospital,** 800 E. 9th Ave. (☎894-2111); free **Internet access** at the public library, 325 Library Ln. (☎894-3027); and **post office,** 300 Main St., in the middle of town (open M-F 9am-3pm), or 1507 N. Date St. (open M-F 8:30am-5pm). **Postal code:** 87901.

ACCOMMODATIONS & FOOD. Riverbend Hot Springs Hostel (HI-AYH) ❶, 100 Austin St., can be reached from I-25. Take exit 79, turn right, and continue 1.5 mi. to a traffic light. Turn left at the light, then immediately turn right onto Cedar St. and follow it down to the river and the blue building at the road's bend. Use of on-site mineral baths and a meditation cove are free for guests. Though years of wear are starting to show, Riverbend is reason enough to stop in T or C—many travelers plan to spend a night and end up staying a week. (☎894-6183; www.nmhotsprings.com. Kitchen and laundry. Reception open 8am-10pm, call ahead for late-night arrivals. Tepees or dorms $14, non-members $16; private rooms $30-48; tent site $10, non-members $12.) The **Charles Motel and Spa** ❷, 601 Broadway, offers simple and clean accommodations. The large rooms have kitchenettes, A/C, and cable TV. There are also mineral baths on the premises. (☎894-7154 or 800-317-4518; www.charlesspa.com. Singles $39; doubles $45.) **Campsites** at the nearby **Elephant Butte Lake State Park** ❶ have access to restrooms and cold showers. (Primitive sites $8; developed sites with showers $10, electricity $14.)

Nearly all of T or C's restaurants are as easy on the wallet as the baths are on the body. For groceries, try **Bullock's,** at the corner of Broadway and Post. (☎894-6622. Open M-Sa 7:30am-8pm, Su 8am-7pm.) **La Hacienda** ❷, 1615 S. Broadway, is well worth the short drive out of the center of town. Arroz con pollo (rice with chicken, $7), and breakfast chorizo con huevos (sausage with eggs, $5) make this the best Mexican food around (open Tu-Su 11am-9pm). The popular **La Cocina** ❷, 1 Lake Way Dr. (look for the "Hot Stuff" sign above N. Date St.), also pleases with huge portions of Mexican and New Mexican food, including chimichangas ($7). A Carrizozo cherry cider ($1.50) will surely slake your thirst. (☎894-6499. Open daily 10:30am-10pm.) **Hot Springs Bakery Cafe** ❷, 313 Broadway, located in a turquoise stucco building, has an outdoor patio and cactus garden. Pizzas go for $7-14. (☎894-5555. Open Tu-Sa 8am-3pm.) **Bar-B-Que on Broadway** ❷, 308 Broadway, serves plentiful breakfast specials that start at $2.50 and hearty lunch entrees running $5-8, as well as local gossip. (☎894-7047. Open M-Sa 7am-4pm.)

NIGHTLIFE. Raymond's Lounge, 912 N. Date St., next to the Circle K, is T or C's rock 'n' roll bar. (☎894-4057. Free pool Th night. Draft beers $1.50. Open M-Sa 11am-2am, Su noon-midnight.) The **Pine Knot Saloon,** 700 E. 3rd Ave., just past the curve on 3rd St. towards Elephant Butte, is a vintage Western saloon adorned with photos of John Wayne. (☎894-2714. Karaoke Th, live music on weekends.) **The Dam Site,** just past the **Elephant Butte Dam** on Rte. 51, is a bar and grille with an outdoor patio, offering spectacular views of the lake and surrounding mountains. (☎894-2073. Live music Sa afternoon Easter to Labor Day. Dinner entrees $7-19, drafts $3. Open Su-Th 11am-9pm, F-Sa 11am-10pm; bar open F-Sa until midnight.)

SIGHTS & OUTDOORS. Mineral baths are the town's main attraction; locals claim that the baths heal virtually everything. The only outdoor tubs are located at the **Riverbend Hostel,** where four co-ed tubs abut the Río Grande (bathing suits must be worn). Access to the baths is $6 per hr. for the public (10am-7pm), but complementary for hostel guests (7am-10am and 7pm-10pm). Five miles north of T or C, **Elephant Butte Lake State Park** features New Mexico's largest lake (take Date St. north to a sign for Elephant Butte; turn right onto 181 and follow the

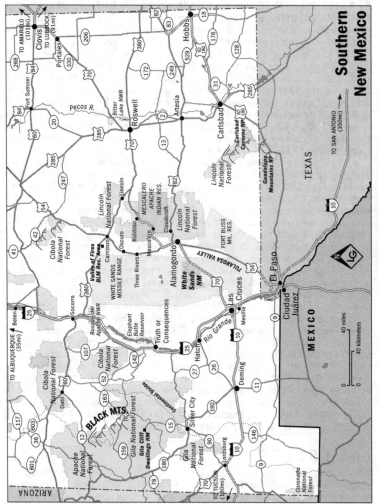

signs). A public works project dammed up the Río Grande in 1916 after the resolution of a major water rights dispute between the US and Mexico. The resulting lake is named after the elephantine rock formation at its southern end. The park has sandy beaches and a marina. (Cars $4, bikes and pedestrians free.) **Sports Adventure,** on the lake at the end of Long Point Rd., north of the town of Elephant Butte, rents jet skis. (☎744-5557 or 888-736-8420. Rentals start at $35 per 30min.) **Marina del Sur** rents motorized boats of all kinds. (☎744-5567. Must be 18+ and have a valid driver's license to rent. Jet skis $35 per hr., pontoon boats $30 per hr., ski boats $45 per hr., 3hr. minimum and deposit on all rentals.) There is a **Visitors Center** at the entrance to the park with a small museum on the area's natural history. (☎877-664-7787. Open M-F 7:30am-4pm, Sa-Su 7:30am-10pm.) An easy 1.6 mi. nature trail begins in the parking lot just past the Visitors Center.

🔁 DAYTRIP FROM TRUTH OR CONSEQUENCES: BOSQUE DEL APACHE NATIONAL WILDLIFE REFUGE. The damming of the Río Grande in the early decades of the 20th century destroyed the wetlands that were once winter feeding grounds for migratory waterfowl. In 1939, Franklin Roosevelt created Bosque del Apache in an effort to recreate these lost wetlands. At the end of every summer, 7000 acres of land are flooded to provide a fertile resting ground for 20,000 sandhill cranes, 30,000 snowgeese, and countless other waterfowl. The peak season for bird-watching is November through February, and the best times of day are sunrise and sunset. During the **Festival of the Cranes**, held every November, over 5000 bird-watchers descend on the Refuge to attend talks and embark on tours. To reach the Refuge, take I-25 to exit 124 at San Marcial, head east down a well-maintained gravel road for ½ mile, and then go north on Rte. 1 for 8 mi. (Open 1 hr. before sunrise to 1 hr. after sunset. $3 per car.)

A 15 mi. scenic **auto loop** takes visitors past the prime bird-viewing locations. The loop also makes an excellent bike trail. Within the wildlife refuge are a number of hiking trails, ranging from easy to strenuous. The **Canyon Trail** is a moderately difficult 2.5 mi. hike through the northern tip of the Chihuahuan Desert. It begins by winding through a dry river bed and passes a natural rock arch on its way to an overlook with a view of the Río Grande and the refuge wetlands. The **Chupadera Trail** is the most challenging hike in the refuge. A 9.7 mi. round-trip, it leads to the summit of 6195 ft. Chupadera Peak, which stands nearly 2000 ft. above the valley floor. Three and a half miles from the trailhead, the trail enters a stunning red canyon created by volcanic activity. From the summit, you can see the northern shore of Elephant Butte Lake to the south, White Sands Missile Range to the east, and the town of Socorro to the north. The sprawling **Visitors Center** offers detailed brochures with maps for all hikes within the park. Its collection of art and sculpture inspired by the local waterfowl makes it worth a visit. (☎835-1828; www.friendsofthebosque.org. Open M-F 7:30am-4pm, Sa-Su 8am-4:30pm.)

Eight miles north of the Wildlife Refuge along Rte. 1 lies the attractive, small village of **San Antonio.** The **Owl Bar and Cafe ❶** at the main intersection in town is notable for its famous green chile hamburgers ($3) and its old wooden bar, once owned by Conrad Hilton, the town's most famous resident. (☎835-9946. Open M-Sa 8am-9:30pm.) A couple blocks south of the Owl on 4th St. is a beautiful **adobe church** with blue and yellow glass windows. Three and a half miles farther south of San Antonio on Rte. 1 is the **Bosque Birdwatchers RV Park ❶.** (☎835-1366. Tent sites $10, with electricity $12; for 2 people $12/$14. Showers $2.)

LAS CRUCES
☎**505**

The second largest city in New Mexico, Las Cruces is situated in the fertile Río Grande Valley, 32 miles north of El Paso and the Mexican border. No one knows exactly how the town got its name. Some say the name comes from the crosses erected to commemorate the deaths of traders heading north to Santa Fe along the Camino Real and of locals killed during Apache raids. Others hold that it is a Spanish rendering of "the crossroads," as this site marked the junction of the north-south Camino Real with the east-west Butterfield Trail in the 18th century. Today, Las Cruces marks the intersection of I-25 and I-10. There isn't much to do in Las Cruces, but historic Mesilla, just 3 miles to the southwest, has interesting shops, restaurants, and a thriving art community. The rugged Organ Mountains tower over the city to the east, offering chances to hike, mountain bike, and camp.

🔲🔁 ORIENTATION & PRACTICAL INFORMATION. The city is framed by **I-25** to the east and **I-10** to the south. East to west, the major north-south streets are **Telshor Boulevard** (I-25), **Main Street,** and **Valley Drive.** Lohman Ave. runs east-west through the heart of the city, while University Ave. forms the southern boundary, leads east to the Organ Mountains, and is the easiest route to the historical Mesilla plaza. **Greyhound,** 490A N. Valley Dr. (☎524-8518), on the west side of the city, sends buses to **El Paso** (45min., 10 per day, $10) and **Albuquerque** (6½hr., 3 per day, $40). Buses operated by **Road Runner Transit** (☎541-2500) service the Las Cruces area. Adults $0.50, children $0.25. The **Convention and Visitors Bureau,** 211 N. Water St. (☎541-2444), is open M-F 8am-5pm and offers maps and brochures. Other services include: **police,** 217 E. Picacho Ave. (☎526-0795; **emergency,** ☎911); **Memorial Medical Center** (☎522-8641), on Telshor Ave. at University Ave.; and the **post office,** 201 E. Las Cruces Ave. (☎524-2841). **Postal code:** 88001.

⌂ ACCOMMODATIONS. Cheap motels dot Picacho Ave. to the west of Valley Dr., within walking distance of the bus station. **However, this area is not very safe at night, so be careful when walking alone.** Other motels cluster around the exits from I-10 and I-25. The **⧉Lundeen Inn of the Arts Bed and Breakfast ❹,** 618 S. Alameda Blvd., one block west of Main St., is worth the premium price. This beautifully decorated, 100-year-old adobe mansion serves as both a guest house and an art gallery. The spacious rooms are named after area artists, and each has a private bath, A/C, cable TV, and a minifridge. Reservations are absolutely necessary. (☎526-3327 or 888-526-3326; www.innofthearts.com. Reception 8am-10pm. Singles $58-64; doubles $77-85; suites with kitchen $125. Discounts for AAA, AARP, and students.) For a cheaper room, **Day's End Lodge ❷,** 755 N. Valley Dr., just a couple blocks from the bus station, offers simple accommodations with A/C, heating, and cable TV. (☎524-7753. Singles $25; doubles $28-33.) If you are looking for a scenic place to pitch your tent, drive east on Rte. 70 for about 15 mi. and turn left on Aguirre Spring Rd. to reach the **Aguirre Spring National Recreation Area ❶,** on the eastern side of the Organ Mountains. (☎525-4300. Entrance gate open mid-Apr. to mid-Oct. 8am-7pm, mid-Oct. to mid-Apr. 8am-6pm. Vault toilets, water available at campground host's site. $3 per vehicle.)

❏ FOOD. The food in Las Cruces revolves around fast-food and chain restaurants, but there is a slew of interesting places to dine in nearby Mesilla. **La Posta ❷,** one block from Mesilla plaza at 2410 Calle de San Albino, is a favorite among camera-toting tourists and Billy the Kid, Kit Carson, Douglas MacArthur, and Pancho Villa before them. The menu has a full range of New Mexican food, with combination plates

HEAT: IT'S WHAT'S FOR DINNER

Whether cooked in fiery dishes or offered as a novelty hot sauce in tourist shops, the chile pepper is the icon of New Mexican cuisine. Its spicy flavor comes from the chemical *capsaicin,* which resides not in the seeds, as many believe, but in the pod's membranes and the soft tissue that supports the seeds. The chemical is thought to be an evolutionary adaptation to prevent mammals from eating the pods. Unable to taste *capsaicin,* birds eat but can't digest the seeds, thus helping with their dispersal; mammals, who can digest the seeds, taste the heat and avoid chiles entirely.

In the summer, farmers' markets brim with chiles of all kinds. All told, New Mexico produces about 100,000 tons of chiles each year, the most in the US. Most common is the New Mexico green chile, with a 6 in. pod and a firm, crisp texture, but chiles range from fat, orange *habañeros* to skinny, red *de arboles* to the stubby, green *jalapeño.* The *habañero* is the undisputed king of heat, its orange variety topping out at eight times the heat of a regular *jalapeño.* Its juice can actually blister bare skin. When the fire hits, the best remedy is milk or yogurt; the chemical *casein* in dairy products helps prevent the tongue's nerves from sensing *capsaicin.* Resist the urge to reach for water—it will only help the fire spread.

for $8. (☎524-3524. Open Su-Th 11am-9pm, F-Sa 11am-9:30pm.) **El Comedor ❷**, 2190 Avenida de Mesilla, is also worth a look. Understated and plentiful, the menu includes, among other dishes, a traditional Mexican stew for $7. (Open M-Th 8am-8pm, F-Sa 8am-9pm, Su 9am-3pm.) In Las Cruces, try **International Delights ❶**, 1245 El Paseo, in the corner of the Albertson's shopping center. With a relaxed atmosphere, long hours, and a full selection of coffee drinks ($1-3) and sandwiches (falafel $4.50), it provides a cozy haven from Las Cruces's suburban sprawl. (Open M-Th 7am-6pm, F-Sa 7am-midnight, Su 7am-10pm.)

◪ ⚞ SIGHTS & OUTDOORS. Though Las Cruces is the demographic center of the area, Mesilla, only 3 mi. away, is the cultural center. When the US acquired the land in 1854, Mesilla became an important stop on the road between San Antonio and San Francisco. By the 1880s the town was as wild as any other in the West; it was here that Billy the Kid was tried for murder and sentenced to hang in 1881. Today Mesilla looks much the same as it did then, and most of the adobe buildings around the central plaza date back 150 years. On the plaza, the **Visitors Center,** 2348 Ave. de Mesilla, shows a short video on the town's history. (☎647-9698. Open daily 9:30am-4:30pm.) Presiding over the plaza is the majestic **San Albino Church** (☎526-9349), originally built in 1855. On November 2-3, residents recognize All Saints Day with the Día de Los Muertos (Day of the Dead) Celebration with tables on the plaza, adorned with pictures of their deceased relatives and their favorite foods.

The **Organ Mountains** to the east of Las Cruces offer great opportunities for hiking, mountain biking, and rock climbing. On the western slope of the Organ Mountains, **Dripping Springs** and **La Cueva Trails,** both easy, 1 mi. hikes, are accessible by Dripping Springs Rd. The Dripping Springs Trail leads to the ruins of a resort and the "weeping wall" at Dripping Springs. La Cueva leads to an archaeological site that is associated with the ancient Mogollon culture. For more info, check at the **A.B. Cox Visitors Center.** (☎522-1219. Open daily until 5pm.) The entrance gate to the park closes every day at 5pm. On the eastern slope of the Organ Mountains, **Aguirre Springs** is farther from Las Cruces, but the hiking is more challenging. The **Pine Tree Loop Trail** is a moderate 4.5 mi. hike that climbs nearly to the base of the rock formations. The **Baylor Pass Trail** is a 6 mi. hike to the top of 5500 ft. Baylor Pass. From the top, one can see Las Cruces and the Río Grande Valley to the west and White Sands National Monument to the east.

Las Cruces provides some decent mountain biking opportunities as well. The **A Mountain Trail** is a moderately difficult ride around the base of the hill at the east end of the New Mexico University's campus. The trail takes its name from the "A" formed by the white stones that adorn the mountain's east face, which is visible from most of Las Cruces. The BLM maintains the longer, more difficult **Sierra Vista Trail,** which rises into the Organs. Check with bike shop **Outdoor Adventures** for more information on these and other trails in the area. (☎521-1922. Open M-F 10am-6pm, Sa 10am-5pm.)

SILVER CITY ☎505

In its heyday, Silver City was a raw, wild place. It spawned the famous outlaw Billy the Kid, and brown historical markers scattered around town point out the sites of his home, his school, his first bank robbery, and his first jailbreak. Unfortunately, buildings dating from Billy's Wild West days are few; an 1890s mudslide swept away most of downtown Silver City, producing the trench that downtown Big Ditch Park commemorates. Dating from the turn of the 20th century, the current downtown is surprisingly vibrant for a town of this size, but Silver City's attraction for most visitors is its distance from civilization and proximity to the undisturbed wilderness of Gila National Forest.

■■ ORIENTATION & PRACTICAL INFORMATION. Silver City is about 50 mi. off I-10 and easily reached by state roads. Rte. 90 links the city with **Lordsburg** on I-10 near the Arizona border, U.S. 180 stretches from **Deming** on I-10 through Silver City to northeastern Arizona, and Rte. 152 leads east to **Truth or Consequences** (p. 421). **U.S. 180 (Silver Heights Boulevard)** and **Hudson Street (Route 90)** make up the backbone of the city's street grid. Around the center of town, College Ave. bisects Hudson St. and leads to the **University of Western New Mexico.** A few blocks south, Broadway runs parallel to College Ave. and leads through downtown. One block west of the main drag, Bullard St. contains galleries, health food stores, New Age herb shops, cafes, and various services. **Enterprise Rent-A-Car** has an office at 1455 U.S. 180 E. (☎534-0000. 21+ with credit card and valid driver's license. Open M-F 8:30am-6pm.) **Silver Stage Lines** (☎800-522-0162) has bus service twice daily to Silver City from the El Paso airport (round-trip $59). **Las Cruces Shuttle Service** (☎800-288-1784) runs daily trips to: **Deming** (3 per day; $23 one-way, $35 roundtrip, additional person $15); **El Paso** (3 per day, $40/$60/$25); and **Las Cruces** (3 per day, $33/$50/$20). Both pick up passengers from the corner of N. Bullard St. and Broadway.

The **Chamber of Commerce/Visitors Center**, 201 N. Hudson St., is near the intersection with Broadway. (☎538-3785. Open M-Sa 9am-5pm.) Other services include: **Laundryland,** 407 N. Hudson St. (☎538-2631; open daily 7:30am-9:30pm); **Gila Regional Medical Center,** 1313 E 32nd St. (☎538-4000); free **Internet access** (1 hr. max.; sign up in advance) at the **public library,** 515 W. College Ave. (☎538-3672; open M, Th 9am-8pm, Tu-W 9am-6pm, F 9am-5pm, Sa 9am-10pm); **emergency:** ☎911; and the **post office,** 500 N. Hudson St. (☎538-2831; open M-F 8:30am-5pm, Sa 10am-noon). **Postal code:** 88061.

■■ ACCOMMODATIONS & FOOD. Now without a hostel, Silver City accommodations begin in the $30 range for those not willing to camp. Chain motels and other inexpensive lodgings flank U.S. 180 on the east side of town. A half-block from Bullard St., ■**Palace Hotel ❸,** 106 W. Broadway, has beautiful, antique-styled rooms that hail from 1882, though only five of them are at the cheap end of the spectrum. Reservations are absolutely necessary in the summer. (☎388-1811. Small rooms $35, doubles $47, additional person $5; suites $57.) Two solid options are the **Copper Manor Motel ❷,** 710 Silver Heights Blvd. (☎538-5392 or 800-853-2916. Rooms $38-52), and the **Drifter Motel and Cocktail Lounge ❸,** 711 Silver Heights Blvd. (Motel: ☎800-853-2916. Rooms $38-52. Lounge: ☎538-2916. Live music F-Sa. Open daily 5pm-1:30am.)

On the culinary side of things, the **Piñon Cafe and Bakery ❷,** 603 N. Bullard St., offers tasty continental cuisine and an extensive beer and wine menu. (☎534-9168. Open M-Th 8am-9pm, F-Sa 8am-11pm, Su 8am-8pm. Lunch $5-8, dinner $11-15.) The colorfully decorated **Jalisco Cafe ❷,** 100 S. Bullard St. at Spring St. in the heart of downtown, serves heaping portions of spicy Mexican food with a unique jalapeño guacamole. (☎388-2060. Open M-Th 11am-8:30pm, F 11am-9pm, Sa 11am-8:30pm. Meals $5-8.) The bright, high-ceilinged **Olde World Bakery and Cafe ❶,** at the corner of Bullard and Broadway, is by far the best spot for breakfast or lunch in Silver City. Danishes ($1.50), stacked cold-cut and vegetarian sandwiches for $3.25-6. (☎534-9372. Open M-Sa 7am-5pm. Outdoor seating available.)

■■ SIGHTS & OUTDOORS. For a view of the Wild West, try the **Billy the Kid Historical Walk.** It starts at the corner of Hudson St. and Broadway; follow the arrows to take the stroll. Art enthusiasts will find a respectable collection of galleries on Yankie St., one block north of Broadway at Bullard St. Silver City houses the headquarters for the **Gila National Forest.** The main forestry station is on the 32nd Bypass Rd. off U.S. 180 east of town. The station provides excellent maps of the forest and its wilderness areas, as well as having info on various outdoor activities in the region. (☎388-8201. Open M-F 8am-4:30pm.) Its proximity to the national forest makes Silver City the base for a variety of outfitting operations. The **Gila Hike and Bike Shop,** 103 E. College Ave., rents mountain bikes and cross-country skis for exploring Gila and the surrounding foothills, repairs bikes, sells outdoor equipment, and provides maps of the area. (☎388-3222. Open M-F 9am-5:30pm, Sa 9am-5pm, Su 10am-4pm. Bike rentals first day $20, 2nd day $15, 3rd day $10, each additional day $5; cross-country skis $12 per day.) **Continental Divide Tours,** run by one of the Hike and Bike guys, runs van, hiking, and biking tours in the Gila area. (☎534-2953. 4hr. tour $50, full-day $110.)

GILA NATIONAL FOREST ☎505

The Gila National Forest encompasses hundreds of miles of hiking trails through mountains, canyons, and forests. This area includes more wilderness than any other national forest in the Southwest, and if that's not enough, it abuts Apache-Sitgreaves National Forests in Arizona. Rugged, mountainous terrain makes it ideal for extended and intense backpacking trips.

⁊ PRACTICAL INFORMATION. Three **ranger stations** serve the Gila National Forest: one in **Silver City** (p. 426), one near **Mimbres** along Rte. 35, and another northwest of Silver City on U.S. 180 by **Glenwood.** The **Visitors Center** near the cliff dwellings also contains thorough information about hiking and other activities in the area. The Silver City station is the regional headquarters, dispensing recreation info and maps of the entire area. Dispersed camping is allowed without permit anywhere in the forest—the only exception may be sensitive areas of the designated wilderness, where seasonal limitations may take effect. Ask rangers for details. More accessible than wilderness expanses, there are a few maintained campgrounds in the area. 38 miles north of Silver City and 4 mi. south of the Cliff Dwellings Visitors Center, the free **Grapevine ❶** and **Forks Campgrounds ❶** provide toilets, but no designated sites. A scant ½ mi. from the Visitors Center, the **Scorpion Campground ❶** features more services (water and flush toilets in summer, picnic tables, and grills) but has no fee. North of Lake Roberts on Rte. 35 is the **Mesa Campground ❶**, which also has water and toilets but charges $7 per night.

⚐ HIKING & BACKPACKING. The colossal Gila National Forest is singular in that the entire forest exists as one contiguous chunk. As a result, the trails are as close to endless as you'll find. The only limits to backpacking trips in the forest are your creativity and stamina. A brief glance at a topo map will get your mind swimming with ideas for a week-long escape. Although the trails are many, major routes are few, and so a consultation with a park ranger might help narrow down the possibilities. Horses are allowed on most trails. A number of popular trailheads lie along the length of Forest Rd. 15 to the Cliff Dwellings. Many of these trailheads offer both day hiking and backpacking alternatives. Some of the day hiking opportunities in the Gilas are a bit more established.

The **Gila River Trek** (17 mi. round-trip, 1 long day or 2) departs from the Sapillo Trailhead just south of the junction with Rte. 35. It crosses canyon country for its first leg before following the Gila River north and east 10 mi. to link up with Forest Rd. 15 near Grapevine Campground. The first leg traces Spring Canyon Trail (#247). The initial ascent is a short climb and after a 5 mi. descent, the trail hits the Gila River. The final 10 mi. are along the river, which represents a reliable water source year-round. This hike is scenic but not strenuous, though be advised that it requires many crossings of the river in water up to 4 ft. There are also great hikes up the West and Middle Forks of the Gila with much shallower crossings.

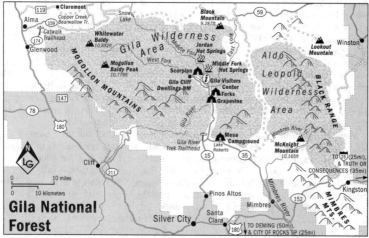

Gila National Forest

The Catwalk Trail, an 18 mi., 1-3 day loop, begins at the Whitewater Picnic Area near Glenwood. Reaching the trailhead involves a 60 mi. drive from Silver City along U.S. 180 N; signs mark the turnoff clearly. The first length crosses into Whitewater Canyon in an intriguing way: a remnant of the mining industry, a steel-grate catwalk is suspended along the side of the Canyon above a rushing creek surrounded by steep cliff faces on either side. Even for those unwilling to walk the full hike, this first section merits a quick stroll. Good bouldering awaits inside the canyon, accessible from either end of the catwalk. Cross over the catwalk (less than 1 mi.) and follow Trail #207. This flat route continues to trace Whitewater Canyon. After 5 mi., Winn Canyon branches south and Trail #179 follows it for 1.5 mi. to Spider Saddle, an intersection of several trails. Take Trail #181 farther south (which is strenuous as it leaves one canyon to enter another) and begin the return via 8 mi. of the South Fork Trail (#212), hugging the south fork of Whitewater Canyon. The recreation area requires a $3 parking fee and closes at 6pm. Leave a note on your dash giving an approximate time of return to avoid being ticketed.

To get to the **Mimbres River Trail** (28 mi., 2-3 nights), take Rte. 35 to Forest Rd. 150 Go 8 mi. and park at the Continental Divide Trail parking lot. Enter the wilderness at the sign for the Mimbres River Trail. The first leg is 13 mi. up the Mimbres river to the Reeds Peak Lookout Tower. The return is 13 mi. along the Continental Divide Trail. Water is available only on the first segment of the trail.

◪ OTHER OUTDOOR ACTIVITIES. In the Gila Wilderness, many outdoors pursuits await those willing to traverse this vast and little-traveled area. Much of it is designated wilderness, but not all—the trails available for mountain biking are fewer but still plentiful. **Rock climbing** is permitted in select parts of the forest, and many of the canyons make for good **bouldering.** Use caution and common sense at all times. If you intend to use tackle or gear on the canyon walls, check with the rangers for seasonal or territorial restrictions. The Gila National Forest can get hot in the summer, and the most convenient location for a cooling dip is **Lake Roberts.** Located just south of the intersection with Forest Road 15 on Rte. 35, the lake is wildly popular with fishermen. The facility also has a boat ramp and picnic area.

Due to the active subterranean geology of the area, a variety of **hot springs** bubble up in the Gila Wilderness. One of the easiest to find is **Middle Fork Hot Springs.** Conveniently located ½ mile up the well-marked trail that stretches north from the

National Monument Visitors Center, it's popular and sees consistent use. The water here comes out of the main spring at about 130°F, so stick to the shallow pools where it cools down a bit. **Jordon Hot Springs,** more of a lukewarm springs, can be reached on the Middle Fork Trail from TJ Corral Trailhead north of the Visitors Center. From TJ, it's a 4.5 mi. hike overland to the middle fork of the Gila River and then 1.5 mi. upstream. A map is recommended for this route. The canyon is narrow at points and can suddenly fill during flash flooding. Check with rangers before entering the canyon, and for directions to more out-of-the-way hot springs. **Warning: The hot springs are inhabited by an amoeba that causes meningitis.** Under normal conditions the risk is very slight so long as you do not immerse your head, mouth, or nose, but again, checking with rangers is a good idea.

Much of the Gila National Forest, including almost all of the area around the Gila Cliff Dwellings, is designated wilderness and, as such, is off-limits to mechanized vehicles, including mountain bikes. That said, there is great **biking** in the area. The region around Glenwood, north of Silver City on U.S. 180, falls outside the wilderness area and thus accommodates bikers. **Gila Hike and Bike** (p. 427) in Silver City is the closest outfitter, providing rentals, information, and shuttles.

Copper Creek/Bearwallow Trail (10 mi. round-trip), following Forest Rd. 119 from Claremont to Bearwallow Park, is not a loop but rather an out-and-back trip. To reach the beginning, head north of Glenwood approximately 7.5 mi. to Forest Rd. 119. Turn right and drive 10 mi. to Claremont, where you switch from four wheels to two. Stick to 119 to stay on track; the roads are well marked, so this shouldn't be difficult. The trail gains nearly 3000 ft. along its course, and passes through forests, canyons, and abandoned, turn-of-the-century mining ruins. Seasonal creek beds pass the road, but Turkey Springs, near the middle of the ride, is the only reliable water source. The area is mostly abandoned during the summer but is a popular hunting locale during the fall. In those months, be careful and wear orange.

GILA CLIFF DWELLINGS NATIONAL MONUMENT   ☎ 505

The mysterious Gila Cliff Dwellings National Monument preserves over 40 stone and timber rooms carved into the cliff's natural caves by the Mogollon tribe during the late 1200s. About a dozen families lived here for some 20 years, farming on the mesa top and along the river. During the early 1300s, however, the Mogollon abandoned their homes for reasons unknown, leaving the dwellings as their only trace.

From Silver City, the Cliff Dwellings are reached via 44 mi. on **Forest Road 15** through Piños Altos. From San Lorenzo, **Route 35** leads 26 mi. and ends 19 mi. south of the monument at an intersection with Forest Rd. 15. Though both roads are narrow and winding, Forest Rd. 15 is somewhat steeper and more difficult. Both roads require 2hr. for safe passage. Road conditions can be impassable in winter; pay close attention to the weather and the road surface.

The **Visitors Center,** at the end of Rte. 15, shows an informative film and sells various maps of the Gila National Forest. (☎536-9461. Open daily 8am-6pm, off-season 8am-4:30pm.) The picturesque ½ mi. round-trip hike to the dwellings begins past the Upper Scorpion Campground. Rangers give short interpretive tours through the cliffs at 11am and 2pm. A trail guide ($0.50) can be purchased at the trailhead or Visitors Center and is recommended for understanding the site. (Dwellings open daily 8am-6pm, off-season 9am-4pm. Entrance fee $3, under 12 free.) A variety of commercial cabins, campgrounds, and recreation sites are sporadically distributed along Rte. 35; smart shoppers will take advantage of the cheaper **services,** such as groceries and gas stations, in Silver City.

The nearest accommodations can be found at the comfy **Grey Feathers Lodge ❸,** 20 mi. south at the intersection of Forest Rd. 15 and Rte. 35. Drawing as many as 4000 hummingbirds on some summer weekends, the Grey Feathers Lodge is a perfect place to kick back, relax, and bird-watch. (☎536-3206. Singles $40-45; doubles $45-50; suites $65-75.) The adjoining **cafe** ❶ offers sandwiches ($3-7) and ice cream ($1.25 per scoop).

SOUTHEASTERN NEW MEXICO

White sand dunes, ponderosa pines, caves, aliens, and the atomic bomb have somehow all carved out a niche in this idiosyncratic pocket of the Southwest. Some of the country's most enigmatic history, coupled with outdoors opportunities in the Lincoln National Forest, Sacramento Mountains, and Tulorosa Basin, make this region one that appeals to a wide variety of travelers. Be prepared for the unusual, the unexpected, and maybe even the uncanny.

ALAMOGORDO   ☎505

Alamogordo is Spanish for "fat poplar," a fitting description for this rapidly growing community of 30,000. Much as the area's poplar trees suck up water flowing down from the Sacramento Mountains, Alamogordo feeds on the region's military bases. As a tourist destination, the city has little charm, but many visitors pass through on the way to White Sands National Monument and other area attractions.

▪▪ **ORIENTATION & PRACTICAL INFORMATION.** Alamogordo lies 86 mi. north of El Paso (p. 447) on U.S. 54 and just 16 mi. west of the mountain town of Cloudcroft (p. 433). White Sands Blvd. (U.S. 70/54) and 10th St. are the main avenues of commerce. **Greyhound,** 601 N. White Sands Blvd. (☎437-3050), in cooperation with **TNM&O Coaches,** has service to **Albuquerque** (5hr.; 3 per day; M-Th $36, F-Su $38) and **El Paso** (1hr.; 4 per day; M-Th $21, F-Su $23). The **Visitors Center** offers standard info at 1301 N. White Sands Blvd. (☎437-6120. Open daily 9am-5pm.) The **Lincoln National Forest Office,** 1101 New York Ave., is a great resource for planning a hiking or camping trip in the Sacramento Mountains. (☎434-7200. Open M-F 7:30am-4:30pm.) **Outdoor Adventures,** 1516 10th St., rents bikes and offers advice on where to ride in the area. (☎434-1920. Open M-F 10am-6pm, Sa 10am-5pm. Bikes $20-25 per day.) Other services include: the **police,** 700 Virginia Ave. (☎439-4300); **emergency** (☎911); **Gerald Champion Regional Medical Center,** 2669 Scenic Dr. (☎439-6100); free **Internet access** at the public library, 920 Oregon Ave. (☎439-4140; open M-Th 10am-8pm, F 10am-5pm, Sa 11am-5pm, Su 1-5pm); and the **post office,** 930 12th St. (☎437-9390. Open M-F 8:30am-5pm, Sa 9am-noon.) **Postal code:** 88310.

▪▪ **ACCOMMODATIONS & FOOD.** The **Alamo Inn** ❷, 1450 N. White Sands Blvd., is one of the many budget motels lining White Sands Blvd. (U.S. 70). Its plain rooms have cable TV, A/C, and an outdoor pool. (☎437-1000. Singles $26; doubles $35.) **Oliver Lee State Park** ❶, 10 mi. south of town on U.S. 54, has excellent camping facilities with clean showers (tents sites $10; hookups $14). There are two nearby hostels: the **Mountain Park Hostel** ❶ (p. 433), 12 mi. east in Cloudcroft, and the **High Desert Hostel Ranch** ❶ (p. 435), 40 mi. north in Oscuro.

Maximinos ❶, 2300 N. White Sands Blvd. has breakfast burritos for $2.50 and the popular chicken mole goes for $6. (☎443-6102. Open Tu-Sa 8am-2pm and 5-9pm, Su 8am-3pm.) **Dave's Pizza** ❷, 415 S. White Sands Blvd., is a family-run Italian restaurant with good homemade pasta ($6-9) and pizza. (☎437-2505. Open M-Th 11am-10pm, F-Sa 11am-midnight.) **Plaza Pub,** 1004 N. White Sands Blvd., is a laid-back local hangout, offering a respectable menu of local and microbrewed beers ($3-4) and free pool. (☎437-9495. Open M-Sa 11:30am-10pm, Su noon-7pm.)

NEW MEXICO

◙ **SIGHTS.** In addition to its contributions to the space program, this region of the country is known for its pivotal role in the development of weapons of mass destruction. 65 miles northwest of Alamogordo, the **Trinity site** was the location of the world's first atomic bomb detonation on July 16, 1945. The heat of the explosion caused the desert sand to melt and form a green glass dubbed Trinitite. Part of the original trinitite has been preserved, but otherwise the area is now barren. The Alamogordo Chamber of Commerce organizes two tours annually to the site, on the first Saturdays of April and October. (☎437-6120 or 800-826-0294. Call ahead for details.) **The New Mexico Museum of Space History,** 3198 S.R. 2001 off Scenic Dr., displays artifacts from the history of space exploration in both the US and former USSR. An impressive garden of rockets and missiles, including a World War II-era V2 rocket, awaits outside. The facility also houses the International Space Hall of Fame and an IMAX dome theater. (☎437-0318. Open daily 9am-5pm. $2.50, children $2, seniors $2.25, under 4 free. IMAX films daily 11am-5pm, $6, children $4.50, seniors $5.50, under 4 free.)

WHITE SANDS NATIONAL MONUMENT ☎505

Situated in the Tularosa Basin between the Sacramento and San Andres Mountains, the world's largest dunes formed as rainwater flushed gypsum from nearby peaks into Lake Lucero. As desert heat evaporated the lake, left-behind crystals became blindingly white dunes. These drifts create the look of arctic tundra, but don't be fooled: the sun assaults the shadeless with an unbearable light and heat— be prepared with protective clothing and eyewear, heavy-duty sunscreen, and plenty of water. Trekking or rolling through the dunes can provide hours of mindless fun or mindful soul-searching; it's particularly awe-inspiring at sunset.

■▪ ▮ **ORIENTATION & PRACTICAL INFORMATION.** White Sands lies on Rte. 70, 15 mi. southwest of Alamogordo (p. 431) and 52 mi. northeast of Las Cruces (p. 424). Rte. 70 is prone to closures due to missile testing at the nearby military base. Delays can run up to 1hr.; call the park **Visitors Center** to check the status of Rte. 70 closures. The center itself has a small museum with an introductory video and a gift shop. (☎479-6124. Park open daily June-Aug. 7am-10pm, last entrance 9pm; Sept.-May 7am-sunset. Visitors Center open daily June-Aug. 8am-7pm; Sept.-May 8am-5pm. Park admission $3, under 16 free.) The nearest **grocery store, ATM, post office, hospital,** and **Internet access** are in Alamogordo. In an **emergency,** call ☎911. For more info visit the park web site (www.nps.gov/whsa).

▮ **CAMPING.** The only way to spend the night inside the park is to camp at one of the **backcountry campsites ❶.** Ten daily permits for the sites ($3 per person in addition to the park entry fee) are available on a first-come, first-served basis. The sites have no water or toilet facilities and are not accessible by road, requiring up to a 2 mi. hike through the sand dunes. Campers must register in person at the Visitors Center and be in their sites before dark. Campfires are prohibited, but stoves are allowed. Sleeping amid the white dunes can be an extraordinary experience, but plan ahead because sites fill up early on full-moon nights. Occasionally, the sites are closed due to missile range launches. The closest campgrounds with amenities are at **Oliver Lee State Park ❶** (p. 431) and **Aguirre Springs ❶** (p. 425). The park does not offer indoor lodging, but motels and restaurants abound in Alamogordo (p. 431). Affordable hostels await in Oscuro (p. 435) and Cloudcroft (p. 433).

◙▮ **SIGHTS & OUTDOORS.** The 8-mile **Dunes Drive** is a good way to begin a visit to White Sands. However, really experiencing the uniqueness of the monument means getting out of your car and taking a walk across the dunes. Off-trail hiking is permitted anywhere in the eastern section of the park. Anyone considering a backcountry hike should bring a compass and map, as it is easy to get lost in the vast sea of seemingly uniform gypsum dunes.

The only **wheelchair-accessible trail** in the park is the **Interdune Boardwalk,** an easy ¼ mi. walk above the sand. The best hike in the park is the **Alkali Flat Trail,** a moderately strenuous 4.6 mi. loop through the heart of the dunes to the parched, salty lakebed of Lake Otero. The trail is marked by white posts with orange reflective tape. Do not hike the trail in strong winds, when blowing sand reduces visibility and makes it very easy to lose the trail. Bring lots of water and protect yourself from the intense sunlight.

There is a free, guided **sunset stroll** every evening (call ahead), and on summer nights, a park ranger gives an **evening talk** on various topics (June-Aug. 8:30pm). On **full-moon nights** in the summer, the park stays open late (until 11pm, last entrance 10pm), and a guest speaker or performer takes the stage at 8:30pm. A **star talk** takes place most Fridays during the summer at 8:30pm. During the **Perseid Meteor Shower** (usually the 2nd week of Aug.), the park stays open until midnight.

CLOUDCROFT ☎505

At 9000 ft. in the Sacramento Mountains, it is easy to forget that you are still in New Mexico and not the Pacific Northwest. The Ponderosa Pines that blanket the mountainsides were big business for loggers 100 years ago. Today, with the timber industry gone to the real Pacific Northwest, the vast Lincoln National Forest protects the trees so hikers, bikers, and campers can enjoy the spectacular scenery. Due to its high elevation, temperatures are always cool in Cloudcroft, making for comfortable summers with chilly nights and white, snowy winters. The town's temperament is as agreeable as its climate. Even with the influx of summer tourists, Cloudcroft's 750 full-time residents maintain a genial small-town atmosphere.

■ ⁊ ORIENTATION & PRACTICAL INFORMATION. Cloudcroft is 16 mi. east of Alamogordo (p. 433) on U.S. 82. Most of the town's shops and restaurants are either along James Canyon Hwy. (U.S. 82), or Burro Ave. one block to the north. Cloudcroft has **no public transportation.** The **Chamber of Commerce,** 1001 James Canyon Hwy., dispenses information from inside a log cabin. (☎682-2733. Open M-Sa 10am-5pm.) The **Lincoln National Forest Office,** 61 Curlew Pl., just across U.S. 82 from the gas station, is a great resource for info about hiking and camping in the area. (☎682-2551. Open June-Aug. M-Sa 7:30am-4:30pm; Sept.-May M-F 7:30am-4:30pm.) The nearest **laundry** is at the **High Rolls General Store** (☎682-2955), 5 mi. west of town along U.S. 82. Other services include: the **police,** 201 Burro Ave. (☎682-2101); **emergency** (☎911); free **Internet access** at the public library, 90 Swallow Pl. (☎682-1111); and the **post office,** 20 Curlew Pl. (☎682-2431. Open M-F 8:30am-5pm, Sa 9:30-11:30am.) **Postal code:** 88317.

⁊ ⁊ ACCOMMODATIONS & CAMPING. There are quite a few options for lodging in Cloudcroft. The premier budget accommodation in town is the new **Cloudcroft Mountain Park Hostel ❶,** 1049 U.S. 82, 5 mi. west of town between mile markers 10 and 11. This hostel stands on 27 acres adjacent to Lincoln National Forest and has a living room, kitchen, and a large front porch. Pets are allowed, and there are free pickups from the Alamogordo bus station. At the time of publication, this hostel was still under construction and slated to open at the beginning of 2004; for up-to-date info, consult the Visitors Center. (☎682-0555. Wheelchair accessible. Dorms $17; private rooms $34.) The **Alta Vista Motel ❸,** 1605 James Canyon Hwy., has the cheapest motel-style rooms in town. (☎682-2221; www.cloudcroft-motel.com. Rooms $50. Reservations accepted by email.) Another option, attractive mainly to families and groups, is to rent a **wood cabin** in the forest outside of town. These cabins generally come with fireplace, TV, and full kitchen, running about $60-100 for 2-8 people. Rates are highest in summer and during the ski season; reservations are advised, especially during peak season. **The Spruce Cabins** ❸ (☎ 682-2381) and **The Cabins at Cloudcroft** ❸ (☎ 682-2396) are two good bets, or call the Chamber of Commerce for other options.

Camping under the tall pines of **Lincoln National Forest** is not to be missed. The six national forest campgrounds within a 4 mi. radius of Cloudcroft offer drinking water and pit toilets, but do not accommodate RVs. **Silver, Saddle,** and **Apache** (all ❶), 3 mi. north on Rte. 244 from U.S. 82, are popular for their shower access (sites $11). The other three campgrounds are **Pines** ❶ (on Rte. 244, 1 mi. north of U.S. 82; sites $8), **Sleepy Grass** ❶ (1½ mi. east of Cloudcroft on U.S. 82; sites $9), and **Deerhead** ❶ (2 mi. south of town on U.S. 130; sites $9). All campgrounds are open mid-May to mid-October. **Backcountry camping** ❶ is free in the national forest. **Bluff Springs** ❶, on Río Penasco Rd., is one of the more trafficked sites because it's next to a stream and a waterfall. Inquire at the Forest Office for more info.

⬜ FOOD. There are few restaurants in Cloudcroft. The friendly **Western Bar and Cafe** ❷, on Burro St., is a popular dive known for the best breakfast in town. At night, it becomes the main bar. The steak Diane ($11) is fantastic. (☎ 682-2445. Open daily 6am-9pm; bar open M-Sa 9am-2am, Su noon-midnight. Cowboy karaoke on alternate W and Sa. Breakfast special $3-5, dinner entrees $6-11. Cash only.) The **Cookshack** ❷, on U.S. 82 in the center of town, is a great spot for a quick lunch or dinner. (☎ 682-9920. Open daily 11am-7pm. BBQ Plate $6.50. Cash only.) For basic supplies, head to the **Mountain Top Mercantile and Grocery,** 105 James Canyon Hwy. (☎ 682-2777. Open daily 7am-8pm.)

⚡ OUTDOORS. With miles of hiking trails, plenty of mountain bike routes, challenging rock climbing, and even downhill skiing, the Sacramento Mountains have plenty to offer any outdoorsman. The Lincoln National Forest Office in town is a good place to get your bearings before heading off into the wilderness.

The hiking trails in the mountains could keep an avid hiker busy for months. For a complete list of hikes, purchase the *Lincoln National Forest Trail Guide* at the Forest Office in Cloudcroft ($15). The **Osha Trail** (2.5 mi. round-trip) begins 1 mi. west of Cloudcroft off U.S. 82 and offers brief views of White Sands, the Tularosa Basin, and the village of Cloudcroft. Another easy day hike is the **Cloud-Climbing Rail Trail** (2.2 mi. round-trip), a jaunt that passes two large railroad trestles. The trailhead is on U.S. 82 at the western side of town in the Trestle Recreation Area.

The **mountain biking** near Cloudcroft is hailed as some of the best and most challenging in the region. All Lincoln National Forest trails are open to bikes. **High Altitude Outfitters,** on Burro St. in Cloudcroft, sells bike equipment and gives advice on area trails. (☎ 682-1229. Open June-Sept. daily 10am-6pm; Oct.-May W-M 10am-5pm.) Bikers have to share the Rim Trail with other recreational users, but it is still the most popular area ride. The Forest Service has maps of other interesting trails.

Rock climbers scale the cliff next to the U.S. 82 tunnel, 6 mi. west of town. For beginners and those eager to learn, local climbing instructor **Leroy Lewis** (☎ 430-2987) takes climbers of all skill levels for half-day and full-day trips.

TULAROSA VALLEY/U.S. 54   ☎ 505

The Tularosa Valley, a wide expanse of desert, dunes, fractured lava flows, and plains, stretches between the San Andres Mountains to the west and the Sacramento Mountains to the east. Because of its bleakness and flat terrain, the military claimed much of the valley and built the White Sands Missile Range and, to the south, Fort Bliss. The eastern side of the valley nestles up to the foothills of the Sacramento Mountains and traces the path of U.S. 54. The short stretch of highway accesses ancient artworks, fractured lava beds, and an out-of-the-way hostel on its 60 mi. run between Alamogordo and Carrizozo.

THREE RIVERS PETROGLYPHS & ENVIRONS. Seventeen miles north of Tularosa and 30 mi. north of Alamogordo (p. 431), **Three Rivers Petroglyphs** represents one of the largest displays of rock art in the Southwest, with over 21,000 inscriptions. The art was left by the Jornada Mogollon Indians who lived in the area 1000 years ago. The petroglyphs are accessible via a 1 mi. trail that ascends a small rocky ridge. An interpretive pamphlet, available at the trailhead, explains some of the more distinctive designs. The **BLM ●** permits camping on the gravel parking lot; facilities include water and toilets. (☎585-3457. Park open sunrise-sunset. Visitors Center open daily 9am-4pm. Admission $2; camping $2.)

Eight miles past Three Rivers Petroglyphs on Forest Rd. 579 is the **Three Rivers Campground ●** in Lincoln National Forest. Sites ($8) have pit toilets and potable water. The **Three Rivers Trail** starts at the campsite and climbs 4000 ft. into the **White Mountain Wilderness Area** in the Lincoln National Forest. The strenuous hike (6 mi. one way) follows a stream most of the way and offers great views of Sierra Blanca, White Sands, and the Malpais Lava Flow. Many do this hike as part of a **backpacking** trip through the White Mountain Wilderness. Contact the Lincoln National Forest offices in Alamogordo (☎434-7200) or Ruidoso (☎257-4095) for more info.

OSCURO. The **High Desert Hostel Ranch ●**, the most unique accommodation in southern New Mexico, sprawls 15 mi. south of Carrizozo. The 88-year-old orange adobe ranch house is comfortable and friendly, offering weary travelers respite from life on the road. The ranch's 240 acres feature an orchard, an organic vegetable garden, plenty of land for hiking, and stunning sunsets behind the San Andres mountains. Guests enjoy access to all the food in the kitchen and a vast living room with TV. The hostel is in the tiny hamlet of Oscuro, a flag stop on the **Greyhound** route from El Paso to Albuquerque ($24 one-way from either city; one per day from Albuquerque, two per day from El Paso); call ahead for a free pickup. The hostel is 1 mi. east down a dirt road from the 108 mi. marker on U.S. 54; follow the signs. (☎648-4007. www.oscurohostel.com. Free laundry. Dorm beds $14; private doubles $27; triples $32. Cash or traveler's checks only.)

CARRIZOZO, VALLEY OF FIRES, & ENVIRONS. Fifteen miles north of the hostel is the quaint town of **Carrizozo.** Peddling coffee and sandwiches, **Carrizozo Joe's ●**, 113 Central Ave., also supplies the area's only public **Internet access.** (☎648-5637. Open M 7am-6pm, Tu-W 7am-2pm, Th-F 7am-6pm, Sa 8am-3pm. Free 15min. with purchase or $5 per hr.) **Sierra Blanca Brewing Company,** 503 12th St., offers free tours and tastings at its small facility. (☎648-6606. Open M-F 8:30am-4:30pm, call ahead for tours.) **Sturges Market,** on U.S. 54, sells the town's only groceries. (☎648-2125. Open M-Sa 8:30am-7pm.)

The old gold-mining village of **White Oaks,** 5 mi. north of Carrizozo on U.S. 54 and 8 mi. east on Rte. 349, used to be the second largest town in New Mexico; now it's a ghost town with 24 residents. The main reason to stop in White Oaks is to visit the 120-year-old **White Oaks Saloon,** with its infamous "No Scum Allowed" sign out front. (☎648-9915. Open M and W-Sa 10am-9pm, Su noon-9pm. Beer $2.25.)

A volcanic eruption 1500 years ago caused lava to flow south into the Tularosa Basin, covering over 125 sq. mi. To see the fractured lava beds, visit the **Valley of Fires Recreation Area,** 4 mi. west of Carrizozo on U.S. 380. The .7 mi., wheelchair-accessible **Malpais Nature Trail** allows visitors to tread the volcanic terrain. The park has a **campground ❶** with showers. Sites grant no shade other than small pavilions over the picnic tables but have great views of the valley. (☎648-2241. Park open 24hr. Visitors Center open daily 8am-noon, 1-4pm. Vehicles $5, bikes or pedestrians $3. Camping: primitive sites $5, developed sites $7, full hookups $11.)

RUIDOSO   ☎505

During the summer months and again in ski season, a West Texas twang buzzes through the streets of Ruidoso, the premier summer and winter resort destination in southern New Mexico. In the summer, thousands of tourists, mostly Texans, flock here to fritter away their money at the casinos and the racetrack. In the winter, nearby Ski Apache, an impressive low-latitude ski area, is the major draw. Though it is possible to escape to the woods during the summer, the peaceful spring and fall months offer an even quieter opportunity to explore the trail system of the Lincoln National Forest and the White Mountain Wilderness.

▉ 🛈 ORIENTATION & PRACTICAL INFORMATION. Ruidoso sits at 7000 ft. in the Sacramento Mountains, 46 mi. northeast of Alamogordo (p. 431) and 75 mi. west of Roswell (p. 438). **Sudderth Drive** (Rte. 48) is the town's main drag. U.S. 70 passes east of downtown and leads to Ruidoso Downs. **Greyhound,** 138 Service Rd. (☎257-2660), sends buses to **Alamogordo** (1hr.; 3 per day; M-Th $10, F-Su $11) and **Albuquerque** (6hr.; 2 per day; M-Th $40, F-Su $42). The **Chamber of Commerce,** 720 Sudderth Dr., doles out the requisite visitor info. (☎257-7395 or 800-253-2255. Open M 9am-5pm, Tu-Th 8:30am-5pm, F 8:30am-4:30pm, Sa 9am-3pm; May-Aug. additionally Su 9am-1pm. Info available 24hr. from a touch screen in the lobby.) For more info on the Sacramento Mountains area, check out the informative **Billy the Kid Scenic Byway Visitors Center,** 841 U.S. 70W, just east of the racetrack. (☎378-5318. Open daily 10am-5pm.) The **Lincoln National Forest Smokey Bear Ranger Station,** 901 Mechem Dr., has the area's outdoors info. (☎257-4095. Open June-Aug. M-Sa 7:30am-4:30pm; Sept.-May M-F 7:30am-4:30pm.) Services include: **Becker's Mountain Laundry,** 721 Mechem Dr. (☎257-7667; open M-Sa 8am-8pm); the **police,** 1085 Mechem Dr. (☎258-7365); **emergency** (☎911); **Lincoln County Medical Center,** 211 Sudderth Dr. (☎257-8200; free **Internet access** at the public library (☎259-3704. Open M-Th 9am-6pm, F 9am-5pm, Sa 9am-1pm); and the **post office,** 1090 Mechem Dr. (☎257-7120. Open M-F 8:30am-5pm, Sa 8:30am-noon.) **Postal code: 88345.**

🛈 ACCOMMODATIONS. Because of nearby hostels in Oscuro (p. 435) and Cloudcroft (p. 433), many budget travelers eschew overnight visits to Ruidoso. Motels clustered around the intersection of U.S. 70 and Rte. 48 offer rooms for $40-70, but most jack up prices between June and August. It is not impossible for this town to completely sell out on a busy weekend like July 4th. The **Apache Motel ❷,** 344 Sudderth Dr., is the best buy in town, with large, comfortable rooms, many with futons and fully-equipped kitchens. (☎257-2986 or 800-426-0616. Singles $35-40; doubles $40-56.) The **Nob Hill Lodge ❸** on U.S. 70, west of Rte. 48 and across from the Super 8, has newly renovated and refurnished rooms with cable TV and A/C. (☎257-9212. Singles $30-55; doubles $40-65. 10% student discount Sept.-May.) The invading Texans rent cabins, and so can you, although it's only a good deal if you have a family or large group. Expect to pay $50-120 per night for a cabin with a fireplace, TV, and full kitchen. Though located in town, **Sierra Blanca Cabins ❸,** 217 Country Club Dr., has a quiet and picturesque spot beside a creek (☎257-2103).

Those in search of the real woodsman's experience should head to the number of national forest campgrounds northwest of Ruidoso, all with pit toilets and no running water. **South Fork ❶** is the only campground with drinking water and flush toilets (sites $10). To reach it, drive north 11 mi. on Rte. 48; turn left and follow

Forest Rd. 107 for 5 mi. Call the Smokey Bear Ranger Station (see **Practical Information,** p. 436) for information on other campsites. Campgrounds are generally open from May to October.

FOOD. Restaurants are everywhere in Ruidoso, with the highest density on Sudderth Dr. in the downtown area between Mechem Dr. and Paradise Canyon Rd. Vegetarians stampede to the **Terraza Camanario ❷,** 1611 Sudderth Dr., which has the most authentic Mexican food in town. (☎257-4227. Enchiladas $6; Mexican steaks $7-8.) Surrounded by rustic furniture, vegetarians and carnivores alike nosh on tasty wraps ($5-6) at **River's Edge Eatery ❶,** 2404 Sudderth Dr. (☎630-5394. Open Th-Tu 10am-5pm.) **Pasta Café Italian Bistro ❸,** 2331 Sudderth Dr., offers a varied Italian menu in a tasteful atmosphere; before and after meals, diners relax on the pleasant patio or in the cigar bar. White tablecoths adorn tables, but jeans are OK. Veal parmagiana ($13) and Red Snapper Veracruz ($15) are favorites. (☎257-7867. Dining room open Su-Th 11am-9:30pm, F-Sa 11am-10:30pm; lounge open daily 11am-12:30pm.)

SIGHTS. Much of Ruidoso's summer activity revolves around wagering money. **Ruidoso Downs,** 4½ mi. east of town, is one of America's top horseracing venues. The All-American Futurity is the biggest paying quarterhorse race in the country, forking out $2 million annually. (☎378-4431. Races late May-early Sept. Open Th-Su.; Th-F races start at 3:30pm, Sa-Su 1pm. Free.) The **Hubbard Museum of the American West,** just east on U.S. 70 from Ruidoso Downs, is affiliated with the Smithsonian and has exhibits on chuckwagons, stagecoaches, saddles, guns, and Native American crafts. The building also houses the Ruidoso Downs Hall of Fame. (☎378-4142. Open daily 10am-5pm. $6, seniors $5, children $2.)

OUTDOOR ACTIVITIES. During the winter, skiing is king. Eighteen miles northwest of Ruidoso, **Ski Apache,** off of the Sierra Blanca Peak, is southern New Mexico's best ski area. Eleven lifts, including New Mexico's only gondola, serve 55 trails (20% beginner; 35% intermediate; 45% advanced) on 750 skiable acres. The base of the mountain is a whopping 9600 ft. above sea level, and the top of the highest lift reaches 11,500 ft. (☎336-4356, 24hr. snow report 257-9001; www.skiapache.com. Open late Nov.-early Apr. 8:45am-4pm. Snowboards welcome. Annual snowfall 185 in. Full day $45-49, half-day $31-34, under 13 $29-32/$20-22.)

The Lincoln National Forest around Ruidoso is one of the most beautiful areas of the Sacramento Mountains, and during the summer, hiking is a great way to escape the racing and gambling crowds. Beginning at the entrance to Ski Apache, the 6 mi. round-trip hike up **Lookout Mountain** (11,600 ft.) leads to the highest point in the national forest. Take Trail 15.5 mi. to Trail 25; turn left and then turn left again on Trail 78, which leads to the top of Lookout Mountain. On a clear day, you can see all the way to the Gila Mountains in the west and the Sangre de Cristo Mountains to the north. The 21.1 mi. **Crest Trail** is an unforgettable backcountry hiking route into the heart of the White Mountain Wilderness Area. To reach the trailhead, drive north on Rte. 48; turn left and go 1 mi. on the road to Ski Apache. Turn right on Forest Rd. 117 and follow it 5.5 mi. until you see a sign for the trail.

For a great view of the Sacramento Mountains that doesn't involve much hiking, drive to the **Monjeau Lookout,** a granite fire tower built in the 1930s by the Civilian Conservation Corps. To visit the lookout, drive north from Ruidoso and turn left on Rte. 532; after 1 mi., turn right onto Forest Rd. 117 and follow it for 6 mi. The gravel Forest Road 117 has stellar views but becomes rocky near the top. Four-wheel-drive and/or experience driving rough roads is recommended, and the drive should not be attempted in inclement weather.

OH, BILLY!

_awrence Murphy owned the only general store in Lincoln in the .870s. When John Tunstall and Alexander McSween opened a rival store in 1878, Murphy saw red, and his assistant James Dolan had Tunstall killed. One of Tunstall's men, William H. Bonney, vowed to get revenge. Bonney, a.k.a. **Billy the Kid,** rounded up a posse called the Regulators who wreaked havoc in Lincoln, killing Tunstall's assassins along with the sheriff, a friend of Dolan. Dolan's men fought back, burning McSween's house with his family inside. McSween himself was shot unarmed on the doorstep as he came out to propose a truce. Billy the Kid, then only a peach-fuzzed teenager, escaped and spent the next two years on the run.

The new Lincoln sheriff, Pat Garrett, finally caught up with Billy in nearby Ft. Sumner, and he was subsequently put on trial for killing the sheriff. Sentenced to hang, Billy was in jail awaiting execution in Lincoln on April 28, 1881 when he made his famous escape. While in the outhouse, he grabbed a pistol hidden by an accomplice, burst out, and killed one of his two guards. In a famous scene, Billy then killed his other guard with the man's own shotgun and fled on a horse. Less than three months later, Garret caught up with Billy again, and this time he did not give the slippery Kid a chance. Garret shot him dead, and so ended the saga of Billy the Kid.

Mountain biking is popular on the trails of the national forest but is not allowed on the trails of the White Mountain Wilderness Area. The 3 mi. **Perk Canyon Trail** is a favorite with locals. From the traffic circle in Ruidoso, take Upper Canyon Rd. 1 mi. to Ebarb St., turn right and then left onto Perk Canyon Rd. **Smokey's Revenge** is a singletrack course with a huge variety of terrain. Turn east off of Mechem Dr. at the Forest Service office onto Cedar Creek/Sam Tobias Rd. and look for the course on the right. **High Altitude Outfitters,** 2316 Sudderth Dr. (☎257-0120), rents mountain bikes for $25 a day or $20 for 2hrs. and offers advice and maps.

⚡ **DAYTRIP TO LINCOLN.** Little has changed in Lincoln (northeast of Ruidoso on U.S. 380) since the days of Billy the Kid and the infamous "Lincoln County War" of 1878. The town's buildings have not been Disney-fied, making Lincoln one of the best preserved Wild West towns in New Mexico (the bullet hole from Billy's gun is still in the wall at the bottom of the staircase in the Courthouse). The **Lincoln Visitors Center,** on the west side of town, has a comprehensive museum and shows a video about the Lincoln County War. (☎653-4025. Open daily 8:30am-4pm.) Buildings open to the public include the Courthouse, Dr. Wood's House, the Tunstall Store, and the Montano Store. The buildings are essentially museums, preserving the Lincoln of yore. (Open daily 8:30am-4:30pm. $6.)

The small town of **Capitan,** located some 12 mi. west of Lincoln on U.S. 380, is famous for being the "birthplace" of Smokey the Bear. The muscular, axe-toting icon we now know actually began as an orphaned cub found by firefighters in 1950. **Smokey Bear Historical Park** has a small museum telling the story and a park housing Smokey's gravesite. (☎354-2748. Open daily 9am-5pm. $1, children $0.50.) But don't just stop for Smokey: every July 4th weekend, the annual Old West Ranch Rodeo and Smokey Bear Stampede is held out at the fairgrounds. If you want to grab lunch on the way, **Downtown Deli ❶,** 101 Lincoln, is just down the street; try a Piquante chicken with cucumber dill sauce, Asian slaw, and chipotle aioli for $5. (☎354-0407. Open M-Tu 11am-3pm, W-Sa 11am-3pm and 5pm-9pm.)

ROSWELL   ☎505

With giant, inflatable Martians advertising used cars, streetlights donning painted-on pointy eyes, and flying saucers adorning fast-food signs, one thing is certain: aliens have invaded Roswell. Located 76 mi.

north of Carlsbad, Roswell is a celebration of extra-terrestrial life and the mania that accompanies it. The fascination began in July of 1947, when an alien space-craft reportedly plummeted to the earth near the dusty town. The official Army press release reported that the military had recovered pieces of some form of "fly-ing saucer," but a retraction arrived the next day—the mysterious wreckage, the brass claimed, was actually a harmless weather balloon. Everyone admits that something crashed in the desert northwest of Roswell on that fateful night over 50 years ago. Was the initial Army admission just a poor choice of words by some P.R. hack or a crack in the facade of an elaborate cover-up?

ORIENTATION & PRACTICAL INFORMATION. Aside from its extrater-restrial peculiarities, Roswell is a fairly normal town. The intersection of **2nd Street** (Rte. 70/380) and **Main Street** (Rte. 285) is the sun around which the Roswell solar system orbits. To reach Roswell from Albuquerque, head 89 mi. south on I-25 to San Antonio, then 153 mi. east on U.S. 380. **Greyhound,** 1100 N. Virginia Ave. (☎622-2510), in conjunction with TNM&O, runs buses to **Albuquerque** (4hr.; 2 per day Tu-Sa, 1 on Su; M-Th $36, F-Su $38) and **El Paso** (4½hr.; 3 per day; M-Th $41, F-Su $44). **Pecos Trails Transit,** 515 N. Main St., runs buses all over town. (☎624-6766. M-F 6am-10:30pm, Sa 7:10am-10pm, Su 10:30am-7pm. $0.75, students $0.50, seniors $0.35.) The cheery and helpful **Visitors Center** is at 426 N. Main St. (☎624-0889 or 623-5695. Open M-F 8:30am-5:30pm, Sa-Su 10am-3pm.) Laundry machines adorn **L&W Kwick Wash,** 211 S. Union Ave. (☎627-8257). The **public library,** 301 N. Pennsylvania Ave., has free **Internet access.** (Open M-Tu 9am-9pm, W-Sa 9am-6pm, Su 2-6pm.) In an **emergency,** call ☎911 or the **Roswell Police Department,** ☎624-6700. The **post office** occupies 415 N. Pennsylvania Ave. (☎623-7232. Open M-F 7:30am-5:30pm, Sa 8am-noon.) **Postal code:** 88202.

ACCOMMODATIONS & FOOD. Budget motels line both Main St. and 2nd St., but the chain motels that have settled on Main St. north of downtown tend to be pricier than the options on 2nd St. The **Budget Inn West ❷,** 2200 W. 2nd St., has recently remodeled rooms to include A/C, telephones, and refrigerators, as well as a pool. (☎623-3811 or 800-806-7030. Singles $28-38; doubles $35-50.) **The Belmont Motel ❷,** 2100 W. 2nd St., has clean, newly refurnished rooms with fridges, micro-waves, cable TVs, and A/C. (☎623-4522. Singles $20-$27; doubles $30-39.) **Bottom-less Lakes State Park ❶** has camping along the shores of seven beautiful, natural lakes. To reach the park, drive 12 mi. east on Rte. 380, then 5 mi. south on Rte. 409 and follow the signs. (☎624-6058. Tent sites $10, full hookups $18.)

Fast-food restaurants are as prevalent in Roswell as allusions to alien life, and they are concentrated along N. Main St. and W. 2nd St. Side streets are home to less commercial budget eateries. **Albertson's Supermarket** is at 1110 S. Main St. (☎623-9300. Open daily 6am-midnight.) Just around the corner from the UFO Museum, the **Crash Down Diner ❶,** 106 W. 1st St., is an out-of-this-world-themed res-taurant, albeit with standard fare. Try a Starchild burrito creation ($5.75), a "hun-gry alien" sub ($3-5), or an "unidentified" burger ($4). A giant alien mural covers the wall, and even the salt and pepper shakers are shaped like aliens. (☎627-5533. Open M-Sa 8am-6pm, Su 8am-6pm.) **Tia Juana's ❸,** 3601 N. Main St., is the kind of funky Tex-Mex restaurant that the big chains try to imitate. Try the chili rubbed ribeye for $15, or refresh yourself with something from the huge margarita menu for $5-8. (☎624-6113. Dining room open M-Th 11am-9:30pm, F-Sa 11am-10pm, Su 11am-9pm; bar open daily 11am-10pm.) **Peppers Bar and Grill ❷,** 500 N. Main St., serves American and Mexican food indoors and on a mist-cooled outdoor patio. (☎623-1700. Apr.-Oct. F-Sa live music; DJ spinning on the patio W. Dining room open M-Sa 11am-10pm, bar open 11am-midnight.)

ALIENS WANTED

Roswell, New Mexico is nothing if not UFO crazy, and every year on the Fourth of July weekend this town officially goes berserk. Billed as the world's largest gathering of ufologists," the **Roswell UFO Festival** defies the conventional motif of barbecues and fireworks, drawing thousands of people from all over for a weekend of lectures and discussions about UFOs, extraterrestrial life, and other paranormal phenomena.

For those less interested in the (quasi-)academic investigations of alien life, the festival means an opportunity for a good old-fashioned fiesta, albeit with an alien theme. Outside the lecture halls, the streets overflow night and day with people and even pets dressed as alien life-forms, culminating in a parade that transforms into a dance party. A carnival touches down at the local fairgrounds, thousands of locals and visitors (from Earth only, so far) participate in a 5km "UFO Chase" road race, even the holiday fireworks are UFO-themed. Recently the festival has taken on an artistic dimension with showings of Sci-Fi films, a music festival, and displays of art inspired by UFOs and close encounters.

Between the visiting ufologists and those just looking for an off-beat good time, accommodations tend to fill up for the festival, so make reservations early. For more information, visit the website: **www.uforoswell.com.**

◉ ♪ SIGHTS & ENTERTAINMENT. Believer or skeptic, most visitors will find the alien side of Roswell entertaining, if not rather enlightening. During the first week of July, the **UFO Festival** commemorates the alleged close encounter, drawing thousands to the area for live music, an alien costume contest, and a 5km "Alien Chase" race. With a plastic flying saucer above its storefront, the popular **International UFO Museum and Research Center,** 114 N. Main St., dedicates itself to telling the story of what supposedly happened near Roswell in 1947. Exhibits contain testimonials and newspaper clippings about the 1947 alien contact incident, as well as chronicling alien sightings from all around the world. Some visitors may remain skeptical of the research center's scholarly credentials, but the museum's backers say the reading rooms and archives are completely legitimate. In any case, it's the best of the alien research center bunch. (☎625-9495. Open daily 9am-5pm. Free. Audio tour $1.)

If you can tear yourself away from Roswell's alien mania, head to the **Roswell Museum and Art Center,** 100 W. 11th St., which showcases works by area artists Peter Hurd and Henriette Wyeth. The museum also features the laboratory of Robert Goddard, the Roswell resident who invented the liquid-fueled rocket. The center has a **planetarium** running shows frequently during the summer. (☎624-6744. Museum open M-Sa 9am-5pm, Su 1-5pm. Free. Planetarium shows $3, call ahead for schedule.)

To cool off on a hot summer day, head to **Bottomless Lakes State Park** (for directions, see **Accommodations,** p. 439). The seven lakes in the park were formed when several underground caves collapsed and filled with water. Swimming is allowed at Lea Lake at the southern end of the park, and a short hiking trail provides one of the area's only opportunities to experience the desert landscape up close. (☎624-6058. Visitors Center open June-Aug. daily 9am-6pm; Sept.-May 8am-5pm.)

CARLSBAD   ☎505

In 1899, townsfolk decided to name their agricultural settlement Carlsbad after the Karlsbad Spa in the former Czechoslovakia, hoping to attract tourists to the area's natural springs. In a twist of fate, the splendors of Carlsbad Caverns became known in the 1920s, and tourists flocked here. Carlsbad itself is a fairly dull city of 25,000, but it makes a good base for exploring the area. Folks from all over descend on Carlsbad at the end of September for the International Bat Festival.

🔣🔢 ORIENTATION & PRACTICAL INFORMATION. Carlsbad stands at the intersection of U.S. 62/180 and U.S. 285, 166 mi. northeast of El Paso, TX (p. 447) and 278 mi. southeast of Albuquerque (p. 378). **Canal Street** is the main downtown thoroughfare. South of downtown, Canal St. becomes National Parks Hwy. (U.S. 62/180). **Carlsbad City Air Terminal** (☎887-1500), south of downtown on U.S. 62/180, offers flights to Albuquerque on Mesa Airlines. The **Greyhound Station,** 1000 S. Canyon (☎887-1108. Open M-F 7:30-11:30am and 1:30-4pm, Sa 8:30-10am), has service to **El Paso** (3hr., 2 per day, $32) and **Albuquerque** (6hr., 2 per day, $46). The **Chamber of Commerce,** 302 S. Canal, has basic tourist info. (☎887-6516. Open M 9am-5pm, Tu-F 8am-5pm, Sa 9am-4pm.) The **National Park Service Information Center,** 3225 National Parks Hwy., has brochures and other resources for nearby parks. (☎885-5554. Open June-Aug. daily 8am-4:30pm, Sept.-May M-F 8am-4:30pm.) Services include: **police,** 405 S. Halagueno St. (☎885-2111); **emergency** (☎911); **Carlsbad Medical Center,** 2430 W. Pierce St. (☎887-4100); **Clean Corner Coin and Laundry,** 521 S. Canal St. (☎885-1183; open daily 7am-9pm; last wash 8pm); **public library,** 101 S. Halagueno St., with free **Internet access.** (☎885-6776; open M-Th 10am-8pm, F-Sa 10am-6pm, Su 2-6pm); **24hr. ATM,** 111 N. Canal St; and **post office,** 301 N. Canyon St. (☎885-5717. Open M-F 8am-5pm, Sa 10am-1pm.) **Postal code:** 88220.

📷🌲 ACCOMMODATIONS & FOOD. A slew of budget motels line U.S. 62/180 south of downtown. The **Stage Coach Inn ❷,** 1819 S. Canal St., is the nicest of the lot with an outdoor pool, indoor jacuzzi, and laundry. Comfortable, clean rooms have A/C, cable, and refrigerators. (☎887-1148. Singles $34-40; doubles $36-47. 15% AAA and AARP discount.) For a cheaper room, try the **Park View Motel ❷,** 401 E. Greene St., just across the Greene St. Bridge on the right. Clean, cinderblock rooms have A/C, cable, microwaves, and refrigerators, with a swimming pool outside. (☎885-3117. Singles $23; doubles $30.) The **Carlsbad RV Park and Campground ❷,** 4301 National Parks Hwy. (☎888-885-6333), 4 mi. south of town, has two wooden camping cabins with a full-size bed, two bunk beds, and A/C ($30; linen not provided). Low-privacy tent camping ($14.50) is also available. All guests have access to showers and a swimming pool.

Food options in Carlsbad are decent for a town of its size. The atmosphere of the **No Whiner Diner ❷,** 1801 S. Canal St., complete with a whiners' room, makes it Carlsbad's unique dining option. The food is standard diner fare. (☎234-2815. Open Tu-Th 11am-2pm, 5-8:30pm; F-Sa 11am-2pm, 5-9pm. Burgers $5.25, pasta $7-9, chicken-fried steak $8.) For down-home Western barbecue, check out **Red Chimney BBQ ❷,** 817 N. Canal St. Dinners ($7-8) come complete with meat (turkey, chicken, spare ribs, or pork), beans, bread, and salad. (☎885-8744. Open M-F 11am-2pm, 4:30-8:30pm.) Stop at **Albertson's Supermarket,** 808 N. Canal, before heading off for a daytrip. (☎885-2161. Open daily 6am-11pm.)

🔳🎷 SIGHTS & OUTDOOR ACTIVITIES. The **Carlsbad Museum and Art Center,** 418 W. Fox St. next to the library, houses a collection of New Mexican art and artifacts. Highlights include pueblo pottery, paintings by the Taos Ten, and an 1858 Wells Fargo Stagecoach. (☎887-0276. Open M-Sa 10am-5pm. Free.) The **Waste Isolation Pilot Plant,** 4021 National Parks Hwy., 40 mi. east of Carlsbad, is a deep repository for long-term disposal of radioactive waste. Curious visitors can travel ½ mile underground to tour the disposal facilities. If you are pressed for time, visit the info center and learn all about nuclear waste. (☎800-336-9477. Open Tu and Th 9am-11am. Call a month in advance to schedule a tour.)

If the desert has ever come across as ugly and barren, a trip to the beautifully maintained **Living Desert Zoo and Botanical Garden,** 4 mi. north of Carlsbad on U.S. 285, will restore its image. The 1.3 mi. walking tour takes visitors through different desert environments and offers great views of Carlsbad and environs. Javelinas, deer, mountain lions, numerous desert birds, and many types of cacti populate the park. (☎887-5516. Open June-Aug. daily 8am-8pm, last entry 6:30pm; Sept.-May 9am-5pm, last entry 3:30pm. $4, children $2.)

Outdoor activities abound in the Carlsbad area. The **National Park Service Information Center** is a good general resource for hiking, backpacking, and climbing. The **La Cueva Trails,** southwest of town, form an extensive system of mountain bike paths for riders of all levels. Bikers should stop by **The Bike Doc,** 304 W. Orchard Ln., for maps and guides to these and other area trails. (☎887-7280. Open Tu-F 10am-6pm, Sa 10am-5pm.)

Sitting Bull Falls, 42 mi. west of Carlsbad, offers a pleasant respite from the desert sun. To get there from Carlsbad, drive north 12 mi. on U.S. 285, turn left onto Rte. 137, and after traveling 23 mi. turn right onto Forest Rd. 276. Most people come just to bathe in the cold spring water at the foot of the waterfall at the end of the road. There are 16 mi. of hiking trails in this area of Lincoln National Forest. **The Bowl,** above the parking lot, is a popular **rock climbing** spot. A 1 mi. hike along Trail 68a (Sitting Bull Falls Trail) leads to **The Grotto,** a natural spring with a deep pool alongside a rocky cave. A popular 10 mi. loop, including the Sitting Bulls Falls Trail and the Overlook Trail, takes hikers past a few different mountain springs. Primitive camping along the trail is free with permission from the ranger. Remember to take lots of water and watch out for prickly cacti. This is mountain lion country, so exercise caution. Free maps and hiking info are available in Room 159 of the Carlsbad Federal Building, 114 S. Halegueno St. (☎885-4181. Open daily 8am-7pm. $5 per vehicle.)

CARLSBAD CAVERNS NATIONAL PARK ☎505

In 1898, Jim White, a 16-year-old Texan cowboy, thought he saw smoke coming from the top of a hill while riding through southern New Mexico. When he got closer he realized that what he thought was smoke was actually millions of bats emerging from a fissure in the ground. With only a kerosene lantern to light his way and a ball of string to trace his path, White began the first thorough exploration of the cave. What he found beneath the earth's surface was nothing short of spectacular: underground rooms, delicate stone draperies, natural sculptures, and millions of stalagmites and stalactites.

The limestone rock that composes the outer walls of the Carlsbad Caverns are the lithofied remains of the same Capitan Reef that forms the spine of the Guadalupe Mountains. Beginning several million years ago, rainwater seeped through cracks in the reef, slowly dissolving the limestone. Meanwhile, oil and gas deposits below the reef began to leak hydrogen sulfide gas upwards into the atmosphere. When the hydrogen sulfide met the rainwater, highly corrosive sulfuric acid formed. This acid ate through huge amounts of limestone rock to create the vast chambers of Carlsbad Caverns.

While Jim White may have been the first white man to explore the caves, he was certainly not the last. By 1923, colonies of tourists clung to the walls to see the newest national monument, and by the end of the decade, an "underground lunchroom," elevator, and electric lighting all had been added to the main cave. Today, over 1000 light bulbs and 19 miles of wires help illuminate the cave's features for its 600,000 annual visitors. The developed Carlsbad Cavern is the main tourist attraction, but some of the other 93 caves in the park are more spectacular and remote. The largest in the park, Lechuguilla Cave, is off limits to the general public, but several other undeveloped caves are accessible by ranger-guided tours.

AT A GLANCE: CARLSBAD CAVERNS NATIONAL PARK

AREA: 46,427 acres.

FEATURES: The Big Room, King's Palace, Slaughter Canyon, Lechuguilla Cave.

HIGHLIGHTS: Touring the self-guided Big Room, climbing through Lower Cave, exploring rugged Slaughter Canyon Cave.

GATEWAYS: White's City and Carlsbad (see p. 440).

CAMPING: No developed campgrounds. Backcountry permits are free.

FEES & RESERVATIONS: There is no park entrance fee. Big Room entrance $6. Other cave tours $8-20. Reservations highly recommended (p. 444).

ORIENTATION & PRACTICAL INFORMATION

The closest town to the park is **White's City,** on U.S. 62/180, 20 mi. southwest of the much larger **Carlsbad** and 6 mi. from the park Visitors Center. Flash floods occasionally close these roads; call the park for the latest road conditions. **El Paso, TX** (p. 447) is the nearest major city, located 150 mi. west beyond the **Guadalupe Mountains National Park** (p. 452).

The borders of the park include the subterranean limestone chasms, but above ground large canyons lead up towards the crest of the Guadalupe Range. The park itself has two entrances. The northern entrance lies just west of White's City and leads to the main cavern system and the Walnut Canyon Desert Drive. The southern entrance is accessible by Rte. 418 and leads to Slaughter Canyon Cave, Yucca Canyon, and North Slaughter Canyon Trail.

Greyhound, in cooperation with **TNM&O Coaches** (☎887-1108), runs four buses per day between El Paso, Texas and Carlsbad ($37). The buses will also make a flag stop at White's City. **Caverns Visitors Center** has plenty of trail maps and organized tour information. (☎785-2232. Open daily 8am-7pm; late Aug. to May 8am-5:30pm. Entrance fee $6.) Make reservations by phone through the **Guided Tour Reservation Hotline** (☎800-967-2283) or on the web (http://reservations.nps.gov). White's City, just outside the park on U.S. 62/180, provides most major services for travelers to the area, such as **laundry, gas station, grocery store,** and **ATM.** In an **emergency,** call ☎785-2232 or 911. White's City's **post office,** 23 Carlsbad Caverns Hwy., resides next to the Best Western gift shop. (☎785-2220. Open M-F 8am-noon and 12:30-4:30pm, Sa 8am-noon.) **Postal code:** 88268.

> **WHEN TO GO.** The main attraction of the Carlsbad Caverns National Park is the elaborate cave system, which remains about 56°F all year. Above ground, the weather heats up in the summer to temperatures over 100°F. Most visitors flock to the caves in the summer for the natural air conditioning. To avoid the crowds, visit during the mild fall.

CAMPING

Cheap motels and chain hotels abound in Carlsbad (p. 441). Sleep closer to the park at **White's City Resort RV Park ❷,** outside the park entrance, which has water, showers, and a pool. (☎785-2291 or 800-228-3767. Tent sites with full hookup $20.) Though the national park doesn't have an established campground, **Guadalupe Mountains National Park,** 32 mi. south on U.S. 62/180 has nice sites ($8). **Backcountry camping ❶** in the wilderness of Carlsbad Caverns National Park is free; get a permit at the Visitors Center.

🔵 SUBTERRANEAN SIGHTS

There are two ways to get down into the **Big Room:** the steep but paved and hand-railed 1.3 mi. walk through the **natural entrance** or taking the **elevator** down 75 sto-ries. The natural entrance route is spectacular and should only be skipped by visitors short on time or hesitant to walk 1.3 mi. downhill. Walking down into the cave from the natural entrance, one will see the cave much as the early explorers did. Once inside, the self-guided Big Room is the main attraction. Most of this walk is wheelchair accessible. The Big Room is over 600,000 sq. ft., roughly the size of 14 football fields. Inside this room are many fascinating cave formations including **Rock of Ages, Bottomless Pit, Painted Grotto,** and **Giant Dome.** While the park does maintain adequate lighting in the Big Room, visitors may find the tour more enjoy-able if they also bring a flashlight of their own, as many formations are only dimly lit. (Natural entrance open June to mid-Aug. daily 8:30am-3:30pm, mid-Aug. to May 8:30am-2pm. Big Room open June to mid-Aug. daily 8:30am-5pm, mid-Aug. to May 8:30am-3:30pm. $6, age 6-15 $3. Audio tour $3.)

The caverns adjacent to the Big Room are only accessible by ranger-guided tour. Use the web site or the hotline (☎800-967-2283) for reservations. The most fre-quently offered tour, the **King's Palace Tour,** passes through four of the cave's low-est rooms and some of the most awesome anomalies. (1½hr. tours every hr. 9-11am and 1-3pm. $8, Golden Age Passport holders and ages 6-15 $4. Advance reservations required.) Other guided tours in the Big Room include a lantern tour though the **Left Hand Tunnel** (daily; $7) and a ladder tour of the **Lower Cave** (M-F; $20, bring gloves and four fresh AA batteries.)

Tours of the undeveloped **Slaughter Canyon Cave** present a more rugged spelunk-ing experience. A reliable car is required to get there, as there's no public transpor-tation. The parking lot sits 23 mi. down Rte. 418 (an unpaved road) several miles south of the main entrance to the park on U.S. 62/180. The cave entrance is a steep, strenuous ½ mile from the lot—allow yourself 45 min. for the walk. Ranger-led tours traverse difficult and slippery terrain; there are no paved trails or handrails. Bring at least a two D-cell flashlights and sturdy shoes. (2hr. tours; June-Aug. twice daily, Sept.-May Sa-Su only. $15, Golden Age Passport holders and ages 6-15 $7.50. Call the Visitors Center at least 2 days ahead to reserve.) Tours of **Hall of the White Giant** and **Spider Cave** require crawling and climbing through tight passages. *Let's Go* does not recommend these tours for claustrophobes. Bring gloves and four fresh AA batteries.(☎800-967-2283. Tours Sa 1pm, 4hr. $20. Call at least a month in advance to reserve. These tours depart from the Visitors Center lobby.)

Visitors can also explore some of the park's caves on their own. Free permits are available by mail one month in advance. For a permit application write: Super-intendent, Carlsbad Caverns National Park, 3225 National Parks Highway, Carls-bad NM, 88220; or call ☎505-785-2232, ext. 363 or 368 and leave your name, address, and phone number. Vertical caves such as **Chimney Cave** and **Christmas Tree Cave** require spelunking equipment and are only for experienced cavers. **Ogle Cave** involves a fun rappel, but because of the fragile environment, visitors to Ogle Cave need a ranger guide and must pay $15 per person. **Goat Cave, Lake Cave,** and **Corkscrew Cave** are horizontal caves and require no special equipment or technical training, but visitors are advised to observe proper caving technique by carrying at least three light sources per person, using proper protective equipment, and advis-ing someone of their plans and expected return time.

Plan your visit for the evening to catch the magnificent bat flight. The flight, during which hungry bats storm from the cave at a rate of 6000 per minute, follows a ranger talk. (May-Oct. daily just before sunset, call the Visitors Center for exact time.)

⚠ OUTDOOR ACTIVITIES

Opportunities for driving, hiking, biking, and camping abound. The park offers a 9.5 mi. **scenic drive** through the Chihuahuan Desert. An interpretive brochure (available at the Visitors Center) explains the vegetation and scenery along the route, which otherwise resembles the drive into the park. This trail is also good for an easy, non-technical **mountain bike** ride. For those less mechanically inclined, the park includes 33,125 acres of designated federal wilderness. **Hiking** trails are rarely used, making Carlsbad Caverns a great spot to find solitude on the trail. The **Rattlesnake Canyon Trail** (6 mi. round-trip) makes for a fun day hike. The trail begins at marker #9 of the Desert Loop Scenic Dr. and descends into Rattlesnake Canyon. For an overnight backpacking trip, consider hiking the **Yucca Canyon Trail** or the **Guadalupe Ridge Trail.** The Yucca Canyon Trail is a strenuous 11 mi. hike one way up to a ridge in the Guadalupe Mountains; the Guadalupe Ridge Trail is a strenuous 11.3 mi. hike one way to Putnam Cabin on the northwest boundary of the national park. Hikers often use this trail as the last leg of a week-long backpacking trip from Guadalupe Mountains National Park to Carlsbad Caverns (p. 442). Hiking and backcountry camping require free permits from the Visitors Center. Bring lots of water; there are no reliable water sources in the backcountry.

NEW MEXICO

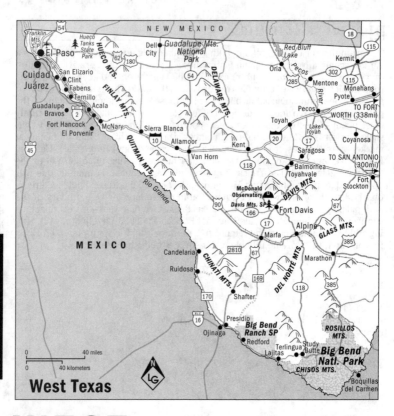

West Texas

0   40 miles

0   40 kilometers

WEST TEXAS

Hundreds of miles from Dallas's Trinity River and even farther from the rolling hills and bright lights of Austin, West Texas offers a look at a sincere, unpolished side of the Lone Star State. Populated by prickly-pears and yuccas, rattlesnakes and mountain lions, the desert plains and jagged mountains of West Texas suggest that much of the land remains untamed. Moreover, the region is a summertime pressure cooker, with temperatures reaching, and occasionally exceeding, 110°F. The relative lack of development makes the region popular with both savvy and novice outdoorsmen. The otherworldly Big Bend National Park is a haven for bikers and backpackers, while Hueco Tanks draws climbers and the remote Guadalupe Mountains invite adventurers looking for solitude. For those more used to the urban jungle than the desert wilderness, the Panhandle treats visitors to an unspoiled view of Americana, and El Paso offers excitement and easy access to south-of-the-border fun.

⚑ HIGHLIGHTS OF WEST TEXAS

MCKITTRICK CANYON. In the **Guadalupe Mountains** (p. 452), this canyon fosters lush vegetation that turns a striking red in November.

HIKING IN BIG BEND. In summer, the **Chisos Mountains** (p. 458) provide premium vistas at relatively mild temperatures. In winter, the Río Grande affords riverside hiking.

CLIMBING AT HUECO TANKS. Some of the best **bouldering** (p. 451) anywhere awaits visitors to this park outside of El Paso.

EL PASO ☎915

The largest of the US border towns, El Paso boomed in the 17th century as a stop-over on an important east-west wagon route that followed the Río Grande through "the pass" (*el paso*) between the Rocky Mountains and the Sierra Madre. Today, the El Paso-Ciudad Juárez metropolitan area has nearly three million inhabitants. That number steadily increases due to a proliferation of cross-border enterprises fueled by the North American Free Trade Agreement (NAFTA). Nearly everyone in El Paso speaks Spanish, and the majority are of Mexican descent. After dark, activity leaves the center of town, migrating toward the suburbs and south of the border to raucous Ciudad Juárez.

☐ TRANSPORTATION

Flights: El Paso International Airport (☎780-4749), 10 mi. northeast of downtown. Sun Metro bus #33 runs to the city center. Major airline service, including **American** (☎800-433-7300), **Delta** (☎800-221-1212), and **Southwest** (☎800-435-9792).

Trains: Union Train Depot, 700 San Francisco St. (☎545-2247), 2 blocks west of the civic center complex. **Amtrak** runs trains to **Tucson** (6hr., 3 per week, $43-145) and **San Antonio** (12½hr., 3 per week, $116-225).

Buses: Greyhound, 200 W. San Antonio (☎532-2365), near the Civic Center, has daily service to: **Albuquerque** (5½hr., 3 per day, $38); **Tucson** (6hr., 12 per day, $37); **Dallas** (12hr., 11 per day, $54); **Los Angeles** (16hr., 15 per day, $41). **El Paso-LA Bus Lines,** 720 Oregon St. (☎532-4061), on the corner of 6th Ave., is significantly cheaper than Greyhound and offers service to major destinations in the Southwest: **Albuquerque** (4hr., 3 per day, $20); **Las Vegas, NV** (1 per day, $45); **Phoenix** (4 per day, $35).

Public Transportation: Sun Metro (☎533-3333) leaves from San Jacinto Plaza and other locations. $1, students $0.50.

Taxis: Checker Cab (☎532-2626).

Car Rental: Budget (☎778-5287), with locations at 4024 N. Mesa and the airport. **Enterprise** (☎779-2260), also at the airport.

◼ ☒ ORIENTATION & PRACTICAL INFORMATION

San Jacinto Plaza, at the corner of Main and Oregon, is the heart of El Paso. **Interstate 10** runs east-west and **U.S. 54** into the city from the north. El Paso is divided east-west by Santa Fe Ave. and north-south by San Antonio Ave. **Although El Paso is ranked as one of the safest cities in the US, tourists should be wary of the streets between San Antonio and the border late at night.**

Visitor Information: 1 Civic Center Plaza (☎544-0062; www.visitelpaso.com), at Santa Fe and Mills in the small round building. Purchase tickets here for the **Border Jumper Trolley,** a guided trip that crosses the border and makes 8 stops in Ciudad Juárez.

CROSSING THE BORDER. The easiest way to cross the border is to walk. Take the north-south #8 or 10 green trolley operated by Sun Metro to Stanton Bridge, the last stop before the trolley turns around (every 20min.; M-F 6:15am-8:30pm, Sa 7:45am-8:45pm, Su 8:45am-7:55pm; $0.25). Do not confuse the green trolley with the more expensive Border Jumper Trolley. Two roads cross the Río Grande: **El Paso Avenue,** a crowded, one-way street, and **Stanton Avenue,** a parallel road lined with stores and restaurants. Walk to the right side of the Stanton Bridge and pay the $0.25 fee to cross. Daytrippers, including foreign travelers with multi-entry visas, should be prepared to flash their documents of citizenship. US citizens need proof of citizenship or a driver's license. Non-US citizens must have either an I-94 form or a passport. If you are planning to venture more than 22km into Mexico's interior, you need a **tourist card,** which costs about $20. Get one at the immigration office to your right as you enter Ciudad Juárez. To **re-enter** the US, cross the Stanton Bridge near the large *"Feliz Viaje"* sign. Be ready to answer questions posed by border guards and to show a valid visa or proof of citizenship. Once in El Paso, wait at the bus stop on the right-hand sidewalk just across from the bridge. The north-south bus runs M-F 6:15am- 8:45pm, Sa 7:40am-8:45pm, and Su 8:45am-7:45pm. Either the #8 or the 10 bus will return you to downtown El Paso. **Driving** to and from Mexico, vehicles are charged $1.50 each way and may require a permit.

(☎544-0061. Runs 10am-4pm daily. $12.50, children $9.) Parking ($3) is available in the Convention Center parking lot, which is located directly underneath the Visitors Center. Open daily 8am-5pm.

Mexican Consulate: 910 E. San Antonio (☎533-3644), on the corner of Virginia. Dispenses tourist cards. Open M-F 8:15am-4pm.

Currency Exchange: Valuta, 301 E. Paisano (☎544-1152), at Mesa St., is open 24hr. Conveniently near the border and also open 24hr. is **Melek,** 306 E. Paisano (☎534-7474), next to Valuta. Most of the banks in the downtown area have **24hr. ATMs**.

Police: 200 Campbell St. (☎577-5000). **Emergency:** ☎911.

Hospital: Providence Memorial Hospital, 2001 N. Oregon St. (☎577-1700).

Internet access: The **public library,** 501 N. Oregon St. (☎543-5433), has free access. Open M-Th 8:30am-8:30pm, F-Sa 8:30am-5:30pm, Su 1-5pm.

Post Office: 219 E. Mills (☎532-8824), between Mesa and Stanton. Open M-F 8:30am-5pm, Sa 8:30am-noon. **Postal code:** 79901.

ACCOMMODATIONS & CAMPING

The places to stay in El Paso are much safer and more appealing than the accommodations in Ciudad Juárez. Several good budget hotels can be found downtown, near Main St. and San Jacinto Square.

El Paso International Hostel, 311 E. Franklin (☎532-3661), between Stanton and Kansas in the Gardner Hotel. From the bus station walk up Santa Fe and turn right on Franklin. From San Jacinto Park, walk 2 blocks north to Franklin, turn right, and head east 1½ blocks. Located in the 80-year-old Gardner Hotel, the best budget accommodation in El Paso takes great pride in meeting the needs of backpackers. Dorms open only to those with HI, HA, ISIC or student ID (also to teachers with ID). Clean, 4-bed, single-sex rooms, a full kitchen, a large lounge with cable TV, and self-service laundry. Check-out 10am. Dorms $15, HA Members $14. Sheets $2. Towels $0.50. ❶

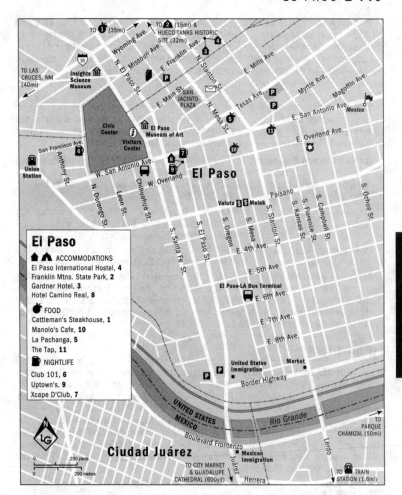

El Paso

♠♠ ACCOMMODATIONS
El Paso International Hostel, 4
Franklin Mtns. State Park, 2
Gardner Hotel, 3
Hotel Camino Real, 8

🍖 FOOD
Cattleman's Steakhouse, 1
Manolo's Cafe, 10
La Pachanga, 5
The Tap, 11

🎷 NIGHTLIFE
Club 101, 6
Uptown's, 9
Xcape D'Club, 7

Gardner Hotel, 311 E. Franklin (☎532-3661; www.gardnerhotel.com). Built in the 1920s, this is the oldest continually operating hotel in El Paso. John Dillinger stayed here in 1934. All rooms have phones and cable TV. Singles with shared bath $20; doubles with shared bath $30; with private baths start at $40. ❷

Hotel Camino Real, 101 S. El Paso (☎800-769-4300). In the center of downtown at El Paso and San Antonio. This is El Paso's most posh and historic hotel. With doormen, every amenity you could ask for, and a beautiful Tiffany glass dome in the lobby, the Camino Real is the best place in El Paso to spend a little extra money. Singles $89-159; doubles $104-174; suites $275-1000. ❺

Hueco Tanks State Historic Site (☎849-6684), 32 mi. east of El Paso. Offers camping 7 days a week. Water and showers; no charcoal or wood fires. Call to reserve a site. Campers must arrive at the park one hour before close. Tent sites $10; entrance fee $4 per person. For more info on Hueco Tanks, see p. 451. ❶

Franklin Mountains State Park (☎566-6441). Drive west on I-10 to the Trans-Mountain Road exit; the park entrance is on the left just before the road climbs into the mountains. Because of the campground's proximity to the city, campers should guard belongings carefully and take safety precautions. Sites are primitive; no water or electricity. Reservations recommended. Tent sites $8; park entrance fee $3. ●

🔲 FOOD

There's no shortage of good Mexican food in downtown El Paso, and prices are generally cheap. If it's a burger you crave, El Paso's fast food joints cluster around Stanton and Texas. Many downtown restaurants close on the weekends.

The Tap Bar and Restaurant, 408 E. San Antonio (☎532-1848), is dimly lit but has excellent Mexican food. Don't mind the mirrored walls or the waitresses' skimpy dresses. Delicious burritos ($1.75-4), enchiladas ($4.25), and grilled shrimp in garlic ($9). Open M-Sa 7am-2am, Su noon-2am. ●

Manolo's Cafe, 122 S. Mesa (☎532-7661), between Overland and San Antonio, offers cheap food in a spartan setting. Menudo ($2), burritos ($1), and generous lunch specials ($4) are standard fare. Open M-Sa 7am-5pm, Su 7:30am-3pm. ●

La Pachanga, 222 Texas Ave. (☎544-4454), between Mesa and Stanton. Serves fine sandwiches ($2.50) and excellent fruit smoothies ($2). Open M-Sa 8am-5pm. ●

Cattleman's Steakhouse (☎915-544-3200), located on the grounds of the Indian Cliffs Ranch. Take I-10 east to exit 49 and go north 5 mi. This place is considered El Paso's finest in steak. A 35min. drive is all that separates you from famous steaks and other Southwestern favorites. For a splurge, try the 2 lb. T-bone steak at $28. Open M-F 5-10pm, Sa 12:30-10pm, and Su 12:30-9pm. ❺

🎵 NIGHTLIFE

Most nightlife seekers follow the younger drinking age across the border to Ciudad Juárez. Still, there remain several viable options north of the Río Grande. **Club 101,** 500 San Francisco, is El Paso's oldest club, drawing a vibrant crowd with its three dance floors and party scene. (☎544-2101. W-F 18+, Sa 21+. Cover $5. Open W-Sa 9pm-3am.) **Xcape D'club,** 209 S. El Paso St., sits downtown in a beautifully restored theater and caters to a chic Latin crowd. (☎542-3800. Open F-Sa 9pm-2am.) If it's the weekend and you're in the mood for sizzling jazz in an upscale setting, stop by **Uptown's** in the historic Camino Real Hotel, 101 S. El Paso St. (☎800-769-4300. Open F-Sa 9:30pm-1:30am.)

👁 SIGHTS

Most visitors to El Paso are either stopping on the long drive through the desert or heading south to Ciudad Juárez. For a whirlwind tour, hop aboard the Border Jumper Trolleys, departing from the tourist office. Historic **San Jacinto Plaza** swarms with daily activity, brims with historical sites. To take in a view of the Río Grande Valley, head northwest of downtown along Stanton and make a right turn on Rim Rd. (which becomes Scenic Dr.) to reach **Murchison Park,** at the base of the ridge. The Park offers a commanding vista of El Paso, Ciudad Juárez, and the Sierra Madre Mountains that is particularly impressive at night. The **El Paso Museum of Art,** 1 Arts Festival Plaza, is one of the largest art museums in the Southwest, with over 5000 works of art and a recently renovated building. Particularly extensive are the holdings of 19th- to 20th-century Southwestern art and 18th- to 19th-century Mexican colonial art. (☎532-1707. Open Tu-Sa 9am-5pm, Su noon-

5pm. Free.) On Rte. 28 at a small airport in Santa Teresa, NM, 16 mi. west of El Paso off I-10, stands the **War Eagles Air Museum,** displaying 29 historic aircraft, mostly from WWII and the Korean War. (☎505-589-2000. Open Tu-Su 10am-4pm. $5, students and children free, seniors $4.)

⚑ OUTDOOR ACTIVITIES

North of downtown El Paso, **Franklin Mountains SFtate Park** (24,000 acres) is the largest urban wilderness park in the US. Flora include Yucca, Pincushion Cactus, and the Barrel Cactus. Mule deer and mountain lions are among the park's diverse fauna. The **Visitors Center** is in McKelligon Canyon on the east side of the Franklin Mts. To reach the Visitors Center from downtown, take Scenic Dr. east and turn left onto Alabama St. The canyon and Visitors Center are a couple miles down on the left. (☎566-6441. Open summer M-F 8am-8pm.) The Tom Mays section of the park is accessible only from the west side of the Franklin Mts. Try any of the activities in this section of the park: hiking, mountain biking, and rock climbing. In the summer heat, any physical activity demands frequent hydration. (Park open June-Sept. daily 8am-8pm; Oct.-May 8am-5pm. $3 entrance fee.)

HIKING. Beginning from Sneed's Cory, **West Cottonwood Spring** is a moderate 1.6 mi. round-trip hike to a spring with an amazing view of the valley. Also from Sneed's Cory, the **North Mt. Franklin Trail** is a difficult 9 mi. round-trip to the top of 7200 ft. Mt. Franklin. Allot at least 5hr. for the trek. The **Aztec Caves Trail,** a steep 1.3 mi. round-trip, takes about 2hr.; to reach the trailhead, take the second right after the fee station. One of the easier hikes in the park is **Upper Sunset,** a 1.2 mi. walk along the western edge of the mountain, with benches along the way for admiring the view. *(The trail begins just after the fee station on the left side of the road.)*

MOUNTAIN BIKING. Biking in the park caters to intermediate and advanced riders. A number of loop trails vary in length up to 16 mi. For equipment rentals and trail info for the park and nearby areas, call or visit **Crazy Cat Cyclery,** 2625 N. Mesa. *(☎577-9666. Open M-Sa 10am-8pm, Su 10am-6pm. Bikes $15 per day.)*

ROCK CLIMBING. Make the first right after the fee station to reach **Sneed's Cory,** the primary site in the park for **rock climbing.** A diagram of routes and boulder problems, along with their difficulty ratings, is available at the ranger station. **Hueco Tanks State Historical Park** (p. 451) is a premier bouldering and climbing spot.

OTHER ACTIVITIES. In the Franklin Mountains, the **Wyler Aerial Tramway,** northeast of downtown on the corner of Alabama St. and McKinley Ave., leads to the top of 5632 ft. Ranger Peak. The third tramway of its kind in the US, it was built in 1960 to serve TV and radio antennas. On a clear day, you can see 7000 sq. mi. from the top—all the way to the Guadalupe Mountains and Ruidoso, NM. *(☎562-9899. Open M and Th noon-6pm, F-Su noon-9pm. Ticket sales stop 1hr. before closing time. $7, children $4.)* The truly gutsy should consider a trip to **Skydive El Paso,** next to the War Eagles Museum in Santa Teresa, NM. *(☎505-589-4506. Skydives Sa-Su. $135 per person. Training starts at exactly 7:30am—come late and you don't jump.)*

HUECO TANKS STATE HISTORIC SITE   ☎915

Located 32 mi. east of El Paso on U.S. 180/62, this out-of-the-way site features unique geological formations and great rock climbing opportunities. The park's name is actually redundant: *hueco* is the Spanish word for "natural rock basin that stores water," a meaning echoed in the English equivalent, "tank." The park's outcrops formed when molten magma intruded into older sedimentary layers over 34 million years ago. After overlaying sedimentary rocks eroded, the resistant igneous rock, syenite, remained, forming the *huecos* and bubbly rock mountains that rise 300 ft. from the desert floor.

Hueco Tanks is a **rock climber's paradise.** There are climbs of all difficulty levels, and the park is known as one of the best bouldering sites in the world. Technical climbers should purchase John Sherman's book, *Hueco Tanks Climbing and Bouldering Guide*, available in El Paso bookstores and at rock climbing outfitters. A great resource for people interested in technical climbing is the **Hueco Rock Ranch,** located just outside the park grounds. To reach the Ranch, look for the sign on the main road into the park. Turn left there, take the first right, and make a left when that road ends. The Ranch is about 200 yds. ahead on the left. Knowledgeable staff will customize a day of rock climbing to meet a visitor's individual needs. Rock Ranch staff have access to all areas of Hueco Tanks, including those closed to the general public. Call ahead to reserve guides. The Rock Ranch also offers camping with showers for $5 per person. (☎855-0142; www.routfitters.com. Bouldering $10 per person per day, multi-pitch $110, top rope $60.)

The challenging scramble to the top of **North Mountain** is a rewarding venture that requires only a modicum of cardiovascular fitness and no technical rock-climbing accessories. Those who reach the summit will see a wide variety of desert flora and fauna and enjoy a spectacular view.

From El Paso, take U.S. 62 east from El Paso for 24 mi. Turn left at the sign for the park, and continue another 8 mi. to the park entrance. The state park consists of three mountains. The North Mountain is open to the public for climbing and hiking, but no more than 70 people may be on the mountain at once. Once full, the park closes its gates and no one can enter until someone leaves. Call the **state parks department** (☎512-389-8900) to reserve a spot before coming to the park; last-minute visitors can contact the park within 24 hours of arriving to see if space is available. This is particularly important for visits during weekends and holidays. Visitors are allowed on the **West Mountain** and **East Mountain** on guided tours only. (Park office and tours ☎849-6684. Park open Oct.-Apr. daily 8am-6pm; May-Sept. M-Th 8am-6pm, F-Su 7am-7pm. Tours June-Aug. W-Su 9am and 11am; Sept.-May W-Su 10am and 2pm. Tours often available during the week for visitors who call at least 10 days prior to visiting; subject to guide availability. Calling in advance is recommended for all tours. Access $4; children free.)

GUADALUPE MOUNTAINS ☎915

The Guadalupe Mountains are the highest and most remote of the major West Texas ranges. The peaks are remnants of the ancient Capitan reef that formed 225 million years ago along the edge of a vast inland sea and covered much of what is now western Texas and southeastern New Mexico. After the sea receded, the reef was buried under layers of sediment until major block faulting and erosion excavated and exposed the petrified remains 26 million years ago. Hikers in the high Guadalupes are thus treading on the same rock layer that forms Carlsbad caverns.

Mescalero Apaches inhabited this land for three centuries until they were forcibly relocated to reservations in 1880. Upon their departure, ranching was taken up by a group of hardy latter-day pioneers, who barely eked out a living. In 1921, wealthy oil geologist Wallace Pratt took a fancy to the area. He bought up large tracts of land, which he eventually deeded to the government for the establishment of a national park. A long time in the making, the park finally opened in 1972.

Guadalupe Mountains National Park accommodates a particularly wide variety of flora and fauna. Drivers can glimpse the park's most dramatic sights from U.S. 62/180: **El Capitan,** a 2000 ft. high limestone cliff, and **Guadalupe Peak,** the highest point in Texas at 8749 ft. Roadside views notwithstanding, the Guadalupe Mountains are a true wilderness; no roads penetrate the center of the park. The only way to appreciate the magnificence of these mountains is to get out of the car and hit the trails. As always, anyone hiking alone should let someone know her/his destination and expected time of return.

AT A GLANCE: GUADALUPE MOUNTAINS NATIONAL PARK	
AREA: 86,190 acres.	**GATEWAYS:** El Paso (p. 447); Carlsbad (p. 440).
FEATURES: El Capitán, Guadalupe Peak, McKittrick Canyon, "The Bowl."	**CAMPING:** Park campgrounds $8; free permit required for backcountry camping.
HIGHLIGHTS: Hiking to the "Top of Texas," fall leaves in beautiful McKittrick Canyon, seeing Williams Ranch.	**FEES AND RESERVATIONS:** Entrance fee $3 per person.

ORIENTATION & PRACTICAL INFORMATION

There are only three park entrances accessible by car. In the southwestern portion of the park, **Pine Springs** is the main entrance and contains park headquarters, a Visitors Center, and a campground. **McKittrick Canyon** lies only a few miles farther on U.S. 62/180. The **Dog Canyon** campground on the north side of the park is 2hr. by car from Pine Canyon, accessible via Rte. 137 from Carlsbad, NM. The park lies 110 mi. east of El Paso (p. 447) and 55 mi. south of Carlsbad, NM (p. 440) on U.S. 62/180. **TNM&O Coaches** (☎505-887-1108) may stop at Pine Springs on its route between Carlsbad, NM (2½hr., $26) and El Paso if you call ahead and ask the driver nicely. The **Pine Springs** (☎828-3251; open June-Aug. daily 8am-6pm, Sept.-May 8am-4:30pm) and **McKittrick Canyon** (open Apr.-Oct. daily 8am-6pm; Nov.-Mar. 8am-4:30pm) **Visitors Centers** have park info and permits. For additional info, check the web site (www.nps.gov/gumo), call the Visitors Center, or write to Guadalupe Mountains National Park, HC 60, Box 400, Salt Flat, TX 79847.

There are very few services within the park itself. **Gas** is available at the **Nickel Creek Cafe,** 5 mi. north of Pine Springs. (☎828-3295. Open M-Sa 7am-2pm and 6-9pm. Cash only.) **White's City, NM,** 35 mi. northeast on U.S. 62/180, has the nearest **post office, ATM, laundry,** and **24hr. gas station.** The nearest hospital is **Carlsbad Medical Center,** 2430 W. Pierce St. (☎887-4100), in Carlsbad .

WHEN TO GO. Most people visit in the spring or fall when temperatures are moderate. Many visitors come just for the fall leaves in McKittrick Canyon. Snow can stick to the highest peaks in the winter, and summers bring oppressive heat to the surrounding desert plains.

CAMPING & FOOD

The park's two simple campgrounds, **Pine Springs ❶,** just past park headquarters, and **Dog Canyon ❶,** at the north end of the park, have water and restrooms but no hookups or showers. No wood or charcoal fires allowed. (☎828-3251. Tent sites $8. Reservations for groups only.) Dog Canyon is accessible via Rte. 137 from Carlsbad, NM (72 mi.), or by a full-day hike from Pine Springs. After-hours info is posted on the bulletin board. Get a free **backcountry camping** permit at the visitors center. None of the 10 backcountry sites in the park has water or toilets. Backpackers should carry at least a gallon of water per day and pack out trash, including toilet paper.

The park's lack of development is attractive to backpackers, but it creates some inconveniences. **Nickel Creek Cafe ❶,** 5 mi. north of Pine Springs, is the only restaurant near the park. The friendly owner serves Mexican food ($3-5), burgers ($4),

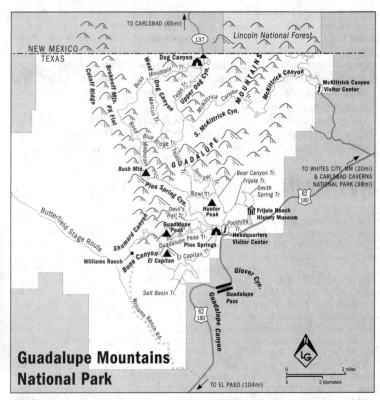

TO CARLSBAD (65mi)

Lincoln National Forest

NEW MEXICO
TEXAS

Dog Canyon

West Dog Canyon

Cutoff Ridge

Brokeoff Mts.

Px Flat

Bush Mountain Tr.

Tejas Tr.

Upper Dog Cyn.

McKittrick Canyon

McKittrick Canyon

McKittrick Canyon

Marcus Tr.

Bush Mountain Tr.

S. McKittrick Cyn.

Blue Ridge Tr.

Tejas Tr.

G U A D A L U P E

M O U N T A I N S

McKittrick Canyon
Visitor Center

Bush Mtn.

Juniper Tr.

TO WHITES CITY, NM (20mi)
& CARLSBAD CAVERNS
NATIONAL PARK (38mi)

Bear Canyon Tr.
Frijole Tr.

Smith
Spring Tr.

62
180

Pine Spring Cyn.

Bowl Tr.

Hunter
Peak

Frijole Ranch
History Museum

Butterfield Stage Route

Shumard Canyon

Devil's
Hall Tr.

Guadalupe
Peak

Foothills
Tr.

Headquarters
Visitor Center

Williams Ranch

Bone Canyon

Guadalupe Peak Tr.

Pine Springs

El Capitan

El Capitan Tr.

Salt Basin Tr.

Williams Ranch Rd.

Glover Cyn.

Guadalupe Canyon

Guadalupe
Pass

62
180

Guadalupe Mountains National Park

N

0 --- 2 miles

0 --- 2 kilometers

TO EL PASO (104mi)

---

and beer. (☎828-3295. Open M-Sa 7am-2pm and 6-9pm. Cash only.) White's City, 35 mi. north of Pine Springs, offers a handful of restaurants and a small **grocery store.** (Open May-Sept. daily 7am-10pm. Oct.-Apr. 7am-8pm.) For more restaurants and the nearest supermarket, visitors must travel 55 mi. north to Carlsbad.

◎ SIGHTS

The remote Guadalupe Mountains were the locale of many late 19th- and early 20th-century ranching efforts. The still-standing ranch buildings are the only nearby sights. Just up U.S. 62/180 from Pine Springs is **Frijole Ranch,** a restored ranch house with a history museum inside. Hours vary depending on the availability of volunteer staff. The only road into the interior of the park is a 7.3 mi. dirt road that begins 8.3 mi. west of Pine Springs on U.S. 62/180 and leads to the **Williams Ranch** at the base of a 3000 ft. cliff on the west side of the Guadalupe Mountains. The road is only open to high-clearance, four-wheel-drive vehicles. Visitors must get the key to the gate at the Pine Springs Visitors Center.

▧ HIKING & BACKPACKING

With 80 mi. of established trails and low visitation figures, Guadalupe Mountains National Park is a hiker's heaven. Most trails in the park begin at the Pine Springs Campground. Backpackers have plenty of options for multi-day hiking trips. Trekking from Pine Springs to the McKittrick Canyon Visitors Center is an arduous 20 mi. hike by the shortest route, but there are any number of possible alternate routes and side trips. One interesting backpacking route follows the Tejas Trail from Pine Springs all the way to the Dog Canyon Campground and then returns via the Bush Mountain Trail. The 24 mi. loop goes through the heart of the Guadalupe Mountains and includes the summit of Bush Mountain (8368 ft.), the second highest peak in Texas. Free backcountry camping permits are required.

Dehydration and weather are the most pressing safety concerns for hikers. **There are no reliable water sources in the backcountry; pack plenty of fluid.** In the high country, watch the weather closely. Strong winds often blow through; take a windbreaker on any hike and be careful at high elevations if the wind is gusting.

Guadalupe Peak (8.4 mi. round-trip, 5-7hr.), at 8749 ft., is the highest mountain in Texas, and many people hike this trail as an ego-booster. The well-marked climb can be tough on the lungs in parts. From the Pine Springs Campground, the route ascends quickly and affords views of the Permian Basin to the east. At the summit is a monument erected in 1958 to commemorate the 100th anniversary of the first transcontinental mail route, which passed through Pine Springs. From the top, the expansive Chihuahuan Desert stretches to the east, south, and west. White splotches to the southwest are salt flats, and on a clear day the Davis Mountains are visible 125 mi. to the southeast. Hikers should be prepared for strong winds at the top.

Devil's Hall (4.2 mi. round-trip, 3-5hr.). A moderate hike, the trail starts at Pine Springs, winds through the Chihuahuan Desert, then drops into a dry stream bed after 1 mi. Maples, oaks, and pines shelter the stream bed. The trail leads to a series of rocky steps known as the Hiker's Staircase and ends between the vertical stone walls of Devil's Hall. Cairns (stacks of rocks) mark the trail in its more difficult-to-follow sections.

Smith Spring Trail (2.3 mi. round-trip, 1-2hr.), a short, easy trail; a good choice for those with limited time. The trail begins at the Frijole Ranch House, the park's first permanent building. Bearing east, the trail passes Manzanita Spring, where the US cavalry destroyed a cache of Mescalero Apache supplies in 1878. The trail terminates at Smith Spring, a favorite watering spot for area wildlife, especially around sunrise and sunset.

McKittrick Canyon (2.3-10.9 mi. one way). The canyon lures hikers with the lush vegetation growing alongside McKittrick Stream. During the last two weeks of Oct. and the first week of Nov., people drive hundreds of miles to see the maple leaves turn brilliant shades of red. From the McKittrick Canyon parking lot, the spectacular scenery requires at least a 2 mi. jaunt up the trail. Wallace Pratt's cabin stands 2.3 mi. from the trailhead, and the most beautiful section of the canyon lies beyond the cabin. Day hikers should consider hiking to the Grotto Picnic Area, 3.4 mi. from the parking lot. Backpackers will probably stop at the backcountry campsite 7.4 mi. from the trailhead. The trail runs all the way to Dog Canyon (1-2 days) or Pine Springs (2-3 days).

The Bowl Loop (9 mi. round-trip, 5-7hr.). This route grants hikers a chance to see the flora and fauna of the Guadalupe high country. Visitors will be surprised to find a dense, coniferous forest full of deer and elk, remnants of an earlier time when much of western Texas was blanketed in trees, not desert. From Pine Springs Campground, start on the Tejas Trail, then take the Bowl Trail to the summit of 8368 ft. Hunter Peak. The spectacular view from the summit stretches in all directions. Continue down the mountain on the Bear Canyon Trail and then Frijole Trail. Many visitors choose to do this hike as an overnight, sleeping at the Pine Top campsite, about 4 mi. up the trail.

ALPINE ☎432

Alpine is the seat of Brewster County, the largest and most sparsely populated county in Texas. While there is little to see in the town itself, it makes a great stopover en route to Big Bend National Park (p. 458). Labor Day weekend brings

HIKING PARK TO PARK. If the idea of jumping back in the car to drive from Guadalupe Mountains National Park to Carlsbad Caverns (p. 442) doesn't suit you, don your pack and spend 5-7 days hiking the 60 mi. stretch to Carlsbad along the spine of the Guadalupe Mountains. The trip can be completed in either direction and is most pleasant in the spring or fall. The route lacks any reliable water sources, and strong winds and heavy thunderstorms are constant threats. Contact either national park for more info and trail conditions.

attracts tourists to the Alpine Balloon Rally and the nearby Marfa Lights Festival. Sul Ross State University is the main fixture of Alpine. The school is known for its rodeo team, one of the best in the nation. The university also hosts an annual **Cowboy Poetry Festival** on the first weekend in March. The festival includes three days of recitations by cowboys and cowgirls, along with a celebrity rodeo, music, and plenty of hearty Western cooking. Also at the university, on the first floor of Lawrence Hall, is **Museum of the Big Bend,** a small gallery with exhibits on the history and art of the Big Bend region. Every April the museum shows a special cowboy art exhibit. (☎837-8143. Open Tu-Sa 9am-5pm, Su 1-5pm.)

Alpine lies at the junction of U.S. 90 and Rte. 118. Most of the town's accommodations and restaurants are along U.S. 90, which splits into **Holland Avenue** and **Avenue E** in the downtown area. The **Amtrak** station (☎800-872-7245), at the highway junction, runs trains to **El Paso** (5hr., 3 per week, $32) and **San Antonio** (8hr., 3 per week, $113). **Greyhound,** 601 East Ave. E (☎837-5302), runs buses to **El Paso** (3hr.; 1 per day; M-Th $39, F-Su $41.50) and **San Antonio** (9hr.; 3 per day; M-Th $59, F-Su $63). **Alpine Auto Rental,** 414 E. Holland, next to the Sonic, will rent cars for a trip to Big Bend. (☎837-3463. From $36 per day, $0.10 per mi. 21+ with valid driver's license and proof of insurance.) Tourist info is available at the **Chamber of Commerce,** 106 N. 3rd St. (☎837-2326. Open M-F 9am-6pm, Sa 10am-2am.) **Emergency:** ☎911. **Police:** 309 W. Sul Ross (☎837-3486). **Medical Services: Big Bend Medical Center,** 2600 N. Rte. 118 (☎837-3447). The **public library,** 203 N. 7th St., has free **Internet access.** (☎837-2621. Open M 9:30am-8pm, Tu-F 9:30am-5:30pm, Sa 10am-1pm.) **Post office:** 901 W. Holland. (Open M-F 8am-4pm, Sa 10am-1pm.) **Postal code:** 79830.

A glut of cheap motels is located east of downtown on Rte. 90 near Sul Ross State University. The nicest budget accommodations in town are at the **Antelope Lodge ❷,** 2310 W. Rte. 90, 2 mi. west of Rte. 118. Each room occupies half of a small cottage and has a kitchenette, A/C, cable TV, and desert art on the wall. (☎837-2451 or 800-880-8106; www.antelopelodge.com. Singles and doubles start at $35.) Some of the cheapest rooms in town are at **Motel Bien Venido ❷,** 809 E. Holland Ave., two blocks west of the university. The rooms have A/C, cable, and private baths. (☎837-3454. Singles $28, doubles $34.) The **Woodward Ranch ❶,** 16 mi. south of Alpine on Rte. 118 (☎364-2271), has primitive campsites along a mountain stream with oak trees ($10; no bathroom facilities), or less scenic sites with bathrooms and showers ($15). Stop at the **Food Basket,** 104 N. 2nd St. (☎837-3295), to stock up on food before heading to Big Bend. **La Tapatia ❶,** 202 W. Holland Ave., is a pleasant Italian-style cafe where coffee drinks are $1-3 and fresh panini sandwiches run $6-7. (☎837-2200. Open M-Th 8:30am-6pm, F-Sa 6:30am-10pm.) **Penny's Diner ❶,** 2407 E. Holland Ave., east of downtown on Rte. 90 by the Oak Tree Inn, is a great spot to tank up before or after a long drive, serving up sandwiches ($4-5), burgers ($5), and big salads ($5.25), as well as breakfast all day. (☎837-5711. Open 24hr.) At night, the **Railroad Blues,** 504 W. Holland Ave., is the place to hang your hat in Alpine. Pick your poison from among 118 brands of beer from 80 countries, 33 types of wine, and a special house sangria. Live music Friday and Saturday nights ranges from rock to reggae. (☎837-3103. 21+. F-Sa cover $5-7. Open M-F 4pm-midnight, Sa 4pm-1am.)

FORT DAVIS & THE DAVIS MOUNTAINS ☎432

Life is quiet in Fort Davis. Although this town of 1400 gets a fair amount of tourist traffic, it manages to eschew traffic lights, chain motels, franchise restaurants, and even numbered street addresses. Instead, wooden buildings adorn downtown's main drag and tall tales bordering on Old West mythology fill the air of the town's lazy, mom-and-pop establishments. The highest town in Texas at 5000 ft., Fort Davis lies at the foot of the scenic Davis Mountains. Renowned for wonderful stargazing opportunities, this rounded range offers a greener, gentler alternative to the rugged desert peaks of Big Bend and the Guadalupe Mountains.

■☐ **ORIENTATION & PRACTICAL INFORMATION.** The town sits in the Davis Mountains at the junction of Rte. 17 and 118. The roads merge to form the main street of the town and then diverge again south of the courthouse. Tourist info is available at the **Chamber of Commerce** in the center of town just behind the Limpia Hotel. (☎426-3015. Open M-F 9am-5pm.) Next door, the **public library** has free **Internet access.** (☎426-3802. Open M-F noon-6pm.) To contact the **sheriff,** call ☎426-3213. The closest **medical facility** is Big Bend Regional Medical Center in Alpine. The **post office,** 500 N Sergeant Gonzales, is at Memorial Square. (☎426-3914. Open M-F 8am-4pm.) **Postal code:** 79734.

☐☐ **ACCOMMODATIONS & FOOD.** Private rooms in Fort Davis are pricier than in larger towns nearby. Camping is more economical, and the mountain scenery beats wallpaper. But if you insist, **Stone Village Motel ❸,** on Rte. 118 between the courthouse and the fort, has the cheapest rooms in town, with A/C, heat, and cable TV. (☎426-3941 or 800-649-8487. Singles $45, doubles $50.) The best place to pitch your tent is in nearby **Davis Mountains State Park ❶,** 5 mi. north of town. (☎426-3337. Primitive sites $6, with water and showers $8; entrance fee $2. Gates close at 6pm in summer, 5pm in winter.) The **Drugstore ❶,** on Rte. 118 in the center of town, serves large, thick milkshakes ($3), and a $5 hearty breakfast special. (☎426-3118. Open daily 8am-4pm.) **Pops Grill ❶,** Hwy. 17 near the vet clinic, serves great burgers ($3.30) and offers take-out. (☎426-3195. Open daily 9am-9pm.) For groceries, try **Baeza's Thriftway,** on Rte. 118 across from the fort (☎426-3812).

◙ **SIGHTS.** In town, the **Fort Davis National Historic Site** incorporates the restored buildings of the original 19th-century fort, named after Jefferson Davis. The **Visitors Center** has a video and summer history programs. (☎426-3224. Open June-Aug. daily 8am-6pm; Sept.-May 8am-5pm. $3, children free.) Operated by the University of Texas, the **McDonald Observatory,** 17 mi. north of Fort Davis on Rte. 118, is the most publicly accessible research observatory in the world. Every year, 120,000 visitors are tallied, and a new Visitors Center was finished in 2002 to accommodate the traffic (open daily 9am-5pm). Visitors can view images of the sun through a filtered telescope and take daily tours of the facility. The most popular program at the observatory is the **Star Party.** Every Tuesday, Friday, and Saturday evening visitors look through telescopes at star clusters, planets, and far-away galaxies. Also available are guided tours of the Observatory's two largest telescopes, offered daily at 11:30am and 2:30pm. (☎426-3640 or 877-984-7227; www.mcdonaldobservatory.org. Check web site for updated schedule; hours seasonal. $5, children $4, family $15. Star Party $8/$7/$25. Telescope tours $7/$6/$22.) At the end of a bumpy dirt road 4 mi. south of town on Rte. 118, the **Chihuahuan Desert Research Institute** promotes the scientific and public understanding of the geology, flora, and fauna of the Chihuahua Desert. Visitors can tour the cactus gardens, 20-acre arboretum, and Visitors Center exhibits, or hike the **Modesta Canyon Trail** to a series of springs. (☎364-2499; www.cdri.org. Open M-F 9am-5pm, Apr.-Sept. Sa 9am-3pm. $2, children under 12 free.)

WEST TEXAS

⚠ OUTDOOR ACTIVITIES. High up in the scenic mountains, 5 mi. north of town on Rte. 118, **Davis Mountains State Park** shelers an abundance of wildlife, miles of hiking trails, amazing scenic vistas, and a great campground. Wildlife in the park include javelinas, grey foxes, and ring-tail cats. Mule deer are abundant and tend to dart across the roads, so be careful when driving, especially at night. A 3 mi. scenic drive takes visitors to the highest point in the park and a great view of the Davis Mountains. The **Fort Davis Trail** is a moderate 4.5 mi. one-way hike that begins behind the interpretive center and leads over the mountains to the Fort Davis National Historic Site. Hikers will need to pay an entrance fee at the Historic Site. The **Limpia Canyon Trail** is the most challenging hike in the park. The trail is 6.5 mi. one-way and takes hikers through a canyon and up to a scenic lookout, 600 ft. above the valley floor. There are six primitive campsites near the top of the trail with no water or bathroom facilities. Campers should reserve a site in advance and must check in with the park office before beginning the hike and again upon returning. A newer, unnamed trail offers a 3.5 mile round-trip hike or mountain bike ride with excellent views. For more info about recreation in the park, contact the park office. (☎426-3337. Hours vary. Entrance fee $3, seniors $2, children free.) A 75 mi. **scenic drive** loop along Rte. 118 and Rte. 166 whisks tourists through the entire Davis Mountain Range. From the town of Ft. Davis, drive north on Rte. 118. At 6791 ft., the point where the highway passes the McDonald Observatory is the highest elevation on the Texas Highway system. Thirteen miles past the Observatory, turn left at the intersection onto Rte. 166. Sawtooth Peak and then Mt. Livermore (the second-highest peak in Texas) will be visible on the left as the road leads south. To return to town, continue along Rte. 166 and turn left on Rte. 17.

BIG BEND
NATIONAL PARK   ☎432

Early Spanish travelers called the region *el despoblado*, "the unpopulated land." However, evidence suggests that Native American tribes inhabited this land as early as 8500 BC and as late as the 18th century, when the Mescalero Apaches displaced the Chisos Indians. Interest in the area grew at the onset of the 20th century when valuable mineral deposits were discovered, and a number of mining operations opened in the park. In the 1920s, though, a hot springs resort opened near Boquillas Canyon and established Big Bend as a tourist attraction. It was purchased by private landholders and then donated to the federal government in 1944 as Big Bend National Park. Today, the park's remote location in western Texas and the scarcity of nearby tourist facilities help keep visitors to a minimum. About 325,000 came to Big Bend last year, most of whom flocked to the Chisos Mountains and the Río Grande. Off the beaten path, vast expanses of empty desert basins and mountain ranges lure the intrepid traveler seeking untrodden ground.

AT A GLANCE: BIG BEND NATIONAL PARK	
AREA: 801,163 acres.	**GATEWAY TOWNS:** Alpine (p. 455), Terlingua, Marathon, Study Butte.
FEATURES: Río Grande, Chisos Mountains, Sierra del Carmen.	**CAMPING:** Park campgrounds $10; free permit required for backcountry camping.
HIGHLIGHTS: Hiking on the South Rim Trail in the Chisos Mountains, rafting the Santa Eleña Canyon, cruising the Ross Maxwell Scenic Drive.	**ENTRANCE FEES:** Weekly entrance pass for vehicles $15; pedestrian, bike, or motorcycle $5; yearly pass $20.

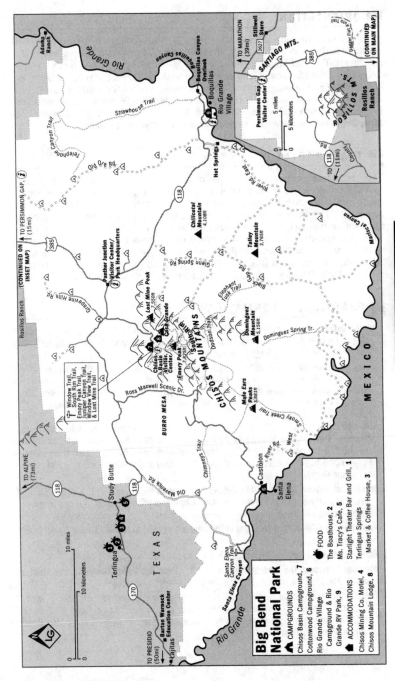

WEST TEXAS

Big Bend National Park

CAMPGROUNDS
Chisos Basin Campground, 7
Cottonwood Campground, 6
Rio Grande Village
Campground & Rio
Grande RV Park, 9

ACCOMMODATIONS
Chisos Mining Co. Motel, 4
Chisos Mountain Lodge, 8

FOOD
The Boathouse, 2
Ms. Tracy's Cafe, 5
Starlight Theater Bar and Grill, 1
Terlingua Springs
Market & Coffee House, 3

TO ALPINE
(73mi)

TO PRESIDIO
(50mi)

Barton Warnock
Education Center

Lajitas

Terlingua

Study Butte

170

118

T E X A S

Ross Maxwell Scenic Dr.

Window Trail,
South Rim Trail,
Emory Peak Trail,
Juniper Canyon Trail,
Window View Trail,
& Lost Mine Trail

Panther Junction
Visitor Center/
Park Headquarters

385

118

CONTINUED ON
INSET MAP

TO PERSIMMON GAP,
(15mi)

Rosillos Ranch

Grapevine Hills Rd.

Old Ore Rd.

Telephone Canyon Trail

Strawhouse Trail

Rio Grande

Adams
Ranch

Boquillas Canyon

Boquillas Canyon
Overlook

Boquillas

Rio Grande
Village

Hot Springs

River Rd. East

Chilicotal
Mountain
4,108ft

Glenn Spring Rd.

Elephant Tusk Trail

Talley
Mountain
3,765ft

Black Gap Rd.

Dominguez
Mountain
5,156ft

Dominguez Spring Tr.

Lost Mine Peak
7,550ft

Casa Grande

Chisos
Basin
Visitor
Center

Emory Peak
7,825ft

SOUTH
RIM
CHISOS MOUNTAINS

Dodson Trail

Mule Ears
Peaks
3,881ft

Smoky Creek Trail

West River Rd.

Castolon

Santa
Elena

BURRO MESA

Chimneys Trail

Old Maverick Rd.

Santa Elena
Canyon Trail

Santa Elena Canyon

Rio Grande

M E X I C O

Mariscal Canyon

TO MARATHON
(39mi)

Stillwell
Store

Persimmon Gap
Visitor Center

SANTIAGO MTS.

ROSILLOS MTS.

Rosillos Ranch

2627

Dagger Flat Auto Trail

385

CONTINUED
ON MAIN MAP

TO U.S. 118
(11mi)

5 miles

5 kilometers

10 miles

10 kilometers

▄ ORIENTATION

There are three developed areas in the park: **Río Grande Village** in the south, the **Chisos Basin** in the center of the park, and the **Castolon/Santa Eleña Canyon** area in the southwest. The best hiking is found in the Chisos Mountains. The other two locations are on the Río Grande and cater more to those viewing or running the river. Much of the rest of the park is wilderness, dominated by flat Chihuahuan Desert and volcanic mountain ranges. Just west of the park lies **Terlingua,** a mellowed-out, historic ghost town (the name is Spanish for "three languages"), and **Lajitas** and **Study Butte,** two sand-swept hamlets with a few restaurants and motels.

▐ TRANSPORTATION

There is no transportation service into or around the park. **Amtrak** goes to Alpine (p. 455), 103 mi. north of the park entrance, where **car rentals** are available. Three roads lead south from U.S. 90 into the park: from Marfa, U.S. 67 to Rte. 170; from Alpine, Rte. 118; from Marathon, U.S. 385 (the fastest route). There are two **gas stations** within the park, one at **Panther Junction** (☎477-2294; open Sept.-Mar. daily 7am-7pm; Apr.-Aug. 8am-6pm; 24hr. credit card service), next to the park headquarters, and one at **Río Grande Village** (☎477-2293; open Mar.-May daily 9am-8pm; June-Feb. 9am-6pm). On Rte. 118, about 1 mi. from the western park entrance, the **Study Butte Store** also sells gas. (Open 24hr. Credit cards only.)

▐ PRACTICAL INFORMATION

Visitor information: The park web site (www.nps.gov/bibe) is a great resource for planning a trip to Big Bend. For more info, write to the Superintendent, Big Bend National Park, P.O. Box 129, Big Bend National Park, TX 79834.

Park Headquarters (☎477-2251), at Panther Junction, 26 mi. south of the northern park boundary. Open daily 8am-6pm. A **ranger station** (☎477-2225; closed June-Oct.) awaits at Castolon.

Visitors Centers: Persimmon Gap, where U.S. 385 enters the park (☎477-2393; open daily 8am-5pm); **Chisos Basin** (☎477-2264; open daily 9am-4:30pm); and **Río Grande Village** (☎477-2271; usually closed June-Oct.).

Groceries: Stores selling food and camping supplies are located near all three campgrounds: **Río Grande Village** (☎477-2293; open daily 9am-5pm); **Chisos Basin** (☎477-2291; open daily 9am-7pm); and **Castolon** (☎477-2222; open daily 10am-6pm). For a larger selection of food go to the **Study Butte Store** (☎371-2231; open daily 7am-9pm).

Bank: The nearest **ATM** is at the **Quicksilver Branch Bank** (☎371-2211). The Lodge, restaurant, stores, and gas stations in the park all accept credit cards, but camping fees must be paid with cash.

Laundry: The only laundry facilities in the park are at the Río Grande Village Store. Open daily 9am-5pm.

Emergency: ☎477-2251, then press 9. If no answer, dial ☎911.

Medical Services: The closest medical facility is the **Big Bend Family Health Center** (☎371-2661), 2 mi. west of Study Butte on Rte. 170.

Post Office: Main office (☎477-2238) in Panther Junction, next to Park Headquarters. Open M-F 8am-4pm. Chisos Basin office is inside the grocery store. Open M-Sa 9am-5pm. Post office accepts general delivery mail addressed to visitor's name, Big Bend National Park, TX. **Postal code:** 79834.

WHEN TO GO. Due to the oppressive summer heat, peak visitation of the park occurs during spring break and winter holidays, but, truth be told, there really isn't a bad time to visit Big Bend. In the summer months, areas along the river are unbearably hot, but hikers can find more pleasant temperatures in the Chisos Mountains. In the winter, when the mountain climate is cold and blustery, the temperature in the lowlands along the Río Grande is more comfortable. The best season for rafting is fall, when river levels tend to be highest, though flash floods can render the river impassable. June to October is the rainy season at Big Bend; bring raingear if you visit. Thunderstorms can roll in quickly, so keep an eye on the sky to avoid lightning danger, especially in the mountains.

▌ ACCOMMODATIONS & CAMPING

The three developed campsites within the park do not take reservations and are run on a first-come, first-serve basis. During Thanksgiving, Christmas, March, and April, the campgrounds fill early; call park headquarters (☎477-2251) to inquire about availability. **Free backcountry camping** in the park requires a permit from one of the Visitors Centers. Nearly all areas of the park are open to backcountry camping. A number of sites are accessible by paved roads, but many lie dirt roads requiring four-wheel-drive or a hike. In the Chisos Mountains pit toilets accompany some sites. Backcountry campsites have no water; plan ahead and bring your own. Consult a park ranger before setting off on an overnight trip.

Chisos Mountains Lodge, in the Chisos Basin (☎477-2291; www.chisosmountainslodge.com), 10 mi. from park headquarters. It's expensive, but it's the only motel-style shelter within the park. Reservations are a must for high season; the lodge is often booked a year in advance. Singles $73; doubles $78, additional person $10. ❹

Chisos Mining Company Motel, on Rte. 170 (☎371-2254), ¾ mi. west of the junction with Rte. 118. Provides clean rooms with A/C and an offbeat atmosphere. Life at this gateway to Big Bend is welcoming enough to skip staying in the Basin. Singles $37; doubles $45-55; 5-6 person cabins with kitchenettes $60. ❷

Chisos Basin Campground, 5400 ft., has 65 sites with running water and flush toilets. Stays cooler than the other sites in the summer. $10; 14-night maximum stay. ❶

Río Grande Village Campground, 1850 ft., has 100 sites near the only showers in the park. Flush toilets and water are also available. $10; 14-night maximum stay. ❶

Cottonwood Campground, 2170 ft. More primitive than the other options, Cottonwood's 35 sites offer only pit toilets and prohibits generators. $10. ❶

Río Grande RV Park, 1850 ft., at Río Grande Village. Provides 25 full hookups, the only ones in the park. $18.50 for up to two people; $1 per additional person. ❶

▌ FOOD

Chisos Mountain Lodge Restaurant, in the Chisos Mountain Lodge (☎477-2291). The only dining in the park. Breakfast buffet $6.75, lunch sandwiches $4-8, dinner entrees $6-15. Open daily 7-10am, 11:30am-4pm, and 5:30-8pm. ❷

Ms. Tracy's Cafe, on Rte. 118 just south of the intersection with Rte. 170 (☎371-2888). Has outdoor seating and decorative cacti. Ms. Tracy serves eggs, hamburgers, burritos and a number of vegetarian entrees. Open Oct.-May daily 7am-9:30pm; June 7am-2pm; July-Sept. 7am-5pm. ❶

WEST TEXAS

EIGHT-LEGGED FREAK

think it first really hit that I was
ar away from a Tower Records or
a CVS when I tried to get my
change out of the motel's pay
phone and retrieved two legs.
"Push for Coins" should have read
"Push for Dead Black Widow Spider" (I pulled out the rest of the
body): had it been alive, I imagine
would've screamed like a seven-
year-old Whitney Houston. No, it
was earlier than that. The day I
drove into Study Butte, outside
Big Bend, I nearly ran over a red
licorice shoelace about three feet
long: I later learned it was a non-
venomous coachwhip. I was to be
tested night after night by like-
minded suicidal furries hell-bent
on painting my right front tire: a
full-scale coordinated carni-
valesque game of Don't-Whack-a-
Mole. Five roadside jackrabbits
who had lost everything in the
stock market chose this method of
death but met with no success.
With any luck, my swerving con-
vinced them not only to reinvest
themselves in the Chisos Mountains skyline but to reinvest in
telecommunications and office
furniture. At least the javelinas
(black peccaries) give you fair
warning. They run out a full fifteen
yards ahead and in threes, giving
you ample time to avoid trimming
their backsides.

(Continued on next page)

Terlingua Springs Market and Coffee House, between Study Butte and the ghost town on Rte. 170 (☎371-2332). A laid-back coffee shop and organic market that's a perfect place to hang out while you're on the relaxed schedule locals like to call "Terlingua Time." Open daily 10am-7pm. ❶

Starlight Theater Bar and Grill, off Rte. 170 in Terlingua's historic ghost town (☎371-2326), 7 mi. from the park entrance. Upbeat joint with healthy portions of inventive Tex-Mex ($7-16) and live music on weekends. Food served daily 5:30-10pm; bar open Su-F 5pm-midnight, Sa 5pm-1am. ❸

The Boathouse, in the ghost town (☎371-2219), has a gourmet chef, nightly specials ($8-13), and the Zenternet cafe hawking Internet access at $2 per 15 min. Open Su-F 5pm-midnight, Sa 5pm-1am. ❸

⚑ HIKING

There are 200 mi. of hiking trails in the park, from 30min. nature walks to extended backpacking trips. Park rangers at the Visitors Centers are happy to suggest hikes and sights; the *Hiker's Guide to Big Bend* ($2), available at Panther Junction, is a good investment. Those hiking in the Chisos Mountains should purchase the topographical *Chisos Mountains Trail Map* for $1 at the Visitors Center. The number one safety hazard in the park is dehydration: **always carry at least a gallon of water per person per full day of desert hiking, if not more.** Also, anyone hiking alone should let someone know his/her destination and expected time of return. Sneakers can be worn on very short hikes, but proper footwear is absolutely crucial for more strenuous hikes. When hiking or backcountry camping, be sure to pack out all trash and bury all human waste 6 in. deep in the ground.

▨ **Window Trail** (5.2 mi. round-trip, 2-3hr.). From the Chisos Basin parking lot, this popular hike runs down from the Chisos Lodge to a U-shaped rock formation called the Window. The trail follows the natural drainage of the basin and passes a wide variety of desert flora and colorful, otherworldly rock formations. In rainy months the Window becomes a 200 ft. waterfall. A side trail toward Oak Spring, 0.3 mi. from the Window, has great views down into the desert and up toward the Chisos. During the summer, the best time to hike this trail is in the early morning or at sunset. Some people begin this hike next to site #52 in the Basin Campground, shaving 1.2 mi. off the round-trip distance.

Santa Elena Canyon (1.7 mi. round-trip, 1½hr.). Starting at a trailhead at the end of the Ross Maxwell Scenic Drive, this spectacular trail takes hikers through a

1500 ft. high limestone canyon carved by the Río Grande. The trail begins by crossing Terlingua Creek; most of the year the water is shallow and hikers can easily wade across. **Do not attempt this hike after heavy rains when the water is high and the current is strong.** On the other side of the creek the trail climbs upward to a view of the canyon, slopes down to the river's edge, and continues along the canyon floor before ending at a rock wall.

Window View (0.3 mi, 20min.). A short, paved loop from the Chisos Basin parking lot with benches along the way. Watching the sun set through the Window is a must for all visitors to Big Bend National Park, though the view from here does not compare to that available on the Window Trail. Wheelchair accessible.

Lost Mine Trail (4.8 mi. round-trip, 3-4hr.). This moderately strenuous hike that goes into the Chisos Mountains begins at Panther Pass (not Junction), which is located at Mile 5 of the road that leads up into the Chisos Basin. The trail passes below Casa Grande and climbs 1100 ft. to a vantage point high above Juniper Canyon. Those pressed for time or sapped of energy can hike to the impressive Juniper Canyon Overlook, 1 mi. from the trailhead.

South Rim (13-14.5 mi. round-trip, 7-10hr.). The South Rim of the Chisos Mountains, 2500 ft. above the Chihuahuan Desert, offers the most impressive views in Big Bend National Park. On a clear day, you can see the Río Grande's path through the Chihuahuan Desert, mountain peaks in Mexico nearly 50 mi. to the south, Santa Eleña Canyon 20 mi. to the west, and the Sierra del Carmen Mountains 30 mi. to the east. 2 trails from the Chisos Basin parking lot lead to the South Rim, Laguna Meadow (6.5 mi. one-way), and Pinnacles Trail (6.4 mi. one-way). Most hikers ascend the Laguna Meadow trail and descend the steeper Pinnacles Trail. Once at the South Rim, the 3.3 mi. loop to the east is a must-do for its panoramic views of rolling desert hills 1500 ft. below. (Closed Feb. 1-Jul. 15 for peregrine falcon nesting season.) The descent on the Pinnacles Trail follows a series of rainwater pools through the high woodlands of Boot Canyon and overlooks Casa Grande and the Chisos Basin. For those who choose to do the South Rim as an overnight hike, primitive campsites are located along the trail.

Emory Peak (4.5 mi. one-way, 5-8hr.). At 7825 ft., this is the highest mountain in the park, and one of the tallest in Texas. From the Basin Trailhead in the parking lot, take the Pinnacles Trail 3½ mi. to the Emory Peak Trail. The summit is a mile from this junction, and reaching it requires scrambling up a rock wall. **Be very careful climbing up the rocks: serious accidents have occurred here.** Dedicated hikers will be rewarded

(Continued from previous page)

Yes, the circle of life is indeed a bloody wonder: out here, it can be more of a hexagram than a circle. The bugs that fly past your ears in Big Bend and at the Guadalupe Mountains sound like loud FM static and if challenged, could probably benchpress a toaster oven. Texas insects aren't so much living organisms as abstract ideas like annihilation, desperation, and desire (her name is June).

Some are sapphire blue and appear to be fashioned out of blown glass; others are clearly pure titanium and recall scenes from *Critters 4*. Still others have filed applications to be included in the mollusk family, and one insect I had coffee with has started a ska band called St. Vincent and the Grenadines. Still you need to stay in harmony with your natural surroundings: fear the beetle, die by the beetle. Repeat after me: as I walk through the valley of the shadow of Guadalupe, I shall fear nothing on four legs. The scorpions are nothing you'd tickle under the chin, but admire it for its own relentless force. If your spirit is at ease, foraging deer walk three feet to your side in the Chisos Basin, mother and child, no questions asked. Even the hawks wheeling in the blue sky over Boquillas Canyon will pose for photos you'll need to title "Hawk and Moon." Some will even be kind enough to ask you to dinner: declining the offer requires ducking.

–Jonathan Sherman

with a 360-degree view from the top. Combine Emory Peak with a hike to South Rim for a 15 mi. round-trip. There are bearproof lockers at the trailhead for backpackers who want to leave their packs behind for the peak hike.

▲ OTHER OUTDOOR ACTIVITIES

BACKPACKING. Big Bend offers numerous backpacking opportunities to those willing to rough it in the desert. One of the more popular multi-day hikes is the **Outer Mountain Loop** (31.6 mi., at least 3 days; includes the **Dodson Trail** among others). This trail promises a variety of scenery, from the woodlands of the High Chisos Complex to the scrub and cacti of the Chihuahuan Desert. It begins at the Basin trailhead, climbing up to Emory Peak and the South Rim as side trips, then loops around and travels 16 mi. through the desert below South Rim. Water is often scarce on this trail, but there are opportunities to cache water in advance via car. There are also several possible overnight routes through the Chisos, but longer hikes are limited by the small size of the Chisos area and the fact that all water must be carried in with you. All backcountry camping requires a permit, available at any park Visitors Center. **Desert Sports** and **Big Bend River Tours** (see **River Running**) each provide day and overnight guided hiking trips.

RIVER RUNNING. The awesome canyons and blue waters of the Río Grande are best appreciated on a trip down the river. Luckily Big Bend is a river running hotspot. The National Park Service has jurisdiction over the entire 118 mi. of river along the southern boundary of the park, as well as an additional 127 mi. downstream of the park known as the **Río Grande Wild and Scenic River.** Until 1899, these 235 mi. of the Río Grande were considered impassable to boats. An 1852 surveying expedition floated an unmanned boat through Santa Eleña Canyon, only to find splintered pieces of wood at the other end. Today, because of extensive damming, only those with the necessary knowledge and experience can navigate the river.

There are three main river canyons within the park boundaries. Near the western end of the park, **Santa Eleña Canyon** is a 20 mi., two-to-three-day trip with a 7 mi. stretch confined by 1500 ft. limestone walls. Two miles into this canyon is the Rock Slide, a Class IV rapid when the water level is high. **Mariscal Canyon** is a 10 mi., one-day trip through 1400 ft. canyon walls. The rapids within this canyon are Class II-III. **Boquillas Canyon,** along the eastern edge of the park, is a 33 mi., three-to-four-day journey through 1200 ft. walls. The rapids here do not exceed Class II, making Boquillas a good choice for rafters with less experience. Another easy, one-day trip is **Colorado Canyon,** in **Big Bend Ranch State Park** (p. 465), upstream of the national park. The **Lower Canyons** downstream of the Big Bend wind through 137 mi. of rugged desert and deep canyons. Floating the Lower Canyons can take seven to ten days depending on the distance and amount of side hikes. River conditions at Big Bend change vastly from day to day, which can affect both the difficulty of the rapids and the amount of time necessary to float sections. The most consistent water levels are in the fall rainy season, but even then the river can be raging one day and calm the next.

There are three options for river trips: bring your own equipment, rent equipment from an outfitter, or go on a guided trip. Those tackling the river on their own must obtain a permit from the Visitors Centers at Persimmon Gap, Panther Junction, or Río Grande Village. Boaters should buy the detailed river guide available at park headquarters. Inflatable rafts are much safer than canoes because they bounce off rocks and canyon walls. In Terlingua, **Desert Sports** rents rafts and canoes starting at $40 per day. (☎371-2727 or 888-989-6900; www.desertsportstx.com.) Guided tours start at $125 for a daytrip. In Terlingua off Hwy. 170, **Big Bend River**

Tours rents canoes ($45 per day) and inflatable kayaks ($35 per day). Guided trips: half-day $62, full day $130, less for larger groups. (☎371-3033 or 800-545-4240; www.bigbendrivertours.com.) Both offer **shuttle service** for downriver pick ups.

For those without river experience, a guided trip is the safest option and generally runs $100 per person per day. Desert Sports, Big Bend River Tours, and Texas River and Jeep Expeditions and Far-Flung Adventures (☎371-2633 or 800-839-7238; www.farflung.com/tx), in Terlingua, offer single- and multi-day canoe and kayak trips through the park's canyons (also specialty trips with area chefs and musicians; call well in advance for reservations). For each of these guided trips, a minimum of two people is required to start a separate scheduled trip.

MOUNTAIN BIKING. Bikes are allowed on all roads in the park, both paved and unpaved. **Old Ore Road** (26 mi. one-way, 4-6hr.) is perhaps the best ride in the park. Start at the Dagger Flat Auto Trail, halfway between Persimmon Gap and Panther Junction; from here the trip is mostly downhill. The road is rough but the views are spectacular with the Chisos Range to the west and the Sierra del Carmen to the east. Another good route is **Glenn Springs Road** to **River Road** (25 mi., 3-4hr.) starting about 6 mi. south of Panther Junction and ending up near Río Grande Village. For a less technical ride, consider biking the **Ross Maxwell Scenic Drive** and **Old Maverick Road Loop** (56 mi. round-trip, 5-6hr.). All but 13 mi. of this loop are paved, and bikers can stop at Santa Eleña Canyon for a breather and a few snapshots. **Desert Sports** (see **River Running**) rents mountain bikes ($25 per day).

ROCK CLIMBING. Although the mountains and canyons of Big Bend have plenty of exposed rock faces, much of the rock is sedimentary and too soft for climbing. Nonetheless, the park offers a few decent rock climbing spots. Many climbers frequent **Indian Head,** on the northwest border of the park, 6 mi. northeast of Terlingua. Another spot is the top of the **Lost Mine Trail,** which offers 5.8 and 5.9+ pitches. For the location and ratings of climbing routes and bouldering problems, check out *A Climber's Guide to Big Bend* at Park Headquarters. Hand-drills are allowed only with approval of the superintendent, but permission is rarely granted. Only white chalk with oil-based additives may be used.

SCENIC DRIVING. There are only five paved roads in the park. Of these, the best sight-seeing is along the **Ross Maxwell Scenic Drive,** a 30 mi. paved route from the western edge of the Chisos Mountains that leads down to the Río Grande and Santa Eleña Canyon. The 8 mi. drive that winds its way up into the **Chisos Basin** is also quite rewarding. However, the most spectacular drives in the park are unimproved, only accessible to four-wheel-drive jeeps and trucks. **River Road,** a 51 mi., 6-8hr. drive, skirts along the Río Grande from Castolon to the Río Grande Village. Another good drive is the 26 mi. **Old Ore Road,** which travels along the western edge of the Sierra del Caballo Muerto. Those interested in driving the backroads of Big Bend should purchase the guide to backcountry roads at the Visitors Center for $2. For visitors without their own four-wheel-drive vehicle, **Big Bend River Tours** (p. 464) offers backcountry jeep tours ($65 per person for a half-day).

BIG BEND RANCH STATE PARK ☎432

This 470 sq. mi. state park adjoins the National Park and was a private ranch until the state of Texas bought the land in 1988. Today, the state operates the ranch as a state park. The rarely visited park is a hidden jewel that can provide backcountry solitude for those that find the National Park too crowded and developed. Its territory includes mountains, waterfalls, and a number of sites of interest to geologists and archaeologists, as well as vast stretches of the Chihuahuan Desert and the Río Grande. Within the confines of the state park, the 50 mi. **El Camino del Río Scenic**

Drive follows Rte. 170 along the Río Grande from Lajitas to Presidio. Named by *National Geographic* in 1985 as one of the prettiest drives in the US, the road winds through mountains, canyons, desert, and farmland. Allow 1½hr. to drive the route, plus additional time for stops.

The most accessible hiking trails in the park begin from Rte. 170. The **Closed Canyon Trail**, 1.4 mi. round-trip, winds through the walls of a narrow canyon carved by a tributary of the Río Grande. The **Rancherías Canyon Trail** leads 4.8 mi. one-way along the canyon floor to 70 ft. Rancherias Falls. **Flash floods can occur on either canyon trail; check with rangers to make sure conditions are safe.** The **Rancherías Trail** is a 19 mi., two-to-three-day backpacking trail into the canyon country of the Bofecillos Mountains. An interpretive guide available at the Visitors Center provides extensive information about the flora, fauna, and geography encountered along this trail, making it an interesting and informative trip for those unfamiliar with the area. There are three primitive camping areas with pit toilets located along Rte. 170. Hikers spending a night in the backcountry must obtain a backcountry permit from the Warnock Education Center. The **Horse Trap Trail** is a 5 mi. loop open to hikers and bikers. It departs from just south of the Sauceda Ranch and loops through the old ranch country, with great scenery along the way. Hikers will find the terrain easy, while some sections are fairly challenging on a bike.

The park borders a 21 mi. stretch of the Río Grande with plenty of good **rafting.** Between the Colorado Canyon river access point and the takeout at the town of Lajitas there are several Class II-III rapids and three other access points for trips lasting an afternoon to three days. **Colorado Canyon** on the upper portion makes an easy day trip with beautiful deep canyon views, while the trips on the lower portion can catch some good white water at **Fresno Rapids** when water levels are high. For oufitters, see **River Running** p. 464.

The **Barton Warnock Education Center,** 1 mi. east of Lajitas on Rte. 170, has a big desert garden and an excellent interpretive exhibit on the geology and natural history of the Big Bend region. The Visitors Center sells multi-use permits ($6) for hiking, camping, and river access and has trail and river maps. (☎424-3327. Open daily 8am-4:30pm. Exhibit $3, children $1.50.) **Ranch headquarters** at Sauceda in the park interior is at the end of a 29 mi. gravel road. The historic **Ranch House** ❷ (☎229-3416) has private rooms ($50 per person) or bunks ($20 per person) in the hunting lodge. Reservations for rooms and meals are essential. The ranch also rents bikes and offers horseback tours. The road to Sauceda makes a great mountain bike ride, and there are many hiking trails that begin near park headquarters.

INDEX

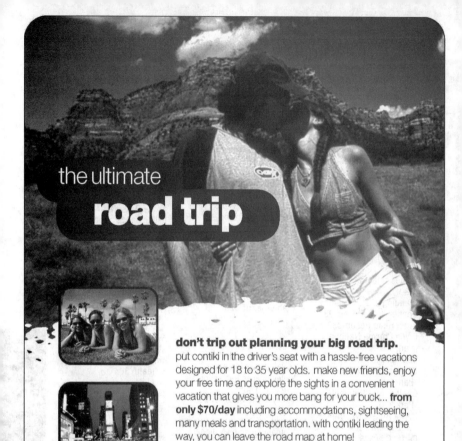

MAP INDEX

MAP LEGEND

Park	Water	Desert	
Hospital	Airport	Hotel/Hostel	14 Forest Road
Police	Bus Station	Camping	207 State Road
Post Office	Train Station	Food	56 U.S. Road
Visitor Information	Parking	Nightlife	70 Interstate Highw
Border Crossing	Park	Primitive Campsite	Freeway
Embassy/Consulate	Church	Shelter	Paved Road
Site or Service	Mission	Ranger Station	Unpaved Road
Internet	Pueblo	Mountains	4-Wheel Drive Ro
Museum	Ruins	Butte	Trail
Library	Ski Area	Pass	The Let's Go
Pedestrian Zone	Trailhead	Waterfall	compass always points NORTH